FROM THE HOME OF

MARTHA STEWART'S
HOMEKEEPING HANDBOOK

MARTHA STEWART'S
HOMEKEEPING HANDBOOK

The Essential Guide to Caring for Everything in Your Home

CLARKSON POTTER/PUBLISHERS
NEW YORK

ALSO BY MARTHA STEWART
Entertaining
Martha Stewart's Quick Cook
Martha Stewart's Hors d'Oeuvres
Martha Stewart's Pies & Tarts
Weddings
Martha Stewart's Quick Cook Menus
The Wedding Planner
Martha Stewart's Christmas
Martha Stewart's Gardening
Martha Stewart's New Old House
Martha Stewart's Menus for Entertaining
The Martha Stewart Cookbook
Martha Stewart's Healthy Quick Cook
Martha Stewart's Hors d'Oeuvres Handbook
Martha Stewart's Baking Handbook

Copyright © 2006 by Martha Stewart Living Omnimedia, Inc.,
11 West 42nd Street, New York, NY 10036

A list of photograph credits appears on page 724.

All rights reserved.
Published in the United States by Clarkson Potter/Publishers,
an imprint of the Crown Publishing Group,
a division of Random House, Inc., New York.
www.crownpublishing.com
www.clarksonpotter.com

Clarkson N. Potter is a trademark and Potter and colophon
are registered trademarks of Random House, Inc.

Library of Congress Cataloging-in-Publication Data
is available upon request.

ISBN 13: 978-0-517-57700-4
ISBN 10: 0-517-57700-3

Printed in the United States of America

Design by William van Roden

10 9 8 7 6 5 4 3 2 1

FIRST EDITION

TO ALL MOTHERS AND DAUGHTERS,
FATHERS AND SONS
WHO HAVE A ROOM, AN APARTMENT,
OR A HOME TO CARE FOR

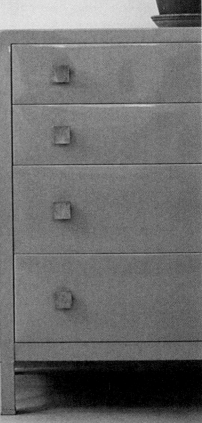

CONTENTS

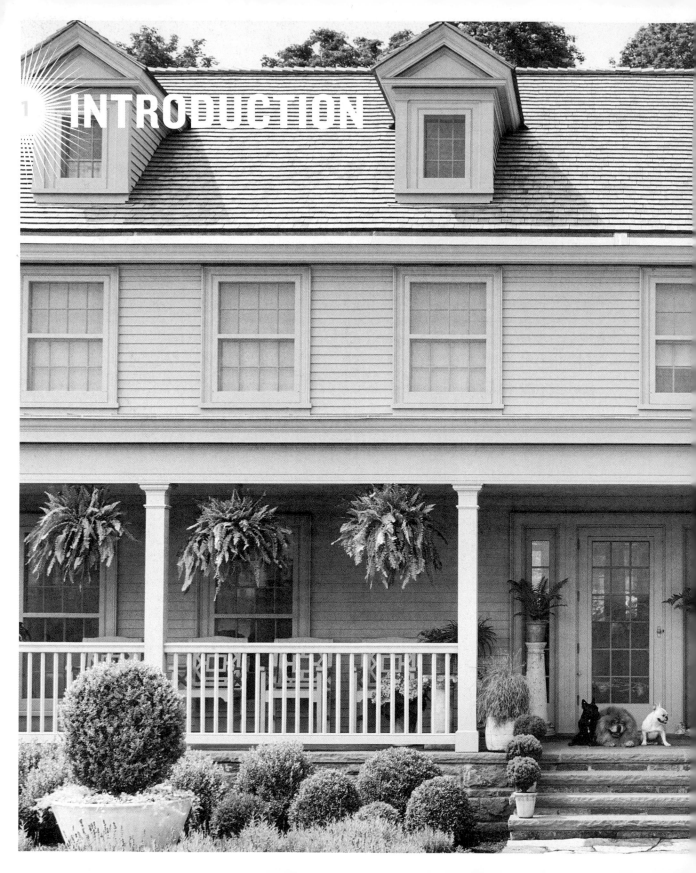

INTRODUCTION

I STARTED COMPILING MY RESEARCH and information for this book many years ago, when I first realized that homekeeping, homemaking, and housekeeping were my favorite subjects. Every day I was faced with the myriad challenges of running and maintaining my home on Turkey Hill Road, a complex old house set on four very lush and landscaped acres.

There were always problems—puzzles to be solved and solutions to be discovered. When I installed a marble tile floor in one of the bathrooms I had to learn how to clean the surface and maintain the glow. I had to learn how to polish the nickel hardware in the powder room, never having had such a finish anyplace before. I had to figure out how to iron antique linens, and seal stone floors, and grout around the shower. My New York apartment, a small but lovely pied-à-terre in a prewar building on Central Park, posed even more complex problems for which I needed guidance and solutions. I knew that I was like so many of you, wanting to do many of these small chores myself, not wanting to call in a handyman, knowing that I could not rely 100 percent on my husband to do every little thing that popped up many times a day. I knew that if I needed a modern *Mrs. Beeton's Book of Household Management*, so did you.

I received my first copy of *Mrs. Beeton's Book of Household Management* in 1961, the year I married, and one hundred years after the first copies were published in England. I was entranced with the size of the book and with its contents. Always fascinated with vintage books on all subjects having to do with home and garden, I found this one especially charming and curious. Who was Mrs. Beeton, and why would she compile so huge a compendium of useful recipes and household facts? I have since discovered that Isabella Beeton was the young wife of a well-to-do publisher whose idea it was to create a vast and useful "encyclopedia" for every homemaker, to make "mis-management" of one's home an undesirable thing.

Mrs. Beeton, aided by a large staff of employees and generous friends, published the compilation in 1861; its many editions cover topics such as general household work, including labor-saving instructions, laundry work, household hints, and many recipes; medical and nursing chapters; and even legal advice for ordinary household occurrences. Waste was always to be avoided, the household staff was to be trained and managed, the nursery should face a "southery" direction, and spaghettis and macaronis were always to be cooked in boiling, not tepid or simmering, water so that starch particles would burst while cooking.

French cookery, Jewish cookery, and Indian cookery are addressed, with delicious, mouthwatering recipes. How to carve a roasted beef, a hare, or a ham is examined, described, and explained in detail with excellent illustrations. And if one reads the "Home Doctor's ABC," many common ills can be tended to as a result. In more than 1,680 pages, Mrs. Beeton managed to educate and inform a great number of homemakers for decades.

So fascinated was I with Mrs. Beeton that I wondered if authors in other countries had espoused similar treatments of "household management," and I started looking. I found a wonderful tome, *A Woman's Book,* published in Edinburgh around the end of the nineteenth century. It contained even more detailed information on preservation of food, butchering, laundering, and equipment for the home than the Beeton encyclopedia, but was very similar in tone and scope.

I also came across another massive work, 1,238 pages long, published in America in 1845, entitled *An Encyclopedia of Domestic Economy,* written by Thomas Webster, assisted by Mrs. Parkes, with notes and improvements by D. Meredith Reese. A precursor to Mrs. Beeton's book, it includes vast amounts of information about everything from "warming domestic edifices" to "economy of the laundry." "The toilet and subjects connected," "practical household details," "artificial illumination," and so much more about the domestic residence of the nineteenth century are treated with thoughtfulness and respectful attention to detail.

Another English work, published early in the twentieth century, is *The Concise Household Encyclopedia.* It contains, in alphabetical order, thousands of entries pertaining to the home: materials and their uses and preparations, bathroom fixtures, instructions for card games, leaded windows, household signs, and even a how-to for stenciling.

To me, these books were unusual and actually cutting edge in the way they treated the subject matter of the house, the home, and living in general. It was enlightening to find out that these books were very, very successful, some selling millions of copies to avid homemakers so in need of help in establishing, running, and maintaining households. Another discovery was that these books did not target one demographic, but many. It mattered not at all whether one was married or single, lived in a mansion or a cottage, in a few rooms or many. What mattered was that the information was useful and practical and clearly presented, covering a very broad number of topics so that it was indeed encyclopedic in nature.

I started working on this book myself, gathering information, writing an outline, and formulating the way the book would look, the way it would be used, and the way it would be organized. During the ensuing years we have covered homekeeping in our various magazines, and many of those articles—on laundry, organizing, and even stain removal—are still extremely popular with our readers. (Our "Ask Martha" columns alone have generated hundreds of answers to reader queries about household dilemmas.) Because of the scope of this book, and because I really wanted the content to be as comprehensive as possible, a team was formed to complete the research and the manuscript. So this book, not unlike the antique volumes preceding it, is a team effort, the result of the hard work of many people with curious minds, excellent research skills, and their own homekeeping experiences to draw upon.

I like to think we've come close to answering just about any question you might have, and sincerely hope that the information in this book can enrich your life—for taking care of a home is rewarding work indeed.

Martha Stewart

THE KITCHEN AT BEDFORD

HOW TO USE THIS BOOK

WHEN THE FIRST ISSUE OF *MARTHA STEWART LIVING* was published in 1990, I could not have begun to anticipate how wide-ranging our readers' home-keeping concerns would be. Since then, we have discovered new solutions to age-old problems, brought in experts to advise us on very specific questions about very specific concerns, and experimented with all the new (and not so new) home-care products. Over the years, I've brought these lessons home with me, too, which has made me more organized and made my homes better cared for and maintained.

HOUSEHOLDS ARE BUSY PLACES, works in progress where there is always something needing immediate attention and always something more that can be done. With that in mind, I have organized this book to address the tasks at hand and also to address the "more that can be done" for when you have the time and the inclination to go beyond the essentials.

It starts with the big picture—an examination of every room and everything you will find within each. The twelve chapters in the "Room by Room" section take you on a tour through the house, focusing on the surfaces and furnishings you might find in any room, and offering strategies for their care and maintenance. Starting with the kitchen, the central staging area in any home, these chapters open with space-planning practical advice, followed by the golden rules of organizing. This information is intended to help contain your belongings and make each room clutter-free and functional. Relevant homekeeping concerns particular to each room are explored in depth—so stain-removal basics appear in "Laundry Room," the best way to clean grout in "Bathroom," and easy sewing repairs in "Utility Spaces." The equipment essential to each room is also addressed, so if you are considering what kind of bathtub to install during a bathroom renovation or whether a gas or electric range would best suit your style of cooking, you will have the information necessary to make such an investment with confidence.

Consider the "Throughout the House" section of the book a master class on how to clean. Here you will find simple, clear instructions for the basic techniques needed to clean any household object or surface. The five fundamentals—dusting, wiping up, sweeping, vacuuming, and mopping—that constitute the core of any weekly household schedule are covered in "Routine Cleaning," with detailed descriptions of the best tools and equipment for each task. Look to these cleaning-specific chapters for photo glossaries of dusters, brushes, brooms, cloths, sponges, and vacuum cleaners, along with tips for their efficient use and care. Beyond "Routine Cleaning" lies "Periodic Maintenance," which encompasses all you need to know to perform those less frequent but nonetheless crucial chores, including scrubbing, waxing and polishing, and maintaining the surfaces that are found in every room of the house—walls, ceilings, woodwork, windows, and floors.

So many of the systems in a house are invisible—the vents and pipes and wires we depend upon for heat, water, and light, for example. Included in the "Comfort and Safety" section are explanations of the multiple hidden systems that keep a home functional. No one needs to become a master electrician or plumber to learn how to check these systems on an ongoing basis. The instructions found here for making small repairs and adjustments will give you a sense of control over this important aspect of homekeeping. Beyond these repairs and maintenance recommendations, there's advice on how to prepare for emergencies, how to choose the best air and water filtration systems, even how to create the most nurturing environment for your pets. A checklist of monthly and seasonal reminders to keep these systems in good working order appears on page 559, to supplement the regular homekeeping calendar that opens the "Room by Room" section, on pages 23–29.

Since the average American changes residence about a dozen times in his or her lifetime, a section on how to move from one home to another begins on page 678. Included are a moving timetable, box-packing tips, and advice on how to ensure the most comfortable arrival at your new home.

Besides the everyday furnishings and surfaces that make up a home, there are those unique objects that give rooms personality and express a sense of style. The substances that make up these things are explained in the "Materials Guide," a comprehensive reference that includes brief descriptions and care and storage recommendations. Look to this handy, alphabetically arranged guide whenever you are curious about how to handle an unusual household material, from abalone to zinc.

Throughout this book, suggestions are given for particular cleaning products and tools. These are the things we have discovered in our research—whether over the years at home or in the course of compiling this book—that perform well, time and again. These favorites are mentioned within the text, where appropriate, but you'll also find them in one convenient list in "Sources" on page 721, with buying information for each.

Before you make your way through the book, take a moment to familiarize yourself with household cleaners, examined in detail in "Cleaning Products 101," the section immediately following this one. We so often take for granted the things we use to mop and scrub, but it's worth getting to know what's in the products we use every day so we can use them more efficiently.

I hope you will turn to this book every time a homekeeping need, question, or concern arises. I hope, too, that the information in these pages will encourage you to look at your home in a whole new way, and turn it into the place you have always wanted it to be.

CLEANING PRODUCTS 101

AS YOU WALK DOWN THE AISLES of your grocery store, you may have a hard time imagining that people once cared for their floors, windows, and clothes without the aid of commercial products. They made soap from tallow and ashes, and cleaners from lemon juice, borax, vinegar, and baking soda. Before the advent of the myriad products we take for granted today, a homemaker had to have a basic understanding of the chemistry of cleaning in order to keep a tidy house. She would have been familiar with the bleaching properties of lemon juice, the disinfecting power of vinegar, and the grease-cutting abilities of baking soda. She would have known that a tablecloth stained with blueberries would require very different treatment than one marred by gravy. Homekeeping generations ago was as much a science as an art.

BECAUSE OF THE CONVENIENCE OFFERED by many new products, much of that knowledge has faded. But it's just as important today as it was a century ago to understand how cleaning products work. Because there are so many products to choose from, cupboards can quickly become cluttered, and confusion about which products to use can abound. A little knowledge about ingredients and their individual properties can help remedy that. Armed with a few facts, you can confidently choose the cleansers, polishes, and detergents that will allow you to clean more effectively and efficiently.

HOW TO READ LABELS

The most important thing you can do before choosing a cleaning product is also the easiest: Read the label. As with food, the labels on household cleaners sometimes seem to be written in a language all their own. Once you are familiar with the vocabulary, however, you can glean a great deal of information from them. A label usually includes the following:

THE TYPE OF PRODUCT
Cleaning products fall into two categories: all-purpose cleaners, designed for multiple surfaces; and specialty cleaners, for specific materials, including glass, tile, metal, wood, and carpets. No matter what kind of cleaner you use, you must read the entire label, especially the small (and easily overlooked) type. For example, a stainless-steel polish might be designed for use on pots and pans, but not on appliances. A floor cleaner may work on wood and vinyl, but not on stone. Heeding the information in small print will help you avoid damaging the surfaces you're trying to maintain.

DIRECTIONS FOR USE
This information explains how much product to use (and whether it needs to be diluted), what sort of cleaning cloth or tool to use, and whether the treatment should stand for any length of time to emulsify dirt. Using more than the recommended amount won't ensure cleaner surfaces—it will only waste product and money and possibly do more harm than good. In fact, in some instances you can probably use less than the recommended amount. The only way to know for sure is to experiment.

INGREDIENTS
Manufacturers are not required by law to disclose ingredients unless they're disinfectants (meaning they kill microorganisms such as bacteria, viruses, and fungi) or known to be hazardous (a determination made by the U.S.

Occupational Safety and Health Administration). Products with disinfectants will have an Environmental Protection Agency registration number (or numbers) indicating that the disinfectant meets the agency's guidelines. Keep in mind that when ingredients are listed, they are not necessarily listed in descending order of predominance as they are on food labels.

SAFETY INFORMATION

Products that contain chemicals known to be hazardous carry a warning that includes a list of potential risks, guidelines for safe usage, and first-aid instructions. The following words indicate a product is hazardous: "warning," "caution," "poison," and "danger." The latter two indicate the highest hazard level. A hazardous product is toxic (it can cause illness), flammable (it can cause a fire if exposed to a flame or spark), corrosive (it can eat through materials including skin), and/or reactive (it can ignite or create a poisonous vapor if mixed with another product). Wear rubber gloves and work in a well-ventilated area whenever you see one of these words on a label; also wear eye protection with any product labeled "poison" or "danger."

STORAGE GUIDELINES

Household cleaners often require specific storage conditions both to maintain their effectiveness and for safety's sake. For example, powdered detergents, such as automatic dishwashing detergents, don't clean as well if they clump, so they need to be stored in a dry location. Aerosols, which are highly flammable, must be stored away from heat sources. Always check this information before storing a cleaning product.

DISPOSAL GUIDELINES

Drain cleaners, oven cleaners, floor-wax strippers, and other products that contain hazardous ingredients often require special arrangements for disposal, which are noted on labels. Keep in mind that many communities will not allow garbage haulers to pick up hazardous products with the regular trash. Check with your local sanitation department for guidelines. They may require that you wait for a hazardous-waste pickup or that you drop off such items at a special collection site. Hazardous products should never be poured down drains or storm sewers.

Manufacturers often note whether a product's packaging can be recycled. When it comes to plastic containers, not every community accepts every type, however, so before putting a container in the recycling bin or taking it to a drop-off site, note the number on the bottom of the container (each number indicates a different type of plastic). Consult your sanitation department to learn whether they accept that number; if they don't, you'll have to throw out the container with the regular trash.

CLEANING PRODUCT INGREDIENTS

Cleaning products today are remarkably complicated, in part because they are designed for the ever more diverse array of materials in our homes and also because we demand a great deal from them. We expect them to lift stains with a minimum of scrubbing, to kill germs without smelling strongly of chemicals, to cut grease without damaging a sleek stainless-steel counter or polished wooden cabinet. In order to meet these requirements, a product may contain a long list of chemical ingredients. Most of these ingredients, however, fall into one of these categories:

ABRASIVES

Small particles—usually minerals—in liquid or powder form that scour away soil. Particles are rated according to the Mohs' scale, which measures the relative hardness of minerals. The scale goes from talc (number 1) to diamonds (number 10). Silica, which is rated 7, and feldspar, which is rated 6, are the abrasive components usually found in household cleansers. Baking soda (sodium bicarbonate), rated 2.5, is a gentler alternative to commercial cleansers.

BLEACHES

Whitening, brightening, and stain-lifting chemicals in laundry products, scouring liquids and powders, and tub and tile cleaners. Chlorine bleach is sometimes listed as sodium hypochlorite. Besides being a whitener, it is a disinfectant that kills bacteria, viruses, and fungi. Oxygen bleach is a less toxic alternative to chlorine bleach, but it does not have the same disinfecting power. It may be listed as hydrogen peroxide, sodium perborate, or sodium percarbonate.

BUILDERS

Chemicals in detergents and other cleaners that soften water by binding together minerals so they don't interfere with the action of surfactants.

ENZYMES

Proteins added to laundry and dishwashing detergents that break down dirt and protein-based, oily, and starch-based stains.

FRAGRANCES

Chemicals added to most household cleaners and laundry products to mask the odor of chemical ingredients during use and to leave behind a pleasant scent.

SURFACTANTS

Chemicals in detergents and many other cleaning products that make water spread rather than bead, so it clings to surfaces to better emulsify, or dissolve, dirt. Surfactants also help soil particles stay suspended in water so they aren't redeposited on the surface or fabric being washed. Most surfactants are derived from petroleum.

SOLVENTS

Substances—usually liquids—that dissolve other substances. Solvents used in household products—called organic solvents because they are carbon-based—are made from either petroleum or plant materials. They are useful for cutting grease. Common household solvents include acetone, ethanol, isopropyl alcohol, d-limonene, mineral spirits, naphtha, and turpentine. Waxes, furniture polishes and strippers, rug cleaners, spot cleaners, glass cleaners, and degreasing products generally contain organic solvents. Most organic solvents are toxic (a label may not indicate a product contains a solvent, but may list one of the ingredients above); it's essential when using them or products containing them to wear rubber gloves and work in a well-ventilated area.

THE PH SCALE

The lessons learned in chemistry class actually come in handy when choosing household cleaners. All solutions have a pH, and in the case of the products we use to wash dishes, floors, and clothes, the pH level helps determine what kind of dirt and stains they're best at removing. The pH scale ranges from 0 to 14, with 7 being neutral. Levels below 7 are acidic; levels above 7 are alkaline.

Household cleaners, laundry detergents, and dishwashing detergents are alkaline because alkaline solutions effectively cut through grease, oil, fats, proteins, and other common household dirt—in short, organic substances. Tub, tile, and toilet cleaners are often acidic, since acids are best for dissolving calcium, one of the minerals commonly left behind by hard water, and rust—in short, inorganic substances.

Dishwashing liquids labeled "Gentle" or "Mild on Hands" often have a pH close to 7 and are ideal for day-to-day cleaning. Products designed for stone surfaces (which can be damaged by either acidic or alkaline products) also generally have a neutral pH.

Products with pH levels at the extreme ends of the scale are corrosive and require rubber gloves, eye protection, and good ventilation.

Product labels don't usually list pH levels, but you can often learn what they are by looking at a product's material safety data sheet (MSDS), which you may be able to find online or get from the manufacturer.

PH LEVELS OF COMMON HOUSEHOLD CLEANERS

Cleaning Product	pH level	Cleaning Product	pH level
Chlorine bleach	13	Baking soda	9
Ammonia	12	Dishwashing detergent	6.5–9
Oven cleaner	12	Vinegar and lemon juice	3
Tub and tile cleaner	12	Toilet cleaner	3
Borax	10		

HEALTHIER CHOICES

Many people are conditioned to believe a house is not clean unless it smells of chemicals (in fact, nothing indicates a clean house more than a complete absence of odor other than fresh flowers or food cooking). Because of this, a lot of us tend to use cleaners that contain ingredients that are far stronger than necessary. But in doing so, you risk not only wear and tear on the surface or material you're cleaning, but polluting the air inside your house as well as the planet. According to the Environmental Protection Agency, concentrations of volatile organic compounds—chemical-laden gases emitted by a variety of household products that can have short- and long-term health effects—are ten times higher inside the home than outside.

Fortunately, there are more products on the market that are better for your health and the environment than ever before—and these products are more effective than they used to be, too (although they often still require more elbow grease than conventional products). But because health and environmental claims are minimally regulated, you need to be vigilant about checking labels to ensure products are delivering what they promise. Claims such as "environmentally friendly," "natural," and "biodegradable" don't necessarily mean a product is free of harmful chemicals. Here are the indicators a product will have less impact on your health and the planet's:

☐ Buy from manufacturers that readily disclose a full list of ingredients, and choose products whenever possible without hazardous ingredients. The Consumers Union, a nonprofit product-testing organization, recommends avoiding the following, all of which pose health and environmental risks: alkylphenol ethoxylates (AEPs); antibacterials; ammonia; butyl cellosolve, also known as ethanol, butyl glycol, ethylene glycol, and monobutyl; chlorine bleach; d-limonene; diethanolamine (DEA) and triethanolamine (TEA); disinfectants; fragrances; hydrochloric acid; naphtha; petroleum-based ingredients and surfactants; phosphates, which are generally found only in automatic dishwashing detergents; lye, also known as sodium hydroxide; and sulfuric acid.

☐ Choose products labeled with specific claims, rather than general ones. The term "environmentally friendly," for example, which has no widely accepted definition, is only meaningful if it is accompanied by an explanation, such as "This product has no air-polluting potential." The phrase "100 percent plant-based surfactants" is more meaningful than "natural," since petroleum-based ingredients and surfactants are, strictly speaking, natural. "This product will biodegrade in four to six days" is more meaningful than "biodegradable" since most everything biodegrades eventually (although some may take many years). The more specifically a term is qualified, the better you'll be able to judge a product's merits.

☐ Be aware of meaningless claims. Many products are prominently labeled "phosphate free" even though phosphates, which are damaging to waterways and aquatic life, haven't been used in household products, except automatic dishwashing detergent, since the mid-1990s. Likewise, products labeled "CFC free" are no more environmentally friendly than other products, since ozone-depleting CFCs, or chlorofluorocarbons, were banned from consumer aerosols in 1978.

☐ If you're concerned about a particular product's health or environmental impact, you can get more information on its ingredients by calling the company's customer-service department (the company's name, address, and phone number will be printed on the label). You can also look up the product on the National Library of Medicine's Household Products Database (www.householdproducts.nlm.nih.gov) or search online for a product's material safety data sheet (MSDS), which will contain information on hazardous ingredients.

CLEANING WITH KITCHEN STAPLES

Although there's a commercial product tailored to most every task, you can still make your house sparkle with just a few simple supplies, many of which are probably already in your cupboards. Mixing your own cleaners is not only inexpensive, it means that you will also know exactly what you're using. With a little extra effort (you're probably going to have to scrub a bit harder), you can replace many commercial cleaners with homemade ones. Here are the basics:

☐ Mild dishwashing liquid is excellent for removing spills that water won't budge. Make a simple all-purpose cleaner by mixing 2 cups water with 2 tablespoons dishwashing liquid in a spray bottle; use it on countertops and other hard surfaces. It's also good for removing greasy fingerprints from doorframes and other painted woodwork. Be sure to rinse your sponge or cloth often and wipe again to eliminate any detergent residue.

☐ Baking soda is good not only for deodorizing the refrigerator and freezer, but for a variety of cleaning tasks. Baking soda has scrubbing power but won't scratch surfaces. To scrub away kitchen stains or clean the oven, mix a paste of 3 parts warm water to 1 part baking soda. Make a bathroom cleanser by mixing a dishwashing liquid with baking soda until you have a thick paste.

☐ Distilled white vinegar and lemon juice are both excellent for cleaning, deodorizing, and mild bleaching. Both are acidic and can be used to eliminate soap scum. Soften mineral deposits on faucets by covering for several hours with a paper towel soaked in either. Make a window and mirror cleaner by mixing 1 part vinegar and 1 part water. This solution also works well on most wood floors finished with polyurethane.

CLEANING-PRODUCT GUIDELINES

☐ Always try the least-toxic products first before moving to something stronger. When cleaning the oven, for example, start with baking soda and water before using a commercial spray oven cleaner containing lye, which is highly corrosive.

☐ Buy only as much product as you plan to use within a month or two. Products can lose effectiveness if they sit for long periods.

☐ Keep products in their original containers so you'll always have access to instructions for effective use and safe disposal.

☐ Never mix cleaning products. Combining chlorine bleach with either ammonia or acidic products such as tub and tile cleaner, for example, results in deadly fumes. Mixing acidic and alkaline substances will mute the effect of both, as will mixing chlorine and oxygen bleaches. For this reason, you should always take care to thoroughly rinse surfaces after cleaning them.

☐ Always store cleaning products out of the reach of children and pets.

UNIVERSAL CLEAN KIT

For routine cleaning, less is more. You actually need very few products to clean any given room (too many can make your house smell like a hotel). Although there will certainly be instances where specialized cleaners are necessary, the list of products below will suffice for most tasks. Gather them in a caddy so you can transport them from room to room as you work.

☐ An all-purpose cleaner, such as Mrs. Meyer's, or a solution of 2 tablespoons mild dishwashing liquid, such as Ivory, and 2 cups water in a spray bottle

☐ A mildly abrasive cleanser, such as Bon Ami

☐ Glass cleaner, or a solution of 1 part white vinegar and 1 part water in a spray bottle

☐ Rubber gloves

☐ Lint-free white cloths

☐ Medium-bristled scrub brush

ROOM BY ROOM

EVERY HOME IS UNIQUE. Each one is a reflection of its era, its locale, and most significantly, the tastes and lifestyle of its occupants. Despite the differences, however, there are a host of cleaning and maintenance concerns particular to each room that never change. All kitchens, for example, share a primary function—the preparation of meals—which necessitates that surfaces, whether granite or ceramic tile, be kept immaculate. Similarly, although no two bedrooms look quite the same, each one promises retreat, comfort, and rest, which dictates that linens be laundered weekly to keep them fresh and welcoming. In the chapters that follow, each of which delves deeply into the care of a specific room or area of the house, these fundamentals are addressed, as are the specific techniques for cleaning the materials you're likely to encounter within each room—be it crystal in the dining room or porcelain enamel in the bathroom.

Deciding when and how often to clean each room depends on your habits, the size of your family, and your lifestyle. Once upon a time, the many tasks necessary for keeping a house clean adhered to a rigid schedule. Washing, ironing, dusting, and mopping were each undertaken on a prescribed day during the week, ensuring that cleanliness and order prevailed at all times. Today, given the many work and family obligations most of us have, creating a cleaning schedule can be a challenge. It's not impossible, though, with a little planning.

The first step to crafting a workable cleaning calendar is to define tasks that need to be accomplished weekly, monthly, on a seasonal basis (fall, winter, spring, and summer), and during an annual spring cleaning. Use the following lists as a general guideline, and tailor them as your lifestyle dictates—decreasing or increasing frequencies as needed. Creating a personal calendar—either manually or electronically—will give you a sense of control over what might otherwise seem overwhelming (doing so should also make it easier for everyone in the family to pitch in with housekeeping chores).

Once you have a list that suits you and your home, you can decide how to parcel out the tasks. You might find it easiest to set aside several hours one day a week to accomplish your weekly cleaning, or to do it in shorter bursts over several days each week. Once a month, devote a couple of extra hours to deep cleaning, such as vacuuming baseboards. And once a season, particularly in the spring, schedule several full days to attend to more-involved projects, such as washing windows, shampooing carpets, or cleaning out closets. Experiment until you find the system that works best for you. Keep in mind, too, that housework is a chore that, once done, allows for flexibility and enjoyment in other parts of daily life.

SIX THINGS TO DO EVERY DAY

Get into the habit of completing these basic tasks daily. With just a few minutes' work, you'll easily be able to keep chaos at bay.

① **MAKE THE BED**
Tidiness begets tidiness. A crisply made bed makes the whole room seem more orderly, which makes it less likely that you'll let other things—such as clothes and papers—pile up around it.

② **MANAGE CLUTTER**
Whenever you leave a room, take a quick look around for anything that isn't where it should be. Pick it up and put it where it belongs. Insist that everyone in the household do the same.

③ **SORT THE MAIL**
Take a few minutes to open, read, and sort mail as soon as you bring it inside. Keep a trash bin near your sorting area for junk mail. Drop other mail into one of four in-boxes: personal correspondence, bills, catalogs, and filing.

④ **CLEAN AS YOU COOK**
Instead of filling the sink with pots and dishes, wash them or put them in the dishwasher as you prepare a meal.

⑤ **WIPE UP SPILLS WHILE THEY'RE FRESH**
Whether it's tomato sauce on the cooktop or makeup on the bathroom counter, almost anything is faster and easier to remove if you attend to it immediately.

⑥ **SWEEP THE KITCHEN FLOOR**
Every evening once you've finished washing up after dinner, sweep the floor. This will keep tough-to-clean dirt and grime from building up, which will make the weekly mopping much quicker.

WEEKLY HOMEKEEPING

KITCHEN
- ☐ Wipe surfaces, including sink, countertops, the outside of the ventilation hood, refrigerator and cupboard doors, top of refrigerator, appliance exteriors, shelves, and furniture
- ☐ Wipe the inside of the oven, microwave, and toaster oven
- ☐ Flush drain with boiling water
- ☐ Discard foods and beverages past their prime
- ☐ Dust light fixtures
- ☐ Wipe the inside and outside of trash and recycling bins
- ☐ Vacuum and mop floor

DINING ROOM
- ☐ Dust surfaces and objects, including furniture and light fixtures
- ☐ Vacuum upholstery and floor

LIVING ROOM
- ☐ Fluff and rotate sofa cushions
- ☐ Discard magazines and catalogs on coffee or side tables; store those you want to keep
- ☐ Dust surfaces and objects, including furniture, light fixtures, and electronics
- ☐ Vacuum upholstery and floor

HOME OFFICE
- ☐ Sort through in-boxes: pay bills, file paid bills and paperwork
- ☐ Dust surfaces and objects, including furniture, light fixtures, and electronics
- ☐ Empty trash bin
- ☐ Vacuum floor

LIBRARY
- ☐ Dust the tops and spines of books, shelves, and light fixtures

ENTRYWAYS, STAIRS, AND HALLWAYS
- ☐ Dust staircase banisters, furniture, objects, and light fixtures
- ☐ Wipe mirrors
- ☐ Launder machine-washable throw rugs and runners
- ☐ Vacuum stairs and landings
- ☐ Vacuum and mop floors

BEDROOMS	☐ Change and launder sheets and pillowcases ☐ Fluff pillows and comforters ☐ Discard magazines and catalogs on side tables; store those you want to keep ☐ Dust surfaces, including furniture, objects, and light fixtures ☐ Empty trash bins ☐ Vacuum floors
BATHROOMS	☐ Clean toilets, bathtubs, showers, and sinks ☐ Wipe mirrors ☐ Change and launder bath mats, towels, and washcloths ☐ Dust light fixtures ☐ Empty trash bins and wipe the insides and outsides ☐ Vacuum and mop floors
THROUGHOUT THE HOUSE	☐ Wipe hand and pet prints from windows and glass doors ☐ Vacuum vents

MONTHLY HOMEKEEPING

KITCHEN
- ☐ Wash ventilation hood filters
- ☐ Discard food in the freezer that's past its prime

LIVING ROOM
- ☐ Vacuum fireplace screen

BEDROOMS
- ☐ Launder duvet covers, pillow protectors, mattress pads, and shams

BATHROOMS
- ☐ Wipe tub and shower surrounds
- ☐ Scrub grout
- ☐ Wipe insides of medicine cabinets

CLOSETS
- ☐ Dust shelves and storage bins
- ☐ Vacuum floors and baseboards

UTILITY SPACES
- ☐ Vacuum floors
- ☐ Wipe insides and outsides of trash and recycling bins

THROUGHOUT THE HOUSE
- ☐ Vacuum window treatments, moldings, and windowsills
- ☐ Dust portable and ceiling fans
- ☐ Wipe interior and exterior doors and trim
- ☐ Wipe switch plates
- ☐ Wipe telephones
- ☐ Flush drains with vinegar, boiling water, and baking soda
- ☐ Buff waxed stone, masonry, concrete, and wood floors

SEASONAL HOMEKEEPING

KITCHEN
- ☐ Replace baking soda in refrigerator and freezer
- ☐ Clean ovens
- ☐ Wipe kitchen ceiling
- ☐ Wipe the inside of the refrigerator
- ☐ Remove contents of cabinets and clean interiors
- ☐ Clean hanging pot rack and polish copper
- ☐ Organize pantry, discarding expired food

LIVING ROOM
- ☐ Sweep out fireplace
- ☐ Clean leather furniture

LIBRARY
- ☐ Rotate stacked books to prevent warping

BEDROOMS
- ☐ Turn mattresses
- ☐ Vacuum mattresses, box springs, and bed frames
- ☐ Launder pillows

THROUGHOUT THE HOUSE
- ☐ Wipe baseboards and moldings

SPRING HOMEKEEPING

KITCHEN
- ☐ Vacuum refrigerator grill and coil
- ☐ Wipe the inside of the freezer

LIVING ROOM
- ☐ Rotate heavy curtains, rugs, and throws for lightweight ones

BEDROOMS
- ☐ Replace cool-weather bedding with warm-weather bedding
- ☐ Launder or dry-clean blankets

BATHROOMS
- ☐ Discard expired cosmetics, beauty products, and medications

HOME OFFICE
- ☐ Clean out files
- ☐ Review and update insurance policies, contracts, and household inventories

CLOSETS
- ☐ Reorganize closets, giving away unwanted items
- ☐ Replace cool-weather clothing with warm-weather clothing

UTILITY SPACES
- ☐ Remove lint from the hose attached to the back of the clothes dryer
- ☐ Clean the attic and basement, giving away or discarding unwanted items
- ☐ Vacuum and mop attic and basement floors

OUTDOOR SPACES
- ☐ Scrub porch ceilings and walls
- ☐ Scrub porch floors, decks, patios, the driveway, and walkways
- ☐ Scrub outdoor furniture, umbrellas, and awnings
- ☐ Wash light-fixture covers
- ☐ Clean gutters

THROUGHOUT THE HOUSE	☐ Vacuum and wipe walls and ceilings ☐ Shampoo wall-to-wall carpets and area rugs with backings ☐ Send area rugs without backings out for professional cleaning ☐ Steam-clean upholstery ☐ Dust radiators ☐ Reseal stone surfaces ☐ Reseal grout ☐ Launder machine-washable window treatments ☐ Dry-clean non-machine-washable window treatments ☐ Take books off shelves, dust shelves and books ☐ Polish metal door and window hardware ☐ Oil window and door hinges ☐ Wax wood furniture ☐ Wax wood, stone, concrete, brick, and unglazed tile floors ☐ Strip and rewax vinyl and linoleum floors ☐ Wash windows and window screens ☐ Remove, wash, and store storm windows

AND IN THE FALL...

LIVING ROOM	☐ Rotate lightweight curtains, rugs, and throws for heavier ones
BEDROOMS	☐ Replace warm-weather bedding with cool-weather bedding ☐ Launder or dry-clean blankets
CLOSETS	☐ Replace warm-weather clothing with cool-weather clothing
OUTDOOR SPACES	☐ Scrub porch ceilings and walls ☐ Scrub porch floors, decks, patios, the driveway, and walkways ☐ Scrub outdoor furniture, umbrellas, and awnings ☐ Wash light-fixture covers ☐ Clean gutters

THE KITCHEN AT BEDFORD

KITCHEN

MORE AND MORE, LIFE AT HOME revolves around the kitchen—to me, it's the most inviting, interesting, and important room in the house. I love gathering people in my kitchen to talk, eat, drink cappuccino, and even cook with me. In every home I have ever had, the kitchen has been the center of activity, the place where people naturally tend to congregate. It comes as no surprise, at least to me, that the kitchen is usually the first room to undergo renovation after a new home is purchased, and that it's the room with more homekeeping concerns than any other.

My parents' original kitchen in New Jersey had just a tiny cooking area, a breakfast nook, and a pantry. It was cramped, with little light, and as a family we had long outgrown it before we renovated it eleven years after moving into the house. I have remodeled many kitchens since then, paying close attention to all the fine details, building upon the knowledge I gained during that original remodeling job, which we carried out with painstaking care and a very limited budget. We took every single inch of space into account, and considered many possible kinds of cabinetry and hardware. That renovated kitchen became even more the center stage for our family life. It was where we sat down to eat, do our homework, play games, and share important moments, such as opening acceptance letters from colleges. The kitchen was light and bright, as are my memories of it.

In the thirty years I lived in my Federal farmhouse on Turkey Hill Road in Westport, Connecticut, the kitchen was renovated twice. There was our original renovation when we first moved in, and a more recent remodeling, when the original pine floors actually began to wear out. That initial renovation was historic for me. It was the first real kitchen I designed, and my husband built it. The cupboards were handmade of sycamore wood, cut from our town in the Berkshires, and there were two small work islands. I chose a commercial Garland range, installed beneath a copper hood that we made ourselves, and set the kitchen table near the existing 1805 fireplace, which had an adjacent beehive oven. I hung wicker baskets from the exposed wooden ceiling joists, and the result was homey, warm, and friendly.

KITCHEN STOOLS AT SKYLANDS, MY HOUSE IN MAINE, ACCOMMODATE GUESTS OF VARIOUS HEIGHTS.

The newer version is much lighter and more organized. I added beautifully made double skylights, and many glass-fronted cupboards framed in fine poplar wood stained white. The new floors are pumpkin pine, installed to match the rest of the house. (Actually, the pine was a mistake. That wood is too soft for a kitchen, and is already wearing thin.) The cupboard doors are glazed with restoration glass, some clear, some pale green. The exposed joists were covered with a plaster ceiling, and now, instead of baskets overhead, copper pots hang from a large rectangular rack. The new work counter is honed marble, and so is the new kitchen table, which seats eight. It is not a large kitchen, but it functions much more smoothly, and, finally, I have drawers and cupboards for all the "stuff."

The kitchen is above all a place to celebrate the rituals of cooking and eating.

Not long ago, I moved to a new place in Bedford, New York; I live in a restored 1925 "fancy" farmhouse. I was able to incorporate everything that I've learned before into a wonderful new kitchen. It is large and light, and virtually everything in it—the open shelving for my dishes and glasses, the bases of the islands and table, the walls and woodwork—is painted a color called Bedford Grey that was inspired by a piece of Italian stationery I fell in love with. There are lots of lovely details, such as cabinet fronts embellished with specially dyed (Bedford Grey, of course) sycamore veneer, white marble countertops, and beautiful old white marble floors. But it is the color, the rich, neutral hue, that makes the biggest impression. It makes the kitchen feel calm, no matter how many tasks are being performed.

A kitchen is a working room, after all, and I designed this one to be especially efficient and welcoming. The room is planned around stations, or zones, for specific tasks, such as baking, prepping ingredients for cooking, even making a really good cappuccino. I still have pots and pans suspended from a rack over the island (now they are stainless steel), and all my other supplies and ingredients are similarly accessible, well organized in cupboards, in large refrigerators with glass doors, and in a small adjacent room known as the servery. This intimate space also happens to be where guests tend to gather to sip a glass of wine, or sit on stools, when I prepare dinner.

For a kitchen table, I am partial to a counter-height surface with stools to sit on—that's what I have at Skylands, my house in Maine, and now in Bedford, too. The extralong marble-topped table in Bedford is an excellent spot for an informal meal, with friends or on my own. I also use it for working, for crafting, for reading—just about anything. Whether it's a small counter with a couple of stools, a little breakfast nook, or a full-size table, a comfortable place to sit and to eat and to talk is so important in any kitchen.

OPEN CROCKS FILLED WITH KITCHEN UTENSILS—WOODEN SPOONS, PASTRY BRUSHES, WHISKS, AND MORE—KEEP EVERYTHING TOGETHER AND ACCESSIBLE.

LAYOUT BASICS

Four basic layouts dictate the design of most kitchens: the one-wall or galley, the corridor (which has counters and/or cupboards along two walls), the L-shape, and the U-shape. Regardless of the layout, every kitchen needs space for each of the functions that take place within it: storing food, tableware, flatware, cookware, and utensils; mixing and preparing food; cooking; cleaning up; and eating, if space allows it.

Kitchens function best when there are at least 36 inches between the most frequently used surfaces, such as kitchen islands and countertops, for example. Aisles are most comfortable when they are 42 inches wide or, if more than one person cooks at a time, 48 inches wide. For the sake of safety and comfort, you should have easy access to appliances and cupboards, minimal steps between work areas, and few large spaces to navigate. Many design professionals rely on recommendations from the National Kitchen and Bath Association (NKBA), some of which are noted below. Keep these in mind if remodeling or building anew.

WORK AREA DIMENSIONS

THE FOOD STORAGE AREA
The refrigerator is generally the main food storage area, and requires between 15 and 18 inches of counter space just next to it (the handle side, if applicable), to hold grocery bags and other foods you're preparing to store.

THE PREPARATION AREA
For the myriad tasks required to prepare meals—chopping, stirring, mixing, and more—$3\frac{1}{2}$ to 7 feet of counter space, with all of the necessary tools, including pans, bowls, and cooking utensils nearby, is ideal. Counters should be 24 inches deep, with a minimum of 15 inches of clearance below cabinets or shelving. If you wish to add a serving center, you will want another 3 to 7 feet of free counter space for bowls, trays, and other serve ware.

THE COOKING AREA
A range or cooktop requires at least 12 inches of counter space on one side, and 15 to 24 inches on the other side, as a landing space for hot pots and pans. Make sure that a microwave oven has at least 15 to 18 inches of counter space on the right side, assuming the door is hinged on the left side, for the same purpose.

THE CLEANUP AREA
It's best to allow 18 to 30 inches on one side and 4 to $4\frac{1}{2}$ feet on the other side of the sink to stack the things that need washing or rinsing. If you have a dishwasher, give yourself plenty of room—at least 20 inches from the front edge of the open dishwasher door to the nearest surface—for easy access.

THE EATING AREA (OPTIONAL)
Allow 3 feet or more between a dining table and the nearest wall, to allow enough room to pull chairs away comfortably. Leave at least $3\frac{1}{2}$ feet between any counter edge and the dining table. A dining nook functions better if it's accessible from both sides of the table, so that the first one in doesn't have to be the last one out. A bar counter with stools should have a comfortable overhead—a foot or more to function well. And stools should be of comfortable height for each family member, so that everyone can perch and still eat, or drink, or read and write.

DINING NOOKS

A breakfast nook is a charming addendum to any kitchen, cozy and personal. The first nooks to appear in the United States were in houses influenced by the Arts and Crafts Movement of the late-nineteenth and early-twentieth centuries, which popularized built-in furniture. Thanks to Sears, Roebuck and Co. and other companies that sold many thousands of prefabricated house-building kits by mail, nooks were commonplace by the mid-thirties. A breakfast nook—usually comprising two settles (enclosed benches) flanking a table at a window between the dining room and the kitchen—made the morning meal more convenient for the American housewife. But the nook beckoned all day long, and so it often became the nerve center of a house. Over time many nooks were lost to kitchen modernization, but they are still welcome features in any space.

THE KITCHEN TRIANGLE

Many kitchen layouts are based upon the work triangle, referring to the configuration of range or cooktop, refrigerator, and sink. If you decide, when building or renovating a kitchen, to create such a triangle, make sure that the total of all three legs measures no more than 26 feet, with each leg measuring between 4 and 9 feet (measure from the center-front of each surface). Also, avoid having any leg of the triangle intersect any other kitchen area, such as an island, by more than 12 inches. This arrangement ensures easy, comfortable access and saves steps when preparing, cooking, and serving meals.

KITCHEN CLEANING BASICS

Basic kitchen and cleaning supplies include the following:

- ☐ Mild dishwashing liquid
- ☐ All-purpose household cleaner
- ☐ Mild abrasive cleanser
- ☐ Baking soda
- ☐ White vinegar
- ☐ Glass cleaner

- ☐ Fresh sponges and older, used sponges for cleaning the oven
- ☐ A supply of soft, clean white cloths
- ☐ Kitchen brushes (pot and pan scrubbers and bottlebrushes)
- ☐ Rubber gloves

- ☐ Stainless steel, copper, and aluminum cleaners/polish
- ☐ Scouring pads (white nylon, the least abrasive, and green nylon, which is more abrasive, for tough jobs)
- ☐ Paper towels
- ☐ Microfiber cloths
- ☐ Toothbrush

KITCHEN CLEANING KIT

Cleanliness is not just a virtue in this most frequented of rooms, but a necessity. The storage, preparation, and serving of food demand the highest standards of neatness and order. Keeping this room pristine, of course, demands old-fashioned elbow grease. But some simple organization will make the task much easier.

Start by corralling cleaning supplies (see the list of basics, opposite) in a bin or a bucket, and store them in a cupboard under or near the sink. To protect the floor of the cupboard, line it with parchment paper or rubber matting from the hardware store and replace or clean it as necessary.

ORGANIZING

There is no single right way to order a kitchen; the trick lies in finding the way that works most efficiently for you. Employing the basic organizing concepts below can help you tailor a system to suit your needs and practices. A well-organized kitchen will make meal preparation—and planning—easier and more enjoyable. If your cupboards are filled to overflowing or you frequently have to rummage through drawers to find things, it's time to impose order. Here's how:

GOLDEN RULES OF KITCHEN ORGANIZATION

1. Store things where you use them. Pots and pans are best kept near the range or cooktop; mixing bowls near the countertop you use for food preparation; plates, glasses, and flatware near the dishwasher.

2. Group like items together—store all bakeware in the same cupboard, all wooden spoons in the same ceramic crock, all spices in the same drawer.

3. Store your most frequently used items in the most accessible places. Keep things you use most often at eye level; store heavy items below waist level and infrequently used items on high shelves (keep a step stool within easy reach for such items) or in another area of the house. For example, if you use your oversized turkey platter only once a year, you don't need to store it in the kitchen at all. Instead, stow it on a high shelf in the garage or basement.

4. Declutter yearly. Take an inventory of all utensils, cookware, and dishware annually. Get rid of unnecessary duplicates, items that are damaged beyond repair, or things no longer used.

5. Keep small kitchen items in containers, see-through bins if possible, with neat, easy-to-read labels.

CABINETS

There are three types of kitchen cabinets: wall (or upper) cabinets, base (or lower) cabinets, and pantry (or tall) cabinets. To function well, a kitchen should contain the following:

☐ Spacious wall and base cabinets. Aim for at least 50 square feet of storage. With many models of cabinetry, this means about 6 feet of wall and base cabinets.

☐ Generous drawer space. You'll want at least one drawer per base cabinet and at least 11 square feet of storage.

☐ Wall and base cabinets in the preparation area, for cutting boards, mixing bowls, and other utensils

☐ Base cabinets in the cooking area, for pots and pans (if not on a rack)

☐ Wall or base cabinets in the eating area, for serving pieces and table linens

☐ A base cabinet under the kitchen sink, known as a sink base cabinet (see below), for cleaning tools and supplies

☐ At least one separate wall, base, or tall cabinet designated as a pantry, to hold food items (for more on the pantry, turn to page 128).

STANDARD KITCHEN CABINET SIZES

WALL CABINETS
These are 12 inches deep and 12 to 36 inches high. Widths range from 9 to 48 inches; cabinets are manufactured in 3-inch increments. The most common widths are 12, 15, and 18 inches.

PANTRY CABINETS
These are 12 to 24 inches deep and 84, 90, or 96 inches high. Widths range from 9 to 36 inches; cabinets are manufactured in 3-inch increments.

BASE CABINETS
These are 24 inches deep and 34½ inches high. With a counter installed on top, a standard base cabinet is 36 inches high. Depending on your height, you might choose to install the countertop higher or lower. Widths range from 9 inches to 48 inches; cabinets are manufactured in 3-inch increments. There are four types of base cabinets:

Standard Base
This common type of cabinet has a shallow drawer above a door, with shelves inside for storage.

Drawer Base
With three or four drawers, this cabinet is useful for organizing and storing utensils and other small items.

Sink Base
A sink base may have one false drawer or a small tilt-out drawer for sponges and cleaning supplies, with doors and an open storage area below.

Corner Base
Made just for corners, this cabinet often has a lazy Susan inside to make it easier to access items.

CABINET ACCESSORIES

Storage capacity can be significantly increased in any cabinet with the use of simple accessories. Housewares stores are teeming with racks, bins, and baskets designed to use every square inch of space.

BASKETS AND BINS
Use them to contain small items that might otherwise create clutter, such as spices, dish towels, or cleaning supplies.

DRAWER ORGANIZERS
Divide flatware or utensils within drawers. Arrange separate components to fill a drawer or look for expandable one-piece units.

LAZY SUSANS
These multitier turntables are handy for organizing condiments, spices, or vitamins and can make the most of corner base cabinets and storage spaces.

PULL-OUT BASKETS
Install plastic or wire baskets on gliders in base cabinets to ease access to pots, pans, or cleaning products.

SPICE RACKS
Contain spice bottles on wire racks that sit in wall cabinets, fit into drawers, or are mounted on walls.

STACKING SHELVES
Utilize cabinets top to bottom by placing plastic-coated wire shelves in between shelves to double storage capacity.

STORAGE STRATEGIES

It's not the amount of room you have that matters, but how you manage it. Saucers are often stacked, for example, and then topped with piles of cups, which simply don't pile up very well. The result is a lot of unused space. Instead, store cups and saucers the same way they are used: saucer, cup, saucer, cup. They not only look better but also can be safely stacked higher, and when you pull out a cup and saucer, they are ready for use. Here are other ideas to help you make the most of the space you have:

BOWLS, POTS, AND PANS

Nest them to conserve space. Place paper plates or sheets of paper towels in between layers to prevent scratching (use nonabsorbent coated paper plates between cast-iron pans, which tend to retain traces of oil).

FRAGILE TRAYS AND PLATTERS

Stack them by size, with the biggest ones on the bottom and the smallest on top. Leave a few inches between stacks to avoid the possibility of chipping pieces when pulling them out and putting them back. Stack like shapes together—round platters in one stack, oblong platters in another. You can also lean platters against the back wall of a cabinet (secure them using rubber bumpers) and stack plates in front.

NONBREAKABLE FLAT ITEMS

Store cutting boards and baking pans upright, by installing tension rods vertically between shelves.

GLASSWARE, DINNERWARE, AND SERVING PIECES

Group by pattern, collection, or function—for example, all transferware in one group and Fiesta ware in another, or everyday glasses on one shelf with special-occasion stemware on another. Stack no more than four to six plates together (anything that has been repaired should always be kept on the top, or not stacked at all) and store glasses upright to protect rims.

UTENSILS

Group wooden utensils in one crock, stainless-steel ones in another. Line up crocks next to the cooktop, for easy access.

CABINET CARE

Of course, it's as important to keep cabinets tidy as it is to be well organized. Because kitchen cabinets are placed precisely where some of the messiest work in the home occurs, they soon show the effects of grease, food spills, and moisture.

   To minimize dirt and grime on the inside of cabinets (and protect dishes and glassware), always line shelves and drawers: easily replaced parchment paper for the cabinet under the sink, for example, and vinyl board cover liners (made of a resilient rubbery substance) in the knife drawer to help keep the knives from sliding. Here are other liners and their uses:

KITCHEN SHELVING
A busy kitchen needs shelves for cookbooks and narrow shelving for often-used spices, oils, and condiments (don't store these items over a cooktop, however, as heat can cause oil to turn rancid and herbs and spices to lose their flavor). Items that are used less frequently, or are intended for display, can be placed on shelves over a window or doorway, about 1½ feet below the ceiling, or almost anywhere else where you can find a bit of spare space. Be sure to measure anything you intend to stow on shelves before building or installing them to ensure they're the correct depths.

TYPES OF SHELF AND DRAWER LINERS

ADHESIVE
The traditional inexpensive adhesive plastic shelf liner is difficult to handle and remove. (See instructions for removing, below.) Look for low-tack versions.

CEDAR
Because of the repellent properties of cedar, natural cedar liners are suitable for storage areas where pantry moths and other insects can be a concern, such as where you keep spices, dry goods, or kitchen linens.

CORK
Available in rolls several feet in length, cork provides a resilient surface that cushions fragile items such as glassware. It also resists mold and mildew.

FELT
Line drawers containing silver and silver-plate flatware with felt that has been treated with antitarnishing agents.

RUBBER
Resilient and nonslip, rubber grips small items to hold them in place. Because it contains sulfur, which causes corrosion, however, it is not a good choice for drawers containing silverware.

HOW TO REMOVE ADHESIVE SHELF LINERS

There are several solvents that will dissolve shelf-liner adhesive. From mild to strong, these include rubber-cement remover, acetone, and turpentine. Start with a mild product; if it doesn't work, move to something more potent. Carefully pull up a corner of the liner with a paint scraper or razor blade. With a natural-bristle paintbrush, dab solvent beneath the paper while tugging on the corner. Working quickly, continue brushing and pulling until the liner comes off. You may need to use a scraper to peel back the liner, but keep in mind that this can gouge the surface of the shelf. Once you have removed the liner, sand any remaining adhesive with a fine- to medium-grit sandpaper.

If you're not able to lift the liner using the technique above, try paint stripper. Apply it to the entire surface of the liner using a paintbrush, and leave it on for about half an hour (follow the manufacturer's instructions); use a scraper to loosen the liner. Wipe residual stripper off the surface with a damp sponge, then sand.

When using any solvent, work in a well-ventilated area and safeguard the surrounding surfaces by taping down kraft paper. (If you are working with paint stripper, use plastic drop cloths.) Cross-ventilate the area by opening all doors and windows. Wear goggles and chemical-resistant gloves, and never work near a source of high heat, sparks, or flames, such as a clothes dryer or gas stove.

HOW TO CLEAN CABINET HARDWARE

Grime builds up quickly on cabinet doors, especially around handles, and that buildup can be particularly stubborn. Typically, though, a good cleaning with mild dishwashing liquid and water, as part of your regular routine, is all that's required to undo the damage and prevent further buildup.

The best way to clean tough grime, however, is to remove the hardware itself. Unscrew it, and soak it in warm, soapy water for thirty minutes (while you wipe down the cabinets); scrub lightly with a soft brush if necessary. Let hardware dry completely before replacing it.

HOW TO CLEAN GLASS-FRONT CABINETS

Wipe glass with a solution of 1 part white vinegar to 1 part warm water, or any cleaning products designed for glass, carefully following the manufacturer's instructions. Never use abrasive cleaning tools or sponges, which could scratch or dull the finish.

HOW TO CLEAN CABINET BOXES AND DOORS

For all cabinets, the approach you take will depend largely on the material, although gentle treatment is best. As part of your weekly cleaning routine, wipe cabinet exteriors with a soft, damp cloth or a damp microfiber cloth. Try a mixture of several drops of mild dishwashing liquid in a bucket of warm water, applied with a soft cloth or sponge, before working your way up to anything stronger. For stubborn stains, wipe with an undiluted all-purpose cleaner. Whatever product you use, always read the label carefully, follow all instructions, and test a small area inside a door—where any mishaps will be inconspicuous—before tackling the fronts of your cabinets. Rinse surfaces thoroughly with a clean, damp cloth after washing. To avoid streaking, dry with a clean, absorbent cloth.

At the beginning of each season, clean the insides of cabinets, first removing everything within, including liners if possible; wipe interior sur-

---

GOLDEN RULES OF CABINET CARE

1. Always spray or apply cleaners to a damp cloth rather than the cabinets themselves.

2. Never use abrasive cleansers or scouring pads or other abrasive tools, which can permanently dull finishes.

3. Avoid products containing silicone, which can damage finishes.

4. Avoid cleaning products that are strongly alkaline (such as ammonia) or acidic (such as basin, tub, and tile cleaners) or chlorine bleach, all of which can damage finishes.

5. Avoid polishes containing petroleum solvents, which are toxic and flammable.

6. Avoid furniture spray polishes and creams and products containing wax, which can cause a buildup of film.

7. Never hang wet dish towels over the door of a sink or other base cabinet, which can cause permanent water damage.

8. Protect cabinets from heat damage by removing drawers and doors of cabinets adjacent to or above the oven when using the oven's self-cleaning feature.

faces with the mild dishwashing liquid solution mentioned above. After washing, wipe interiors well with a clean, damp cloth. Dry completely with a clean absorbent cloth before replacing liners and the cabinets' contents. For specific care guidelines for cabinets, by material, see the chart below.

CABINET MATERIALS AND THEIR CARE

The four most common cabinet materials are wood, laminate, thermofoil, and stainless steel. General care is the same for all, but treatments of scratches and stains differ for each.

WOOD

Cabinets can be made of many different wood varieties, including maple, birch, and cherry. Often, cabinet boxes and doors are covered in a veneer bonded to lesser-quality woods or medium-density fiberboard rather than being made of solid wood. Wood cabinets are usually finished with either a tough, clear coating that seals and protects the wood or a painted finish.

Special Considerations Do not apply oil to sealed or painted wood cabinets. The oil will not penetrate the finish and will attract dust and grime. Camouflage superficial scratches with shoe polish or a wax fill stick designed for repairing furniture in a color that matches the original finish. Deep scratches will necessitate refinishing.

LAMINATE (ALSO KNOWN AS MELAMINE)

Made of layers of kraft paper impregnated with plastic, laminate veneers are generally bonded to wood or medium-density fiberboard to create cabinet boxes and doors.

Special Considerations Stains on laminates with a matte and granular texture can be treated with a paste of baking soda and water to draw the stain out. Do not rub, as baking soda is abrasive. Do not use baking soda on laminates with a glossy texture. Camouflage superficial scratches using a repair kit made specifically for laminate cabinets, available at home centers or from cabinet retailers. Deep scratches cannot be repaired; you will need to replace the cabinet door.

THERMOFOIL

This is made of medium-density fiberboard coated with a layer of vinyl. Unlike laminate cabinet doors, which are generally flat, thermofoil cabinet doors often have raised- or recessed-panel designs. Because the vinyl layer is extremely thin, it can be bonded to more intricate shapes than laminate can.

Special Considerations Camouflage superficial scratches using a repair kit made specifically for thermofoil cabinets, available at home centers or from cabinet retailers. Deep scratches cannot be repaired; you will need to replace the cabinet door.

STAINLESS STEEL

Made of an alloy of steel and chromium, stainless-steel veneers are bonded to wood or medium-density fiberboard to create cabinet boxes and doors.

Special Considerations Always wipe in the same direction as the grain. Water stains can be treated with a commercial stainless-steel spray. Stainless steel with a smooth finish shows water marks and fingerprints more than stainless with a brushed finish. Although stainless is durable, it will scratch and dent. Superficial scratches can be polished out with a light-duty (white) nylon pad. It's essential that you polish with the grain; polishing against it will create more damage. Dents are usually not repairable; you will need to replace the entire cabinet door.

COUNTERTOPS

A generous expanse of counter is essential for preparing food, keeping dishes and platters at the ready, and housing small appliances used every day. Keep counters clear and clutter-free, and always work neatly, wiping up spills and messes as they happen. Use the least accessible counter space for storage first. If upper cabinets are positioned over only one section of the counter, then you will be unlikely to chop in that limited space, which makes it better for storage than a wide-open stretch of counter.

Keep the small appliances you use regularly, such as a coffeemaker, a toaster, and a standing mixer, on countertops. Group like items together; arrange the coffeemaker, toaster, and a tray of breakfast condiments together, for example, to create a breakfast station. Stow the small appliances you use only periodically, such as the waffle iron, in cabinets.

Set up a countertop workstation near your cooktop. The tools you will reach for again and again—wooden spoons, spatulas, ladles, and so on— should be nearby, separated by type and stored in crocks or glass jars. You can also arrange small bottles of olive oil, vinegar, and bowls of salts and peppers on a tray that is easy to move from place to place and will contain spills and drips. (Larger bottles of oil and vinegar should be stored in a cool, dark place, and used to replenish the smaller containers as needed.) Similarly, set up a "sink station" by placing sponges, brushes, and soaps on small plates, which can be easily moved to clean underneath them, and the contents can be regularly removed to clean the plates themselves. Decant liquid dishwashing detergent into an attractive glass bottle, such as a cruet or an unusual flea-market find, and attach a pour spout. Buy detergent in bulk, and refill the glass bottle as needed. Wipe the spout and bottle after you pour any soap out of it, to keep the spout clog-free and the bottle from getting slippery. Or use a plain plastic squeeze bottle, which won't break. Keep hand soap in a dish to protect your sink. Or, use liquid hand soap in its own dispenser; there's no gummy soap dish to clean. Keep nylon scrubbing pads rinsed and dry in a metal or glass dish. Designate one small crock for brushes and scrubbers. Vegetable brushes and scrub brushes must be washed and rinsed after use.

The wall area between the countertop and the upper cabinets, known as the backsplash, can also provide extra storage space. Consider installing a rail with hooks or a pegboard to hold frequently used gadgets that can get lost in a drawer. Situate electrical outlets—which for safety's sake should be grounded three-prong outlets—along the backsplash to accommodate small appliances (on islands, outlets are generally installed below the countertop).

KEEPING A COUNTERTOP TRAY FILLED WITH SEASONINGS—INCLUDING A VARIETY OF SALTS AND GROUND PEPPER— ELIMINATES THE NEED TO GO BACK AND FORTH TO THE CABINET WHILE COOKING.

SMALL DISHES HOLD SOAPS AND SPONGES BY THE SINK, AND DISHWASHING LIQUID IS DECANTED INTO A PRETTY GLASS BOTTLE WITH A POUR SPOUT.

CUTTING BOARDS

It's a good idea to get in the habit of using cutting boards every time you prepare food. They go a long way toward keeping countertops clean and long-lasting. There are, however, a few things to keep in mind about the boards themselves, especially in terms of food safety.

While wooden boards are ideal for slicing (and even serving) bread and cheese, the USDA recommends nonporous plastic boards for cutting raw meat or poultry because they are easier to sanitize than wooden boards. (Although glass boards are also nonporous, avoid them as they can ruin knives.)

At a minimum, designate one board for fresh produce and another for raw meat, poultry, and seafood. This will prevent cross-contamination. Keep the guidelines on the following page in mind as well.

NOTES ABOUT CUTTING BOARDS

Carving meat
Choose a board with a channel running around the perimeter to prevent meat juices from spilling onto the countertop.

Slicing bread
Dedicate a separate wooden board for this task. Serrated bread knives tend to create deep grooves, which can make the surface uneven and difficult to use for other tasks.

Chopping onions and garlic
Reserve a separate plastic or wooden board for this task so garlic and onion flavors, which tend to linger, don't transfer to other foods.

CUTTING BOARD SAFETY

The number one safety concern regarding cutting boards is cross-contamination, which happens when bacteria such as *E. coli* is transferred from meat to raw foods, such as lettuce or tomatoes, by way of a cutting board or work surface. Both wood and plastic boards are generally safe if used and maintained properly—that is, cleaned after every use.

THE GOLDEN RULES OF CUTTING BOARD CARE

1 After each use, wash plastic boards in the dishwasher. Clean wooden boards with hot water and mild dishwashing liquid; dry completely. Scrub them periodically with coarse salt, a natural abrasive, and lemon juice, which kills odors and has bleaching properties. Rinse well with a clean, damp cloth after cleaning with lemon juice, as the acid can damage wood. Do not put wooden boards in the dishwasher or soak them; they can crack, split, and develop mold.

2 To keep wooden boards from drying out, rub them with food-safe mineral oil, which can be found in hardware and home-supply stores. Oil brand-new boards once a week for a month, then every month for a year, or whenever the wood feels parched. Rub the oil in with fine steel wool and wipe off the excess after five minutes.

3 Once cutting boards develop deep scratches, hard-to-clean grooves, or cracks—all of which can harbor bacteria—replace them.

MOBILE KITCHEN CARTS

If you're short on counter space, consider a mobile kitchen cart. Department and kitchen-supply stores carry a variety of styles, sizes, and price ranges. Look for a cart with wheels that are easy to maneuver, have a locking option, and won't damage your floors. Consider whether the extra surface space will be used for food preparation, storage, or as a serving area whenever necessary. The top, at work height, which is usually about 36 inches from the floor, should be made of a material that complements your countertops, whether stainless steel, butcher block, or tile.

HOW TO CARE FOR COUNTERTOPS

The care recommended for countertops and backsplashes differs according to the material (turn to pages 48–53 for specifics). If you give these hard-working surfaces the appropriate care, they will serve you well for years.

☐ Never cut directly on countertops, no matter what the material. Use cutting boards instead.

☐ Protect countertops, even heat-resistant stone ones, from hot pots and pans. Burn marks are permanent on most surfaces. Always use trivets (with rubber feet to prevent scratches) or insulating pads under hot pots and pans.

☐ Wipe up spills immediately with a clean, damp cloth, and treat stains as soon thereafter as possible—the faster you address them, the more successful you will be in removing them.

☐ Place coasters under glasses and bottles (including cooking oil bottles) to prevent ring marks, particularly on stone surfaces, from which they can be difficult to remove.

☐ Never pound or tenderize meat directly on countertops; the impact from a metal or even wooden mallet may gouge or crack countertops, particularly laminate ones. Always pound on top of a cutting board.

☐ Avoid strongly abrasive scouring powders and cleaning tools, such as steel wool, which will scratch almost any surface. Mildly abrasive cleansers, such as Bon Ami, and nylon pads should be used sparingly; if countertops have a polished finish, they should not be used at all.

THE KITCHEN HAS
BECOME THE MODERN HUB OF MY HOME,
AND IT IS CERTAINLY
WHERE I SPEND MOST OF MY TIME.

A CORNER OF THE KITCHEN AT SKYLANDS

COUNTERTOP MATERIALS

BUTCHER BLOCK

Maple and oak butcher blocks are the most common woods for countertops, although other hardwoods such as cherry, walnut, and mahogany are also used. Rock maple is traditional for chopping surfaces because it is hard yet won't damage knife blades. Butcher-block counters are available in several configurations: as wide planks (also called flat-grain) or narrow strips glued together, or end-grain butcher block, made from hundreds of small wood squares laminated together. Wide planks are more apt to warp than narrow strips or end-grain blocks. Butcher block is finished with either mineral oil or polyurethane. Mineral oil prevents the wood from warping and drying out, but will not prevent stains. Polyurethane provides an impenetrable plasticlike coating.

HOW TO CLEAN

Wipe with a damp cloth and mild dishwashing liquid. Rinse well with a clean, damp cloth. A cloth dampened with fresh lemon juice or white vinegar may remove or lighten stains, and deodorize a surface finished with mineral oil.

Pros Easy to maintain; can be sanded and reoiled or resealed as needed; looks warm.

Cons Prone to water and stain damage; must be oiled or sealed periodically to prevent drying out and reduce porosity; burns easily and absorbs odors.

Do Apply polyurethane to counters around the sink, since moisture causes wood to crack and split.

Don't use vegetable or olive oils to treat wood, as they can turn rancid; use only food-grade mineral oil.

Periodic Maintenance Once a month, or when oiled countertops begin to look dry, reapply oil (never oil butcher block that has been sealed with polyurethane). Place a bottle of food-grade (nontoxic) mineral oil into a bowl of hot (not boiling) water, then rub a generous amount of oil onto the surface with a soft, clean cloth, working with the grain; reapply after the wood soaks up the oil. Continue until the wood stops absorbing oil. Wipe off excess oil, then let the countertops dry for at least six hours or, ideally, overnight, before using.

Repair/Restore Badly scratched or stained counters can be sanded smooth, then treated with oil or polyurethane. Use a fine-grit sandpaper (grade 220 to remove stains and 400 to smooth), sanding with the grain of the wood, before reapplying a finish.

CERAMIC TILE

Ceramic tiles are made from a variety of materials and methods, and offer a range of design possibilities. The most common, traditional glazed tile, is made from clay fired at extremely high temperatures. Its tough, glasslike surface is nonporous, although the grout that holds the tile in place is extremely porous.

HOW TO CLEAN

Wipe with a damp cloth and mild dishwashing liquid. Rinse well with a clean, damp cloth. Tackle tough stains with a mildly abrasive cleanser such as Bon Ami and a soft cloth or a paste of baking soda and water. Grout can be cleaned with nontoxic oxygen bleach, then lightly scrubbed and rinsed.

Pros Available in many colors, textures, and prices; glazed tile doesn't stain; resists heat and moisture.

Cons Uneven counter surface; installation requires time and attention to detail; tiles can easily chip, scratch, or crack; grout stains easily; tough on dishware and glasses.

Do Consider dark grout when installing tile, as it will show fewer stains than a light one. Treat grout with a sealer to reduce porosity.

Don't use vinegar or anything acidic as a cleaner. It can damage the glaze and harm grout.

Periodic Maintenance Seal grout twice a year with a penetrating grout sealer.

Repair/Restore Damaged tiles can be replaced by a professional tile installer.

CONCRETE

To create countertops, concrete is mixed with pigment, then poured into molds on-site, or precast in a workshop. After it is troweled smooth, it takes several days to dry and harden; it must then be sealed to guard against stains. Concrete counters can be as thick as desired, although anything more than 4 inches could strain supporting cabinets and floors.

HOW TO CLEAN

Wipe with a damp cloth and mild dishwashing liquid. Rinse well with a clean, damp cloth. Although a sealer offers protection, spills still must be wiped up immediately with a damp cloth or sponge to prevent staining. Acidic foods and cleaners will etch the surface; cooking oil will leave a mark. Use coasters to prevent ring marks.

Pros Heat- and scratch-resistant; can be tinted in a wide range of colors; can be molded into different shapes to accommodate integral sinks, drain boards, and decorative edging.

Cons Expensive and heavy; cracking is common; because it is very porous, it stains if not well sealed; tough on dishware and glasses.

Do Reapply sealer when drops of water no longer bead on the surface.

Don't use abrasive pads or cleaners, which can abrade the sealer, making staining more likely.

Periodic Maintenance A coat of food-safe paste wax (available from some concrete installers and online retailers), applied on top of the sealer, can add an additional layer of protection.

Repair/Restore Hairline cracks are just part of the aging process. Repairing more serious damage depends on the size of the damaged area. Small chips might be repairable; larger ones might necessitate countertop replacement. Either way, consult a contractor; concrete repairs are not do-it-yourself jobs.

ENGINEERED STONE

This relatively new countertop material is a composite of rock aggregate (which makes up 90 percent of its mass), resin, and pigments. Engineered stone is sold under brand names including Zodiaq and Silestone. Available in dozens of colors, it is nonporous and scratch-resistant. The most common (and most durable) engineered stone is made from quartz particles. Because these stones do not contain fissures or veins, the strength of a slab may be more consistent throughout than that of a natural stone. That consistency also makes seams easy to match.

HOW TO CLEAN

Wipe with a damp cloth and mild dishwashing liquid. Rinse with a clean, damp cloth.

Pros Easy to maintain; resistant to stains, heat, scratches, and acid; sealing is generally not required; color consistent throughout, so scratches are less noticeable than with other materials.

Cons Expensive; less natural-looking than marble or granite.

Don't clean with chlorine bleach or products containing chlorine bleach, which can mar the color of the stone.

Periodic Maintenance None.

Repair/Restore Any damage must be repaired by a countertop professional; consult an engineered-stone installer for advice.

COUNTERTOP MATERIALS (CONTINUED)

GRANITE

A popular countertop choice because of its appearance and durability, granite is a siliceous stone made from an extremely hard volcanic rock. It is available in a range of colors and is often flecked with bits of minerals that produce a salt-and-pepper look. There are two types: consistent, which has the same pattern throughout, and variegated, which has veins.

HOW TO CLEAN

Dust once or twice a week with a soft cloth, and wipe periodically with a cloth dampened in warm water and a bit of pH-neutral cleaner formulated for stone (available from stone suppliers).

Pros Heat-resistant; beautifully colored; luxurious; each slab of granite is unique; good surface for working with pastry dough, since it doesn't conduct heat.

Cons Expensive; requires regular maintenance, including periodic sealing; stains; can crack; can be tough on dishware and glasses; variegated granite pieces hard to match.

Do Reapply sealer when drops of water no longer bead on the surface.

Don't use soap, detergent, all-purpose cleaners, or citrus-based cleaners—products that are too alkaline or acidic can etch stone. Don't use abrasive powders or dusting sprays, which can damage the surface.

Periodic Maintenance If the polish dulls, it can be revived with a commercial polishing agent (available from stone suppliers), but this should not be done more frequently than every three or four years, and the counter should be resealed afterward.

Repair/Restore If there are deep stains or there's erosion, the stone will have to be rebuffed and resealed by a stone professional.

MARBLE

Marble and other stone countertops are beautiful, and they generally outlast all other kitchen surfaces. But because it is a calcareous stone, marble is softer and more porous than granite. Its permeability makes it susceptible to scratches, chips, and stains, and its luster can be dulled if not properly cared for. Many homeowners choose to confine it to an island or a baking center.

HOW TO CLEAN

Dust once or twice a week with a soft cloth, and wipe periodically with a cloth dampened in warm water and, if necessary, a bit of pH-neutral cleaner formulated for stone (available from stone suppliers).

Pros Holds up to heat; beautiful and luxurious; ideal for rolling out dough, since it doesn't conduct heat.

Cons Expensive; must be sealed to protect it from stains; requires regular maintenance; very soft, so it scratches and etches easily; can be tough on dishware and glasses.

Do Reapply sealer when drops of water no longer bead on the surface. Protect marble from acidic foods; vinegar, lemon, and tomato will etch it instantly.

Don't use soap, detergent, all-purpose cleaners, or citrus-based cleaners—products that are too alkaline or acidic can etch stone. Don't use abrasive powders or dusting sprays, which can damage the surface.

Periodic Maintenance See Periodic Maintenance for granite, above.

Repair/Restore For stains such as rust marks or oil spots, try a poultice treatment (for more on poultice treatments, turn to page 55). If marble is badly stained or starting to erode, the stone will have to be rebuffed and resealed by a stone professional.

PLASTIC LAMINATE

The most common—and usually most affordable—countertop choice, laminates are made of multiple sheets of kraft paper, like that used for grocery bags, and plastic resins. Brand names include Formica and Wilsonart. The layered paper creates dark edges, which are visible where two pieces of laminate meet. More expensive plastic laminates—known as color-through laminates—retain the surface color throughout the layers, so nicks and scratches are less noticeable, and there are no dark seams. Laminate countertops are available in granular, matte, or glossy finishes and sold premolded with rounded edges or in sheets, which are glued onto a plywood form on-site.

HOW TO CLEAN

Wipe with a clean, soft cloth and a mild dishwashing liquid and water, then wipe away streaks with a clean, damp cloth. Treat stains with a paste of 3 parts baking soda to 1 part water; do not rub, as doing so could mar the surface. Wipe away paste with a clean, damp, soft cotton cloth, and then rinse with clean water. (Some stains, such as food dyes or coffee and tea stains, will not disappear right away, but may with repeated cleanings.)

Pros Inexpensive; sturdy; resists scratches, scuffs, burns, and other normal wear and tear; available in many colors and patterns; easy to clean.

Cons Not stain- or scratch-proof; can be impossible to repair if damaged by burn marks and deep scratches; seams show; potentially costly end finishing and edge choices.

Do Rinse laminate surfaces after cleaning; even a small amount of detergent residue can cause damage—any moisture the residue comes into contact with can reactivate it, and result in etching.

Don't allow water to pool—if it seeps into seams, it can cause swelling.

Periodic Maintenance None.

Repair/Restore Repair superficial scratches and small chips with laminate-repair paste, available at home-supply stores in a variety of colors (or you can mix the paste to match your countertop). If the laminate has begun lifting off the substrate below, reattach it with contact cement.

SLATE

Traditionally used to make durable rooftops and walkways, slate can be formed into kitchen counters that are at once classic and modern. It comes in deep greens, blues, grays, and purples, and has a matte surface and a distinctive cleft pattern. Although it is less porous than granite or marble, and less prone to staining, most stone professionals recommend sealing slate to be on the safe side.

HOW TO CLEAN

Dust once or twice a week with a soft cloth, and wipe periodically with a cloth dampened in warm water and, if necessary, a bit of pH-neutral cleaner formulated for stone (available from stone suppliers).

Pros Heat-resistant; timeless, natural style; luxurious.

Cons Expensive; brittle; scratches and chips easily; tough on dishware and glasses.

Do Reapply sealer when drops of water no longer bead on the surface.

Don't clean with abrasive cleansers or dusting sprays, which can damage slate (and other natural stones).

Periodic Maintenance Aside from sealing, none.

Repair/Restore Slate is less susceptible to etching from acidic cleaners and foods than other stones. It does scratch easily, however. Small scratches can be sanded away with fine sandpaper. If your slate countertop cracks, the entire countertop will have to be replaced. Consult a general contractor for advice on how to deal with the damage.

COUNTERTOP MATERIALS (CONTINUED)

SOAPSTONE
Named for its smooth, soapy touch, soapstone is composed of mineral talc, quartz, and other minerals. It starts out light gray in color but darkens significantly as it ages. (Frequent applications of mineral oil hasten the darkening process.) It is used for science laboratory counters because of its resistance to acids and alkalis, which means that chemicals or cleansers won't cause it to deteriorate. Soapstone is both softer and less porous than granite.

HOW TO CLEAN
Wipe with a cloth dampened with water and mild dishwashing liquid.

Pros Rich, deep color; smooth feel; doesn't stain easily; very resistant to heat.

Cons Expensive; requires regular maintenance; may crack and darken over time; scratches and chips easily; hard on dishware and glasses.

Don't apply any type of sealer to soapstone.

Periodic Maintenance After the initial installation, you will need to apply mineral oil over the entire surface often. Apply weekly to monthly until the counter stops darkening, which can take a year or more. After that, reapply mineral oil about every six months.

Repair/Restore Remove small scratches with fine sandpaper or try rubbing them out with mineral oil. If the stone cracks, the entire countertop will need to be replaced. Consult a general contractor to assess the situation.

SOLID SURFACING
Solid-surface countertops, including the brand names Corian and Avonite, are a blend of acrylic polymers and materials derived from natural stone. To form countertops, the composite is poured into molds. Counters are generally about half an inch thick, although usually thicker on edges, which can make the counters appear deeper. Solid-surfacing simulates marble, granite, or other hard stone. It is widely considered to be the lowest-maintenance luxury countertop material and is often recommended for busy kitchens because of its durability and lack of porosity. Solid surfacing is sold in matte and glossy finishes.

HOW TO CLEAN
Wipe with a damp cloth and then towel-dry. Treat spills or light stains with mild dishwashing liquid or an ammonia-based cleaner. Remedies for tougher stains depend on the finish: On matte (nonshiny) finishes, use an abrasive cleanser and a nylon scouring pad. Semigloss surfaces require a mildly abrasive liquid cleaner (such as Soft Scrub, which is recommended by Corian's manufacturer) or a solution of 1 part bleach to 10 parts water, and a white scouring pad.

Pros Available in a wide range of colors; seamless; stain-resistant; low maintenance; holds up well to abrasives; scratches can be sanded out; can incorporate integrated sinks.

Cons Expensive; looks less natural than stone.

Don't On solid surfacing with a high-gloss finish, don't use anything harsher than a mildly abrasive liquid cleaner and a sponge.

Periodic Maintenance None.

Repair/Restore Treat minor damage, including scratches, stains, scorches, and minor impact marks, with a light abrasive cleanser or a nylon scouring pad as described above. For difficult residues and stains, use a commercial spray cleaner made specifically for solid surfacing (available at home-supply stores).

STAINLESS STEEL

Stainless-steel countertops are heat-resistant, extremely durable, and easy to keep clean. Because stainless countertops are built to measure, there are no seams to trap dirt and bacteria. Most health codes mandate it in commercial kitchens. Although stainless steel can scratch, over time the scratches mesh, forming a soft patina. Stainless-steel counters should be at least $\frac{1}{20}$ inch thick ($\frac{1}{16}$ inch is preferred) to prevent them from denting and buckling. (To learn more about the gauge of stainless steel, turn to Stainless-Steel Sinks, page 59.)

HOW TO CLEAN

Wipe with a soft cloth and a few drops of mild dishwashing liquid, or a dry microfiber cloth (without cleaner). You can also use a gentle abrasive powder such as Bon Ami. Buff the surface dry after cleaning. Most hardware stores and home-supply stores sell spray cleaners specifically for stainless steel; they effectively remove fingerprints and water marks.

Pros Resists rust, corrosion, and common household stains; withstands heat; easy to maintain; can incorporate integrated sinks; resists acids and oils.

Cons Expensive; can be noisy; may dent; shows fingerprints and water marks.

Do Always wipe with the grain.

Don't let it come in contact with chlorine bleach, which can pit the surface.

Periodic Maintenance Deep scratches or dents may be impossible to remove, but minor, everyday scratches can be camouflaged by rubbing with a nylon abrasive pad. Start with a gentle pad, and work in the same direction as the existing grain. Switch to a more abrasive pad if necessary. If you create an area that looks different from the rest of the counter, gently rub the changes in with a feathering stroke to help them blend. You can also hand-polish the entire counter to blend the finish.

Repair/Restore Deeper scratches require more aggressive treatment; consult a metal fabricator (look in the Yellow Pages to find one) for repair recommendations.

ZINC

Zinc is shiny like stainless steel when it is new, but it develops a warm, soft patina with time and wear. It has long been formed into restaurant countertops, sinks, and bars, and can lend an old-fashioned look to any residential kitchen. For durability, choose zinc countertops that are at least $\frac{1}{20}$ inch thick (preferably $\frac{1}{16}$ inch).

HOW TO CLEAN

Wipe surface with a solution of warm water and mild dishwashing liquid, then rinse well and towel-dry thoroughly.

Pros Heatproof; can incorporate integrated sinks; develops a warm glow over time.

Cons Scratches easily; can look industrial; shows fingerprints and watermarks.

Don't use cleaners that are highly alkaline (such as ammonia) or acidic (such as vinegar), both of which can cause damage.

Periodic Maintenance To minimize tarnishing, apply a thin coat of food-safe paste wax (with a clean, lint-free cotton cloth, preferably a diaper), available from online retailers.

Repair/Restore If dull or corroded, rub with number 000 steel wool.

PROTECTING STONE SURFACES

The stones most often used for countertops can be divided into two categories: siliceous stones and calcareous stones. Granite, slate, and soapstone are all examples of siliceous stones. Marble is a calcareous stone.

In general, siliceous stones are more durable and easier to maintain than calcareous stones, which are extremely vulnerable to etching from common household products, including citrus juices and citrus-based cleaning products, acidic cleaning products (including vinegar), alkaline cleaning products (including ammonia), shaving cream, alcoholic beverages, soda, perfume, nail-polish remover, ketchup, mustard, vinegar, hair- and body-care products containing EDTA (a common chemical additive), rock salt, toothpaste, drain openers, and toilet-bowl cleaners.

Although siliceous stones are less prone to etching and damage from these substances, they are by no means impervious to them. To keep any stone counter looking its best, take care to protect it from these substances.

SEALING STONE SURFACES

A penetrating sealer is the best defense against stains on almost any natural stone countertop. These products, also known as impregnators, penetrate the surface to offer stain resistance from within the stone itself. They are sold at stone suppliers and hardware stores, and are easy to apply at home.

First, though, you must determine whether or not your countertop needs to be sealed, since not all stone surfaces do. Begin with this simple test: Place a drop of water on the surface. If after several minutes the area below the water becomes dark, the stone is porous and requires a protective sealant; if the color remains the same, then sealing is optional. To be safe, you should conduct a few tests in different (inconspicuous) spots on the counter, and wait twenty-four hours before you begin treatment to ensure that test areas are dry. (Water spots must dry completely before sealing, or they will become permanent.)

To prepare the stone for sealing, clean it thoroughly with water and a pH-neutral cleaner formulated for stone; wipe with a clean cloth and let dry completely, which will likely take several hours. Tape off adjacent areas that you don't want to treat in order to protect them from splashes. Using a clean white towel, apply sealer evenly to the surface, saturating it thoroughly. Take care to keep the sealer from getting into any open joints. Following the manufacturer's instructions, let the sealer stand for several minutes before removing excess with a clean, dry towel. The sealed stone will not be stain-proof, but the sealer will have filled in the pores, therefore slowing down the time that it takes a stain to set (and giving you more time to wipe up a spill when it happens). When drops of water no longer bead on the surface of the countertop, you'll need to reapply sealer. You may need to reseal annually or even less frequently depending upon use.

POULTICE TREATMENTS

Available at hardware and home-supply stores, poultices are powders specially formulated for treating deep-set stains (especially oil and rust) on marble and other types of stone. Begin by mixing the powder into a paste according to package directions, until it has the consistency of peanut butter. (Some stores carry ready-to-use poultice pastes, which are convenient if you don't want to mix your own.) Apply the paste to the stained area, overlapping the stain by at least 1/4 inch. To retain moisture, attach plastic wrap to the stone to cover the poultice (using painter's tape, which is low-contact). The paste can take twelve to twenty-four hours to dry completely. Remove the plastic and check that the paste has dried. (As the poultice dries, it draws the stain out.) Once dry, scrape the paste off and rinse the area with a damp, clean cloth. Examine the stain. If you are satisfied, follow the poultice treatment with a stone sealer (see above). You can reapply the poultice if the stain remains, but if after several applications the stain doesn't disappear completely, consult a stone-restoration specialist or your stone supplier.

A NOTE ABOUT HONED, POLISHED, AND TUMBLED STONE

Honed stoned typically looks and feels "soft" and has low reflectivity. Polished stone looks and feels "mirrorlike" with a high-gloss surface. Any stone that is referred to as tumbled will have a more porous finish than polished or honed stone. It is lightly tumbled (in a machine that actually bounces the stones in a barrel) to achieve an uneven matte surface that is not as smooth as honed.

COUNTERTOPS MADE OF MARBLE OR OTHER TYPES OF STONE SHOULD HAVE A PENETRATING SEALER APPLIED AS A DEFENSE AGAINST STAINS.

A CLEAN KITCHEN
SINK IS A TOUCHSTONE OF
GOOD HOMEKEEPING.

KITCHEN SINKS

With all the activity and traffic it attracts, the kitchen sink is arguably the central workstation of the entire house. It should be welcoming, with the necessary accoutrements nearby. It must also be kept immaculate, not only for aesthetic reasons but for essential issues of sanitation as well. Plates and glasses should not be allowed to pile up there during the day, the drain should be kept free of bits of food, and any deposits of detergent or cleaning products should be wiped away at once. The danger of mixing cleaning supplies with food at the kitchen sink is reason enough to keep it absolutely pristine.

If you wipe out the sink with a damp cloth or sponge every time you use it and clean it well after preparing meals, a sense of cleanliness will pervade everything around it. Likewise, you should attend to dirty dishes as soon as possible; leaving them piled in the sink is unsanitary as well as unsightly. If you absolutely cannot get to them right away, at least scrape the dishes of food and rinse them under hot water.

HOW TO CLEAN THE KITCHEN SINK

The kitchen sink requires daily, gentle cleaning. For routine care, wipe with mild dishwashing liquid, warm water, and a soft cloth.

As a general rule, do not scrub any sink with scouring powder containing chlorine bleach, ammonia, or hydrofluoric acid and never use steel wool, stiff brushes, or abrasive pads, unless so directed by the manufacturer. These products will damage the surface of most sinks. To guard against stains, attend to all leaks immediately. This is especially important if you have a granite or marble sink, as mineral-laden water will turn both surfaces brown.

For deep cleaning, wipe with a mildly abrasive cleanser, such as Bon Ami, and a soft cloth. To remove heavy buildup of soap scum or mineral deposits, follow the instructions on page 65.

ABOUT SPONGES AND DISHRAGS

Do you know that the FDA forbids sponges in commercial kitchens because of the risk of contamination from such bacteria as salmonella, *E. coli,* and staphylococcus? If you choose to use sponges in the kitchen sink area, keep them very clean, and store them in a very clean soap dish. Designate specific sponges for specific tasks—dishes, countertops, and so on—and don't substitute one for another. Wash sponges in the washing machine, not the dishwasher, or sterilize them by soaking for a minute in 3 cups water mixed with 2 tablespoons chlorine bleach. Rinse well. Discard sponges when they start to disintegrate or take on a foul odor. (For more on sponges, turn to page 487.)

Terry dishrags, also called bar mops, can be used instead of sponges; rinse thoroughly and wring out after each use and change them daily. Launder them with your regular white loads.

ABOUT POT FILLERS

Kitchen-sink depths generally range from 6 inches on the shallow end to about $10^{1/2}$ inches for a deep, apron-front sink. Deeper sinks are helpful for filling large stockpots with water, although it takes quite a bit of water to fill the basins for washing dishes, which can be wasteful.

You can install a wall-mounted pot filler for this purpose instead. Most wall-mounted pot fillers, which are installed in the wall behind the cooktop, have a double-jointed spout that extends to 24 inches. The faucet can fold against the wall or be extended—and the joint will allow it to bend—to reach different burners. Typically the faucet is connected to the cold water supply, but some are connected to both the cold and hot water supply. There are often two shut-off valves, one where the faucet is mounted to the wall, and one near the spout. Pot fillers may also be mounted in the counter next to the cooktop.

KITCHEN SINK MATERIALS

COPPER

Copper sinks develop a deep luster over time. This patina, which is actually a protective barrier that forms naturally, ranges from pink to green to brown, and takes about a year to develop a warm nut color. To keep this natural look, nothing is required other than gentle cleaning, described on page 57. If you want to keep the copper shining like new, however, it requires diligent, careful polishing. Some copper sinks come with a clear lacquer coating to protect the shiny appearance, but as the coating wears away, professional resurfacing is necessary.

Pros Warm, rustic look; antibacterial properties.

Cons Expensive; scratches easily; hot pots and pans can damage the surface; too much polishing can wear away the metal.

Special Considerations To shine, select a commercial polish that's specially formulated for copper, such as Red Bear, and follow the manufacturer's directions, making sure to test in an inconspicuous spot before proceeding. Don't use polish on sinks coated with lacquer.

ENGINEERED STONE

See Engineered Stone countertops, page 49.

FIRECLAY

Fireclay is created when clay containing large amounts of quartz and feldspar is fired at extremely high temperatures. The intense heat vitrifies the clay and fuses the glaze to the surface. The resulting material is durable, nonporous, and capable of withstanding high temperatures. Fireclay is a variation of vitreous china (see below right).

Pros Because the surface is very hard and nonporous, it resists damage like rust and discoloration caused by most cleansers and chemicals.

Cons Expensive.

Special Considerations None.

MARBLE

See Marble countertops, page 50.

PLASTIC

Plastic sinks are made from acrylic resin, fiberglass, or polyester.

Pros Inexpensive; many color options; some acrylic models are available with "built-in" germ-fighting materials.

Cons Not very stain-, scratch-, or heat-resistant; nicks and cuts are common.

Special Considerations None.

PORCELAIN ENAMEL

This term is used to describe sinks made of either porcelain enamel steel or porcelain enamel cast iron. The enamel is a fired-on opaque glassy coating, which is fused to a metal base. Sinks made of this material are commonly found in older homes.

Pros Can be buffed to a shine.

Cons Stains can be hard to treat; the enamel can chip with heavy impact.

Special Considerations Acidic substances such as vinegar and citrus juices can etch porcelain enamel, even if the sink is acid-resistant. Immediately wipe up spills with a damp sponge and mild dishwashing liquid.

VITREOUS CHINA

Traditionally found in bathrooms, vitreous china sinks are increasingly installed in kitchens. Vitreous china is a hard, nonporous, glazed clay material similar to fireclay.

Pros Available in a variety of colors.

Cons Hardwater can cause stains; boiling water can be damaging; can chip or crack.

Special Considerations If you live in a hard-water area, frequent cleaning with water and a mild dishwashing liquid is recommended.

SOAPSTONE

See Soapstone countertops, page 52.

SOLID SURFACING

See Solid Surfacing countertops, page 52.

STAINLESS-STEEL SINKS

These are the most common kitchen sinks. They are affordable and easy to install and maintain. They won't chip, although they will show scratches over time. But stainless steel, an alloy of steel, chromium, and nickel, can also amplify noises such as those caused by dripping faucets and clanging silverware, so it's important to consider the gauge when choosing a stainless-steel sink. The gauge refers to the thickness of the material; the lower the gauge, the thicker it is. A gauge of 18 percent chromium is considered optimal (inexpensive sinks can range to a gauge as high as 24 percent). High-quality sinks are also described as 18/10 or 18/8—which means 18 percent chromium and either 10 or 8 percent nickel (which prevents corrosion and adds shine). For care information, see Stainless-Steel countertops, page 53.

SINK INSTALLATION STYLES

Kitchen sinks are either single bowl or double or triple bowl; the latter two allow you to wash dishes in one bowl while using the other for food prep. Bar sinks, which are smaller and deeper than standard kitchen sinks, are often installed as secondary sinks in an island or butler's pantry. All three types can be installed in the following ways:

APRON FRONT

Deeper than other sinks, apron fronts have an exposed front that may project beyond the front of the surrounding cabinetry. Apron-front sinks usually don't have decks, so faucets are mounted in the countertop or on the wall above the sink.

INTEGRAL

Fabricated out of the same material as the countertop, integral sinks are particularly hygienic because there are no seams between the two surfaces, making for easy cleanup. Grooves can be routed right in the countertop near the sink to create a built-in drain board. Because it can be molded, solid surfacing is particularly well suited to integral sink installations. Faucets are mounted in the countertop or on the wall above the sink.

UNDERMOUNT

The installation of an undermount, or submount, sink presents some challenges. The sink sits below the surface of the counter, so it looks more integrated than a sink with a lip. Crumbs and spills can be brushed directly off the counter and into the sink. Undermount sinks cannot be used with laminate countertops, because the edge remains exposed; this style of sink is most common with counters made of stone or solid surfacing. Faucets are mounted in the countertop or on the wall above the sink.

SELF-RIMMING

Self-rimming sinks, also known as top-mounted or drop-ins, have a lip that sits on the countertop, and are held in place by clips or screws mounted under the counter. Although the installation is simple, the lip makes cleanup of spills and crumbs more difficult. Most stainless-steel sinks are installed this way, as are many sinks set into laminate countertops, since the lip protects the cut edge, which can swell when wet. Faucets and accessories, such as sprayers, are generally mounted on the sink deck, a lip with predrilled holes that extends behind the sink toward the backsplash.

FAUCETS

Faucets are susceptible to soap buildup, mineral stains, and smudgy fingerprints, and the best all-around care is preventive. Every time you've finished using the sink, rinse the faucet with water and blot dry, to prevent the white mineral stains that may be left behind when water evaporates.

To remove a buildup of mineral deposits, mix 1 part white vinegar with 1 part water and apply with a soft cloth. If necessary let the solution soak in before you wipe it off, then rinse and dry again. Use vinegar sparingly, as it can damage faucet finishes over time. There is usually an aerator in your faucet, which is a small metal screen, that can also become clogged with mineral deposits; keep it clean by soaking it in white vinegar. To remove the aerator from the faucet, unscrew the ring at the end of the spout.

The body of a faucet is generally made from one of three materials: brass, which is the most durable and most expensive; die-cast zinc-alloy, which costs less than brass and delivers good quality; and plastic, which is the least durable option. Each of these materials is coated with a decorative finish, such as chrome. Finishes on plumbing fixtures, traditionally applied using a plating process, may also be coated with an additional clear finish to prevent discoloration and keep metals such as brass, which tarnishes, shiny. These finishes must be treated gently.

To create a more durable surface than traditional plating finishes, many manufacturers treat fixtures with Physical Vapor Disposition (PVD). Used on metals from brass to platinum, PVD is a protective coat applied with a molecular bonding process. The resulting finish permanently resists tarnish, scratches, and rust. Though PVD-treated faucets cost about 25 percent more than those with plated finishes, many come with a lifetime guarantee, so they will never need to be retreated, as traditional plated fixtures will. PVD finishes are considered better for the environment, as no toxic wastes are produced in their manufacture.

HOW TO CLEAN THE FAUCET

Although newer PVD-finished faucets are more durable than plated faucets, they both require very gentle care. Wipe with mild dishwashing liquid, warm water, and a soft cloth. Do not use abrasive pads. Buff any water spots with a soft cloth. Clean seams and crevices with a soft toothbrush. Avoid cleaners containing ammonia, bleach, abrasives, or other strong chemicals. Also avoid products that say they remove rust or contain hydrofluoric or phosphoric acid.

HOW TO CLEAN PORCELAIN KNOBS

Never use abrasive cleaners, sponges, or brushes. Clean with a solution of mild dishwashing liquid and water, or with glass cleaner. Rinse well with water afterward, and dry with a clean cloth.

DRAINS

To keep your drain running freely, flush it with boiling water once a week. Boil one gallon of water, pour half down the drain, wait a few minutes, and then pour in the rest. Twice a year, flush drains with baking soda and vinegar, following the directions on page 62.

The cardinal rule when it comes to keeping drains clear is this: Never pour grease down the drain. Animal fats cause the fats in soap to congeal, clogging the drain. Pour it instead into a disposable glass jar, milk carton, or metal container; once the grease has solidified, discard it into the trash.

KITCHEN FAUCET FINISHES

BRASS

An alloy of copper and zinc. Often coated with a clear finish to prevent tarnish.

Special Considerations Unless you want to spend a lot of time polishing, a brass faucet should be coated with either an epoxy or a PVD finish. Otherwise it will lose its shine and tarnish quite easily.

COPPER

A reddish metal that can be coated or uncoated.

Special Considerations If copper is uncoated, you may prefer to let a patina develop rather than polish regularly. Simply wipe with lukewarm water and mild dishwashing liquid. If you want to keep your copper faucet polished, select a commercial polish, such as Red Bear Copper and Brass Polish, that's specially formulated for copper and follow the manufacturer's instructions, making sure to test in an inconspicuous spot before proceeding.

BRONZE

An alloy of copper and tin.

Special Considerations If bronze is uncoated, you may prefer to let a patina develop rather than polish it regularly. Lukewarm water and mild dishwashing liquid will clean off light soiling and smudging. To shine, use a commercial polish that's specially formulated for bronze and follow the manufacturer's instructions, making sure to test in an inconspicuous spot before proceeding.

ENAMELED PLASTIC

A popular alternative to metal faucet fixtures, enameled plastic faucets are available in colors that can be coordinated with the rest of the room.

Special Considerations Enameled plastic scratches easily, so it is not the best choice for an active household.

NICKEL

A silvery white metal that resists tarnish.

Special Considerations Nickel doesn't tarnish but it will darken with age, and can develop water spots quite easily. Remove them with a soft cloth and a nonammoniated glass cleaner.

CHROME

A mirrorlike finish treatment, chrome does not tarnish or corrode, but the underlying metal can, causing pockmarks. To prevent corrosion from worsening, never break pockmarks.

Special Considerations Although chrome-plated fixtures are widely available and very durable, you still need to clean them regularly to keep them from losing their shine. Wipe with warm water and mild dishwashing liquid.

STAINLESS STEEL

An alloy of steel, chromium, and nickel that's highly resistant to rust, stains, and corrosion. Water spots are common, however.

Special Considerations Though faucet fixtures are easy to maintain, they can begin to dull over time and with wear. Use an all-purpose cleaner or a commercial stainless-steel cleaner. Apply polish along the grain (stainless steel often has a brushed finish), rinse immediately, then polish dry.

Wipe all greasy pans with
a paper towel before
washing. Always keep
the strainer basket clean.
Fine mesh drain screens,
sold at home centers,
hardware stores, or
plumbing supply stores,
catch more than tradi-
tional baskets do, and are
available in several sizes.

TREATING CLOGGED DRAINS

Liquid drain openers are often made with caustic chemical compounds,
so pouring them down the drain is cause for environmental concern. There
are, fortunately, several ecologically friendly alternatives worth trying.

First, pull out and clean the stopper. If that does not help, use an ordinary funnel-cup plunger to flush away the clog. Fit the plunger's cup into
the drain, and plunge vertically to keep water from spraying out the sides.
Do not worry about working rapidly; just make sure you have created a
strong seal (if your sink has an overflow hole, plug it with a small rag or
sponge). It may take ten to fifteen minutes to loosen the blockage, so
don't quit if results are not immediate. If your problem is in a double-bowl
sink in the kitchen, first plug one drain with a wet rag or sponge and hold
it securely before you start plunging the other.

If plunging doesn't clear the clog, try adding a solution made with
basic kitchen supplies. Pour ½ cup baking soda down the drain; follow
with ½ cup vinegar, then cover the drain (and overflow hole) tightly with a
drain plug or wet rag. Allow this mixture to sit for five minutes while the
vinegar and baking soda work to break down any fats into salt and a harmless gas. Next, flush the drain with boiling-hot water from a teakettle (the
spout is important because you can safely pour and avoid scalding yourself).

Various enzymatic drain openers also dissolve clogs safely, including
a product called Super Digest-It, which consists of freeze-dried blocks of
bacillus bacteria. These microorganisms literally eat the material interfering
with your plumbing, turning it into carbon dioxide and water.

If plunging and natural drain openers fail, try using a drain auger, also
known as a snake (available at hardware and home-supply stores). Slowly
feed this tool—a length of thin steel coil—down the drain in a twisting motion. Once you feel the coil reach the blockage, steadily push through it;
then pull the auger back and forth to loosen the clog and expand the hole.
When the blockage is broken, try plunging again; then run the water for
a few minutes to clear up the rest.

GARBAGE DISPOSALS

In-sink garbage disposals, also known as food disposers, are convenient,
efficient, and ecologically sound; food scraps don't end up in a landfill, but
are shredded into fine particles and sent to the sewage system, which is
equipped to treat and even recycle waste. There are two kinds of disposals:
With a batch-feed model, you fill the disposal and insert a stopper to
turn it on; the more popular continuous-feed model is activated with an

electrical switch, and you can add food waste as it runs. It's a good idea to refer to your owner's manual for instructions specific to your model, but there are a few basic guidelines for all types:

☐ Always run cold (never warm or hot) water with each use of the disposal; hot water will dissolve fat and grease—as the water flows down the pipes, it starts to cool and a film of grease begins to build on the inside of the pipes, leading to a clog.

☐ Run the disposal each time you place food in it; food left sitting in a garbage disposal will cause odor.

☐ Insert food waste loosely; never crowd it or jam it into the disposal. If you overload the disposal, it will stall. Most are equipped with overload protectors, however, to prevent the motor from getting damaged.

☐ The disposal is for food waste only; never use it for materials like paper, plastic, or metal, or harsh chemicals such as lye or drain-pipe cleaners.

☐ Process vegetable skins (including potato) in small quantities with a forceful flow of water to help them run through the system.

☐ Some hard materials, including small bones and fruit pits, can be processed; in fact, this is often recommended, as it creates scouring action inside the grinding chamber that keeps it clean and fresh. Large bones should not be placed in the disposal, however.

☐ Avoid putting fibrous foods, such as cornhusks, artichokes, rhubarb, and celery, in the disposal; they can cause jamming.

☐ A properly cared for garbage disposal should stay clean, but you can always freshen and deodorize it by grinding citrus peels or vinegar ice cubes in it.

HOW TO CLEAR A CLOGGED DISPOSAL

1. Turn the power switch to the Off position.

2. Disconnect the power at the main fuse or circuit breaker.

3. Remove the stopper or the splashguard.

4. Check the interior of the hopper, using a flashlight if necessary, for objects that will not grind properly, such as glass or metal, shells, large bones, plastic, or aluminum. Use long-handled tongs to remove any such objects.

5. NEVER put your hand into the disposal.

6. Once you've safely removed the obstruction, turn the power on and reset the button on the disposal unit. Flush the disposal well with cold water.

DISHWASHING BY HAND

There are times when you have to rely on hand-washing your dishes, and there are ways to cut down on water and energy consumption while doing so. Washing the dishes properly—in a plastic dish tub, rather than one at a time under the tap—will not only save water and energy but also save time in the long run. To begin, set yourself up for washing dishes by putting everything you need in place so that you don't drip suds all over while looking for a pot scrubber or dish towel. To catch drips, place a baking sheet under your drying rack. Look for sheets with 1-inch vertical sides to prevent runoff from seeping onto your countertop. And since they're made of metal, they resist mildew better than a rubber tray or a dish towel.

A NOTE ABOUT WATER CONSERVATION

When run at full capacity, a dishwasher relies on only a fraction of the energy, water, and detergent that it takes to clean the same-size load of dirty dishes by hand. Some studies estimate that the dishwasher uses half the energy and only about a sixth of the water. Dishwashers manufactured since 1994 are particularly energy- and water-efficient.

HOW TO WASH DISHES BY HAND

☐ Scrape food from dishes with a rubber spatula. You'll scratch dishes less with a rubber spatula than with metal utensils.

☐ Rinse every dish with hot water, then stack by type.

☐ To conserve water, fill a large plastic bin or tub with hot, soapy water. (One or two squirts of dishwashing liquid—do not use automatic dishwasher detergent—should be sufficient to clean one load. This is much more economical than squirting dishwashing liquid directly onto a sponge.) The hotter the water, the more likely glass and silver will dry without spots and streaks. Don't overload the tub; you may risk chipping or breaking your dishes.

☐ If you're not using a tub, line the sink with a rubber or plastic mat for protection should a glass or plate fall. For particularly fragile items, line the sink with old, soft bath towels and skip the rubber gloves as they tend to be more slippery than bare hands.

☐ Wash one piece at a time. Rub the dish with the cloth or sponge while revolving it with the other hand, working from the center of the dish outward (or inside out, for glasses), then back again inward. Turn the dish over and repeat. Scrub stuck-on foods with a dish brush.

☐ Wash dishes in this order: crystal, glassware, clear glass plates, other plates, flatware, serving ware, then the greasiest serving dishes and finally pots and pans. Start with the least soiled dishes and end with the greasiest. (If you wash the greasy things first, the grease will remain on the sponge and leave a residue on everything else.) When in doubt about the cleaning power of the dishwater, drain the tub and start again fresh. Adding more dishwashing liquid to dirty water will not boost the cleaning power of the water.

☐ Stack washed dishes by the side of the sink or in the empty bowl of a two-bowl sink. Once you have five or six pieces, and before the suds dry, rinse under hot running tap water. Start with the back of the plate or the outside of the glass, rinsing the eating or drinking surfaces last.

☐ Place items on a dish rack to air dry, or dry with a clean dish towel.

SPECIAL CIRCUMSTANCES

☐ Starches and dairy products get gummier in hot water, so use cold water on dishes with these types of residue. You can soak them for a few minutes to loosen residue, but don't let them sit for any length of time (bacteria grows quickly).

☐ Wash or at least rinse china teacups soon after you have finished with your coffee or tea, so that stains will not have time to set.

☐ Bottles are easier to clean if you soak denture cleaner in them overnight and then scrub them with a narrow nylon bottlebrush.

ESSENTIAL DISHWASHING SUPPLIES

☐ Rubber gloves
☐ Plastic dish tub
☐ Nylon and plastic scouring pads
☐ Dish brush
☐ Dishwashing liquid

☐ Baking sheet and dish rack or wire mesh cooling rack
☐ Rubber spatula
☐ Clean, dry dish towels (a half dozen or more, depending on the number of dishes)

☐ Dish cloth or sponge, which should be used only for washing dishes (to avoid spreading germs to dishes, do not use it to mop up spills on counters or floors)

A NOTE ABOUT DISHWASHING LIQUID

Dishwashing liquids are detergents, which are made with synthetic ingredients. Because fats, the natural ingredients used in soap, were in short supply during World War I, detergents were developed to keep up with the demand for cleansers. As it turned out, detergents did a better job than soap in dissolving the oils and grease that cause bits of leftover food to adhere to plates. Detergents also worked better than soap in hard water, and largely supplanted soap by the 1950s.

Detergent suds actually serve an extraordinary purpose. Once you've washed a plate with deter-gent, the suds gather and suspend the tiny particles of soil, keeping them away from the newly cleaned surface. As the suds diminish, so does the cleaning power of the detergent. Suds also help keep the dishwater hot; without them, the water will cool faster, further reducing the detergent's cleaning power.

If you're observing a buildup of scum in the sink after washing dishes, it doesn't mean you're using too much detergent. In fact, you're probably not using enough detergent to prevent fats from adhering to the sink. Try using a little more next time.

SALT CLEANSER
Because salt is absorbent and a natural abrasive, it is an excellent antidote to grease. Rub salt into especially dirty pots and pans with a dry sponge, until greasy residue is gone.

WASHING POTS AND PANS

Whether it is a frying pan or a roasting pan, made of enamelware or cast iron, the sooner you wash a pot or pan after using it, the better. And bear in mind that you will have an easier time cleaning your pots and pans if you take a few easy steps *before* using them.

☐ Line the bottom of roasting pans with aluminum foil, especially when roasting meat, which produces a lot of fat.

☐ Line baking sheets and cake pans with parchment paper.

ESSENTIAL TOOLS FOR WASHING POTS AND PANS

☐ Dishrag or sponge

☐ Dish rack (place in a baking sheet, to catch drips)

☐ Nylon and plastic scouring pads

☐ Pot scrubber

☐ Rubber spatula

DRYING DISHES, POTS, AND PANS

Let dishes, pots, and pans air dry if possible. If the water you rinsed them with is hot enough, it should evaporate almost immediately. Towel drying is obviously effective, but you must make sure that the towels you use are dry and clean before starting, and you should replace the towels often with fresh ones as they get damp. A damp towel is a prime breeding ground for germs. Wash and dry all dish towels promptly after you are finished with them, and keep plenty on hand for the next round.

HOW TO WASH POTS AND PANS BY HAND

All pots and pans, except for those made of stainless steel, should be washed by hand rather than in the dishwasher. Here's how:

1. Line the sink with a rubber or plastic mat so the bottoms of pots do not mark or damage the sink.

2. Scrape food with a rubber spatula.

3. If the pot or pan is especially greasy, wipe it out with a paper towel.

4. Rinse each pot or pan under hot water and set to the side of the sink.

5. Fill a plastic tub or the sink with hot water and a few squirts of dishwashing liquid.

6. Wash one pot or pan at a time, tackling stuck-on food with a pot scrubber or a plastic or nylon pad (the exception to this rule is nonstick cookware, which should not be cleaned with abrasives of any sort).

7. A mildly abrasive cleanser, such as Bon Ami, can effectively clean stainless-steel and aluminum pots and pans. Don't use it routinely, however, as over time it can create a fine network of scratches.

HOW TO WASH ESPECIALLY DIRTY POTS

For especially dirty pots (not burned, but coated with baked-on food):

1. Fill the pot with water and ¼ cup powdered dishwasher detergent or baking soda.

2. Bring the mixture to a boil; remove from the heat and let the pot soak for an hour.

3. Scrape the pot with a nonabrasive utensil, such as a wooden spoon or a rubber spatula.

4. Wash as described above.

HOW TO WASH BADLY BURNED POTS

For badly burned pots (without nonstick coatings):

1. Fill the pot with cold water and 2 or 3 tablespoons salt.

2. Let the pot soak overnight.

3. In the morning, slowly bring the water to a boil. The burn marks should disappear. If, however, the burns are especially harsh, you may need to repeat this process several times before they vanish.

4. Wash as described above.

CLEANING OF POTS AND PANS, BY MATERIAL

ALUMINUM	Prolonged exposure to hard water or alkaline foods, such as potatoes, will darken aluminum. To clean a pot or pan with these dark gray or black stains, scour it with a nylon pad, following the grain of the metal as you rub, to prevent scratching. For severe darkening, simmer a mixture of 2 tablespoons cream of tartar per quart of water for ten to fifteen minutes. After simmering, polish the pan with a nylon pad or a mildly abrasive cleanser and a cloth. Rinse and dry. To remove lime deposits from the interior of an aluminum teakettle or coffeepot, boil equal parts water and white vinegar for ten to fifteen minutes (or longer depending on how heavy the deposits are).
ANODIZED ALUMINUM	After sautéing or frying, wash with a light-duty nylon pad and a mildly abrasive powder such as Bon Ami. Although these pans do not need to be seasoned before using, they must be kept scrupulously clean; any oily residue can cause foods to stick.
CAST IRON	Cast iron needs careful treatment to prevent rust. The porous surface is partly sealed by factory grinding and polishing, but cast-iron pans need to be seasoned before first use and periodically thereafter. Seasoning seals the surface, preventing rust as well as the transfer of metallic tastes to food. To season, rub well on all surfaces with vegetable oil and place the pan in a 300°F oven for one hour. Let the pan cool, then wipe away excess oil. To clean a seasoned pan, wipe with only hot water and a sponge or soft cloth. Never use detergent, which strips cast iron of its seasoned surface. If you have burned food in a cast-iron pan, boil a little salt and white vinegar in it, then dry it on top of the stove over a low flame, or scrub with coarse salt and a cloth. Wipe immediately with a clean cloth, then brush the interior of the pan with another thin coating of vegetable oil to preserve the seasoning. Wipe gently before storing in a dry place; stack by layering paper towels (or paper plates) between pans to prevent scratching. Leave off any lids to prevent mustiness and moisture buildup. If storing a cast-iron pan for any length of time, consider coating it first with food-grade mineral oil instead of vegetable oil, which will turn rancid.
COPPER	Although the tin linings of copper pots should be allowed to tarnish (the darker color helps absorb heat), the exteriors can be polished. You can achieve a soft "restaurant glow" by applying a mixture of salt and lemon juice or white vinegar, but a pot won't gleam without commercial polish (Red Bear Copper Cleaner, for example) and elbow grease. To clean especially dirty copper pots, fill with water and 2 tablespoons dishwashing liquid or baking soda for each cup of water; bring the mixture to a boil, let the pot soak, and then scrape it with a nylon mesh pad. Avoid metal utensils, abrasive cleaners, and steel-wool pads, which can leave pits and scratches.
ENAMELED STEEL OR ENAMELED CAST IRON	After washing with a light-duty nylon pad and water, towel-dry pans immediately to prevent rust around rims.
NONSTICK PANS	Clean with a soft sponge and water; never scour a nonstick surface with abrasive brushes or pads, which can damage it. If there are any scratches or signs of flaking or peeling, throw out the pot or pan.
STAINLESS STEEL	It's best not to soak stainless steel, since it will pit. Instead, rub with white vinegar or lemon juice and a soft cloth to remove stains.

KITCHEN LINENS

When it comes to linens, there are specific fibers for specific jobs. For drying glassware, lint-free towels and flour sacks are ideal. For dishes and pots and pans, a terry-cloth or flat-weave cotton dish towel works fine. Terry-cloth bar mops come in handy for blotting up spills on counters and floors. Keep these separate from towels you use to dry dishes.

To keep the kitchen clean and minimize the spread of bacteria, all towels and dishrags must be washed, dried, and changed daily. Otherwise, you could be transferring germs, which are easily absorbed by kitchen linens, from one surface to another when you prepare food and wipe up afterward. Make it a habit to collect kitchen linens once you've cleaned up after dinner, and place a fresh supply on the countertop for the next morning. (For more information on laundering kitchen linens, turn to page 157.)

TYPES OF KITCHEN-LINEN WEAVES

Flat weave
Also known as plain weave, these smooth towels are not very absorbent, but they are good for lint-free drying of glassware.

Flour sack
Though flour is no longer commonly sold in pure-cotton sacks, the material is still used to make absorbent kitchen towels. Because they're lint-free, they're ideal for drying glassware.

Jacquard
This cotton fabric has an intricate design woven into it. It is also lint-free, so it works well for drying glassware.

Terry cloth
Sometimes known as bar towels or mops, this looped cotton fabric is extremely absorbent. It is good for drying pots, pans, and other large items.

Waffle
The honeycomb pattern on these cotton cloths makes them especially absorbent, so they are good for pots, pans, and other large items.

TOP-QUALITY
APPLIANCES MAKE THE
KITCHEN FUNCTION
WELL, WHICH MAKES
WORKING IN THE KITCHEN
A PLEASURE.

MAJOR APPLIANCES

Appliances are the kitchen's furnishings. They are also, for the most part, big-ticket items, investments meant to last for a long time. In order for them to do so, it is worthwhile to keep them clean and perfectly maintained, and to follow appropriate safety measures. For example, do you clean the grill on the bottom of your refrigerator annually? If not, you are making the motor work harder, thereby shortening the life of the machine.

Because appliances vary from manufacturer to manufacturer, model to model, it's essential to read and understand the instructions for using and caring for each. Keep all owner's manuals together in a loose-leaf binder, each in its own waterproof plastic sleeve. Manuals for newer appliances offer "troubleshooting" sections, useful if a problem arises later on, as well as toll-free numbers for questions. If you have misplaced the manual, search for the information on the Internet, where almost every manufacturer provides parts lists and prices for replacements and repairs—and in some cases, downloadable manuals. Also keep your warranty information handy. You will want to reference it to see what your warranty covers, and does not cover, and for how long.

Sooner or later, most appliances will break down and need to be replaced. If you love to cook or bake, then a top-quality cooktop and oven should be on your wish list. But "top quality," depending on what you need, does not have to mean "top dollar." Even entry-level appliances are much higher in quality than they used to be.

ABOUT WARRANTIES

All new appliances come with a manufacturer's warranty, which serves as an assurance the appliance in working order, and that it should last for a fixed amount of time, usually one year. Should the appliance prove faulty or need repair in that period, the manufacturer usually agrees to repair or replace the appliance at no extra charge. Appliance warranties are available in two types, full and limited.

Warranty cards, enclosed with the owner's manual, contain a series of questions for the consumer to fill out. Beyond the basic information, such as name, address, date of purchase, and the serial and model numbers of the appliance, many of the questions are more personal, including inquiries about your income, family size, and purchasing preferences. These questions are designed to collect valuable marketing information. You should be careful about answering them, however, as they can put you at risk of identity theft and fraud.

Federal law states that if your appliance comes with a full warranty, you are not obligated to return the warranty card. It's not a bad idea to return it, though, especially if the manufacturer ever needs to reach you in the event of a recall or safety alert; just restrict your answers to the basic questions. If you choose not to return the card, keep it with the original receipt and the owner's manual for the warranty period, should the appliance need repair within that time. Limited warranties, which are much more common, are not activated until the consumer returns the warranty card, but you don't have to fill in anything other than your name, address, date of purchase, and product number.

EXTENDED WARRANTIES

As the name implies, these agreements extend the coverage period for an appliance beyond the expiration date of the manufacturer's warranty. Though an extended warranty may sound like a good investment when you purchase your appliance, the Federal Trade Commission recommends that consumers consider a few things before buying one. An extended warranty won't guarantee that the product will last longer, of course, but only that the company you purchase the policy from promises to service or repair the appliance during the extended period. Do a little research on repairs, since an extended warranty could cost as much as the repair itself, making it essentially worthless. Check with your credit card company as well, since some companies automatically extend the manufacturer's warranty, at no extra charge, if you buy an appliance with their card. And bear in mind that if you purchase an extended warranty, you won't get to decide who does the repair—the company who holds the policy will make that decision.

RANGES

A good range, cooktop, or oven can elevate cooking to a high art, and it's well worth comparing models carefully when selecting new ones. There are many considerations, including the cost, the upkeep, the performance, the safety features (particularly with small children in the household), and the energy source (gas or electric).

A range has a cooktop and an oven, both of which generally use the same type of energy, whether gas or electric. A dual-fuel range is usually a model that has a gas cooktop and an electric oven; these ranges are more expensive than single-fuel appliances. The ovens in most ranges today—both gas and electric—are self-cleaning (meaning they use very high heat to turn spills into ash that is easy to clean), and manufacturers have made great strides in designing cooktops with fewer crevices to trap grease and dirt. Special features on modern ranges are numerous—from interchange-able, or modular, griddles and grills to warming drawers to high-powered burners designed for wok cooking.

To the uninitiated, all ranges may look more or less the same. There are, however, several different kinds, each of which is designed for a specific type of installation (see below). They measure from 24 inches to 48 inches in width.

RANGE TYPES

FREESTANDING
This range isn't tucked between cabinets or appliances, so its sides are finished. It stands on the floor (not on a cabinet base), and usually has its controls on a back panel.

SLIDE-IN
This range is designed to fit in between two cabinets and has a lip along each side that overlaps the countertop. Like a freestanding range, it rests on the floor. It does not have a back panel, however, and the sides are unfinished. Controls are on the front of the appliance.

DROP-IN
Drop-in ranges are made to fit between cabinets or appliances, so their sides are not finished. They usually stand a few inches off the ground, on top of a low cabinet base. Controls are generally on the front of the appliance.

HIGH/LOW
A high/low range has an oven above the cooktop as well as one below. The top may actually be a microwave oven with a vent hood.

COOKTOPS

Installing a separate cooktop and oven can be an attractive and practical option, though it may be more expensive than installing a range. It allows you the flexibility of putting each appliance where it's most convenient. The cooktop can be installed in an island, for example, while the oven (or ovens) can be installed at eye level in a tall cabinet. It also allows you to mix and match energy types—a gas cooktop, for example, and an electric oven, which many seasoned cooks prefer for baking. As with ranges, some cooktops are manufactured with modular grills or griddles, woks, or even deep fryers that can replace burners. Cooktops measure from 30 to 36 inches wide.

FUEL TYPES

Ranges and cooktops can be powered by either gas (natural gas or propane) or electricity. Each type of power has its own benefits and drawbacks.

GAS BURNERS

Because they allow you to turn heat on or off with a quick flick of the wrist, gas burners give you more precise control over temperatures than other fuel types. Kitchens with gas appliances must have proper ventilation, however, to reduce the risk of air pollution caused by gaseous fumes. The appliances also require a gas line, which if your house is not already plumbed with one, can be costly and impractical to install. Your local gas company can provide information. You could choose to use propane, also known as liquefied petroleum gas, instead of natural gas, by either purchasing a propane tank or renting one from a gas company. Since most appliances are made to run on natural gas, you will need to buy an LP gas converter as well.

Older gas appliances often have continuously burning pilot lights, also known as standing pilot lights. Modern appliances have what's called an intermittent ignition system, which is electronic: Electricity makes a spark that ignites the burner (and can use 30 percent less gas than models with standing pilot lights). Modern gas appliances also generally have sealed burners, rather than the open burners and drip pans found on older models, which makes it easier to clean up spills.

ELECTRIC COIL BURNERS

Electric burners maintain low, even heat better than their gas counterparts. And though many people think they are slow to respond, a large electric burner can boil water more quickly than a gas burner. One of their major drawbacks is that you can't control temperature exactly, since burners take time to heat up and cool down. Electric ranges tend to cost less than gas ones, but it can cost more to operate an electric appliance over time.

A NOTE ABOUT BRITISH THERMAL UNITS (BTUs)

Gas burners are measured in British Thermal Units, or BTUs. The higher the BTU capacity, the hotter the burner (or oven) can get. A BTU is the amount of heat required to raise the temperature of 1 pound of water by 1°F. When comparing gas ranges, consider the relative BTUs of each burner. Most have one or two large, high-power burners (about 12,500 to 15,000 BTUs per hour), one or two medium-power burners (which have a maximum of 9,000 BTUs per hour), and a small burner (about 5,000 BTUs per hour). The BTU rating of propane is higher, meaning it burns hotter than natural gas. Most appliances are fitted with a mechanism to adjust for this, so your range will have the same BTU rating whether it burns natural gas or propane.

There are three other types of electric burners in addition to the traditional coil. Radiant, halogen, and magnetic induction elements are all concealed by a glass ceramic surface. Patterns on the surface indicate the presence of heating elements below. Glass ceramic cooktops have a smooth, continuous surface that is particularly easy to care for (although it's best to wipe up spills promptly after the surface has cooled). They look clean and uncluttered, though they are vulnerable to scratches, particularly if you vigorously shake pots and pans directly on the surface itself. It can also be difficult to tell at a glance whether burners have cooled down (some models have small indicator lights noting if the cooktop is still hot). Here's how the three types function:

RADIANT

Also known as ribbon elements, these work in a similar way to the familiar black electric coils but they usually do not heat as quickly.

HALOGEN

As the name suggests, halogen elements work like the lightbulbs—but generate more heat, of course. Glass tubes filled with halogen gas warm in an instant, giving off a glow.

MAGNETIC INDUCTION

Magnetic induction cooktops don't get hot, but they do rely on magnetic energy to create heat when pots are placed on top of them. The pots must be made of a metal that can be magnetized, such as cast iron or steel. Magnetic induction offers excellent control and heats faster than gas or electric. It's also the most expensive of the electric elements since many models are European-made.

HOW TO CLEAN PORCELAIN ENAMEL COOKTOP SURFACES

Clean with a soft cloth and an all-purpose cleaner. Avoid heavily abrasive cleansers, abrasive pads, and steel wool. Porcelain surfaces may etch or discolor when a spill is high in sugars or acids; these spills should be wiped up as soon as possible. Never wipe a hot porcelain surface with a wet cloth, however; cracking or chipping may result. If a pot boils over, turn down the heat to the lowest temperature that will allow it to continue cooking, and after the cooktop surface cools down, wipe the surface clean with a damp sponge. Loosen baked-on spills with a paste of baking soda and water. For very dirty surfaces, use a commercial stovetop cleaner, available at home-supply stores. If the surface of a porcelain enamel range gets chipped, camouflage damage with appliance touch-up paint from a hardware store.

HOW TO CLEAN A RANGE OR COOKTOP

1. Always consult the owner's manual before cleaning.

2. After each use, as soon as the appliance is cool, wipe down the cooking surface, including burners and grates. The sooner you get to spills, the fewer cleaning products and less elbow grease you'll need. Grease and food spatters will be more difficult to remove once the range or cooktop is reheated.

3. To clean burned-on food spills from grates, place the grates on a large plastic bag or on newspaper in a well-ventilated area or outside. Carefully spray with commercial oven cleaner (follow the manufacturer's instructions). Let stand for several hours or overnight. Wash grates in hot soapy water (wearing rubber gloves). Rinse thoroughly and dry before replacing.

4. To clean the control knobs, first remove them: Turn to the Off position and pull them straight off. Wash knobs in mild dishwashing liquid and warm water. Do not soak them or use any cleaners containing ammonia or abrasives, which could remove the graphics from the knob. Dry thoroughly and replace them by pushing firmly onto the stem.

HOW TO CLEAN STAINLESS-STEEL COOKTOP SURFACES

Wipe with a sponge and a few drops of mild dishwashing liquid, or a commercial stainless-steel spray cleaner. Be sure to dry thoroughly afterward with a clean cotton or microfiber cloth; otherwise, any residue will cause streaking. To remove encrusted materials from stainless steel, soak the area with a towel dampened with hot water to loosen the material and then gently scrape with a rubber spatula. For tough stains, use a commercial stainless-steel spray, making sure to polish with the grain.

HOW TO CLEAN GLASS CERAMIC COOKTOP SURFACES

Wipe clean with a damp cloth (you may also wash with a mild dishwashing liquid; just avoid using excessive amounts of water). These surfaces scratch easily—even the gritty particles in a dirty sponge can cause damage. Wipe up any messes, particularly sugary spills, before they solidify. If spills do harden, carefully remove them with a razor blade. You can also use a commercial cleaner formulated specifically for glass ceramic cooktops, available at home-supply stores. To protect the surface, use only smooth-bottomed pans and keep them as clean as possible. Don't slide pans or metal utensils across the cooktop. Never cook on a broken or cracked cooktop. Cleaning solutions and spillovers may penetrate the surface and create a risk of electric shock.

HOW TO CLEAN ELECTRIC COIL BURNERS

Food spills frequently fall into the metal bowl beneath the burner. Usually made of chrome, these bowls look like stylish drip catchers, but their real job is to reflect heat onto the bottoms of pans. Do not line these bowls with aluminum foil or place them in the dishwasher, as they may discolor. Keep them as clean as possible since burned-on stains and heat discoloration make them less effective reflectors. Food spills sometimes make their way underneath these bowls, but most models have hinged tops to allow easy access. Clean with hot, soapy water.

HOW TO CLEAN GAS BURNERS

Gas burners sometimes become clogged. The ports—the small holes around the burners where gas is ignited—become blocked with food particles or cleaning products, resulting in a sparse flame or no flame at all. Use a pin, piece of wire, or opened paper clip to clear the ports (never use a wooden toothpick, as the tip could break off and make the clog worse). Do not attempt to enlarge or distort the ports while clearing them, and use care around the igniter; the burner may not light if the igniter is damaged, soiled, or wet. Use a damp, not wet, cloth for cleaning. This will prevent water from entering the gas tube opening. If you have an older range with a standing pilot light, turn off the gas valve first. See the owner's manual (or search for it online) for instructions. After cleaning, relight the pilot, if necessary, according to the manufacturer's instructions. Any removable range parts, such as griddles and burner grates, can be soaked in hot water and mild dishwashing liquid while you clean the rest of the range.

CLEANING A GAS STOVE

Clear clogged gas ports by inserting a pin, paper clip, or piece of wire in holes. Remove the knobs, grates, and reflector bowls for a thorough cleaning in hot water and mild dishwashing liquid. Lift up the hinged stove top to wipe up spills that find their way beneath burners.

COMMERCIAL VS. COMMERCIAL-STYLE RANGES

There are important distinctions between commercial and commercial-style ranges. Commercial-style ranges look similar to their professional cousins, with heavy grates, substantial knobs, and sleek stainless-steel finishes. They may also feature high-heat burners, warming lights, and griddles, all of which are standard on restaurant ranges. Unlike restaurant ranges, however, commercial-style ones are insulated. The walls of commercial ranges are uninsulated and they can get as hot on the outside as on the inside, which is a danger to bare hands and wood cabinetry. As such, commercial ranges must be installed with wider-than-normal clearances, and surfaces around the range must be flame-proof (sheathed with materials such as stainless steel, brick, or tile). Many local codes may also require a ventilation hood, and may even require a built-in sprinkler system. Considering that most insurance companies will not insure a residence with a true commercial range, it's understandable that demand for commercial-style ranges, with many of the same features but few if any of the same safety concerns, arose in the mid-1980s. Those safety features more than justify the higher price of commercial-style ranges, which can cost up to a third more than true commercial models.

OVENS

The principles of oven cooking are simple: Food is heated by hot air (baking) or infrared radiation (broiling). Ovens generally have two heating elements: the baking element on the bottom of the oven and the broiling element on the roof of the oven. The elements work separately, except during preheating, when they work simultaneously. Wall ovens work in the same way as the ovens in ranges. Wall ovens measure from 24 inches to 30 inches wide.

CONVENTIONAL OVENS

During baking in a conventional oven, the heating element at the bottom of the oven heats the air inside the cavity. That air rises and transfers its heat to the food; cooler air then sinks to the bottom of the oven and the cycle begins again. This natural process can be relatively slow and inefficient, and results in inconsistent heating within the oven.

CONVECTION OVENS

A convection oven accelerates the conventional baking process with a fan and sometimes a third heating element (models that have the third element are called true, European, or third-element convection ovens). Heat is distributed more evenly throughout the oven by the fan, which helps food

A NOTE ABOUT CONVERSION FOR CONVECTION OVENS
There is no equation you can apply to a recipe to yield cooking times or temperatures for a convection oven. A good rule of thumb is to reduce your baking time by 20 to 30 percent at the same temperature, *or* to lower the recommended temperature by 25°F. About 10 minutes before the recommended cooking time has expired, check for the traditional cues to doneness. Don't expect significant time savings on recipes with cooking times of fifteen minutes or less.

bake faster (up to 25 percent less time) and reduces the energy needed to operate the oven.

Many commercial kitchens and bakeries use convection ovens, not only because they save time and energy, but because they bake and roast foods more evenly and consistently than conventional ovens. Meats often emerge juicier than with conventional cooking because when moisture rises to the top of a roast, it is quickly turned into a crust by the hot, circulating air. The same air, however, is unsuitable for delicate dishes such as soufflés or quiches. The convection feature can be turned off on most models, allowing you to cook conventionally.

COMBINATION OVENS

Combination ovens are wall ovens that combine a conventional or convection oven with a separate microwave oven above it.

POSITIONING OVEN RACKS

For both gas and electric ovens, use the middle rack for the majority of dishes, such as cakes, cookies, and casseroles. The lowest rack is best for pizza and artisanal breads—the bottoms will be crunchy but not the tops. If your broiler is inside the oven, use the top rack for broiling. Whenever possible, try to use a single rack at a time, without crowding it, to promote air circulation. If you have multiple pans in the oven—for two cake layers, say—place one in the upper third of the oven and one in

HOW TO CLEAN OVEN DOORS

To clean the inside of the oven door, wipe the completely cool door thoroughly with a solution of water and mild dishwashing liquid, or 1 part water and 1 part white vinegar. Do not use abrasive pads, which will scratch the glass. Do not allow water or cleaner to get on the door gasket; both can cause the gasket to deteriorate. If you make a habit of wiping the door every time you use the oven, you will never have to battle with greasy buildup or burned-on stains.

HOW TO CLEAN OVENS, BY TYPE

CONVENTIONAL OVENS
Conventional ovens require periodic scouring, but you should use store-bought oven cleaners with caution. Most contain lye to remove burned-on, greasy deposits. Lye and its fumes are not safe on all surfaces and can be hazardous to children and pets. If you choose to use it, always wear rubber gloves, goggles, and a dust mask; ventilate the area thoroughly by opening windows; protect the floor with newspapers; and cover the light and heating elements inside the oven with foil. Always read product labels carefully, since some cleaners are not meant to be used in gas ovens. Turn off the gas supply before cleaning if you have an oven with a standing pilot light.

SELF-CLEANING OVENS
Self-cleaning ovens use very high heat (up to 900°F) to turn spills into ash that is easily cleaned with a damp cloth. You must remove the oven racks during the cleaning cycle because the heat can affect the metal, discoloring it and making it difficult to slide racks in and out. Never use commercial oven cleaners on a self-cleaning oven.

CONTINUOUS-CLEANING OVENS
Continuous-cleaning ovens are coated with a chemical that causes food spills and spatters to dissolve, but at a lower temperature than self-cleaning ovens. This action takes place automatically when baking or roasting. Never use commercial oven cleaners on a continuous-cleaning oven, as they can damage the oven walls.

the lower third, and rotate halfway through baking. It's also wise to test the oven temperature with an oven thermometer. If you find a disparity between the oven's setting and the actual temperature, you'll have to adjust for the difference each time you set the oven. If there's a significant difference, call an appliance-repair professional to recalibrate the system.

AN ALTERNATIVE TO COMMERCIAL OVEN CLEANERS

For very dirty ovens, sprinkle the contents of a small box of baking soda onto the floor of the oven and add enough water to make a thick paste. Spread the paste thickly on dirty surfaces, and leave overnight. Scoop away remaining material with a small squeegee or plastic spatula. Rinse and wipe clean with a damp cloth.

VENTILATION HOODS

Cooking produces smoke, smells, and often grease and gases that need to find their way out of your kitchen. A ventilation system clears the kitchen of these by-products by expelling them outdoors through metal ducts or filtering them through an activated charcoal filter (a ductless charcoal system should be installed only when it is impossible to vent fumes outdoors, such as in apartments). Using the fan while cooking, especially while cooking on high heat, will keep the kitchen more comfortable, reduce humidity and odors, and help minimize greasy buildup on cabinets, walls, and ceilings. Depending on municipal building codes, the layout of your kitchen, and your personal design preferences, you can choose between an updraft and a downdraft ventilation system.

UPDRAFT

Updraft hoods are positioned over a range or cooktop. A fan draws the air upward and through a filter. There are many different styles of hoods—from compact models that are built into an upper cabinet to sleek stainless-steel chimney-style hoods that make dramatic design statements.

DOWNDRAFT

Downdraft systems are built into the base cabinet behind the cooktop or integral to the range or cooktop itself. They exhaust air by drawing it downward. Downdraft units are either fixed or retractable, the latter meaning you can raise them with the touch of a button while cooking and lower them when you're done. Downdraft systems are good for island installations, where installing a hood overhead wouldn't work. They do not exhaust the steam from taller pots and pans very well, however, and will not catch anything that's not right by the vent.

HOW TO CLEAN OVEN RACKS

Soak dirty oven racks for several hours in warm, sudsy water to loosen grease, then scrub with a brush or scouring pad. You can also spray them with commercial oven cleaner, slide them into a garbage bag, and let them sit for several hours. Rinse thoroughly before drying.

HOW TO CLEAN BROILER PANS

Many gas ovens have a broiler element and pan housed in a drawer below the main oven. Keep this area clean by washing the pan thoroughly in hot, soapy water after each use; doing so will also help prevent grease fires.

HOW TO CLEAN VENTILATION HOODS

Once a week, wipe down the outside of the hood with hot, soapy water and a soft cloth; do not use steel-wool pads or abrasive cleansers that will scratch the surface. Rinse with a hot, damp cloth and wipe dry. Grease will build up quickly if this task is neglected. Stainless-steel hoods can also be cleaned with commercial stainless-steel spray. Wipe in the direction of the grain.

Once a month, remove the filters and soak them in hot water and dishwashing liquid (do not use ammonia or ammonia-based products, which can discolor the metal). Brush lightly with a plastic scrub brush to dislodge greasy particles. Rinse filters in hot water and let dry thoroughly before replacing. Many filters can also be safely cleaned in the bottom rack of the dishwasher, although they can become discolored as a result; check the care manual for instructions.

ABOUT CFM AND SONES

All ventilation systems have what's called a CFM rating, which quantifies the cubic feet of air a fan can move per minute. The higher the CFM, the more powerful the system. The National Kitchen & Bath Association recommends a minimum CFM of 150 for all surface cooking appliances. For a commercial-style range with powerful burners, the hood should have a rating of 300 to 600 CFMs. When considering CFM, it's also important to consider the size of your kitchen. For example, if you have a 200-square-foot kitchen with 8-foot ceilings, you have 1,600 cubic feet of air. If you install a ventilation hood with 150 CFMs, the fan is going to clear the air in the room every ten and a half minutes. Increase the CFM from 150 to 1,000, and the air would clear every 1.6 minutes, which would probably mean too much air circulation. Ultimately, you should choose a hood that falls in between those two extremes, and clears the air every five or six minutes.

Ventilation systems often have a sone rating as well, which quantifies the noise level. The Home Ventilating Institute recommends that kitchen ventilation fans should not be louder than 9 sones. By comparison, the noise emitted by a refrigerator equals about 1 sone, normal conversation is about 4 sones, and a jet plane landing is about 256 sones.

MICROWAVE OVENS

Microwaves cause the water, fat, and sugar molecules in food to vibrate, which creates heat. Because the food is heated directly, the cookware and the interior of the oven generally do not get hot. These appliances are useful for quickly defrosting and warming, but not for browning or crisping foods. To remedy this, some manufacturers offer microwaves with a convection feature, which circulates hot air around food to brown it and seal in juices. Others incorporate halogen light to accomplish the same thing. Microwaves with sensors measure the amount of moisture inside food and adjust power levels accordingly (the oven automatically shuts off when it senses that the food is cooked). If you are primarily interested in reheating foods or making popcorn, you won't need these advanced features—all you'll need is a turntable, which helps foods heat more evenly.

WIPING THE MICROWAVE
AFTER EACH USE WILL
KEEP FOOD RESIDUE FROM
BUILDING UP.

Microwaves come in a variety of sizes, from compact to large. Capacity can range from 0.7 cubic foot to 2 cubic feet (a capacity in the range of 1.6 cubic feet is most popular). Most ovens sit on the countertop, but some are mounted over the range (and can include a ventilation fan) or are installed at eye level in a tall cabinet. Over-the-range and built-in models are considerably more expensive than countertop models.

HOW TO CLEAN A MICROWAVE OVEN

To prevent sticky or greasy stains from forming, always cover food with a paper towel before cooking or reheating anything in the microwave.

PLASTIC INTERIORS

- ☐ Wipe stains with a soft cloth or sponge and a solution of warm water and mild dishwashing liquid, then plain water.
- ☐ If that isn't enough, clean with 1 or 2 tablespoons of baking soda in a quart of water.
- ☐ For caked-on residue, heat water in a microwave-safe dish on High for three minutes; let stand for five minutes (with door closed), and then wipe the interior.

- ☐ For odors, clean with a baking soda solution, wipe surfaces dry, and leave the door open for a few hours. If the smell persists, stir 6 tablespoons baking soda or ½ cup lemon juice into a cup of water. In a microwave-safe dish, heat the mixture on High for two to three minutes. Then leave the door open for a couple of hours.

STAINLESS-STEEL INTERIORS

- ☐ Use a nylon scrubber and a mildly abrasive cleanser such as Bon Ami. Rinse with a clean, damp cloth and dry completely.

OTHER PARTS

- ☐ Clean doors with a solution of water and mild dishwashing liquid, or a mildly abrasive cleanser such as Bon Ami and a sponge or soft cloth.
- ☐ Wipe control panels with a barely damp (not wet) cloth; moisture behind the panel could ruin the oven.

MICROWAVE SAFETY

Most dishware made today comes with manufacturer's instructions for use and care, typically including information on whether it is suitable for the microwave. Sometimes the words "microwave safe" are printed on the bottom of the dish, meaning it will not sustain damage in the microwave. Such information is rarely available for older dishware. In this instance, you will have to do a little investigating.

Most metal-free glass, china, and pottery can be used in the microwave oven. Clear-glass Pyrex, which can withstand very high temperatures of heat, is ideal for microwave cooking as well as for use in the oven, freezer, or refrigerator. Some colored Pyrex, though, which was manufactured between 1947 and the late 1980s, has metallics in its paint and is therefore not microwave safe.

It is never safe to put anything made of or containing metal in the microwave; not only will the food it contains fail to heat, but the reaction between the metal and the microwaves could cause a spark. So it is important to examine any dishware for metal, including gold or silver decorative trim, or a metallic glaze.

If your dishware is old or delicate, a family heirloom, or a valuable collectible, you might still want to avoid putting it in the microwave. In such a case, you are always better safe than sorry: Avoid extreme heat—including the microwave, the oven, and the dishwasher.

You should also avoid using plastic of any sort in the microwave. When plastic is heated, there's a danger of potentially harmful chemicals leaching into food. The label "microwave safe" on plastic means only that it won't melt or sustain damage in the microwave.

A NOTE ABOUT ENERGY STAR LABELS

An Energy Star label means that an appliance meets strict energy-efficiency guidelines set by the EPA and the U.S. Department of Energy. There are more than forty different categories of Energy Star–labeled products, from appliances to home electronics and lighting. Because they use less energy, these products should save you money in the long term on your utility bills. Dishwashers with an Energy Star label use less water and 25 percent less energy than conventional models.

DISHWASHERS

Dishwashers today are remarkably sophisticated, with thick insulation that cuts down dramatically on noise, adjustable racks, and a variety of settings, from Rinse Only to heavy-duty Pots and Pans cycles. Some of the newer dishwashers are almost silent, and with some models, you can even skip prerinsing dishes.

Generally, dishwashers have three cycles: a Light cycle, which is suitable for lightly soiled china and crystal; a Normal cycle, for moderately to heavily soiled dishes and glassware; and a Scrub or Pots and Pans cycle, for heavily soiled dishes and cookware. More expensive models may have an Economy or Speed cycle, which is shorter and uses less water and power than a Normal cycle; it's suitable for medium soil. Many dishwashers today have sensors that evaluate the amount of grease in the rinse water, and choose the appropriate cycle accordingly.

Most dishwashers measure 24 inches wide (though there are models as wide as 30 inches), 34 inches high, and 24 to $26\frac{3}{4}$ inches deep. Compact and portable dishwashers are 18 inches wide, with the same range in height and depth as regularly sized models. Some manufacturers also offer even smaller dishwashers designed to fit into a drawer or sink. These units typically accommodate four or five complete place settings. The drawer units can be stacked and used simultaneously or individually, depending on the number of dishes you need to wash.

ABOUT DISHWASHER NOISE

Manufacturers do not have a consistent rating system to quantify how noisy a dishwasher is. Some use decibels (actual noise) and some use sones (perceived noise, as defined on page 80). Any decibel rating lower than 60 is quiet, with 43 being about the quietest currently available (that's about 4 sones). Construction affects noise level. The quietest dishwashers, including many European models, have their motors mounted directly to the base pan rather than to the tub. Machines with motors and pumps attached to the tub are significantly more noisy, since the tub magnifies sound.

A dishwasher's noisiness also depends on its filtration system. Less-expensive machines use food-disposal grinders to reduce large bits of food, and spray arms to clean out its filters during the Rinse cycles. They are generally louder than dishwashers with removable filters that are cleaned by hand.

HOW TO COMBAT CLOUDINESS ON GLASSWARE

If you find cloudy spots on glasses after running them through the dishwasher, first test whether it is only temporary, as a result of hard water.

Dampen a soft cloth with vinegar and rub the cloudy area. If the vinegar removes the cloudiness, you're in luck. To remove the film, put the glasses back in the dishwasher for a Normal Wash; stop the dishwasher at the beginning of the final Rinse cycle and set 2 cups white vinegar in a measuring cup on the bottom dish rack. Once the cycle is done, run another cycle to remove the traces of vinegar. In the future, use a liquid rinse agent to prevent further filming. If rubbing with vinegar does not remove the etching, the damage is permanent. Prevent damage to other items by minimizing the amount of detergent and using a lighter, shorter cycle.

HOW TO LOAD THE DISHWASHER

1. Since heat and hot water are generally more intense on the lower rack than the upper rack, pots, plates, utensils, and other heavy-duty wash jobs should go on the bottom rack.

2. Load as much as you can without having things touch. Stagger or overlap small plates.

3. Delicate dishes and glassware should be placed in the upper rack.

4. Place everything in the upper rack facedown; everything in the lower rack facing the center.

5. Cooking utensils should be lying down on the bottom or top rack, not in the cutlery bin.

6. Don't place items over the prongs on the upper rack. Glasses and mugs should go in the rows between the prongs while bowls should be placed down in the center.

7. Forks and spoons should be placed in the cutlery bin alternately (some handles up, some down, if possible) so they don't nest.

WASHING SILVER IN THE DISHWASHER

Most experts agree that hand-washing sterling silver and silver plate is preferable because it's gentler, but silver can go in the dishwasher; it would take a long time and many washings for damage to occur. The most important thing to remember is to keep stainless steel out of the dishwasher if you put sterling or silver-plate pieces there. The two metals will react with each other, causing irreparable damage to both finishes. Also, if you are concerned about damaging a vintage piece, wash it by hand to be on the safe side (never use steel wool). Wash newer pieces (as long as they don't fall into any of the categories listed on page 87) in the machine, especially if doing so encourages you to use and enjoy your silverware more regularly. Just wash and dry any new silverware by hand after the first few uses, to prevent spotting. After that, you should be able to wash it in the machine, but remember to use less detergent than normal and don't run the Dry cycle. All silver should be removed from the dishwasher just after the rinse cycle and dried by hand with a soft cloth, since the heat of the machine can cause detergent residue to bake onto the surface of the metal, leaving it dull or discolored.

HOW TO CARE FOR THE DISHWASHER

Once a week, clean the dishwasher door panel with a soft, lightly dampened cloth and dry thoroughly. Stainless steel can be cleaned with a commercial stainless-steel spray. To clean the control panel, use a lightly dampened cloth (excessive moisture can damage the panel) and dry thoroughly. Dishwasher interiors are either stainless steel or plastic. Stainless is generally impervious to stains; plastic is more vulnerable. Here's how to deal with a stained plastic tub interior, as well as with mildew and white film buildup:

RUST STAINS

Iron and manganese in the water usually cause rust. It can also come from a rusty water heater or rusty water lines. You can check for iron and manganese content by having an analysis done by a water treatment equipment company or testing laboratory. To find a local facility, contact your local Cooperative Extension System Office (a complete list of local offices is available at www.csrees.usda.gov/Extension/index.html). They should be able to tell you how to obtain a sample of your water and send it in for analysis. (For more information on testing your water, turn to page 606.)

☐ To remove stains, try a commercial rust treatment, such as RoVer Rust Remover.

☐ As a preventive measure, ask a plumbing contractor to install a filter that can aid in the control of rust.

BROWN STAINS

Probably caused by a calcium or iron buildup.

☐ Use citric acid (also known as sour salt) in liquid form, available at some large grocery stores (it was once widely used for canning) and many health food stores; you can also purchase it from some online retailers. Empty the dishwasher, fill the detergent cup with citric acid, and run a complete cycle. Run the dishwasher through a second cycle without the crystals but with detergent.

MILDEW

☐ To remove mildew from the interior or gasket, mix 1 part chlorine bleach to 10 parts water, or mix 1 gallon water with $\frac{1}{2}$ cup ammonia.

☐ Then wipe with a cloth or sponge, wearing rubber gloves. *Note:* Never mix bleach and ammonia; doing so will result in dangerous, potentially lethal fumes.

☐ Run the dishwasher through a Rinse cycle to remove any residual cleaner.

RED STAINS

Most likely caused by a tomato-based product.

☐ The stain may be permanent but should fade over time with repeated washings.

☐ Staining can be minimized by removing any excess sauce from your dishes before loading the dishwasher.

GREEN STAINS

Caused by detergents that contain dye or color pigments.

☐ Switch to another detergent.

WHITE FILM BUILDUP

Caused by hard minerals and over time can cause damage to other components of the dishwasher.

☐ Install a water-softening system. You can temporarily remove the buildup by using citric acid, as directed above, under "Brown Stains."

GETTING THE MOST OUT OF YOUR DISHWASHER

DO

□ Use only automatic dishwashing detergent in the dishwasher—never use soap, laundry detergent, or dishwashing liquid; they are too mild and will cause the machine to make too many suds.

□ Experiment with different brands and types of detergent to find the one best suited for your machine and your local water conditions. There are two types of dishwasher detergents available: granular and liquid. Granular is the more traditional form. Boxes should be kept tightly closed and stored in a dry place (not under the sink since it's usually too warm and damp). Old and caked detergent will not clean as well, since it won't dissolve and activate properly, and will leave behind a sandy deposit. Liquids and gels won't cake, but can separate with age, which can cause excessive suds in soft water.

□ Use only the recommended amount of detergent—too much can leave behind a residue, and too little can result in dirty dishes, which in turn leads to another Wash cycle and wastes water and energy.

□ To save water and energy, run only full loads. If the dishwasher is partially full, use the Rinse-Hold cycle to remove odor-causing foods. This is more economical than rinsing dishes by hand, which can waste up to 20 extra gallons of water per load or 6,500 gallons per household each year.

□ Use a rinse aid (either in the automatic rinse dispenser or, if your dishwasher doesn't have one, in solid form, which you can hang from the upper rack). Rinse aids lower the surface tension of the rinse water so it sheets off dishes and glasses, and droplets don't form. This translates into few water spots. Rinse aids are particularly helpful if you have mineral-rich hard water. They also help dishes dry faster, which can be helpful when using the Energy-Saving Dry cycle or air-drying dishes.

□ Dry dishes on the lowest temperature setting; hotter temperatures can leave spots on glassware.

□ If you have a European dishwasher, you may need to clean out a filter periodically; check the care manual for instructions.

DON'T

It's safe and efficient to wash most of your dirty dishes in the machine, but bear in mind that many kitchen tools and serving pieces should never be placed in the dishwasher. If in doubt about a particular piece, keep it out of the dishwasher. Do not put the following items in the dishwasher:

☐ Acrylic

☐ Adhesive-joined pieces

☐ Aluminum, including anodized aluminum

☐ Antiques

☐ Blown glass

☐ Brass

☐ Bronze

☐ Cast iron

☐ China with metallic decoration

☐ Crystal

☐ Disposable plastics not labeled "dishwasher-safe"

☐ Flatware with bone, plastic, or wood inlays or handles

☐ Gold-plated flatware

☐ Iron

☐ Knives

☐ Many nonstick pots and pans (check manufacturer's instructions first)

☐ Milk glass

☐ Pewter

☐ Rubber tools

☐ Tin

☐ Wooden spoons

☐ Don't spill dry dishwasher detergent on flatware; it can cause dark spots.

☐ Don't use detergents containing chlorine, to avoid the release of chlorine fumes in the kitchen while running the dishwasher.

☐ Don't jam too many pieces into the silverware basket; overcrowding can cause items to become scratched.

☐ Don't mix sterling or silver-plate and stainless-steel flatware in the dishwasher, even when using the Rinse-Hold cycle. If the metals come in contact with each other, a reaction between the two metals can damage both finishes. (Since most knives, including sterling ones, have stainless-steel blades, keep them away from other silver pieces, too.)

REFRIGERATORS

Refrigerators don't cool food; rather, they remove heat and moisture from an enclosed space, just like an air conditioner. They also slow the growth of bacteria. Most refrigerators have two compartments: one for freezing and one for chilling. Although they appear to be separate, in most models, they share the same air (all of which is cooled by a single system), which is transferred from one compartment to the other by a gatelike device called a baffle. That's why storing an uncovered dish of pasta redolent with garlic in the refrigerator will eventually result in ice in the freezer compartment with the same flavor.

Refrigerators can account for up to 25 percent of household energy costs. Although new models are much more energy efficient, it's still wise when making a new purchase to look for the Energy Star label, which means the appliance meets government standards for low energy consumption (for more information on Energy Star, turn to page 82). When considering capacity, which is measured in cubic feet (manufacturers give a number that encompasses both the refrigerator and freezer), a good rule of thumb is to allow 12 cubic feet of space for the first two members of the family and 4 cubic feet for each additional member.

Wiping up spills as they occur and quickly checking the contents daily to see if anything needs to be thrown away or replaced will keep the refrigerator clean and smelling fresh. Here are a few more guidelines:

CARING FOR YOUR REFRIGERATOR

1. Plug your refrigerator (and freezer, if it's separate) into a grounded outlet; never use an extension cord.

2. Cover food in airtight wrap. The refrigerator (and freezer) draws moisture out of food, whether it's lettuce or an uncovered bowl of leftovers. Even eggs, with their porous shells, will stay fresher longer when refrigerated in their cartons. (For more on food storage, turn to page 130.)

3. Never store foods or other items on top of the refrigerator, which can be warm, particularly bottles of cooking oil, which turn rancid when exposed to heat.

4. Keep the refrigerator three-quarters full to ensure it runs at optimum efficiency for the lowest cost. This allows plenty of room for air to circulate, and also allows cold items to "hold the cold," keeping the temperature stable when the door is repeatedly opened.

5. Neutralize odors by placing an open box of baking soda in the refrigerator. Stir the powder up from time to time to refresh it. Replace the box every three months, or sooner if your nose tells you it's time. Mark the box with the date it was opened.

6. When discarding an old refrigerator (or freezer), remove the door for public safety.

REFRIGERATOR STYLES

TOP-FREEZER MODELS

This style still dominates the refrigerator/freezer market, and is the one you are most likely to find in most American kitchens. Its popularity is due largely to an affordable price and easy set-up. Wide shelves (top-freezer models range from about 24 to 36 inches wide) allow easy access, even to items in the back, though you do have to bend to reach anything on the bottom. The capacity for these models ranges from 10 to 27 cubic feet.

SIDE-BY-SIDE MODELS

These appliances have a refrigerator and freezer both placed at eye level. Their narrow doors are particularly convenient in kitchens with tight spaces, although it can be difficult to store anything large, like a Thanksgiving turkey, on the shelves. Side-by-sides are generally 30 to 35 inches wide, with a capacity of 19 to 30 cubic feet. They are usually more expensive and less energy-efficient than top-freezer models. Many people prefer these models because of available special features such as built-in ice and water dispensers and temperature-controlled bins.

BOTTOM-FREEZER MODELS

Though these models still represent a small part of the American refrigerator market, they are gaining in popularity. They are more expensive, with a smaller capacity (usually up to 22 cubic feet), but their set-up offers many benefits. Because the refrigerator portion is at eye level, you don't have to bend to reach the most commonly used items. The freezer compartment, often with a pull-out basket, sits below the refrigerator. They are generally 29 to 36 inches wide.

BUILT-IN MODELS

These refrigerator/freezers are designed to fit flush with kitchen cabinets and counters, and are often sold with trim kits so you can attach a front panel that matches the cabinetry. Built-ins contain side-by-side compartments and are about a foot taller than conventional models, since the compressor is at the top rather than the bottom of the appliance. Because of the shallow depth, you sacrifice some storage space. Built-ins are generally 36 to 48 inches wide, with a capacity of 20 to 30 cubic feet.

A NOTE ABOUT CRISPER AND DELI DRAWERS

Some refrigerators offer a high-humidity crisper drawer for produce. It works by permitting less air to circulate within the drawer, thereby drawing out less moisture. You can mimic this feature by wrapping produce in slightly damp paper towels and then placing it in a plastic bag, which will keep air out and moisture in. Meat or deli drawers are generally kept at a slightly colder temperature than the rest of the refrigerator.

HOW TO KEEP THE REFRIGERATOR CLEAN

DAILY	☐ Wipe up spills immediately, before they have a chance to dry. ☐ Ensure everything that goes into the refrigerator is immaculate. Always wipe off the rims of jam jars, salad dressing bottles, and ketchup containers before storing them. ☐ Check for spoilage and throw out foods and beverages that are past their prime. ☐ Place anything likely to drip or leak, such as defrosting meat or cartons of berries, on a rimmed plate.
WEEKLY	☐ Wipe doors, including edges, and top of refrigerator with a cloth dampened with mild dishwashing liquid and water. Pay special attention to the areas around the handles, which can harbor sticky fingerprints. ☐ For a stainless-steel surface, use commercial stainless-steel spray and wipe in the direction of the grain.
SEASONALLY	☐ Turn off the power at the circuit breaker or fuse box. ☐ Put food in a cooler and remove glass shelves and crisper drawers to bring them to room temperature so there's no danger of them cracking when you wash them. ☐ Wipe the interior with a solution of 2 tablespoons baking soda and 1 quart hot water. Rinse with a damp cloth, then dry with a clean towel. Do not use soap or detergent; they can leave behind fragrance, which will be absorbed by food. Do not use abrasive cleansers, ammonia, or bleach. ☐ To remove caked-on residue, rehydrate by liberally applying the baking soda solution mentioned above with a wet towel. Leave the door open, and let the residue soak in the solution for ten minutes, or until it starts to crack or soften (reapply if necessary). Wipe the stain away with a clean, damp towel. If the stain won't come off, repeat the process with a mildly abrasive, chlorine-free household cleanser such as Bon Ami; dilute 1 tablespoon cleanser in 1 pint hot water to avoid scratching plastic surfaces. ☐ Soak shelves and bins in a solution of 2 tablespoons baking soda for every quart warm water. Do not wash in the dishwasher. Dry thoroughly before replacing. ☐ Clean the door seals, which can collect crumbs, with hot water and mild dishwashing liquid; dry thoroughly with a clean cloth. Check the seals periodically. An improper fit can cause cold loss and temperature fluctuations. ☐ Clean the drip pan or tray (also known as a defrost pan), which holds water from the continual process of defrosting, if your refrigerator has one. You'll have to remove the base grill first to look for the pan; it often sits on a set of black condenser coils. Before pulling it out, check to see if there's liquid in it. If so, soak it up with paper towels (wear rubber gloves and a dust mask first in case the water is moldy). When the pan is dry, pull it out and examine it for signs of mold. Wash the pan with warm, soapy water; if it's moldy, follow with a 1-to-10 solution of bleach and water. Dry thoroughly and vacuum the area around the pan before replacing it. To clean a fixed drip pan, wrap an absorbent cloth around the head of a clean long-handled brush or a clean paint roller and secure the cloth with rubber bands. Dampen it with warm soapy water and clean the pan. Wipe with a clean cloth and let air-dry before replacing the grill.

REFRIGERATOR-GRILL CLEANING

As a refrigerator pulls the heat out of the storage cavity, it vents it slowly and evenly into the kitchen through condenser coils. A buildup of dust around these coils acts like insulation and keeps the coils from releasing heat, which shortens the life of the machine.

These coils, which look like bedsprings, are usually at the bottom of the refrigerator, under the grill, although they also may be located at the top or in the back. Twice a year, or more if you live in a particularly dusty climate, clean the coils, either by vacuuming with the crevice attachment or by using a refrigerator coil brush (a long, thin brush capable of getting into tight areas), available at home centers and hardware stores. Be sure to shut off the power at the circuit breaker or fuse box beforehand.

ELIMINATING REFRIGERATOR ODORS

Regular maintenance and storing leftovers in airtight containers are the best ways to prevent odors. Even so, you may still be plagued with smells from time to time. To combat them, turn off the power at the circuit breaker or fuse box and remove the contents of the refrigerator (put in a cooler). Prop the door ajar, and clean the refrigerator with the baking soda and water solution noted opposite. If an odor still persists, turn the refrigerator back on, and try any of the following. (Avoid strong commercial odor-control products as their scent may contaminate foods and also permeate the plastic interior.)

☐ Spread a box of baking soda onto a rimmed baking sheet, and leave it in the refrigerator, with the door closed, until the smell goes away.

☐ Spread fresh coffee grounds on a tray, and leave it in the refrigerator, with the door closed, until the smell goes away (the lingering coffee smell will eventually dissipate).

☐ Place activated charcoal (available at drugstores or pet shops) on a tray, and leave it in the refrigerator for a few days, with the door closed and the temperature set on Low, until the smell goes away. Refresh charcoal (if odors persist) by placing it in the oven at 350°F for twenty minutes.

☐ Spread ½ inch of unscented chlorophyll cat litter in a shallow pan. Leave it in the refrigerator with the door closed until the smell is gone.

A NOTE ABOUT REFRIGERATOR TEMPERATURE

The temperature control in your refrigerator should be set between 37° and 40°F, and that in your freezer to between 0° and 5°F. If you want everything inside to be colder, adjust the setting in the refrigerator section, not in your freezer. Cold air originates in the freezer. A very high setting (meaning low in temperature) there will only cause the machine to close the baffle between the two sections so that the cold air stays in the freezer, leaving ice cream rock hard and drinks too warm.

FREEZERS

Freezers were introduced to consumers in the 1920s and 1930s, and since then long-term storage of otherwise perishable food has been a reality in our homes. Although some foods, such as potatoes (unless mashed), citrus fruits, mayonnaise, cream fillings, cream, cooked egg whites, and sour cream, don't freeze well, virtually any food can be frozen.

A frost-free freezer, which, as the name implies, never has to be defrosted, has three basic parts: a timer, a heating coil, and a temperature sensor. The timer turns on the heating coil, which is wrapped among the freezer coils every six hours or so. The heater continues to melt the ice off the coils until the sensor registers that the system's temperature has risen above 32°F, then shuts off the heater. Heating the coils requires energy, and also cycles the food in the freezer through temperature changes. Because of this, most large chest freezers, which are often placed in a basement or garage for extra storage, require manual defrosting. They preserve food longer and consume less power.

FREEZER TIPS

1. Neutralize odors by placing an open box of baking soda in the freezer to absorb stale odors; replace it every three months. (Mark the date when it was opened on the box.)

2. Store all foods in air-, moisture-, and vapor-proof containers and wraps specifically designed for the freezer. (For more information on wraps, turn to page 141.)

3. Trapped air can affect the flavor and texture of frozen foods, so you should try to force as much air as possible from containers before sealing them tightly and freezing them.

4. If you plan to store fresh meats and poultry in the freezer for more than two weeks, use freezer wrap to cover the original packaging, and label the wrap with the contents and date.

5. To keep the freezer working effectively, don't add too many things to it at once. Doing so can temporarily reduce the freezing capability and raise the temperature of already-frozen foods.

6. Put packages in the coldest part of the freezer first (against the walls or bottom of the compartment, not in the freezer door). Allow adequate room between items for cold air to circulate.

HOW TO DEFROST A FREEZER

Freezers that are not frost-free will need to be defrosted at least once or twice a year. As a general rule, when the frost reaches a thickness of ¼ inch, or when ice crystals form on packages, it's time to defrost.

1. Empty the freezer and transfer food to a cooler.

2. Turn off the power at the circuit breaker or fuse box.

3. If you have an upright model, place towels inside the bottom of the unit to catch any drips, or use drip pans.

4. Let the frost melt naturally, which can take several hours, or place a pot of boiling water on a heat-proof surface, such as a trivet or pot holder, inside the freezer to speed up the process.

5. Do not pry off ice with a spatula or other tool. You may puncture the lining of your freezer.

6. Once the freezer is defrosted, follow the directions for freezer cleaning on page 94.

7. Dry the freezer with a towel and switch the power on. Allow it to return to its original temperature (which should take up to thirty minutes) before replacing food.

HOW TO DEFROST FOOD SAFELY

The safest way to thaw food is to do it slowly in the refrigerator, where the temperature can be kept consistently at 40°F or colder. Small items such as steaks may defrost as quickly as overnight, whereas larger items, such as a turkey, can take several days. Dangerous microbes in food are inactive at this temperature, and if unused portions of the food are not exposed to higher temperatures, they can be safely refrozen.

If you must defrost frozen items more quickly, you can do so, but the food will have to be cooked before you can safely refreeze it. Place the food in a resealable, leak-proof plastic bag. Immerse the bag in cold water, and change the water every thirty minutes, checking frequently to make sure it remains cold. You can also use the microwave to defrost food more quickly. Once the food is thawed in either of these manners, it should be cooked immediately. The cooked food can then be refrozen for later use.

Of course, beyond the safety issues, there are quality issues to consider. Each time food freezes, it loses moisture, which helps impart flavor and texture. To avoid this problem, try freezing ingredients in small batches that can be used completely at one time.

A NOTE ABOUT ICE MAKERS

If your freezer has an ice maker, stir the ice up at least once every few days. This circulates air, keeping the ice fresher, and prevents clumping. If you don't use much ice, empty the ice bin once a month so the machine will make new ice; ice that sits for long periods can pick up odors from the air that circulates through both the freezer and the refrigerator.

HOW TO KEEP THE FREEZER CLEAN

Because the freezer contains foods that are generally well wrapped or sealed when they go into it, the freezer is less vulnerable to spills and drips than the refrigerator. Nonetheless, there are a few simple maintenance chores that will keep the freezer fresh and clean.

DAILY	☐ As with the refrigerator, everything you put into the freezer should be immaculate—wipe drips and smudges off ice cream cartons and plastic storage containers.
MONTHLY	☐ Check packaged foods for expiration dates and throw out anything that's past its prime.
ANNUALLY	☐ Turn off the power at the circuit breaker or fuse box; put food in a cooler. ☐ Remove shelves or bins to bring them to room temperature so there's no danger of them cracking when you wash them. Once they're at room temperature, soak them in a solution of 2 tablespoons baking soda for every quart warm water. Do not wash them in the dishwasher. Dry thoroughly before replacing them. ☐ Wipe down the interior with a solution of 2 tablespoons baking soda and 1 quart hot water. Rinse with a damp cloth, then dry with a clean towel. Do not use soap or detergent to clean the freezer; they can leave behind fragrance, which will be absorbed by food. Do not use abrasive cleansers, ammonia, or bleach on any part of the freezer. These agents can scratch, crack, or discolor surfaces. ☐ To remove caked-on residue, begin by rehydrating it in the baking soda solution mentioned above. Apply the solution liberally to the residue with a wet towel. Leave the freezer door open, and let the residue soak in the solution for ten minutes, or until it starts to crack or soften. If necessary, reapply the solution. Once the stain has softened, wipe it away with another clean, damp towel. If the stain won't come off, repeat the process with a mildly abrasive household cleanser—one that does not contain bleach, such as Bon Ami—and hot water. Dilute 1 tablespoon cleanser in 1 pint water to avoid scratching the freezer's plastic surfaces.

ABOUT FREEZER BURN

Freezer burn refers to the rough, dry, often discolored patches that sometimes appear on the surface of frozen food; it affects both flavor and texture but does not make the food unsafe to eat. Freezer burn occurs when the dry air in the freezer causes the moisture in the food to evaporate, leaving it dehydrated. To prevent freezer burn, do your best to keep the food from coming into contact with the drying air: Always wrap food tightly, eliminating as much air as you can. Wrap food once in plastic or foil, then again in a heavy-duty freezer bag; note the contents and date with a felt-tip pen.

IF YOU KEEP EVERYDAY
APPLIANCES ON YOUR
KITCHEN COUNTERTOP,
USE FELT GLIDES
UNDERNEATH THEM TO
PROTECT THE SURFACE.
THIS WILL ALSO MAKE
THEM EASY TO SLIDE BACK
AND FORTH.

SMALL APPLIANCES

The small appliances you keep in your kitchen are an indicator of who you are as a cook, and the kinds of cooking and baking that most entice you. Like major appliances, small appliances such as food processors, standing mixers, and juicers can also be investments that endure, as long as they're well cared for and maintained. If your food processor isn't chopping as well as it used to, it may not be worn out; it may just need a new blade. If your standing mixer sounds "rough," it may need new motor brushes. Watching out for these maintenance details will help keep your small appliances in top working order.

CLEANING SMALL APPLIANCES

☐ Always consult your user's manual before cleaning any appliance.

☐ First unplug and cool the appliance.

☐ Wipe with a cloth dampened with mild dishwashing liquid and water, and dry with a soft cloth or paper towel. Baking soda is also an excellent all-purpose cleanser for most appliances. If you choose to use spray cleaners, never spray them directly on appliances.

☐ Do not allow any moisture to come in contact with electrical parts. Never immerse any appliance or any part of an appliance in water unless specifically labeled "immersible" in the care guide.

HOW TO CLEAN SMALL APPLIANCES, BY TYPE

BLENDER

Wash the blender jar and the cover in warm, soapy water; rinse and dry thoroughly or place in the upper rack of a dishwasher. Wipe the motor base clean with a damp cloth; do not submerge it in water or place in the dishwasher. Wash the cutting assembly, gasket, and locking ring in warm, soapy water as well. Rinse and dry thoroughly. For stuck-on residue, pour $\frac{1}{2}$ cup water and $\frac{1}{3}$ cup baking soda into the blender jar; run the blender briefly before disassembling and washing.

COFFEEMAKER, AUTO DRIP

Wipe the exterior with warm sudsy water to cleanse it of oils and residue, then rinse and dry. Place coffeemaker carafes in the top rack of a dishwasher. Avoid placing them on the bottom rack because the plastic handles may melt. To avoid breakage, never rinse a hot coffeepot with cold water. When brewing becomes sluggish, fill the carafe with equal parts water and white vinegar. Pour into the reservoir and turn the machine on. When several cups have run through, turn the machine off and let it sit for an hour. Turn the machine back on; when the cycle is complete, discard the vinegar and water in the carafe. Run clean water through the machine a few times to remove any traces of the vinegar.

COFFEEMAKER, ESPRESSO MACHINE

Wipe with a damp cloth. Do not use abrasive cleansers or steel wool, which could damage the surface of the metal. Follow manufacturer's instructions for cleaning nozzles.

COFFEEMAKER, MANUAL DRIP OR FRENCH PRESS

Allow delicate glass carafes to cool to room temperature before washing by hand with water and mild dishwashing liquid. Never wash warm glass pieces with cold water, which can cause breakage. Wash metal and plastic parts with water and mild dishwashing liquid.

COFFEEMAKER, STOVETOP ESPRESSO

Wash by hand in warm, soapy water. Do not put in the dishwasher as the dishwasher detergent may alter the surface of the metal. Do not use abrasive products or steel wool. Replace the top only after all parts are thoroughly dry.

COFFEE/SPICE GRINDER

Clean grinders by pulverizing bread or uncooked white rice in them; both will pick up any lingering coffee or spices. If you have any residue or aromas left behind by nuts, grind 1 tablespoon of baking soda, and wipe thoroughly.

FOOD PROCESSOR

Wash all removable parts by hand or in a dishwasher. If washing by hand, use warm, soapy water; rinse and dry thoroughly. Never use scouring pads or abrasive cleansers. Avoid letting the knife blade or disks soak in water for any length of time. To prevent cutting yourself, use a nylon brush to clean the knife blade and reversible disks. If washing in the dishwasher, place the blade and disks in the upper rack. Wipe the base with a damp cloth and dry thoroughly. If necessary, use mild dishwashing liquid to remove stubborn stains. Do not immerse in water.

HAND MIXER

Eject the beaters and whisks. Wash them in hot, soapy water or place in the dishwasher. Dry thoroughly before storing. Clean the unplugged mixer and cord with a damp cloth. To remove stubborn stains, use a sponge or cloth moistened with mild dishwashing liquid and water. Follow by wiping the surface with a damp, clean cloth. Do not use abrasive cleansers as they can damage the finish.

TOASTER

Unplug it once cooled, carry it to the sink, pull down the crumb tray knob or turn the toaster upside down, and let the crumbs fall into the sink. (If you don't have a garbage disposal, empty the tray over a garbage can.) Wipe the crumb tray with a damp cloth or sponge and snap shut. Wipe the exterior with a soft cloth dampened with mild dishwashing liquid. Chrome surfaces can be wiped with a cloth dampened with nonammoniated cleaner.

ELECTRIC JUICER

Remove all parts; wash the cover, reamer, strainer, pitcher, and any other moving parts in hot, soapy water. Use a bristle brush to remove any pulp. Do not wash in the dishwasher. Wipe the base with a damp cloth or sponge.

TOASTER OVEN

Wipe spills or spatters after each use. Wash racks in warm soapy water. If the inside of the toaster has a nonstick coating, wipe it with a damp soft cloth. On a bare metal interior, use a nylon scrubbing pad. To avoid scratching surfaces (or making it more difficult to clean the next time food cooks on), use nothing more abrasive than a light-duty (white) nylon pad. Some toaster-oven interiors may look rough and feel gritty, indicating a continuous-clean surface that automatically burns off food residue. Do nothing more to this type of surface than wipe it with a damp soft cloth. Since most toaster ovens have plastic or painted steel exteriors, use only a mild dishwashing liquid. If burned food discolors the paint on a toaster oven, a degreasing cleaner may minimize the discoloration, but nothing removes it entirely. Chrome surfaces can be wiped with a cloth dampened with window cleaner.

STANDING ELECTRIC MIXER

Wash beaters by hand unless you know they are stainless steel. Many stand mixers have beaters made of brushed aluminum, which automatic dishwasher detergent discolors. Beaters that look plastic may actually be aluminum with a nonstick coating and should not be washed in the dishwasher, either. Wipe the base with a damp cloth or sponge. If the vent is clogged, loosen the dirt with a toothpick or toothbrush, and then vacuum it.

WAFFLE IRON

Brush grids with a soft plastic brush or wipe gently with a paper towel while still warm (but not hot) to remove crumbs. Don't wash the grids with water or even wipe them with a damp cloth or sponge, or you will remove the layer of seasoning. However, if a waffle iron without a nonstick finish begins to stick or becomes stained, wash the grids with warm suds, rinse, wipe dry, and reseason with unsalted butter or canola oil. Clean the outside surfaces by wiping them with a damp sponge or cloth. Do not use harsh or abrasive cleansers or tools that may mar the surface.

ESSENTIAL SMALL APPLIANCES

FOOD PROCESSOR

This is a must-have for prepping all sorts of ingredients, blending pie crust dough, kneading bread dough, and pureeing vegetables and soups.

TOASTER OR TOASTER OVEN

Look for a toaster with slots wide enough for bagels and thick, hand-cut slices of bread, and clean it often to keep it crumb-free. A toaster oven has the advantage of using less energy than it would take to heat up the oven for something small like a pizza slice.

COFFEE/SPICE GRINDERS

If you do a lot of cooking, invest in two: one for coffee beans, and another for whole spices and peppercorns. Mark each one with a label to avoid mixing them up.

BLENDER

Choose one that's at least 500 watts so it's powerful enough to crush ice, as well as blend smoothies and puree soups. You should be able to move it easily between kitchen and bar. A handheld immersion blender, with a rotary blade and variable speeds, is also useful; it is immersed directly into a pot of soup or bowl of fruit to puree it.

MIXERS, HAND AND STANDING

A standing mixer with paddle and whisk attachments is indispensable if you enjoy baking; a grinder attachment is helpful if you don't have a food processor. A hand mixer is convenient when space is limited or when you need to beat something over a bowl of cold or hot water.

COFFEEMAKERS

Depending on your tastes and preferences, choose one (or more) of several types: automatic drip, electric espresso machine, French press, manual drip, and stovetop espresso makers. Although an espresso machine may seem like an expensive investment, it can save you money in the long run if you drink cappuccino or lattes every day.

SPECIALTY SMALL APPLIANCES

SLOW-COOKER

This countertop appliance consumes less energy than an oven, and allows you to do all the prep work hours before eating. Because it cooks foods slowly at a low temperature—usually between 170° and 280°F—the machine coaxes flavor from less expensive cuts of meat.

MINI FOOD PROCESSOR

This is ideal for jobs too small for the standard-size food processor, such as chopping nuts and herbs, and for making your own mayonnaise and pureeing small batches of food for babies.

WAFFLE IRON

Great for those who enjoy homemade waffles. It also doubles as a sandwich press. Unless it has a nonstick surface, you need to season a waffle maker before using it for the first time (follow manufacturer's instructions).

CITRUS PRESS

For making your own fresh juices from citrus fruits. This manual version can rest on the countertop if you enjoy fresh juice every morning. Electric versions are useful if you need to squeeze large quantities of juice.

PRESSURE COOKER

Pressure cooking is a quick and healthful way to prepare roasted meats, whole chickens, vegetables, and stews.

RICE COOKER

This machine cooks rice perfectly, and keeps it warm once it's done; it also doubles as a vegetable steamer.

ICE-CREAM MACHINE

For making delicious homemade ice creams, gelatos, and sorbets. It's a great investment if you like to entertain.

STORAGE SOLUTIONS

A stainless-steel grab bar and several S-hooks will turn a few square feet of ceiling or wall space into a convenient rack for kitchenware. Grab bars are better than towel bars for the job because they support more weight. Look for them, in sizes from 12 to 32 inches long, at surgical supply stores. S-hooks are available at most hardware stores.

HOW TO CLEAN A HANGING POT RACK

A hanging pot rack will need a thorough cleaning a couple of times a year. Remove everything that is hanging from it and wipe down the rack with a cloth dampened with hot water and a solvent-free degreaser. Wash and dry any pots and pans to remove grease and dust. Regularly using an exhaust fan while cooking will help to reduce this problem.

COOKWARE

With so many shapes, sizes, and special uses for pots and pans, not to mention variations in quality and cost, the selection process itself can feel overwhelming. There is no single rule for choosing pots and pans, and many fine cooks like to mix and match metals.

You can tell a lot from scrutinizing a pot. It should be heavy but comfortable to hold. Handles should be easy to grip, securely fastened to the pot with rivets, and tilted slightly to provide protection from the heat for the cook. Pot lids should fit securely.

When selecting pots and pans, think of the purpose the pan is meant to fill in your cooking repertoire. Be practical, buying good-quality pots and pans for the way you cook now, and adding specialty items only when you discover you need them. If poached salmon is your specialty, then you would want a high-quality poacher, but if you've never poached a fish in your life, don't buy one until you're ready to experiment. Choose pots and pans with ovenproof lids and handles, if possible, for quick and easy transfer of dishes that need to go from cooktop to oven. Study the pros, cons, and maintenance issues inherent in the metals available, to make your decisions wisely, because the right cookware greatly enhances the pleasure (and success) of cooking.

COOKWARE MATERIALS

ALUMINUM

Aluminum is the most heat-conductive metal after copper. It is durable and heats quickly, but if the metal is thin, the pan will warp easily and heat unevenly. Untreated aluminum is reactive, meaning it can also affect the taste and color of certain foods, particularly acidic ones like tomatoes. Some types are dishwasher-safe, but check with the manufacturer first; if it is not dishwasher-safe, it will turn black.

ANODIZED ALUMINUM

This is aluminum that has been treated to become nonreactive and is also much stronger than regular aluminum. The anodizing process hardens the surface, making pots and pans relatively easy to clean, and scratch- and stick-resistant. It is not dishwasher-safe.

CAST IRON

Cast iron provides excellent heat conductivity and is good for cooking at high temperatures. It is exceedingly strong and durable but reacts with acidic foods (therefore, it is not ideal for making sauces), is slow to heat, and is very heavy. Seasoning your cast-iron pan will make cleaning easier and will also help keep it from rusting. (For information on how to season a pan, turn to page 68.) It is not dishwasher-safe.

COPPER

An excellent heat conductor, copper is often considered the ultimate material for cookware. It spreads heat quickly and loses it quickly, making it ideal for cooking delicate foods, such as sauces. Most copper pans are lined with an inert metal such as tin or stainless steel to prevent the reaction between copper and acidic foods that can leach into foods and result in verdigris poisoning. Copper also tarnishes easily and must be hand-washed and polished regularly to retain its shine. Use a product specifically formulated for copper, such as Red Bear Copper and Brass Polish.

ENAMELED CAST IRON

This cookware material shares the characteristics of plain cast iron but is nonreactive. It has a glassy surface that protects the metal from rust. The surface can chip easily, however, and doesn't lend itself to sautéing. It is recommended for long, slow braising or simmering. Enameled cast-iron pans can be used on the stovetop or in the oven. Because they retain heat longer than other types, the pans are ideal for keeping foods hot for serving. Enameled pans don't need to be seasoned and are easy to clean, though they are not generally dishwasher-safe.

NONSTICK

A nonstick coating may be applied to any metal, but is most commonly applied to aluminum. Nonstick pans allow you to cook without using a lot of oil, which is helpful for cooks concerned with fat and calorie intake; the pans are also easy to clean. Protect the surface by using plastic, rubber, or wooden utensils instead of metal. Avoid cooking over high heat with nonstick pans, and never heat an empty pan. If any scratches or flaking appears, discard the pan immediately to prevent any unsafe chemicals from leaching into your food. Nonstick pans are generally not dishwasher-safe.

STAINLESS STEEL

Nonporous, noncorrosive, and nonreactive, stainless steel resists denting and scratching. Its heaviness also helps guard against scorching. It is not a particularly heat-conductive metal on its own, however. High-quality stainless-steel pans have a copper or aluminum core. A copper core will be more expensive, but it is worth the price, as it allows the pan to heat to a higher temperature, and is more responsive to changes when the heat level is lowered or raised. Stainless steel is dishwasher-safe, but it should never be put in the machine with anything made of sterling silver or with silver plate.

ESSENTIAL POTS AND PANS

These are the basic pans you should purchase for your kitchen, individually or as part of a starter set. Later, you can build a collection as your needs expand.

STRAIGHT-SIDED, COVERED SAUCEPANS
Choose a 2½-quart size, for reheating soups and pasta sauces and cooking oatmeal, and a 4-quart pan, for making soups and boiling small amounts of pasta.

STOCKPOT
An 8-quart pot is essential for boiling pasta and vegetables and making chilis or stews.

SAUTÉ PAN, COVERED
Use a 10-inch pan for sautéing meats, fish, and vegetables, and for making sauces, frittatas, and stir-fries; a slope-sided pan is preferable for scrambling eggs or frying one or two burgers.

GRILL PAN
Useful for grilling meats, fish, and vegetables on the stovetop year-round, without adding fat. The raised ridges add grill marks, and allow grease to drip below the food as it cooks.

DUTCH OVEN OR BRAISER
A 6-quart model is best for braising meats and vegetables, as well as for making pot roasts and stews such as coq au vin and boeuf bourguignon.

ROASTING PAN AND RACK
Indispensable for roasting meats, poultry, fish, and vegetables. Choose one made of heavy-gauge stainless steel, with sturdy handles. Non-stick racks are easier to clean.

SPECIALTY COOKWARE

As you experiment with recipes and cooking techniques, you may discover other pans and cooking equipment that come in handy. Here are a few of the most useful:

WOK
Ideal for stir-frying and hot-smoking; the rack can also hold foods for steaming. The round-bottomed shape evenly spreads heat, so food cooks rapidly.

CHEF'S PAN, COVERED
A 3-quart pan is perfect for making risottos, sauces, and ragouts.

OVAL GRATIN DISH
This practical baking dish holds fruit crisps and cobblers, casseroles, gratins, and baked pastas such as macaroni and cheese.

OVAL OMELET PAN
Add an oval pan to your collection if you like to make omelets. It's also useful for flank steaks and other long pieces of meat or poultry.

NONSTICK SAUTÉ PAN
This pan is useful when you want to reduce the amount of fat you are cooking with. Besides enameled cast iron, nonstick pans are available in lightweight materials.

A FEW MORE SPECIALTY ITEMS

LARGE STOCKPOT
A 12-quart pot is handy for making stocks, steaming corn on the cob, and boiling lobsters.

SMALL SAUCEPAN, COVERED
A 1-quart pan is practical for melting butter, making caramel, and steaming milk for lattes.

STEAMER INSERT
Chinese bamboo steamers can be stacked to steam multiple foods at once. A collapsible metal steamer is great for cooking vegetables.

DOUBLE BOILER
A double boiler makes easy work of melting chocolate and preparing delicate cream sauces and custards.

FISH POACHER
Available in stainless steel or copper, this is a covered, elongated oval pot for poaching fish.

PAELLA PAN
Paella, a Spanish specialty, is cooked in and served straight from these wide, round, and shallow pans.

BAKEWARE

The best bakeware, which includes commercial-grade, evenly weighted pans and baking sheets, will make a world of difference to your success with baking recipes. A springform pan that doesn't spring properly will not do its job, and a warped baking sheet won't produce evenly baked cookies. The more you bake, the more you will begin to understand bakeware.

Most bakeware is made from the same materials and finishes as cookware. Professional bakers tend to prefer heavy-duty aluminum sheets, with small rims on the short sides only, for making cookies, and round pans in graduated sizes for layer cakes.

Bear in mind that dark pans conduct heat differently from light-colored ones, so you will have to experiment and adjust baking times and oven temperatures to allow for the difference. Always check on a baked item ten to fifteen minutes before the time suggested in the recipe, and continue checking at five-minute intervals thereafter. It takes only a few minutes for something to go from perfectly baked to overdone.

It's always wise to purchase the best-quality tools you can afford. When you're still using them years from now, you'll be glad you spent a little more.

BAKEWARE MATERIALS

ALUMINUM
Heavy-duty aluminum is best for all-around baking because it won't rust or buckle. It is also relatively inexpensive, and conducts heat beautifully.

CAST IRON
Cast iron retains heat very well but takes a long time to warm up. Therefore, always preheat a cast-iron baking pan before pouring the batter into it. And like other cast-iron pans, season it first. (For instructions, turn to page 68.)

PORCELAIN
Porcelain and ceramic pans look attractive and are wonderful to use as serving vessels for quiches and soufflés. Ramekins and crème brûlée molds are also usually made of porcelain because it's nonreactive and can take high heat.

STEEL
The best steel items to use for baking are those lined with tin, which is an excellent heat conductor. However, these pans can rust if they are not thoroughly dried after being washed. (Put it in a low oven to dry after washing.) If your tinned-steel pan does rust, clean it gently with a nylon pad.

GLASS
Glass gets hot quickly and retains heat well. Therefore, the outside of pastry baked in a glass pan can be ready before the inside is cooked through. To avoid this, reduce the oven temperature by 25°F, as you would for nonstick or dark-colored pans. For pies, clear glass dishes allow you to monitor the bottom crust as it browns.

NONSTICK
Nonstick bakeware has a black coating that readily absorbs the heat of the oven and creates dark, crisp crusts on baked goods. While this can be an asset for breads, it's not ideal for cakes, cookies, and other delicate desserts. To inhibit a dark crust, set the oven temperature 25°F lower than the recipe calls for.

ESSENTIAL BAKEWARE

LOAF PANS
For quick breads, pound cakes, yeasted sandwich breads, and meatloaf. Choose glass or metal versions, or both if you bake a lot.

PIE DISHES
Glass and ceramic work well and are perfect for pies with acidic fruit, which can react with some metals. The most common diameter is 9 inches, but 8- or 10-inch pans are versatile options. Deep-dish pans are useful if you bake frequently.

ROUND CAKE PANS
The most common are 9 inches across and 2 inches deep, with straight sides. You should have two, for making layer cakes; this size is compatible with most recipes. Avoid nonstick cake pans, as they can cause the crust to darken too much.

SPRINGFORM PAN
This features a clamp to release the side of the pan from its bottom. Use it for cheesecakes and tortes; it can also double as a tart pan. Invest in a heavy-duty, nonreactive pan with a protruding lip, which keeps thin batter from leaking through.

COOKIE SHEETS
Large ones are most efficient, but make sure they're several inches smaller than the inside of your oven so air can circulate around them. Half-sheet pans and jelly-roll pans have sides and are therefore not interchangeable with cookie sheets. While many people use pans with sides for baking cookies, pans with open sides are better: Cookies brown more evenly on a surface that allows for heat circulation. Heavy-duty aluminum sheets are best, as they heat quickly and evenly, and they don't rust or buckle. If you like your cookies crisp, avoid insulated sheets, which don't absorb enough heat to allow for sufficient browning. Line the cookie sheets with parchment paper or a nonstick baking mat such as Silpat for easy removal and cleanup.

BUNDT PAN
A ring-shaped cake pan used most often for pound cakes and coffee cakes. Choose one made of professional-grade aluminum.

MUFFIN PANS
If you like to bake muffins and cupcakes, a good combination is two or three standard 12-cup muffin pans, two jumbo pans, and two mini muffin pans (great for hors d'oeuvres such as mini quiches). You can also use flexible silicone "pans," which are nonstick and easy to clean, and are useful for parfaits and frozen mousses, too.

SQUARE AND RECTANGULAR PANS
Use 8- or 9-inch square pans for brownies, gingerbread, and other bar cookies and cakes, and 13 by 9-inch pans for sheet cakes and baked savory dishes like lasagna.

ESSENTIAL BAKING TOOLS

PASTRY BLENDER
A wood-handled tool with sturdy, rounded wires or blades for cutting butter into a flour mixture for scones and pie dough.

COOLING RACKS
Raised racks allow air to circulate around baked goods as they cool. Look for racks made of stainless-steel mesh, with feet on the bottom. Avoid plastic racks and those with bars in only one direction (small items won't sit level on them).

OVEN THERMOMETER
This is crucial for bakers, since an inaccurate oven temperature reading can ruin a baking project.

ROLLING PINS
The classic American rolling pin is called a baker's pin. It's very comfortable to use and has handles to give a firm grip. A wide 3-inch center barrel means fewer strokes are needed when rolling. Look for a 12-inch-long rolling pin with tightly sealed joints between the handle and barrel to protect the inside from flour, and stainless-steel ball bearings inside, which make the pin glide easily. One pin should suffice, but if you are an avid baker, you might start collecting other types. Marble pins are ideal for rolling out pastry, since they stay cool, but they are also a lot heavier and harder to wield than wooden pins. French pins, constructed of solid wood, without handles, allow you to distribute pressure more evenly over the barrel, making it easier to roll dough extra thin.

BISCUIT CUTTERS
Choose one set in graduated sizes; they come in round, square, and fluted shapes, and can double as cookie cutters.

NONSTICK BAKING MATS
Made of rubberized silicone, these mats are great for baking cookies or meringues that might stick to a cookie sheet. They are well worth the initial cost, since, unlike parchment paper, they are extremely long lasting, and can be reused many times. Silicone mats can withstand high oven temperatures, and since they are nonstick, are easy to clean. Don't put silicone mats in the dishwasher; wipe them with a sponge and dry them flat so they retain their shape.

COOKIE CUTTERS
Copper cookie cutters last longer than aluminum ones, and hold dough shapes better, too. They can also be displayed decoratively.

PASTRY BRUSHES
(with ermine or boar bristles, in $\frac{1}{2}$-, $\frac{3}{4}$-, 1-, and 2-inch sizes) Use these to apply glazes to pies, cakes, and fruit tarts; brush excess flour from rounds of dough or countertops; and sweep crumbs from cakes before icing.

PLASTIC-LINED PASTRY BAGS
Reusable bags with plastic couplers and metal tips are useful for decorating cakes and cookies.

SPECIALTY BAKING EQUIPMENT

FLAN RINGS
Made of stainless or tinned steel, and used primarily to bake tarts (set on baking sheet first).

MADELEINE MOLD
To make the shell-shaped cakes of French pastry shops; they are traditionally made of tinned steel, though nonstick versions are available.

SOUFFLÉ DISH
A 2-quart dish made of porcelain, with straight, ridged sides and flat bottom, will work for most soufflé recipes.

BRIOCHE MOLDS
These fluted pans are used to bake the classic French bread, and come in several sizes.

TART PANS
Choose from round or rectangular shapes, with fluted rims and removable bottoms.

RAMEKINS
For individual-size cakes, custards, bread puddings, and frozen mousses, as well as pots de crème and crème brûlées.

TUBE PAN
Used primarily for angel food cake; look for one made of a light-colored metal, with feet.

ROTATING CAKE STAND
This turntable is essential if you like to decorate cakes.

THE MORE YOU COOK,
THE MORE YOU'LL
WANT A COLLECTION OF
KNIVES SUITED
TO A VARIETY OF PURPOSES.

KNIVES

Special knives for special tasks abound, but a few well-made, well-maintained, multipurpose knives are all that most cooks need. A good knife will feel that it belongs in your hand. The blade and handle will have a finely weighted balance that is comfortable to work with. The extra weight causes the blade to tip forward as you use it, saving your arm muscles from providing the downward thrust.

Traditionally, most knives were made of carbon steel, invented centuries ago and valued for the fine, long-lasting edge it gives to cutting tools. Carbon steel is prone, however, to rust and corrosion, which means it must be dried immediately after washing to prevent rust; remove any rust that does develop with a nylon pad. Stainless steel, invented in 1914, never rusts, but it does not sharpen well. The best compromise—high-carbon stainless, introduced after World War I—produces the best knives, which are rust-resistant and also retain a very sharp edge. Different knives have different amounts of carbon in them; knives with a higher carbon content will be sharper and stay sharper longer than those with less. A high-carbon stainless knife is an excellent investment; with the right care, it should last a lifetime.

ANATOMY OF A KNIFE

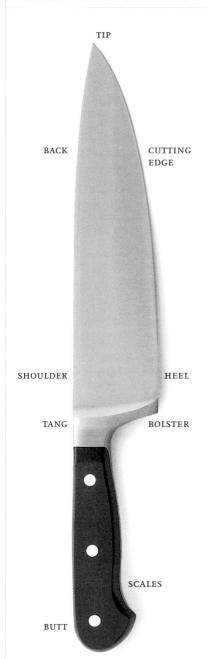

TIP

BACK

CUTTING EDGE

SHOULDER

HEEL

TANG

BOLSTER

SCALES

BUTT

TIP

Use the pointed end of the knife for piercing, precision cutting, and slicing scallions, mushrooms, and other small foods. Treat it with care—never, for example, use the tip of the knife for prying something open.

CUTTING EDGE

This side of the knife blade has been ground to a very thin, very sharp point. It is used, of course, for most types of cutting and slicing. The edge dulls just a bit with every use, and must be honed and sharpened regularly. (For instructions, turn to page 111.)

BACK

Also referred to as the spine, this side of the blade is thicker and blunter than the cutting edge. You may steady it with the heel of your hand or grip it with your fingers as you work.

HEEL

When using the blade's base, known as the heel, you can get better leverage than when using the tip, making this the part of the blade for heavy-duty cutting, such as through a chicken-bone joint or a dense, hard root vegetable.

BOLSTER

The bolster is the thick metal section between the blade and the handle. It used to be found only on forged blades (those hand-hammered from metal), but some manufacturers today are attaching bolsters to machine-stamped blades. The bolster provides a knife with both balance and stability, making it easy to use and comfortable to hold.

SHOULDER

This is where the blade thickens as it meets the handle. In kitchen knives, it keeps chopped items from moving back toward the hand as they pile up.

TANG

This is the part of the blade that extends into the handle. High-quality knives generally have a full tang, which means the metal extends all the way to the butt of the knife, and is cut to the same shape as the handle (which is riveted to or molded around the tang). A full tang gives a knife durability and balance.

BUTT

The back end of the knife is known as the butt. On a knife with a full tang and riveted handle, the tang is visible at the butt, between the two pieces of the handle.

SCALES

The pieces used to make a knife handle are called scales. (For more on choosing handle materials, see page 110.)

KNIFE-HANDLE MATERIALS

When buying knives, pay as much attention to the handle as to the blade. A fine-quality handle—the right one for you—will be smooth and feel comfortable in your hand so you can work without getting tired or having your hand cramp up. For safety, the handle should be made of a slip-proof material. Here are some other things to consider when making your choice.

HORN AND BONE

These natural materials are beautiful and feel good to hold. However, they are porous and therefore vulnerable to damage if not cared for properly. Moisture, heat, and light can cause cracking and fading. These materials are also not as hard as some others, and may develop nicks and scratches with use. Always wash knives with horn or bone handles by hand and dry immediately (never put them in the dishwasher or let them soak). Store them in a dry, dark place with a stable temperature.

METAL

Stainless-steel handles are sleek, attractive, and durable. However, they feel hard in the hand and are not the easiest to grip when wet.

PLASTIC-IMPREGNATED WOOD

Combining wood and plastic gives the best qualities of these two materials, so you have a handle that looks and feels good (like wood) but is durable (like plastic). Plastic-impregnated wood is not porous and generally gives a secure grip.

RUBBER

Handles made of rubber are particularly good for wet hands, but they are not common on excellent-quality knives.

TEXTURED OR MOLDED PLASTIC OR COMPOSITION

This type of handle is non-porous and easy to clean (however, all knives stay in the best condition when washed by hand, so having a dishwasher-safe knife isn't necessarily an advantage). Plastic can become brittle with age. If the surface isn't sufficiently textured, plastic handles can be slippery.

WOOD

Natural wood is always beautiful in a kitchen and a pleasure to use. Rosewood, which is resistant to splitting and cracking, is a traditional favorite. Wood feels secure in the hand even when wet, and can last for many years if cared for properly. It is porous and reacts to changes in its environment, however, such as fluctuations in temperature and humidity; when it expands and contracts, the parts of the knife can loosen or separate. Wood can also dry out and crack and become scratched or gouged. To prevent these problems, look for sealed wood, or treat an unsealed-wood handle regularly with a protective coating of mineral oil. Always wash a wood-handled knife by hand and never leave it submerged in water.

BLADE MATERIALS

Most knife blades are made of some form of steel. All knife steel is subjected to high temperatures to harden it, then tempered by being reheated at a lower temperature to make it less brittle. Steel blades may be stamped or forged. Traditionally, knives have been made by forging—a time-consuming process of melting, molding, heating, and pounding a piece of metal into the desired shape before it is sharpened and tempered. Many of the world's leading makers continue to craft their knives in this way, and most culinary professionals believe these knives are the finest available. Stamping, whereby knives are cut from a sheet of metal much as cookies are cut from dough, is a less expensive alternative to forging. At their best, stamped knives can compete with the performance of a good forged knife, though they may not withstand as many years of heavy use.

HOW TO HONE AND SHARPEN A KNIFE

The factory-made edge on any new knife starts to dull as soon as you put the knife to use. As a result, the sharpness of your kitchen knives depends very much on how you maintain them. There are two basic maintenance methods: regular straightening and conditioning of the edge, known as honing; and after a while, creating a brand-new, sharper edge. Knowing when to sharpen versus when to hone is a simple matter: If you can no longer restore the edge with a steel, the blade needs to be sharpened.

HONING

A sharpening steel is a metal rod with a finely ridged surface. Despite the name, a sharpening steel does not sharpen a knife as much as it resets, or realigns, the edge. Under a microscope, a dulled edge appears to have misaligned teeth, which catch as you cut. Ten strokes on each side of a steel are usually enough to reset the knife edge before using it again.

KNIFE BLADE MATERIALS

CARBON STEEL
This material, a mix of iron and carbon that was invented hundreds of years ago, still sharpens the most easily and holds the finest, longest-lasting edge. It is also inexpensive. However, carbon steel rusts, stains, and darkens when it comes into contact with humidity and acidic ingredients—slice an orange with a carbon-steel knife, and the fruit and the utensil may become discolored.

CERAMIC
Ceramic blades are at once very hard and somewhat fragile. They are made of a material called zirconium oxide, which is second only to diamonds in terms of hardness. They will not rust, stain, or react to foods, and they keep their sharp edge for long periods of time—routine sharpening is not required. However, they are not flexible, and can chip or even break. When they do eventually need to be sharpened, the task must be done by a professional. Ceramic knives are also relatively expensive.

HIGH-CARBON STAINLESS STEEL
This metal (an alloy of steel, molybdenum, vanadium, chromium, and nickel) has become—by far—the most popular material for kitchen knives, and with good reason: It combines the advantages of carbon steel (its ability to take a sharp edge) and stainless steel (its resistance to rusting and discoloration). It is also known as no-stain steel.

STAINLESS STEEL
Since its invention in 1914, stainless steel, an alloy that includes chromium, has been popular for many applications in the kitchen and around the house because it is hard and doesn't rust or corrode. However, it has fallen out of favor for knives as it is difficult to sharpen to a keen edge.

TITANIUM
Manufactured from titanium and carbides, this material is lighter and more flexible than steel. It is also resistant to corrosion and wear, and retains its edge very well.

A fine steel produces a smoother finish, though honing is faster on coarse steel. Any steel can be used horizontally or vertically. Here's how:

If steeling vertically, anchor the steel in a damp towel, then place the heel edge of the knife behind the steel at a 20-degree angle (to find 20 degrees, hold the knife edge perpendicular to the steel at a 90-degree angle, then tilt the knife halfway up for a 45-degree angle, then approximately halfway up again). Pull the entire blade down the length of the steel until you reach the tip, then place the knife in front of the steel; repeat.

To steel a knife horizontally, hold the knife in the cutting hand with its blade perpendicular to the steel, which is held in the other hand. Find a 20-degree angle, and move the knife across the steel from heel to tip. Turn the knife over; repeat. Ten strokes on each side are usually sufficient.

There is no need to use a lot of force or to work quickly. And since the steel does not remove much metal from the blade, you need not worry about overdoing it. After you finish honing the blade, wipe it dry to remove any clinging metal particles. Since a steel is magnetized to attract particles, store the steel separately from knives.

A SHARPENING STEEL IS
USED TO REALIGN,
OR RESET, THE CUTTING
EDGE OF A KNIFE.

SHARPENING

Keep in mind that you can actually damage your knives if you try to sharpen them at home without being sure of your technique. If in doubt, have your knives professionally sharpened. Check the Yellow Pages for knife sharpeners, or try hardware stores or sporting goods stores. Beware of sharpeners (either professional or at-home models) that heat the knife to a point at which it throws off sparks. This can actually remove too much metal, and reverse the tempering process that lends the knife hardness. Once a knife is distempered, it will no longer take or hold a sharp edge.

A knife can be sharpened several times a year on a stone. A rectangular Carborundum block with medium-coarse and medium-fine grit is most common for home use. Before using, cushion the stone in a damp towel, lubricate it with food-grade mineral oil, and orient it vertically. Start with the coarse side up; lay the heel of the blade on the bottom right-hand edge of the stone. Sharpen the entire edge by holding the knife at 20 degrees with one hand while guiding the blade with the other. Turn the knife over; repeat, starting with the heel of the blade on the lower left-hand edge of the stone. After ten to twenty swipes on each side, use the fine-grain side to hone the edge.

A RECTANGULAR
CARBORUNDUM BLOCK
WITH COARSE- AND
FINE-GRAINED SIDES CAN
BE USED TO SHARPEN
KNIVES AT HOME.

ELECTRIC AND MANUAL SHARPENERS

If you do decide to sharpen at home, electric and manual sharpeners are quick and easy to use—you just draw the cutting edge through a slot in the machine, which is built around a pair of abrasive tools (usually rods or wheels) that are set at a fixed angle. Many people prefer them to stones because they take the guesswork out of sharpening, so they can be less intimidating. These days, at-home knife sharpeners are vastly improved over previous models (including those found on the backs of electric can openers). You still have to choose one carefully, though, for the sake of keeping your knives sharp longer. Single-stage models are the least expensive, but you're better off with a multiple-stage sharpener. These two- and three-stage models are usually equipped with fine and coarse abrasive elements, which break the sharpening process into different steps. Some also include a slot for polishing, or stropping, the knife edge to finish it. Abrasive materials can vary, and may include diamond, carbide, and ceramic.

HOW TO STORE KNIVES

Storing knives properly helps them to maintain their edges. An in-drawer knife tray, with slots for different blade and handle sizes, keeps knives from colliding, which dulls and damages their finely honed edges. Vinyl board covers (available at art supply stores) have a slightly rubbery surface that also keeps sharp implements from being jostled around in the drawer, and wipes clean easily. Cut a piece of the cover to fit the bottom of a drawer using a ruler and a utility knife; anchor it in place with double-sided tape. Knife guards can further protect knives stored in a drawer. Countertop wooden blocks, with slots for different knife sizes, and wall-mounted magnetic strips offer other storage options.

HOW TO CLEAN KNIVES

It is best to wash and dry knives by hand, as washing them in the dishwasher can dull the blades or damage the handles. Rub off any stains with a clean wine cork dipped in mild dishwashing liquid; a mixture of coarse salt and lemon juice or vinegar also works well. Don't let knives soak, as their handles can shrink. Dry immediately.

JAPANESE CERAMIC KNIVES

These supersharp ceramic knives are designed to slice micro medallions of meat and seafood, and to carve meticulous garnishes. Unlike most European and American knives, Japanese knives are sharpened on only one side and are available for both left- and right-handed wielders. Use a *nakiri* or *nasuba* for vegetables; a *deba* for fish, meat, and poultry; a *funayuki* for boning; and a *yanagi* for slicing. A *takobiki* (with a 24-inch blade) is used by professional sushi chefs.

KITCHEN CUTLERY

CHEF'S KNIFE

SANTOKU-STYLE KNIFE

PARING KNIFE

SERRATED KNIFE

KITCHEN SHEARS

POULTRY SHEARS

SLICING KNIFE

CLEAVER

BONING KNIFE

CHEF'S KNIFE

Featuring a broad, substantial blade with a curved bottom and a width of at least 2 inches, a chef's knife is designed to steady the rocking motion when chopping firm vegetables, distinguishing it from others. The flat side of the knife can be used for crushing herbs, garlic, and spices. Choose either an 8- or a 10-inch blade, whichever you are most comfortable with.

SANTOKU-STYLE KNIFE

Created in Japan as an all-purpose knife, the *santoku bocho* is sharp on both sides, creating a V-shaped cutting edge like that on the knives used predominantly in the West. It is similar to a traditional chef's knife, except it has a shorter, broader blade that is thinner in width, so it cuts effortlessly through dense vegetables. It has a straight cutting edge like a cleaver but curves up slightly at the tip. Some versions have a granton edge—evenly spaced indentations along the blade that keep food from sticking and reduce friction.

PARING KNIFE

A 3-inch or shorter knife that provides enough flexibility for peeling, cutting, coring, and shaping fruits or vegetables or thinly slicing cheese and vegetables. Ideal for small, delicate jobs such as deveining shrimp and trimming green beans.

SERRATED KNIFE

Also called a bread knife, it has a scalloped blade (or serrated edge, hence the name) that saws easily and cleanly through hard crusts as well as tender crumbs. Because it is designed to be used in a sawing motion, a serrated knife is also very useful for making clean cuts through foods such as tomatoes that might otherwise fall apart under the pressure of a slicing knife. They are ideal for cutting anything with a rind or skin such as squash or eggplant; they are also good for cutting cold roasts. Buy a knife with at least an 8-inch blade, or longer if you favor large, rustic loaves of bread.

KITCHEN SHEARS

For multiple kitchen tasks, including snipping herbs and trimming vegetables; keep a set in the kitchen and avoid using regular household scissors as a substitute.

POULTRY SHEARS

Designed to cut through bones and joints, these specialty shears feature curved blades and a spring-bolt hinge. They are especially handy for spatchcocking, or partially deboning and butterflying a bird, which makes easy work of grilling a whole chicken.

SLICING KNIFE

At least 10 inches long and 1 inch or less wide with either a pointed or a round tip, it is used to very thinly slice fruits as well as raw and cooked pieces of fish and meat, or for carving roasts, chicken, and ham.

CLEAVER

Available in a range of lengths and weights for various uses: a small 1-pound model is sufficient for cutting through poultry bones and chopping vegetables; a medium 2-pound cleaver with a 6-inch blade will handle most other kitchen jobs.

BONING KNIFE

The narrow and flexible blade of a 5- to 6-inch boning knife wiggles between meat and bones, allowing you to trim off fat, tendons, or cartilage easily. Stiff boning knives are good for beef while flexible boning knives are better for poultry.

AS YOUR COLLECTION OF
KITCHEN TOOLS
GROWS, CAREFULLY EDIT
OUT THOSE YOU DON'T
USE. YOU'LL END UP WITH
A COLLECTION
WELL-SUITED TO THE WAY
YOU COOK.

TOOLS AND GADGETS

The right assortment of kitchen tools can reduce preparation time, and also improve the flavor, texture, and presentation of the food you are preparing. The proper tools can also be a pleasure to master and work with. Quality tools perform better and seldom need replacing, which saves money over the long term. These include stainless-steel measuring cups with long handles; silicone basting brushes, which never shed their bristles; and lots of wooden kitchen tools, constructed of smooth hardwoods rather than pine, which does not wear as well over time. The most functional kitchen tools are often the old-fashioned ones that have not been improved upon in generations—a classic mortar and pestle, for instance. So choose wisely now, adding new tools only when you are sure you need them, and more than likely, you will also have chosen well for later.

DRY VS. LIQUID MEASURING CUPS

Many experienced cooks rely on instinct when it comes to measuring, adding a pinch of this or that, estimating tablespoons and cups. But in many recipes, baking in particular, success depends on precise measurements. That is why there are measuring cups for dry ingredients (usually a nesting set of cups with handles) and liquids (usually a clear glass cup with a spout).

If you were to measure a dry ingredient like flour in a liquid measuring cup, you would have to give the cup a good shake in order to have the top of the flour line up with the marking on the cup. Even so, the flour wouldn't be perfectly level, and you would also have eliminated some of the air in the flour, making it more compact and throwing off your measure. Instead, gently fill the dry measuring cup, without shaking or packing, then scrape a straight edge such as the back of a knife or other flat tool along the top, removing excess flour and making the flour perfectly level. You should also use dry measuring cups for ingredients like shortening and peanut butter, which would be impossible to level in a liquid measuring cup. It's worth seeking out dry measuring cups (and spoons) in sturdy, easy-to-clean stainless steel, which is not as likely to crack as plastic or to dent as cheaper metals; dents do affect accuracy.

Liquid measuring cups have the amounts marked on the side. To measure liquids, pour the ingredient into the spouted cup, and place it on a flat, level surface; look at it at eye level to be sure you have the correct amount. Looking into the cup from above is not as accurate. Liquid measuring cups made of heat-resistant glass (such as Pyrex) can last a lifetime, while plastic cups probably won't.

CARING FOR WOODEN TOOLS

Wooden tools are attractive and reliable, and with proper care can outlast the hardest plastics. Since wood is a poor conductor of heat, wooden utensils can be easily handled when stirring something in a hot pot. For the best, and safest, results, however, keep the following things in mind:

☐ Because wood is absorbent, soaking wooden tools or putting them in the dishwasher will saturate them, and make them more likely to mildew before drying out completely. Instead, clean wooden tools by hand, using hot, soapy water and a dish brush. A cloth dampened with a solution of 1 part chlorine bleach to 10 parts water can occasionally be rubbed across the surface to sanitize the wood, which should then be thoroughly rinsed and dried.

☐ Not all wood is created equal. Cheaper tools and utensils are typically made of soft wood, such as pine, which will not withstand regular use in a kitchen. Buy good-quality, smooth hardwood tools with no jagged edges.

☐ Wood tends to hold strong odors and flavors, so use separate tools for different jobs. For example, don't stir your pasta sauce with the same wooden spoon that you use for cookie dough.

☐ Store wooden tools in a cool, dry spot—again, too much moisture can breed mildew. To keep the wood from drying and cracking, condition it every few months by applying nontoxic mineral oil (available at kitchen-supply and specialty stores for use on salad bowls and butcher block); this will also create a barrier over the wood grain, slowing absorption of water and food odors. Apply the oil with a fine steel-wool pad.

HOW TO CLEAN A BOX GRATER

After using a box grater, let it soak in warm water to loosen stuck-on bits of food. Then use a stiff brush rather than a sponge, which will rip on the teeth. A toothbrush or toothbrush-shaped brush, available at hardware stores, works well; the small brush and long handle give you a lot of control—and help you keep from scraping your knuckles on the grater. You might also spray the grater very lightly with cooking spray before using it, which should make it easier to clean.

BASIC TOOLS AND GADGETS

BASTING BRUSH

For brushing pan juices onto roasts and grilled meats. Silicone brushes retain their shape and color, withstand heat up to 800°F, do not absorb flavors, and do not shed. Also, they are easy to clean and can even go in the dishwasher.

BENCH SCRAPER

Useful for loosening bits of dough from a work surface as you knead, and for neatly dividing mounds of dough such as that used to make scones or biscotti. The flat surface can also help transfer chopped ingredients from a cutting board to a bowl or pan.

BOWL SCRAPER

An inexpensive rounded plastic gadget used for scraping dough or batter from a mixing bowl and transferring it to a work surface or a pan; especially helpful for a large amount of dough, when a flexible spatula is too small.

CITRUS PRESS

For quickly extracting lemon or lime juice for vinaigrettes, marinades, and cocktails. Its handheld size makes it perfect for small amounts of juice.

CHEESECLOTH

For straining stock, enclosing herbs in bouquets garnis, and draining yogurt to make cheese. Soaked in butter or wine, a piece of cotton cheesecloth can also help keep turkey moist and tender while roasting.

CITRUS REAMER

This is also for quickly juicing lemons and limes, but made of a sturdy, single-piece wood or metal design. Over a bowl, twist the reamer into half a lemon or lime; allow the juice to drip into the bowl.

CUTTING BOARDS

For chopping and all manner of food preparation. Use wood for fruit and vegetables; plastic for raw meat and fish; and a separate board for garlic and onions (to keep their flavors from seeping into other foods). Ideally, you should have one or two larger boards with plenty of room to work on and one or two small boards for slicing fruits or vegetables one at a time. (For more on cutting boards, turn to page 45.)

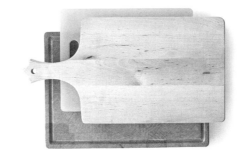

CITRUS ZESTER

This handled tool has four small holes that are used to remove long strips of zest from citrus fruit, while leaving bitter white pith behind.

MICROPLANE GRATER (OR RASP)

The tiny, razor-sharp teeth of a microplane grater also removes zest from citrus fruit. The tool can also be used for grating hard cheeses such as Parmesan, Pecorino, and Romano, or for grating chocolate and whole nutmeg.

VEGETABLE PEELER

Choose a U-shaped model with a steel blade, for peeling vegetables and fruit, shaving cheese, and making chocolate curls.

FOOD MILL

For pureeing fruits and vegetables; usually comes with three interchangeable disks, with holes in graduated sizes, so you can choose the thickness of your puree. Because the food mill removes skin and seeds, it's excellent for soups and sauces; you can also use it in place of a ricer to make fluffy mashed potatoes.

COLANDER

A metal, plastic, or porcelain enamel perforated bowl for draining and rinsing pasta or cooked vegetables. The holes are larger than those in a strainer, and may form a decorative pattern. Most have a base or feet and two looped handles. They come in several sizes; select more than one if you do a lot of cooking. You could also use graduated footed strainers for many of the same tasks.

CHINOIS

Used to strain stocks and vegetables, a chinois is constructed of very fine stainless-steel mesh in a cone-shaped basket. Soups and sauces strained in a chinois have a velvety smooth texture.

BASIC TOOLS AND GADGETS (CONTINUED)

ICE-CREAM SCOOP

For more than just making perfect scoops of ice cream, these come in varying sizes and are ideal for measuring equal amounts of cookie doughs and other batters. Look for one that is mechanical, and dip it in warm water between scoops to help it release more easily.

GRATERS

Use an all-purpose four-sided box grater for grating cheese (coarse or fine) and slicing and shredding vegetables (for cleaning instructions, turn to page 117). A handheld grater is convenient for table use.

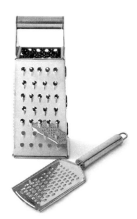

LIQUID MEASURING CUPS

Choose transparent glass cups with clearly marked lines and spouts, for measuring and pouring liquid ingredients. Remember to measure liquids at eye level.

MANDOLINE

For quickly slicing vegetables paper thin; the blade also adjusts to create julienned vegetables or the waffle pattern on *gaufrette* potatoes. Japanese mandolines, like the ones pictured, are made of plastic and are a less expensive alternative to the traditional stainless-steel French model.

DRY MEASURING CUPS

For accuracy in cooking, especially baking, choose a graduated, stainless-steel, long-handled set; be sure they fit easily into the mouths of your dry-ingredients jars and canisters.

MEASURING SPOONS

For small amounts of both liquid and dry ingredients. When working with dry ingredients, level the top with a knife. As you pour a liquid ingredient into the spoon, don't hold it over a mixing bowl, since it's so easy to spill; measure over a separate bowl or the sink to contain spills instead. If you can, invest in two sets, so that while you're cooking one can be used for liquid ingredients and one for dry ingredients, minimizing cleaning between measurements. Stainless-steel spoons are the most durable.

MELON BALLER

For making spheres of ripe melon such as cantaloupe or honeydew; it's also useful for carving the core from a halved apple or pear, stemming a tomato, or picking the seeds from a watermelon.

MIXING BOWLS

For myriad kitchen tasks. Choose one set of stainless-steel and one set of tempered-glass bowls. Nested bowls are best for storage and also for making ice baths. Glass mixing bowls can be used in the microwave, for quickly melting butter or chocolate.

GARLIC PEELING TUBE

For easing off the skin of garlic cloves. Place a clove into the pliable rubber sleeve, then press and roll on a hard surface.

MEAT-TENDERIZING MALLET

The waffled side is for tenderizing inexpensive cuts of meat like flank steak; the flat side is for pounding meat thinner. Pound evenly, and not too hard, between sheets of parchment or wax paper.

PASTA MAKER

For rolling out fresh spaghetti, linguine, lasagna, and many other pasta shapes from homemade dough. Also useful for rolling out very thin doughs like those for crackers and some Italian pastries.

PIZZA WHEEL

Primarily for slicing pizza and other flatbreads; can also be used to cut lattice strips from pie dough, or to trim the edges of rolled-out cookie dough.

MORTAR AND PESTLE

For crushing garlic, dried chiles, and whole spices into fine pastes (which retains all the moisture and flavor) and rubs. Many cooks prefer to pound their own pesto with this tool, rather than making it in a food processor.

BASIC TOOLS AND GADGETS (CONTINUED)

SALAD SPINNER

For drying salad greens quickly and gently after washing. It also makes an efficient storage container for washed and dried lettuce, keeping it crisp and fresh for days.

SCALE

For weighing ingredients; especially useful for baking recipes that call for ingredients in weights rather than measures. Look for a digital scale that includes metric weights, for easy conversion of European recipes.

SIEVES

For removing lumps from dry ingredients such as flour or confectioners' sugar, and straining certain soups or sauces; look for sturdy mesh that won't stretch or bend. Choose sieves in several sizes and levels of coarseness (fine, medium, and coarse).

SPATULAS, METAL AND SILICONE

Silicone spatulas are great for folding cake batters or transferring them from bowl to baking pan. They are heatproof up to 800° F, won't pick up or impart flavors from other foods, and are safe to use on nonstick pots and pans. A set of three (1-, 2-, and 3-inch) heatproof silicone spatulas is ideal. The most useful metal spatulas are wide offset stainless steel, for flipping pancakes or patties; long offset, for spreading batters in pans; and long flat, for icing cakes. Other helpful tools include a fish spatula, with a flexible slotted blade, and a wedge-shaped cake server.

THERMOMETER, CANDY

For making syrups, jams, or jellies, when accuracy is crucial to success. It can usually double as a deep-fat thermometer, although you should buy two if you do either activity with any sort of frequency. It should be long enough to reach into a deep pot, and will often be attached to a flat metal backing, which makes it easier to handle and to read.

THERMOMETER, MEAT

For testing the internal temperature of cooked meats. These have a thin, 4- to 5-inch-long stem that is inserted into the roast, and a dial on the end that indicates the temperature. There are two models: one is inserted into the meat before it goes into the oven; the other, called an instant-read or rapid-response thermometer, is inserted near the end of the cooking time; it is never left in the meat as it cooks. Always insert deep into the thickest part of the meat, without touching a bone, which can result in an incorrect reading.

WOODEN SPOONS

The most essential tool for mixing everything in the kitchen— from sauces to soups to salads. Flat wooden spoons with angled bottoms are great for getting at a pan's edges when making custards and thick sauces.

TIMER

For monitoring cooking time. It's a good idea to invest in one even if your oven has a built-in timer. Some digital models allow you to time a few jobs at once.

WHISKS

For beating egg whites, smoothing sauces, and "sifting" dry ingredients together in a mixing bowl. Look for one with fine spokes that wiggle when you shake the handle; the best whisks are stainless steel and weighted for strength and comfort. They are dishwasher-safe. The most versatile whisk to have on hand measures 3 to $3\frac{1}{2}$ inches across at the widest point, and is more elongated than a balloon whisk. A cut-off whisk is the best tool for making spun sugar, as for a *croquembouche*. You might also consider a mini whisk (8 inches), handy for quick vinaigrettes, marinades, and glazes; and a flat whisk (12 inches), which works beautifully to deglaze corners of pans and to go around the inside of a saucepan when cooking custards and puddings.

TONGS

Select 12-inch tongs for myriad kitchen tasks such as turning meat when browning or roasting, lifting vegetables out of hot water, and grilling. Look for heavy-duty, professional-grade tongs; a long-lasting spring allows for easy storage.

WHO WOULD HAVE
GUESSED
THERE ARE SO MANY
SIZES AND SHAPES OF
WIRE WHISKS?
WITH EXPERIENCE,
YOU CAN DISCOVER WHICH
IS MOST USEFUL
FOR A SPECIFIC TASK.

THESE ARE MY FAVORITE ASIAN COOKING TOOLS, INCLUDING AN "UNI" OPENER, A SESAME SEED TOASTER, AND A WHITEBAIT FRYER STRAINER.

THE PANTRY

Every home needs a place in which to store food safely. It may be a small room on its own, such as you would find in many older houses. Or you may have to create it with shelving wherever you can find space, out of direct sunlight and away from heat sources. A closet, a small hutch, a freestanding cupboard, or even a bookcase can all be converted into pantry space.

Stock your pantry based on your cooking habits or by season—this can help in your shopping and meal-planning efforts. What you store in your pantry is up to you, but there are rules about how to store certain things for safekeeping. Flour, sugar, grains, beans, and other dry goods should be transferred from their packaging into widemouthed jars (for easier scooping) with airtight lids to protect against pests. Always note the date of purchase on the jar. If you keep multiples of any product on hand, organize them so that the first ones purchased will be the first ones used. Keep empty jars and containers on hand for stocking new items.

Optimum conditions for a pantry call for good air circulation, low humidity, dim lighting, and cool temperatures. Use a thermometer to test the temperature, and also an instrument called a hygrometer, available at hardware stores, to test the humidity. Food does best when stored at temperatures below 68°F, and at a humidity level of no more than 60 percent. This means keeping foods and oils away from cabinets near the cooktop, oven, or dishwasher. Install a simple fan if necessary. If you live in a climate that gets hot and humid, store flours, grains, nuts, and seeds in the freezer.

Pristine countertops, an immaculate sink, and sparkling-clean appliances are all signs of a well-kept kitchen. But the ultimate hallmark of homekeeping in the kitchen is the food you prepare, serve, and eat there, which all begins in the pantry, wherever you create it.

STOCKING A PANTRY

No pantry, however beautifully designed, is complete until it's fully stocked. For quality and economy, it helps to shop well in advance from a master list of ingredients. Once you've done that, you'll rarely need to substitute what you happen to have on hand for what a recipe really calls for.

The chart on the opposite page includes the basic components of any well-stocked pantry. The pantry is also a convenient place to store nonfood items if you have the room, such as cookware, trays and baskets, liquor, stepladder, candles, matches, lightbulbs, and pet treats (in a sealed jar).

DRIED BEANS, PASTA, AND GRAINS STAY ORGANIZED AND EASY TO FIND WHEN STORED IN THE PANTRY IN AIRTIGHT CLEAR GLASS JARS.

WHEN TRANSFERRING RICE FROM A BOX INTO A JAR, TAPE THE INSTRUCTIONS FOR COOKING THAT TYPE OF RICE TO THE INSIDE OF THE LID.

WHAT TO KEEP IN A PANTRY, AND FOR HOW LONG

BAKING STAPLES

Pure vanilla extract and other extracts, vanilla beans, baking soda, baking powder, unsweetened and semisweet dark chocolate, Dutch-process cocoa powder, unflavored gelatin, dry yeast, cornstarch—store ingredients in airtight containers, away from heat and light sources. Extracts will last several years; leavenings lose their potency after about one year, and should be discarded on their expiration dates.

CANNED AND BOTTLED ITEMS

Italian plum tomatoes, tomato paste, green and black olives, olive paste, anchovies, anchovy paste, capers, chickpeas, black beans, hot sauce, mustards, Italian oil-packed tuna, low-sodium chicken broth, canned fruits, chutneys, fruit jam. Heed expiration dates; otherwise, most canned and bottled goods, such as preserves, pickles, and relishes, can be kept, unopened, for up to one year. Once opened, glass bottles should be refrigerated; transfer unused canned goods to airtight containers and refrigerate for three or four days. This is especially important for canned acidic foods such as tomatoes or pineapples; once the interior of the can is exposed to air, the acidity is likely to cause rust. If you do see rust on an opened can of food, the can and food should be discarded.

DRIED PASTA

Assorted shapes including spaghetti, penne, rigatoni, fettuccine, lasagna, orzo, couscous—dried pasta can be stored in its original packaging until opened, then transferred to airtight containers. They are best used within one year of purchase.

FLOURS

Unbleached all-purpose white, whole wheat, cake (not self-rising), and almond—store wheat flours in airtight containers at room temperature up to one year. Choose containers with wide mouths for easy scooping and measuring. Freeze almond and other nut flours up to six months.

GRAINS, RICE, DRIED BEANS

Quick-cooking polenta; stone-ground cornmeal; oats; Arborio, long-grain white, medium- to long-grain brown, and basmati rice; green lentils du Puy; black-eyed and split peas; black, pinto, and cannellini beans; flageolets—dried items, with the exception of cornmeal, can be stored in the pantry up to one year. To discourage pests, keep cornmeal in the freezer, for up to one year.

NUTS AND DRIED FRUIT

Pecan and walnut halves; pine nuts; peanuts; cashews; almonds; hazelnuts; raisins; golden raisins; currants; dried apricots, dates, and figs; sun-dried tomatoes. To discourage nuts from turning rancid, store them in the freezer for up to six months. Dried fruits can be stored at room temperature six months to a year but last longer in the refrigerator; keep them well sealed to preserve freshness and prevent stickiness.

OILS

Extra-virgin olive, canola, vegetable, peanut, and corn; specialty oils such as toasted sesame and white truffle—store vegetable oils in the original bottles, unrefrigerated, in a cool, dark place up to six months. Refrigerate nut oils (such as walnut oil), and use within three months.

SPICES AND SEASONINGS

Most spices will lose their potency after about a year, but their flavor will deteriorate faster if stored improperly. Keep them in airtight, light-proof containers, away from heat. Choose an accessible drawer or cabinet or a wall-mounted rack (do not hang it above the cooktop).

SUGARS AND OTHER SWEETENERS

Granulated white, superfine, light and dark brown, and confectioners' sugar; light corn syrup; molasses; pure maple syrup; honey—humidity can make solid sugars lumpy, so keep them in well-sealed containers in a cool, dry spot. Double-wrap brown sugars to keep them moist. Store syrups at room temperature in their original containers up to one year.

VEGETABLES

Store only hardy vegetables such as potatoes, onions, garlic, and dried wild mushrooms in your pantry. Potatoes should not be refrigerated; keep up to two weeks' worth in baskets or bins in a cool, dry, dark, well-ventilated spot. Do not store them in plastic, which can encourage mold. Keep onions, shallots, and garlic in the pantry (do not refrigerate) up to one month, and dried mushrooms for several months. Store each vegetable in a separate basket or bin; it's especially important to keep potatoes and onions apart since they can cause each other to spoil.

VINEGAR

Aged balsamic, cider, white wine, red wine, rice wine, and sherry—keep all types of vinegar in their original bottles, and store them in a cool spot up to one year.

FOOD STORAGE

Long before it actually spoils, food begins to lose quality. Over the centuries, cooks have learned to slow this loss by cooking, curing, smoking, drying, and canning. The method most recently developed, and considered the best for many foods, is refrigeration, because the cold air in the refrigerator retards the action of enzymes that first ripen, and then rot, vegetables and fruit. It also slows the growth of bacteria that are present in all raw foods.

The right handling is almost as important as the right temperature. Bruises on apples and cracks in eggs can admit bacteria, and even the dry air of the refrigerator does damage, pulling moisture from a wedge of cheese or a stalk of celery. To prevent this, almost everything should be covered or well wrapped before it goes into the refrigerator, and absolutely everything must be totally covered for the freezer. Here are the best ways to store food in the refrigerator to keep it at the peak of freshness:

MEAT, POULTRY, AND SEAFOOD

You can leave meat and poultry in plastic-wrapped supermarket trays, according to the United States Department of Agriculture (USDA). But put the tray on a plate or in a plastic bag to keep juices from leaking onto other foods. Meat can be frozen in these packages, if wrapped with heavy foil or airtight freezer bags. The best environment for these perishable foods is on the bottom shelf of the refrigerator or in a deli or meat drawer that's set between 29° and 34°F. (Keeping them on the bottom shelf also prevents juices from dripping onto other foods.) Wrap leftovers and cold cuts well in plastic wrap, and double-wrap in foil. Seafood should be used the day it's bought, and wrapped to keep fishy odors from escaping and tainting dairy products.

EGGS

There's no reason to take eggs out of the cardboard or foam carton they're sold in. Store the carton in the body of the refrigerator, not the egg-keeper built into the door. (Eggs kept there are bounced about and bathed with room-temperature air every time the door swings open.) Refrigerated eggs stay fresh for about three or four weeks after they're put in cartons. A number code on most boxes tells the packing date, with 1 meaning January 1 and 365 meaning December 31. Hard-cooked eggs, unpeeled, will keep in the refrigerator for a week.

DAIRY PRODUCTS

With the carton top closed to keep out odors, milk usually stays fresh for a few days after the "sell by" date. Milk can also be frozen, then thawed in the refrigerator; it may be grainy but is still safe to use in coffee or in cooking. Butter, like milk, should be kept wrapped or covered to protect it from refrigerator odors. The butter compartment is usually warmer than the rest of the refrigerator, to keep butter spreadable, and there is sometimes a gauge that lets you control the temperature there. Double-wrapped in plastic and foil, butter can be frozen for six to nine months. Some hard cheeses last months; softer ones, only a few weeks once they're opened. How long

STORAGE SAFETY CHART FOR MEAT, FISH, EGGS, AND DAIRY

Product	Variety	In Refrigerator 40°F/5°C	In Freezer 0°F/−18°C
FRESH MEAT	Beef, ground	1–2 days	3–4 months
	Steaks and roasts	3–5 days	6–12 months
PORK	Chops	3–5 days	4–6 months
	Ground	1–2 days	3–4 months
	Roasts	3–5 days	4–6 months
CURED MEATS	Lunch meat	3–5 days	1–2 months
	Sausage	1–2 days	1–2 months
	Bacon	7 days	1 month
FISH	Lean (such as cod, flounder, sole)	1–2 days	Up to 6 months
	Fatty (such as salmon, mackerel, bluefish)	1–2 days	2–3 months
CHICKEN	Whole	1–2 days	12 months
	Parts	1–2 days	9 months
	Giblets	1–2 days	3–4 months
DAIRY PRODUCTS	Cheese	3–4 weeks	n/a
	Milk	5 days	1 month
	Ice cream, frozen yogurt	n/a	2–4 months
EGGS	Fresh in shell	3 weeks	n/a
	Hard-boiled	1 week	n/a

SOURCES: FOOD MARKETING INSTITUTE FOR
FISH/DAIRY; USDA FOR OTHER FOODS

your cheese will last depends entirely on its variety and how it's stored. Since the conditions that most higher-end cheese stores maintain are difficult to re-create, try to buy only the amount of cheese that you will use immediately. High humidity (65 percent to 75 percent) is important for cheese—more important, in fact, than the actual temperature (though 55°F is the ideal). Keep cheeses in the crisper of the refrigerator, wrapped in cheesecloth, parchment paper, or the wrapping used by the cheese store. Completely enclosing the cheese in plastic wrap does not let it breathe. If this is the only material you have on hand, leave the rind exposed so air can reach the cheese. Cheese can be very strong-smelling and can impart its aroma to other foods (it can also absorb odors), so if you want another layer of protection, put it in a plastic container with holes poked in the lid.

STORAGE TIPS FOR FRUITS, VEGETABLES, AND HERBS

□ Cold air slows the process by which fruit first ripens and then deteriorates, which is why hard pears are left out to ripen, then refrigerated to keep them from getting too soft.

□ Although the conventional wisdom is not to refrigerate bananas, it is okay to do so. The skin will blacken, but the fruit inside remains good. Green, unripe bananas will mature in 4 to 6 days on the countertop, while green-yellow ones should ripen in 2 to 4 days. To speed ripening, store bananas in a brown paper bag at room temperature. Keep the bag out of direct sunlight.

□ Almost all vegetables benefit from chilling. (Tomatoes, which are actually fruit, should not be refrigerated, unless they are in danger of going bad. See chart on pages 136–137.) To keep vegetables from drying out, put them in the crisper drawer or in plastic bags, which act as individual crispers. Mushrooms, however, should never be kept in plastic; use paper bags for them.

□ Store fresh herbs in the refrigerator crisper drawer (except basil, which turns black), with the stems wrapped in damp paper towels, or stick the stems in a glass of water, with a plastic bag tenting the leaves. To store basil, first rinse it well, and set on paper towels to dry. Pat gently to absorb excess moisture. Wrap basil in damp paper towels, and place in resealable plastic bags. Store in the refrigerator for up to five days.

□ Transfer canned vegetables to a lidded container once the can is opened, to prevent them from acquiring a tinny taste, and keep them in the refrigerator.

OTHER FOOD STORAGE TIPS

CRACKERS AND BREAD

Crackers do well in dry refrigerator air but bread is more complicated. Wrapped, soft-crusted breads, such as supermarket loaves, muffins, pitas, quick breads, and doughnuts, can be refrigerated, especially in a hot, humid climate where mold can be a problem if breads are left on the counter. They may feel stale, but they soften at room temperature. Tortillas should always be kept, well wrapped, in the refrigerator. Refrigerate a crusty loaf from a bakery, however, and the dry crust will soften as it draws moisture from the interior of the bread. Store hard-crusted bread, loosely wrapped, at room temperature, preferably in a bread box; or wrap it in foil and resealable plastic bags for the freezer. (For more on bread boxes, turn to page 138.)

COFFEE

A perishable, coffee is best purchased only within two weeks of use. And keep just a week's supply in an airtight container in a dark, cool, and dry spot such as a cabinet. Coffee beans and grounds should never be kept in a refrigerator. If you like to buy grounds in bulk, keep a week's supply on-hand and store the rest of the grounds in the freezer, dividing them into one-week portions among airtight plastic freezer bags. Never return coffee to the freezer once you bring it to room temperature, and do not store grounds in the freezer for more than one or two months.

TEA

There are four things that will harm tea—air, light, moisture, and heat. Since all of these variables can affect its taste, store tea in an airtight container in a dark, dry, cool place. It is also extremely absorbent, so avoid storing tea near items with strong odors such as spices or garlic.

WINE

Unless you have a bottle of twenty-five-year-old Burgundy, you can happily drink half a bottle at dinner, seal it with a vacuum recorker, a simple device that forces air out of the bottle, and keep it at room temperature. Champagne cannot be recorked; the best way to keep an open bottle of Champagne is to insert a metal Champagne stopper and refrigerate. Disregard the myth that Champagne keeps in the fridge if you put a silver spoon in the neck of the bottle. For more on storing wines, turn to page 178.

TOFU

Once opened, it should be kept in a tray of water, completely submerged; rinse and change the water every day. Use within a week.

A NOTE ABOUT STORING COOKED FOOD

Putting a pot of steaming-hot soup or stew in the refrigerator will make the temperature inside soar, so first cool the food quickly by lowering the pot into a sink full of ice water and stirring often. Cooked food should be refrigerated as soon as possible: The USDA rule is not to leave perishable food out for more than two hours.

HOW TO STORE CONDIMENTS

Ketchup, mustard, mayonnaise, jam, and chocolate syrup should all be refrigerated once they're opened. Because they're highly processed and not very perishable, they will keep for a long time, losing texture and taste before safety. Wipe the bottle clean after each use, and discard anything that develops a foul odor or changes color.

FRUIT STORAGE GUIDELINES

Product	In Refrigerator 40°F / 5°C	Other Considerations
APPLES	1 month	☐ Apples give off ethylene, which speeds the ripening of many green vegetables; store in a separate refrigerator compartment, or in a sealed plastic bag. ☐ Freshly picked apples will taste better if you keep them at room temperature.
AVOCADOS	2–4 days	☐ Will ripen on counter in 4–7 days; to speed ripening, place in a paper bag and store at room temperature for 2–4 days. ☐ Once ripe, avocados can be preserved by placing them in the refrigerator. ☐ To keep sliced avocados from turning brown, rub lemon or lime juice onto the exposed flesh and wrap tightly in plastic.
BERRIES (BLACKBERRIES, BLUEBERRIES, CURRANTS, RASPBERRIES, STRAWBERRIES)	2–3 days	☐ Highly perishable. ☐ Remove damaged berries to help prevent the spread of mold. ☐ Store unwashed in a shallow container, not a plastic bag, to allow air to circulate. ☐ Wash just before eating.
CHERRIES	2–3 days	☐ Highly perishable. ☐ Store unwashed in a shallow container, not a plastic bag, to allow air to circulate. ☐ Tend to absorb odors; store separately, if possible. ☐ Wash just before eating.
GRAPEFRUIT	2 weeks	☐ Will stay fresh at room temperature for about a week. ☐ Store in crisper drawer.
GRAPES	3–5 days	☐ Best to eat right after purchase. ☐ Remove any spoiled fruit. ☐ Store unwashed, in a perforated plastic bag, in the crisper. ☐ Wash just before eating.
LEMONS AND LIMES	2 weeks	☐ Will stay fresh at room temperature for several days; refrigerate if storing longer. ☐ Keep out of bright sunlight.

Product	In Refrigerator 40°F / 5°C	Other Considerations
MANGOES	2–3 days	☐ A green mango will ripen within a week at room temperature; to speed ripening, place in a paper bag out of direct sunlight. ☐ Store only ripe mangoes in the refrigerator.
MELONS	5 days–1 week (whole); 3 days (cut)	☐ Despite their hardy appearance, melons are quite perishable. ☐ Melons will ripen in a few days at room temperature; to speed ripening, place underripe melons in a pierced paper bag. ☐ Keep ripe, uncut melons away from other fruit so that the ethylene does not affect the other fruit's ripening. ☐ When storing cut melon in the refrigerator, leave the seeds in to help keep it fresh.
ORANGES	2 weeks	☐ Stay fresh at room temperature for about a week. ☐ Store in crisper drawer.
PEACHES AND NECTARINES	3–5 days	☐ Highly perishable. ☐ Will ripen, at room temperature, within 2–3 days; to speed ripening, place in a paper bag out of direct sunlight. ☐ Store ripe peaches and nectarines in the crisper drawer.
PEARS	3–5 days	☐ Lose moisture quite rapidly. ☐ To ripen, store at room temperature for 2–3 days. ☐ Store when ripened in the crisper drawer.
PINEAPPLE	2–3 days	☐ Best to eat soon after purchase. ☐ Store in a perforated plastic bag in the refrigerator.
PLUMS	3–5 days	☐ Highly perishable. ☐ Store at room temperature to ripen; to speed ripening, place in a paper bag out of direct sunlight. ☐ Store ripe plums in a plastic bag in the crisper drawer.
TOMATOES		☐ Store at room temperature; they should keep for about a week. ☐ Chill tomatoes only if they are in danger of going bad.

VEGETABLE STORAGE GUIDELINES

Product	In Refrigerator 40°F / 5°C	Other Considerations
ARTICHOKES	1 week	☐ Store, unwashed, in a plastic bag. ☐ If the stems are still attached, place them in a container of water, then refrigerate.
ASPARAGUS	3–4 days	☐ Keep moist, especially the tips, to prevent the asparagus from rotting; a plastic bag helps retain moisture. ☐ Place upright in a glass with an inch of water, or wrap the stem ends in a damp paper towel, then refrigerate.
BEETS	2–3 days	☐ If beets have greens, cut them off before storing. ☐ Store beets unwashed and loose in the crisper.
BROCCOLI	3–5 days	☐ If left unrefrigerated, becomes woody and fibrous. ☐ Store unwashed in an open or perforated plastic bag; moisture will encourage spoilage.
BRUSSELS SPROUTS	3–5 days	☐ Place unwashed sprouts in a paper bag in the crisper.
CABBAGE	1 week	☐ Store in the crisper, sealed in a perforated plastic bag. ☐ Never wash cabbage before storing—it will hasten deterioration.
CARROTS	2 weeks	☐ Very hardy. ☐ Wrap in paper towels or keep in a perforated plastic bag. ☐ If your carrots have greens, cut them off before storing; otherwise, the greens may hasten spoilage.
CAULIFLOWER	3–5 days	☐ If left unrefrigerated, becomes woody and fibrous. ☐ Store unwashed in an open or perforated plastic bag; moisture will encourage spoilage.
CELERY	1 week	☐ Store in a plastic bag in the crisper.
CORN	1–2 days	☐ Best if eaten immediately; becomes starchy after it's picked. ☐ Shuck just prior to cooking; the husk helps protect the kernels.
CUCUMBER	1 week	☐ Store unwashed and loosely wrapped in a plastic bag. ☐ Some cucumbers are covered with an edible wax that helps protect them from moisture.

Product	In Refrigerator 40°F / 5°C	Other Considerations
EGGPLANT	1–3 days	☐ Highly perishable. ☐ Whole eggplant will last longer out of the refrigerator, but in a cool place. ☐ If storing cut eggplant in the refrigerator, wrap in plastic and place in the least cool section of the refrigerator.
GREEN BEANS	3–5 days	☐ Best eaten immediately. ☐ Refrigerate unwashed and tightly wrapped in plastic.
GREENS (COLLARDS, KALE, SPINACH, SWISS CHARD)	3–4 days	☐ Wrap in damp paper towels and store unwashed in a perforated bag.
LETTUCE (ARUGULA, ICEBERG, MESCLUN, ROMAINE)	1 week	☐ Store unwashed in a perforated or loosely closed plastic bag. ☐ Leaf lettuces, arugula, and mesclun will last only 2 to 3 days.
MUSHROOMS	2–3 days	☐ Store in a paper bag. Storing in plastic will cause moisture condensation, which accelerates spoilage. ☐ Place a lightly damp paper towel in the bag to keep them moist.
ONIONS, GREEN	3–4 days	☐ Place in a plastic bag and store unwashed in the crisper.
PEAS (SNOW AND SUGAR SNAP)	2–3 days	☐ Fairly perishable and will decrease in flavor if stored for too long. ☐ Store in a plastic bag in the refrigerator.
PEPPERS	3–5 days	☐ Store unwashed in a perforated bag in the crisper.
RADISHES	1 week	☐ Store in a plastic bag in the crisper. ☐ Remove tops from radishes before storing.
RHUBARB	3–5 days	☐ Wilts quickly. ☐ Store in the crisper drawer, wrapped in plastic.
ZUCCHINI	4–5 days	☐ Store in a plastic bag in the crisper.

SOURCE: USDA

FOOD CONTAINERS

BREAD BOXES

Homebaked and crusty store-bought loaves are best wrapped in plastic, wax paper, or cloth and then stored in a bread box (make sure bread is completely cool before storing). Keep your bread box on a countertop. High storage spaces—on top of the refrigerator, for example—are too warm, and the bread will soon mold. Refrigerators slow mold from growing, but they may also dry out bread and make it taste stale sooner than it does when kept at room temperature. (Exceptions include high-moisture breads such as English muffins and brioche.) In particularly hot, humid weather, bread can be refrigerated after two or three days in order to retard mold growth. If you need to keep bread longer than it will keep in the bread box, wrap it airtight and freeze. It will maintain its quality for up to three months. Frozen bread keeps only the freshness it had when put in the freezer, so freeze fresh-baked bread as soon as it has cooled completely. A bread box should be made of moisture-resistant material that cleans easily, such as enameled metal. Wash it weekly with scalding water (more often in warm weather) to kill mold spores before they affect your bread. Use a solution of baking soda and water rather than detergent to clean the inside surfaces; any fragrance may transfer to the bread. Dry the bread box thoroughly after cleaning.

CERAMICS

Small ceramic dishes are useful for keeping salt and pepper on hand as you cook, and for storing leftovers. Be careful about storing, serving, and eating foods out of ceramics, however, since some glazes contain harmful lead. Since 1980, the FDA has required that any new ceramic products made with unsafe glazes sold in the United States are labeled as such; by law, they should say, "Not for Food Use—May Poison Food." Avoid storing anything acidic in a ceramic container, and also beware of ceramics that are from other countries or made in the United States before 1980, as they may contain lead. Ceramics cannot be heated in a broiler or on a cooktop and must be labeled "ovenproof" and "microwave safe" to be used to heat food.

PLASTIC

Lidded plastic containers are convenient for leftovers, soups, and other foods to be stored in the refrigerator and freezer. They can be washed in the dishwasher, on the top rack only. Do not, however, heat food in plastic, even plastic labeled "microwave safe," and always let hot foods cool before putting them in plastic. When plastic is heated, it may leach potentially dangerous chemicals into food. Throw out or recycle visibly damaged,

I LIKE TO MAKE GIFTS OF FOOD
FOR FRIENDS. AN ANTIQUE
RACK, FOR STORING PAPER AND
CELLOPHANE BAGS,
AND AN OLD-FASHIONED PAPER
CUTTER LOOK GOOD ON
THE COUNTER AND PROVIDE
ME WITH EASY ACCESS
TO WRAPPING MATERIALS.

A KITCHEN COUNTER AT TURKEY HILL

GLASS STORAGE BOTTLES AND JARS

An assortment of glass jars and bottles can be used to store infused oils and vinaigrettes temporarily, or dry goods such as crackers and grains for longer periods. Use caution when storing anything perishable, however, and follow all safety guidelines when canning foods at home.

stained, or unpleasant-smelling plastic containers due to some concern that chemicals may also leach from scratches. Do not reuse plastic containers intended for one-time use, such as yogurt tubs. Contact your local government recycling or waste-management office (look for the telephone number in the blue pages of your phone book) to find out what plastics are recyclable in your community (not all communities accept all types). Disposable plastics are generally labeled on the underside with a number; your waste-management office will tell you what numbers it accepts.

METAL

Small airtight metal canisters are excellent for storing spices, since they keep out flavor-robbing light. Larger metal containers are good for storing coffee, tea, and dry staples such as flour and sugar.

GLASS

Lidded glass containers are ideal for storing all sorts of foods—in the pantry, the refrigerator, and even the freezer. They are preferable to plastic containers because they are easier to clean, particularly when it comes to greasy residue, and will last for years, making them a much more economical choice. Before subjecting any glass container to the extreme temperatures of the freezer (or oven), however, be sure it is intended for this purpose. Brands such as Pyrex, for example, are specially designed for use in the freezer and oven. Ordinary glass will crack. If in doubt, leave it out. Most glass containers, unless they have a metallic trim or finish, are safe to use in the microwave.

ABOUT REFRIGERATORWARE

In the late 1930s, when many homemakers still used iceboxes, companies like Westinghouse and General Electric stocked their new refrigerators with colorful machine-molded glass containers. The lidded vessels became known as refrigeratorware; many were stamped with the appliance company's name on the bottom or lid. Their appeal endured through the fifties and sixties, and today these neat, space-saving vessels are highly collectible, prized not only for their streamlined, modern design, but also for their utility. Popular brands include Fire-King—which manufactured green glassware known as Jadeite—McKee, and Hall China.

TYPES OF FOOD WRAPS

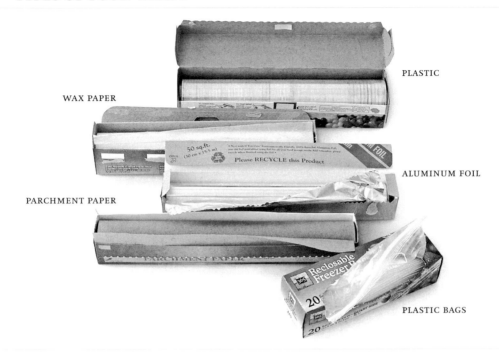

PLASTIC

WAX PAPER

ALUMINUM FOIL

PARCHMENT PAPER

PLASTIC BAGS

PLASTIC

Clings best to glass and ceramic dishes, not rubber or plastic. Do not use to cover hot foods, as the plastic could cause condensation. Use in the refrigerator, to protect foods from absorbing and releasing odors; wrap foods for the freezer once in plastic, then place in a resealable plastic bag. Do not use plastic wrap in the oven or microwave. Heating plastic releases potentially harmful chemicals.

WAX PAPER

This is tissue paper with a coating of paraffin. Secure it to a table or countertop to create a nonstick work surface, and use it to wrap sandwiches. Place on the surface of custards, puddings, pastry creams, and curds to prevent a skin from forming. Never expose wax paper to the heat of an oven or microwave.

ALUMINUM FOIL

Foil is good at preventing the loss of moisture in food. It makes no difference which side—shiny or matte—touches food. Heavy foil is versatile; it can be used in the freezer, and heavy-duty foil bags are useful as temporary storage for hot food. It can be used in the oven but not in the microwave.

PARCHMENT PAPER

Parchment paper, which is grease-proof and silicone-coated, is an excellent bakeware liner. Use it as well for cooking *en papillote*, a classic French technique for "steaming" food inside of a paper package, and for covering foods in the microwave. It's not recommended for food storage. Freezer paper is kraft paper coated with plastic. It's more durable than plastic or parchment paper.

PLASTIC BAGS

Resealable bags can be used to store almost all foods, though cheeses are best stored in paper. Lightweight plastic bags are fine for short-term storage of sandwiches and other lunchbox items. For freezer storage, use freezer bags, which are heavier than conventional storage bags. Place plastic- or foil-wrapped packages in plastic bags, labeled with date and contents, before freezing. Do not heat or microwave food in plastic bags; heating plastic can release potentially harmful chemicals.

RECIPE STORAGE

A good collection of cookbooks is indispensable. Organize them by subject matter—all baking books together, all books on French cuisine together—and if you choose to store them in the kitchen, protect them from excessive heat and humidity by keeping them away from the cooktop, oven, and sink. Protect from spills and spatters while cooking by propping the book open on a cookbook stand, which holds open the recipe page you are using.

As part of your weekly cleaning routine, dust cookbooks with a duster or dry paintbrush. Follow with a damp cloth or sponge to remove any sticky residue or food smudges, if necessary. For paperbacks, use a soft eraser and rub very gently, especially on colored covers.

Anyone who likes to cook knows how quickly loose recipes—clipped from newspapers and magazines, printed off the Internet, handwritten by a friend—can accumulate. Without an efficient filing system, you are sure to lose track of some. However you store them, it's important to divide recipes into categories that make sense to you. So in addition to the basics—hors d'oeuvres, soups, beef, vegetables, desserts—you should have sections that correspond to the way you cook and entertain. This may mean a category just for tomatoes, sandwiches, dips, your children's favorite foods, or dishes that work well for a buffet.

Keeping loose recipes pristine may be impossible, but protecting them from food spatter and grease is not: You can laminate recipe cards, then cut them into uniform sizes and corral them with loose-leaf rings. This way, they are always accessible, and any food spills can be wiped away. Color-coding the paper your recipes are printed on is an additional organizing step: orange for side dishes, yellow for appetizers, blue for desserts, for example. You might also choose to slip loose pages of recipes clipped from magazines and newspapers into clear plastic sheet protectors, available at any office supply store, then collect the sheets in a loose-leaf binder. Or you can copy the clippings onto heavier stock paper before slipping them into sheet protectors.

Yet another option is to scan recipes into the computer to store in a database or on a disk. Also available are several computer cookbooks on CD-ROM, which come with recipes and allow you to enter your own, as well as recipe storage software that can find recipes based on nutritional characteristics. These programs allow you to choose recipes for a dinner party, calculate the quantity of ingredients you'll need, and calculate costs. Many will also perform nutritional analyses, create shopping lists, and track diet progress. Best of all, you can often download this software to a PDA, so it's easy to access when you're at the grocery store.

PLASTIC SHEET
PROTECTORS KEEP RECIPE
CARDS NEAT
AND PROTECTED FROM
FOOD STAINS.

If you're an avid cook, keep a food journal in a blank book. This is a place to record recipes that you make up and want to remember, issue dates and page numbers of recipes in magazines that you don't want to snip from, and notes about recipes: "Reduce the amount of salt in the gazpacho next time." Jot down meal and party menus, noting which cookbooks or files recipes came from, as well as wines, guest lists, and seating arrangements. This way, you can look through past menus when creating new ones. The journal will also serve as a keepsake that you will enjoy reading years from now, and passing on to the next generation of cooks in your family.

COOKBOOK FAVORITES

Cookbooks that contain instructional illustrations, helpful lists of measures and equivalents, nutritional information, and some of your all-time favorite recipes are always a smart choice. The following is a list of my favorite cookbooks; some are sure to become yours.

JOY OF COOKING
Irma S. Rombauer and Marion Rombauer Becker. Indianapolis and New York: Bobbs-Merrill Company, 1975.

MASTERING THE ART OF FRENCH COOKING
Julia Child, Louisette Bertholle, and Simone Beck. New York: Knopf, Volume 1, 40th Anniversary Edition, 2001.

MASTERING THE ART OF FRENCH COOKING
Julia Child and Simone Beck. New York: Knopf, Volume 2, 1970.

ESSENTIALS OF CLASSIC ITALIAN COOKING
Marcella Hazan. New York: Knopf, 1992.

ITALIAN FOOD
Elizabeth David. New York: Penguin, 1999.

FRENCH COUNTRY COOKING
Elizabeth David. New York: Penguin, 2001.

CAFE BOULUD COOKBOOK
Daniel Boulud. New York: Scribner, 1999.

THE NEW MAKING OF A COOK
Madeline Kamman. New York: Morrow Cookbooks, 1st Edition, 1997.

LA VARENNE PRATIQUE
Anne Willan. New York: Clarkson Potter, 1989.

LA TECHNIQUE
Jacques Pepin. New York: Crown, 1976.

LA METHODE
Jacques Pepin. New York: Crown, 1979.

ON FOOD AND COOKING
Harold McGee. New York: Scribner, 2004.

BEARD ON BREAD
James Beard. New York: Knopf, 1995.

THE DINING ROOM AT TURKEY HILL

DINING ROOM

WHEN I FIRST MOVED INTO MY HOUSE in Bedford, I entertained often, sometimes hosting several large dinner parties in a week. I hadn't yet decorated the formal dining room, so I used the large family room I call the brown room for my dinners. It has two large marble-topped tables I designed; when they're put together, I can easily seat twenty-five people, which is a true luxury.

What fun it has been to use so many of my collections of tableware for the table settings, to walk down to the greenhouse to select some very special plants or flowers for the centerpieces, and to go through my collection of fine table linens looking for just the right napkins.

I particularly enjoy entertaining at Skylands, my house in Maine. The dining room there is large, with windows on three sides. It is a room that evokes a different era, and a different way of life. When Edsel Ford and his family built Skylands early in the twentieth century, all meals were eaten in the dining room. There were servants to make the meals, serve them, and clean them up. I am told that the family and their guests seldom ventured into the realm of the kitchen! Today, the kitchen contains a large table that I use for informal suppers, and the dining room is used for formal, sit-down dinners or formal lunches, as well as for luxurious breakfasts when we sit at a smaller breakfast table in an alcove, with windows perfectly situated for watching the sunrise.

Of course, times and tastes and styles have changed, and many modern homes and apartments don't have separate dining rooms at all. Instead, there may be an area off the living room or kitchen that's designated for eating. This type of space is perfect for informal daily meals. But remember, with the addition of fine linens, candles, flowers, and your very best china, you can transform even the tiniest corner into an elegant place for entertaining. Ideally, your supplies—your china, silver, and linens—would

THE FORMAL DINING ROOM AT SKYLANDS, ABOVE, ACCOMMODATES MANY GUESTS. AT LILY POND LANE, RIGHT, I OFTEN SET UP A TABLE FOR CASUAL DINNERS IN AN ALCOVE JUST OFF THE KITCHEN.

be stored in a sideboard or china cabinet in the dining area. But if you don't have space there, make room in your kitchen cabinets and drawers. Or, for the items you use only rarely, consider a storage system such as the quilted, zippered containers made for china and stemware, which will keep them safe and clean. Just be sure to keep everything accessible—you'll be much

You can transform the tiniest corner into an elegant place for entertaining.

more likely to use your fine belongings if you keep them at the ready—for they should be used and enjoyed and admired often.

For me, because I entertain a great deal, and love to collect dishes and flatware, to arrange flowers, and to celebrate special occasions, setting the table is always a creative endeavor—and a pleasure. I start by choosing a theme, which might be a color palette, flowers that are in the garden, or a decoration for a holiday, and then I select the linens, glassware, dishes, flatware, and centerpieces accordingly. My goal is always to set an inviting table, one that surprises my guests and feels just right for the occasion.

LAYOUT BASICS

The centerpiece of any dining room is a table—as generously sized as the space will allow—surrounded by chairs. Although that's all you really need to make the room functional, a china cabinet and sideboard can be useful additions, allowing you to conveniently store your collections of fine china, silver, crystal, and linens where you use them.

A china cabinet or hutch is a high cabinet consisting of a top section with shelves, often protected by glass doors, and a bottom section with shelves concealed by solid doors. You can easily convert an armoire into a china cabinet with the addition of shelves.

A sideboard is a low cabinet, often consisting of drawers (sometimes lined with antitarnish silver-cloth) for flatware, and shelves concealed behind solid doors. Sideboards also provide an extra serving surface, which can be a boon during large holiday gatherings and an ideal spot to lay out a buffet. A low dresser can serve the same purpose.

Make sure the shelves of any piece you use to store and display your fine dish- and glassware are sturdy and that the cabinet itself isn't in a high-traffic area where it will be bumped or even shaken by a slamming door. Open shelves are fine; dust won't harm china (nor will sunlight and fluctuations in temperature or humidity), but dusty pieces will need to be cleaned more frequently, which is one way accidents happen.

Allow at least 36 inches between chairs and a china cabinet or sideboard as well as walls. This will allow enough space for your diners to pull back comfortably from the table. Allow at least 42 inches if the space behind the chair is a traffic route.

WOOD FURNITURE

Bare wood is absorbent and marks easily, so furniture is sealed with a finish when it's manufactured to protect it from scratches and spills, to give it shine, and to enhance its natural beauty and color. A finish is any clear coating that is either "on the wood," which means it sits on the surface, or "in the wood," which means it soaks into the wood in such a way that you can still see and feel the grain of the wood. Many finishes require more than one coat to provide protection. Most commercially manufactured furniture made since the 1930s is finished with clear lacquer, which is a hard, durable, and flexible coating that is scratch-resistant and impervious to most household cleaners and spills. Vintage and antique pieces, on the other hand, are often finished with varnish, oil, or shellac, which is less durable than lacquer and benefits from a yearly coat of wax.

COMMON WOOD FINISHES

LACQUER

A clear water- or solvent-based finish that creates a hard, durable, and flexible coating. Lacquer is preferred by commercial manufacturers because it dries quickly, reducing the chances that airborne particles get caught in the finish. This is the finish most commonly used on furniture. The term "lacquer" also refers to the technique of applying multiple layers of varnish and polishing them to a sheen. For more on this finish, which is generally found on antique furniture, turn to page 708.

PAINT

The practice of painting wood furniture began as a way to protect the wood and make inexpensive but useful items look valuable. Western craftsmen learned to imitate Asian lacquer's mirrorlike finish in the seventeenth and eighteenth centuries by using various combinations of varnishes and powdered pigments. Their diverse techniques came to be known collectively as "japanning." Often, a layer of plain varnish would have been painted over the finished pieces to protect them. Modern pieces may be painted with either alkyd or latex paint.

PENETRATING OIL

Unlike other finishes, which coat the surface of wood, a penetrating oil finish does just what the name implies: It seeps into the wood and permeates the fibers. Tung, linseed, Danish, teak, and mineral oils are commonly used to finish furniture. These oils create a soft, natural-looking luster but do not offer as much protection as lacquer, polyurethane, or varnish. Oil finishes are often found on Danish modern pieces from the 1940s and 1950s.

POLYURETHANE

A water- or solvent-based finish available in a range of sheens. Polyurethane is actually a type of varnish that is made with a polyurethane resin to create a more protective and durable finish that is resistant to both water and alcohol.

SHELLAC

A resin made from the secretions of the Coccus lacca bug, which is indigenous to Thailand and India. French polishing, a high-gloss finishing technique that was used in the nineteenth and early twentieth centuries, is achieved by applying successive thin coats of shellac and denatured alcohol. Shellac is often found on furniture made between the nineteenth century and the 1930s.

VARNISH

A combination of oils and resins that produces a glossy finish. The primary downside of varnishes is that they are slow drying, which can allow dust and dirt time to settle and damage the finish. Durable alkyd urea varnishes were common before lacquer became a popular finish in the 1930s.

PREVENTIVE CARE

Fine wood furniture, even a valuable antique, does not need to be reserved for special occasions as long as it's treated with care. Here's how to ensure your wood furniture will remain beautiful for years to come:

☐ Do not place furniture near heat sources, including warm-air registers, radiators, or fireplaces.

☐ Wipe up spills immediately.

☐ Use coasters for both hot and cold drinks.

☐ Use place mats or lay a tablecloth before dining.

☐ Place a mat or trivet under warm dishes.

☐ Add an extra layer of protection to a dining table with a ½-inch pad. Standard-size pads are available at housewares stores or you can have one custom made (look in the Yellow Pages under "Dining Room Furniture" or search the Web using the words "dining table pad").

☐ Place vases on saucers.

☐ Place potted plants on saucers or in cachepots.

☐ Avert scratches by affixing self-adhesive rubber pads or felt to the bottoms of vases and collectibles.

☐ Store table leaves in protective bags in the same environment as your table. Storing them in a basement or garage where temperature and humidity can fluctuate can cause them to shrink or swell.

ROUTINE CARE

Regular polishing of wood furniture—using one of the many liquids, creams, or aerosols designed to dispel dust or generate a shine—is unnecessary and can even be damaging. Many of these products contain silicone, an oily substance that attracts more dust than it gets rid of. After years of use, silicone will cloud many finishes, and there is no quick fix; the piece will eventually require refinishing. You should also refrain from applying furniture oils (unless the furniture was originally finished with a penetrating oil), which will not penetrate a sealed surface. For all wood furniture, dusting is the only necessary maintenance. Simply wipe wood furniture weekly with a lamb's-wool duster, or soft cloth lightly dampened with water (for more on dusting, turn to page 482). If a surface is particularly dirty or sticky, dampen the cloth with a solution of water and mild dishwashing liquid, wring it out, and wipe the surface well, being careful not to saturate the wood. Rinse the cloth often and follow with another cloth and clean water. Always wipe dry with a soft, clean cloth.

**STEADYING
A WOBBLY CHAIR**
Once they've done their duty as wine-bottle stoppers, corks can come in handy in the dining room. They are a simple solution to an exasperating problem: an unsteady chair. Simply cut a slice of cork horizontally from the top end with a bread knife and secure it to the underside of the troublesome leg with wood glue. Be careful when slicing—since your measurement will be an educated guess, you'll want to have enough cork left over for a second try.

KEEP WOOD FURNITURE
CARE SUPPLIES—
MINERAL SPIRITS, SHOE
POLISH, LACQUER STICKS,
AND SOFT CLOTHS—
TOGETHER IN AN EASILY
ACCESSIBLE KIT.

ALLOW CANDLE WAX TO
HARDEN ON A
TABLETOP BEFORE USING
A CREDIT CARD TO
REMOVE IT.

PERIODIC MAINTENANCE

Waxing wood furniture has been on the list of household chores for hundreds of years, but today is often avoided or skipped altogether. It shouldn't be. Waxing—which puts a barrier between the finish and the elements—is still the simplest and most effective way to care for vintage and antique wood furniture. (New furniture finished with lacquer or polyurethane does not need to be waxed, since these finishes are plasticlike and extremely durable.) Furniture can be waxed once or twice a year and rewaxed when buffing no longer restores the sheen. In a pinch, a dining room tabletop can be waxed and the legs left for next time. Or a few minutes can be spent rewaxing and buffing the often-grabbed areas around the handles on the china cabinet.

QUICK FIXES

SCRATCHES AND NICKS

They can't be repaired, but they can be camouflaged. Shoe polish, more opaque than tinted paste wax, offers easy coverage for an overused tabletop or frequently kicked table legs. It's also reversible: If you don't like the way it looks, you can remove it with mineral spirits. Place a small amount of polish in a color that matches the surface you're treating on a soft cloth and rub it into the scratch until it disappears. Permanent color from a lacquer stick is adequate for furniture that won't have another generation of owners, but do not use it on a valuable piece or an antique.

CANDLE WAX

Scrape it off using a credit card, plastic spatula, or flexible dough scraper (don't use anything made of metal) and buff the excess away with a soft cloth. To harden soft wax (from a fresh drip), place ice cubes in a plastic bag and rest the bag against the wax. The hardened wax can then be scraped away easily using the method above.

RINGS LEFT BY GLASSES

A white ring means that moisture or heat has disturbed a wax finish and the spot just needs rewaxing. Rub it with mineral spirits, apply wax, and buff. A ring darker than the wood, however, has permeated the finish and requires professional treatment by a furniture refinisher.

HOW TO WAX A TABLE

① Wipe the table with a soft cloth dampened with water and mild dishwashing liquid. If a piece is especially dirty (a new flea-market find, for example), use a mild solvent such as mineral spirits or odorless paint thinner. Test an inconspicuous area to make sure the solvent doesn't damage the finish. If the finish remains unchanged, dampen a soft cloth with the solvent—use it straight, but sparingly—and rub it over the wood.

② Apply a paste wax, such as Butcher's Wax, which is available in hardware stores and supermarkets, with a cotton rag folded into a square pad. According to some conservators, it's best to avoid cream or liquid waxes. Although easier to apply, they sometimes contain unnecessary ingredients that can damage some finishes. Apply a thin, even coat to a few square feet at a time, covering every inch of wood.

③ If the piece has carved or detailed molding, apply the wax with a new toothbrush (or an old one reserved for this use) using circular motions.

④ Allow wax to dry for ten to twenty-five minutes. If you don't wait long enough, you'll wipe the wax right off. If you wait too long, it will be difficult to buff out. In that case, simply add more wax to soften the existing coat.

⑤ Buff with a clean cloth, turning it frequently, and try to remove all the wax. When the rag slides rather than drags, you're done.

CHAIRS

In standard dining room chair sets, there are two chairs with arms for the ends of the table and four to six, depending upon the length of the table, that have no arms, for the sides. (If you have a roomy table, however, there's no reason all the chairs can't have arms.) The chair height generally ranges from 17 inches to 19 inches, which goes well with tables that have a height of 28 inches to 30 inches. Keep in mind that chairs do not have to match the table, or even one another, for that matter. Mixing and matching styles and materials can actually give the room a greater sense of style. Just make sure that the table and chairs share the same level of formality. To protect wood floors, glue felt squares to the bottoms of chair legs so they glide easily and do not scratch the wood.

CARING FOR UPHOLSTERY

Vacuum upholstered dining room chairs weekly using the upholstery attachment and crevice tool. When spills occur, blot them immediately with a white cotton towel or white paper towel. If the spill results in a stain, check the underside of the chair or inside a zippered cushion to see if there are cleaning instructions. If not, turn to page 193 for spot-removal solutions and for more on caring for upholstered furniture.

REMOVING WAX FROM UPHOLSTERY

Although a dry cleaner should remove wax from delicate fibers such as silk, for durable fabrics such as cotton, you can try to clean them yourself. First, let the wax cool on its own or hasten the process by placing an ice cube in a resealable plastic bag on top of it. Once firm, carefully scrape off as much wax as you can using your fingernail or the dull edge of a butter knife. If the wax is on a cushion cover that can be removed, take it off and place several layers of damp paper towels on each side of the fabric, ironing over the paper on a low setting; the wax should be absorbed by the towels. Apply a fabric stain remover to eliminate any lingering residue (check for colorfastness first in an inconspicuous spot, then follow label instructions on the spot remover); blot with clean paper towels before laundering. If the wax hardened on a fragile material, do not attempt to remove it yourself by scraping; take it to a dry cleaner instead. And if the cushion covers can't be removed, ask your dry cleaner to recommend a tailor who can remove the stuffing so you can have the cover treated separately.

CARING FOR CANING AND RUSH

Regularly vacuum cane and rush work with the dust-brush tool. To clean stains, use a solution of a few drops of mild dishwashing liquid diluted in warm water. Don't clean cane or rush with powerful abrasives or acidic or alkaline cleaners. Rub gently with a soft-bristled brush or a soft cloth dampened in the dishwashing solution, then rinse by wiping with a cloth dampened in plain water. Dry with a second clean cloth. Indelible stains generally occur where the protective shellac finish has worn away, allowing stains to penetrate deep into the fibers. Reapplying shellac is inadvisable because it is thinned with a drying agent that is more damaging than simply leaving a stain untouched. Excessive dryness can also cause breakage. Regular mistings with plain water one to two times every month in very dry environments will keep these materials from drying out. Spray a brief, fine mist about 2 feet above the surface; do not saturate. Only mist the top, never underneath.

PROLONG THE LIFE OF A CANED CHAIR BY DUSTING WEEKLY AND LIGHTLY MISTING ONCE OR TWICE A MONTH.

SETTING THE TABLE

The word "etiquette" comes from the French word for "label" or "ticket." In the eighteenth century, visitors to court were given a small card, an *estiquette,* with written or printed instructions on how to behave. Today, hostesses and diners alike could use just such *estiquettes,* describing how to lay a table properly as well as how to navigate the resulting assortment of forks, spoons, and glasses. Fortunately, the principles of setting a table—whether casual or formal—are simple, and the very configuration of china, flatware, and stemware also guide diners effortlessly through the meal.

The cardinal rule of table setting is this: Place the silverware on the table in the order it will be used, from the outside in. The fork for the first course is the farthest to the left, and the knife that goes with it is farthest to the right (with the blade facing the plate). Any spoons needed before

TWO TYPICAL PLACE SETTINGS

EVERYDAY DINING

A classic, informal place setting begins with a dinner plate only when soup or another first course is served. Dinner plates are not on the table when guests take their seats if there is no first course. Of the five basic flatware pieces, only the teaspoon is left off the table; it will arrive with coffee or tea, placed at the saucer's edge. A water glass (placed over the knife) and single wineglass are set, suggesting that one wine will accompany dinner. A folded cloth napkin adds a touch of elegance.

SPECIAL-OCCASION DINING

This formal place setting includes a charger and is set for European dining, where the salad follows the main course. From the left, forks are for fish, main course, and salad. From the right are the soupspoon, fish knife, and dinner knife. Above the charger are a dessert spoon and dessert fork. Stemware forms a triangle: The water glass sits above the dinner knife, the white-wine glass is to its right, and the red-wine glass is above them. The bread-and-butter plate and butter knife sit above the forks.

dessert are placed to the right of the plate, among the knives. Dessert silverware rests horizontally above the plate or is brought to the table after the meal. Stemware is placed above the knives; salad plates rest to the left of the forks, with the butter plate just above. The napkin, generally folded into a rectangle, is placed in the center of the plate or charger, to the left of the plate, underneath the forks, or to the left of the forks.

Although these guidelines might seem arbitrary, reasons both practical and historical underpin the accepted arrangement of table items. Case in point: Because most people are right-handed, knives and glasses are placed on that side and forks are put on the left, where they can be used to steady the meat while the stronger hand does the cutting. Glasses for water and white wine are placed closer to guests than those for red wine because they are provided first (the water glass should be filled before guests are seated; and white wine should be poured after guests are seated, as it is typically served before red, to complement the lighter starter courses).

A hostess who masters the basics can create a thousand variations by mixing and matching tableware patterns. There are a couple of rules of thumb when it comes to creating a successful mix: Maintain a single level of formality (don't pair casual Bakelite flatware with elegant lusterware plates, for example) and make sure tableware from different eras share similar lines and proportions.

SERVICE ETIQUETTE

Proper service etiquette is rarely discussed and even more rarely put into practice today. We pass platters around the table, serve ourselves from buffets, and even invite guests into the kitchen to help with preparations. This relaxed approach works fine most of the time, but when serving a formal dinner, some rules still apply:

☐ Serve guests from the left.

☐ Remove dishes from the right or left depending on which is more convenient for the guest.

☐ Fill glasses from the right, leaving the glasses in place during pouring.

☐ Fill wineglasses only halfway. This leaves room for aeration and it creates space in the glass for the bouquet to collect.

☐ Before serving dessert, clear the table of everything except glasses, which should remain until after guests have left the table. If dessert flatware was not placed above the dinner plate when the table was set, bring it to the table on a tray, along with coffee cups and saucers.

HOW TO USE A CHARGER

Purely for decoration, a charger, also known as a service plate, is an oversized plate—generally 12 to 14 inches in diameter—meant to serve as a placeholder on a formal table. Dinner is never served on a charger, although it is permissible to set a first course or a soup bowl on it. The charger is removed, along with the first course, before the main course is served.

A NOTE ABOUT SALTCELLARS

The saltcellar, a small, open container for holding salt at the table, is a charming holdover from the pre-saltshaker years. Place one at each setting (anywhere above the dessert utensils) or between two settings for guests to share. Diners can pinch the salt with their fingers or scoop it up with the tip of a knife. When a single cellar is to be used by several people, include a tiny spoon; be sure to offer a pepper mill as well. If you don't own any cellars, several pairs of salt and pepper shakers set between guests will do.

TABLE LINENS

Draped with a white damask cloth and topped with folded napkins, your dining table signals that an elegant meal is on the way. Covered with bright stripes or checks, it's ready for an indoor picnic. Set with a pair of place mats and matching napkins, it invites brunch for two. Experimenting with linens is one of the most effective and inexpensive ways to transform the look of your dining room. The basics—tablecloths, napkins, place mats, and runners—can be mixed and matched. Some combination of these elements can make up a set, and not all your sets will consist of the same pieces.

TABLECLOTHS

A tablecloth should match the shape of your table: round, oval, square, or rectangular. When it is draped over your table, it should have at least an 8-inch drop on all sides. For a formal look, you'll want a 24-inch drop. For the most dramatic look, use a cloth that reaches all the way to the floor.

NAPKINS

White cotton or linen dinner napkins will see you through any occasion, be it casual or formal. Depending on how you entertain, buy napkins in sets of seven, nine, or thirteen; use the extra napkin to line the breadbasket. Rotate them in and out of use, so they maintain a consistent appearance.

PLACE MATS

Place mats are appropriate for both casual and formal dining. Use these linens instead of a cloth to show off a pretty tabletop. A set of twelve will come in handy for a dinner party as well as a buffet where the mats mark the spots for platters. Place mats should be larger than your plates for both aesthetic and practical reasons. Antique place mats are narrower than today's typical 13-by-19-inch rectangle and 15- or 16-inch round, making them suitable only for smaller dinner plates.

RUNNERS

Table runners are both decorative and practical. These lengths of fabric are wonderful accessories for a table, whether or not it's set for a meal. A runner can overhang the edge of a table by a few inches or extend almost to the floor. When dining, use the runner as a spot for serving dishes, candles, and condiments. Or use two runners down opposite sides of the table instead of place mats or a tablecloth.

COMMON WEAVES

Linen, cotton, and synthetics are woven in a number of different ways, and each weave produces a different kind of fabric. Common weaves used for table linens include:

Plain

The simplest and most common of all weaves. Each filling yarn passes alternately over and under each warp yarn, producing a strong, stable fabric. Can be heavy or light. Organdy, which is a translucent, crisp cotton, is one example of a plain weave.

Jacquard

A pattern woven directly into the fabric. Damask and brocade are examples of Jacquard weaves.

Sateen

Yarns are interlaced in such a way that there is no visible pattern. The result is a smooth-textured fabric with a subtle sheen.

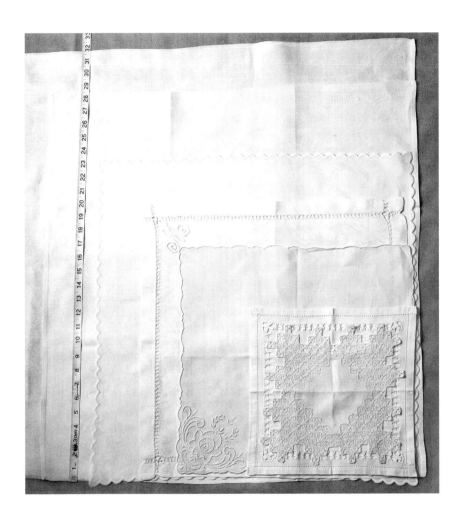

CARING FOR LINENS

No matter the material, weave, or embellishment, all table linens benefit from the following care:

☐ Blot big spills promptly, then flush with cold water and a mild dishwashing liquid.

☐ Launder immediately after use, using an oxygen-based bleach if suitable for the fabric (check the care label information). Use warm water rather than hot water, which can shrink the fibers.

☐ Do not use fabric softener, which can weaken delicate fibers and reduce absorbency, which is especially undesirable with napkins.

NAPKIN SIZES

There are many napkin sizes that suit a number of different purposes:

Cocktail napkins are usually 5 inches square.

Luncheon napkins are 10 to 13 inches square.

Dinner napkins are typically 22 to 24 inches square.

COMMON EMBELLISHMENTS

Linens are often trimmed with delightful details besides monograms. Common forms of ornamentation include:

Cutwork

Embroidery in which the design is outlined in a buttonhole stitch and the material inside the stitching is cut away.

Hemstitching

A stitch usually bordering a hem that is characterized by small open rectangles. It's created when several parallel threads are caught together in groups.

Picot

A row of small loops sewn along the edge of a table linen.

☐ Make sure there are no spots before putting linens in the dryer—the heat will set a stain. For more on stain removal, turn to page 374.

☐ Dry linens on low heat and remove them from the dryer while still slightly damp. Overdrying linens can weaken the fibers.

☐ Dry-clean linens with fancy trim, such as beading.

STORAGE

Clean, pressed linens (for instructions on how to iron linens, turn to pages 402 and 406) should be folded neatly, in as few folds as possible, depending on your storage space. Keep linens in cupboards or drawers that are well ventilated, clean, and dry. Wooden shelves or drawers should be painted or lined with shelf paper (wood can stain fabrics over time). Here are some additional tips for keeping your table linens table-ready:

NAPKINS

Keep sets of napkins together. Acid-free tissue is an excellent storage material that helps prevent fabric from yellowing. For sets that you use infrequently, stack napkins and wrap them loosely in tissue, as you would a present. Attach an adhesive label to the top of the bundle identifying the contents. For napkins you use often, simply wrap a sleeve of tissue around the stack and secure the bundle with an adhesive label on which you've written the number of napkins in the set.

TABLECLOTHS

Few things are more nerve-wracking than taking a creased cloth out of a drawer and having to iron it before a dinner party. To keep tablecloths smooth, you can store them on a roll rather than folding them flat. Completely wrap a large cardboard tube (a mailing tube or wrapping-paper roll both work well) with a couple of layers of acid-free tissue paper. Then carefully wrap an ironed cloth around the layers of paper. Depending on the width of your cloth, you may need to fold it lengthwise before rolling it. Cover with acid-free tissue paper and store the roll horizontally. This technique also works well for table runners—smaller tubes, such as those from aluminum-foil packages, are good for this purpose. You can also hang tablecloths over sturdy hangers, placing a sheet of acid-free tissue between the rod and the cloth. Protect the cloth with another sheet of tissue (never store linens in plastic dry-cleaning bags, which can cause fabrics to yellow) or protect a group of cloths with a canvas garment bag. For information on linen closets, turn to page 355.

HOW TO REMOVE WAX FROM TABLE LINENS
Allow wax to harden before you attempt to remove it. When wax is frozen, it becomes even more brittle and is easier to remove, so either place the linens in the freezer or rub with an ice cube wrapped in a plastic sandwich bag. Once the wax is hard, gently flake it off with a dull butter knife. Do not scrape since this may damage the fibers. The dyes used in colored candles may leave behind a stain; if an oily spot remains, have the item dry-cleaned.

THE MOST USEFUL,
THE MOST PRACTICAL, THE MOST
BEAUTIFUL—I USE THESE
EXPRESSIONS OVER AND OVER AGAIN
WHEN DESCRIBING WHAT
A STORAGE SOLUTION SHOULD BE,
WHETHER FOR FINE LINEN
TABLECLOTHS LIKE THESE, OR CHINA,
SPICES, OR MIXING BOWLS.

TABLE LINENS STORED AT SKYLANDS

TABLECLOTH SIZE CHART

Table Shape	Table Size	Number of People	Tablecloth Size
Square	28 × 28″ to 40 × 40″	4	52 × 52″ square
Round	36 to 48″ diameter	4	60″ round
Rectangle/Oval	28 × 46″ to 40 × 48″	4–6	52 × 70″ rectangle/oval
Round	42 to 60″ diameter	6	70″ or 72″ round
Rectangle/Oval	36 × 60″ to 48 × 72″	6–8	60 × 84″ rectangle/oval
Round	64 to 76″ diameter	6–8	90″ round
Rectangle/Oval	36 × 78″ to 48 × 90″	8–10	60 × 102″ rectangle/oval
Rectangle/Oval	36 × 96″ to 48 × 108″	10–12	60 × 120″ rectangle/oval

TYPES OF TABLE LINEN FABRICS

COTTON

Soft, beautiful, and affordable, cotton is also very durable, and can stand up to repeated launderings since cotton fibers are stronger when they're wet than when they're dry.

Care Most cotton fabrics are machine-washable and dryer safe (check care labels). Except in the most casual circumstances, you'll need to iron cotton.

LINEN

A generic term for all types of cloth used in the home, linen is also the name of a specific fabric, woven from flax fibers and considered extremely luxurious. It is stronger than traditional table fabrics (it is two to three times as strong as cotton). However, it is typically the most expensive table-linen fabric.

Care Some linen is machine-washable and dryer safe (check care labels). Linen requires a thorough pressing to keep it looking its best.

SYNTHETIC BLENDS

These are durable and require little upkeep. They do not feel as good as cotton or linen and may also be less absorbent. Polyester blends may pill with repeated use.

Care Machine-washable and dryer safe; no ironing needed.

CHINA

"China" is a general term for ceramic tableware, whether made of earthenware, stoneware, or porcelain. All ceramics are clay that has been hardened by fire. The clay is mixed with minerals to form a body or paste that can be molded and kiln-fired. Ceramic bodies are of two types: porous earthenwares and nonporous stonewares and porcelains. Everyday china is generally earthenware or stoneware. The term "fine china" generally refers to thinner porcelain or bone china.

China is usually sold in four- or five-piece place settings. A standard five-piece place setting consists of a 10-inch dinner plate, a slightly smaller salad plate, a bread-and-butter plate (or in more contemporary patterns, a soup bowl), and a cup and saucer. A four-piece setting substitutes a mug for the cup and saucer. A basic set of serving pieces consists of a serving platter, an open vegetable dish, a creamer, and a covered sugar bowl.

CARING FOR CHINA

Wash all china as soon as possible after each meal. Acidic foods, such as tomatoes and citrus fruits, and sulfur-based foods, such as mayonnaise, tartar sauce, and eggs, can mar the glaze and color of china not rinsed

COMMON PLATE SIZES

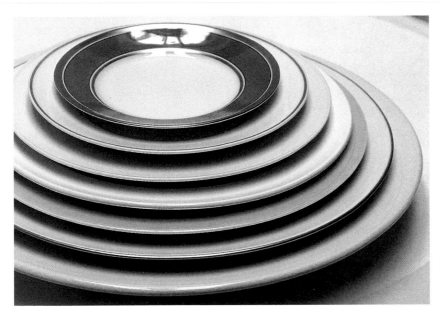

The basic place setting includes the bread-and-butter, the salad, and the dinner plates, although those who entertain frequently may also want luncheon and dessert plates, which are appropriately scaled to the smaller portions they hold, as well as chargers or service plates.

BREAD-AND-BUTTER 6″
DESSERT PLATE 7″
SALAD PLATE 8″
LUNCHEON PLATE 9″
DINNER PLATE 10″
SERVICE PLATE 12″
CHARGER 13½″

soon after eating. Rinse coffee and teacups right away, as well, to prevent staining. In addition, be sure to rotate dinnerware, so that each piece receives the same frequency of use. This will ensure that each piece in your set maintains a consistent appearance over time. Vintage and antique pieces were not made to withstand the heat of the dishwasher, so older china should be washed by hand. Although newer pieces may technically be machine-washable, they may also begin to show signs of wear after repeated machine washings, so you may want to hand-wash pieces of value.

HAND-WASHING

To prevent scratching and chipping, remove rings and other jewelry and wash flatware and cookware separately. Avoid abrasive pads and gritty cleansers; use a soft brush and mild dishwashing liquid instead.

DISHWASHING

To avoid the risk of scratching, load the pieces so that they do not touch each other. Do not allow aluminum utensils to touch china; black marks will appear on white china that comes in contact with aluminum during washing (you can polish them away with a mildly abrasive cleanser such as Bon Ami). Do not overload the dishwasher. Use the Short Wash or China and Crystal cycle. For more on washing dishes, turn to page 83.

STORING CHINA

China should be stored with care to avoid chips or scratches in the glaze.

PLATES, BOWLS, AND SAUCERS

When dishes are stacked, the bottom of one can scratch the one beneath it. Place a cushion between them to reduce the risk. Paper plates, coffee filters, and felt rounds are just right for cradling plates, bowls, and saucers without adding bulk. Alternate dishes and inserts.

CUPS AND MUGS

Store these rim side up to guard against chipping. Cups and mugs can also be hung from cup hooks, but do not hang antiques or pieces that have been repaired. Store-bought coated wire racks can add shelves in between shelves to double the number of pieces you can store.

LIDDED PIECES

Top-shelf storage may keep your best china away from kitchen bustle, but it can create a hazard when lidded pieces are pulled from their high perch. Fasten lids with waxed twine so they do not fall off. First, place the lid upside down inside the vessel, then wrap twine in a figure eight around both vessel handles and over the lid. Tie the twine gently to finish.

FELT ROUNDS ARE IDEAL FOR CUSHIONING STACKED FINE CHINA.

TYPES OF CHINA

EARTHENWARE

Fired at a low temperature, earthenware is a fragile, heavy dinnerware. It is the least durable ceramic and chips easily. It is also usually the least expensive and, because of its low firing temperature, capable of the brightest color. Majolica, faience, delftware, and slipware are all varieties of collectible glazed earthenware.

Care Many pieces are dishwasher-safe (look at the bottom of a piece or check with the manufacturer), but anything of value should be washed by hand.

STONEWARE AND PORCELAIN

These are fired at higher temperatures, which produces a harder and more impervious ceramic. Porcelain is distinguished from stoneware by its whiteness and translucency, which result from its clay (a white clay called kaolin) and the inclusion of minerals (usually feldspar and quartz).

Care Many pieces are dishwasher-safe (look at the bottom of a piece or check with the manufacturer); however, handpainted, metal-trimmed, or vintage or antique pieces should be washed by hand.

BONE CHINA

A type of porcelain with ash from actual bones as the predominant ingredient, which makes the clay body particularly white. Fired at high temperatures, it is thin and lightweight but very durable.

Care Many pieces are dishwasher-safe (look at the bottom of a piece or check with the manufacturer); however, handpainted, metal-trimmed, or vintage or antique bone china should be washed by hand.

HOW TO REPAIR BROKEN CHINA

1. Wash pieces in warm, soapy water; rinse well.

2. Let pieces dry for several hours, then arrange on a work surface.

3. Determine in what order you will join the pieces (for example, start with the pieces near the center and work outward).

4. Use a fast-drying, water-resistant epoxy. Swab the common edges with acetone (which will ensure the pieces are clean of oil and dirt).

5. Place a thin, even bead of epoxy along one edge.

6. Join the two pieces and adjust for a close fit.

7. Remove excess epoxy by wiping it away with acetone-soaked cotton swabs.

8. Place tape across the joint to hold pieces in place until the glue has cured. If the design is fragile, apply tape to the back of the joint as well.

DISPLAYING CHINA

Plates on display in a dining room or dining area reinforce the purpose of the room, and are lovely set off on their own as decorative pieces of art. What is more, they can fit cozily into small spaces, over a door or window, for example, or in between two windows. Plates can be mismatched and hung in a grouping, but the display will look better if the plates you use are all of a piece or in the same category, such as brown transferware, for instance, or lusterware.

GROUPING CHINA BY TYPE AND COLOR MAKES FOR A PLEASING DISPLAY.

To display plates upright in a cabinet, use Museum Putty (available in most hardware stores), to hold them in place. This off-white putty is good for keeping the edges of standing plates from slipping on shelves or holding vases in a fixed position.

If you are going to hang plates on the wall, do so with great care. Plate hangers, available at housewares and hardware stores, are adjustable; the package label should indicate the size of the plates the hanger can accommodate. Some plate hangers can scratch or chip the plate and, in the case of antique or delicate plates, the pressure of the hanger can cause an old, well-repaired crack to resurface. You can avoid this by placing a tiny wad of cotton over the "claws" of the hanger, then securing it with a small piece of clear fish-tank tubing, which serves as protective padding.

Plate easels are another display option. Make sure the easel is the appropriate size for the display piece and use a couple of small pieces of Museum Putty to secure the plates to the easels.

FLATWARE

Knives, forks, and spoons, as witnesses to family meals and celebrations, have been regarded as heirlooms since table silver was first made into sets in the late seventeenth century. The basic set of flatware (the name given to the utensils used for eating and serving food) consists of a five-piece place setting: a dinner knife, dinner and salad forks, a soupspoon, and a teaspoon. For a formal dinner, you'll need extra salad forks and teaspoons; the former are used for first courses and dessert, and the latter are used for both dessert and coffee. Butter knives, fish forks, and round-bowled soupspoons are also useful additions.

A BASIC SET OF FLATWARE
INCLUDES
A SALAD FORK, DINNER
FORK, DINNER KNIFE,
TEASPOON, AND
SOUPSPOON.

During the Victorian era, it became fashionable to have a special utensil for every purpose, and some silver patterns offered as many as 130 different pieces per place setting. Some pieces, like an aspic spoon or a sardine fork, are quaint reminders of a bygone era, while others are practical, albeit luxurious, even today. The tines of a lemon fork are splayed to release a generous spritz of juice; the dull blade of a fish knife flakes the delicate flesh perfectly. If you invest in pieces like fruit forks, oyster forks, iced-tea spoons, and cheese knives, you'll certainly find uses for them—and it doesn't have to be what they were originally intended for.

Similarly, there are serving pieces for almost any imaginable task, from poking pickles, to ladling soup, to spreading caviar. The basics, however, include a large serving spoon, a serving fork, a pierced serving spoon, a serving ladle, a sugar spoon, and a butter knife.

TYPES OF FLATWARE

Most flatware is made of one of three materials: stainless steel, silver plate, or sterling silver.

STAINLESS STEEL

Most casual flatware is made of stainless steel, an alloy, or mix, of steel (which is itself a combination of iron and carbon), chromium, and nickel. As the name implies, it stains less easily than other metals, making it ideal for the wear and tear of daily dining. The chromium lends stainless steel its hardness, resistance to heat, and ability to resist corrosion. The nickel imparts shine and luster, as well as hardness. Stainless flatware is often labeled either 18/10 or 18/8. The first number refers to the percentage of chromium; the second to the percentage of nickel. The higher the percentage of nickel, the higher the quality of the flatware.

Care Dishwasher-safe. Although stainless steel is highly resistant to stains, it can be damaged by prolonged contact with eggs, vinegar, and acidic foods, so rinse promptly after dining. Use the minimum recommended amount of detergent and avoid detergents with lemon, which can harm the finish. Do not wash stainless-steel pieces with items made of aluminum, silver plate, or sterling. Never let flatware soak overnight in water. If spots remain after washing, polish them away with a paste of water and baking soda. If your flatware looks dull, an application of stainless-steel polish (available at silversmiths and hardware stores) may restore the luster.

SILVER PLATE

Silver plate, a less-expensive alternative to sterling, is made when a base metal, such as nickel silver (an alloy of copper, nickel, and zinc) or brass, is coated with a thin layer of 100 percent silver.

Care Dishwasher-safe; however, opt for the gentlest detergent you can find and reduce the amount you normally use in order to decrease the risk of damage. Don't run the Dry cycle and remove and dry with a clean, dry cloth immediately. Knives, especially older ones, shouldn't go in the dishwasher; the joint between the blade and handle could loosen. Repaired flatware could also break in the dishwasher. Most important, *never* put silver plate in with stainless steel; a reaction between the two metals can cause damage to both finishes. Avoid prolonged contact with eggs, vinegar, and acidic foods, which can tarnish, pit, and corrode silver-plated flatware. Never let flatware soak overnight in water.

STERLING SILVER

Flatware with the "sterling" mark stamped on it is 92.5 percent pure silver (the rest is an alloy, usually copper, which adds durability). Until the Industrial Revolution, all silver was made by hand; today, most silver is cast using a process that dates from the nineteenth century. The best thing you can do for your silver—whether it's new or a family heirloom—is to use it. The more often you do, the less you'll need to polish it. In addition, with years of use, the mesh of fine lines and scratches that result creates a rich and desirable luster, called a patina.

Care If the prospect of washing your silver by hand prohibits you from using and enjoying it, by all means put it in the dishwasher. There are a few caveats, however. As with silver plate, use the gentlest detergent you can find and reduce the amount used to decrease the risk of damaging the patina. Turn off the Dry cycle and remove and dry silver with a clean, dry cloth immediately. Don't put old knives in the dishwasher and *never* wash sterling silver alongside stainless steel. Repaired flatware could also break in the dishwasher. Avoid prolonged contact with eggs, vinegar, and acidic foods. Never let flatware soak overnight in water.

TYPES OF KNIVES

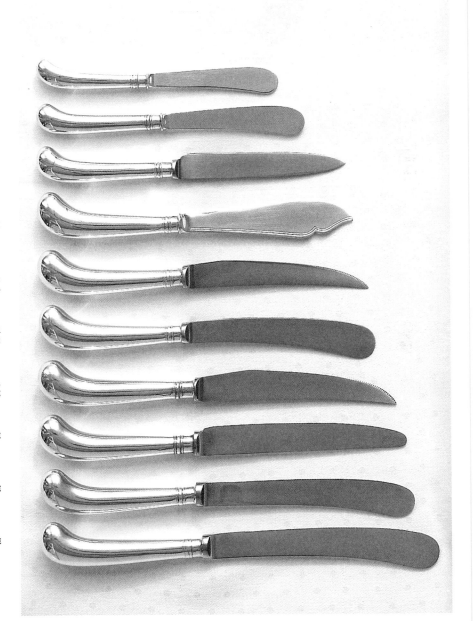

BUTTER KNIFE

CHILD'S KNIFE

FRUIT KNIFE

FISH KNIFE

STEAK KNIFE,
SMALL

LUNCHEON OR
DESSERT KNIFE

STEAK KNIFE,
LARGE

DINNER KNIFE

DINNER KNIFE

TABLE KNIFE

TYPES OF FORKS

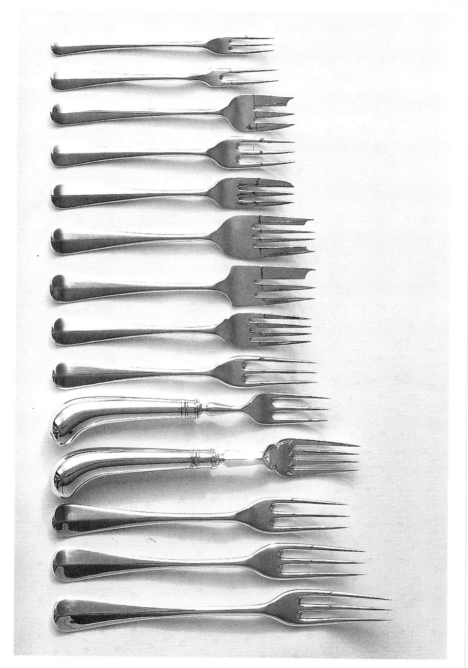

SEAFOOD FORK

SNAIL FORK

OYSTER FORK

CHILD'S FORK

PASTRY FORK

FOUR-TINED
SALAD FORK

THREE-TINED
SALAD FORK

FOUR-TINED
DESSERT FORK

THREE-TINED
DESSERT FORK

THREE-TINED
FISH FORK

FOUR-TINED
FISH FORK

LUNCHEON FORK

THREE-TINED
DINNER FORK

TABLE FORK

TYPES OF SPOONS

MUSTARD SPOON

CHILD'S
DEMITASSE SPOON

BABY SPOON

EXTRA-SMALL
TEASPOON

SMALL TEASPOON

ICE-CREAM FORK

ICE-CREAM SPOON

TEASPOON

LARGE TEASPOON

FRUIT SPOON

BOUILLON SPOON

CREAM
SOUPSPOON

SAUCE SPOON

ENGLISH DESSERT
SPOON

LARGE SOUPSPOON

LARGE ICED-TEA
SPOON

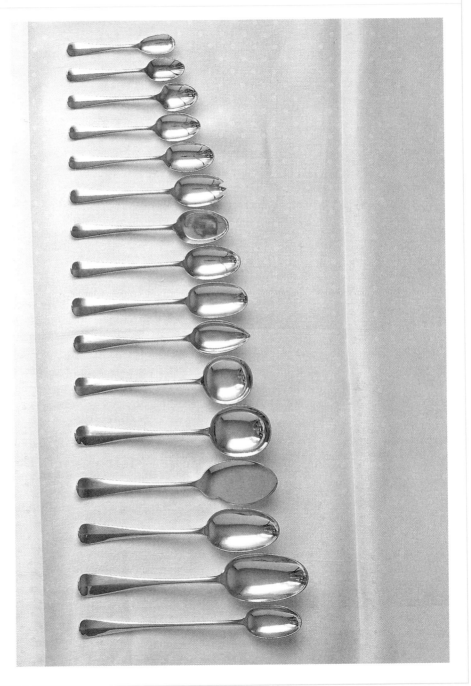

HOW TO POLISH SILVER

Acids from your hands, sulfur from foods such as eggs and Brussels sprouts, sunlight, smoke from the fireplace, and even compounds released by cupboards and drawer liners all conspire to dull silver's glow. But keeping tarnish at bay isn't really so difficult. Regular use is one of the best solutions. When a good polishing is called for, just follow these simple steps. Keep in mind, however, that silver should be polished only occasionally—before a holiday gathering, for example. Although silver is sturdy, it scratches easily and is worn away a bit with every polishing.

1. Work in a well-lighted area on a nonporous surface. To prevent dents and scratches, pad your work area with an old towel.

2. Protect your hands (and the silver you're polishing from the oils and acids on your skin) by wearing white cotton gloves.

3. Before applying polish, inspect the piece for a previous polishing pattern. This is usually circular on hollowware and lengthwise on flatware. Polish in that pattern with a light touch, following the silver polish's label instructions and avoiding areas where different materials meet.

4. Start with a polish-imbued cloth or liquid polish designed specifically for silver. If this proves inadequate, move on to a paste or cream. Apply with a 100 percent cotton flannel cloth or a cellulose sponge. Use a soft toothbrush or wooden cuticle stick wrapped in cotton on monograms and ornate designs. Don't worry about removing every bit of tarnish in the crevices of an intricate or ornate pattern—the darkness is what allows the pattern to really stand out. Don't be tempted to use acid baths, called silver dips, which are far too harsh.

5. Rinse the piece when you're finished, being sure to remove all the polishing compound, then dry with a soft cotton cloth.

HOW TO CLEAN BONE- AND IVORY-HANDLED CUTLERY

Bone is a delicate, porous material and must be treated carefully to keep it from warping or absorbing dirt. It is sometimes mistaken for ivory, which is heavier and more prone to cracking. Over time, both bone and ivory develop a pleasing yellow or brown patina; however, they can both be discolored fairly easily. Here's how to care for both:

1. Don't immerse in water, and never put bone- or ivory-handled pieces in the dishwasher.

2. Wipe the blades with a damp, soft cloth and mild dishwashing liquid, but avoid wetting the handles and seam between the blade and the handle; on antique pieces, animal glues were often used and they can weaken in water.

3. Wipe handles with a damp cloth and dry. If they require a more thorough cleaning, use mild dishwashing liquid sparingly.

4. Always use soft, white cloths, since bone and ivory can pick up dyes from fabrics.

5. Store in a cool, dry spot, away from direct sunlight; heat and humidity can cause shrinking and swelling.

HOW TO STORE FLATWARE

For everyday use, store your flatware in a drawer that's been outfitted with a multi-compartment cutlery tray or individual boxes sized to hold your collection. Group like things together. To prevent scratching, line the tray or boxes with a resilient liner made of industrial felt, cork, or ribbed plastic. Do not use a rubber liner, as it can cause some metals to tarnish.

To store silver or silver plate pieces you use only occasionally, place them in protective flannel bags treated with a tarnish inhibitor, available from housewares stores or jewelers. Never store flatware in plastic bags, which trap moisture, or wrapped in rubber bands, which contain damaging sulfur. Rotate place settings in and out of use to ensure the entire set retains a consistent appearance over time.

GLASSWARE

A good drinking glass is a pleasure to use. It feels just right in your hand and can dress up any meal. It can be all-purpose, or for one use only—wine lovers know a properly shaped glass can amplify the richness of a Bordeaux, for instance, or keep Champagne from losing its fizz.

Regardless of shape, all glass is made from the melding together of sand with ashes, lead oxide, and ground limestone. The fewer imperfections and trace elements in the sand, the more colorless the glass will be.

The two basic methods for making glass are blowing and pressing. The finest handmade glasses are made with metal blowpipes. A clump of molten glass at the end of a long pipe is coaxed into a bubble by the breath of the blower. Today, of course, in this age of mass production, this process is often done by machine. Pressed glass, which tends to be thicker than blown glass, is made when molten glass is poured into a mold. Unlike blown glass—which is uniformly smooth inside and out—pressed glass usually has a raised pattern on the outside. Depression glass from the 1930s is a typical example of pressed glass, as is the dinner tumbler with paneled sides, a classic on the American table for generations.

EVERYDAY GLASSWARE

One of the most important qualities of a basic drinking glass is durability. A glass with a beaded lip is stronger than one with a straight edge; pressed glass is more durable than blown glass.

When replacing drinking glasses, keep in mind that high-quality glass is clear and colorless. Lesser-quality materials can give glass a grayish tinge. Inspect glasses to make sure there are no flaws, such as bubbles.

CARE

Because most drinking glasses are made to go in the dishwasher, caring for them is easy. Hard water, however, may leave deposits on glasses, causing a cloudy film. To prevent this, use the minimum recommended amount of detergent, run the machine on the Delicate or Normal cycle (avoid the Heavy-Duty or High-Temperature setting), and try a rinse aid.

CRYSTAL

Crystal is simply glass to which red lead oxide has been added. Lead makes glass more durable and exceptionally brilliant. Fine drinking glasses often contain small amounts, but full-lead crystal must contain at least 24 percent. The term "crystal" has come to refer to all superior-quality glassware. True crystal, however, has an unmistakable shine and tone—if you tap the edge of the glass with your finger, it will ring like a bell.

EVERYDAY GLASSES
An everyday-glass wardrobe might include a tall, wide glass for water, an all-purpose medium-sized tumbler (also known as a cooler, which is handy for milk or lemonade), a tall glass for iced tea, and a smaller juice glass.

CARING FOR CRYSTAL

Liquids left in crystal can cause stains, so empty and rinse glasses soon after use. Even though many dishwashers have a setting for crystal, it's best to wash fine glassware by hand; the heat and detergent can etch and cloud the glasses over time. Long-stemmed glasses can also topple over during the wash cycle and break or chip. Before hand washing crystal, remove rings and bracelets. Line the sink with a towel and fill it with hot, soapy water. Wash glasses one at a time with a soft cloth. Rinse and dry with a lint-free cloth that has not been laundered with fabric softener, which can leave a residue; drip drying can create water spots.

To smooth a very small chip in a glass, you can use a sanding tool called a jeweler's belt stick. This process is simple, but no matter how careful you are, there is still a risk of breakage. Begin by wetting the stick and lightly rubbing it over the chip, then coat the area with clear nail polish. The chipped area will feel and look better, although it will not be perfect. For pieces that you value, have a professional polish the rim.

TYPES OF CRYSTAL EMBELLISHMENTS

ACID ETCHED
For a frosted effect that's more shallow than engraving, an artisan coats crystal with an acid-resistant resin, then cuts the design through the coating with a metal stylus. The glass is then dipped in acid; when the resin is removed, the design is revealed.

COLORED
Metal oxide can be added, in the form of a powder, during manufacture to give crystal color. Layered, or encased, crystal is formed from two layers of glass: one colored and one clear. When the top layer is cut, the underlayer is revealed, creating a two-tone design.

CUT
The lead in crystal makes it soft enough to cut. Designs are ground into the glass using iron wheels. Smaller wheels of lead, wood, cork, or rubber are used to refine and polish.

ENGRAVED
Designs are cut freehand using a variety of copper disks. The engraved areas have a matte, clouded finish, but they can also be polished clear.

BARWARE

A perfect home bar—with its attendant array of glasses—is different for every hostess, since it will reflect both her tastes and those of her guests and friends. In addition to stemmed glassware designed for wine, Champagne, and cordials (see opposite page), the basic bar should include eight to twelve old-fashioned glasses, also known as rocks glasses. They hold 8 to 10 ounces and are suitable for all mixed drinks. Other useful additions: highball glasses, which are taller than rocks glasses and are traditionally used for juice-based drinks; Y-shaped martini glasses, also known as cocktail glasses; and beer, or pilsner, glasses. Even if you don't serve many cocktails, these shapes come in handy for other beverages and can make a wonderful presentation for an array of appetizers and desserts.

STEMWARE

Fine stemware pieces come in different shapes to enhance the qualities of the drinks they're meant to hold. Depending on how you entertain, it's useful to have eight to twelve of each. Although many glass manufacturers make specific glasses for every major wine type, for the majority of consumers it would be difficult and a needless expense to stock your cupboards with that many varieties. Three basic types of glasses will suffice for all of your wine needs: a glass for white, a slightly larger glass for red, and a flute for sparkling wine. If cost or space is an issue, a good, all-purpose wineglass—one that is clear in color, with a thin rim and an ample bowl—can be used for both white and red still wines. The ideal size for a 4-ounce serving of red or white wine is a 10- to 12-ounce glass, which allows room for swirling to help the flavor to evolve.

CARE

Most new everyday barware is made to go in the dishwasher (crystal, vintage, and antique barware should be washed by hand to prevent clouding or etching). To prevent hardwater spots, use the minimum recommended amount of detergent, run the machine on the Delicate or Normal cycle (avoid Heavy-Duty or High-Temperature settings), and try a rinse aid.

STORAGE

Store all glassware—everyday and special occasion—upright. The rim is the most delicate part of any glass and is the most vulnerable to chipping. Avoid nesting glasses, which can cause scratching. To further safeguard glassware, line shelves with a resilient liner such as cork or ribbed plastic.

SAFETY OF LEAD CRYSTAL

In general, pregnant women and children should avoid drinking from lead-crystal glasses; for most everyone else, the risk is minuscule if lead crystal is not used regularly. Lead quantities in newer pieces are relatively low, and even with older crystal, the liquid doesn't stay in the glass long enough for the lead to pose any danger. Decanters can be another story: If wine or another beverage is stored in a crystal decanter, the lead can leach out into the liquid in significant quantities. Because of this, manufacturers either no longer use lead in their decanters, or they seal the inside with a protective coating to prevent leaching. If you have a crystal decanter and are not sure of its age or lead content, stay on the safe side and don't use it to store beverages.

TYPES OF STEMWARE

WATER
This widemouthed goblet has a large bowl.

BORDEAUX
This glass is smaller than the Burgundy glass, and is suited to serve hearty red wines, such as Cabernets.

BRANDY SNIFTER OR BALLOON
This piece has a tulip-shaped bowl with a round belly and narrow "chimney" that funnels aroma to the nose. The shape also tones down any harsh alcoholic qualities and is a good choice for serving all types of brandy, including Cognacs and Armagnacs. The balloon should not be too large, as it is not optimal for releasing the bouquet. Professionals usually choose a brandy snifter that is 4 inches deep.

FLUTE
Made just for Champagne, the tall, slender silhouette reduces the wine's surface area, slowing the bubbles from dissipating.

WHITE WINE
Because white wines are best enjoyed chilled, the bowls are smaller than Bordeaux glasses. White-wine glasses also have narrower openings, which help concentrate the delicate scents.

BURGUNDY
A very large, balloon-bottomed glass that can be used to serve both Burgundy and other delicate reds, such as Pinot Noir. The extra space allows the bouquet to gather.

CORDIAL
This is the smallest type of glass, intended for apéritifs and after-dinner drinks.

THE BAR

The tradition of serving cocktails at home has its roots in Prohibition, when people sought out private places to drink. By the time the law was repealed in 1933, the living room bar was well on its way to becoming an institution. By the 1950s, it seemed every home had one. Today's home bar is often simpler than its predecessors. But regardless of the size of your bar, the bare essentials include wine, beer, and vodka, with gin as a close runner-up. These four staples will satisfy the majority of guests and allow a hostess to offer a satisfying array of choices. Ounce for ounce, beer is still the most popular alcoholic beverage in the United States, especially in summer, when entertaining tends toward outdoor events. And vodka has been America's favorite spirit since 1976, when it surpassed whiskey.

If you favor dinner parties, consider adding apéritifs and after-dinner liqueurs to the basic repertoire noted above. Sherry, Lillet, and Campari are all elegant starters, and less taste-bud numbing than more potent mixed drinks. After-dinner drinks, such as port, Cognac, and Armagnac, and cordials such as eau-de-vie, can be consumed alone or with coffee.

If your entertaining style tends toward cocktail parties, you'll need a bar suited to the preparation of mixed drinks, with a variety of liquors, mixers, and garnishes. (Consult the checklist below.) Allow a pound of ice for each guest, as well as three drinks and three napkins, for a two-hour party.

LIQUOR AND BEVERAGE CHECKLIST

Most liquors keep indefinitely in a cupboard, but port, vermouth, and wine will spoil if left at room temperature once opened and must be refrigerated.

- ☐ Hard liquors: vodka, gin, whiskey (Scotch, Irish, bourbon, or rye), rum
- ☐ Wine
- ☐ Beer
- ☐ Vermouth (sweet and dry)
- ☐ Tequila and triple sec, for margaritas

- ☐ Mixers and soft drinks, including soda water and tonic, cola, ginger ale, and a variety of juices
- ☐ Apéritifs
- ☐ Brandy or Cognac
- ☐ Cordials such as eau-de-vie
- ☐ Bitters, Worcestershire and Tabasco sauces, grenadine and flavored syrups, for cocktails and soft drinks

- ☐ Fresh garnishes, such as lemons, limes, and mint
- ☐ Bottled garnishes, such as maraschino cherries, olives, and cocktail onions
- ☐ Nonalcoholic wine and beer
- ☐ Sparkling cider
- ☐ Seltzer or sparkling mineral water

BAR TOOLS CHECKLIST

BASICS

- ☐ Bottle opener and corkscrew
- ☐ Ice bucket and tongs or scoop
- ☐ Cocktail shaker
- ☐ Paring knife and cutting board for preparing garnishes
- ☐ Long-handled cocktail spoon
- ☐ Jigger marked with levels (for example, ½ ounce, 1 ounce)
- ☐ Slotted spoon or strainer

OPTIONAL

- ☐ Swizzle sticks
- ☐ Peeler or zester to make citrus twists
- ☐ Champagne stoppers, wine-bottle vacuum stoppers, pour spouts
- ☐ Bartender's guide
- ☐ Muddler
- ☐ Blender

WINE AND ENTERTAINING

When determining how much wine to buy for a dinner party, figure on a half bottle per person. If the party is going to last more than three hours or you plan to serve multiple courses, plan on more. If the party is on a Sunday evening or a weeknight, guests will likely consume a bit less.

All wine (still and sparkling) should be stored in a cool, dry place (never on top of the refrigerator or above the cooktop) with a steady temperature, away from direct sunlight and other sources of heat, such as a radiator or vent. If storing wine for more than a few weeks, rest bottles on their sides; the wine moistens the cork, which expands to maintain an airtight seal.

If you don't plan to serve white and sparkling wines right away, keep them at room temperature. Before serving, chill for about an hour in the refrigerator. To chill wine quickly, plunge the bottle into a bucket of ice water—a half hour in ice water is equivalent to two hours in the refrigerator. Resist the temptation to put wine into the freezer to chill: It's too easy to forget about it, only to remember it too late, once the cork has popped.

Opened bottles of wine can be recorked and refrigerated for three to five days. Before drinking red wine, let it return to room temperature. Sparkling wines can be kept for one or two days; to preserve the bubbles, use a vacuum stopper (available at wine shops and housewares stores).

Wine actually tastes better when it has a bit of breathing room and space in the glass for aromas to gather. So instead of pouring to the rim, fill glasses no more than halfway, then occasionally top them off.

YOU CAN CHILL
A BOTTLE OF WHITE WINE
BY PLUNGING
IT INTO A BUCKET OF
ICE WATER FOR THIRTY
MINUTES.

A NOTE ABOUT THE BUTLER'S PANTRY

The word "pantry" brings to mind the closet off the kitchen where the flour and canned soups hide, but in grand old houses, there was often a second pantry, known as a butler's pantry. Located between the kitchen and dining room, often with a door leading to each room, these spaces were designed as storage and staging areas where food could be warmed, dishes that had been cleared from the table could be stacked, wine could be decanted, and a family's collection of fine china and silver could be safely tucked away. Today, with the hostess serving as both head cook and butler, these spaces, though rare, are no less practical.

If you are fortunate enough to have a nook or closet in between the kitchen and dining room, you can convert it into a butler's pantry by adding shelves for china and glassware and a countertop work surface. Depending on the amount of space you have available, a warming drawer, undercounter wine refrigerator, and sink are other useful additions. Even if you don't have room for a built-in pantry, you can make entertaining large groups easier by pressing a rolling cart into service. Use it to bring food to the table and again to clear dishes after the meal has ended.

LONG-TERM WINE STORAGE

Whether you own many bottles or just several, storing your wine properly will ensure that it always tastes its best. The ideal temperature is between 55° and 58°F, and the best relative humidity for your wine is between 60 and 75 percent, so choose storage space with those numbers in mind. The area should also be out of direct sunlight, in a space with good air circulation that's free from movement and vibration (don't store bottles near stereo speakers, for instance).

If you have a large or valuable collection, invest in a climate-controlled wine refrigerator. They are widely available and reasonably priced. Generally, they're the size of a regular undercounter refrigerator and range from hundreds to thousands of dollars, depending on capacity and other features. If you own many bottles, you might also consider keeping a wine inventory. There are a number of software programs that allow you to index your collection and alert you when wines reach maturity. These programs allow you to track the wines you own or have tasted, and will store winery information, tasting notes, transactions, market values, bottle locations, and label pictures. These software programs often have an online component, where you can access winery information and also export the data to a PDA.

A REFRIGERATED UNDER-
COUNTER DRAWER IS
IDEAL FOR
A SMALL COLLECTION OF
WHITE AND
SPARKLING WINES.

CANDLES

Few things have the power to transform a room like candlelight—or to transform it so easily and inexpensively. At the crack of a match, even the most modest dining room can become glamorous, warm, and inviting.

Candles consist of wax and a wick, but may also contain colorants, fragrances, and additives. Candles are most often made of paraffin, a petroleum by-product. However, beeswax, a natural wax derived from the hives of honeybees; vegetable waxes, such as soy wax; gels made of mineral oil; and synthetic waxes are also frequently used to manufacture candles.

The cleanest-burning candles are those that are undyed and unscented. Soy candles are naturally odorless and do not produce soot; beeswax candles emit a natural honey scent. It's best to avoid strongly scented candles altogether in the dining room—their fragrance will compete with the delicious aromas of your food and wine.

BURNING TIPS

Here's how to keep candles burning bright and clean.

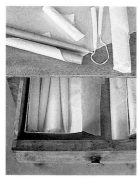

KEEP WICKS CENTERED
WITH A SPOON HANDLE.

☐ Cut wicks to ¼ inch in length before lighting. The longer the wick, the larger the flame, the more the soot.

☐ Protect candles from drafts, which can create a large flame that can shorten the life of the candle, as well as cause it to melt in a lopsided manner (which can eventually cause it to collapse).

☐ Protect candles from light and heat. Placing them on a sunny windowsill or in an overheated room can cause them to soften and droop.

☐ Keep wicks centered in pillar candles. Off-center wicks can cause uneven burning, leading to spills and resulting in misshapen candles. To recenter, extinguish the flame, then insert a spoon handle alongside the wick and press it back into place.

STORING CANDLES

Wrap sets together in tissue paper and stow them in a cool, dry drawer. To keep delicate tapers from damage, wrap them in tissue paper and slip them into cardboard paper-towel tubes. Store the tubes in a drawer.

☐ Limit burning time of pillar candles. Pillars should burn for approximately the same number of hours as the diameter measures in inches. For example, a candle that's 3 inches wide should burn for no more than three hours. Otherwise, the wax is likely to pool around the wick and bury it, ruining the candle. You can burn tapers as long as you want if they are not smoking or dripping excessively.

☐ If a wick is drowning in its own wax, score the candle with a sharp knife all the way around, ½ inch from the top. Cut the candle through, taking care not to sever the wick.

REMOVING WAX FROM CANDLEHOLDERS

It's easiest to remove wax when it's warm. Whenever possible, peel off the fresh drippings as soon as possible after you blow out the candles. If the wax has cooled, try these techniques:

HOT WATER

If the candleholders are waterproof, run them under hot tap water and remove the wax by hand.

FREEZING

Wax will shrink after a few hours in the freezer, making this a good technique for cleaning votive holders. The stubborn coating of wax inside the votive should pop right out. (To prevent the wax from sticking in the first place, fill votive holders with 1/2 inch of water before inserting candles.)

After melting or freezing, any remaining residue should come off with a gentle scrubbing.

HOW TO REMOVE SOOT STAINS

Soot stains are composed primarily of carbon, which is difficult to remove from any surface. Start by putting a drop cloth under the surface you're going to clean. Next, vacuum the stained area, using the dust-brush tool. Next, go over the area with a cleaning product called a dry sponge. Specifically made for use on painted walls and ceilings, wallpaper, acoustical ceiling tile, and other surfaces that might be damaged by moisture, dry sponges are made of soft, foamlike rubber. You can find them at many hardware stores and janitorial-supply houses. Gently rub the stained area with the sponge, moving it around as it becomes saturated with soot. Do not wet the sponge, or you'll end up with a mess.

If this method does not remove the stain, try washing with an all-purpose cleaner and warm water, drying thoroughly with soft, clean cotton cloths. But first, test a small spot, preferably in a corner, to make sure you won't be removing the paint along with the stain. If your ceiling is textured (with a spray-on acoustical finish), you'll face an extra challenge because such surfaces are especially hard to clean. You may need to hire an acoustical ceiling professional to respray the surface.

A SPLASH OF WATER IN VOTIVE HOLDERS WILL MAKE CLEANUP EASIER.

EXTINGUISHING A CANDLE

To ensure you do not spray the melted wax when putting out a candle, try this technique: Place your index finger between the flame and your lips—as if saying "shhh"—and gently blow.

THE LIVING ROOM
AT LILY POND LANE

LIVING ROOM

THE LIVING AREAS IN A HOUSE—the living room, family room, and den—are simultaneously intimate and public. These are the spaces where family members gather and relax, and where guests spend time when they visit. These are also the rooms that tell the world who we are: The furniture and rugs, the paintings and mirrors on the walls, the mementos and photographs arranged on the tables, and the books in the bookcases all have a story to tell.

Each of us uses these spaces differently, depending on how we live and how the rooms are dictated by the layouts of our homes. My living room at Turkey Hill, for example, is delightfully old-fashioned, an excellent retreat for quiet, reflective time (although there have been plenty of occasions when I've transformed the space into a party room—holidays, for instance, and my sister Laura's New Year's Eve wedding). At Bedford, I also have a formal living room—it's a true parlor, a genteel space painted a surprising, bright, almost intense shade of green that I based on a swatch of Japanese linen the color of green tea. The paneled walls are painted with a faux-bois pattern and hung with gilt mirrors, the sofas are upholstered in different green and gold Fortuny fabrics, and there are a chandelier and sconces. Guests enjoy this restful room, for cocktails and hors d'oeuvres before dinner or coffee afterward.

Living areas aren't just for entertaining—these are the rooms where families play games, read, do homework, and watch movies and television. I still recall when we got our first TV in Nutley, New Jersey, which Dad decided to install in the living room wall. Where to position it? He settled himself into his favorite easy chair while I drew a string across the room and marked the place on the wall where he would be able to view the screen most comfortably. Suddenly, our living room became the family room; as a result, we used the room differently, even sitting and stretching out on the furniture in a new way.

If your living areas need to be flexible spaces like this, to be used for different purposes and occasions, keep this in mind when decorating. If you watch television and entertain in the same room, consider housing the television in an attractive piece of furniture, such as an armoire, so it is not always on view. If children play in that room, have baskets or bins tucked into cupboards so you can put away their toys.

The lighting from fixtures and lamps should also be flexible, to accommodate all the activities for which you want to use the space. You cannot read or play Scrabble in a warm, dim glow that might be just right for after-dinner conversation, nor can you watch a late-night movie with the lighting that will work for Scrabble. Adaptable lighting will go a long way to make the room welcoming for any number of uses.

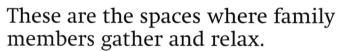

These are the spaces where family members gather and relax.

It is also important to consider the room or area's natural light when positioning the furniture, books, and electronic equipment. The fabric on upholstered furniture will fade with exposure to direct sunlight, as will any artwork not covered by UV-filtering acrylic glass. Similarly, books, CDs, and DVDs should be stored out of direct sunlight, or protected from it with window treatments that can block out the light when necessary. Balance the welcoming brightness of a sunny room with what your equipment needs in order to stay in top working condition, even if it means doing a little rearranging to keep the sun away from the things it will harm over time.

Many of the things in these living areas are valuable to us—family photos, for instance, or an oil painting that's been passed down through generations. And the furnishings tend to be pieces we invest in and expect to last many years, such as sofas and side tables. These items require a particular regimen of both routine and periodic cleaning, to stay looking their best. When everything is clean and organized, these parts of the home will feel inviting, warm, and, ultimately, ready for living.

LAYOUT BASICS

Before the advent of television, many American families spent their evenings gathered around the fireplace, which was not only a literal source of warmth before the luxury of central heating, but the symbolic heart of the home. In older houses, the fireplace was often the focal point of the living area and the nexus around which furniture was arranged.

In many homes today, the fireplace has been supplanted by the entertainment center, especially in living areas devoted to casual family gatherings rather than formal entertaining. Organizing these rooms depends solely on how you use them. If the room is primarily for watching television, choose a comfortable sofa with several easy chairs all arranged for optimal viewing. If, on the other hand, the room serves as a space for social occasions, as in more formal living spaces, you'll want an intimate arrangement of furnishings placed close enough together to encourage conversation and a few easily moveable pieces, such as stools or ottomans, that will allow you to add extra seating for large parties. For your guests' comfort, make sure there is a table within convenient reach of every seat. Whether casual or formal, pulling furniture away from walls and toward the center of the room will make the space seem more cozy and inviting.

SPACE-PLANNING FUNDAMENTALS

Regardless of how you use your living areas, allow for the proper clearances to ensure the room functions comfortably.

- ☐ Allow 36 inches for traffic lanes in busy living areas, or 24 to 30 inches if the room is formal or seldom used.

- ☐ Leave enough room between the sofa and coffee table (about 14 to 18 inches) to allow for easy access and to ensure your knees don't bump furniture once you're seated. Don't allow so much, however, that you or your guest will have to reach to set down a glass.

- ☐ The best angle for television viewing is within 45 degrees of the straight-on view; the distance from television to seating depends on the screen size. The larger the screen, the more distance you'll need. It's generally most comfortable to allow between three and six times the width of the screen.

- ☐ For closets, allow clearance in front that equals the width of the doors if they swing open, or 36 inches to view the closet's interior if doors slide or fold open.

- ☐ If you have a desk in the room, you will need to allocate 36 inches for standing room while opening drawers, and 42 to 60 inches to pull out the chair.

THE TOOLS FOR CREATING
A FURNITURE PLAN ARE
AVAILABLE AT OFFICE- AND
ART-SUPPLY STORES.

DRAWING A FURNITURE PLAN

Before you strain your back lifting and rearranging heavy sofas and armoires to create optimum comfort and functionality in your living areas, adopt the decorator's method of mapping out a furniture plan. It will allow you to test the arrangements in as many ways as you can imagine, and create a reference tool to carry with you on shopping expeditions.

Begin by roughly sketching the outline of the floor on a piece of plain paper, indicating fixed features, such as doorways, alcoves, radiators, and built-in shelving. Next, add dimensions to this sketch. With a tape measure, work your way around the room, from corner to corner, at baseboard level. (Taking readings from the walls could give you an inflated measure of the floor area.) Mark each dimension next to the appropriate detail on your sketch. Once you've circled the room, add the placement and width of windows, and the locations of outlets, light fixtures, vents, and air conditioners. (These features will affect furniture placement.)

Now you're ready to create the scale drawing. Although architects and decorators often use $\frac{1}{4}$-inch scale (meaning $\frac{1}{4}$ inch on the drawing represents 1 foot in real life), $\frac{1}{2}$ inch works best for amateurs; the larger the drawing, the easier it is to envision what's represented. At $\frac{1}{2}$-inch scale, the plan of a 16-by-21-foot room fits on a single $8\frac{1}{2}$-by-11-inch sheet of $\frac{1}{2}$-inch graph paper, with a slight margin for notations. (You can download $\frac{1}{2}$-inch graph paper from a number of sites on the Internet; search for "graph paper.") To transfer the measured sketch to the paper, use a ruler as a guide for creating straight lines and the grid to maintain 90-degree corners and to dictate line length. For inches, mark portions of the boxes. You can eyeball some of the fractions, but you're better off using an architect's scale if you can. This special kind of ruler, available at some office-supply stores, lists feet and inches translated to scale.

Next, measure the width and depth of the furniture, rugs, lamps, and other items you're arranging. Transfer the measurements to graph paper in the proper scale—a circle template or compass will help with items that have curved edges—and label each piece. For adjustable furniture such as reclining chairs, use their maximum sizes with all movable parts extended, but add dotted lines to indicate the smaller space the furniture occupies when folded. Finally, cut out the shapes and start to move them around within the drawing, testing various arrangements. Keep the clearance guidelines on page 185 in mind. When you've found an arrangement that suits you, trace it for a permanent record. Add fabric and paint swatches and a few snapshots and you'll have a compact summary of your room to take with you wherever you go.

FURNISHINGS

SOFAS

A sofa is usually the dominant piece of furniture in any living room, surrounded by easy chairs and case goods (an industry term used to describe furniture, usually made of wood, that provides storage), such as armoires, as well as a coffee table and side tables.

The sofa generally sets the decorative tone and it also must be well suited to your lifestyle, the dimensions of the room, and the level of formality your decor demands. Manufacturers often combine elements of traditional styles—the Bridgewater, Chesterfield, Chippendale, Lawson, Sectional, and Tuxedo (pictured on page 189)—and then add their own decorative flourishes.

A sofa's construction—the frame, springs, and padding—deserves as much attention as its style. A high-quality piece is worth the investment—a well-built sofa can last for decades; and as your tastes evolve, it can be reupholstered or slipcovered, leaving the sturdy underlying construction intact.

FRAMES

The best sofa frames are kiln-dried hardwoods (typically oak, maple, or ash), joined by blocks or dowels or by the tongue-and-groove technique. The joiners themselves are often reinforced with screwed-in or glued-on corner blocks. Frames that are made from layered hardwoods or engineered wood and merely stapled together are not as durable but will probably cost less. Opt for a sofa with legs that are screwed in or attached with dowels and screws; legs that are glued in place are more likely to become wobbly.

SPRINGS

Eight-way hand-tied springs offer the most support, limiting depressions or sags in the cushions; these springs are securely tied with twine to all adjacent springs. Sinuous springs are S-shaped wires that run from the front of the frame to the back. These give a little less support, but are not necessarily of lesser quality; instead, they are often used to achieve a sleek look in low sofas and modern styles. Frame padding, usually polyester or cotton batting, is the buffer between the frame and the upholstery fabric.

CUSHIONS

Back cushions can either be attached to the frame (aptly called an attached-pillow back), fit to the back but not attached (loose-pillow back), attached to the inside back with a zipper or seam (semiattached), or scattered along the sofa's back (multipillow, or scatter back). Some sofas don't have cushions at all; these "tight-bound back" sofas have plenty of frame padding instead. The seat can either be loose (with unattached cushions) or tight (upholstered without separate cushions). A sofa commonly has one, two, or three seat and back cushions, and choosing among them isn't just a matter of design. Single seat cushions are often rather firm and benchlike (with no crevices to trap crumbs or change). A two- or three-cushion seat is often softer and more cushioning.

For cushions, down is the softest filling as well as the costliest; down cushions are also quick to look untidy and require frequent fluffing to retain their shape. Polyester fill, used primarily in seat cushions and throw pillows, has a good "memory," meaning the cushions will spring back to their original shape after you sit on them, with little to no fluffing. This convenience can also make them less comfortable than cushions filled with foam or down. Like polyester, foam filling has a good memory and is often used in the seat cushions, but it is available in a wider variety of densities and prices. In general, the denser the foam, the firmer the cushion. Many cushions are filled with a combination of feathers and down, or made with a polyester or foam core surrounded by a layer of down, or down and feathers. The latter type combines the good memory of foam or polyester fill with the comfort and luxuriousness of down, at an accessible price.

HOW TO BUY A SOFA

A sofa is one of the biggest furniture purchases you're likely to make, and will be with you for years to come. So it's important to choose carefully. Before you start looking for a new sofa, you must first determine where it will go. Since sofas come in varying silhouettes and sizes, knowing your room's dimensions will keep your search focused. If you've made a furniture plan (see page 186), you can figure out exactly how much room you have to work with. Otherwise, first choose a spot in your room for the sofa and measure the length, accounting for any area that shouldn't be blocked, such as a vent or a hallway. Then measure the depth of the space, keeping in mind where you might position a coffee table or an ottoman. Make a note of the ideal height, too, if the sofa will be placed under a window or another architectural element. And also be sure to measure the doors, halls, or stairways a sofa will pass through upon delivery to be sure it will fit.

Consider how you will use your sofa. If it's going to be for entertaining friends for cocktails, you may want a formal style with firm cushions that make sitting down and getting up easy. If it is for a family room, where you might gather to watch television or play games, look for spacious, cozy cushions and low, padded arms, which can double as headrests. If you live in an apartment with limited space, your sofa should be able to accommodate a variety of functions.

UPHOLSTERY BUYING TIP

When you order custom curtains, slipcovers, or upholstery, ask for recommendations for easy-care fabrics. And once you've made your choice, request written care instructions.

CLASSIC SOFA STYLES

BRIDGEWATER

This English-style sofa, with its tight-bound back, row of tidy seat cushions, and low-slung arms, is all graceful curves. The legs in front are slightly higher than the ones in back so the sofa has a subtle tilt that complements its angled back.

CHESTERFIELD

The tufted upholstery, nail-head trim, and rolled arms that may reach as high as the back give the dignified Chesterfield a distinct personality. Though hardly casual, it's not just for the library, either. With its impeccable detailing, it would be at home in almost any formal living area.

CHIPPENDALE

The Chippendale is a genteel style that traces its origins to eighteenth-century England. Also called a camelback because of the unique curve to its silhouette, this sofa has high rolled arms and straight, exposed legs that are fit for the most formal room.

LAWSON

The Lawson sofa, with its neatly rolled arms and plump back and seat cushions, has a somewhat formal feel but is inviting and comfortable enough for a more casual family room.

SECTIONAL

Sectional sofas are often an amalgamation of sofa styles and run the gamut from sleekly modern to cozy and casual. Legs are sometimes exposed, sometimes skirted (a more relaxed look). They are ideal for family rooms and invite lounging and napping.

TUXEDO

This sofa is characterized by clean lines and angles, and it has the perfect silhouette for a modern setting. firm, boxy cushions and slim, squared-off arms that are the same height as the back make it excellent for sitting and chatting or for curling up with a book, but you'll need an extra pillow to support your head if you want to lie down.

Comfort is another important factor. Consider the depth of the seat cushion in relation to your own height: If it's too deep, your feet may not reach the floor; if it's too shallow, you won't be able to settle in. Check whether the arms are a good height for the use you have in mind, whether the angle of the back offers enough support, whether the cushions are as soft or as firm as you like, and whether the sofa seats enough people comfortably.

Fabrics range widely, from durable cottons, denims, and synthetics to fragile silks and delicate velvets; your choices depend largely on the function of the room as well as your color palette. If you have a very busy household, especially one with children or pets, choose a sturdy, washable material that can withstand a lot of wear and tear. Natural-fiber options include cotton, wool, and linen, all of which are generally resilient, though they might require more maintenance than synthetics. If you expect the sofa to get constant use, or if stains are a concern, a synthetic may be your best option. Leathers are durable and look good as they are broken in, although they can be expensive and are not as easy to clean as many other materials. Microfiber fabrics are made out of man-made fibers many times smaller than natural ones and as a result, have an extremely soft hand. They are also so stain-resistant that a liquid spill may simply bead up and roll off. They are very sturdy and will not wrinkle easily.

Solid colors may be more versatile than patterned fabrics when it comes to decorating, but patterns may hide spots and imperfections (as do

A NOTE ABOUT FABRIC PROTECTORS

Many new upholstered items sold in this country are treated with a "stain guard" that helps them resist common household substances. A furniture dealer may give you the option of having a piece treated for an extra cost, or the piece might be upholstered already with fabric that was treated by the textile manufacturer. Although the treatments offer convenience and ease of care, there are a few health considerations to consider before choosing to bring stain-treated fabrics into your home.

These treatments often contain perfluorocarbons (PFCs), which some research has linked to birth defects and a variety of cancers when inhaled or absorbed through the skin. Although the Environmental Protection Agency has not released definitive findings on the toxicity of PFCs, a number of consumer groups have issued strong warnings about these chemicals and advised consumers against their use, whether on pretreated fabrics or as a spray-on additive.

If you live in a household with small children or anyone whose health is compromised, it's probably wise to opt for an untreated piece. Instead, choose a durable fabric that will hold up to stains and, when stains do occur, try natural treatments before moving on to anything containing harsh chemicals. (For more on removing stains from upholstery, turn to page 195.)

loose cushions that can be turned over). Texture plays a big role in durability as well: Jacquard, twill, and chenille styles will hide indentations and spills better than flat, smooth weaves, which are best suited to rooms that get little wear and tear. Finally, if you worry about stains, purchase slipcovers, or have them made, in a fabric that is easy to clean.

SOFA BEDS

A sofa bed can transform your living room into an instant guest room, but not all sofa beds offer a good night's rest. And although no sofa bed will be as comfortable as a standard mattress, there are some things you can look for to make it worth the investment. In general, the thicker the mattress, the more comfortable it will be. A quilted cover is a sign of a high-quality mattress, as is a warranty of five years or more. Some manufacturers offer sofa beds with an air mattress designed to be used on top of the regular mattress for added comfort, or you can buy a separate inflatable topper. Sofa beds constructed with spring coils inside the frame provide more support for a mattress than do frames made of nylon webbing. The familiar metal-tube framing is standard, though the shapes and styles of frames vary from one manufacturer to the next. For ultimate support, choose frames made of wooden slats.

UPHOLSTERED CHAIRS

Like sofas, the best chairs have frames made of kiln-dried hardwood that are joined with either dowels or with glue, staples, and corner blocks. A frame made with glue or staples alone will not prove stable in the long run.

When it comes to upholstered chairs, design and style terms are used inconsistently. An easy chair refers to any upholstered or padded chair suitable for lounging. Chairs constructed of springs and cushions were originally introduced in the nineteenth century, although their structure then and today is often patterned after chairs of the eighteenth century.

Many of the same considerations apply when choosing a chair as when selecting a sofa. Before making a purchase, research all of the details about a chair's basic construction—frame, springs, and padding—while also taking into account the stylistic features that make a chair feel comfortable for you and appropriate for your living space. Ask yourself the following questions: Is the padding too hard, too soft, or just right? Does the chair fit my particular build? If you are long-legged, choose a higher seat. Also bear in mind the height of the arms, the pitch of the back, and the support under your knees; they should all harmonize with your body.

SOFA-BED BUYING TIP
To determine the quality of the sofa bed, open it on the showroom floor. That way, you can see whether or not it's easy to maneuver, and with what amount of effort. Lie down on the mattress to see if you can feel the springs or frame against your back—a common drawback of poorly constructed sofa beds. Ask the dealer about special features; some styles have a headrest or a compartment in which to stow bed linens or pillows. Then fold the bed back up, put the cushions in place, and take a seat—it is just as important that a sofa bed be comfortable when you're sitting on it as when you're sleeping on it.

CLASSIC CHAIR STYLES

BERGÈRE
This chair, which is well suited to formal interiors, takes its inspiration from a French design popular during the reigns of Louis XIV and XV. It consists of a wooden frame (often embellished with carved detail), closed sides, and a generonsly proportioned seat. Bergère chairs can either be upholstered or have cane work backs and sides.

SLIPPER
Despite some claims that this chair's low-slung shape resembles that of a shoe, it was named for its function, not its form: Its proximity to the ground (thanks to low legs, which are often concealed by a skirt) makes it easier to remove shoes than do chairs of conventional height.

WING
This chair is named for the winglike pieces that grace its sides. Elements of the chair are found in an old French type known as the confessional, but the modern version is believed to have evolved in England and America after 1750. Theories abound as to the purpose of the wings, which may have been designed to protect the occupant from drafts.

CLUB
A plush, low-backed chair, often with boxy proportions. The arms, which are often rolled, are ample, inviting relaxation. Club chairs are well suited to casual settings.

BARREL
The curvaceous, barrel-like back is the distinguishing feature of this chair, which can have either an exposed wooden frame, lending it a formal air, or be entirely upholstered, which imparts a more casual appearance.

HOW TO CARE FOR UPHOLSTERED FURNITURE

☐ If you have a particularly busy household, especially one with children or pets, you should vacuum cushions and chair and sofa frames twice a week with the upholstery tool. Otherwise, vacuuming once a week should be fine.

☐ Fluff and rotate cushions after they are vacuumed; this helps keep their fillings evenly distributed and ensures even wear.

☐ Once a week, lift cushions off sofas and chairs, and use the upholstery and crevice tools to vacuum the deck (the area under seat cushions and the nooks and crannies).

☐ Once or twice a month, gently beat the dust out of cushions with your hands; take the cushions outside first, so dust doesn't settle on floors.

UPHOLSTERY CARE LABELS

When it comes to cleaning the fabrics used for upholstery, draperies, and slipcovers, it can be difficult to figure out the proper products to use. Often, manufacturers will sew care labels in an inconspicuous spot. These labels will be marked with a letter indicating what type of cleaning agent (or agents) is recommended.

W

WATER-BASED CLEANING AGENT
Spot clean the upholstered fabric using the foam of a water-based cleaning agent, such as a mild detergent, or a commercial nonsolvent upholstery shampoo. Use it sparingly and avoid overwetting the fabric, which can leave a permanent mark. Apply the foam with a soft brush in a circular motion. After the upholstery fabric dries, vacuum it.

S

WATER-FREE SOLVENT
Spot clean the upholstery with a mild, water-free solvent or dry-cleaning product. Use sparingly and in a well-ventilated room. Never use a water-based solvent cleaner, which could cause spotting or excessive shrinkage.

WS

WATER-BASED OR WATER-FREE AGENT OKAY
Spot clean using either a water-based or solvent-based upholstery cleaner.

X

CLEAN ONLY BY VACUUMING OR LIGHT BRUSHING
No cleaner is safe.

UPHOLSTERY FABRICS CARE GUIDE

PLAIN-WEAVE LINEN AND COTTON (CANVAS, CHINTZ, DENIM, GINGHAM, SAILCLOTH, TICKING, AND TOILE)	Curtains, slipcovers, and other removable items are cold-water machine-washable, as long as they are preshrunk and colorfast (test by rubbing a damp white washcloth gently on a discreet area, such as a hidden seam, to see if any color comes off). For items that are not preshrunk or color fast, hire an upholstery-cleaning professional or have items dry cleaned. Glazed fabrics, such as chintz, should never be ironed because heat damages the shiny finish.
SILK (CREPE, TAFFETA, AND SATIN)	These should be dry-cleaned. Satin, which can be woven from pure silk, rayon, acetate, or polyester has a lustrous face and a dull underside. Iron only the dull side. Harsh sunlight is an enemy of silk, so if used for draperies, it should be lined with satin backing. Position silk-upholstered furniture out of direct sunlight, or protect it with cotton slipcovers.
RAYON	Although rayon itself is washable, it is often sized with coatings that are water-soluble. Professional cleaning is best unless a care label directs otherwise.
JACQUARDS (BROCADE, DAMASK, MATELASSÉ, TAPESTRY)	Any such pattern, which is created by a weave, requires mild washing. For cotton and linen, use the Gentle cycle on the washing machine. If the fabric contains silk, dry-clean only. Before laundering, mend, clip, or point out any loose threads to a professional upholstery cleaner.
PILE FABRICS (CHENILLE, CORDUROY, VELVET, VELVETEEN)	If made of preshrunk cotton, these can be machine washed in cold water (test for colorfastness as with plain weaves). Be mindful of sharp objects, which can snag fabric and destroy construction. Pile fabrics made of acetate, polyester, or rayon should be professionally cleaned. In either case, never iron these fabrics, because piles flatten easily from moisture and pressure and can't be repaired.
WOOL	Dry-clean only. When vacuuming, be careful not to rub vigorously since wool is very difficult to repair once it is torn.

LEATHER UPHOLSTERY

Leather is made from animal hides that have been tanned. During the tanning process, the hides are softened, dyed, and protected. There are generally two grades of upholstery leather: Top-grain, which is the top layer of the hide, and split leather, which is the lower layer made into suede or into inexpensive leathers that are sometimes embossed with imitation grain. Leather upholstery generally falls into one of three categories:

PIGMENTED

Pigmented leather, also called protected or coated leather, is the most common type of leather found on furniture. It is covered with a pigmented opaque finish that hides imperfections. Unlike aniline or nubuck leathers, liquids will not penetrate or mark pigmented leather.

ANILINE

Aniline leathers are colored with aniline dyes that penetrate the surface of the leather and are sometimes coated with a clear, protective finish. Because the dye does not camouflage the natural imperfections found on hides, it's suitable for use only on fine-quality hides. Water drops will darken this surface; spots disappear once the leather dries.

NUBUCK

Nubuck is a napped leather. It is similar in appearance to suede, but comes from the grain rather than the flesh side of the hide.

HOW TO CARE FOR LEATHER UPHOLSTERY

☐ Keep it at least 2 feet away from heating vents or radiators, which will dry leather out.

☐ Protect the upholstery from sun from windows or skylights, which will cause fading.

☐ Dust weekly with a dry microfiber cloth or the dust-brush tool attachment on your vacuum.

☐ To keep wrinkles to a minimum, turn and fluff cushions weekly.

☐ Never use soaps, detergents, dusting sprays, furniture polish, solvents, or oils.

☐ Blot spills immediately with a soft, dry white cloth. To remove a stain, blot with a white cloth dampened with lukewarm water. Do not rub. Allow to air-dry (never hasten the process with a hair dryer). For stubborn stains, such as ink, call a professional leather upholstery cleaner.

☐ Every three to six months, depending upon use, clean with commercial leather cleaner, such as Leather Master.

☐ Never place newspapers or magazines on the upholstery; inks may bleed onto the leather, causing permanent damage.

COFFEE TABLES

Many living rooms feel uncomfortable, even unbalanced, without a coffee table. The height of a coffee table should be dictated by its function: For drinks or displaying objects, the best height is usually parallel to or slightly lower than a sofa's or chair's seat, which is about 18 inches; for writing or eating, it can be as high as 28 inches. If it is too high or low, you won't be comfortable reaching for a magazine or setting down a cup of coffee. If magazines or books are stacked on top of the table, it's important to rotate them once a week. As part of your weekly routine, remove the stacks and clean the table below. Discard outdated magazines and swap out older books for newer ones.

If you have a small living area, you may want to consider nesting tables in lieu of a coffee table. Nesting tables are usually three or four matching tables, in graduated sizes, which stack tidily one on top of another. They are extremely versatile. You can either draw them out, telescope fashion, to form a large display area with several levels or move them around separately. Ottomans and even groupings of small side tables can also function as coffee tables.

NESTING TABLES
OFFER FLEXIBILITY IN
SMALL SPACES.

ARMOIRES

A functional armoire for the living room should be deep and wide enough to house your television and have enough shelf space for all of the attendant audiovisual equipment. A removable back panel is useful if your television happens to be a bit deeper than the armoire's interior, and double-hinged doors that fold flat against the sides or that slide into the sides of the armoire will make television viewing easier, especially in a small room. Additionally, a versatile armoire will have adjustable shelves, so that you can easily configure it to accommodate your sound system, video equipment, as well as CDs, videos and DVDs, and video game equipment. Small details like built-in power strips and grommets (holes) to accommodate wires and plugs also make for ease of use.

CARING FOR WOOD FURNITURE

Dust and vacuum all furniture and floor coverings at least once or twice a week, depending on traffic. Always dust from top to bottom, and do so before you vacuum floors. Dust tabletops and any objects displayed on them, such as picture frames and decorative boxes; window trims; the mantelpiece; lamp shades; and furniture legs. For more on dusting, turn to page 482. For more on vacuuming, turn to page 496. For more on waxing, turn to page 520.

FIREPLACES

Everybody loves a fireplace—an architectural anachronism that still has the power to warm us, body and soul. But as anyone who moves into a house or an apartment so equipped soon realizes, a crackling fire on the hearth is only part of the magic: A fireplace is also an aesthetic tableau. The mantelpiece sets the stage, and a melange of objects—andirons, fender, screen, tools, grate—completes the picture.

Up until the middle of the nineteenth century, log fires were an important part of domestic life. But fireplaces eventually gave way to heating stoves and, later, to furnaces in the basement. The Victorian era was the last time in which fireplaces were still routinely built into the principal rooms of city houses. By 1900, their function had become largely decorative. Today, fireplaces are a great luxury, enhancing a home's value and appeal.

A FIREPLACE MANTEL
AND SURROUND,
LIKE THIS NINETEENTH-
CENTURY FRENCH ONE,
CAN SET THE DECORATIVE
TONE FOR A ROOM.

TYPES OF FIREPLACES AND HEATING STOVES

WOOD BURNING

Traditionally found in older homes, wood-burning masonry fireplaces are built directly into walls. They often have large mantels and elaborate stone or brickwork around them. The masonry is designed to absorb heat, then radiate it back into the room.

Pros Attractive; offers many options for mantels; emits a pleasing wood scent; wood is a renewable resource; will work during power outages; increases the value of a home.

Cons Can be two to three times the price of factory-built fireplaces; is difficult to install when remodeling an existing house; is not the most effective heat source, as masonry allows too much heat out of the chimney; requires constant attention when a fire is going; creates ashes to be disposed of; requires storage space for wood.

Maintenance Clean out the ashes after every fire (for more, see page 204) and have the chimney checked regularly for creosote (a by-product of combustion), the buildup of which can cause a chimney fire; if there is a buildup of $\frac{1}{8}$ to $\frac{1}{4}$ inch, it's time for a cleaning (see page 203 for information).

GAS

These models are powered by natural gas, and can be easily converted to run on liquid propane as well (some even have built-in converters), both of which are the cleanest-burning fossil fuels. Gas fireplaces are typically made of metal casing with ceramic logs inside, and come in three types: top-vent, direct-vent, and vent-free. Top vents are usually installed inside an existing wood-burning masonry fireplace, using the existing chimney as an exhaust vent. A direct-vent model consists of two pipes that lead outside of the house—one that pulls in combustion air while the other pushes out exhaust. Vent-free models, as the name implies, do not require any venting. Many homeowners report that vent-free models provide the best heat.

Pros Fire is ignited by simply flipping on a switch; no ashes to dispose of or soot to clean; generally fuel efficient; affordable; may operate during power outages, as long as you can bypass the automatic pilot switch to light the unit directly; can be placed on nearly any wall or in the center of a room.

Cons Needs a gas line to the house for natural-gas models; logs and flames can seem artificial; does not emit that cozy wood-smoke smell.

Maintenance Manufacturers recommend an annual inspection by a gas-fireplace professional to check for carbon-dioxide leaks and proper log position, to replace ember bed material, and to touch up the interior firebox paint. The glass, firebox, heat exchanger, and air-intake areas should also be cleaned, and all settings and connections checked at this time.

WOODSTOVES

Most commonly made of porcelain, soapstone, or cast iron, the fireboxes of woodstoves are entirely self-contained. The stoves have an attached chimney, which vents outside of the home. Some homeowners will place a woodstove inside a masonry fireplace and use the chimney as a vent. Most new, EPA-certified woodstoves provide a nearly smokeless burn, producing maximum heat while using about one-third less firewood than the older pot-bellied models. Because newer models produce about 90 percent less smoke and particulate matter than older stoves, they also produce far less creosote. This, in turn, virtually eliminates the danger of a chimney fire and reduces the frequency with which the flue pipe and chimney will need to be cleaned.

Pros Uses renewable resources (wood); will work when the power goes out.

Cons Requires storage space for wood; requires close attention because you can't just shut them off at will; gets very hot, and can be a danger for small children; the ashes have to be disposed of.

Maintenance Clean out the ashes regularly and check for creosote buildup—when you have $1/8$ to $1/4$ inch, you must remove it to prevent a chimney fire. (For more information, turn to page 204.)

PELLET-BURNING STOVES

More energy-efficient and environmentally friendly than woodstoves, this type of stove burns pellets that are made from a variety of materials, including sawdust, waste paper, corn kernels, and dried cherry pits. They burn cleanly, and can be inserted into a fireplace or purchased as a freestanding unit. A feeder device inserts pellets into a combustion chamber; pellets are stored before being used in a hopper.

Pros Releases fewer pollutants into the air than wood-burning stoves; can be vented directly to the outside; needs refueling only once a day.

Cons Requires electricity, which can become expensive; has a lot of working parts that may require more maintenance than woodstoves.

Maintenance Check and clean the flue vent weekly, and inspect fans and motors monthly. To reduce the chance of rust, remove pellets from the hopper at the end of the heating season.

ELECTRIC

Electric fireplaces operate exclusively on electricity and require no vent, so they can be placed anywhere in a room. They are an option for apartments and condominiums without chimneys, or for anyone who might want to take their fireplace with them when they move.

Pros Easy to install; portable; doesn't need a chimney; smokeless; less expensive to operate than gas or wood-burning fireplaces; can be moved from room to room; heat radiates quickly and can be turned off at will; remains cool to the touch, so it's safe for children and pets; no soot or ashes to clean.

Cons Can seem artificial; no wood-smoke scent.

Maintenance Electric fireplaces require virtually no maintenance besides dusting.

FIREPLACE ACCESSORIES

Fireplace screens add beauty to a wood-burning fireplace, but more important, they act as a barrier between the fire and your living area, thus
protecting the floor and any adjacent furnishings from sparks and cinders.
Always use a screen when burning wood to keep flying embers at bay.
Screens also act as an effective obstacle, for both wood- and gas-burning
fireplaces, against young children or pets from coming in contact with the
flames. Similarly, fenders (low curbs fashioned from metal) prevent a burning log from rolling out of the hearth. To protect your home's exterior, install a spark arrester, a mesh device designed to keep sparks from escaping
the chimney opening, landing on the roof, and causing a roof or attic to
catch fire. They also keep animals and small objects from making their way

TYPES OF ACCESSORIES

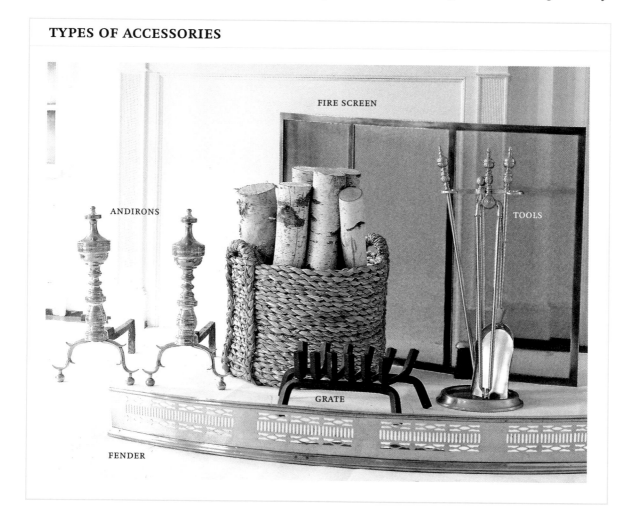

FIRE SCREEN

ANDIRONS

TOOLS

GRATE

FENDER

through the chimney and into the fireplace, as well as discourage back-drafts and downdrafts. Spark arresters are available at most hardware stores, woodstove and fireplace suppliers, and from some online retailers. You can also ask a chimney installer or brick mason to obtain and install one for you.

ANDIRONS

Andirons, also referred to as firedogs, hold the logs in place inside the firebox. The elevated logs, in turn, receive more air, which allows for better combustion as they burn. These can be used in place of grates.

GRATES

Fireplace grates also hold the logs above the floor of the firebox, and can be used in conjunction with andirons or on their own. They help a fire burn longer, hotter, and more efficiently, while also protecting the floor of your fireplace and keeping it clean. Grates are usually made of either cast iron or steel; the heavier the grate, the stronger it is and the longer it will last. Matching the appropriate size grate with the fireplace is particularly important, as this will help the fire burn more efficiently. To determine the appropriate size, measure the width of the front and back of the firebox, as well as its depth. The grate should be 6 inches smaller than the width of the firebox in both the front and back and at least 3 inches shallower.

TOOLS

The individual pieces (shovel, tongs, poker, and brush) are used to stoke the fire, add and turn logs, and sweep away the ashes afterward.

WOOD-BURNING FIREPLACE BASICS

TINDER

Tinder should consist of a highly flammable material, since it is the first thing to catch fire. It can be composed of brown bags, twisted newspaper, applewood chips, dried hemlock and birch twigs, birch bark, and the feathery tips of dried pine branches. (Don't use paper with colored inks, such as magazines or wrapping paper, which can leave a flammable residue on the inside of the chimney.) Tinder is used to ignite the kindling, which is slower to catch fire but once it does will burn long enough to set fire to the logs.

KINDLING

Kindling, such as pine and birch twigs, is placed on top of the tinder. It will stay ablaze long enough to set fire to the logs. Dry corncobs, pinecones that are well dried and free of sap, and fatwood (highly flammable resin-laden sticks from coniferous trees) are also good fire starters.

FIREWOOD

Firewood must be properly dried before use. Freshly cut, or "green," wood is still full of water; besides burning unevenly, damp wood produces more smoke and ash than dry wood. Tiny radial cracks along the cross-sections of a split log indicate that wood is fully dry and ready to use. Hardwood logs, which come from broad-leafed deciduous trees, are ideal. (The term describes the type of tree rather than the relative hardness or softness of the logs.) Hickory, oak, maple, ash, beech, and birch are good choices (birch is great because it leaves no ash); for fragrance, try logs from cherry, pear, and pecan trees. Softwood logs, which come from needle- and cone-bearing trees such as pine and spruce, burn very quickly and should only be used for tinder and kindling. Their resin never burns off completely; it also pollutes the air and collects on chimney walls. High levels of creosote (a substance that results when wood is burned) in your chimney can leave an unpleasant odor as well as be flammable. (For more on the various types of firewood, turn to page 473.)

WOODEN KITCHEN MATCHES

Wooden kitchen matches, or long-handled fireplace matches for deep hearths, are better than paper matches, which burn too fast, and don't allow the tinder to ignite before the match burns out. Be sure to store matches far enough away from the fire (at least 3 feet) in order to eliminate the chance of them igniting.

ORGANIZING FIREWOOD

Firewood is sold by the cord, which equals 128 cubic feet and measures 4 by 4 by 8 feet. When you bring home a cord or more, remove several logs and place them in baskets or other containers beside the hearth, so they are on hand during the fire-building season; stack the rest of the wood outside. (For more on stacking wood, turn to page 472.)

MANUFACTURED FIRE LOGS

Manufactured fire logs, designed to be a low-emission and convenient alternative to natural firewood, are made either entirely from sawdust or from a combination of sawdust and wax. Those that contain wax are not meant for use in a closed stove, or in EPA-certified woodstoves or fireplaces. Here are some other guidelines to keep in mind when using them:

☐ Read and follow the manufacturer's instructions before lighting a manufactured log. Most fire logs are Underwriters Laboratories (UL) Classified and are suitable for use only in traditional open-hearth fireplaces; never use one in a woodstove or a woodstove fireplace insert.

☐ Always leave glass fireplace doors open while burning a manufactured log unless the instructions indicate otherwise. Doors can be closed after the log has stopped burning in order to keep the warm air in the house. Leave the damper open until the ashes are cool.

☐ Manufactured logs are conveniently designed to eliminate the need for adding more fuel to a fire. Therefore, burn only one log at a time; burning more than one could result in too large or too hot a fire.

☐ Never use fire logs as starter materials for a wood fire; they provide more fuel than is necessary.

☐ Since fire logs tend to soften while burning, always place them on a supporting grate. A lack of adequate support may result in log breakage, flare-up, or reduced burn time.

☐ Unlike firewood, manufactured logs do not require constant tending, since they are designed to burn in a controlled manner. Using tongs or pokers can actually cause a fire log to break apart prematurely, exposing more surface area to the air, increasing the burn rate, and resulting in a briefer fire.

☐ Manufactured logs leave significantly less creosote in chimneys than firewood. Although, depending upon burning conditions, a small amount of carbon or graphitelike material may be deposited in the chimney instead. Follow instructions for cleaning the fireplace, below.

MAINTENANCE

It is essential to hire a chimney sweep for a professional cleaning of your firebox and chimney at least once a year. Spring is an ideal time for this; after winter's fire-building season has ended, a professional checkup of your fireplace will prepare it for the next season. Look in the Yellow Pages under "Chimney" for a specialist in your area, or ask your local fire department for a recommendation.

There are two things you should be mindful of when cleaning your fireplace: creosote and soot. Creosote is a brown or black residue that appears on the inner surface of the flue liner. When wood is burned slowly, it produces tar and other organic vapors, which combine with expelled moisture to form creosote. Excessive creosote is often the result of a restricted air supply (which can occur if the damper is left partially closed) and the burning of firewood that's not sufficiently dry. Creosote is *highly* combustible and is the main cause of most chimney fires. You can remove it from the firebox periodically (see the following page for instructions), but don't attempt to remove it from the chimney yourself. Again, hire a chimney sweep to tend to it at least once a year.

Soot is a carbonized deposit of fine black particles that can gather and collect anywhere in your home. Extreme care must be taken when removing soot; it can stain very quickly if moistened while cleaning.

Take the time to examine your fireplace for any damage, buildup, and wear, especially cracks or loose mortar in the chimney area, cracks or disfiguring in the chimney liner, and loose brick or mortar around the fireplace. Other hazards include animals residing within the chimney and birds nesting in or around the chimney opening. Proper inspection will help eliminate these problems. Call a chimney sweep immediately if you suspect you have any of them.

CARE GUIDELINES

☐ Always keep a whisk or hearth broom and metal dustpan on hand to capture stray embers. Handle the broom with a quick flicking motion to transfer embers onto the dustpan without igniting the bristles. Deposit embers back into the fireplace.

☐ Clean the firebox (the area of the fireplace in which the grate sits and the fire is built) after each fire, especially if you use your fireplace only occasionally; air currents in the room can draw out ash, contributing to dust and grime. Make sure that the fire is completely out and that all coals have had time to cool down completely, which may take up to a day, before cleaning. Sweep all ashes and coals into a coal hod (a metal bucket with a handle and lid made specifically to contain ash and prevent it from blowing out as it is carried outdoors for disposal). Never collect ashes in a garbage bag or can; a fire can start this way, because embers can smolder for days. Take the bucket outside, away from the house, in case any coals are still hot enough to catch fire. Leave it for at least a day, to make sure all embers have died. Ashes can be deposited onto flowerbeds around the garden (they are beneficial to roses and other flowers), but they should never be added to a compost heap.

☐ Remove all traces of creosote, the black or brown residue left behind by fires, from the firebox. It usually has the consistency and stickiness of tar, but it can also be hard and shiny. Brush creosote off the inside of the firebox with a stiff-bristled plastic brush (using a long, angle-handled brush will make it easier to reach the back of the fireplace without having to crawl inside), and discard in it the trash, taking care that it is not warm or hot before doing so.

☐ The damper, which regulates and controls the flow of air inside the chimney, can also become encrusted with creosote, soot, and ash buildup. To gauge its cleanliness, open and close the damper several times. It should move freely, while fitting snugly against the smoke shelf. Watch for any debris that may restrict the airflow and remove it with either a chimney or fireplace brush.

☐ Clean the flue with a hard-bristle chimney, or specially made flue, brush. The flue, the pipe that runs between the fireplace and the chimney, is another common area for creosote buildup and should be routinely checked and maintained.

☐ To remove dust from brick and the mantelpiece, vacuum with the dust-brush tool. Designate a separate vacuum brush specifically for this job so that there is no chance of transferring ash and creosote onto other household items.

☐ Fireplace doors made from tempered or safety glass should be cleaned regularly of soot and creosote to help improve the transfer of heat and prevent damage. Clean doors between fires, when they are cool, with a solution of 1 part water and 1 part white vinegar.

HOW TO REMOVE SOOT FROM FIREPLACE SURROUNDS

Soot is carbon-based, so try dry methods of cleaning before moving on to wet methods. (When carbon gets wet, it creates a sludgelike substance that is much harder to remove than when it is dry.)

1. Start by vacuuming the stained area using the dust-brush tool, which will remove loose surface particles. Never rub with a cloth or rag, as the pigments from the soot will only spread and smear.

2. Go over the area with a "dry sponge" (specifically made for use on painted walls, wallpaper, lamp shades, or anything that might be damaged by moisture), rubbing the stained area in even, light strokes in one direction. Always start at the top and work down. Do not wet the sponge for cleaning, which can lead to smearing or staining. Refrain from wringing out the sponge or cleaning it with water after using it which will only alter its chemical treatment.

3. After removing the bulk of the soot, wipe the stained area with a cloth dampened with an all-purpose cleaner and warm water, if necessary. (First test a small area to be sure that you won't be removing any paint.) Make certain to dry the area thoroughly with a soft, clean cotton cloth.

For more on soot stains, see the opposite page.

HOW TO BUILD A FIRE

Firewood should be dried for six months to a year to be in the best condition. If the logs are freshly cut, they will burn unevenly, produce a lot of smoke, and won't smell very good.

1. If your fireplace has an adjustable damper, open it all the way. Begin by crumpling single sheets of newspaper or other tinder into grapefruit-size balls, or twist them into batons, and place one or two underneath the grate or in between the andirons on the floor of the firebox. Place strips of newspaper on top of this pile.

2. Lay six to twelve pieces of kindling in a crisscross pattern on top of the crumpled newspaper on the grate or in between the andirons. Leave spaces between the sticks for air circulation.

3. Place a couple of thin, split logs on top of the tinder and kindling. Remember to arrange logs and paper loosely so air can circulate.

4. Light the newspaper or other tinder with a long match. Within seconds, the tinder should catch fire, followed by the kindling. When the fire is established and the small split logs are burning steadily, add two more small logs and one larger log, leaving at least an inch between them so the flame can "breathe." As the warm air rises up the chimney and into the room, cool air is sucked up into the spaces between the logs, fanning the flames. Don't overfeed the fire. Placing too many logs on the fire at once can either smother the fire or cause it to blaze out of control. Flames should consume the area immediately surrounding the logs but should not burn more than a few inches above it. Fires that burn too wildly also have the potential to "pop" and emit sparks as well as send burning embers up the chimney and onto the roof.

5. A fire will cease on its own provided that you are not adding fuel to it. Leave the fire alone and allow the ashes to cool completely before removing them. Keep in kind that you should never leave a fire unattended.

ELECTRONICS

As with computer equipment in your office, the electronics in your living room generate static and are prone to attracting dust. The best way to keep dust from accumulating on these items is to store them in an entertainment center with doors. Dusting the casing of your television, audio, and video equipment weekly with a damp, lint-free cloth should keep dust and grime at bay. Solvents in common cleaners will damage plastic casings and television screens, so for more thorough cleaning you should generally use only a lint-free cloth dampened with a solution of water and a few drops of mild dishwashing liquid. Electronics stores also sell antistatic wipes specifically made for cleaning the screens and casings of these components. When cleaning beyond minor dusting, it is always a good idea to unplug electronics. Keep the following considerations in mind, which will extend the life and performance of your electronics:

☐ Review your owner's manuals for specific instructions on cleaning and maintenance of all electronics.

☐ Keep electronics out of direct sunlight and away from sources of extreme heat, such as heaters or radiators, and out of areas with high humidity or dust. All of these elements can damage internal parts.

☐ Never block or cover ventilation holes on electronic equipment, especially with soft materials, such as cloth or paper. The holes help keep the unit from overheating. For the same reason, never stack components on top of one another—unless they are specifically made to be stacked.

☐ Dust your TV screen with only a lint-free cloth dampened with water or an antistatic wipe. Paper towels can be used to dust the casings of equipment, but may scratch television screens with an antiglare coating. The solvents in cleaning products can damage television screens, as well as the screens on handheld devices, such as PDAs and MP3 players. Use only a lint-free cloth moistened with water or a mild cleaning solution (such as a few drops of dishwashing liquid in a gallon of water), or antistatic wipes.

☐ Never spray water or any sort of cleaner directly onto electronics. Instead, spray liquid onto a cloth, then use the cloth to wipe the component.

☐ DVD, CD, and cassette players can be cleaned two ways: with a cleaning kit from an electronics store (which usually consists of a CD cleaner disk and brush), or by using a can of compressed air, available at office-supply stores. Read the specific instructions on cleaning kits or compressed air.

☐ Never push foreign objects into a VCR, DVD player, or other equipment.

☐ Dust that has collected in the nooks and crannies of components can be dislodged with a burst of compressed air.

☐ If you spill liquid directly onto any electrical equipment, stop using it immediately, unplug it, and consult a customer service representative.

☐ Never use a conventional vacuum cleaner to clean dust from electronics. It can create more static and harm your components. Hardware and electronics stores sell antistatic vacuums that are safe to use.

☐ If one of your electronics seems to be malfunctioning, there may be dust inside the component interfering with its operation. Take the machine to an electronics store to have it serviced.

LCD AND PLASMA SCREENS

Liquid crystal displays (LCD), otherwise known as flat-panel screens, and plasma screens are extremely delicate. Never use glass cleaners or detergents on either type of screen. Electronics stores sell specific plasma and LCD cleaning kits, which usually consist of a soft pad with a spray. When cleaning either type of screen, make sure the television has cooled completely; if you clean the screen's surface when it is still warm you could leave permanent streaks on it. LCD screens are softer and more delicate than plasma screens, so it is particularly important never to use pressure when wiping them.

SPEAKERS

Generally, all you'll need to do to maintain speakers is dust them with a lamb's wool or feather duster. To remove stains or scuff marks, wipe the unit with a lint-free cloth dampened with water or a very mild solution of a few drops of dishwashing liquid and water, or with antistatic wipes. Most cloth coverings on speakers can be removed and dusted or rinsed in the sink, but check your owner's manual for specific instructions. Do not touch the inside of the speaker. Use a can of compressed air to dislodge dust.

CORD MANAGEMENT

To organize the multiple electrical cords from your television, audio, or video equipment, mount a power strip with a surge protector inside your entertainment center, so that the only cord that has to travel to the outlet is that of the strip. Organize the wires by binding them in Velcro straps or threading them through a plastic tube, both sold at hardware and electronics stores. Another option would be to mount a coated wire basket, which is also available at hardware and electronics stores, beside the strip. Bundle lengths of wire with twist ties and arrange them neatly in the basket. Attach tags to identify which machines each wire comes from.

A NOTE ABOUT OVERHEATING
All electronics can get hot when left on for extended periods of time—LCD and plasma TVs are particularly prone to overheating. Never house electronics, especially flat-screen TVs, in a bookcase or a built-in cabinet that is not adequately ventilated. Excessive heat can shorten their life span.

**HOW TO CLEAN
HANDHELD DEVICES**
Use a lint-free cloth or
anti-static wipe to dust
remote controls, PDAs,
cell phones, and MP3
players. A can of com-
pressed air is particularly
helpful for cleaning
the crevices in remote
controls. As with all electronics, the best way to
preserve the life of your
handheld devices is to
keep dust and dirt from
getting inside the ma-
chine in the first place.
Consider covering your
cell phone or MP3 player
with a protective case.

MEDIA STORAGE

It's essential to store CDs, DVDs, records, and audio- and videocassettes in a clean, dust-free area out of direct sunlight. Dust, dirt, and airborne pollutants can collect on these items and damage the respective players. Following a few simple guidelines will ensure that your disks, cassettes, and LPs stay in good working order:

☐ Always store media in cases or protective sleeves.

☐ Always store vinyl records vertically to avoid warping.

☐ When handling, hold CDs, DVDs, and records by the edges. Never touch the tape ribbon on cassettes. Fingerprints can affect the readability of all media and dirt can scratch or damage these items, making them permanently unreadable.

☐ Because cassettes are magnetic, they should never be placed near magnetic fields, such as magnetic closures on entertainment centers.

☐ Use a lint-free, antistatic pad (available at electronics stores) to clean CDs and DVDs. Always wipe in a straight line from the center to outer edge. Don't wipe in circles, which can cause damage. It's nearly impossible to clean VHS or audiocassettes, so prevent them from getting dirty by keeping them in appropriate cases. For instructions on how to clean vinyl records, turn to page 718.

ARTWORK

Whether you have inherited a cherished family portrait or started your own collection of works on paper, photographs, acrylic or oil paintings, or sculpture, the pieces you choose to grace your living room walls (or any walls for that matter) will almost certainly hold pride of place. Properly caring for each piece goes a long way toward preserving it for years to come, and for future generations. Here are some guidelines:

☐ When hanging artwork, a general rule of thumb is to place the center of the work 60 inches from the floor, as most galleries do. You'll need to account for the wire hanger on the back and its distance from the center of the painting when calculating this measurement. Use a picture-hanging hook, available at hardware stores, that is designed for the specific weight of your artwork.

☐ To prolong the life of your artwork, choose its location with care. Although dust is inevitable, paintings, photographs, and sculpture can deteriorate rapidly if exposed to direct sunlight, cold drafts, hot air from a radiator, humidity, smoke, and soot.

☐ Because excessive light levels can cause works of art to darken or fade, protect them from direct sunlight. If you can't find a dimly lit space in your house, keep drapes drawn or cover windows with a film that will lower the light intensity and screen out ultraviolet rays. To protect works on paper, replace glass with UV-filtering acrylic—usually Plexiglas.

☐ Rotate artwork periodically. This is particularly important for very light-sensitive pieces, such as watercolors, prints, and anything on colored paper.

☐ Avoid hanging any artwork over a fireplace, as exposure to soot and smoke can dirty them.

☐ High light levels can result in heat damage; if highlighting work, use incandescent rather than halogen bulbs, which give off too much heat.

☐ Fluctuations in humidity are especially damaging to hygroscopic (water-absorbing) materials such as wood, paper, and fabric. These materials expand when exposed to humidity and contract when dry. These changes can result in cockling, or rippling, of the material.

☐ To provide additional protection against cockling, maintain a constant room temperature.

☐ Mold can pose a problem for artwork subjected to excessive humidity; it can cause reddish brown spots known as foxing. Hang all artwork on

HOW TO CARE FOR SCULPTURE

Dust sculptures made of wood, marble, bronze, and other materials with only a clean, soft paintbrush. Do not use cleaning products.

interior walls to prevent exposure to dampness, especially if you live in an old or poorly insulated house.

☐ Clean frames with either a soft paintbrush or a can of compressed air. Frames that are made of aluminum or lacquered wood should be wiped only with a dry, lint-free cloth. If the frame is made of metal, you can use an all-purpose cleaner, but be sure to spray it onto the cloth first (never directly onto the frame), then wipe the frame.

☐ Avoid touching paintings or photographs with your bare hands. The natural oils in your skin can cause damage.

☐ Prior to moving or hanging a work of art, be sure to remove all jewelry, belt buckles, and the like, so that the work is not accidentally torn or scratched in the process. Always grasp a framed piece from both vertical sides, and never hold it at the top of the frame or by its wire hanger. Avoid bumping the canvas; even the slightest bump can cause future cracking of an oil painting's surface, for example.

DUST DELICATE, CARVED FRAMES WITH A SOFT PAINTBRUSH.

☐ Consult a fine-art restorer if a work of art is damaged or soiled; look under "Art Restoration and Conservation" in the Yellow Pages, or contact the American Institute for Conservation of Historic & Artistic Works (aic.stanford.edu) for an expert in your area. A restorer will be able to accurately assess which materials the artist originally used and, therefore, which cleaning agents would be most appropriate.

☐ Check the front and back of artwork several times a year so that you can remedy problems—whether it's mold or fading—before they become too serious.

ACRYLIC AND OIL PAINTINGS

Acrylic and oil paintings have no protective sheet of glass between them and the elements, so dust and dirt accumulate over time, and mute the colors and details of the painting. Preventive care can help, as can routine cleaning, but sooner or later all paintings need professional cleaning to restore them to their original beauty.

SPRAY THE CLEANING CLOTH, NEVER THE PIECE OF ARTWORK OR FRAME BEING CLEANED.

☐ Before cleaning a painting, first examine it closely to make sure there are no areas where the paint is flaking; brushing a damaged surface can easily dislodge any loose pieces.

☐ Brush the painting very gently with a soft, clean paint brush or duster; move from top to bottom. Do not use cotton cloths, as they may leave lint, which can damage the pigment.

☐ When dusting, take care not to flex the canvas or dislodge paint chips by bumping the painting.

☐ Trying to do anything beyond dusting is risky. Never use any sort of cleaning product on a painting. Even the mildest of detergents can affect or remove certain paint colors if their pH levels are incompatible.

☐ Protect paintings from moisture, which can also cause the canvas to shrink or create cracks in the surface, called crazing.

☐ If shipping a painting or moving it to a new house, never put any sort of plastic or Bubble Wrap against its surface, which can react with the paint. Instead, wrap the painting first in glassine or acid-free tissue paper, then in Bubble Wrap.

WORKS ON PAPER

The general maintenance of photographs, drawings, watercolors, and other works behind glass is much simpler than it is for oil paintings.

☐ The best way to protect photographs and other paper works, is to frame them behind UV-filtering acrylic—usually Plexiglas—rather than regular glass. In addition to filtering the harmful rays, Plexiglas won't shatter if the piece is dropped.

☐ These pieces usually need only a light dusting as part of your weekly routine. If the work is behind Plexiglas sheeting, wipe with a damp, lint-free cloth. Never use a dry cloth as Plexiglas scratches easily and is damaged by the solvents commonly found in window cleaners (such cleaners are fine to use on regular glass). Never spray anything directly onto glass or Plexiglas, however, to avoid the risk of moisture coming into contact with the artwork. Instead, spray water onto a cloth and then wipe.

☐ Have photographs, watercolors, pastels, or other works on paper framed by a specialist in "archival framing," to ensure that the work is completely sealed from dust and moisture behind the frame and glass. Make sure it is matted with an acid-free mat and backing. Better yet, the mat board should be made of 100 percent rag or lignin-free cellulose. Acid can yellow paper over time. Because colored papers often contain acid in them, they are a poor choice for matting.

PIANOS

Pianos need to be cared for more gently than any other furnishings, since mistreatment can damage or change the sound of these intricate, finely crafted instruments. For optimum acoustics, a piano should be placed in a large room with high ceilings. The more space and the less furniture that surround a piano, the better it will sound. Beyond acoustical considerations, there are several other steps you can take to prolong the life of the instrument and keep it in top condition:

KEEP DUST AT BAY BY CLOSING A PIANO'S LID AND COVER WHEN NOT IN USE.

☐ Place the piano near an inside wall (one that adjoins with another room, rather than the outside of the house), away from any heating or cooling sources. Similarly, keep pianos away from drafty windows and direct sunlight, both of which can ruin the finish and lead to severe damage both inside and out.

☐ Extreme fluctuations in relative humidity are also harmful, since they can affect both tone and pitch. In the winter, warm air can dry out the piano's soundboard, causing the piano to go flat. In the summer, moist air can cause the soundboard to expand, causing the piano to go sharp. Moisture can also cause the strings to rust. The ideal environment for a piano is a room where relative humidity is about 50 percent (although some manufacturers give a range of 42 percent to 60 percent). A hygrometer, a small gauge available at hardware stores, will allow you to accurately monitor a room's humidity levels. The ideal temperature is between 68° and 75° F.

☐ Have your piano maintained and tuned by a professional, even if it is rarely played. Pianos usually require tuning twice per year—less often if they are brand-new or in constant use. It may be tempting to let an unused piano go for longer between tunings, but doing so may cause strings to sag and lose their pitch quickly upon retuning.

☐ Keep the lid of your piano closed when not in use, in order to prevent dust from accumulating and becoming lodged between keys. If your piano is older and has ivory keys, leaving the lid open occasionally may slow the yellowing of the keys.

CARE

☐ Older pianos were covered with a variety of finishes, including shellac and varnish. On newer pianos, if you can see the wood grain, it's probably covered with a nitrocellulose lacquer, which gives a satin finish. When cleaning, it's important to follow the grain on this type of finish. A piano with a very shiny finish may be covered with a polyester finish (sometimes referred to as Chinese lacquer), which scratches very easily. (If you're unsure of the finish on your instrument, a piano tuner or restorer may be able to offer insight.) Regardless of the finish, dust the piano weekly to remove fingerprints by using a lightly dampened, lint-free, cotton cloth. If you think it needs something stronger than water, moisten the cloth with a mixture of water and mild dishwashing liquid; wipe afterward with a dampened cloth to remove any residue and polish dry with a clean cloth.

☐ A professional piano restorer should buff out any scratches, whatever the finish. He or she can also advise you about adding additional shine to your piano with specialty products, such as Cory Piano Polish.

☐ Piano keys, whether ivory or plastic, usually just require routine dusting and the occasional wipe with a damp, soft cloth. If the keys are especially dirty, add a few drops of mild dishwashing liquid to the cloth. Do not spray water or cleaner directly onto the keys; any liquid that runs down between them can damage the instrument. You may not want to clean your keys too often. Many pianists find very clean piano keys too slippery, and therefore difficult to play.

☐ If you own an antique piano, the keys may be made of ivory. The use of ivory has been banned in the United States for some years, and today pianos with ivory keys cannot be imported unless it is proven that the keys are more than one hundred years old. For this reason, ivory replacement keys are very hard to come by, so it's very important that you treat them carefully. You can perform the surface cleaning yourself, but if they are very dirty or stained, it's best to have them professionally buffed by a piano restorer; the same is true for wooden keys with an acrylic finish. If the restorer can't rebuff the keys, he or she will probably know of a rebuilding shop that can. To find a restorer (or tuner) in your area, try the website of the Piano Technicians Guild, www.ptg.org.

CLEAN KEYS WITH A CAN
OF COMPRESSED AIR OR A
SOFT PAINTBRUSH.

☐ Use a can of compressed air to clean between keys. You might also use a soft-bristled brush.

☐ A piano tuner can also care for the piano's interior. Schedule its maintenance in tandem with your biyearly tuning. By neglecting to do so, you run the risk of damaging the core of the instrument.

☐ Never wax a piano and avoid putting anything on the piano's lid, such as picture frames or other decorative objects. In addition to scratching or damaging the finish, the objects can alter the sound.

ALEXIS'S HOME OFFICE
IN NEW YORK CITY

HOME OFFICE

THE TERM "HOME OFFICE" MAY BE relatively new, but the concept is not. In the first chapter of her classic *Book of Household Management*, published in 1861, Mrs. Beeton enumerates the duties of the mistress of the house, and makes two pronouncements that are not at all dated: "Frugality and economy are home virtues, without which no household can prosper," and "A housekeeping account-book should invariably be kept, and kept punctually and precisely."

When I was growing up, my mother paid all the bills and kept all the family records. Her home office was a rolltop desk on our sunporch, where she kept a small ledger, a checkbook, and a brown accordion file, which was impeccably organized. Back then, I had a tiny rolltop of my own where I played at running an office. I typed on our old Smith Corona typewriter and cranked the manually operated adding machine.

Today, I have offices in all my homes, tucked into very compact spaces. At Turkey Hill, the office is built into a closet in a sunny room. In East Hampton, I converted a mudroom into my office. And in Bedford, the office is a small built-in desk in the kitchen. A wonderfully functional home office can also be created in the space under a staircase, in an underused corner, in a cupboard—almost anywhere.

THIS WORK AREA
IS IN AN UNOBTRUSIVE
CORNER OF A
KITCHEN. HOLES DRILLED
INTO THE BACK OF
THE CABINET ACCOMMO-
DATE THE CORDS OF
THE COMPUTER, PRINTER,
AND PHONE.

My offices are organized to be as uncomplicated as possible and still have everything I need. In each one I have a good computer with lots of memory, a fax/copy machine, a scanner, a color printer, a phone system with multiple lines, and an intercom.

I bought my first computer in 1982 and, in checking my records, I see that I paid for it in three installments, a total of $6,842—a huge sum of money for me, or for anyone, at that time. I was catering then, and we used the computer for bookkeeping, word processing, filing, and record keeping.

Today, I have offices in all my homes, tucked into very compact spaces.

All of the records from my home-grown businesses are neatly organized in my office storage rooms. I have archives, too, of all my major purchases, tax returns, mortgages, house deeds, and other legal documents; I also keep expired passports, trip logs, diaries, and old calendars.

Even if you do not feel compelled to save and document everything, as I do, there is still an enormous amount of record keeping that goes into keeping a household functioning and up to date, and there are simple ways to organize your personal office space.

The modern desk no longer needs an inkwell and a leather writing pad. It is now essential to have the most up-to-date computer equipment and software. The goal for me is actually the "paperless home" that functions superbly from one desk that is adaptable and practical.

LAYOUT BASICS

In many homes, an empty extra bedroom or guest room can easily be converted into a home office. Yet if you don't have a whole room in which to arrange an office, a closet—even a small one—is a good place to set up a computer, fax machine, and supplies. You can even place an office under the stairs. First determine what the office is going to be used for—work, correspondence, paying the bills, organizing the household, children's homework—and what equipment you will need. Wherever you choose to set it up, the basic requirements of a home office are the same: function, space, and comfort. You will need a desk, a supportive chair, task lighting, file cabinets or boxes, shelves or bookcases, and a power source.

Next, figure out which area of your home best suits your needs while also considering how the placement of your office will affect your household. Make sure that the closet or room will provide enough space for all of your office items and equipment. If you require privacy, then the attic, basement, or an area of the house without a lot of traffic is best. If you will be meeting clients or accepting couriers, then the main floor is ideal.

If you need more work space than your desk allows, an additional surface with a usable countertop, such as a filing cabinet or credenza at a comfortable height (between 27 and 30 inches), can help increase the available area. Choose one of three standard configurations: parallel, L-shape, or U-shape. A parallel arrangement allows you to move easily between the two surfaces, although it's impractical if you need to shuttle back and forth often in order to complete routine tasks. L-shape and U-shape configurations, with additional work surfaces arranged at right angles to the primary work surface, are more practical if you need to perform multiple tasks, such as working on the computer combined with traditional pen-and-paper desk work. L- and U-shape configurations also make it easier to keep everything at your fingertips, allowing you to access necessary documents, files, or equipment without the bother of getting up from your chair.

Of course, you will need to spend some time working in the space to see how well it functions, so set it up in a way that makes sense but remains flexible. If after a month it seems that the arrangement isn't as comfortable or functional as you would like and needs rethinking, move furniture and files around and try again. There are no hard-and-fast rules when it comes to home office arrangement—only what works best for you.

THIS WELL-EQUIPPED
WORK AREA OCCUPIES
AN UNUSED SPOT
BENEATH THE ENTRYWAY
STAIRS.

EQUIPMENT AND WIRING

You can accomplish most tasks in the home office with a computer, printer, scanner, fax machine, telephone, and paper shredder. Fortunately, most equipment has become so sleek and slim that your home office doesn't have to be consumed by bulky machinery and heavy cords in order to function. In fact, there are now many so-called all-in-one machines that combine printing, scanning, copying, and fax capabilities, which saves a tremendous amount of space.

Once you have your electronic needs taken care of, make sure that your office has all of the necessary wiring. You will need electrical outlets (and more than likely, power strips/surge protectors), telephone outlets, and data access equipment, which will provide a connection to the Internet. If you have a cable modem, you will need cable access; if you have a dedicated service line (DSL), you will need a phone jack near the computer.

To set up a wireless network, you'll likely need an Internet broadband connection such as a cable or DSL modem, a router, and a wireless card installed in your computer. Make sure that a password is required to log on to your wireless connection, so that no one can share it beyond the people you've allocated; without a password, it's much easier for hackers to get to your information. And be aware that a wired connection is the safest one.

WIRE MANAGEMENT

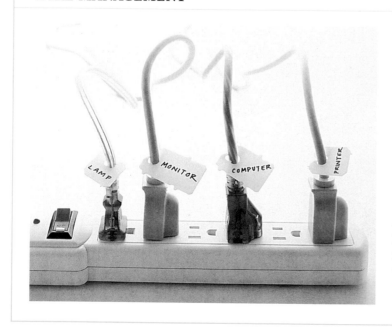

No matter how streamlined your equipment, you will still have multiple cords and wires to contend with. But they need not become a tangled mess. At the minimum, you can mount a power strip to the underside of your desk so the only cord that has to travel to the outlet is that of the strip. Then mount a coated wire basket (available at housewares and office-supply stores) beside the strip. Bundle lengths of wire with twist ties and arrange neatly in the basket. Attach tags to identify which machine each wire comes from (bread-bag tags work well).

A NOTE ABOUT ERGONOMICS

A comfortable home office promotes not only efficiency but also good health and good work habits. If your chair is rigid and uncomfortable, the keyboard is poorly positioned, or the monitor has a distracting glare because of poor lighting, you will be less inclined to accomplish all that you would like to in the space and you may also experience back and neck pain.

Take ergonomic guidelines into account as you outfit your office. Ergonomics is the study of the relationship between people and furniture and equipment. Ergonomicists study the physiological stresses that can result from poorly functioning workspaces, such as fatigue and hasty decision making, and look for ways to make people more comfortable.

The degree to which you adopt the study's tenets depends on how many people will use the space and how often. An adjustable chair is less important in an office used by a single person than in one shared by a family. Likewise, if an office will be used less than an hour a day, ergonomics are not terribly important; if it is used for four hours or more a day, they're essential. For more information, visit Cornell University's ergonomics website: ergo.human.cornell.edu.

DESKS

A desk can be any table you choose, as long as the work surface is sturdy and spacious enough to hold office equipment and still leave room for paperwork. The industrial metal desks that were ubiquitous in offices from the 1930s through the 1970s are particularly functional. They tend to have roomy drawers and generous writing surfaces, easily accommodating com-

YOU CAN SPRUCE
UP VINTAGE METAL OFFICE
FURNITURE LIKE THIS
DESK AND CABINET
BY HAVING IT PAINTED AT
AN AUTO-BODY SHOP.

puters and telephones, as well as bills, newspapers, and magazines. Regardless of style, the recommended height for a desktop is 30 inches from the floor; obviously, you can adjust this figure to suit your stature.

For ease of movement, position the telephone on the left side of the desk if you're right-handed and on the right side if you're left-handed. Keep the area under your desk clear of clutter so you can stretch your legs.

COMPUTERS

When positioning your computer, bear in mind that guidelines depend upon the type of computer you use. Desktop computers, with a separate monitor and keyboard, are preferable as primary computers because you can position them in such a way that they allow you to keep your head and neck in a neutral position, which reduces the likelihood of aches and pains. Laptop computers, on the other hand, which can be adjusted only minimally, are not an especially good choice for prolonged, daily use.

DESKTOPS

Center your computer monitor and keyboard in front of you, with the monitor's top casing 2 to 3 inches above eye level. Tilt the monitor back 10 to 20 degrees. A no-glare screen will reduce eyestrain; use an optical glass antiglare filter where needed. Also, keep the monitor no more than an arm's length away from you while you are seated. Use a document holder whenever necessary, preferably one that sits in line with the monitor. If you are installing the computer in a closet, make sure you leave the proper amount of clearance for ventilation and heat dispersal around the central processing unit and monitor (check the owner's manual for specific guidelines). Failure to do so could jeopardize the life span of the computer. The same goes for other office equipment.

LAPTOPS

For occasional use, sit in a comfortable chair and position the computer on your lap so your wrists are as flat as possible. Angle the screen so that you can see it without craning your neck or straining your eyes. For full-time use, position the laptop on a desk. Elevate it on a monitor pedestal so the monitor's top casing is 2 to 3 inches above eye level, and tilt the screen back 10 to 20 degrees. Attach a separate keyboard and mouse, either to the computer itself or via a docking station, and place them on the work surface or on a keyboard tray. This will allow you to maintain a neutral posture.

KEYBOARDS

The keyboard should rest at or below elbow level when you're sitting (about 27 to 30 inches from the floor, depending upon your height), with arms and elbows relaxed and close to the body and forearms parallel to the floor. Wrists should be kept flat and straight in relation to forearms when using the keyboard or mouse. A sliding keyboard drawer attached to the underside of the desk is optimal, as long as it is stable and doesn't bounce. Although wrist rest pads were once believed to reduce the stress placed on wrists from frequent keyboard users, more-recent ergonomic studies have found their use unnecessary.

PRINTERS

The printer you select for your home office depends on the kind of tasks you'll be using it for.

LASER

Laser printers, although more expensive than inkjet printers, are less expensive to maintain over time. They're the best bet if you're printing a large volume of documents (more than 10,000 pages a month), because of their speed.

INK-JET

Ink-jets produce high-quality printouts and are a smart choice if you have less printing to do. Inkjet cartridges can be expensive, however, and you may end up spending more on them than on the printer itself.

PHOTO

Ink-jets can also print high-quality photos besides functioning as all-purpose printers. If you print a lot of digital photographs, however, you may want to consider a dedicated photo printer. They are specifically designed to print on photo (glossy) paper and may allow you to print the equivalent of a contact sheet with thumbnail images so you can choose which photos you want to print in a larger format, which will save paper and ink. They may also allow you to print directly from your camera's memory card rather than your computer.

MULTIUSE

Multiuse printers include a scanner, copier, and fax in one compact unit. These models are especially useful where space is limited.

HOW TO RECYCLE PRINTER CARTRIDGES
Don't just throw old ink cartridges into the trash; it's not good for the environment. Many companies that sell cartridges take them back for recycling; check with your local office-supply store which may provide drop-off bins. Another option is to call your local trash handler and ask them what their rules are for cartridge disposal.

A CHAIR WITH A FIVE-
PEDESTAL BASE ON
WHEELS PROVIDES THE
MOST MOBILITY.

CHAIRS

Comfort is the most important criterion when selecting home-office seating. A chair should be sturdy, with sufficient padding and support to allow you to sit in it comfortably for several hours or more. If limited space means that you must borrow a chair from your dining room or kitchen to sit at the computer, at the very least make sure that you place a firm cushion behind your lower back. High-density foam cushions offer the best form of lumbar support.

For a chair that resides permanently in the office, ergonomic principles are crucial. Look for one that adjusts for height and tilt while also providing firm lumbar support. The seat should fit your shape, allowing even distribution of weight; ideally, the seat will be at least 1 inch wider than your hips and thighs on either side. If you have too little room, you may sit too far forward, which won't give your back adequate support. Choose a chair that will recline and support your back in various positions; a reclined seated posture of 100 degrees to 110 degrees is preferable to a 90 degree upright position. Make sure the cushioning and contouring are ample so that you are still comfortable after sitting in the chair for an hour or two. Look for a chair with a five-pedestal base on wheels, for maximum mobility; a swivel option is also useful. If the chair has armrests, they should be broad, contoured, cushioned, comfortable, and preferably adjustable for height as well.

The chair is the right height for you if your feet rest on the floor and your upper body is aligned with your monitor, keyboard, and mouse. If your feet don't reach the floor and you can't adjust your chair, use a footrest.

LIGHTING

Adequate lighting is essential in a home office. Improper lighting makes work tiresome and causes eyestrain. Table lamps and flexible-arm lamps provide the best task lighting. Flexible lamps should be positioned just below eye level to focus light directly on your work surface. Never overilluminate your work area, however, or you will create too much contrast between it and the surrounding room. To minimize shadows, consider placing a light on both sides of your desktop. Never place a computer monitor against a bright window or facing one, which can make the screen appear washed out; use shades or blinds to block out light from the window.

FOCUS LIGHT
DIRECTLY ON YOUR WORK
SURFACE WITH A
FLEXIBLE-ARM LAMP.

ORGANIZING BASICS

The key to any home office—large or small, traditional or modern—is to keep it organized. If the space is orderly, you will always be able to find what you're looking for and will more readily finish your projects.

COMPUTERS

Take time to organize your computer and all of the data stored there. Files left on the desktop drain memory and can slow down your computer. Create folders and subfolders to organize your documents. Be sure to store your documents separate from the applications that created them.

In the event of a computer crash or virus, you may lose valuable data. That's why it's important to regularly back up any word-processing documents, e-mail, digital photographs, graphics, or other irreplaceable files you wish to save. Backed-up data should be stored externally, meaning in a format that is not on your computer. There are several formats to choose from:

ZIP

A disk drive you plug into your computer. It copies files onto a Zip disk, which can store hundreds of megabytes' worth of data.

CD

If your computer has a built-in CD-RW (meaning "read-write" drive), you can copy, or burn, files onto a CD for storage. CDs can store up to 700 megabytes of data. If your computer is not equipped with a built-in drive, you can buy an external drive.

DVD

If your computer has a built-in DVD-RW (meaning "read-write" drive), you can copy, or burn, files onto a DVD, which can store gigabytes of data, more than either Zip disks or CDs. If your computer is not equipped with a built-in drive, you can buy an external drive.

ONLINE

For a monthly fee, you can store backed-up files on an online storage site.

Whichever storage method you choose, label all disks clearly and legibly, including the date and time of the backup. Never erase an earlier backup before you are sure that you've completed a more recent one.

The frequency with which you back up your files depends on usage. If you use the computer daily, you should probably back it up daily. For occasional users, once a week should suffice.

DESKS AND SHELVES

A tidy work surface is essential to a productive home office. Ample supplies should be close at hand. Keep pencils sharpened and staplers and tape dispensers filled. Similarly, discard dried-out pens and anything else that has lost its ability to function.

Store small items such as pens, pencils, erasers, scissors, and paper clips in containers. Keep desk drawers stocked with extras of the supplies you use frequently, including tape, staples, rubber bands, adhesive notes, ink cartridges, stationery, and index cards. Dividing trays will prevent an organized drawer from becoming a "junk" drawer. You should also have on hand an electronic label maker, a calculator, a calendar with plenty of space to write on, and a clock.

Keep shelves organized by storing magazines and catalogs in magazine holders, photographs in boxes or albums, and memorabilia and supplies in storage boxes. Choosing matching boxes will ensure components stack efficiently and look neat and attractive.

A NOTE ABOUT ANTIVIRUS SOFTWARE
If you don't have anti-virus software installed on your computer, invest in some. Scan and de-fragment your hard drive at least once a month using utility software. Visit a website such as www.mcafee.com for more information on computer security and software downloads.

KEEP DESK DRAWERS
IN ORDER BY CORRALLING
SMALL ITEMS
IN BOXES AND TINS.

CREATING A REFERENCE LIBRARY

You can customize your office reference library and suit your own needs, but the following list is a handy starting point.

☐ Business and residential telephone books

☐ Dictionary

☐ Thesaurus

☐ Atlas

☐ Encyclopedia(s)

☐ Almanac

☐ General desk reference, such as the *New York Public Library Desk Reference*

☐ Medical reference, such as the *Merck Manual of Medical Information*

☐ Style guides for writing (*The Chicago Manual of Style,* Strunk and White's *Elements of Style, Columbia Guide to Standard American English*)

☐ Reference guides to your computer and its programs

☐ Any reference books on special subjects related to your field of work or other interests (i.e., *Food Lover's Companion,* a biographical dictionary, a book of quotations)

DISPOSING OF COMPUTER HARDWARE

New computers are constantly being surpassed by the next generation. But before you toss out a less-than-state-of-the-art model, consider giving it to a school or nonprofit organization who often welcomes donations of equipment; you might get a tax write-off for such a contribution.

If your computer is too old to be of use, it may be ready for the trash. But you should not simply throw it away with your regular garbage. Computers contain toxic materials such as lead, and many states classify discarded computers as hazardous waste. As a rule, hardware should be disposed of like a television set or other household appliance; call your local environmental protection agency for details on the rules in your area.

Before getting rid of your computer, however, you will need to erase all of your personal files; just dragging them into the trash is not enough to protect you. There are one or two disks that originally came with the machine that will restore the original system by overwriting all of your documents on the hard drive. If you have used your computer for personal finances or other sensitive material, consider downloading an application that will erase all of your private files and passwords; you can find this software online by using the keywords "clean drive" in a search engine.

COMPUTER CLEANING KIT

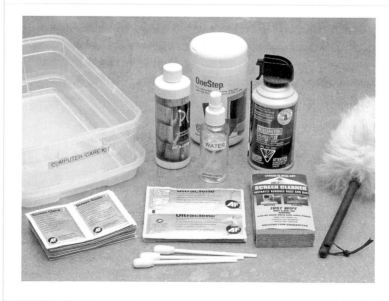

- ☐ Soft, clean, lint-free cloths (such as a diaper)
- ☐ Dry screen-cleaning sponge
- ☐ Disposable screen-cleaning wipes
- ☐ Lamb's-wool duster
- ☐ Can of compressed air
- ☐ Cotton swabs
- ☐ Spray bottle of 1 drop mild dishwashing liquid mixed with 1 quart water
- ☐ Spray bottle of distilled water
- ☐ LCD or plasma cleaning kit

CLEANING ELECTRONICS

A weekly dusting will help keep the items on your desk—telephone, pencil sharpener, portable docking stations, chargers, tape dispenser, and stapler—clean. Don't forget to vacuum the office weekly as well, and give your equipment a proper cleaning to keep it in top condition.

HOW TO CLEAN A COMPUTER

Electrical equipment generates static, which means your computer is prone to attracting dust. As part of your weekly cleaning routine, dust the computer and any accessories such as printers or scanners. Use a gentle duster, preferably one made of lamb's wool (never use a standard vacuum cleaner on electronics as it can cause static, which can damage components). If too much time passes between dustings, a little extra maintenance might be required. The first step is to check your computer owner's manual. The technique explained below is very gentle and could probably be used safely on any computer, but only your manual can explain whether your particular machine may need special care. Always turn off your computer before you clean it.

THE CASING

Dampen a lint-free cloth with the dishwashing solution mentioned in the box on the opposite page. Fold the cloth once or twice and wipe all surfaces—including the vent grille in the back, which often gets clogged with dust—to remove grime. Use cotton swabs to clean nooks and crannies.

THE MONITOR

Some desktop monitors use a cathode ray tube (CRT), while flat-screened monitors and handheld devices use more delicate liquid crystal displays (LCD), plasma, or other image-projection technology:

CRT Spray plain water on a microfiber cloth so it is only slightly moistened—not dripping—then wipe the screen. (Never spray anything directly onto any part of the computer as it can leak into the housing; likewise, never use solvents.) Polish afterward with a fresh, clean cloth. You can also use a dry screen-cleaning sponge or a disposable screen-cleaning wipe.

LCD AND PLASMA Use a soft cloth and a spray specifically designed for either type of screen. Electronics stores sell such products. Make sure the screen has cooled completely; if you clean the screen while it's still warm, you could leave permanent streaks. Apply as little pressure as possible (using too much pressure can disturb the gel in the screen and damage it).

HOW TO CLEAN A TELEPHONE

At least once a month, do the following:

The phone body

Moisten a cloth with the dishwashing liquid solution (see box, opposite) and wipe the surface of the telephone. For hard-to-reach spots, such as the spaces between raised numbers, use cotton swabs dipped in rubbing alcohol. Be careful not to get any liquid near the hook-switch, speaker, or other openings.

The handset

Clean the handset with a cloth soaked with rubbing alcohol; since this is the part of the phone that touches your face, it is important to disinfect it. Do not pour alcohol directly onto the phone. You can also use premoistened, disinfectant wipes on the handset.

The cord

To clean a dirty cord, remove it from the phone, and dampen a cloth with water and a few drops of mild dishwashing liquid. Rub the cord down with the cloth, and dry with a second cloth. Make sure the cord is absolutely dry before you reattach it to the phone.

**HOW TO CLEAN
PRINTERS AND
SCANNERS**
Treat your printer and
scanner with the same
care you give your com-
puter. Never allow water
or liquid of any kind to
come into direct contact
with either. Spray a cloth
with cleaning solution
or water first, then wipe
the equipment to re-
move any dust or dirt.
Unfortunately, any dam-
age caused by spills
will likely be irreparable,
and you will have to re-
place the equipment.

THE CENTRAL PROCESSING UNIT (CPU)

Consult your user's manual regarding how to open its case. Dust the interior without touching the circuit board. If you have a laptop, don't try to
open it. Use compressed air to blow dust from the keyboard.

THE KEYBOARD

Using the extension tube on a can of compressed air, spray air in short
bursts between the keys; avoid long bursts, which may produce condensation. Turn the keyboard over and gently shake it to loosen any lingering
dust, and spray again with compressed air if necessary. Wipe the keys and
keyboard casing with a cloth dampened with the dishwashing solution.
If you have spilled something on your keyboard, try to get off as much of
the liquid as possible. Most desktop keyboards have removable keys (consult
your user's manual for instructions). Use a soft, damp, lint-free cloth to
gently remove the spill from underneath and around the keys. Use distilled
water; hard water may leave behind a thin deposit of minerals.

THE MOUSE

First flip the mouse over and remove the disk that holds the ball; you may
need to push gently on the disk or use a coin to twist it and turn to snap
it out. Remove the ball, and rub it with a detergent-dampened cloth to remove any dust. With a cotton swab barely dampened with water, gently
wipe the rollers inside the mouse; replace the ball; and close it.

THE CORDS

Beginning at one end, wrap a cloth dampened with dishwashing solution
around a cord and slide it to the other end. Give the cords a few minutes to
dry completely before reconnecting them to all the various components.

MANAGING PAPER

As well organized as your home office may be, nothing presents more of a
maintenance challenge than the enormous amount of paper that finds its
way into the space. Set up a system for managing paperwork, and you'll go
a long way toward keeping your office under control.

IN-BOXES

Considering the volume of mail that can accumulate on any given day, one
in-box might not do the trick. Try a system of four in-boxes: for personal
correspondence, bills, catalogs, and papers to file.

BULLETIN BOARDS
Everyone needs a place to tack important reminders and invitations, as well as postcards and mementos. I installed a bulletin board on the back of the door when I set up my first "office in a closet" at Turkey Hill many years ago; it has functioned well for me ever since. As a rule, invitations and reminders should be discarded as soon as the relevant dates have passed. Go over the contents of the board weekly to determine what needs to be added or rotated off.

PERSONAL CORRESPONDENCE

Unless a piece of personal correspondence holds sentimental value, you should discard it once you've answered it. If you decide it's worth keeping, move it to a bulletin board to display it for a while. File it if you've established a very orderly system for other such correspondence, and even then you should make it a regular habit to go through such files annually.

BILLS

Since bills need to be paid in a timely manner, they deserve an in-box of their own. Write the due date on the outside of the envelope as a reminder. Go through the in-box of bills at the beginning of each week and pay anything that's due in the week ahead, then move the bills themselves into a designated accordion file once paid. (For more information on how to set up a bill-filing system, turn to Bill Storage on page 233.)

CATALOGS

Catalogs and magazines can share an in-box. Toss old catalogs into the recycling bin as new ones arrive, or simply tear out relevant pages and keep those in the in-box, especially if you can view the catalog and order products online. Likewise, discard old magazines weekly as new ones arrive, unless you consider them keepsakes; in that case, you should have an ample supply of matching magazine holders set up on a bookshelf wherever you are most likely to read and enjoy the publication.

PAPERS TO FILE

The final in-box is for papers that need to be filed, such as insurance papers, retirement account statements, or investment documents. Make a point to go through this box on a weekly basis and move the papers into their relevant long-term storage files (for more on what needs to be filed and for how long, see What to Keep, opposite).

MINIMIZING PAPER

The best way to manage the amount of paper that comes into your home is to stop some of it before it gets there and to scan some of it so it can be stored electronically.

REDUCING JUNK MAIL

The first step to minimizing junk mail is to sign up for the "do not mail" service available from the Mail Preference Service (MPS) of the Direct Marketing Association (DMA). For no charge, you can send a letter or postcard to the MPS with your name and address, and the information will be provided to direct marketers, who will be asked to exclude you from their mailing lists. (You can also register online for a nominal processing fee.) Your mailing information should remain on this list for five years. Although you may still receive mail from nonmembers of DMA as well as from companies you already do business with, including local merchants, professional and alumni associations, political candidates, and officeholders, you will see a sizable drop in the amount of junk mail you receive after signing up for the service. For complete details, visit the consumers' assistance page of the DMA's website at www.dmaconsumers.org. Keep in mind that you'll have to reregister if you move.

Another way to cut down on unwanted mail is to regularly check the "opt out" box whenever you fill out a new credit-card application or purchase anything online. As you get close to completing such applications or transactions, be on the lookout for boxes that automatically sign you up for updates, specials, bonuses, or deals, and as often as possible, check the box that indicates you refuse all such offers. Otherwise, you may begin to see a steady increase in the amount of mail—both paper and electronic—that you receive.

SCANNING

Of course there are still pieces of mail and other paper that we have to deal with in order to keep the home running smoothly. But just because the paper has come into the home and been managed accordingly doesn't mean it needs to continue to take up storage space. That's why you might consider scanning receipts, business cards, magazine articles, and newspaper clippings into your computer. You can then store the information electronically and discard the paper. Convenient hardware and software on the market allow you to scan and organize your receipts in a searchable database by vendor, date, and IRS deduction category.

BILL STORAGE

The easiest way to keep track of paid bills is to arrange them, by month, in a thirteen-pocket accordion file (use the thirteenth pocket for tax documents, such as W-2s). At the end of each year, simply replace the accordion file with a new one, and use the previous year's file to prepare your taxes. After that, you can go through each month to decide what items might be discarded or at least scanned (See What to Keep, below), and hang on to whatever else needs to be stored in that file until the requisite number of years has passed.

THIS SPECIALTY SCANNER IS DESIGNED SPECIFICALLY FOR RECEIPTS, AND HELPS MINIMIZE PAPER IN THE HOME OFFICE.

WHAT TO KEEP

FOR ONE YEAR
Paid bills for food, clothing, and other discretionary expenses; utility and telephone bills; copies of canceled checks for non-tax-deductible items; and insurance policies against which no claims have been filed.

FOR AS LONG AS THEY ARE ACTIVE
Contracts; mortgage records; real-estate deeds; home-improvement receipts; paid bills for insurable purchases such as furniture, appliances, jewelry, and art; investment buy/sell information and stock or bond certificates or statements; and vehicle titles.

FOR SEVEN YEARS
Personal income-tax records, including all supporting documentation for each line of information on your tax forms. This includes W-2 forms, interest- and investment-income statements, receipts, insurance policies against which you have filed a claim, bank and credit card statements, and canceled checks for all deductible expenses such as charitable contributions and child-support payments.

INDEFINITELY
Birth certificates, immigration papers, passports, wills, tax returns, and marriage and divorce papers. Decide which of these documents should be kept in a safe-deposit box. File originals and copies separate from each other.

**A NOTE ABOUT
TAX RETURNS**
The statute of limitations
with regard to how long
the IRS has to decide
whether or not to audit
you is three years from the
day you file a tax return.
If for some reason the IRS
suspects that you may
have underreported in-
come, however, that statute
increases to six years. More
important, if you neglect
to file a return, or if fraud
is suspected, there is no
time limit on when the IRS
may conduct an audit. You
should, therefore, retain
tax returns indefinitely, but
can shred the paper docu-
mentation after seven years.
Or you can scan the re-
turns and store them electronically, discarding the
return and the paperwork.

LONG-TERM PAPER STORAGE

The best way to arrange files containing legal documents, tax records, and financial statements for long-term storage is also the most common— in alphabetical order. Most filing cabinets have at least two drawers, which you can organize according to your needs. If you don't have room for a piece of furniture devoted entirely to file storage, substitute plastic bins or cardboard, metal, or straw file boxes. Label all file folders, and never pack your filing cabinet (or bins or boxes) so tightly that papers or materials are not easily retrieved. Once a year, or whenever files become too fat, weed out anything you can, and replace worn-out file folders with new ones.

SAFEGUARDING LEGAL DOCUMENTS

Although computers have taken over many record-keeping tasks, it is still extremely important to protect your personal documents. First, gather all your legal documents, including property deeds, car title, will, and birth certificate; your financial records, including the numbers of your bank accounts, credit cards, investments, loan papers, IRAs, and 401(k) plans; your property- and life-insurance policies; and official documents, such as your passport, citizenship papers, and Social Security card. Then make copies of them all. Separate the originals from the duplicates; organize the copies for reference in a file in your home office, and place the originals in a safe-deposit box or fireproof safe or cabinet.

INSURANCE

Whether you own or rent your home, you will need some basic insurance to protect your property and possessions in the event of unforeseen circumstances. Most policies pay for damage to your home from events such as fire, theft, and windstorms. They reimburse you for the actual cash value, minus depreciation, or for the cost of replacement.

HOMEOWNER'S INSURANCE

Homeowner's insurance will generally cover the contents of your household for 50 to 70 percent of the insured value of your home. So if you insure your home for $200,000, you are automatically guaranteed coverage for the contents of $100,000 to $140,000. A higher premium will grant you more coverage. Bear in mind that a replacement-cost policy will provide more protection than actual-cash-value coverage, but the insurer will want proof that you replaced the item before it will pay your claim. Another possibility is that the company might offer to replace the property instead of paying you the cash outright, but in this case, the choice is usually up to the policyholder.

RENTER'S INSURANCE

This type of insurance covers your possessions (but not the physical building) against loss for either actual cash value (minus depreciation) or replacement cost. Because this insurance covers only your belongings, it is relatively inexpensive compared to homeowner's insurance.

SUPPLEMENTAL INSURANCE

Depending on the location of your house and everything contained within it, you might need additional insurance to protect yourself against particular circumstances not covered by your regular policy. Flood and earthquake insurance are examples of supplemental coverage. If you own valuable jewelry or artwork, you should think about purchasing extra coverage to protect those assets, as a typical policy might limit coverage of such items to a couple thousand dollars.

FLOOD INSURANCE

If a flood is caused by something within the confines of the house, like a broken water pipe, the damage will be covered by a basic homeowner's insurance policy. A typical homeowner's policy will also cover damage due to wind, as in the case of a hurricane, and other types of natural disasters as outlined in the basic policy. Supplemental flood insurance, however, is necessary to cover the costs of damage to a home caused by overflowing creeks, water that gushes down hillsides, or storm surge from a hurricane. The National Flood Insurance Program (NFIP) offers flood coverage in many areas. Although the federal government provides the coverage, you purchase it from a commercial agent. Prices range depending on where you live, and to what degree a flood is likely. In most designated flood areas, flood insurance is required in order to get a mortgage when you purchase a home. These policies offer replacement costs for structural damage but only actual cash value, minus depreciation, for anything contained within the home.

EARTHQUAKE INSURANCE

Damage caused by earthquakes is generally not covered by basic homeowner's and renter's insurance, although a standard homeowner's policy can be supplemented by what's known as an earth movement endorsement. The term refers to a broad category that encompasses not just earthquakes, but landslides, mudslides, mudflows, sinkholes, or any other movement that involves the sinking, rising, or shifting of earth. The deductible for such policies usually amounts to 10 to 25 percent of a structure's policy limit, although in recent years the deductible rates have been increasing. In addition, many insurance companies have begun to demand a property inspection before a policy is granted.

JEWELRY AND OTHER VALUABLES

This supplemental insurance remains common, largely because the personal property coverage on most homeowner's insurance policies is capped for valuables (generally at at $1,500 for jewelry and $2,500 for silver), with a deductible of nearly half that amount. And, if the loss or damage of a valuable, such as jewelry, occurs anywhere outside of the confines of the home, the coverage decreases. One way to supplement your homeowner's insurance is with an endorsement or floater policy. A blanket policy covers an entire collection. This type of policy will allow you to put a price on an entire group of objects—say, $20,000—although individual pieces may not be insured for more than $2,500 each. Obviously, this is not suited for a collection in which a piece might be worth more than the per-item limit. A replacement policy, which is significantly more expensive, covers whatever it will cost to replace each item. When considering whether or not to insure your valuables, bear in mind that their value can fluctuate, and have the items in question reappraised every three to five years.

MAKING A HOME INVENTORY

If you don't already have one, make a list of all your accumulated goods, from cherished antiques to sporting equipment, and their value. Begin by taking an inventory of any articles that might be difficult or expensive to replace in the event of a burglary, fire, flood, or other catastrophe. This will help you decide how much insurance protection you will need to adequately cover your belongings.

A HOME INVENTORY
CAN HELP YOU
GET CLAIMS SETTLED
MORE QUICKLY.

Go through the entire house, listing objects in every room. Unlikely valuables might be found in the kitchen (a set of chef's knives), the garage (a riding lawn mower), or the bedroom (an heirloom silver clock). Also include on the list the serial numbers of televisions, bicycles, electronics, and other applicable items. Attach a receipt or an appraisal for each item to approximate its value.

Without such documentation, it can be hard to prove an object's worth after it has disappeared. A home inventory will enable you to plan and forecast your replacement needs. Complete the inventory with photographs (or videotape footage) of the objects. Organize the lists, appraisals, and photographs in a binder, or shoot digital photographs and store the images on a disk, and keep the inventory in your safety-deposit box or a fireproof safe.

I HAVE DESIGNED MANY
HOME OFFICES, AND THEY ALL SHARE
SIMILAR SOLUTIONS TO
THE CHALLENGES OF MAKING AN
OFFICE LOOK GOOD,
BE EFFICIENT AND USEFUL, AND FIT
INTO THE SPACE AVAILABLE.

THE HOME OFFICE AT LILY POND LANE

STORING PHOTOGRAPHS

The National Archives and Records Administration advises storing photographs in a cool, dry, dark spot, where conditions will remain consistent. The ideal environment for photographs has a relative humidity of between 35 and 50 percent and a temperature that stays between 65° and 70°F. Basements and attics are not recommended for photo storage. The moisture often present in those areas causes photographs to stick together and promotes mold growth. Excessive dryness may cause photos to shrink, crack, or curl. Light, especially ultraviolet and fluorescent, can break down images. Keep photographs covered with materials noted on the opposite page.

Photographs should also be protected from contact with fingerprints, tape, glue, ink, rubber bands, paper clips, dust, and chemical fumes. Handle prints and negatives along the edges—and handle them as little as possible. Dirt, dust, and oils from fingerprints can damage your photos. Wear cotton gloves when handling valuable photographs.

PHOTO ALBUMS

Photo albums were long considered the ideal way to display photographs, and they still enjoy pride of place as permanent records of joyful events such as weddings, births, and memorable vacations. Although they are not as convenient as boxes for photo storage, you may still want to compile albums, especially for milestone events, and keep them on display for guests and family members. If so, choose archival-quality albums that are photo-safe, acid-free, and PVC-free, to prevent the photographs from disintegrating over time. If the photographs hold especially sentimental value, consider making two copies of each. That way, you can keep one set stored in an archival-quality box, for future generations, and keep the other in the album for more immediate access and enjoyment.

PHOTO BOXES

If you group photographs in a box, first make sure that fragile ones are protected individually in plastic sleeves or envelopes made from acid-free materials designed for photo storage. The National Archives and Records Administration further recommends the following:

☐ Store photographs 8 by 10 inches or smaller, glass negatives, and magic lantern slides vertically on their long edges.

☐ Store photos larger than 8 by 10 inches or those with brittle or torn edges flat in small stacks inside boxes. They won't have the rigidity to support their own weight if stored vertically, so they will bow.

A NOTE ABOUT LIGNIN

Lignin (also spelled "lignen"), a chemical compound most commonly derived from wood, is used to strengthen paper so it can withstand printing and writing. But the compound breaks down over time, releasing acids that can cause paper to turn brown. These same acids can destroy storage boxes and can cause photographs to deteriorate. For those reasons, look for an archival-quality paper labeled lignin-free when storing photographs or anything else of value.

PHOTO STORAGE GUIDELINES

DO

☐ Use acid- and lignin-free paper (see A Note About Lignin, opposite), photo corners, backings, and boxes.

☐ Use uncoated pure polyethylene, polypropylene, or polyester (also called Mylar) plastics that do not damage photographs. Archival-quality materials such as these are available from photographic suppliers and online retailers.

☐ Handle prints along edges.

☐ Choose enameled metal shelves or cabinets for storing your photographs, if possible. They are better than wood, particleboard, or press-board shelves and cabinets, which can release damaging acidic fumes into your photo collection.

☐ Store negatives and transparencies in the same materials as photographic prints.

DON'T

☐ Don't use photo albums with adhesive backings. Over time the adhesive yellows and hardens, making photos hard to remove. The covering can also damage your photos, especially if it is made of poor-quality plastic. As the plastic ages, it can stick to the front of the photo and affect its color.

☐ Don't use PVC (polyvinyl chloride) products, glassine, colored paper, or kraft paper for photographic storage or mounting; these materials generate acids, which can cause photographs to fade and become brittle over time. The inks and dyes in colored papers may also bleed and stain your photos.

☐ Don't secure your photographs with rubber bands. Photos are silver-based and bands contain sulfur, which tarnishes silver.

☐ Don't store photos in envelopes. The adhesive may cause staining and fading of the silver image. If you do decide to use an envelope, the seams should run along the sides of the envelope, rather than down the center.

☐ Don't write on photographs. If placing photos in an album, include information on the enclosure or actual page instead. If you must write on a photo, use an archival pen or marker that won't bleed through the print or rub off on one stored behind it. Felt-tip and ballpoint pens used on the backs of photographs may stain the photo. A soft pencil can also be used, but be sure to write along the edge of the back of the photo and press lightly.

☐ Don't remove valuable photographs (and their adhesive backings) from albums, even if the photos are fading. The risk of damage is too great. Instead, leave the photos in the album, and handle it carefully. If the pages are falling out, dismantle the album and slip each page into an archival-quality clear sleeve (such as one made of Mylar). Photo labs (or copy labs) can reproduce pictures, retouching them on a computer to "repair" rips or restore colors.

□ Store groups of similar-size photos that are all the same type, such as modern 4-by-6-inch color snapshots, vertically or horizontally without plastic sleeves or envelopes; photographs of the same type are usually safe to store in contact with each other.

□ Don't overstuff (or underfill) boxes of photographs. Overstuffing leads to damage when photographs are pulled out or filed away. Underfilling causes the photographic paper to curl and slump.

□ Get in the habit of editing your photo collections regularly and weeding out the bad in favor of properly storing the good. There's no sense taking up valuable storage space with blurry, unrecognizable photos. A well-edited collection will be far more enjoyable over time, and present far fewer storage dilemmas.

DIGITAL PHOTOGRAPHS

Well-priced, easy-to-use digital cameras have revolutionized the way people snap, print, and store favorite photographs. Yet many of the same principles apply in terms of safeguarding the images you wish to keep.

Even if you don't own a digital camera, you may nevertheless wish to digitize your photographic prints by scanning them on a flatbed scanner, for safe and easy access. Once your photos have been scanned, you can view and print them whenever you want without risking damage to the originals. Never throw away your originals even after digitizing them, however; if you lose data on your computer as a result of deteriorated storage media or you are unable to retrieve images because a piece of software becomes obsolete, you will need your original film. Similarly, never dispose of an original digital file of an image once you've printed it. A print is vulnerable to heat, light, and water damage, so it's worth holding on to the original file indefinitely.

STORING DIGITAL IMAGES

Memory cards are used to store digital photographs temporarily on the camera itself, until the image is loaded on a computer hard drive. And although many users stop there, the hard drive is by no means the most secure place to keep digital photos. If the computer crashes, becomes corrupted by a virus, or gets stolen, any images stored there could be lost forever. Instead, use an additional external storage method, such as a CD or DVD, every time you move a group of images from the memory card to your hard drive. Whenever you burn a new CD or DVD of images (you will need a CD or DVD burner), include all relevant information about the photographs, including dates and descriptions of the images, on a label, or simply name the disk and keep a written log of what the disk contains.

A NOTE ABOUT PHOTO PAPER

To produce the best prints as well as prolong the life of your printer, it's important to choose paper specifically designed for photographs and the type of printer you have. There are a number of glossy photo papers suitable for a range of printers, such as laser and ink-jet, as well as an increasing number of affordably priced dedicated photo printers. Failure to use the appropriate paper for your printer can cause inks to smear and images to print poorly, and may even damage the printer itself. Store all photo paper in a cool, dark place; over time, it will degrade if exposed to sunlight or humidity. Archival paper will cost more than standard photo paper, but in the end, it's worth the extra price. This paper, along with archival inks, can help ensure your photos will remain vivid for years to come.

Or, for particularly important files, make an index print of images (a collection of thumbnail photos akin to a contact sheet) on the disk.

Finally, consider online storage, which is a convenient and relatively hassle-free option, although there are often limits to the digital-file sizes. The greatest benefit of this method is its sharing capabilities; your family and friends can easily access your photos without having to open large attachments from e-mailed files.

However you store your digital images, be sure to set up a system of organization that makes them easy to locate whenever you need them—whether it's by date, individual, or season, and stick to that system. Standardize the naming conventions you use to store them on the hard drive, on disks, or online. If you decide to edit or alter the image, it's important to make a copy of the original before doing so.

STORE DISKS CONTAINING
DIGITAL IMAGES
IN SUBDIVIDED BOXES.

PROTECT PRINTS
BY SLIPPING THEM INTO
ARCHIVAL-QUALITY
POLYESTER SLEEVES.

THE LIBRARY
AT LILY POND LANE

LIBRARY

EVERY HOME SHOULD HAVE a good place for books, and lots of places for reading them. You don't need a formal library: The "library" can be a corner of the living room that has a bookcase and an armchair and a reading lamp, or it can be a long hallway lined with shelves, just steps away from that comfortable reading chair, or your own bed with down-filled pillows.

I have a small library at Turkey Hill and another in East Hampton, where I keep my collection of rare garden books, some of which are more than three hundred years old. These are quite valuable, so the room is climate controlled to protect the books—if you have any rare volumes, they do require special care. And at Bedford, I am very fortunate to have a small house on my property that I can devote almost exclusively to my collection of books. It's a delightful and supremely functional place for reading and working, with floor-to-ceiling shelving in some rooms as well as marble-topped islands with shelving underneath, which remind me of my college library.

My books are not confined to libraries, however. I keep stacks of books everywhere, arranged in what I call ordered disorder. In addition to storing books on shelves, I have neat piles of them on the floor. All new books come into my bedroom first, so I can look at them at my leisure or read them in bed. After that, I organize my art books alphabetically by artist and subject. All other books are organized by topic and then by author. I know where everything is, and I can always find the book I'm looking for. This system works for me, but you can devise a system that best suits you and your book collection.

I have recently created a database for all my books, which makes the continued "building" of my collection much, much easier. Great software is available for doing this, and I advise strongly that everyone with more than five hundred personal books create a system to avoid

You can devise a system that best suits you and your book collection.

duplication. No matter how you organize your library, keep in mind the amount of shelf space you have, the heights of the shelves, and the sizes of your books. Then organize by the category or subject (fiction, history, travel) that makes the most sense to you, and group the categories together either chronologically, by author, or by title. Now curl up in that comfy reading chair and you're ready to read.

AN ANTIQUE BOOK STAND
IN MY LIBRARY IN
EAST HAMPTON HOLDS A
VOLUME FROM
MY COLLECTION OF RARE
GARDENING BOOKS.

LAYOUT BASICS

Books add life and character to a room—the titles on the shelves reveal a great deal about the people who chose them. Housing a collection of books in a way that both displays them properly and makes them easily accessible benefits the books as well as the readers in the home. No matter what room or rooms will house your books, there are shelving systems available to maximize the space you have while complementing the decor.

TYPES OF BOOKSHELVES

BUILT-IN
Fixed shelving can add richness to a room. It is ideal for larger rooms and creates the feel of a traditional library. Because it is usually custom-built, you can tailor it to fit your collection as well as incorporate additional storage, such as cupboards.

FREESTANDING
Although not quite as distinctive as built-ins, freestanding bookshelves are inexpensive and offer design flexibility because of their mobility. They can also be dressed up with moldings and painted to match the room. (For safety, freestanding units should always be secured to walls.)

WALL-MOUNTED
Shelves attached to the wall are an ideal way to make use of vertical space in a small room. They work well over desks, in alcoves, or above low entertainment centers, but sturdy brackets are required to ensure shelves can support the weight of books. A floor-to-ceiling installation can be an inexpensive alternative to either built-in or freestanding bookshelves.

BOOKSHELF GUIDELINES

No matter the style of bookshelves you choose, keep the guidelines below in mind. They will ensure that your shelves are convenient and efficient.

☐ To allow easy access to books, units should stand no higher than 84 inches, with the top shelf at 72 to 78 inches from the floor. If you go higher, you will need a library ladder or stool.

☐ Shelf depth is typically 12 inches; 8 inches is fine for most paperbacks, unless they're shelved two deep. A generous shelf doesn't need to be deeper than 15 inches. If you have deep, widely spaced shelves, consider making a 4-inch-high, 5-inch-deep step to create room for two rows of books, with all titles visible.

☐ Space shelves 10 to 12 inches apart, with more room between lower shelves to avoid the appearance of top-heaviness.

☐ Adjustable shelves will accommodate an evolving library. If shelves are to be fixed, measure your books and build the shelves at a variety of suitable heights. Always create more shelves than you think you will need.

☐ Books are very heavy. If you are having units made, discuss the type and quantity of books to be stored with your carpenter (or if you are making a unit yourself, consult the store you are purchasing your materials from) so that the shelf material is the appropriate thickness, and has adequate strength.

ORGANIZING BOOKS

Think about your reading patterns and tastes when arranging your library shelves. Usually, it is best to organize by subject or category (fiction, nonfiction, nature, photography, or American history, for example), and then either chronologically or alphabetically by author within the subject. If you have many oversized art and coffee-table books, you may choose to organize by topic and then by height for a neat appearance. Remember to leave vacant bookshelf space within each category, for future additions. If you have a collection of magazines, store them on bookshelves in rigid magazine-size holders covered with paper or fabric.

There are several software packages available that can help organize and record your collection. If you are an avid collector, look for one that can be downloaded to a PDA; when shopping for new books, you can have all of your titles at your fingertips so you can avoid buying duplicates. If you lend your books, this system will also help keep track of who has what. A simple inventory on index cards is a useful alternative to a computerized catalog.

HOW TO CARE FOR BOOKS

DO

☐ Use bookmarks. Don't lay books facedown or dog-ear the pages. Also, avoid using paper clips, which may rust or crimp the pages.

☐ Stack large or heavy books in piles. Don't stack them so high, however, that reaching for the bottom books will inevitably cause the pile to topple. Make sure to rotate the volumes every other month so that no particular book is subjected to too much pressure. Keep all other books upright, with another book of similar size or a bookend on each side. This will prevent warping.

☐ Keep books clean by dusting the tops and spines with a feather duster weekly. Once a year, take everything off the shelves, and dust shelves and books thoroughly. Fresh air retards deterioration, so the occasional handling of a book is actually good for it.

DON'T

☐ Don't write in your books; pen notations may bleed and obscure text.

☐ Don't store books near a heat source; doing so hastens aging.

☐ Don't subject books to extremes of heat or humidity. Ideally, books should be stored in a room that is no warmer than 70°F, with a humidity level of 45 to 55 percent. Dampness, which promotes mildew and mold and can cockle or wrinkle pages, is the worst enemy of books. Keep mold at bay by running a dehumidifier, shelving books away from damp exterior walls, and keeping bookshelves away from windows. Shelves should be deep enough to promote air circulation, which will help prevent musty odors.

☐ Don't cram books too tightly on the shelves, or you will harm the bindings.

☐ Don't subject leather-bound books to direct sunlight. Dust the spines with a clean, soft cloth and handle them gently; do not oil the leather, as the oil can cause damage.

☐ If a book doesn't lie flat, don't use force to open it wider or you may loosen the binding.

☐ Don't store books on unpainted or unsealed wood, which can release damaging vapors. Either paint shelves with a latex paint or seal with a water-based polyurethane.

PARING DOWN A BOOK COLLECTION

Any book lover with overstuffed shelves knows how hard it can be to decide which volumes to keep and which to give away. Deciding which books to hold on to is strictly a matter of taste. If, for example, you used to be an avid reader of biographies but haven't picked one up in years, you might want to pare down your collection. Take stock of your current and ongoing interests, as well as those you've outgrown, and weed out those books that don't fit. Give away any obviously outdated books—travel books, almanacs, or other specialized works that are frequently updated.

Check with your local library, house of worship, or community groups to see if they collect books for annual sales. Often, schools, nursing homes, and hospitals welcome book donations, so check with those places, as well. You may live in a neighborhood with a used-book store that will either give you cash or credit for any books you've brought them in good condition. There are many websites available to sell books through, too. If you have volumes that you suspect may be valuable, consult an expert such as a librarian or an antiquarian bookseller before donating or selling them.

REPAIRING BOOKS

DRYING WET BOOKS

If your books get wet, there are several steps to repair them. Attend to books with glossy pages first (if pages dry stuck together, they cannot be separated later). If books are muddy, hold them closed and rinse them. Lay a wet book on a clean surface; interleave the pages with white paper towels, replacing them when damp. Interleaving more than 20 percent of the pages may break the binding, but all glossy pages require it. If you wait more than twenty-four to forty-eight hours, mold and mildew will begin to grow. If there are too many damaged books to dry within forty-eight hours, wrap them individually in freezer paper or wax paper. Pack spine-down in plastic bags and put them in the freezer. This prevents further damage until you can dry them. While defrosting, check the pages hourly to see if they can be gently separated and interleaved with paper towels. If the binding is wet, consider taking the book to a book conservator (the conservation department of a nearby library or museum should be able to recommend one).

ERADICATING MOLD AND MILDEW

If mold or mildew has formed, immediately move your books to a drier environment with plenty of air circulation. Do not attempt to clean books until they are dry. Premature cleaning may smear or grind the mold and

HOW TO HANDLE BOOKS PROPERLY

Don't hook your finger over the top of the spine when you pull a book off the shelf. Doing so will loosen the binding. Try this instead: Push in the books on either side of the volume you want, then pull the book out by grasping both sides. As an added benefit, you'll also be able to tell at a glance where to return it.

mildew into the pages and cause stains. Once dry, gently vacuum or dust with a natural-bristle paintbrush. If you notice brown spots, called foxing, the book is probably in an advanced state of decay and the damage is irreparable. Foxing is a chemical reaction that not only stains paper but also contributes to mold and mildew growth and attracts insects.

REMOVING MUSTY ODORS

A musty odor is a sign of mold or mildew somewhere in your book. Using coffee grounds or kitty litter to get rid of a book's odor is a folk remedy that doesn't work well and can actually damage paper. Instead, place the volume in a room with good air circulation, a temperature of about 70°F, and a humidity level of 45 to 55 percent. Stand the book upright, fan out the pages, and leave it for a few hours. Close it (otherwise you risk damaging the spine), and repeat the process the following day. Do this until the smell dissipates, but be aware that the process could take several weeks or months. Interleaving the pages with archival paper that contains zeolites—minerals that absorb odors—is another good option. (MicroChamber Interweaving paper is available from www.conservationresources.com.) Place a sheet inside the cover and at fifty-page intervals within the book (to avoid stressing the binding). For volumes with fewer than fifty pages, place a sheet every ten pages. Close the book, and leave it for up to a month. If the smell has not improved, remove the sheets, replace with new ones, and repeat. Should these methods fail, contact a book conservator.

RARE BOOKS

The greatest threats to old, valuable volumes are mold, bright light (especially the sun's ultraviolet rays), pests, and damage to the structure or binding due to mishandling. Archival materials such as acid-free book boxes and Mylar (archival-quality polyester) sleeves can protect your books while also allowing them to be handled occasionally. You may want to consider wearing white cotton gloves while handling rare and valuable materials. This will help avoid fingerprint oils from coming in contact with the paper.

Many of the same general conditions that apply for the storage of ordinary books are even more important when dealing with rare books.

☐ Ideal conditions for book storage include a constant, moderate temperature of about 70°F with a humidity level of 45 to 55 percent.

☐ Prolonged exposure to bright light causes fading and accelerates the chemical reactions that make a book's pages, bindings, and dust jackets deteriorate.

HOW TO PROTECT BOOKS FROM DUST
Minimize dust by hanging crisp lengths of linen from shelves. This technique, traditionally used in Swedish libraries, also gives a neat appearance to uneven volumes. Measure the length of the shelf, as well as the distance from the shelf above to the top of the shortest book. Add 1 inch to all sides; cut prewashed linen to this size. Hem the bottom and sides by 1 inch. Sew 1-inch-wide twill tape to top edge. Fasten the tape to the underside of the shelf above at six-inch intervals using small nails or upholsterers' tacks.

☐ Book lice or silverfish are occasionally found on books that are stored in an area where humidity levels are high. Book lice are microscopic; silverfish can measure up to ½ inch. Both can, over time, eat holes in paper. Silverfish are also attracted to the paste in cloth bookbinding, which is often wheat-based. If you spot a few insects, first reduce the humidity in the storage area in order to prevent the growth of the mold they feed on. Then isolate and vacuum the affected book. If the problem is more widespread, contact a book conservator for treatment advice. Avoid chemical fumigants. (For more on silverfish, turn to page 674.)

☐ Metal shelving is preferable to wood, since wood can release damaging pollutants. If wood shelves must be used, seal them first with a water-based polyurethane, or line them with glass, acrylic, or sheets of metal to prevent books from coming in contact with the wood. Avoid oil-based paints, stains, and sealers, which can also release damaging fumes.

HOW TO STORE RARE BOOKS

It is always best to use archival-quality materials for long-term storage of any books or documents. The term "archival-quality" refers to materials that are durable and chemically stable. Such materials are generally free of acids, which can weaken and discolor paper; buffered, meaning an alkaline substance has been added to offset any acidity they may come in contact with; and free of lignin, a substance found in trees that binds wood fibers but breaks down over time, releasing acids that can cause paper to turn brown. It's wise to create dust-covers for rare books out of archival paper or polyester, or, if the books are fragile, to keep them in an archival storage box. Regular glassine is not a good choice for covering valuable books; acids emitted by the glassine will eventually cause damage.

To make a cover for a book, open the book flat on a sheet of archival glassine or paper. Trace around the outside of the book, adding a flap to each side nearly as wide as the cover; add 1½ inches to the top and bottom. Set aside the book. Fold the top and bottom edges over, and crease sharply with a bone folder, then wrap the book snugly.

Damaged books should be stored in archival boxes or wrapped in archival paper bound with cotton-twill tape. Boxes support the volume's weight securely, keeping gravity from pulling it apart, while also protecting it from light, moisture, and dust. Never use cellophane tape on pages or bindings; the adhesives will deteriorate faster than the book, and irreparably discolor the paper. Adhesive tapes are also very difficult to remove without risking further damage to the book.

PROTECT RARE BOOKS
WITH MYLAR DUST COVERS.

HIRING A CONSERVATOR

If you have a book with extensive damage, or an antique in need of repair, consult a professional book conservator, who is trained to handle the repair of damaged books and bindings. To determine what steps will be necessary to repair a book, a conservator will examine the structure of the original binding (whether sewn through the folds, sewn over the folds, or adhesive-bound), the type of paper (coated or uncoated), the condition of the paper (strong or brittle), the value, and the potential use.

Good conservators don't try to make an old book appear brand-new. Doing so would detract from its historic and monetary value; instead, conservators treat an antique book as a historical artifact, working by hand and using techniques that are true to the way the book was made. The result is a sturdy volume that can be used and enjoyed, but one that still shows its attractive patina.

To select the professional best qualified to treat your book, contact the conservation department of a nearby library or museum for a recommendation or visit the website of the American Institute for Conservation of Historic and Artistic Works, aic.stanford.edu.

REPAIRING A TORN PAGE IN A RARE BOOK

1. Open the book to the damaged page. Place another book, about the same size as the book you are repairing, on the facing page; put a heavy can on top of the second book to weigh it down.

2. Realign the torn text or image. Place a plastic cutting board under the damaged page so that it extends past the torn page's edge.

3. Working from the bottom up, affix acid-free, nonyellowing archival document-repair tape to the tear so that it goes slightly over the page's edge. Using a bone folder, smooth out wrinkles. Trim excess tape with a utility knife, using a straight-edge as a guide. Document-repair tape is available from art supply stores and online retailers specializing in archival products.

THE ENTRYWAY
AT LILY POND LANE

ENTRYWAYS, STAIRS, AND HALLWAYS

THE ENTRYWAY OF A HOME, whether it's a back entry, or front, should convey a sense of arrival and welcome. At Bedford, I have a pair of console tables flanking the front door in the foyer; on each, I display plants from the greenhouse—the specimens that are looking the most lush or most colorful at the time. The side door is also used a lot for guests—coats can be hung in an open closet, and there is a powder room directly adjacent.

At Turkey Hill, a grandfather clock greets guests with its rhythmic tick-tock, and the sidelights flanking the door have large hurricanes with candles that are lit whenever an evening party is planned. The back door opens into a brick-floored room that is really the back hall, and it is warm and appealing, with coat closet ready. At Skylands, the front hall is a very important "room." Stone-floored, cool, with a soaring ceiling, the hall prepares the guests for the spectacular view in front of them—fir trees, the ocean, and islands beyond.

Even if your front door opens directly into the main living area, the entry area can still be gracious. Above all, it should be clean and free of clutter (in fact, this goes for all entries, not just by the front door). Windows and doors should be sparkling—I know,

I have dogs, and their nose-level smudges have to be wiped away every day. If you don't have a coat closet—I don't at the Turkey Hill front door—make room in the closet nearest to the entry or have a system of hooks and pegs for keeping things organized. If you have school-age children, assign each his or her own area—complete with good-looking name tags—within a shelving unit; the kids can use bins to keep books, accessories like mittens and hats, and small sports equipment neat and tidy.

Here's one thing you'll find by the doors of all of my houses: a basket of folded, fresh towels. They help immensely when it comes to keeping your floors clean. Have them at the ready so you can lay down one for guests to wipe their feet on, or grab one to dry off a pet's wet or muddy paws. I almost always ask guests to remove their shoes as well; they line them up on a towel and put on a pair of slippers or nonskid socks that I also keep by the door. Most people don't mind this at all—and how it saves on wear and tear of the floors!

Hallways should also be clean, clutter-free, and well lit. A long hall makes an excellent "gallery" for artwork and mirrors. At Lily Pond Lane, I display travel photography on high-shelved wainscoting; at Skylands, engravings from a seventeenth-century globe in the Louvre; at Turkey Hill, charcoal landscape drawings. I like sconces for lighting a hallway, as they cast a flattering glow and provide a decorating opportunity in what should be a relatively unadorned space. Most hallways will not accommodate much furniture other than perhaps a small, shallow bookcase or a long, narrow table. All corridors should be unobstructed, for comfort and safety.

Safety is, in fact, a primary concern with staircases. I recently had runners installed on the basement stairs at Bedford; they're made of synthetic sisal that looks good and offers just the right amount of traction underfoot. At Turkey Hill, the stairs are narrower than those in most new houses. Until I had a runner installed and carefully anchored, I was always worried that someone might slip. I also make sure that banisters provide a firm handhold.

I LIKE TO KEEP A BASKET OF SLIPPERS BY THE DOOR FOR GUESTS.

A long hall makes an excellent gallery for artwork and mirrors.

These spaces—the entry, hallways, and stairs—tend to be high-traffic areas, which means they should be swept or vacuumed as often as every day, and given a more thorough cleaning once a week. This regular maintenance will keep them feeling fresh and functional, turning the areas you might think of as pass-throughs into lovely places in their own right.

ENTRYWAY BASICS

In some houses, the front door is the main entrance for the whole family; in others, a back door or a mudroom serves this purpose, and the front entrance is used primarily for guests. Depending on where you live, you may use the entryway to accommodate muddy boots and winter coats; those in warmer climes may use it year-round for gardening gear.

Any entrance will stay cleaner—and make the best impression on visitors—if it is well organized and cared for. If you have an opportunity to choose the flooring, opt for a low-maintenance material that can withstand everyday wear and tear, such as wood, vinyl, or laminate. Avoid choosing a surface that will be too slippery when wet, such as polished stone, or applying treatments, like floor wax, that will make it so. The entryway floor should not be carpeted as it will become too dirty, although a washable throw rug or runner on a slip-proof pad can be added.

Place doormats inside and out, to reduce the amount of dirt that enters the home and to minimize cleaning. The indoor mat should be made of an

HOW TO MAKE A BOOT SCRAPER

To make a simple but effective boot scraper, flank a sturdy mat, such as a coir rug, with upended push-broom heads. Have a sheet of 1-inch-thick marine-grade plywood cut to size at a lumberyard; its width should equal the width of the mat, and its length should equal the length of the mat plus the width of the broom heads. Finish the plywood with marine-grade varnish. With a drill and screws, attach the mat to the plywood from above, and attach the broom heads to the board from below. There should be at least 3 inches of clearance below your door so that it can be opened easily over the mat.

absorbent woven cloth, machine-washable if possible, and the mat outside constructed of a rugged natural fiber, such as coir, to remove grit from the bottoms of shoes. (See the previous page for instructions on how to make a simple boot scraper.)

A bench or chair installed in the entryway will provide a place to sit when removing shoes and boots. Although it's not always practical to have guests remove shoes upon entering your home—during a party, for example, this rule does not apply—floors will stay in better condition the less they are scuffed by shoes. Add a basket of terry-cloth or boiled wool slippers for guests, especially in cold or wet weather. Stow wet boots and shoes in a shallow metal boot tray; you can make your own using a rimmed baking sheet lined with a wire mesh rack, which can be easily washed. An accordion-style wooden wine rack makes a convenient spot for drying wet woolens, and an umbrella stand placed by the door will help eliminate drips on the floor.

ORGANIZING PRINCIPLES

Keeping the entryway organized will result in fewer lost mittens, forgotten mail, and misplaced keys. Efficient, pleasing arrangements of shelves, hooks, pegs, bins, baskets, and bowls make it satisfying to put things away and more likely that everything will find its place. Whether you live in a house or an apartment, a systematic entryway will keep things neat and save you time whenever you have to dash out the door. Here's what you need to ensure that your entryway works:

☐ Space for outerwear. Whether it's in a front hall closet or a series of hooks on the wall, be sure to allow sufficient space for everyone in the household, plus extra space for visitors. Placing an initial above hooks, so each family member has his or her own assigned place, can keep things especially orderly.

☐ A place to set things down temporarily. A demilune (half-round) table or small console, set against a wall, can hold shopping bags and mail while you remove coats and footwear.

☐ A system for incoming and outgoing mail. Letter trays, baskets, and standing racks all work well. Establish a dedicated bin for junk mail, so it can be immediately recycled. File bills and other correspondence in separate in-boxes. (For more on managing bills and filing paperwork, turn to page 230 in "Home Office.")

☐ A spot for keys. Choose a consistent place, such as a built-in hook, to store your own set of keys to avoid mislaying them, and designate another spot for extra sets.

THIS WELL-EQUIPPED MUDROOM HAS HOOKS FOR COATS AND ACCESSORIES, LARGE TRAYS FOR BOOTS AND ICE SKATES, AND SHELVES FOR TOWELS.

A DEMILUNE TABLE MAKES EFFICIENT USE OF A NARROW SPACE BY THE FRONT DOOR.

☐ Bins for things you need on your way in or out. Hang dog leashes and umbrellas on hooks. For everything else, be sure that entryway bins or baskets are sorted and emptied weekly.

☐ A message board. Install a small chalkboard for jotting notes and re-minders. A cloth-covered piece of Homasote board, available at hardware stores and home centers, can hold messages and also display items, such as invitations, postcards, photographs, and other mementos. Add a calendar, mail sorter, and battery-operated clock if space allows.

ENTRYWAY MAINTENANCE

Once a week, as part of your cleaning routine, vacuum and mop entryway floors, dust shelves and sort out bins, and wash throw rugs and runners in the machine if possible. Of course, much depends on the time of year; you may need to increase the frequency during the winter months or whenever mud gets tracked indoors.

IN THIS BACK ENTRYWAY, A BULLETIN BOARD HOLDS SCHEDULES, INVITATIONS, AND A CHALKBOARD.

FRONT HALL CLOSETS

A closet near the front door is useful in any home, but particularly if there isn't a mudroom. Regardless of its size, the hall closet should never be overflowing with sporting gear, beach umbrellas, or vacuum attachments. It is not a substitute for a utility space or broom closet; rather, it's a spot to hang your coats and those belonging to your guests.

CLOSET MAINTENANCE

Dust shelves and vacuum the floor in the hall closet weekly, as part of your regular routine. Twice a year, remove the contents and give the closet a more thorough cleaning; rotate one season's outerwear for the next, and redistribute seasonal accessories. In the spring, for example, move winter woolens to a cedar closet or bins for storage.

HOW TO CREATE EXTRA STORAGE

If you do not have a hall closet, and you have a large foyer, use an armoire; if your space is limited, place a coat stand near the door, or use your wall space by installing either a peg rail or hooks; hang some at waist level for younger residents and visitors.

WHAT YOU NEED IN THE FRONT HALL CLOSET

☐ Rods for hanging coats and jackets; include extra hangers for visitors' outerwear.

☐ Hooks for tote bags, and a hat rack, especially if shelves are shallow.

☐ A rack on the back of the door for additional storage.

☐ Shelves with separate bins for scarves, gloves, and other accessories, and towels to keep mud and dirt from being tracked farther into the house. Make sure all bins are transparent or well labeled, and contain only those things you need as you come in or go out.

☐ If possible, a light that turns on automatically when the closet door opens. Have an electrician install the switch, or look for do-it-yourself fixtures at hardware stores. Keep a flashlight and batteries on hand as well, for emergencies.

STAIRS

A wooden staircase is an attractive feature in any house, but it's easy to overlook the importance of keeping it safe and clean. Take adequate measures to ensure safety, and make staircase maintenance a part of your weekly cleaning routine. (For more on this, turn to page 262.)

CARPETING THE STAIRS

To keep the treads and risers in good condition, and to provide a safe surface, cover wooden stairs with a runner, made either of the same carpet that runs through the hallways, or a solid or pattern that complements your home. Carpeted stairs offer many benefits, including comfort, warmth, noise reduction, and traction to prevent slips and falls; they can turn even the most formal hallway into a more welcoming place. For safety purposes, limit the total thickness of carpeting and padding to ½ inch.

Staircase carpeting has three essential components: padding, carpeting, and edging. Carpeting can cover the entire stairway or run down only the center of the stairs, leaving a few inches of bare wood exposed on either side. There is no formula for determining the ideal runner width. Ready-made runners are generally 26 to 28 inches wide; staircases are usually about 42 inches wide. Decorative hardware—including brackets, rods, and finials—is sometimes used in runner installations.

STAIRCASE COMPONENTS

BALUSTRADE
A balustrade is made up of a row of balusters, or upright posts, between the handrail and the treads. The main function of a balustrade is to prevent falls from the side.

NEWEL POST
The wide upright pillar at the top and bottom of the handrails is known as a newel post.

LANDING
A platform between flights or at the top or bottom of a staircase.

RISER
The riser is the vertical component of a step, which, along with the stringer, supports the treads.

STRINGER
The stringer is the long, diagonal support that runs the entire length of the stairs beneath the treads.

TREADS
The horizontal, flat surfaces that you step on.

AN ENTRYWAY IS
THE FIRST GLIMPSE A GUEST
HAS OF YOUR HOME
AND "WORLD." IT SHOULD BE
WELCOMING, PRACTICAL, AND
UNCLUTTERED.

THE FRONT HALL STAIRCASE AT TURKEY HILL

STAIRCASE CARPETING BASICS

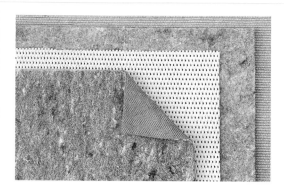

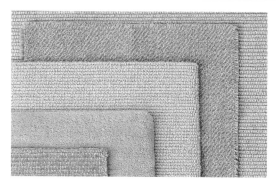

PROTECTIVE PADDING

Synthetic felt padding with latex backing and latex mesh are thin, nonskid pads—good under thicker carpeting or area rugs. A 40-ounce synthetic felt is firm, durable, and comfortable, and is ideal under thin carpet.

CARPETING CHOICES

Cotton is fine for light traffic, but synthetics and wool are longer-lasting choices. Construction affects durability and appearance. A cut-pile is soft and luxurious, but a loop-pile, such as berber, is ideal for high-traffic areas. A combination loop- and cut-pile has the rich texture of a cut-pile, as well as the added durability of a loop-pile. Blanket-weave carpet, an elegant alternative to loop-pile, also wears well.

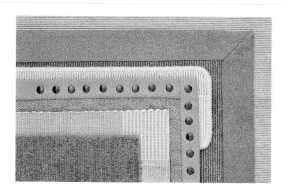

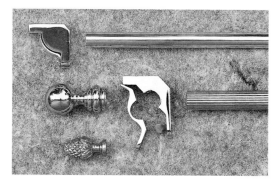

EDGING OPTIONS

Proper finishes prevent carpet from fraying at cut edges. On a French-rolled edge, loops curve over and create a natural-looking finish. A selvage is a plain, woven edge. A tape-bound edge on a blanket-weave carpet is finished with upholstery tacks. A serged edge is a simple binding of looped yarn. Unbleached linen tape creates a wide, decorative edge.

DECORATIVE HARDWARE

Ornamental hardware is optional but can add a decorative accent. Stair rods lend a more traditional look to staircase runners and come in many styles. Brackets are available in chrome or brass (coated to prevent tarnish), either closed at the ends or open to allow for finials. You might also use smooth or fluted rods; or finials in finishes including chrome, brass, crystal, or Lucite.

HOW TO INSTALL A STAIRCASE RUNNER

1. Before the runner is installed, cover the stairs with a durable, 40-ounce synthetic felt padding. Cut padding on each side, to be about ¾-inch narrower than the runner. Staple a piece of padding at the back of each tread, then roll it under the nose of the stair (these front corners were cut at forty-five-degree angles, to avoid bulky edges). Staple the padding in place.

2. Secure the runner to the face of each riser with a staple gun. (Stapling is the safest choice for a thin rug. A deeper pile may call for tacking strips—thin pieces of wood with tacks attached—nailed into the steps.)

3. Use a tool called a kicker to hold the carpet taut while it is stapled to the back of the tread.

4. To finish, screw a brass bracket into place where each tread and riser meet, then close it over the top of the decorative rod.

STAIRCASE MAINTENANCE

Whether you choose to carpet your staircase or not, it is essential to clean it regularly. Here are some guidelines:

☐ Vacuum stairs once a week, or more frequently depending on foot traffic, especially if you have light-colored coverings. (This isn't as much work as it sounds: Instead of vacuuming every inch of the staircase each time, just run the vacuum over the center of the steps, where dirt and wear are concentrated.) Instead of using a full-size vacuum cleaner, which can be cumbersome on stairs, use a lightweight stick vacuum, or a handheld vacuum with a motorized beater-brush attachment. Vacuum stairs more thoroughly once a month.

☐ As part of your weekly routine, dust banisters, removing all fingerprints and smudges from handrails. Use a lint-free cloth; for stubborn grime on sealed or painted wood, dampen the cloth with a solution of 1 part white vinegar and 1 part warm water. Wipe metal with a cloth dampened with a few drops of mild dishwashing liquid and warm water.

☐ Clear stairs of clutter every time you use them. Piles of belongings are not only unsightly but also hazardous. Instead of letting things accumulate, deliver them to their proper places right away.

☐ Fix squeaks on staircases as they arise. First, locate the squeak. If it comes from the front edge of a tread, drive finishing nails at an opposing angle through the tread and into the riser. If the squeak occurs at the rear of the tread, hammer a thin, glue-coated wood wedge into the space be-

HOW TO MAKE BASEMENT STAIRS SAFE

Keep basement stairs visible by adding fluorescent stripes to the treads, about one inch from the edge of the step. Use fluorescent tape, or apply 1 inch stripes of fluorescent paint (both available at hardware stores).

STAIRWAY SAFETY TIPS

☐ Do not use throw rugs on stair landings.

☐ Never wax a staircase.

☐ Tightly attach all stair coverings and ensure they are free of tears and wrinkles. Replace worn or damaged coverings immediately.

☐ Balusters should be spaced no more than 4 inches apart to prevent children from squeezing through or getting stuck in an opening.

☐ Stairwells should be well lit with light switches at the top *and* the bottom of the stairs. Lights should be bright enough to clearly define each step.

☐ The handrail must be sturdy, between 32 and 36 inches above the stair treads, and run for the full length of the stairs.

☐ If you have small children in the house, install safety gates at the top and bottom of all staircases.

tween the tread and riser. (You can buy precut wood wedges or shims from a lumberyard or hardware store, or use leftover wood siding or shingles. Trim wedges with a utility knife so they are flush with the riser, and cover the resulting gap with cove molding.) Loose balusters can be repaired the same way; cut a strip of wood slightly thicker than the widest gap between the top of a spindle and the handrail. Cut the strip into squares, and sand or plane to form wedges. Coat the wedge with glue and knock it into the space between the baluster and banister with a hammer and a block of wood until it is flush with the baluster.

HALLWAYS

Just as you need to clean every room in your home as part of your weekly routine, you must keep the passageways between them spotless as well. In fact, depending on traffic, you may need to clean hallways more frequently than some seldom-used rooms. Clear, uncluttered floor space also helps reduce the likelihood of trips and falls. Here are a few things to keep in mind:

☐ Vacuum hallway floors weekly, whether carpeted or bare. Take care not to run the vacuum into baseboards, which can cause chips and scuffs, and use the crevice attachment wherever necessary.

☐ Clean hallway walls twice a year. You can either use the dusting brush attachment of your vacuum, a dust mop with a newly attached clean head, or a damp, lint-free cloth. For more information on cleaning walls, turn to page 536.

☐ Dust artwork, photographs, mirrors, or decorative objects on hallway walls or shelves as part of your weekly routine. Clean mirrors with window cleaner sprayed on a paper towel or a lint-free cloth. (Never spray directly onto a framed mirror, as the cleaner may seep into the crevices of the frame.) Dust frames with a feather duster, or vacuum with the dust-brush attachment. (For more on caring for artwork, turn to page 211.)

A NOTE ABOUT HALLWAY SAFETY
Sconces provide soft lighting in the hallway, but for safety use several overhead lights, if possible, to create bright paths. If overhead lights aren't possible, use nightlights along the length of the hallway, especially between bedrooms and bathrooms.

A GUEST BEDROOM
AT LILY POND LANE

BEDROOM

BEDROOMS ARE PRIVATE PLACES, and how your own bedroom is set up is a personal matter. Some people, for example, like their rooms to be worlds unto themselves: full-service "control centers" for modern living with a phone and fax system, a computer with Internet access, exercise equipment, and a complete entertainment system, all in place, plus a desk or worktable. My approach to the bedroom is more old-fashioned. I like to use it for reading, occasionally watching TV, and, of course, sleeping. I think of the bedroom as a nighttime place, set up with everything I need to get to sleep and keep me comfortable.

I've always been partial to four-poster beds. In winter, I like to place rugs alongside the bed so I can step out onto something soft and warm in the morning. On each side of the bed there must be a generous nightstand for a reading lamp, books, and a vase for fresh flowers, along with enough space to accommodate whatever else might come in handy, whether it's a phone, an alarm clock, a carafe or bottle of water and a glass, a remote control, or pads and pencils. I have a drop-leaf table with a drawer as a bedside table in Skylands; it's not a traditional choice, but it serves my purposes very well. I can raise the leaf to give myself more night-table space, even pull up a chair if I want to take notes, then lower the drop leaf in the morning. A set of pullout nesting tables next to the bed can be a versatile alternative.

This somewhat minimalist approach (I don't generally keep extraneous furniture or decorative items in the bedroom) would work well in a guest room as well, where you want your visitors above all to be comfortable and have enough space for their belongings. A small vase of fresh flowers on the bedside table is a lovely touch when you have people come to stay.

Storage for clothing and space for dressing are important considerations in a bedroom, as I learned growing up in a big family and then learned again after moving to Turkey Hill, which has few and tiny closets, as is typical in old houses. With such limited space, I learned how to use every square inch. Any bedroom has space that's underutilized, and that can be adapted for storage: under the bed, on the floor beneath hanging clothes, on the closet door itself, in the space above a closet shelf. Organization and clever use of space is the key.

As for the perfect bed, it should be wonderfully comfortable—and that means different things to different people. I prefer an extrafirm mattress. Quality is not subjective, however, and you should always buy the best mattress—and other bedding—that you can afford. It will last the longest and provide you with the most comfort for a good night's sleep. The mattress should have a durable, natural-fiber mattress cover to protect it. Everything that goes on top of that—the fitted and top sheets, the coverlets, blankets, and duvets, as well as pillows with their covers and slips and shams—should be chosen according to how they feel and look, and again, in the best quality possible. Natural materials, such as cotton, linen, wool, and down and feathers, will wear beautifully and feel good, making for an excellent beginning and end to each day.

MY BEDROOM IN EAST HAMPTON HAS A HIGH UPHOLSTERED PANEL AND WALL SCONCES ON EITHER SIDE OF THE BED.

A small vase of fresh flowers on the bedside table is a lovely touch when you have people come to stay.

LAYOUT BASICS

We need our bedrooms for sleep, dreams, love, rest, and recuperation. A sensual, beautiful bedroom can be a nightly pleasure and a daily buffer from life's stresses. As long as you have adequate storage, in the form of closets, dressers, armoires, shelves, or under-bed bins, you can keep floors and surfaces clear, which will make them easier to clean—and keep the room feeling appropriately serene.

When devising a layout, divide the room into zones for each of the bedroom's main purposes: a sleeping area, a clothing storage area, and a comfortable spot for reading. In order for a bedroom to function well, allow for the following clearances:

☐ 18 to 24 inches around the bed, for ease in changing linens

☐ 36 inches in front of a dresser or an armoire to allow enough room to pull out drawers and swing open doors

☐ 36 inches in front of a closet door to allow adequate space for opening doors and maneuvering clothing in and out.

BEDS

A bed generally consists of a frame, which may include a headboard and footboard; a mattress; and a box spring, or foundation. (Platform beds are designed to hold mattresses only, without box springs.) Bed frames, which should be strong and stable in order to keep your mattress set secure, come in a variety of styles.

If you do not have a bed frame with a head- or footboard, you still need a structure to set the mattress on. A Harvard bed frame—a simple metal rectangle mounted on casters—will elevate the mattress and box spring off the floor and also allow you to easily pull the bed away from the wall for changing linens.

When buying a bed, take careful measurements of your bedroom, keeping in mind that you will need at least proper clearance around it (see above). You will also want to consider the height of the tallest person who will be sleeping in the bed and add 6 inches to determine the length you will need (for standard dimensions, turn to page 000). Standard mattress widths are usually available in extralong lengths. Test the bed's sturdiness and balance by pushing against the frame; it should not wobble or creak. Look underneath the bed as well, particularly at the mattress-support system to ensure that it is well constructed. Examine all slats and corner joints, and if the bed is metal, inspect the welds. Joints should be firm and tight.

HOW TO FIX A SQUEAKY BED FRAME

If you have a squeaky wooden bed, examine the frame to determine the problem area. Noisy beds are simply the result of wood rubbing on wood. The possible culprits are headboards, side rails, and slats (which run between the side rails under the box spring). When the slats aren't strong enough, they bow under weight, often creating an uncomfortable surface and noise. Test this by removing the box spring and mattress and by pressing on the slats gently. If they squeak, buy heavier wood for the slats, or simply screw the slats into the side rails. If the problem persists, cut a piece of plywood to the size of the box spring and place it over the slats for extra support, making sure the edges rest on the rails.

If the slats aren't at fault, inspect where the side rails connect to the head and foot of the bed, a possible cause of wobbliness. Usually, plate hooks on the side rails lock into slots in the headboard and footboard; if the connections are loose, fill the space between the side rail and the head post with folded wax paper to stop the bed from shaking. If bolts secure the side rails, try tightening them—they could be loose. Squeakiness can also come from a headboard that is coming unglued. In that case, have a furniture maker or woodworker reglue it. Pay attention to the joints in your bed frame, and you'll be getting a quiet night's sleep in no time.

CREATING UNDERBED STORAGE

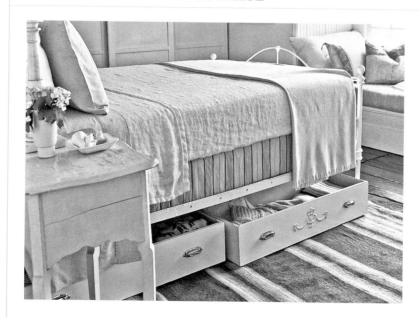

Use the space beneath the bed to store out-of-season clothing or extra bedding. You can easily attach casters to wooden boxes or drawers. Affix drawer hardware or a twill loop to the box or drawer, to make it easy to slide back and forth. Suitcases also make good underbed repositories; store them one inside the other, or fill them with clothes and linens.

BED TYPES

CANOPY

A frame with four high posts at the corners and a tester, or wooden frame, across the top to hold a fabric "ceiling." Canopies work well in large spaces, allowing you to create the feeling of a room within a room.

IRON

A term commonly used to describe beds made of metal (cast iron and wrought iron most often) coated with colored finishes. These frames break down easily for moving and storage and are particularly durable.

SLEIGH

Named for the horse-drawn vehicles they resemble, these beds have solid headboards and footboards that roll outward.

FOUR-POSTER

A bed with a high post positioned at each corner. Now largely decorative, at one time the posts were used to support fabric curtains and upholstered enclosures.

PLATFORM

A flat, hard, horizontal surface meant to support a mattress without a box spring. Platform frames sometimes incorporate storage drawers.

UPHOLSTERED PANEL

A bed with an upholstered headboard. Most panel beds can be purchased with just the headboard or with both the headboard and the footboard.

COVERING A BOX SPRING

Some bed frames leave the box spring exposed. To protect it, and make it more attractive, you can use a box spring cover or dust ruffle, available at linen stores and online retailers, or make your own box spring cover with a fitted sheet instead. Slip the sheet over the box spring, using one that matches those on the bed, or set off a coverlet or duvet by choosing a sheet in a matching pattern or contrasting hue.

A SET OF NESTING
TABLES MAKES A GREAT
NIGHTSTAND, AS IT
ALLOWS FOR MORE SPACE
WHENEVER YOU NEED IT.

NIGHTSTANDS

A bedside table should have a surface large enough to accommodate all of your needs. If sharing a bed, make sure there is a table on each side of the bed. The tables need not match—a late-night reader might use a bookshelf; someone who likes to work in bed might employ a table big enough for a laptop computer.

To maximize storage space in a small bedroom, use a dresser or small writing table as a bedside table. If space is tight, consider nesting tables— during the day, after you move paperwork and other items to your briefcase or desk, the smaller tables can be tucked away, leaving more open floor space. And in spite of the name, nightstands needn't put feet on the floor. A wall-hung cupboard or shelf can meet all your bedside needs and economize on space.

CHESTS OF DRAWERS

In the bedroom, drawers provide storage for more than folded clothes. They can also hold accessories, cosmetics, jewelry, or extra bed linens. If bedroom space is tight, consider a lingerie chest, a tall, narrow dresser with several small drawers. The best way to keep drawers organized is to outfit them with removable partitions and designate each compartment for a group of clothes or accessories.

TO UNSTICK
STUBBORN DRAWERS, TRY
RUBBING WAX FROM
A CANDLE ON THE TOP AND
BOTTOM EDGES
OF THE DRAWERS AND
ALONG ANY SIDES.

☐ Give delicate items such as scarves and jewelry plush support by lining shallow top drawers with velvet. Affix velvet to poster board, cut to size, with archival glue to give it rigidity. The lining will protect items from snagging on the unfinished wood.

☐ Use deep drawers for sweaters and knits (both of which should always be folded rather than hung). Line them with cedar boards to deter moths. If a whole drawer full of cedar creates too strong a scent, try a cedar bag or block of cedar and save the heavy cedar for seasonal storage. The cedar must be fresh in order to be effective; sand wood blocks periodically.

☐ Use small boxes or drawer dividers to organize stockings, socks, pajamas and nightgowns, and T-shirts.

☐ Save a bottom drawer for khakis and jeans. Line this drawer with acid-free paper to protect clothing from splinters and acids in the wood.

ARMOIRES

Armoires often provide ample hanging space, but do not conveniently accommodate shoes, belts, handbags, and folded clothes. You can remedy this problem by fitting one with ready-made closet components from a storage store or home-improvement center. Adjustable shelves stow handbags, stacks of tops and sweaters, and plastic bins for in- and out-of-season shoes. Hooks installed on the insides of doors can hold belts.

LIGHTING

Lighting in the bedroom should be safe and practical as well as create a soothing ambience. This is often best achieved with several kinds of lighting fixtures—an overhead light for general illumination, wall sconces on either side of the mirror for dressing, and table lamps on nightstands for reading, for instance. A wall switch near the door should operate at least one of these sources of light—an overhead fixture or table lamp—so you don't have to stumble around in the dark. Putting a dimmer on this switch will allow you full light for tasks such as dressing or making the bed and softer light for relaxing at the end of the day (for instructions on how to install a dimmer, turn to page 589). Bedside lamps are most convenient for reading when they are adjustable up and down and from side to side. The best reading lamps cast light downward, over your shoulder, and onto reading material. Floor lamps are best avoided in the bedroom—you run the risk of tripping over the cords or knocking them over in the dark.

IF YOUR BEDROOM LACKS ADEQUATE CLOSET SPACE, CONSIDER ADDING AN ARMOIRE; THIS ONE IS IN MY BEDROOM IN EAST HAMPTON.

HOW TO CARE FOR BEDROOM FURNITURE

Considering that you spend one-third of your life in your bedroom, it's worth keeping it free of dust and clutter. This will not only benefit your sense of well-being, but if you happen to suffer from allergies or asthma, it can actually help you get a better night's sleep. Common household dust contains molds, pet dander, pollen, and tiny dust mites—all of which can provoke allergic reactions. Dust surfaces, including dressers, nightstands, shelves, lighting fixtures, and any artwork, and vacuum upholstered furniture with your vacuum's upholstery attachment once a week. For more on caring for wood furniture, turn to pages 147–153.

MATTRESSES

The quest for comfort has led to ever-more sophisticated combinations of materials and increasingly thick mattresses. Years ago, mattresses were about 8 inches high; today, they routinely measure 20 inches thick. Although manufacturers have made forays into alternative types—waterbeds, adjustable air-filled beds, and memory foam, for example—innerspring mattresses, which came into wide use in the 1930s, are still the most common.

BOX SPRINGS AND FOUNDATIONS

Box springs are wooden frames with an internal network of coils or wire. Foundations are wooden frames with support slats. Both are usually upholstered in ticking to match the mattress and their purpose is to elevate, support, and enhance the comfort of the mattress. Mattresses and box springs are usually sold as sets and it's wise to use the box spring recommended by the manufacturer—your mattress's warranty may be voided if you don't.

A well-made box spring will have tightly stitched seams and densely woven fabric around the top and sides to stop wires from poking through. You can usually see the inner construction of a box spring from the underside: Look for evenly distributed coils or slats, which will prevent the mattress from crushing at stress points such as the sides or the center. A box spring should also have corner guards to keep its fabric cover from wearing down and rubbing against the metal corners of a bed frame.

ANATOMY OF AN INNERSPRING MATTRESS

TICKING

Ticking (sometimes called the mattress cover) is the fabric covering the mattress. Ticking is generally made of polyester, latex, or cotton.

QUILTING

Quilting refers to any pattern sewn into the ticking to provide a soft surface. The ticking is often quilted to a urethane foam or other material just below the surface of the mattress pad. Quilting also contributes to firmness and support.

PADDING

Padding (sometimes called the upholstery layers) is made up of various layers of foam and insulating materials placed on top of the inner construction of the mattress.

COILS OR SPRINGS

Coils or springs are below the padding and act as the support system of the mattress. They make up the innerspring core or unit. Mattresses that don't have coils for support generally use high-density foam instead.

EDGE GUARDS

Edge guards are the wire brackets that add support to the sides and ends of a mattress.

AIR VENTS

Air vents are small screens of metal or plastic grommets attached to the sides of mattresses, which allow air to circulate through the mattress.

HOW TO CARE FOR YOUR MATTRESS

DO

☐ Turn your mattress over four times a year, top to toe and side to side, to distribute the wear evenly. Keep track by attaching two tags to the mattress with safety pins. Mark "January" (right side up) and "April" (upside down) on one end, and "October" (right side up) and "July" (upside down) on the other. When the appropriate month rolls around, turn and flip the mattress so that the appropriate month's name is right side up at the foot of the bed. Turning a big bed top to toe can seem like a daunting task, but try this method: Working with one person on each long side of the bed, grab onto the handles and turn the mattress perpendicular to the box spring. Then slide the mattress partially off one side, bringing the end that was at the foot of the bed up, and let the other end fall to the floor so the mattress is standing on one end. Then simply let it fall back onto the bed and turn it back into place, with the end that was the foot now at the head.

☐ Vacuum mattresses and box springs every three months (when you flip your mattress) using the upholstery attachment and, if possible, haul both outside for a day of fresh air.

☐ Strip your bed whenever you go on vacation to air it out.

DON'T

☐ Don't sit on the edge of a mattress; doing so causes the sides to slope.

☐ Don't let children jump on the bed. Not only do they risk serious injury, but also the impact on the mattress can pop buttons, tear the stitching, and damage the filling.

☐ Don't allow your mattress to get wet, which could cause some upholstery materials to compress.

☐ Don't use dry-cleaning fluid of any type to clean your mattress; the chemicals can damage some of the construction materials.

☐ Don't place a board between your mattress and your box spring. The board will interfere with the supporting function of the box spring—and you may not get the proper support that the box spring is intended to give you. If you need extra support, you should consider buying a new mattress set.

MATTRESS DIMENSIONS

Mattresses range from 7 to 20 inches thick. Pillow-top mattresses, which
have a pillowlike layer sewn to the top, offer an extra layer of soft padding.

Mattress	Size	Mattress	Size
Crib	27 × 52″	Extralong full	53 × 80″
Cot	30 × 75″	Queen	60 × 80″
Twin	38 × 75″	King	76 × 80″
Extralong twin	38 × 79.5″	California king	72 × 84″
Full (also known as double)	53 × 75″		

HOW TO BUY A MATTRESS

The general rule of thumb is that a good-quality mattress will last between
eight and ten years. But because each person and each mattress is different,
this is a rough estimate. The quality of the mattress, how it is used and
how often, and the effort you put into keeping it in good shape all combine
to determine its life span. A mattress that has a good number of coils; tight
quilting; and even, sturdy seams will withstand daily wear much better
than a lower-quality product. Obviously, a mattress you sleep on every night
will not last as long as one that is kept in a guest bedroom and slept on only
occasionally. If you also use your bed as a place to read, write, watch television, and so on, it will wear out even more quickly. The shape and weight of
your body will cause your mattress to settle in certain spots over time.

The telltale signs that it's time for a new mattress are hard to miss: If
your bedding sags in spots or looks especially worn, if it creaks, if it feels
bumpy or otherwise uncomfortable to lie on, and especially if it affects your
sleep or leaves you in pain, then you should start shopping for a new one.

In general, people who sleep on their backs tend to prefer firmer mattresses, while those who sleep on their sides or stomachs favor softer ones.

The basic factors to consider when choosing a mattress are size, comfort, support, and durability.

☐ The ideal size depends on who will be sleeping in the bed; the mattress should measure at least 6 inches longer than the height of its occupant(s).

☐ The only way to test for comfort and support is to actually lie on the mattress before purchasing it. First, stretch out on your back and then assume your favored sleeping position. Have your partner do the same. The mattress should support your body at all points and keep your spine in its natural alignment. You may want to consider buying a mattress that is firmer than you are accustomed to, as it will soften with use; if the mattress is *too* firm, however, it will not support your body evenly and may cause you discomfort. The number of coils in a mattress won't necessarily determine how firm the mattress is, because placement of the coils is equally as important as number. The padding also contributes to the firmness. But a good way to judge the coils is the thickness—they should be 13 gauge or lower. (The salesperson or manufacturer may be able to give you that information.) Lower gauges and less padding will make the mattress firmer.

☐ To determine durability, carefully inspect the mattress: The seams should be straight and the quilting should be tight and uniform. There should be no broken threads and the mattress should have sturdy handles for turning. Each innerspring coil should be turned at least five times; tighter coils will make the mattress more supportive and long-lasting.

Most commercially manufactured mattresses contain flame-retardant chemicals, mold and mildew inhibitors, and stain guards to protect the exterior. Some mattresses may also contain formaldehyde, a known human carcinogen. These substances will "off gas," or give off fumes, over time. If you are sensitive to these agents, consider a specialty-mattress maker who uses chemical-free materials.

If you happen to have a vintage bed that will not accommodate a standard-size mattress (dimensions are listed on the opposite page), check with an antique dealer who sells beds. He or she may be able to recommend a custom manufacturer.

Warranties are usually activated automatically from the day you purchase your new mattress. Often consumers will need only their original store receipt and the law label from the mattress to prove their warranty, but be sure to check with your retailer when you purchase your mattress.

BASIC BEDDING

Your bed is a literal and emotional source of warmth. It's a place to rest and restore yourself. The best way to ensure comfort is to think of your bed as a composite of layers, each one adding to your total sense of well-being.

MATTRESS PADS

The most basic layer on any bed is the fitted mattress pad. Its primary function is to protect your mattress from spills and stains, which can be difficult, if not impossible, to remove. Pads can also help keep your sheets in place, especially if your mattress ticking is made of a silky, synthetic fabric. Every mattress, no matter how infrequently it is used, should be covered with one. Mattress pads are also designed to add a layer of softness and comfort. Launder the mattress pad once a month, being sure to heed the instructions on the care label.

The classic quilted pad—made of cotton, polyester, or a silk blend—slips snugly over the mattress. The quilted pad can be filled with down, hypoallergenic synthetic fills, or cotton or polyester batting. There are several other types of fitted mattress pads, including:

☐ Waterproof mattress pads, which are essential for small children or if you have accident-prone pets. Pads with a plush quilted cotton top and waterproof backing are most comfortable.

☐ Electric mattress pads, designed to keep your bed warm to the touch. For safety and convenience, an electric pad should be machine-washable and low voltage to guard against shocks, as well as have an automatic shut-off feature.

MATTRESS TOPPERS

Toppers are intended solely to add softness and comfort. They are often confused with mattress pads, but, in fact, don't protect the mattress and must be covered with a machine-washable classic fitted pad, which should be laundered monthly. (Featherbeds are the exception; they cannot be laundered, but should be spot cleaned the same way as down comforters. See instructions on page 282.)

MATTRESS PADS AND TOPPERS

CHENILLE PAD

WOOL TOPPER

EGG-CRATE TOPPER

MEMORY FOAM TOPPER

CLASSIC QUILTED PAD

FEATHER BED

CHENILLE
Chenille pads create a plush buffer, and the pile wicks moisture away from the body, keeping you dry.

WOOL OR FLEECE
A fluffy wool or fleece topper is a natural insulator; it will keep you warm in winter and cool in summer. Spot clean stains, using a solution of 1 part white vinegar to 3 parts water. Air-dry completely, in sunlight if possible, before replacing on the bed. Do not dry-clean. To freshen, air on a line in the sunshine at least three or four times a year.

EGG-CRATE
Egg-crate (or wavy) toppers provide additional comfort and pressure relief. Rotate to ensure even wear and vacuum with the upholstery attachment monthly. Spot clean with warm water and a mild detergent.

MEMORY FOAM
These toppers offer firm support, are pressure-sensitive, and mold to your body. Vacuum with the upholstery attachment monthly. Treat stains by hand-washing the topper in warm water with a mild detergent. Do not machine-wash or -dry.

QUILTED PAD
The classic fitted pad is designed to protect the mattress and topper.

FEATHER BED
The ultimate layer of luxury, a feather bed is commonly filled with feathers and varying amounts of down for softness, although they can also be stuffed with high-tech downlike synthetics. Air outdoors in the sunshine at least twice a year and shake once a month to keep the feathers evenly distributed.

PILLOWS

When it comes to pillows, people tend to be very picky. Some like them soft, others prefer them firm. Some like to feel propped up while others want to sink in. There are shapes, sizes, and fillings to satisfy every preference.

ABOUT FILL POWER

When choosing a down-filled pillow or comforter, consider the item's fill power, which is a measure of how well it insulates. Because down clusters from different birds range in size, the fill power of down from one type of bird will differ from that of another. The rating is determined based on the number of cubic inches the down takes up. A higher fill power means that the down has more loft, and it will create warmth with fewer down clusters. The rating is given in increments of 50, and can range from 400 to 900. A fill power measure of 600 or higher should indicate high quality. Lower-quality items will contain more feathers and stems, which add bulk and weight rather than warmth. Generally, goose down, characterized by large, fluffy clusters, has a higher fill power than duck down.

A NOTE ABOUT SLEEPING PILLOW SIZES

Basic sleeping pillows come in three densities (soft, medium, and firm) and are available in the following sizes:

Pillow	Size
Standard	20 × 26″
Queen	20 × 30″
King	20 × 36″

SPECIALTY PILLOWS

BODY PILLOW
A long body pillow is great for pregnant women or anyone with a bad neck or back. Sleepers lie on one side and drape one leg over and hug the pillow, which conforms to the body.

BOLSTER PILLOW
Bolster pillows are round, tube-shaped pillows with flat ends. They can be stuffed with a variety of fillings. Their shape is particularly good for supporting the small of the back and the neck.

BOUDOIR PILLOW
A boudoir pillow is a small (usually 12 by 16 inches) rectangular pillow for resting your head.

EURO SQUARES
Euro squares, which most often measure 26 by 26 inches, provide firm support behind sleeping pillows for reading in bed.

NECK ROLLS
Neck rolls are also tube-shaped, but smaller than bolster pillows. Neck pillows are often made of foam and specifically designed to support your neck while sleeping.

WEDGE PILLOWS
Wedge pillows are designed to fit under the bent legs of someone who sleeps on his or her back to alleviate strain on the lower back.

PILLOW FILLINGS

Besides its dimensions, one pillow is distinguished from another by its fill. Each has advantages and disadvantages, depending on the composition, price point, or care.

DOWN

Down comes from the breast of a duck or goose. Most down on the market originates in China, but the best quality is from Europe or Canada. (There's also a rare and extremely fine duck down called eiderdown.) Down and feathers are often associated with allergies, but it's probably not the feathers or down causing the reaction, but rather the dust and dirt on the feathers. In a high-quality pillow, the filling will have been meticulously cleaned, reducing or eliminating the problem. These pillows are more expensive, but their quality justifies the price. Most down can be washed in the machine.

SYNTHETIC (OR FAUX) DOWN

These fills are mostly made of polyester. Different manufacturers have patented their own versions, such as PrimaLoft. The best, which can rival down in price, are made to feel and act like down clusters. Synthetic down provides good support for back sleepers. The better synthetics are now "slickened" with an agent that makes the fibers slide against one another so they feel softer and bounce back after being compressed. Pillows filled with this material can be washed in the machine.

FEATHERS

Pillows filled with feathers are firmer than down, and less costly. Small fluffy feathers make the best fill: They're springy, soft, and don't poke through fabrics as easily as bigger ones. Look for labels that say "Micro Feather" or "Euro Feather." Ticking with a high thread count will also keep feathers from poking out. Most feather pillows can be washed in the machine.

COTTON

An all-natural, nonallergenic fiber that allows air circulation and launders well. (It dries quickly, so it won't get a musty smell.) Although cotton doesn't provide much bounce or loft, it is soft and becomes even softer with repeated use.

WOOL

Wool is another natural fiber that allows for air circulation. The sheared fiber is used as a medium-density pillow filling. Wool-filled pillows can't be washed; air them in the sun at least twice a year.

DOWN/FEATHER

Combinations—in such ratios as 50:50 or 80:20—offer varying levels of firmness and different price points. If a label reads Feathers and Down, there are more feathers than down, and vice versa. Most down/feather pillows can be washed in the machine.

SILK

A lightweight, insulating fill that gives medium to firm support. Silk-filled pillows can't be washed; air them in the sun at least twice a year.

BUCKWHEAT

This fill is used in many Japanese pillows and is good for headaches and neck pain since it conforms perfectly to the contours of your neck. It is made from the discarded hulls of buckwheat, which shift around freely inside the pillowcase. Buckwheat pillows can't be washed.

HOW TO CARE FOR PILLOWS

☐ Fluff pillows daily when you make your bed.

☐ Guard against stains by encasing pillows in machine-washable, zippered pillow protectors; launder protectors once a month. Be sure to place the zipper end of the cover inside the pillowcase first so it's not near your face.

☐ Don't toss extra pillows on the floor when you go to bed. Place them on a sofa or bench to keep them clean.

☐ Whether made of natural fibers (such as down) or synthetic materials (often polyester), most pillows can be washed in the machine. They should be cleaned every three to six months to remove mold, bacteria, and odors. Read the care label for instructions (for more information on laundering pillows, turn to page 279).

☐ Pillows that can't be laundered (such as those made of wool, silk, and some down pillows manufactured before machine-washable ones became common) should be gently spot cleaned with a mild dishwashing liquid (be careful not to saturate the filling) and aired in the sunshine two or three times a year.

HOW TO BUY A PILLOW

No pillow lasts forever. When it's lifeless, flat, badly stained, or can't be fluffed, it's time to replace it. Choose a pillow that will retain its shape while also providing proper support for your neck and spine:

☐ If you sleep on your side, choose a medium-firm to firm pillow filled with a combination of down and feathers, or with silk.

☐ If you sleep on your back, choose a medium-firm pillow with the same fill noted above.

☐ If you sleep on your stomach, choose a soft pillow, such as one filled with down, to reduce neck strain.

☐ Signs of quality include neat, well-filled corners that are not dog-eared. Choose pillows made of silk or cotton with a high thread count; edges should be straight and tightly sewn. The overall appearance should be full, not lumpy or uneven. Check care labels before you buy a pillow to make sure you can easily maintain it.

COMFORTERS

A comforter is a bedcovering with two layers of cloth that contain a filling, such as down, feathers, wool, cotton, or a synthetic material. A duvet is also considered a comforter, but by definition, its filling consists specifically of down or feathers.

One comforter is distinguished from another largely by the properties of its style of stitching, visible on the surface, and by its fill. A comforter is sewn in one of several ways, each of which lends it a different look and keeps the filling inside from shifting and bunching.

Comforters are filled with the same materials used to stuff pillows: down, feathers, synthetic faux down (polyester), silk, cotton, and wool. For more on these various fillings, turn to page 279.

Whatever the filling, comforters come in a variety of weights—light, medium, and extrawarm. For hot weather, many companies now also offer a "blanket" weight, which is an ultrathin layer that gives you cover without heft. Changing comforters seasonally appeals to some people; others, who keep their bedrooms at a consistent temperature, may choose a single weight that works year-round.

TYPES OF COMFORTERS

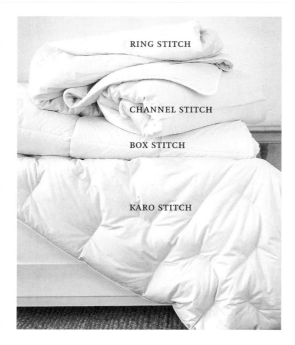

RING STITCH

CHANNEL STITCH

BOX STITCH

KARO STITCH

RING STITCH
Circular seams distinguish the ring stitch.

CHANNEL STITCH
The channel stitch has vertical seams, like swimming lanes, from one short edge to the other.

BOX STITCH
This stitch is a grid of large squares. You'll sometimes see the term "baffle box" in conjunction with box stitch, which means that there's also an interior construction (the baffle)—a fabric wall that gives the down more room to loft.

KARO STITCH
The karo stitch consists of intermittent lines placed perpendicular to one another. This less geometric, less rigid style gives the fill inside room to move and mold to your body.

HOW TO CARE FOR A COMFORTER

☐ Fluff comforters daily, as you're making the bed, to prevent matting.

☐ Guard against stains by encasing your comforter in a machine-washable comforter cover. Launder the cover once a month; if you omit a top sheet and sleep directly under the comforter, launder the cover once a week, with your other bed linens.

☐ To keep a comforter from shifting inside its cover through the night, secure it in place at the corners with ties. Sew two pieces of 2-inch-long fabric tape to all four inside corners of the duvet cover; at each corner of the comforter, push the filler toward the center, and tie the fabric tape around the bunched corner fabric. (Some comforter covers come with these ties.)

☐ Air comforters (without covers) on a line in the sunshine two or three times a year to keep them smelling fresh.

☐ Spot clean small stains with mild dishwashing liquid and water, taking care not to saturate the filling; push the filling out of the way if possible, so you're just treating the fabric casing.

☐ You should not need to launder a comforter if you keep it covered, unless it has been saturated by a spill or an accident. In that case, you will need to take it to a Laundromat and wash it in a large-capacity, front-loading machine or, if it is not machine-washable, to the dry cleaner or a professional cleaner that specializes in down. Keep in mind that repeatedly washing or dry-cleaning down can remove some of its natural oils and reduce loft. As such, it's best not to choose down if you have small children or accident-prone pets. For more on laundering comforters, turn to page 387.

☐ Store comforters for the off-season in cotton or linen bags to keep the dust off. Do not store them in plastic, which can trap moisture and foster mildew growth.

BLANKETS

Blankets and coverlets provide an extra layer of warmth and security. They also make stylish bedspreads in the absence of a comforter. Leaving a folded or draped one atop the bed at all times will make a berth nap-ready. When choosing a blanket for sleeping, first consider its fiber; this will determine its weight, comfort, and the amount of warmth it provides.

HOW TO CARE FOR BLANKETS

The best care is preventive. When making the bed, always fold down the top sheet by several inches to protect the edge of the blanket. This will cut down on wear and tear as you turn down the bed in the evening and make it in the morning. You can further protect Dry-clean Only blankets by layering a machine-washable flat sheet over the top.

BLANKET FIBERS

COTTON
Blankets made of cotton are best for hot weather; because of their open weave, they are lighter in weight than wool and allow better air circulation. Coverlets are typically made from cotton, often with a quilted or Jacquard design. Most can be machine washed.

SILK
Blankets made of silk are soft, lightweight, luxurious, and as warm as cashmere. They generally need to be dry-cleaned.

WOOL
Wool blankets are warmest, but vary in weight depending on the type of wool. Most can be washed by hand, but check the label to be safe. Allow wool blankets to air dry after washing.

Lamb's wool
Lamb's wool is sheared from sheep up to seven months old. It is first clip, and the wool is soft and slippery. All wool clips after the first shearing are called fleece wool. Most lamb's wool blankets can be washed by hand.

Virgin wool
Virgin wool, also known as new wool, is sheep's wool that has not been recycled or reprocessed, so it has not previously been woven, knitted, or felted into a wool product.

Merino wool
Merino wool is fine, strong, and elastic; it comes from the merino sheep. Although the staple (length of the fiber) is short, it is dense, and has excellent spinning and felting properties.

Cashmere
Cashmere is a fine, soft, downy wool undergrowth produced by the cashmere goat, which is raised in the Kashmir region of India and Pakistan and parts of northern India, Tibet, Mongolia, China, Iran, and Iraq. Similar goats are raised in the United States.

Mohair
One of the oldest known textile fibers, mohair is the long, white lustrous hair of the Angora goat, which is native to Turkey.

Alpaca
Alpaca is a hair fiber from the animal of the same name, a member of the South American llama family. It is softer, finer, more lustrous, and stronger than sheep's wool.

BLANKET TEXTURES

Here are definitions to some of the terms you'll see to describe a blanket's feel and appearance:

CHENILLE
Derived from the French word for "caterpillar," this is a special yarn with pile protruding on all sides. It can be made from silk, wool, rayon, cotton, or manufactured fiber filling.

FLEECE
A fabric with a thick, heavy, napped surface, it may be a pile fabric or simply napped, sometimes of a knit construction.

VELOUR
This woven fabric, which comes from the French word for "velvet" (which is derived from the Latin for "hairy"), is finished with a close, dense pile that is laid in one direction. Originally made in wool, it is now made in synthetic fibers as well.

WAFFLE
Also known as honeycomb weave, this is a textured-surface fabric with a pattern of squares or diamonds. The ridges outlining the squares or diamonds are raised above the centers, creating checkered cavities; the back of the fabric is almost the same as the face.

With care, blankets may need to be cleaned only once or twice a season. Many blankets, including wool ones, can be safely washed at home, though dry cleaning is best for vintage blankets. For more information on how to wash blankets, turn to page 392. Pilling can be a problem with any wool item, and there are special pill-removing tools available. (See page 391 for more on removing pills.)

LINENS

Once upon a time, young brides brought assemblages of bed linens called trousseaux to their marriages, often as part of their dowries. Mothers and daughters worked hard for years to prepare a girl's trousseau, which was intended to last a lifetime. By the Victorian era, it was commonplace to have hundreds of linens in the household inventory. Today, a fully stocked linen closet is no longer considered a status symbol, and store-bought sheets have replaced handmade ones. The longing for a beautiful, inviting bed, however, has not waned, nor has the practical desire to keep linens looking as fresh and clean as the day they were made. The feel and quality of sheets and pillowcases depends on the fiber the fabric is made from, and the number of threads woven into each square inch.

ABOUT COTTON

Cotton is comfortable in any season, easy to care for, and affordable, making it the most popular fiber for sheets. In fact, there are several different

A NOTE ABOUT ORGANIC COTTON

Organic cotton is grown without the use of pesticides, insecticides, and defoliants, on land that is certified free of these chemicals. The growth of this crop is healthier for ecosystems and people who harvest the cotton. The care for organic cotton is the same as for conventional cotton products.

types of cotton fibers, each of which has specific characteristics. The main distinguishing feature is the staple or length of the fiber. The longer the staple, the stronger and softer the resulting fabric. When a bed linen is woven from a long-staple cotton, it will usually be noted on the package. Sheets marked simply "100 percent cotton" are generally woven from shorter staple cottons. Below are some other terms used to describe cotton sheets.

COTTON FIBERS

EGYPTIAN COTTON
The longest staple cotton in the world, producing fine, lustrous fabric. It is renowned for its durability and absorbency as well as for generating less lint than other types.

PIMA COTTON
Named after the Pima Indians, who helped raise the cotton in its experimental infancy, it is one of the best quality cottons grown in America. This extra-long staple cotton provides a lustrous, strong, and firm fiber.

SUPIMA
A trademark that appears on products made from 100 percent American pima cotton.

SEA ISLAND COTTON
Considered the finest of all cottons. It's a rare, silky, white, extralong staple cotton grown exclusively in the West Indies and the islands of the Carolinas and Georgia coast.

INTERMEDIATE STAPLE COTTONS
Used for bedding with thread counts up to 230.

SHORT STAPLE COTTONS
These cottons, such as upland cotton, are commonly used in bedding originating from Asia.

ABOUT THREAD COUNT

Most sheets are labeled with the number of threads woven into each square inch of fabric. Along with the type of fiber used, thread count is a useful measure of a sheet's quality. The higher the thread count, the softer and more durable the sheet: Look for a minimum thread count of 200.

Be wary, however, of sheets advertising thread counts higher than 400. Some manufacturers will weave sheets using a double-insertion method, whereby two fine threads are doubled up or twisted together (called plied yarn) to create one thread. For marketing purposes, these threads are counted twice or four times on the packaging. Therefore, a 250-thread-count sheet made of four-ply yarn would be labeled as a 1,000-thread-count sheet.

Linens with lower thread counts are not necessarily of lesser quality. A 250-thread-count sheet made of long-staple Egyptian cotton, for example, will likely feel softer than a 350-thread-count sheet made of a short-staple

OTHER SHEET FIBERS

BAMBOO
A fast-growing plant that doesn't require synthetic fertilizers and pesticides, bamboo is usually mixed with cotton to make sheets. It is naturally antibacterial, very soft, allows for air circulation, and will dry quickly. Wash bamboo fabric just as you would regular cotton.

MODAL
Modal is made from the pulp of beech wood and is often blended with cotton to make sheets and clothing. (The name is a registered trademark of Lenzing, an Austrian company specializing in textiles and plastics.) Modal fabrics are particularly soft and do not retain limestone deposits, which can harden fabric after repeated washings. Wash Modal as you would cotton, in the washing machine.

LINEN
Sheets made of linen are ideal for hot climates because of the fabric's natural tendency to stay cool. They are more expensive than cotton ones, but they can also last for decades if properly cared for. As long as they are preshrunk and colorfast, you can wash linen sheets in the washing machine using the Gentle cycle (with cool to warm water). Colored linen should be washed in cool water only. Use a gentle detergent, such as Ivory Snow or Woolite. Place delicate, embroidered, or fringed linen sheets in a lingerie bag before putting them into the washing machine. Dry linen by hanging or laying it flat. Iron it (on the Linen setting) while the sheets are still damp.

SILK
Silk sheets are durable, but unlike linen, they are best suited to keeping you warm on cold nights. Machine-wash silk sheets in cold water on the Gentle cycle with a mild soap. Never use bleach. You can dry the sheets on a Low setting in the dryer.

SYNTHETIC
Synthetic fibers (polyester, acrylic, and rayon) are resistant to wrinkling, but they are much less comfortable than natural fibers in warm or humid climates due to their low absorbency. A successful blend will possess the most desirable qualities of both natural and synthetic fibers, such as a crisp texture or natural luster with less shrinkage.

cotton. Sheets with lower thread counts do have a higher shrinkage potential, however, and are therefore considered to be less durable than bedding with a higher thread count.

ABOUT WEAVES
The way a bed linen is woven will also contribute to its look, feel, and price. No matter the type, the weave should be firm and uniform. Test by scratching the surface of the cloth. If the threads shift easily, the product may be inclined to develop holes at the seamed edges. You can also hold a sheet to a light and look for any unusually thick or thin areas. If the weave isn't consistent, it will wear unevenly. The chart on the opposite page includes information on the types of weaves you're most likely to encounter in bedsheets.

TYPES OF WEAVES USED TO MAKE BED LINENS

CHAMBRAY

The name of this weave is derived from the town of Cambrai in northern France. Chambray is a plain weave, meaning the warp (lengthwise) and weft (widthwise) threads cross each other one at a time. It is made with a colored warp and white weft thread, usually made of cotton. The fabric is lightweight and often made in a solid color, but also available in striped, checked, and figured patterns.

DAMASK

Damask is woven on a Jacquard loom. Elaborate floral or geometric patterns are woven into the fabric, which is usually made from linen, cotton, wool, silk, rayon, acetate, or other synthetic fibers. The pattern is distinguished from the background by a contrasting sheen and is reversible. In two-color damask, the colors reverse on either side. The fabric is similar to brocade, but flatter.

FLANNEL

A light- or medium-weight fabric of plain or twill weave with a slightly napped surface on one or both sides, flannel has a fuzzy, soft texture. Sheets made of flannel are usually very warm.

JACQUARD

Jacquard is a compound weave, which mixes several warp and weft structures to create a pattern. It is woven on a Jacquard loom and is the most expensive of all types of weaves to produce. Damask, matelassé, and brocade are all examples of Jacquard weaves.

JERSEY

Jersey is a plain fabric that is knitted, meaning the yarns are looped together rather than woven. Like T-shirt material, jersey sheets are soft, breathable, and stretchy.

MUSLIN

Muslin is a plain-weave fabric that must have a thread count of at least 128; in sheets, however, the thread count usually doesn't exceed 160. These types of sheets tend to be rough. The fabric is usually bleached and then finished with very little sizing.

PERCALE

Percale, which is used specifically for sheeting, is a plain-weave cotton fabric with no fewer than 180 threads per square inch. The threads are tightly woven, resulting in a fine texture and finish. Two types exist: those made with carded yarn and those made of combed yarn. Combed-cotton percale sheets, the finer of the two, are smooth, luxurious fabrics with about 200 threads per square inch, and are often called "true percale." Carded-cotton percale sheeting averages 180 thread count. (For more on combed and carded yarns, turn to page 289.)

PLAIN WEAVE

Plain weave, which is synonymous with "flat weave," is the most common weave. The warp and weft threads cross each other one at a time, producing a strong fabric. Voile and percale, which tend to be crisp and allow for air circulation, are examples of plain weaves.

TWILL

Twill weaves, identified by either a diagonal rib or a twill line, produce strong bedding fabrics that have a softer "drape" than those made of plain weaves. They have more cotton fibers exposed on the surface of the fabric so they can be brushed for extra softness.

SATEEN

Sateen weave can be used to make higher-thread-count sheets (although not all high-thread-count sheets are sateen). A sateen weave means that each thread crosses four to eight other threads; as a result, a large number of threads are exposed on the surface of the fabric, lending it a smooth, lustrous sheen. Sateen sheets are usually made of mercerized, combed cotton threads (mercerizing is a process of applying a special finish to strengthen and improve the fiber's shape, luster, and ability to hold dyes). They snag easily, which is why the thread count of sateen sheets is usually higher (the yarns are woven closer together).

SHEET EMBELLISHMENTS

Many sheets are finished with decorative details. These are the most common forms of ornamentation.

EMBROIDERY
Embroidery is made with needle-work stitches using thread, yarn, or other flexible materials. Hand embroidery is a widely practiced craft, but most commercially produced embroidered textiles are made by machine.

HEMSTITCHING
This is a general term for a stitch usually bordering a hem that is characterized by open rectangles. Hemstitching is created when parallel threads are caught together in groups.

LACE
Lace is a delicate ornamental textile made without the aid of a ground fabric (which is used in embroidery). To form the openwork pattern, a network of threads is twisted together either by hand with bobbins and pins, with needles, with hooks, or by machinery. The threads may also be finished by knotting them.

MONOGRAMS
A design composed of letters, typically the initials of some-one's name, monograms are used as an identifying mark. There are typically three ways of showing a three-letter mono-gram. You can make all the letters the same size for your first, middle (or maiden), and last names, reading left to right. Or use a larger center initial for your last name, with a smaller initial for first and middle names on each side. For a cou-ple, use the larger center initial for the common last name, with first initials on each side.

STANDARD SHEET SIZES
Keep the following guidelines in mind when choosing bed linens.

☐ Flat sheets should be at least 24 inches wider and longer than the mat-tress in order to provide an adequate drop on the sides and enough fabric to tuck in at the foot of the bed and fold over the blanket at the head.

☐ Fitted sheets need a "box" deeper than the mattress to avoid midnight tugging. Standard American mattresses are 7 inches to 20 inches deep. Extra-deep sheets to accommodate thicker mattresses are more common in top-of-the-line brands. This is true even for pillow-top mattresses—most manufacturers now account for them with so-called universal-fit fitted sheets, which have more fabric and elastic around the entire edge of the sheet, rather than just at the corners.

☐ Pillowcases should be at least 4 inches longer than the pillow.

☐ Comforter covers should be the same size as the comforter.

☐ Coverlets should be considerably wider and longer than the mattress to allow an adequate drop, although the actual dimensions will depend upon the height of the bed and the presence (or lack) of a bed skirt.

U.S. STANDARD SIZING FOR BED LINENS

	Mattress	Flat Sheet	Pillow	Pillowcase	Comforter, Duvet, and Cover
Crib	27 × 52″	38 × 52″	N/A	N/A	34 × 43″
Cot	30 × 75″	63 × 96″	20 × 26″	20 × 30″	68 × 86″
Twin	38 × 75″	66 × 96″	20 × 26″	20 × 30″	68 × 86″
Extralong twin	38 × 79.5″	66 × 96″	20 × 26″	20 × 30″	68 × 86″
Full (also known as double)	53 × 75″	81 × 96″	20 × 26″	20 × 30″	76 × 86″
Extralong full	53 × 79.5″	81 × 96″	20 × 26″	20 × 30″	76 × 86″
Queen	60 × 79.5″	90 × 102″	20 × 30″	20 × 34″	86 × 86″
King	76 × 79.5″	108 × 102″	20 × 36″	20 × 40″	100 × 90″
California king	72 × 84″	108 × 102″	20 × 36″	20 × 40″	100 × 90″

BED LINEN TERMS

COMBED
A technique usually used with cotton, in which separate fibers are combed to remove the short fibers (or noils), so that the resulting yarn will be composed exclusively of the longer fibers. Combed cotton yarn is made of long-staple cotton and is more even and compact, has fewer projecting fibers, and can be woven into finer counts than carded cotton (which is made of short-staple cotton). Combed yarn produces soft, durable sheets.

MERCERIZED
During the mercerizing process, yarn is immersed in a sodium hydroxide (caustic soda) solution, then neutralized in acid to produce permanent swelling of the fiber. This increases the yarn's luster, strength, and affinity for dyes. The best results are obtained on combed cotton.

CARDED
In order to make thread, cotton must first be processed by a card machine, which separates the fibers and removes impurities. Carded cotton is constructed of short-staple cotton.

RING SPUN
This term describes fiber—usually cotton—that is mechanically twisted (or spun) before it is woven or knitted. The technique produces a strong yarn.

YARN DYED
This means the yarn is dyed before it is woven or knitted, and it is dyed a uniform color. (Other methods involve individual strands that are infused with more than one color at irregular intervals, which creates a more random look.)

RECOMMENDED QUANTITIES OF LINENS

There's no such thing as having too many bed linens (as long as you have adequate space to store them), but having too few is something to avoid. Having multiple sheet sets will also ensure that no one set gets worn out from overuse.

FOR THE MASTER BEDROOM

☐ One topper (an optional layer to add comfort)

☐ Two mattress pads

☐ Three sheet sets (bottom and top sheets, pillowcases or shams)

☐ Two pillows for each person to accommodate any number of favorite sleeping positions

☐ One comforter or duvet

☐ Two comforter covers or, as an alternative, one each of a summer and winter blanket

☐ One bed skirt or box spring cover

FOR EACH ADDITIONAL BEDROOM, INCLUDING GUEST ROOMS

☐ One topper (an optional layer to add comfort)

☐ One mattress pad

☐ Two sets of sheets

☐ Two or four pillows (depending on the bed size)

☐ One comforter or duvet

☐ One comforter cover or, as an alternative, one summer blanket and one winter blanket

☐ One bed skirt or box spring cover

HOW TO CARE FOR SHEETS

☐ Change and launder sheets and pillowcases once a week.

☐ Use warm rather than hot water, which can shrink the fibers.

☐ Keep whites white and stains at bay with oxygen bleach—which is gentler on fabrics than chlorine bleach.

☐ Do not use fabric softener, which can weaken delicate fibers and reduce absorbency.

☐ Check to make sure there are no stains before putting linens in the dryer—the heat will set a stain. For more on stain removal, turn to page 374.

☐ Dry sheets on low heat and remove them while still slightly damp. Overdrying linens can weaken the fibers, and if you plan to iron your sheets, it helps to do so while they are still damp.

☐ For information on how to fold and store sheets, turn to page 355.

HOW TO MAKE A BED

1. If you're using a topper to add a layer of padding, place it directly on the mattress. Protect the mattress (and topper) with a cotton or wool mattress pad that fits snugly over the mattress.

2. Place a fitted sheet over the mattress pad. If using a flat sheet instead of a fitted one, secure it with hospital corners.

3. Lay the top sheet face down (so the right side will be visible when you fold the end over the blanket), with the top edge of the sheet even with the top of the mattress. At the foot of the bed, fold the end under the mattress and make hospital corners. Leave the sides untucked to make it easier to get in and out of bed.

4. If you're using a blanket, add it to the bed after laying the top sheet. The top edge should be about 6 inches from the top of the mattress. Fold the top sheet over the top of the blanket. At the foot of the bed, fold the blanket under the mattress and make hospital corners, keeping the blanket and sheet together. Finish by draping with a comforter (encased in a cover) or a coverlet, and placing pillows at the head of the bed.

HOW TO MAKE HOSPITAL CORNERS

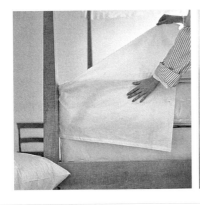  

1. Stand at the middle of one side and pull up the edge of the sheet or blanket a little more than a foot from the corner. Lift up the edge to make a diagonal fold, then lay the fold back onto the mattress.

2. Tuck the hanging edge under the mattress; with the other hand, drop the folded portion and pull it smooth.

3. You can then tuck the hanging portion of the sheet, or let it hang down.

THE GUEST ROOM

Providing overnight visitors with a clean, bright, welcoming place to stay is a pleasure for guests and host alike. The trick is to make guests feel at home, but also away. Guest quarters should be furnished sparsely, but the beds and linens should be as comfortable as those in every other bedroom. In addition, consider stocking your guest room with the following amenities:

ESSENTIALS FOR THE GUEST ROOM

- ☐ A list of helpful details about your home (including notes about where to find extra supplies and toiletries, and instructions for television and stereo equipment and other household systems)
- ☐ A carafe or bottle of water and water glasses
- ☐ Interesting fiction and nonfiction books
- ☐ A local newspaper
- ☐ A list of activities
- ☐ Telephone
- ☐ Alarm clock
- ☐ Bedside fan
- ☐ Flashlight
- ☐ Pad, pencil, and pens
- ☐ Blow-dryer
- ☐ Favorite soaps, shampoos, hand creams, and lotions

SOME OTHER THINGS TO BEAR IN MIND WHEN CONSIDERING GUEST ROOMS

- ☐ Rooms should be personal, attentive, and full of hospitable amenities.
- ☐ Make certain that the room isn't cramped or busy-looking. Space is soothing in an unfamiliar room.
- ☐ Have plenty of extra bedding, especially if you are between seasons. Include a light blanket and a heavy comforter in the closet or chest. Include a throw for afternoon naps.
- ☐ If the floors are wood or stone, place a small rug beside the bed for cold mornings.
- ☐ If there isn't an adjacent private bathroom, leave a set (or sets) of towels in the guest room.
- ☐ If the room has closet space, ensure that it is equipped with hangers and a full-length mirror on the back of the closet door. If not, install hooks on the back of a door.
- ☐ Have a night-light in the hallway en route to the bathroom.
- ☐ Provide adequate lighting, whether it's a bedside lamp or a table lamp with adjustable brightness.
- ☐ If you are going to include reading materials, try to tailor titles to your guests' interests.
- ☐ Include a wastebasket, and make sure that it is emptied before the guest arrives and soon after he or she departs.

I LOVE IT WHEN FRIENDS REMARK THAT THEIR
NIGHT IN ONE OF MY BEDS WAS
"THE MOST COMFORTABLE THEY EVER HAD."
A GUEST ROOM CAN BE SIMPLE OR
FANCY, BUT IT HAS TO BE COZY, CONVENIENT TO A
BATHROOM, AND HAVE A CLOCK, A READING LAMP,
AND, OF COURSE, A WELL-MADE BED.

THE GUEST ROOM AT LILY POND LANE

KEEP NURSERY
FURNISHINGS MINIMAL AT
THE OUTSET, THEN
ADD OR EXCHANGE ITEMS
AS YOUR BABY GROWS.

NURSERIES

Setting up a nursery involves addressing the needs of not one life but three—that of the baby and those of the parents. Keeping a child safe is the primary concern. Dream about decorating the nursery in pleasing colors and fabrics, but first create an environment in which your baby can safely grow and learn about his or her new world.

ORGANIZING PRINCIPLES

We've come a long way from Victorian times when nurseries were placed at a remove from parents so that the baby's nighttime crying wouldn't disturb them. Now, "accommodating parents" means ensuring their proximity to the baby and making Mom and Dad as comfortable as possible.

Newborns can sleep almost anywhere, but for a new parent to grab a good catnap, the nursery needs a small bed or sofa to fully stretch out on, if space permits. Even more vital is a plush armchair or cushioned rocker to lull a baby to sleep. Other useful additions are a lamp on a dimmer, shelves or baskets to hold children's books, a hamper, and a diaper pail.

You'll also need a changing table with shelves or drawers to stow diapers and other supplies (any wide dresser can be made into a changing table by adding a top with sides and a back lip plus a covered pad with a safety strap attached). A small armoire can hold baby's clothes and accessories. Store toys in woven baskets and painted bins.

HOW TO CHOOSE A CRIB

The crib is the only place where your baby is likely to spend time away from an adult's watchful gaze, so take special care to ensure that it offers little opportunity for accident or mischief.

When buying a new crib, look for plain, solid construction, and the Juvenile Products Manufacturers Association (JPMA) seal of approval. Remember, consider safety and functionality before appearance. All cribs should be examined thoroughly. Avoid using secondhand or antique cribs, which might not have the JPMA seal.

Make sure you heed the following guidelines:

☐ Choose a crib that is safe for a newborn as well as an active, ambulatory toddler.

☐ A crib should have tight joints that can't pinch and that prevent the crib from wobbling when the baby is active.

☐ A crib must have side rails that have at least two locking devices that latch securely and will not release by accident.

☐ The corner posts of the crib must be flush with the top of the headboard and footboard or at least 16 inches high. An acorn nut should cover threaded bolts. Loose parts can come free and make a crib wobbly or become a choking hazard. All parts should withstand 20 pounds of force.

☐ The top rails of crib sides, in their raised position, should be at least 26 inches above the mattress support at its lowest position, to make it a challenge for a growing baby to climb out. When checking this height at the store, test the side rail to see whether it can be easily raised and lowered with one hand. When lowered, the crib sides should be at least 9 inches above the mattress support to keep an infant from falling out.

☐ A teething rail is a piece of soft plastic that fits snugly over the top of the crib rail to protect your baby's gums and teeth if she chews on the rail. There should be a teething rail on all four sides of the crib. Avoid vinyl (also known as PVC) rails, which contain phthalate, a substance used in plastic to enhance its flexibility. The use of PVC in toys has been banned by some countries because studies have shown that phthalates can cause liver and kidney disease.

☐ The slats on the sides of the crib must be no more than $2\frac{3}{8}$ inches (about the width of a soda can) apart, to prevent the baby's head from fitting between them.

A NOTE ABOUT CRIB BUMPERS

Padded bumpers, sold as part of most standard crib bedding sets, were originally designed to help protect a baby's head, as well as to keep the baby's arms and legs from sticking through the crib's sides. Now that all new cribs sold in the United States have to meet strict safety regulation codes, including the regulation of slat width, bumper pads are no longer necessary. In recent years, many child-safety advocates, including the American Academy of Pediatrics and the Consumer Product Safety Commission, have recommended the removal of crib bumpers altogether. These groups maintain that crib bumpers pose suffocation risks greater than the risk of injury to the head or limbs on a bumperless crib. (Pillows, thick blankets, and soft toys pose similar suffocation risks, and should also be kept out of the crib whenever a baby is present.)

☐ Make sure mattress supports are properly secured—check by rattling the crib from side to side and thumping on the mattress to see if support dislodges. The mattress should be the same size as the crib, fitting securely on all sides (with no gaps to trap arms or legs). It must be kept at the lowest position once the child can stand.

☐ Inspect cribs for chipping paint, missing parts, wobbly hardware, splinters, cracked or broken slats, and sharp edges or points. Again, avoid second-hand or vintage cribs, which in addition to lacking the JPMA seal might also be covered in lead-based paint, especially if manufactured prior to 1976.

☐ Never place casters on a crib. Babies can rock and move the crib.

CRIB PLACEMENT

☐ Never place a crib—or any other baby furnishings—near windows or window blinds, for several reasons: Curtain fabric and window-blind cords can be a strangulation hazard; children can fall from windows; and full sunlight can cause overheating, even sunburns.

☐ Do not place a crib alongside framed pictures or heavy wall hangings.

☐ Keep lamps and cords away from baby furniture to discourage climbing and tugging.

☐ Keep cribs out of drafts and away from heat registers and radiators.

☐ The American Academy of Pediatrics recommends that all crib toys, including mobiles, be placed or installed well out of a baby's reach. The toy should be removed as soon as a baby can push up on his or her hands and knees or when the baby is five months old, whichever comes first.

THE CRIB MATTRESS

Innerspring mattresses tend to be firmer and wear better over time, but they can also be heavy. Foam mattresses are easier to lift for changing sheets, and usually cost less. If you choose foam, make sure it's dense and firm. If the mattress is too soft, it may conform to your baby's shape and become a suffocation risk. In all cases, the mattress must fit snugly—no more than 1 inch of space between the mattress and crib—so there's no risk of the baby getting caught between the two. It's essential to protect the mattress from moisture with a zippered plastic mattress pad or, as an alternative, a naturally water-resistant merino wool pad.

CHANGING TABLES

A changing table is a central station for almost all baby-care activities and supplies. It's the place where you diaper, dress, and sponge-bathe your baby, as well as administer medications and clip your baby's nails. Whatever the style, the table should be sturdy. Choose one that can accommodate those activities and all the supplies you'll need, and keep it well stocked. A standard changing table consists of a top surface with a railing and open shelving below. Others are designed with doors below the top surface, which are very helpful if you want to conceal the clutter of diapers and toiletries. A third style is really just a changer top that can be secured to a chest of drawers or table; once a baby is toilet trained, the top deck can be cleared so the changing table becomes a dresser.

Here are a few guidelines that can help you choose a safe and efficient changing table.

ATTACH A CURTAIN ON A SWIVEL ROD TO THE CHANGING TABLE SO YOU CAN EASILY CONCEAL DIAPERS AND OTHER NECESSITIES WHEN THE TABLE IS NOT IN USE.

☐ Ideally, a changing table should measure between 36 and 41 inches high, so you don't have to bend or reach unnecessarily. The guardrail should be at least 2 inches high.

☐ Changing tables made of wood are the least likely to sway or tip over.

☐ A cushioned pad and safety belt will help keep your baby from rolling off the changing table. (Although you shouldn't rely on the belt alone to hold your baby in place; never leave a baby unattended on the changing table.) If you buy a changing pad separately, choose one that's contoured, with high sides. It should also have hardware for fastening the pad to the table and a restraining belt. Keep a supply of soft pad covers, which will require frequent laundering.

☐ A changing table should have plenty of compartments for storing things so that you do not take your eyes off the baby. Choose open baskets or boxes, since you'll rarely have both hands free to open lids, and outfit them with easily laundered basket covers. Keep the clothes hamper and diaper pail nearby.

☐ Above the table, tilt a mirror at an angle to reflect down; babies are captivated by their own image, and their preoccupation will increase their patience (and Mom's and Dad's) for diaper changing.

CHANGING TABLE CHECKLIST

- ☐ Baby brush and comb set
- ☐ Burp cloths (cloth diapers are a good choice)
- ☐ Cotton balls and swabs (look for safety swabs, with larger ends that cannot be pushed too far into ears)

- ☐ Diaper-rash cream with zinc oxide
- ☐ Diaper ointment or petroleum jelly
- ☐ Diaper pail
- ☐ Cloth or disposable diapers
- ☐ Clothes hamper

- ☐ Infant nail clippers or scissors
- ☐ Receiving blankets
- ☐ Small toys
- ☐ Tweezers
- ☐ Washcloths and towels
- ☐ Baby wipes

STORAGE SOLUTIONS

With a few shelves and some additional hardware, you can organize all your baby's belongings in a small armoire:

☐ Hang a small cotton or linen bag on a hook on the inside of the armoire door to collect laundry.

☐ Install a pivoting pants rack on the inside of the door to hang lightweight baby blankets.

☐ Keep a clipboard suspended from hooks on the inside of the door, to note doctor's recommendations and your baby's feeding and sleeping schedule.

☐ Hang your baby's clothes according to size; add an extra hook on the inside of the door where you can hang an outfit while you're cleaning and diapering your baby.

☐ Store various items in small simple boxes. Include essential health and grooming items, such as a thermometer, an aspirator, baby analgesic, cotton balls, cotton swabs, a comb, a brush, nail scissors, emery boards, extra diaper-rash ointment, and calamine lotion together. Keep small items such as hats, shoes, booties, and socks in a separate box. Store snap-bottom tees in another box, and bibs and burp cloths in another.

☐ Keep a memorabilia box and a basket of crib sheets and pads on the top shelf of the armoire. Store heavier blankets on the bottom shelf.

☐ Line drawers with shelf paper and fill them with pajamas, folded outfits, and sweaters.

☐ Line the shelves with linen fabric or shelf paper held in place with double-sided tape, and use them to hold clothes in future sizes, extra bed linens, and hooded bath towels.

A WELL-EQUIPPED
ARMOIRE CAN TAKE THE
PLACE OF A DRESSER
AND CLOSET
IN A BABY'S ROOM

CRIB BEDDING

Your baby's bed should be safe and comfortable for him but also practical for you—after all, you'll be changing a lot of sheets in the coming months. The coordinated crib sets available in baby stores are not always the most sensible choice for newborns. Many include fluffy comforters to match the crib sheet and skirt, but since soft bedding is hazardous for babies under twelve months of age (according to the American Academy of Pediatrics and the U.S. Consumer Product Safety Commission), the comforter will be of little use early on. The chart on the following page contains the essentials.

BASIC COMPONENTS OF CRIB BEDDING

CRIB PAD
Lay a quilted, waterproof pad over the plastic mattress cover to make your baby more comfortable.

CRIB SKIRT (OPTIONAL)
Used only for a decorative effect, a crib skirt hangs beneath the mattress like a bed skirt, concealing the construction of the crib frame.

FITTED SHEET
Crib sheets should fit the mattress tightly and have no loose threads or worn elastic. A sheet that can be pulled loose from the mattress poses a tangling hazard for your baby; if after several washings the sheet no longer fits, replace it. Never use an adult sheet on a crib mattress; it can come loose and present an entanglement hazard to young children.

LAP PAD
Placed directly under the baby at bedtime, a waterproof pad can save on sheet changing. The pads are also wonderful for protecting the car seat, your lap, and other spots from accidents.

ZIPPERED PLASTIC MATTRESS COVER
Place it directly over the mattress to keep moisture out and extend the life of the mattress. Or use a water-resistant wool mattress pad.

The American Academy of Pediatrics recommends using a sleeper or other sleep clothing instead of a blanket. If you do use a thin (not thick) blanket, the baby should have her feet at the foot of the crib. The blanket should cover the feet and go no higher than the chest; tuck it securely under the mattress. Nothing should cover the baby's head. Keep in mind, too, that babies and young children do not require pillows to sleep comfortably; pillows can also pose a suffocation hazard.

ABOUT PORTABLE CRIBS AND PLAY YARDS

Since play yards (commonly referred to by brand names such as Pack 'n Play) are used not only for play but also for sleep, the same safe sleeping guidelines for cribs should be followed:

☐ Always put a baby down to sleep on his back with no soft bedding, such as quilts, comforters, and pillows.

☐ Use only the mattress provided by the manufacturer. Do not add additional mattresses in play yards. Children can suffocate in the spaces formed between mattresses or from ill-fitting mattresses.

☐ If using a secondhand unit, check to see that it is in good shape, doesn't have lead paint, and doesn't have any peeling paint. Using a modified or improperly repaired unit can create hazards.

☐ Make sure the top rails of the unit lock into place automatically.

☐ If using a mesh-sided playpen, make sure the mesh is less than $1/4$ inch in size and that it is attached securely.

HOW TO CARE FOR THE NURSERY

Many commercial household cleaners contain toxic ingredients that can be more harmful to babies than the dirt they eradicate. Thankfully, there are now many safer alternatives on the market, which are readily available at health food stores, organic markets, and sometimes even at the super-market. When shopping for safe, gentle cleaning products, keep in mind that label terms such as "nontoxic," "natural," and "biodegradable" don't mean much since the use of these terms is not regulated. Your safest bet is to choose products from manufacturers that make more specific claims— "nontoxic if inhaled or ingested," "plant-based," or "biodegradable in three to five days," for example—and disclose a full list of ingredients on the label. Look for products free of ammonia, chlorine, or fragrance, all of which can cause skin and respiratory irritation. You can, of course, also make your own cleaning products, which not only guarantees safety, but is also economical. Use baking soda to scour, mild dishwashing liquid and water as an all-purpose cleaner, and white vinegar and water on glass.

Regardless of what you use to clean the nursery, it is essential to label everything clearly and store it securely, out of reach in a locked cabi-net (even all-natural agents such as baking soda and vinegar are harmful to children if ingested). In case of accidental ingestion, contact your Poison Control Center.

Since dust mites—microscopic creatures that thrive on dust—can col-lect in floor coverings, always use machine-washable area rugs in the nursery and launder them regularly. Keep the floor clean and vacuum often to eliminate dust. Dust mites, which are second only to pollen in causing allergic reactions, are found in bedding, upholstered furnishings, carpeting, toys, and old clothing. Complete eradication is virtually impossible, but there are some steps you can take to reduce the number in the nursery:

☐ Wash bedding materials, including pillowcases, sheets, blankets, and mattress pads every week in hot water (130°F).

☐ Eliminate or reduce fabric wall hangings.

☐ Purchase stuffed toys that are machine-washable, and wash them regularly.

☐ If your child has allergies, regularly place soft toys in the freezer for twenty-four hours before you wash them, or wash them in hot water.

☐ Install dustable blinds instead of curtains or drapes.

☐ Minimize upholstered furniture and vacuum it weekly.

MINIMIZING HOUSEHOLD TOXINS

Solid-wood furniture can be a wise choice in the nursery. The most significant household sources of formaldehyde, which the Environmental Protection Agency considers a known carcinogen, are likely to be pressed-wood products made using adhesives that contain urea-formaldehyde (UF) resins. Materials containing formaldehyde can release formaldehyde gas or vapor into the air. The pressed-wood products that use UF include particleboard (used as subflooring and shelving and in cabinetry and furniture); hardwood ply-wood paneling (used for decorative wall covering and in cabinets and furni-ture); and medium-density fiberboard (used for drawer fronts, cabinets, and furniture tops), which contains a higher resin-to-wood concentration and emits more formaldehyde than any other UF pressed-wood product. You can reduce formaldehyde levels in your home by ensuring adequate ventilation, moderate temperatures, and lower humidity levels through the use of air conditioners and dehumidifiers.

Carpet adhesives, products made of vinyl, and paints can also contain volatile organic compounds (VOCs), which are substances that release gases and can cause health problems. Opt for area rugs instead of wall-to-wall carpeting in the nursery and use low-VOC paints, available from most paint retailers. (For more on chemical pollutants, turn to page 571.)

NURSERY FIRST-AID KIT

Medical supplies are best kept far from a baby's hands but within your reach. One solution is to mount a storage container on the wall above the changing table. A CD holder or similar small box makes a good receptacle: Paint it to match the nursery's walls, and add cup hooks along the face of it to temporarily hang any jewelry such as rings and watches that might scratch a baby's skin.

- ☐ An illustrated first aid manual, such as *The American Academy of Pediatrics Guide to Your Child's Symptoms*
- ☐ Adhesive tape and gauze pads
- ☐ Alcohol towelettes for cleaning the thermometer and the umbilical cord
- ☐ Antiseptic cream
- ☐ Baby acetaminophen or nonaspirin liquid pain reliever
- ☐ Calamine lotion for bug bites and rashes

- ☐ Child-safe insect repellent
- ☐ Child-safe sunscreen lotion
- ☐ Ear syringe
- ☐ Hydrogen peroxide for minor cuts
- ☐ Medicine spoons, medicine dropper, and/or oral syringe
- ☐ Nasal aspirator and nasal saline drops
- ☐ Rehydration fluid for diarrhea and vomiting
- ☐ Thermometer

NURSERY SAFETY GUIDELINES

DO

☐ Keep the nursery warm, but not *too* warm: The temperature in a baby's room should feel comfortable to an adult, and overdressing of the baby should be avoided.

☐ Install a smoke detector on each level of a house and one in each child's bedroom. You should also have a carbon monoxide detector on each level of the house with one near the sleeping area. (For more on detectors, turn to pages 573 and 653.)

☐ Install a UL-approved night-light that cannot be removed from the outlet except with a screwdriver.

☐ Place drawer stops on all dressers so a growing baby or toddler cannot pull out drawers herself. Ensure that cabinets and windows are equipped with safety locks as well.

☐ Store toys in a chest with a spring-loaded support system, which will support the lid in any position. Avoid using chests with latch lids, which can trap your child inside (it's important to choose a chest with ventilation holes in the event that this does occur), or free-falling lids, which can result in pinched fingers and bumped heads.

☐ Read warning labels to determine whether a toy is age-appropriate or if adult supervision is advised. Infant toys, such as rattles, squeeze toys, and teething rings, should be large enough so that they cannot enter and become lodged in an infant's throat. Check all toys periodically for breakage and potential hazards.

☐ Ensure that decorative cutouts on furnishings are smaller than the width of a baby's finger, and open holes should be too small to catch a child's finger; these spaces can otherwise get a baby caught and tangled.

☐ Keep poisonous and recently fertilized plants well out of reach.

DON'T

☐ Don't let anybody smoke near your baby. Secondhand smoke increases the risk of sudden infant death syndrome (SIDS) as well as colds and other diseases.

☐ Don't use floor lamps in a nursery; they can be knocked over easily. Table lamps should be placed on safe, sturdy surfaces out of reach of a baby's curious hands.

☐ Don't keep bulky toys in the crib or near windows; they can provide a climbing perch for mobile babies.

☐ Don't put your baby to sleep wearing a bib or with a stringed pacifier or propped-up bottle—these all pose choking and strangulation hazards.

KIDS' ROOMS

A child's room ought to be the happiest place in the house—not just for the child who plays there, but for parents as well. It should be safe, clean, well lit, organized, and enough of a blank slate to be adaptable to the child's changing tastes and needs. No seven-year-old wants to live with cute bunny wallpaper appropriate to a toddler. A child's room is always in flux, so the fewer elements that are fixed in the stage of infancy, the better.

Furnishings in a child's room depend on individual needs, but a child's room should have a dresser to store clothing; a child-size table and chairs for art projects, games, and writing; book storage (either shelves, a bench with cubbyholes, or a magazine-style rack); and, later, a desk, chair, and desk lamp for homework.

Make sure all components are within a child's reach. For example, the closet rod should not be too high; dresser drawers should be low and slide easily; light switches and blinds should be easy to operate. For ease of maintenance, the more washable the surfaces, the better. Walls should be painted with a scrubbable paint; all bedding should be machine-washable. Low-pile rugs are easier to clean; machine-washable ones are the most practical choice.

BEDS

When a child is more than three feet tall, the top of the crib rail comes up to the child's chest when standing, or she can climb out of the crib on her own, it's time to move her into a bed. This often happens when the child is between two and a half and three years old. When your child is ready to move to a bigger bed, it's up to you whether you choose a toddler bed (which takes a crib mattress) or a twin bed. For safety's sake, be sure the bed you choose is low to the floor with guardrails attached to the sides of the bed frame, which will help prevent your child from falling out of bed. Padding such as a soft, thick rug or several large pillows on the floor alongside the bed will also offer cushioning. To decrease the risk that your child will become trapped between the bed and the wall, place the headboard—rather than the side—against the wall. And, as with the crib, be sure to keep the bed far away from windows, heating units, dangling cords for drapery or blinds, and plugged-in appliances.

The more simple design the bed, the better. Ornamental beds with elaborate cutouts or protrusions can pose a hazard to your child. Check periodically that the joints of the bed are not loose. Avoid using vintage beds, especially if they may have been manufactured prior to 1976, because of the risks associated with lead-based paint and questionable construction.

ABOUT BUNK BED SAFETY

Although space-saving, bunk beds can also be dangerous for young children. Ensure that the following safety measures are met in order to minimize the danger of falls and other related injuries.

- ☐ There must be guardrails on all four sides of the bed.
- ☐ The spacing between the bed frame and the bottom of the guardrails should not be greater than 3½ inches.
- ☐ The mattress should be at least 5 inches below the top of the guardrail.

- ☐ The ladder must not only be firmly secured to the bed frame but also be the only means of entering and leaving the upper bunk.
- ☐ Never screw hooks or handles onto the bed (or hang things from it) that children can get caught on while playing or entering and leaving the bunk.

- ☐ Children under six (and those who sleepwalk) should not sleep in the top bunk.
- ☐ No more than one person should be in the top bunk at any given time.

HOW TO ORGANIZE TOYS

Teach children to put away their own toys by making it easy for them to use toy-storage containers. Make a set of easy-to-read picture labels for bins and boxes. Divide toys into logical categories, from toy cars to building blocks to dolls, and find an image that suits each. Affix the labels to the top and side of each container. Keep the well-labeled bins together, in a toy chest or an armoire.

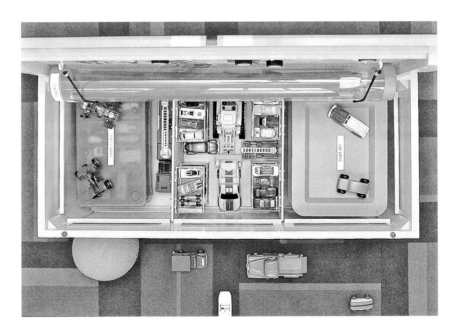

A BATHROOM AT SKYLANDS

BATHROOM

WHEN I WAS GROWING UP, our family of eight shared a single full bathroom, along with two half bathrooms and a powder room off the kitchen. The full bathroom was upstairs and had to be an efficient space, with all of us using it in staggered sequence every morning and night. Sometimes I would stay up late to enjoy a long bath, knowing that the hot water would replenish itself for the rest of the family by morning. Or I would get up early, to savor a few extra minutes of peace.

This is what even the most ordinary bathroom can do: create a sanctuary of privacy and relaxation. You can add all the extras you want, but to me, the amenities that are most easily attained matter more. I like a sink with faucets (mixed hot and cold water—never separate) that never drip, an excellent showerhead with variable settings, a handheld spray shower, fresh towels every day, hooks for hanging robes, flattering lighting over the sink, and ample storage space for toiletries, a hair dryer, brushes, and sundries.

In terms of color, I lean toward white or light for all bathrooms—it feels and looks clean, fresh, and relaxing. Designwise, I am partial to white Italian marble, white subway tiles, and vintage pedestal sinks and fixtures. I also bring the furnishings from other rooms into the bathroom. A chair or bench is always useful; a nightstand with a drawer

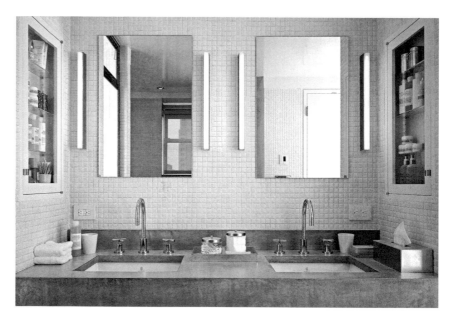

ORGANIZE SMALL ITEMS
IN MATCHING
CONTAINERS TO KEEP
THE MEDICINE CABINET
FREE OF CLUTTER.

and shelf can add more storage. Experiment and see what you can find that will both fit and function well while also adding a touch of warmth and convenience and comfort.

I love to have a neat pile of fluffy, folded bath towels by the tub or shower. Just remember that towels stacked and stored in the bathroom might absorb moisture, and the ones on the bottom may have lost their freshness by the time they come into use (so it's a wise idea to rotate the towels in the stack every few days). Along these lines, good ventilation is an "invisible" but essential feature that makes a bathroom a much more pleasant place; air must be able to circulate so moisture can dissipate, and the more air you can infuse into a bathroom, the better. An exhaust fan as well as good heat and air-conditioning is very important, and a window that opens is essential.

As in the rest of the house, upkeep in the bathroom means day-to-day maintenance as well as weekly cleanings. It's crucial that, for reasons of hygiene and comfort, you stay on top of the schedule in this room. And if you clean regularly, you can use gentler cleaning agents (procrastinate, and you may need harsher products to remove soap scum or mineral deposits). Those gentler cleaners will help your fine fixtures and tiles and tubs last longer—so your bathroom will always be pretty and inviting.

Even the most ordinary bathroom can be turned into a sanctuary of privacy and peacefulness.

LAYOUT BASICS

Baths are second only to kitchens in popularity when it comes to remodeling. Before planning the layout of a bathroom, it's important to remember that certain codes determine the bare minimum space requirements. These regulations will make your bath legal, but not necessarily comfortable. For that reason, many design professionals also heed the more comfort-friendly recommendations of the National Kitchen and Bath Association. Keep the guidelines below in mind should you decide to tackle a bath remodel.

☐ Leave at least 21 inches of clear floor space in front of all fixtures (the toilet, bathtub or shower, and sink), measuring from the front edge; 30 inches is ideal.

☐ Sink height can range between 32 and 43 inches from the floor, depending on the height of the user.

☐ A bathroom with two sinks should allow at least 30 inches between the center line of each, although 36 inches is even more comfortable.

☐ The minimum dimensions for a shower are 30 inches by 30 inches, or 900 square inches, but a comfortable shower with ample elbow room should be at least 400 square inches bigger than that.

☐ Locate the shower controls so they are accessible from both the outside and the inside of the spray zone (so you can adjust them before you step into the shower and while you are showering). Bathtub controls should be similarly accessible and should be located between the rim of the tub and 30 inches from the floor.

☐ If you're planning to install a shower seat, it should not infringe on the minimum interior size of 30 inches by 30 inches. A comfortable height for the seat would be 17 to 19 inches off the floor.

☐ Shower doors should open outward.

☐ The center line of the toilet (or bidet) should be at least 15 inches from the wall or other fixtures, although 18 inches creates a more comfortable perimeter around the toilet. If you're going to place the toilet in a separate room (either inside your bathroom, or adjoining it, European-style), the room must be at least 30 inches by 60 inches, but 36 inches by 66 inches is ideal.

☐ The toilet paper holder should be 8 to 12 inches from the edge of the toilet bowl, and about 26 inches from the floor.

☐ Consider not only an overhead light fixture for overall illumination, but task lighting above the shower, sink, and any other grooming area.

ORGANIZING

The bathroom is, first and foremost, a practical place. Daily rituals here are often rushed, making order essential. Fortunately, these small spaces are among the easiest in the house to tame. If you follow a few simple guidelines, even awkward spaces can function flawlessly.

GOLDEN RULES OF BATHROOM ORGANIZING

☐ Group like things together—store all cosmetics in a washable cosmetics bag or plastic bin (subdivide cosmetics into categories if you have lots), all skin-care products on the same shelf in your medicine cabinet, all shampoos in one spot under the sink.

☐ Get rid of things regularly. Cosmetics have a finite shelf life, as do skin-care products (for specifics, turn to page 313) and medications. Every year, take an inventory, and throw out those items that are expired, you no longer use, or are damaged. There is some concern that flushing expired medications down the toilet can adversely affect the water supply. Instead, ask if your pharmacy has a drug take-back program. If not, throw medicines into the trash; secure them in a garbage bag and make sure it is out of the reach of children or animals who might get into trash bins.

☐ Keep small items in containers. Hair accessories, bottles of nail polish, brushes and combs will all be easily accessible in see-through plastic bins, with neat, easy-to-read labels.

CLEANING SUPPLIES

Cleaning a bathroom well does not mean cleaning a bathroom with harsh chemicals. Many bathroom cleaners contain ammonia, chlorine bleach, or hydrochloric acid, all of which, over time, can damage sinks and faucets, creating tiny pockets of corrosion that ruin finishes and provide perfect hiding places for bacteria and fungi. It's wise to always start with the gentlest cleaning solutions first, such as a pH-neutral all-purpose cleaner like Ivory Liquid or a mildly abrasive cleanser, such as Bon Ami, before moving on to anything stronger.

Bear in mind that it is impossible to completely disinfect a bathroom. Bacteria are some of the most rapidly evolving organisms on earth and are resistant to many commercial antibacterial products. However, regular, gentle cleaning with mildly abrasive cleansers will keep a bathroom clean, fight bacteria, and also preserve bathroom fixtures (especially faucets, doorknobs, and flush handles) for years. Adequate ventilation, too, in the form of a ceiling fan or an open window, will help prevent moisture from building up, which will go a long way toward keeping the room fresh.

BATHROOM CLEANING KIT

Gather the following supplies in a caddy or plastic bin and keep it under the bathroom sink or in a nearby cabinet for easy access:

- ☐ Rubber gloves
- ☐ Paper towels and soft, clean cloths (these cloths should be dedicated to the bath and not used in other rooms in the house)

- ☐ Soft toothbrush
- ☐ Plastic-bristled scrub brush
- ☐ Mild dishwashing liquid
- ☐ Mildly abrasive cleanser, such as Bon Ami
- ☐ All-purpose household cleaner

- ☐ Window/glass cleaner
- ☐ Acidic cleaner, such as white vinegar or Lime-Away, to remove mineral deposits
- ☐ Baking soda to clean drains
- ☐ Toilet brush

STORAGE

Storage in the bath can consist of a medicine cabinet above the sink, a vanity, built-in shelves or drawers, or even freestanding pieces of furniture, such as armoires or chests of drawers, if space allows.

If you're short on storage, look around the bathroom for unused space. You may be able to install shelving over a window, or even over the bathroom door. Small, stacked storage cubes or attractive baskets or bins can fit into a corner or against a wall, and are ideal for stashing extra towels, a hair dryer, and cosmetics. Home centers sell shelving units specially designed to fit around and over the toilet, space that is rarely occupied otherwise. If you have any extra room on the countertop, a few metal, plastic, or ceramic containers can hold cotton balls, swabs, and any other items you like to keep handy.

MEDICINE CABINETS

Space in a medicine cabinet is often limited, so reserve it for things you use every day, such as cosmetics, dental-care products, and hair-grooming products. Medicine, however, should never be stored in the bathroom. The buildup of heat and humidity can cause medicine to lose its potency and perish before the expiration date. Instead, store all medicine in a cool, dry spot and out of the reach of children since most medicine-bottle caps are child-resistant but not childproof.

Organize items by height, and adjust shelves accordingly: tall items all on one shelf, shorter items on another. Place everyday objects at eye level. You can also organize items according to their function, grouping hair products together, for example, or corral small items in ceramic cups.

KEEP ONLY ESSENTIAL TOILETRIES—NOT MEDICATIONS—IN THE MEDICINE CABINET.

If you buy economy-size bottles of body lotion and other toiletries, transfer some to small containers to keep in the bathroom, and store the remainder in a cool place. This will not only get the large bottles out of your way, but will extend the life of the products, as heat and humidity can cause them to break down quickly.

Once a month, remove the contents of the medicine cabinet and wipe out the inside with a cloth dampened with mild dishwashing liquid and warm water. Rinse with a clean cloth and dry thoroughly.

Wipe the mirror weekly with a clean, lint-free cloth (an old T-shirt is ideal) dampened with glass cleaner. Streaks occur when even the merest trace of cleaning product dries on the glass, so be sure to wipe away all of it. Do not let the cleaning product come in contact with the frame or the mirror's edges. This could damage the frame, or moisture could seep behind the mirror, creating black spots or dulling the reflective coating.

COSMETICS AND BEAUTY AIDS

Since cosmetics are high in water content, they provide an ample breeding ground for microorganisms. Eye makeup and brushes that come into direct contact with the eyes are easily contaminated with bacteria, while items containing oil become rancid if exposed to air too often. Cosmetics manufacturers are not required by law to print expiration dates on their products, and there are no hard-and-fast rules to tell if cosmetics have expired. Label each product with the date of purchase or receipt, and discard any cosmetic product if the color or odor changes or if it begins to separate and becomes difficult to apply. Clear out any old and underused products at least once a year. Wash brushes and sponges with mild dishwashing liquid and water about once a month and let dry.

To keep products as fresh as possible, follow these guidelines:

☐ Wash your hands and face before applying makeup.

☐ Keep cosmetics tightly sealed when not in use.

☐ Keep cosmetics out of direct sunlight and away from heat sources (light and heat can degrade preservatives). Storing them at room temperature is ideal.

☐ Don't add water or saliva to a cosmetic to bring it back to its original consistency. Doing so can introduce bacteria.

☐ Don't store cosmetics in the refrigerator, or in your car.

☐ Don't share products.

☐ Discard products as soon as you notice any signs of discoloration, separation, or unpleasant odors.

A NOTE ABOUT MAKEUP TOWELS

Lipstick and mascara can ruin washcloths in short order. Rather than using white or light-colored ones to remove makeup, use dark ones. Have them embroidered with the word *makeup* so their intended purpose is clear to family members and guests alike.

HOW LONG TO KEEP COSMETICS AND BEAUTY AIDS

SKIN-CARE PRODUCTS

Moisturizer
6 to 12 months

Toner
6 to 12 months

Cleanser
6 to 12 months

Choose tubes or pumps (as opposed to jars), which help prevent contamination from microorganisms on fingers.

Exfoliants
6 to 12 months

Oil-based scrubs (like many of the sea-salt ones) last longer than water-based formulas.

Eye cream
6 to 12 months

Look for tubes instead of jars.

Sunscreen
2 years

If it separates or doesn't spread well, replace it. At the beach, keep it covered in a tote bag, out of direct sunlight.

Self-tanner
3 to 6 months

Don't stock up. The self-tanning ingredient dihydroxyacetone oxidizes within a few months, turns brown, and can take on an unpleasant odor.

MAKEUP

Foundation and concealer
6 months

Use sponges or brushes (not fingers) when applying so that you do not contaminate it with microorganisms from your skin.

Eye and lip pencils
3 to 6 months for eyes;
6 to 12 for lips

Sharpen the pencil before each use to clean the tip.

Lipstick
2 to 3 years

If lipstick beads, it means that oils are escaping from the formula, not that it is rancid.

Mascara
3 to 6 months

To prevent contamination, never put down the wand on a counter or tabletop.

Powders (face, blush, or eye)
3 to 6 months for eyeshadow;
6 to 12 for others

Wash applicators monthly; dry before storing.

Applicators (brushes and sponges)
3 to 6 months or longer

Wash sponges used for liquid makeup with soap and water; dry before storing. Replace those used with powders every few months. Cleaned regularly, brushes can last for years; use mild dishwashing liquid and a little water (do not immerse the whole brush, however, to prevent the metal from coming into contact with water).

HAIR PRODUCTS

Shampoo and conditioner
6 to 12 months

Store away from the showerhead so water doesn't get in. If smell or appearance changes, throw out the product. Wipe spills from containers and around them, to prevent buildup.

Styling products
1 year or more

High-alcohol (20 percent or more) gels and other products can last many years.

OTHER PRODUCTS

Lip balm
1 to 2 years

Nail polish
1 year

Don't add remover to bottle to thin polish.

Fragrance
3 years or longer

Store in the refrigerator; if possible, reduce the headspace in a bottle to preserve scent (that is, if you've used half, pour what remains into a smaller glass bottle).

BATHTUBS

Settling in for a good soak is one of life's pleasures. It can be a luxurious start to a leisurely day or a fitting reward at the end of a long week. Tubs come in a variety of shapes, sizes, and materials and run the gamut from utilitarian to glamorous. Understanding the common styles of bathtub—there are three basic types—is useful when shopping for a new one. Similarly, familiarizing yourself with the materials tubs are most often made of can help you make a choice that is suitable for both your budget and lifestyle. It can also help you correctly care for the tubs you already have.

TYPES OF BATHTUBS

SHOWER-BATHTUB COMBINATIONS

The most common type of bathtub is combined with a shower. It is also usually the most shallow of bathtub styles. Shower-bathtub combinations are surrounded by three walls. The walls can be covered in tile or stone or can be integral with the tub. Prefabricated shower-tubs come as one-piece units or in four pieces (the tub plus three walls) and are generally made of acrylic over fiberglass. A standard shower-tub combination generally measures 30 inches by 60 inches. Faucets are usually wall mounted, with the waste and overflow drains mounted in the tub.

Pros Inexpensive; shallow depth makes them easy to get in and out of (a plus for elderly or disabled homeowners).

Cons One-piece units won't fit through narrow bathroom doorways (check the size of your doorway first, or choose a four-piece unit if in doubt); colored acrylic tub/showers can fade after about fifteen years.

DECK-MOUNT

Also known as a drop-in or alcove tub, a deck-mount bathtub is built—or dropped—into its own deck or frame, just as a sink can be placed into a countertop. Decks are custom-built on-site. These deep, comfortable tubs are more luxurious than shower-tub combinations, and are often set against one wall or in an alcove. They are not typically sold with waterproof walls since the shower is generally in a separate stall. The faucets are integrated into the side of the tub. Deck-mount tubs can be found in nearly every shape and size, from oval to square to rectangular; some are even made for two people to soak in.

Pros Deep; luxurious; deck provides a convenient perch for bath accoutrements.

Cons Depth makes them more difficult to climb into and out of, so they are not a good choice for elderly or disabled homeowners; can't usually accommodate a shower; installation is expensive because of the carpentry required to create the deck.

FREESTANDING

The oldest style of bathtub is freestanding, often with a sloped back for comfortable lounging. A freestanding tub may sit on classic claw feet, on a pedestal, or on legs. This type of tub is usually between 4 and 6 feet long, and made of acrylic or porcelain enamel on cast iron or steel. Traditional claw-foot types are either American-style, with holes drilled into the tub for the faucet, or European-style, designed with a hole for the overflow and drain, but no faucet drilling. Faucets are installed in the floor or mounted on the wall, which allows for deep filling.

Pros Plumbing is exposed in floor installations, making for easy maintenance; vintage look; simple to install, doesn't require extra carpentry.

Cons Unless it is installed far from walls, it can be hard to clean the floor underneath the tub; spillover can be a problem, since the bath is not surrounded by a rim or deck; water cools off quickly because there are no surrounding walls to provide insulation (you may need to warm up the room before bathing to minimize this problem).

BATHTUB MATERIALS

ACRYLIC

Acrylic tubs are an inexpensive option. They are made from acrylic sheets that are shaped by a vacuum process and bonded to a fiberglass backing. Acrylic is resistant to cracking, chipping, peeling, fading, and staining.

Pros Nonporous and stain-resistant; available in many colors; scratches can be repaired by sanding the surface and applying a liquid polish designed for acrylic and fiberglass surfaces (available at home centers). To find a reglazer, look up "Bathtubs—Refinishing" in the Yellow Pages.

Cons Scratches easily; lacks a natural appearance; can be more expensive than fiberglass, which it resembles. Colors may fade over time (after about fifteen years).

FIBERGLASS

Affordable, lightweight, and easy to install. Fiberglass tubs are made of molded plastic, with an eggshell-thin layer of pigmented polyester resin (called gel-coat) on the surface and layers of fiberglass added to the back of the gel-coat; you will hear a hollow thud if you thump them. Scratches can be repaired by a professional (check the Yellow Pages under "Fiberglass—Repair").

Pros The most affordable tub choice; comes in a wide variety of colors; nonporous and stain-resistant.

Cons Scratches more easily than acrylic; colored tubs/showers may fade over time.

PORCELAIN ENAMEL

The so-called porcelain coating over a cast-iron or steel bathtub is actually a composition of sand, lime, and sodium bicarbonate fused to the metal shell with repeated firings. These classic, durable, and expensive tubs retain heat the longest but even with the best of care will eventually need reglazing (turn to page 318 for more information). The price can vary depending on the color and gauge (or thickness) of the steel or cast iron underneath—white is usually the least expensive.

Pros Comes in a variety of colors; durable; retains heat.

Cons Is very heavy (more so than any other material) and needs to be well supported.

GRANITE AND SLATE

Both are types of siliceous stone used in custom installations. Granite is made from an extremely hard volcanic rock. Its beauty lies in the quartz, mica, and feldspar crystals that lend it sparkle. There are two types: consistent, which has the same pattern throughout, and variegated, which has veins. Slate comes in deep greens, blues, grays, and purples, and has a matte surface and a distinctive cleft pattern.

Pros Available in a wide variety of colors, grains, finishes, and textures.

Cons Expensive; need to be sealed.

Special considerations Heavy soap scum can be cleaned with a commercial descaling product formulated specifically for stone. Never use products containing hydrofluoric acid—an ingredient in many heavy-duty rust removers—as it can take the gloss off polished granite.

MARBLE AND LIMESTONE

Both are calcareous stones used in custom installations. Marble and limestone are softer and more porous than granite or slate. Their permeability makes them susceptible to scratches, chips, and stains.

Pros Available in a wide variety of colors, grains, finishes, and textures.

Cons More expensive than other materials; marble and limestone are more susceptible to stains and scratches than granite.

Special considerations Heavy soap scum can be cleaned with a commercial descaling product formulated specifically for stone. Never use anything acidic, such as vinegar or orange- or lemon-based cleaners or products containing hydrofluoric acid, as these products will etch the stone.

WHIRLPOOL BATHTUBS

Whirlpool tubs, which are now a standard feature in many newly built houses, are identified with high-end luxury and add to the resale value of a home. These tubs, sometimes mistakenly called Jacuzzis (which is the name of a whirlpool manufacturer), are generally made of acrylic with fiberglass backing, and are equipped with jets that create a bubbling or massaging sensation. Whirlpools are often larger than regular bathtubs, but they are also available in the standard 30-inch-by-60-inch size to fit into typical tub recesses. Whirlpools are generally mounted in a deck, which conceals the mechanical systems. There is usually a removable panel in the deck that allows access to the pump should the unit require repair.

There are two types of whirlpools: air jet and water jet. Air-jet whirlpool tubs have dozens of small holes that shoot air into the tub, creating a gentle, all-over bubbling sensation. A water-jet whirlpool sucks in water from the tub, then shoots it back out through the jets, creating a more vigorous massaging action than the air-jet variety. For this reason, water-jet whirlpools are generally not recommended for young children or people with certain medical conditions.

Most manufacturers of both air- and water-jet whirlpools do not recommend using any sort of bath products (bubble baths, oils, salts) because these materials can promote mold and bacteria if they are not drained completely from the pipes feeding into the tub. Manufacturers also recommend cleaning with a mildly abrasive cleanser.

HOW TO CLEAN BATHTUBS

Even the most durable bathtubs can chip, crack, and dull. Most people tackle cleaning the tub with harsh scouring powder, which is too abrasive to use regularly, and will actually wear away or etch the finish you are trying to clean and protect. Cleansers often contain chlorine bleach, ammonia, or hydrochloric acid, which may corrode finishes and give bacteria a foothold in pitted surfaces. Daily maintenance and gentle weekly cleaning are sufficient to eradicate soap scum.

DAILY MAINTENANCE

After each use, wipe the tub and faucets dry with an inexpensive terry-cloth towel to help remove soap scum and keep mineral deposits from forming. This will save you hours of cleaning time later on. The tub surround—be it acrylic, tile, or stone—will also benefit from a daily wipe-down. Rinse walls with a handheld showerhead (no cleaner is necessary), then run a squeegee or a dry towel over the surface. This will take just a few minutes and will make weekly and monthly maintenance much easier.

WEEKLY MAINTENANCE

Once a week, or more frequently if there are multiple family members using the tub, clean the tub thoroughly with warm water, a mildly abrasive, chlorine-free cleanser, such as Bon Ami, and a cloth or sponge. Never use steel wool, stiff brushes, or strongly abrasive pads, which can damage all tub surfaces. Bathtub rings are usually the result of using oily bath products, which can also make your bathtub quite slippery. Be sure to clean the tub with warm water and a mildly abrasive cleanser every time you use such products. Mildew may call for a mix of 10 parts water to 1 part bleach.

Be sure to scrub the tub strainer during your weekly cleaning routine (clean hair out of the strainer daily), along with rubber drain stoppers. Use a plastic-bristled brush or soft toothbrush and mild dishwashing liquid; these accessories are magnets for mold and mildew.

MONTHLY MAINTENANCE

If you wipe dry the walls surrounding the tub every day, you shouldn't ever be troubled with mildew and will need to scrub them monthly or even less frequently, depending on how many people use the bath. Clean them with warm water, a mildly abrasive cleanser, such as Bon Ami, and a soft brush.

Tile, which lines many tub enclosures, and particularly grout tend to get dirty quickly, because grout is porous and absorbs oils from shampoos, conditioners, and soaps, which can lead to mildew growth. If you remove the mildew before it goes deeper than the grout's surface, the tile won't acquire that grayish tinge that is difficult to scour off. The quick wipe-down described opposite in Daily Maintenance is key. When tile and grout need a more thorough cleaning, scrub with a soft-bristled brush and pH-neutral cleaner (check the label for this designation, which many popular cleaners have); it won't leave a film and is safe for grout, which is easily damaged. If mildew has already built up, use a soft-bristled brush and a cleaner formulated for tile and grout (available at home-supply stores) or a mix of 10 parts water to 1 part bleach. Follow up with a pH-neutral cleaner to remove all the tile cleaner or bleach solution (if the residue mixes with ammonia or an acid such as vinegar, toxic fumes can result). Depending on how dirty the tiles are, you may have to use a fair amount of elbow grease.

Every month or two, give the pipes a good preventive cleaning to keep them clear of grease, oil, and hair clogs. Pour $1/2$ cup baking soda down the drain, followed by $1/2$ cup of white vinegar. The mixture will foam up (let it stand for a couple of minutes to dissolve fatty acids), then pour boiling water down the drain to wash out any clogs. This will not work for tough backups, however, which require a commercial drain cleaner. (Never use drain cleaner immediately after using vinegar; toxic fumes can form.)

HOW TO CLEAN
BATH TOYS

Although tub toys take a
bath every day, that
doesn't necessarily mean
they stay clean. Bacteria
and mildew build up
on them over time. Clean
them once a month: Fill
a bucket or large bowl
with warm water, and
add ½ cup white vinegar
per gallon of water. Soak
toys in the solution
for about ten minutes,
then rub them gently with
a sponge, and let them
dry. Not only is vinegar
inexpensive, unlike
many detergents, but it
is also mostly made up
of acetic acid, which cuts
through dirt buildup
and works as a natural
disinfectant.

HOW TO REMOVE SOAP SCUM

Occasionally, a hazy or crusty film may form on the surface of the tub (as
well as the sink, shower doors, and faucets). The key to removing this layer
of residue—which is formed when calcium and other minerals in hard
water combine with soap—is to use an acidic cleaner. The pH scale measures
acidity or alkalinity on a scale of 1 to 14, with 7 being neutral. Levels above
7 are more alkaline, while levels below 7 are more acidic. Most household
cleaners are slightly alkaline because alkaline solutions cut through grease,
oil, fats, proteins, and other common household soils, but are not particularly effective on soap scum.

White vinegar or a commercial descaling product that contains phosphoric acid, such as Lime-Away (available at hardware and grocery stores),
will cut through this stubborn residue. Always wear rubber gloves when
working with acidic cleansers and rinse completely afterward; acids—
including a vinegar and water solution—left on for too long can damage
the tub surface (particularly porcelain surfaces). They will also corrode
fittings (the industry term for faucets), and etch the glaze on tile. Use
acidic products sparingly, and never use them on marble or limestone.
(Turn to page 314 for instructions on how to remove soap scum from stone.)

HOW TO REMOVE TOUGH STAINS

Iron in water causes rust stains, and the sooner you clean them away, the
better. A heavy-duty cleaner containing phosphoric acid will usually work
on fresh stains (never use products containing phosphoric acid on marble or
limestone, and never use strong rust removers containing hydrofluoric
acid on any natural stone). Apply the cleaner with a damp cloth, rubbing
the surface until the stain fades. Rinse thoroughly and wipe dry with a
soft, clean cloth. Never use chlorine bleach, which will set the stain. For
older stains, try Naval Jelly (a rust inhibitor sold at hardware stores) or
a poultice treatment (for more on poultice treatments, turn to page 55).

Green or blue stains in the tub are usually caused by residue from
cleansers that are not rinsed thoroughly after use. If the surface of the tub
is worn, the dyes used in the cleansers can easily get into the crevices. Chlorine bleach may help lighten a stain, but it can also further dull and discolor the surface, so test first in an inconspicuous spot, and use sparingly.

REGLAZING PORCELAIN BATHTUBS

Porcelain-coated cast-iron tubs came into widespread use in America at the
end of the nineteenth century, and are prized today for their simple style,
generous size, and old-fashioned charm. Cast iron is an alloy, or mix, of
iron, carbon, and other materials that is heated into a liquid state in a blast

furnace, then cast into molds. It is made into cookware and plumbing fixtures, including sinks and bathtubs, because of its ability to withstand and conduct heat without warping.

The smooth coating of a porcelain tub, which is a composition of sand, lime, and sodium bicarbonate fused to the cast-iron shell beneath it with repeated firings, protects the metal from rust and enhances a tub's beauty and comfort. This surface can last as long as five decades, but eventually it will deteriorate, especially if it's mistreated or regularly scrubbed with harsh cleansers. When an enamel surface is porous, stained, or chipped, it needs to be reglazed, which costs less than replacing a tub.

In this process, the tub is thoroughly cleaned to remove any dirt or loose materials; deep nicks and scratches are filled in with fiberglass putty and sanded; then the tub is sprayed with synthetic porcelain. Finally, it is power- and hand-buffed until it is smooth and gleaming.

With proper care, a refinished porcelain tub should last up to fifteen years. Reglazed tubs should be cleaned with mild dishwashing liquid; for tougher stains, use a mildly abrasive cleanser and rinse thoroughly. And be sure to turn off faucets completely and fix leaks promptly, to avoid drips that will burrow into the porcelain. To find a reglazer, look in the Yellow Pages under "Bathtubs—Refinishing."

HOW TO REPLACE CAULK

Caulk is a flexible, waterproof substance used to seal the seams between different materials, such as a bathtub and a tile wall. If the existing caulk in your bathroom is cracked or damaged, replace it immediately. Not only is it unsightly, but water can seep into walls and cause significant damage, and open gaps can be a breeding ground for dirt and bacteria.

Begin by removing any old caulking. Cut it out carefully using a utility knife. Wipe the joints clean before beginning to recaulk. Run fine steel wool lightly through the cleaned-up joints, then wipe the tiles and joints thoroughly with a damp cloth.

A water-based caulk is easiest to clean up. If you don't own a caulking gun, you can buy caulk in a small, squeezable tube. Nip a small bit off the nozzle of the tube at an angle, point it into the joint, and then squeeze a line of caulk from one end of the joint to the other. Wet your finger or the back of a plastic spoon and, starting at the first end, pack and shape the joint. Clean up excess caulk carefully with a wet cloth, or wait for the caulk to dry and trim it with a razor blade. When caulking around a bathtub, be aware that the joint expands when the tub is full of water. To seal the joint when it's at its widest, fill the tub with warm water and kneel in it as you caulk.

A PLASTIC SPOON IS AN EFFECTIVE TOOL FOR SMOOTHING A FRESH LINE OF CAULK.

SHOWERS

Although soaking in the tub is sublime, most people prefer the in-and-out convenience of the shower. Whether combined with the tub or installed in a separate stall, the shower, like the bathtub, is easy to keep sparkling if you spend just a minute or two each day maintaining it.

HOW TO CLEAN SHOWERS

As with the tub, the best care is preventive. Daily maintenance followed by a gentle weekly cleaning will prevent soap scum and damaging mineral deposits from building up, and deter the growth of mold and mildew.

DAILY MAINTENANCE

As with bathtubs, wipe down the walls and floor of the shower with a squeegee or dry towel. Wipe from top to bottom, including the shower door. If stubborn water spots are a problem, you may have very hard water (which also leaves behind accumulations of minerals in appliances, pipes, and faucets, and reduces the effectiveness of detergents). The best way to combat hard water is to install a water conditioner or softener. (For more on water systems, turn to page 592.)

WEEKLY MAINTENANCE

Clean the floor of the shower with warm water and a mildly abrasive cleanser, such as Bon Ami.

Wipe down glass shower doors and enclosures with a glass cleaner and a soft cloth. If your shower doors are coated with a hazy film of soap scum, wipe them with a cloth dampened with white vinegar and rinse thoroughly. Be sure to clean the shower door track as well with a soft toothbrush and mild dishwashing liquid.

Wipe metal frames around doors and enclosures with a cloth dampened with diluted dishwashing liquid. Rinse, and then buff the surface dry with a dry towel. Avoid using ammonia or chlorine bleach, or products that contain these ingredients, which can damage the finish.

MONTHLY MAINTENANCE

Clean the walls the same way you clean the floor each week: with warm water and a mildly abrasive cleanser. Tiled walls, whether ceramic or stone, may require more frequent cleaning because grout, which is porous, is susceptible to mold and mildew. Scrub with a soft-bristled utility brush and a mildly abrasive cleanser or mild dishwashing liquid. If mildew is heavy, use a utility brush and a cleaner specifically formulated for tile and grout (available at home-supply stores) or a mix of 10 parts water to 1 part chlorine bleach.

A NOTE ABOUT STEAM SHOWERS

A steam shower is a conventional shower with an additional steam head located toward the bottom of the shower. The steam creates the feel of a wet sauna. A steam generator, often installed under the bathroom sink, or in a closet or in the wall near the shower, produces the steam that is piped to the steam head. For this type of shower, all surfaces must be impermeable, usually covered in tile. The ceiling should also be sloped, to guide condensation to the wall, and the shower door should enclose the space completely to prevent the steam from escaping. Keep the steam head clear of mineral deposits by wiping it daily; clear clogs with an acidic cleaner such as white vinegar or a descaling product, such as Lime-Away. Never hang anything from the steam head (which would obstruct its operation and possibly damage it).

HOW TO CLEAN SHOWER CURTAINS

Shower curtains are usually in two parts: the outer, decorative curtain, which is not meant to get wet, and the water-repellent liner.

Liners are usually made of vinyl or a lightweight woven synthetic, such as nylon. Cotton canvas and hemp liners are natural alternatives, but they take longer to dry (making them a poor choice for humid climates).

Keeping the liner clean and dry is essential; otherwise mold and mildew will grow in short order. Allow the liner to air dry after each use by shaking off as much water as possible and pulling it closed so moisture can't collect in the folds. Generally speaking, vinyl, synthetic, cotton, and hemp liners can be laundered in the washing machine with hot water and a mild laundry detergent, such as Ivory Snow. Remove the liner from the washer promptly, shake, and rehang (do not put liners in the dryer).

If the care label on your liner does not recommend machine washing (or there is no care label), wash the liner by hand. Take it outside and scrub it down with a solution of 10 parts water to 1 part chlorine bleach and a plastic-bristled scrub brush. Let it sit until any mold or discoloration has faded, then rinse. Shake well and rehang.

Clean the outer, or decorative, curtain according to instructions on the care label every couple of months.

TYPES OF SHOWER AND TUB FAUCETS

TUB-SHOWER COMBINATIONS

Tub-shower combinations are most commonly fitted with a showerhead, hot and cold handles (mounted separately or combined into a single lever), and a tub spout with a diverter, which is a small knob that diverts the water from the spout to the showerhead. Some have a third handle, instead of a diverter on the tub spout, to direct water to either spout or showerhead.

A pressure-balancing tub and shower faucet compensates for fluctuations in temperature (meaning no hot or cold shocks when someone turns on the tap at the sink or flushes the toilet). This feature generally keeps water within a couple of degrees of the original temperature.

SHOWERS Separate showers are generally fitted with a showerhead and hot and cold handles, either mounted separately or combined into a single lever.

TUBS Separate tubs are fitted with a tub filler, which looks like a larger version of a bathroom sink faucet, generally comprising a spout and two handles, each mounted separately. A handheld spray may be mounted next to the tub filler, and can be a great help in rinsing the tub after use.

A NOTE ABOUT SHOWER DOORS

Glass shower doors and enclosures are made of one of two types of safety glass: either tempered or laminated.

Tempered glass
Tempered glass is usually about four to five times stronger than annealed glass (ordinary window glass), but it is still breakable. If it breaks, the pieces are more blunt and less splintery and jagged than those from broken annealed glass.

Laminated glass
Laminated glass consists of two pieces of glass that "sandwich" a tough plastic or resin inter-layer. When laminated glass cracks, the shards tend to stick to the plastic interlayer. Car windows are often made of this type of glass.

TYPES OF SHOWERHEADS

In 1992, the federal government mandated that all showerheads manufactured in the United States restrict maximum water flow at or below 2.5 gallons per minute (before that, standard water flow was 4.5 gallons per minute). Most showerheads manufactured since then aerate the water to create a fuller shower spray.

MULTIPLE-SPRAY
Multiple-spray showerheads have spray options ranging from harder, massagelike water patterns to softer, rainlike flow.

BODY SPRAY
Body spray showerheads are usually set at or below overhead showerhead level and can be adjusted to hit your body at different angles.

HANDHELD
Handheld showerheads have a flexible tube or hose, allowing for a range of motion; they are most often hung on fixed-mount brackets. This type of head is particularly useful for bathing children and pets, as well as cleaning the shower.

RAIN HEADS
Rain heads are wide and round, often mounted on an adjustable arm. They give off a soft spray that feels like a spring shower.

ADJUSTABLE
Adjustable showerheads are mounted on an adjustable arm and can be raised or lowered. This is a good choice if you have people of varying heights using the same shower.

HOW TO CLEAN SHOWERHEADS

If a showerhead becomes clogged with mineral deposits, fill a plastic bag with undiluted white vinegar and place the bag over the head so it is fully submerged; secure and seal the bag with a tightly wound rubber band. Let the showerhead soak overnight and scrub the face in the morning with a toothbrush. If the head is still clogged, you will need to remove it.

If it's an old showerhead, it may be rusted to the pipe. In this case, be gentle when unscrewing it. If you need to use a wrench, be sure to put a cloth between the wrench and the metal to prevent scratches. (It's a good idea to turn off the water supply to the shower, just in case the pipe breaks.)

If it is a low-flow showerhead, remove the perforated plastic flow-restricter disk inside the head, making sure to remember which side faces the waterline. Use a pin to clean out the holes and rinse with water. Next, clean the entire showerhead by soaking it in warm vinegar for an additional four to five hours. After soaking, use a soft toothbrush to scrub away the mineral deposits. Rinse well and reinstall the flow-restricter disk. On older pipes, you may need to clean off any pipe-thread sealant tape, scrub off rust, then put fresh tape over the threads to prevent leaking at the joint between the head and pipe. Screw the showerhead back on.

HOW YOU DESIGN A
BATHROOM—PROVIDING GOOD
VENTILATION, LIGHTING,
STORAGE, AND COMFORT—IS A MATTER
OF PERSONAL TASTE
AND A CHALLENGE WE ALL FACE.

A BATHROOM AT LILY POND LANE

SINKS

The sink is the center of every bath and the orbit around which the other fixtures are organized. It's utilitarian—the place where you wash your hands and face and brush your teeth—but it can also add to the room's ambience and character. The white china sink has long been a favorite in American bathrooms. There are, however, many different materials available, as well as many different sink types.

TYPES OF SINKS

The amount of space available often dictates what kind of sink is installed in a bath. Here are the basic types.

CONSOLE

The basin is supported on legs or set into a countertop that is supported on legs. Often there is an open shelf underneath the sink for towels or toiletries. There is also usually a deck around the sink offering ample room for toiletries. Unlike pedestal sinks, console sinks can be purchased separately from the legs, which allows for a more custom look.

PEDESTAL

A basin that sits on a pedestal, which is mounted on the floor. Pedestals are ideal for small bathrooms and powder rooms, because they take up little space. They don't, however, offer any storage. Pedestals range from 32 to 35 inches high.

WALL-MOUNTED

The basin is attached directly to the wall. Depending on size, this can be a space-saving option.

VANITY-MOUNTED

A cabinet with a countertop, which contains the sink. The counter around the sink offers space for toiletries, and the area below is convenient for storing cosmetics and other grooming products, cleaning supplies, and extra rolls of toilet paper. There are several types of vanity-mounted sinks:

Drop-in (also known as self-rimming)
These sinks fit into an opening cut in the countertop and have a raised rim around the perimeter of the sink. The faucet usually protrudes through a hole drilled into the sink. This is the simplest type of sink to install.

Undermounted
These sinks are mounted underneath the finished opening in the countertop. The faucet is mounted in the countertop or in the wall above the sink. These sinks look sleek, free up space on the counter, and are easy to clean because there is no seam between the sink and counter to collect soap and dirt.

Above-counter
These sinks sit on top of the counter, like bowls. Tall, gooseneck faucets are mounted in the countertop next to the sink, or faucets are mounted in the wall above the sink.

SINK MATERIALS

BRASS
This is an alloy of copper and zinc.

Pros Thicker gauges are very durable; beautiful; creates a custom look.

Cons Scratches easily; dents easily; requires maintenance if you want it to stay shiny; expensive.

Special considerations Stains and tarnish can be removed with a small amount of good-quality commercial brass polish. Minor surface scuffs and light scratches can be removed with a fine, water-based automotive rubbing compound (available at auto-supply stores) followed by brass polish.

FIRECLAY
Created when clay, containing large amounts of quartz and feldspar, is fired at extremely high temperatures. The intense heat vitrifies the clay and fuses the glaze to the surface. The resulting material can withstand high temperatures, and is durable and nonporous. Fireclay is a variation of vitreous china.

Pros Won't rust, fade, or discolor. The hard, nonporous surface offers excellent resistance to most commonly used household chemicals and detergents.

Cons Expensive.

Special considerations Remove stains with any all-purpose soft-abrasive cleanser. Avoid strong abrasive cleansers, which could scratch or dull the surface.

GLASS
Clear, colored, and textured glass is molded into a variety of sink types. They are elegant but delicate, and best suited to bathrooms that get moderate rather than full-time use.

Pros Beautiful.

Cons Fragile, will break, chip, or shatter easily if a heavy object falls on it; sensitive to heat.

Special considerations Wipe with a mild glass cleaner. Wipe dry after every use to prevent water spots. Never use abrasive cleansers or scouring pads, to avoid scratching or dulling the surface. Never pour boiling water directly into a glass sink, which may crack or shatter.

PORCELAIN ENAMEL ON CAST IRON OR STEEL
A fired-on opaque glassy coating, which is fused to either a cast-iron or steel base. Sinks made of this material are commonly found in older homes.

Pros Comes in a variety of colors; looks nice when buffed to a shine.

Cons Stains can be hard to treat; the enamel can chip with heavy impact.

Special considerations Never use anything acidic, such as vinegar or citrus-based cleaners, as these products will etch the porcelain. Use a mildly abrasive cleanser or a paste of baking soda and water to remove soap scum.

SOLID SURFACING
A blend of acrylic polymers and stone-derived materials, which are poured into molds to create sheets that can be molded into a multitude of shapes. Often mistakenly called Corian, which is just one of many brand names.

Pros Comes in a rainbow of colors; can be integrated with the countertop for a seamless installation; stain-resistant; scratches can be sanded out.

Cons Moderately expensive; looks less natural than stone.

Special considerations Wipe with a damp cloth and mild dishwashing liquid or an ammonia-based cleaner. For more on removing stains, turn to page 52.

STONE
For information on stone, turn to page 315.

VITREOUS CHINA
A hard, nonporous, glazed material similar to fireclay.

Pros Durable; easy to clean; available in a variety of colors and shapes.

Cons Will chip if a heavy object is dropped on it; sensitive to heat (will crack if boiling water is poured into it).

Special considerations Never use abrasive cleansers or solvents on vitreous china.

HOW TO CLEAN SINKS

Just like tubs, sinks require regular, gentle cleaning. Depending on use, the bathroom sink will likely need to be cleaned daily with mild dishwashing liquid, warm water, and a soft cloth. (If you have a stone sink, use a pH-neutral cleanser formulated specifically for stone.) This approach will keep your sink looking its best and make certain it is always a welcome place for family and guests.

As a general rule, do not scrub any sink with scouring powder containing chlorine bleach, ammonia, or hydrochloric acid and never use steel wool, stiff brushes, or abrasive pads, unless so directed by the manufacturer. All of these products will damage the surface of sinks. To guard against stains, attend to all leaks immediately. This is especially important if you have a granite or marble sink; mineral-laden water will turn both surfaces brown. For more information on how to deal with these stains, turn to page 318.

Once a week, or as necessary, gently scrub sinks with a mildly abrasive cleanser and a soft cloth. To remove heavy buildup of soap scum or mineral deposits, follow the instructions on page 318.

TOILETS

Although it may not be readily apparent, toilet technology has been steadily evolving. In 1992, Congress passed legislation requiring that all new toilets manufactured for home use consume only 1.6 gallons or less per flush. Every toilet made for home use after January 1, 1994, adheres to this standard.

At first, many of the new toilets didn't function well. Manufacturers simply reduced the tank size from the standard 3.5 or 5 gallons, and hoped the toilets would flush properly. In those early years, there were lots of clogged toilets and double flushing. Since then, the design of the 1.6-gallon toilet has improved, though it still cannot handle extraneous waste materials such as paper towels. The good news, however, is that a family of four using a 1.6-gallon toilet saves about $50 per year on their water bill, compared with the use of older 3.5- or 5-gallon varieties, according to the Environmental Protection Agency. In addition, up to 14,000 gallons of water are saved per year.

Dual-flush toilets, a more recent introduction, are even more efficient than the standard 1.6-gallon type. These toilets, which are more expensive than standard models, have two flush volumes, usually 1.6 gallons for solid waste and 0.8 gallons for liquids.

The majority of residential toilets are gravity fed, meaning water from a tank placed higher than the bowl is forced downward to flush away waste.

Pressure-assisted toilets, most commonly found in public restrooms, utilize pressure from the water-supply system rather than gravity to force water into the bowl. This type of toilet does not have a tank.

Toilet bowls are made of vitreous china, which is a hard, nonporous material that resists stains. There are two standard toilet-bowl shapes: round and elongated. The typical round shape saves space and accommodates many different types of seats. Elongated bowls are oval shaped and considered most comfortable.

TYPES OF TOILETS

TWO-PIECE
This is the most common type. This style is floor mounted on a pedestal and has a separate tank and bowl that are bolted together upon installation.

ONE-PIECE
These toilets have an integral bowl and tank. They are usually more compact than the two-piece variety and tend to be easier to clean because there are few, if any, crevices and seams to trap dirt.

WALL-HUNG
This style, which is common in Europe, is fastened to the wall and has no pedestal. It also appears "tankless," but, in fact, the tank is hidden in the wall. There are three main advantages to wall-hung toilets: They usually have a quieter flush than floor-mounted toilets, take up less space because the tank is hidden, and are easy to clean and to clean around.

HOW TO CLEAN TOILETS

Clean the bowl, exterior, and seat weekly using the following guidelines:

BOWL

☐ Use commercial toilet-bowl cleaners on the inside of the bowl only.

☐ Chlorine bleach is an effective alternative to commercial toilet cleaners. Add ¼ cup to the toilet bowl, let stand a few minutes, brush with a toilet brush, then flush. This will disinfect as well.

☐ One-half cup distilled white vinegar, used the same way as chlorine bleach, is also an effective bowl cleaner. Be very careful never to mix vinegar and chlorine bleach: This combination will result in the release of highly poisonous gases.

☐ To remove a hard-water ring from the inside of the toilet, pour white vinegar into the bowl and let it sit for an hour. Scrub clean and flush.

☐ Do not use in-tank cleaners, which can damage flush valves and other working parts.

☐ Even seldom-used toilets should be flushed regularly, to keep them in optimum working order.

EXTERIOR

☐ Wipe the outside and rim with an all-purpose cleaner and a damp cloth (do not reuse the cloth on any other surfaces in the bathroom besides the toilet, or anywhere else in the house). Be sure not to neglect the bottom of the pedestal where the toilet is bolted to the floor.

TOILET SEATS

☐ Plastic toilet seats: Wipe with an all-purpose cleaner or mild dishwashing liquid and a damp cloth. Don't allow an abrasive cleanser to come in contact with the toilet seat, as it will damage the finish. Wipe any splashes of cleaning solutions from plastic surfaces immediately, especially the bumpers and hinges of the seats.

☐ Wooden toilet seats: Both clear-coated and painted wooden seats should be cleaned with mild dishwashing liquid and water. Do not use abrasives, which can damage the finish. Rinse thoroughly and dry with a soft cloth.

FAUCETS

Bathroom faucets, like kitchen faucets, come in a wide range of styles and finishes. Chrome is still the most popular finish. Here are the basics.

TYPES OF SINK FAUCETS

SINGLE-HANDLE FAUCETS

Single-handle faucets consist of a spout with a lever on top or on the side that controls the temperature. Some require only one hole for installation; others require three. Escutcheons, which are decorative metal plates, can be used to cover unnecessary holes.

WALL-MOUNT FAUCETS

Wall-mount faucets are installed on the wall and can have a spout with an integrated hot and cold handle or a spout and one or two separate handles.

DOUBLE-HANDLE FAUCETS

Double-handle faucets have a spout, plus hot and cold handles. They require three holes for installation. There are three types:

Centerset
Centerset, which measure 4 inches from the center of the left handle to the center of the right handle. The spout and hot and cold handles are mounted together on an escutcheon.

Mini widespread
Mini widespread, which measure 4 inches from the center of the left handle to the center of the right handle. Unlike the centerset design, however, the spout and hot and cold handles are each mounted separately.

Widespread
Widespread, which measures 8 inches from the center of the left handle to the center of the right handle. The spout and hot and cold handles are each mounted separately.

FAUCET FINISHES

Most faucets are made of brass and coated with a decorative finish. Traditionally, these finishes were applied using a plating process and were protected with an additional clear coating. Most manufacturers today, however, create finishes using a technology called PVD (physical vapor deposition). This process bonds the finish to the faucet (as opposed to simply coating it) and can impart the look of brass, copper, platinum, or gold, while simultaneously protecting the coated item from wear and corrosion, even if dented. PVD finishes are generally more durable than traditional finishes.

Polished chrome is the most popular faucet finish and generally the most affordable. In households with lots of activity, brushed, rather than polished, finishes can help hide fingerprints.

BRASS
An alloy of copper and zinc, it's often coated with a clear coating to prevent tarnish from developing.

Special considerations This high-maintenance finish requires frequent polishing to keep it shiny unless it is treated with an epoxy or a PVD finish. Even with constant polishing, uncoated brass will tarnish.

BRONZE
An alloy of copper and tin.

Special considerations If bronze is uncoated, you may prefer to let a patina develop rather than polish it regularly. Lukewarm water and a mild dishwashing liquid will clean off smudging. To shine, use a commercial polish that's specially formulated for bronze and follow the manufacturer's directions, making sure to test in an inconspicuous spot before proceeding.

CHROME
A mirrorlike finish treatment. It does not tarnish or corrode, but the underlying metal can, causing pockmarks. To prevent corrosion from worsening, never break any pockmarks.

Special considerations Fingerprints and water spots will show, although they are easy to remove with a soft cloth and a nonammoniated glass cleaner.

ENAMELED PLASTIC
A popular alternative to metal faucet fixtures. Available in a variety of colors to coordinate with the rest of the room.

Special considerations Scratches easily, so not the best choice in a bathroom that gets a lot of wear and tear.

NICKEL
A silvery white metal that resists tarnish.

Special considerations Nickel will darken with age, and can develop water spots quite easily. Remove them with a soft cloth and a nonammoniated glass cleaner.

STAINLESS STEEL
An alloy of steel, chromium, and nickel, it's highly resistant to stains and corrosion. Water spots are common, however.

Special considerations Though faucet fixtures are easy to maintain, they can begin to dull over time and with wear. Use an all-purpose cleaner or a commercial stainless-steel cleaner. Apply polish along the grain (stainless steel often has a brushed finish), rinse immediately, then polish dry.

PORCELAIN KNOBS
Often found on vintage and vintage-style faucets.

Special considerations Acidic cleaners (such as vinegar) can etch the surface if left on too long.

GOLD-PLATED
A thin layer of gold applied to another metal surface, such as brass.

Special considerations Clean only with warm water.

HOW TO CLEAN SINK FAUCETS

As in the kitchen, faucets are susceptible to soap scum, mineral deposits, and smudgy fingerprints, and the best way to keep them looking pristine is with preventive care. Whenever the sink and faucet get wet, rinse afterward with clean water and blot dry; this will prevent the buildup of mineral deposits that may be left behind when the water evaporates. Wipe weekly with a mild dishwashing liquid, warm water, and a soft cloth or a cloth dampened with glass cleaner. Do not use abrasive pads. Buff any water spots with a soft cloth. Clean seams and crevices with a soft toothbrush. Avoid cleaners containing ammonia, bleach, abrasives, or other strong chemicals. Also avoid products that say they remove tarnish or rust or contain hydrofluoric or phosphoric acid. Although newer PVD-finished faucets are more durable than plated faucets, both require very gentle care.

To remove heavy buildup of soap scum or mineral deposits, wipe faucets with white vinegar or a mildly abrasive cleanser, such as Bon Ami. Use these products sparingly, however.

VENTILATION

Ventilation is essential in any bathroom. If moisture is allowed to build up in the room, mold and mildew will grow on the walls, and the paint or wallpaper may blister or peel.

Bathroom fans (just like kitchen fans) are rated according to how many cubic feet of air they move per minute, which is known as their CFM rating. A bathroom fan should move one CFM per square foot in your bathroom. This means that a 50-square-foot bathroom should have a fan with a CFM rating of 50. Bathrooms over 100 square feet should have two fans, one near the shower and one near the toilet.

Fans also have a sone rating, which measures the sound of the fan. The higher the sone rating, the louder the fan (refrigerators typically run at 1 sone). The ratings for bathroom fans generally range from 1 to 4 sones (one of the biggest reasons people don't use their bathroom fans on a daily basis is that their fan is too loud).

To clean your bathroom fan, first turn off the power to the bathroom at the fuse box or circuit breaker. Remove the fan cover, unplug the fan unit, and pull it out. Using a dry cloth or whisk broom, sweep dust from the cover and unit. Vacuum the fan unit and any dust that you've swept onto the floor using the crevice tool. Wipe the unit with a damp cloth. Once it's completely dry, replace the unit and cover. If the cover is extremely dirty, you can soak it in warm, soapy water for several minutes and gently scrub it with a soft brush, then let it dry completely.

MILDEW

Mildew is a common fungal growth; it shows up as light or dark spots or splotches that eat away at the surface it clings to and it is often accompanied by a musty smell. It likes organic materials best, such as cotton, wool, leather, and paper, and it loves dirt. When you find mildew on tile walls or plastics, it is attacking the dirt on those surfaces rather than the surfaces themselves.

HOW TO PREVENT MILDEW

Mildew thrives in damp, dark, warm, poorly ventilated areas, which is why the bathroom is a prime target. To discourage mildew growth, increase the amount of air circulation and light and decrease moisture.

1. Use fans (during the shower and for roughly thirty minutes after), air conditioners, dehumidifiers, and open windows (unless it's very humid outside).

2. Pull the shower curtain closed when not in use, so water can't sit in the folds, and repair leaky faucets immediately.

3. Spread towels over two hooks to dry, or hang them from rods instead. Where space allows, old-fashioned wooden clothes-drying racks work even better.

4. Wipe shower and tub walls with a squeegee after every use.

ERADICATION

The most effective way to scrub away stains from this pesky fungus is to spray them with a solution of 1 part bleach to 10 parts water. Agitate the solution with a grout or utility brush and let it sit for fifteen minutes. Scrub again, then rinse surfaces thoroughly. (Whenever you work with bleach, make sure there's adequate ventilation, and wear protective rubber gloves and old clothes.)

There are less toxic alternatives to bleach, but they generally require more scrubbing and may not eradicate mildew completely, especially on porous surfaces such as grout. Powdererd oxygen bleach is one such alternative. Although oxygen bleaches are not disinfectants, they have whitening power and can be effective. Mix the powder with water until it becomes a thick paste. Apply it to surfaces with a utility or grout brush, agitate it, and let it sit for an hour or so. Scrub again, then rinse surfaces well. You can also try the same technique (although you don't need to let the paste sit) using a mildly abrasive scouring powder, such as Bon Ami. To discourage mold from growing on shower and tub walls in the first place, try switching from bar soap, which can leave behind a film that attracts grime, to a liquid bath soap.

TOWELS

FOLDING TOWELS

For information on folding towels and keeping the linen closet neat and organized, turn to page 355.

Waffle-weave or plain, pure white or jewel tone, monogrammed or minimalist, your towels function as both the basic equipment and among the most noticeable decorative elements in the bathroom. Many people choose white bath linens or their popular alternatives, beige and off-white, reasoning that they are sure to match any bathroom (they also tend to look good longer since dark colors usually fade). You may want to consider purchasing washcloths in darker colors, however, which will help conceal makeup stains.

Unlike bed linens, whose package labels usually list their per-inch thread count, towel labels are not as specific. A towel that feels "Supreme" or "Luxury" to the manufacturer may not feel that way to you. You have to feel a towel to decide—the weightier it is, the better it will feel. When selecting towels, consider the pile height, loop density, and fiber type.

SIZES AND QUANTITIES

For years, American towels came in standard sizes, like sheets. Now, it's possible to get a bath towel in just about any size imaginable, from about 50 inches long to 70 inches or more. European bath towels are typically wider and shorter than their American counterparts.

Allow for two complete sets of towels for each person in the household and two additional sets for guests. Each set includes a bath towel, a hand towel, and a washcloth. Whether you use bath sheets, which are much larger than bath towels, is a matter of preference. They're not an especially good choice if your bathroom (or climate) is damp, however, as they can take a long time to dry. Allow two bath mats per bathroom.

In addition, it's also useful to have three or six fingertip towels. Also known as guest towels, they are typically smaller than hand towels. They are often embroidered or otherwise embellished and made from flat-woven linen or cotton. They are traditionally set out in groups of three for guests (so they do not, for the sake of hygiene, dry their hands on towels you or your family have already used).

HOW TO CARE FOR TOWELS

Launder washcloths after every use, hand towels every day or two, and bath towels and bath mats every three to four days following these guidelines:

1. Keep whites white and stains at bay with oxygen bleach, which is gentler on fibers than chlorine bleach.

2. Do not use fabric softener, which can reduce absorbency.

3. Check to make sure there are no stains before putting towels in the dryer—the heat will set a stain. For more on stain removal, turn to page 374.

4. Dry towels on medium rather than high heat and remove them while still slightly damp. Overdrying linens can weaken the fibers.

5. Do not iron terry-cloth towels; pressing down the loops will reduce absorbency. Press flat-woven linen or cotton guest towels while they are still damp.

TYPES OF TOWEL FIBERS

COTTON FIBERS
Bath towels are most often made of cotton. There are several different types of cotton fibers. Cottons with a long staple (which describes the length of each individual fiber) are softer than cottons with a short staple.

American upland
Most terry-cloth towels are made of American upland, which has short, sturdy fibers.

Egyptian
Egyptian cotton has the longest staple length, producing fine, lustrous towels. It is renowned for its durability and absorbency as well as for generating less lint than other types.

Pima
Pima cotton, which is named after the Pima Indians who helped develop the cotton, is the best-quality cotton of those commonly grown in America. This extralong staple (ESL) cotton provides a lustrous, strong, and firm fiber. Supima is a trademark that appears on products made entirely from pima cotton.

Sea Island
Sea Island is considered the finest of all cottons. It's a rare silky, white, extralong staple grown exclusively in the West Indies and the islands of the Carolinas and the Georgia coast.

Organic
Organic cotton is grown without the use of commercial pesticides, insecticides, and defoliants, on land that is certified to be free of chemicals.

OTHER TOWEL FIBERS
Bamboo
Bamboo is gaining popularity as a towel fiber. It is a fast-growing alternative crop to cotton that doesn't require synthetic fertilizers and pesticides. The towels created from bamboo fibers are highly absorbent, naturally antibacterial, very soft, and quick-drying.

Linen
Towels made of linen, which is woven from the fibers of the flax plant, are smooth, strong, and are used as hand and guest towels. Like cotton, linen becomes stronger when wet.

TYPES OF TOWEL WEAVES

JACQUARD
Jacquard is a floral or geometric pattern that is woven directly into the towel. The pattern consists of terry loops strategically raised and lowered as the design demands. Used for all sizes of towels, and also for decorative bands, or "dobbies," on other types of weaves.

PLAIN
Plain weave is a smooth weave usually reserved for hand towels, especially linen ones. It is often embellished with hemstitching or embroidery.

PLUSH VELOUR
Plush velour is not as absorbent as terry cloth and is therefore used to blot, rather than rub, water away from the skin. The velvety surface is constructed by shearing the loops after weaving.

TERRY CLOTH
Terry cloth is the most common bath-towel weave. The raised loops provide a soft, plush, comforting texture and excellent absorbency.

WAFFLE
Waffle weave is a sunken square pattern, without loops. It offers an invigorating sensation akin to a massage. These towels are well-suited to damp environments because they dry quickly.

TYPES OF TOWEL EMBELLISHMENTS

DOBBY BORDERS
Dobby borders are the decorative woven bands generally located 2 inches from the top and bottom of towels.

EMBROIDERY
Embroidery is made with needlework stitches using thread, yarn, or other flexible materials. Hand embroidery is a widely practiced craft, but most embroidered towels today are made by machine.

MONOGRAMS
Monograms are embroidered letters. Most any letter style can look good on towels, from three minimalist capital letters to an elaborate twining script. The monogram should be placed on the lower third of each bath or hand towel, a few inches above the dobby border, for maximum visibility when the towel is folded over the towel bar.

SAFETY

Besides keeping medication out of the medicine cabinet (and out of the reach of small children), there are several other precautions that will ensure your bathrooms (frequent sites of household mishaps) are safe for you and your family.

☐ Keep all electrical products, in particular portable appliances such as hair dryers, away from bathtubs and sinks.

☐ All electrical outlets near a water source (sink, laundry, appliances) should have a ground-fault-circuit interrupter (GFCI). These are outlets with "test" and "reset" buttons. GFCIs monitor the flow of electricity through the outlet's circuit. If there is any variation in the current, the GFCI will automatically cut off the flow of electricity, preventing injury.

☐ Use nonskid bathmats to keep the bathroom floor dry.

☐ Install antislip adhesives on the floor of tubs and showers to provide traction and help prevent falls. A rubber bath liner with suction cups on the underside is an alternative, but you will need to scrub it weekly to discourage mildew growth.

☐ Install grab bars if you have someone elderly or with limited mobility in the household. Grab bars are meant to support the weight of a person if he or she is pulling or pushing against it to get on or off a toilet, or in or out of a bathtub. The standard size for a grab bar is $1\frac{1}{4}$ to $1\frac{1}{2}$ inches in diameter, and should be installed $1\frac{1}{2}$ inches away from the wall. Grab bars are made of both plastic and metal, and should be securely screwed into a stud or blocking (which can be added if it isn't already in the wall). Grab bars with a slight texture provide better traction than smooth ones. Keep in mind that towel bars are not substitutes for grab bars.

CLOSETS

DON'T UNDERESTIMATE the importance of having an organized clothes closet—it can actually make every day just a little bit better. Busy mornings are simplified when your garments are accessible and neat, when shoes and bags and belts are in view and within reach. But the perfect closet doesn't happen by accident—it is well researched, well thought out, and well crafted.

For years, I lived with the small closets that are common in old houses, making do with not quite enough space. I learned a lot about organizing closets—small or large ones—when my daughter, Alexis, moved into her New York City loft and worked with a closet consultant, who assessed Alexis's clothing, shoes, and accessories, and her need for out-of-season storage. The consultant then asked lots of questions, things like, "Do you prefer to hang your trousers long from the cuff, waist, or folded?" (If you fold them, there will be room for another rod underneath, thereby doubling your hanging space.) "Do you like to store your shirts boxed or hanging?" (If you box them, you will need more shelf space than you would if you were to hang them.) Now, there are rods for dresses, two sets of rods for trousers and shirts, and drawers with built-in organizers for lingerie, belts, jewelry, and other accessories. There are shelves specifically fitted for the way Alexis likes to keep her sweaters and a surface that works like a counter, which is great for folding clothes or packing.

Anyone can learn from this approach: The key is to start with your own wardrobe, your own habits and needs and desires, then to make your space work for you. Whether you have an expansive or a tiny closet, you can outfit it with shelves and rods and drawers and bins and baskets to make it efficient and attractive. And the transformation of any closet should begin with a fresh coat of paint. Also make sure you have adequate, flattering light in a clothes closet and, ideally, a full-length mirror.

Most of these ideas extend to the other closets in your house. The coat closet, the linen closet, the broom closet—if they're organized and customized to fit their contents, they'll work well for you and be a pleasure to use.

ALEXIS'S CLOSET FEATURES LOTS OF DEEP, WIDE DRAWERS FOR FOLDED ITEMS LIKE SWEATERS AND SHELVES FOR SHOES. GLASS DOORS KEEP THE CONTENTS VISIBLE WHILE ALSO KEEPING OUT DUST.

ORGANIZING BASICS

The promise of a well-organized closet seems as enticing today as a brand-new refrigerator or dishwasher did decades ago. For many, the accumulation of goods has led to a new homekeeping dilemma, which has in turn led to a service economy of its own. There are closet-organizing services and consultants and rapidly growing chains of stores designed entirely to help you sort through the growing mountain of possessions. But there are simple ways to organize your closets so that they are a pleasure to use.

Although you may be convinced that you simply don't have enough closet space, a carefully planned arrangement of shelves, rods, and bins—designed to accommodate your particular belongings—can easily double a closet's storage capacity. And the time, effort, and money you invest in your closets will be repaid in spades. Keeping these private spaces meticulously organized is the key to keeping the public areas of your house neat. Once your belongings—whether a clutch of winter gloves or a stack of sweaters—have a designated shelf, bin, or cubbyhole, tidying up is a snap.

No two closets—or people—are alike, however, so before rethinking yours, it's essential to take the time to identify your needs. You can't begin to organize your closets until you know precisely what you're going to store in them. The following four simple steps will help you determine exactly what your storage needs are and then tailor any closet (or drawer, for that matter) to contain your possessions efficiently.

Start with one closet, and work your way through the whole house, room by room, from there.

SORT

It's easy to let the things you own pile up—but don't let that deter you from digging in and tackling your surplus. If a closet is tightly packed, chances are there are a lot of things in hiding, meaning you haven't used or worn

---

FOUR SORTING PILES

KEEP	**REPAIR**	**DISCARD**	**GIVEAWAY**
These are the items you are sure to wear or use.	Arrange to bring things in this group to the appropriate service shop within a fixed period—say, a week or so.	These are the things that are broken or damaged beyond repair.	Arrange to give these things to either friends or charity. Many charities are happy to accept bags of old clothing and may send a truck to pick them up. Registered 501[c][3] charities will also provide receipts for tax purposes.

them for some time. Thus, you can usually find plenty of items that you don't need: clothes that no longer fit or have gone out of fashion, shoes with broken soles, or a handbag better suited to a friend or family member.

Pull everything out of the closet, and sort items into the four piles mentioned on the previous page: keep, repair, discard, and giveaway. (Be sure to have cardboard boxes or large trash bags on hand—once you're done sorting, you'll need to transport piles to other areas of the house, repair shops, charities, consignment stores, and the trash).

Once everything has been sorted, take a good look at the keep pile and ask yourself a few questions: How long have I had it? Does it still function? Is it a duplicate of something I already own? When was the last time I wore it or used it? Ideally, you'll end up moving a few things to the giveaway pile, creating more space for the things you actually need.

Put the bag or box from your repair pile in your car so you're sure to drop them off within the time frame you've allowed. Contact charities to arrange pickups and call friends to make plans to drop off, or have them pick up, the items in the giveaway pile. Finally, take the items in the discard pile to the trash or recycling bin. All that should be left is the keep pile.

THE CONTENTS OF THESE LINEN-CLOSET BINS ARE EASILY IDENTIFIED— CLOTHESPINS GLUED TO THE BINS HOLD LABELS THAT CAN BE REPLACED WHENEVER THE CONTENTS ARE.

REDISTRIBUTE

The next step is to redistribute the things you're keeping. Re-sort your keep pile, grouping like things together. For example, if you're cleaning out a clothes closet, you might make piles of athletic shoes, dress shoes, sweaters, and T-shirts. Then, take stock of your various piles. Do the items belong in the closet they came out of? It's most convenient to store things where you use them. Would your athletic shoes be better stored in the mudroom, for example, than your bedroom closet? If you're cleaning out a hall closet, would those collapsible beach chairs be more conveniently stowed in the garage? Sketching a floor plan of your home that shows every storage nook, from closets to cabinets to chests of drawers, can be a useful tool in helping you identify the best place to store your belongings. Move piles, as necessary, to other closets or areas of the house.

MAKE AN INVENTORY

Once you've determined exactly what will be going back in the closet you've just emptied, you're ready to put together an inventory of your belongings. Closet consultants actually measure a client's belongings to determine exactly how much space he or she would need to store everything efficiently. You should do the same. Determine how many linear feet of clothing you'll be hanging, or how many shoes, tubes of wrapping paper, or umbrellas you'll be storing. (For clothes, use your winter, rather than summer, volume as a gauge.) Write down the measurements and quantities.

GOLDEN RULES OF CLOSET EFFICIENCY

1. Double up on rods. Two or even three short rods installed one above the other, rather than one high one, will maximize hanging space in one area of the closet for short items like shirts, skirts, and folded trousers. Reserve another area for storage of longer items such as coats and dresses.

2. Opt for adjustable shelves rather than fixed ones. They will allow you to change the arrangement of the closet as your storage needs evolve.

3. Utilize floor space—install shelves or cubbies at the base of a closet and you'll never have to rifle through items strewn across the floor.

4. Use every square inch. Examine the closet closely for potential storage: If the ceiling is high, install shelves above the rods to store items you don't use every day, such as hats, gloves, and other off-season clothing. Walls and the backs of closet doors are also handy spots often overlooked; they can support hooks, Peg-Board (to which you can secure any number of hooks), mirrors, and even built-in bulletin boards and display areas for messages, photos, and other mementos.

5. Keep small items in containers. Corralling like things together in bins, baskets, or boxes is a sure way to minimize chaos.

6. Consider convenience. Heavy items should be stored below waist level; rarely used items, on high shelves. Stash a step stool inside the closet, especially if there are high shelves. A foldaway model will take up little space. Make sure the legs are secure and, if the stool is metal, that there are rubber feet to keep it from sliding.

7. Illuminate the space. If a closet is dark, it will be difficult to locate what you need (as well as to get rid of the things you don't). Consider battery-operated lighting if your closet has no power source. Better yet, have an electrician install recessed ceiling lights that turn on automatically when the door is opened. An incandescent light can also help prevent mildew. (For more on mildew prevention, turn to page 347.)

8. Reassess regularly. To keep your closets functioning optimally, reexamine them every six months. Sort, using the criteria outlined on pages 339–340. If the types of items you're storing have changed, rearrange the shelves, rods, and bins.

CUSTOMIZE

After you've figured out exactly what you're storing by making a written inventory, you can begin to plan the layout of the closet. Use the information you've collected to determine how many rods and shelves you'll need. Refer to this list, too, when purchasing (or repurposing) bins and baskets to store your possessions so you don't end up a bin short or with bins that are the wrong dimensions for their intended purposes. There are, of course, specific concerns for each type of closet, which are detailed on the following pages. Mastering these four steps (sort, redistribute, make an inventory, and customize), however, is the key to creating order in any closet in the house.

A LARGE ARMOIRE—
OUTFITTED WITH SHELVES
AND DIVIDERS,
SEE-THROUGH BINS, AND
HOOKS FOR HANGING—
MAKES A FINE SUBSTITUTE
FOR A CLOSET.

GENERAL CLOSET CARE

Whether a closet is used to store clothing, linens, or cleaning tools and supplies, it's important to make keeping it clean part of your regular routine.

☐ Dust the shelves twice a month, followed by thoroughly vacuuming the closet floors. Vacuuming will help remove insect larvae as well as hair and lint, which can support future infestations. Be sure to vacuum along the edges and baseboards with the crevice tool.

☐ Close closet doors as much as possible to block dust and direct sunlight, both of which can damage clothing.

☐ Keep closets cool and dry. Warm, humid air can cause organic materials— wool, cotton, leather—to mildew. This is why basements are poor storage areas for clothing (clothing is best stored at approximately 70°F and a relative humidity of 50 percent). If you are unsure of the humidity of your closet, test it with a hygrometer, available at hardware stores.

THE CLOTHES CLOSET

ORGANIZING BASICS

How you store your clothes has a lot to do with the way they look when you wear them and how they hold up over time. Organize your clothes well and you'll find that not only will you wear them more often (most people wear 20 percent of their wardrobe 80 percent of the time), but they'll emerge from the closet fresh and wrinkle-free.

The National Closet Group (www.closets.com) suggests the following basic dimensions to help a clothes closet function optimally:

☐ The standard width for a reach-in closet is 72 to 96 inches.

☐ The minimum depth required to hang clothes is 24 inches.

☐ The minimum height required for double-hanging rods is 84 inches. (Mount the top rod at approximately 82 inches from the floor, the lower rod 40 inches from the floor; the chart on page 345 can help you refine these measurements to suit your wardrobe.)

☐ Shelves for folded clothing should be placed about 12 inches apart and should be at least 14 inches deep.

☐ Shelves for women's shoes should be spaced 6 to 7 inches apart; each pair needs at least 7 inches of shelf space.

☐ Shelves for men's shoes should be spaced 9 to 10 inches apart; each pair needs at least 10 inches of shelf space.

MAXIMIZE SPACE BY
PUTTING INFREQUENTLY
USED ITEMS BENEATH
TRAPDOORS LIKE THIS
ONE, WITH SHOES STORED
ON THE TOP.

HANGING VS. FOLDING

One of the first steps in bringing order to a clothes closet is determining what should be hung on rods and what should be folded and stacked on shelves or in cubbies. Follow these guidelines:

ITEMS TO HANG

Organize hanging clothes by category or color and keep extra hangers at the end of the rod for easy access.

☐ Linen, rayon, or all-cotton blouses, on wooden shirt hangers; they're prone to wrinkles.

☐ Slippery silks and satins, on padded hangers; they can slide around in a drawer.

☐ Raw silk, velvet, chiffon, and taffeta, on padded hangers; fabrics are delicate and can crush easily.

☐ Pressed shirts, on wooden shirt hangers, to keep them free of fold marks (although they can also be folded; turn to page 413 for instructions).

HANGER GLOSSARY

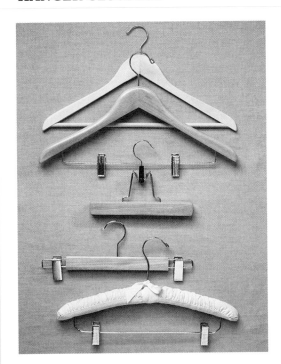

WOODEN SHIRT HANGER
Usually smooth wood, it is slightly curved to follow the natural slope of the shoulders. Keeps shoulders of shirts, jackets, and blazers even with the shoulders of the hanger. Can also fold pants or sweaters over the sturdy rod.

SUIT HANGER
Angled to hold a jacket's shape, with clips below to hold a skirt in place, or a bar for suit pants. As on a wooden shirt hanger, the curved arms are designed to hold the jacket's structure.

CLAMP HANGER
Holds pants by the cuffs without creasing; also useful for hanging multiple skirts made of sturdy fabrics.

CLIPPED SKIRT HANGER
Its movable clips can accommodate various-size pieces.

PADDED HANGER
Designed for delicate items, the soft, rounded arms prevent dents in the fabric. Available with or without clip hangers attached below.

□ Suit jackets and blazers, on wooden shirt hangers or padded hangers with clips attached for skirt or pants; these pieces have definite shapes to maintain. Hang skirts and pants on clip hangers that support their weight evenly across the waistband or cuffs. To store a jacket, drape a folded sheet of tissue around the hanger's neck. Crush more tissue and wrap it inside a tissue sheet to form a tube, and insert one into each sleeve.

□ Pants with creases, on clamp hangers; hang pants from cuffs.

□ Other dress pants, on wooden shirt hangers; use small, circular felt glides, available at hardware stores, to hold folded pants in place.

☐ Pleated skirts and pants, on clipped skirt hangers, to keep the vertical lines crisp; use small squares of felt between the garment and clip to prevent dents on delicate fabrics.

☐ Most dresses, especially tailored styles (but not bias cut or A-line), on wooden shirt hangers, without clips; hang at their full length.

☐ Skirts (except for bias cut or A-line), on clipped skirt hangers; especially for dressy fabrics, hanging is the best way to prevent creases. To prevent dent marks where clips touch fabric, fold two pieces of felt over the waist of the skirt where it meets the clips.

☐ Outdoor jackets and overcoats, on sturdy wooden shirt hangers.

☐ Bathrobes, by the loop on hooks placed on the back of a closet door or on an inner wall; allow to dry completely before hanging in the closet.

☐ Ties, on a tie hanger, although knitted ones should be rolled and placed in a drawer or on a shelf.

☐ Dressy camisoles and lightweight tank tops, on padded hangers. To prevent them from slipping off, sew two buttons onto the hanger's fabric, and position the straps inside of them when hanging.

Use the guidelines at right from the National Closet Group to determine how best to configure rods. These measurements can help you determine how far from the floor to install single rods (for long garments) and how far apart to space double-hung rods (for shorter garments). They can also help you estimate how many linear feet of rod space you'll need. Use your winter items as a guide, and keep in mind that your wardrobe will also change over time. Don't plan for a closet that fits only the things you own now—but one that will accommodate new acquisitions as well.

ITEMS TO FOLD

Keep all folded items in plain view—on shelves or in cubbies—to avoid unnecessary rummaging.

☐ Knitwear: sweaters of all varieties (cashmere to cotton, cardigans and pullovers), plus other knitted tops, pants, skirts, and dresses. If you have shelf space, use hanging canvas sweater organizers or transparent bins stacked on the floor of the closet. If you're tight on space and must hang a sweater, follow the dry cleaner's method: Fold the sweater in half lengthwise (shoulder to shoulder) and drape it over the bar of a sturdy wooden hanger, which will not sag or bend. To protect against creases, slip a piece of tissue paper between the sweater and bar.

HANGING-ROD CONFIGURATIONS: VERTICAL SPACE PER ITEM

Women's blouses
30 to 36 inches

Men's shirts
38 to 39 inches

Women's suit jackets
32 to 42 inches

Men's suit jackets
39 to 42 inches

Pants
46 to 52 inches (by cuff) or 28 to 32 inches (folded)

Dresses
48 to 66 inches

Skirts
34 to 44 inches

Coats
46 to 66 inches

Jackets
40 to 44 inches

HANGING-ROD CONFIGURATIONS: ROD SPACE PER ITEM

Shirts and blouses
1 inch

Pants and skirts
1¼ inches

Dresses, suits, and jackets
2 to 2½ inches

☐ Bias-cut and A-line skirts and dresses. These are best kept folded, as hanging can distort their shapes.

☐ Cotton T-shirts, folded neatly to minimize wrinkles.

☐ Jeans, khakis, and corduroys—any casual pants or shorts in rugged materials. Fold pants in half lengthwise; bring the bottom of the pants up so they align with the top of the back pocket, then bring the new bottom fold up so it is also aligned with the top of the back pocket.

☐ Scarves and shawls. They should be folded, but one or two hanging from hooks can help brighten up a closet space.

☐ Underwear and socks. Keep folded in pullout drawers or trays. Socks can also be kept in coils, lined up in a row. Avoid bunching them together and turning them inside out; although it's convenient for keeping pairs together, it can also stretch them out of shape.

☐ Workout clothes and other sportswear—leggings, bike shorts, yoga pants in fleece, cotton, spandex, or other stretchy synthetics. Keep these in a separate drawer from your other clothes, and like towels and robes, make sure they are completely dry before storing.

CLOSET ACCESSORIES

In addition to hanging rods and shelves or cubbies, you'll want to equip your closet with the necessary accessories. Depending on your needs, check organizing stores and home centers for other specialty closet accoutrements, including shoe drawers, hanging belt or tie carousels, valet rods (to temporarily hold dry cleaning or clothes you plan to steam or air out), or even a hidden safe for jewelry. Here are some conveniences to consider:

☐ Hanging canvas or mesh sweater and shoe bags. They're affordable and easy to add or remove, as your storage needs change.

☐ A pullout shelf for folding. If you have lots of sweaters or other items that require folding, attach a piece of plywood beneath an existing shelf with undermount glides (from a hardware store).

☐ Hooks, for bathrobes, sturdy jackets, and belts. (Don't hang delicates, however, as the fabric can easily retain an impression of the hook.)

☐ A full-length mirror.

☐ A clotheskeeping kit. Space permitting, keep a steamer, lint brush, portable iron, and mini ironing board in the closet. These items are especially useful if your closet is some distance from the laundry area, where those items are usually kept.

AN 8½ BY 11″ CUTTING BOARD MAKES EASY WORK OF FOLDING EVEN STACKS OF CLOTHES.

CLOTHES CLOSET MAINTENANCE

In addition to the closet cleaning guidelines outlined on page 342, here are practices that will keep the clothes in the closet cleaner:

☐ Don't store clothes in dry-cleaning bags. They trap moisture, which can encourage mustiness.

☐ Launder or dry-clean garments before storing them for the season. All stains will set over time and become more difficult to remove. Dirty or spotted clothes are also more attractive to moths (for more on moths and how to prevent them, turn to page 348).

☐ Cover garments you don't wear regularly with zippered fabric garment bags, which will keep the dust off them.

☐ Don't store clothing in regular cardboard boxes as the acids in the paper can cause clothes to yellow if stored too long. Use acid-free boxes and tissue instead: Lay your garment on acid-free tissue and fold the garment and tissue together to prevent creasing. Pack whites and colors into separate containers if possible.

PREVENTING CLOSET MILDEW

1. Use a desiccant such as silica gel packets, available at hardware stores (always keep desiccants out of the reach of children and pets). A bundle of chalk hung in a closet is a good desiccant: Fasten a rubber band around a dozen pieces of chalk, and cover the band with ribbon, allowing extra to loop to over a hook away from clothes or linens. You can keep an open box of baking soda in a closet to help keep it fresh and absorb moisture and odors; replace the box every six months (mark the box with the date when you open it).

2. Ensure everything is clean and dry before putting it away. Leather shoes, in particular, can take a long time to dry; if mildew forms on them, wipe it off with a damp cloth. If that doesn't work, try a one-to-one solution of water and rubbing alcohol, which dries quickly.

3. Install a dehumidifier in or nearby a large closet where there's a lot of moisture. Dehumidifiers extract moisture from the air without changing the temperature of the room. The amount of water a dehumidifier is able to collect depends partly on the relative humidity of the air and partly on the machine's capacity. (For more information on dehumidifiers, turn to page 564.)

4. Install an overhead light fixture. An incandescent lightbulb left on in an unventilated closet may add just enough heat to dry the air. Keep in mind, however, that a compact fluorescent one won't help because it stays cool. To prevent a fire, do not store anything near a bulb.

MOTHPROOFING

Good housekeeping is critical for preventing and controlling moth damage. The best way to prevent infestation is to keep your clothes meticulously clean. Nothing discourages clothes moths more than keeping your woolen items fresh. A few steps taken before you store your clothes for the season can make all the difference in what you find when you remove them: wearable woolens, or unrecognizable, moth-eaten ones.

The two most common types of fabric-attacking moths are webbing and casemaking clothes moths. Webbing moths are common throughout the United States, while casemaking moths are primarily found only in southern states. Both types can fly, and they avoid light. In addition, they try to hide when disturbed, which distinguishes them from pantry pests, which infest flour and grains (for information on pantry pests, turn to page 669). Adult clothes moths are seldom seen, because they prefer dark, undisturbed areas such as closets, basements, and attics and tend to live in corners or folds of fabric. In addition, their cocoons are hard to spot because they incorporate bits of surrounding wool in their construction.

Adult moths themselves won't do any harm, because they don't eat fabric; rather, their eggs hatch into fabric and their larvae feed off of any embedded dirt or perspiration. Clothes damage is actually caused by the larvae of clothes moths and carpet beetles (the latter are more prevalent

MOTHPROOFING TIPS

1. Vacuum closets regularly. Use strong suction and a crevice tool to remove lint, hair, and dust from floor cracks, baseboards, air ducts, carpets, and upholstery.

2. Before packing woolens for storage, wash or dry-clean them; clean synthetics and cottons, too, if you plan to store them with woolens.

3. Brush winter coats—even those that haven't been worn recently. Take them outside on a sunny day and brush the fabric vigorously with a clothes brush, especially under collars and along seams. For extra protection, pack these brushed items separately from any laundered or dry-cleaned items.

4. For short-term storage, reclosable plastic bags or plastic boxes are best for keeping out pests.

5. For long-term storage—years rather than months—avoid plastic containers; they do not allow ventilation, and some plastics may degrade fabrics over time.

6. When storing valuable items (such as furs), consult with a professional textile conservator for guidelines.

7. Make certain that your closets have tight-fitting doors.

than moths in most parts of the United States). Both insects lay eggs in secluded spots where they can find plenty to feed on, whether it's wool, fur, down, shed pet dander, or other animal-based products. Larvae rarely attack frequently worn clothing, but thrive instead on clothes that are hidden away, especially if they are soiled.

Since the females mate and lay eggs all year long, watching out for them is an ongoing process. Here are a few treatments you can try:

PHEROMONE TRAPS

One way to monitor moth infestation (and reduce the amount of larvae) is to hang these traps, used to lure male moths with sex-attractant pheromones. The males get stuck on the surface, keeping them from mating with the females. When you see that there are moths in the trap, it's a sign you have a moth problem.

CEDAR BLOCKS

Cedar contains oils that kill clothes-moth larvae, but it is not effective against carpet beetles. It kills only young moth larvae, not older moths or eggs. Its effect also fades along with scent; you'll need to periodically lightly sand cedar blocks to bring back the scent, or dab cedar oil on them. Lining the closet with cedar is more effective than just using blocks. (For instructions on installing a cedar closet, turn to page 350.)

LAVENDER

Lavender is an old homemaker's staple when it comes to repelling moths. Suspend sachets filled with lavender (and/or laced with its oil) from closet rods or tuck them in your drawers to protect woolens. They will also leave a pleasant scent. Lavender will not, however, kill moth eggs or larvae, so be sure the space is free of them before trying this preventive technique.

A NOTE ABOUT MOTHBALLS AND MOTH CRYSTALS

Because these present so many drawbacks, you're better off not using them. Both contain pesticides that can be harmful to people and pets. Since mothballs and moth crystals work by releasing fumigant gas, they must be used in tight-fitting containers, rather than in closets or drawers, to be effective. To dispose of mothballs you've already used, take them to a licensed hazardous waste handler or save them for a hazardous waste collection program. (Check with your local sanitation department for details.) The EPA classifies both paradichlorobenzene and naphthalene, ingredients in moth balls and moth crystals, as hazardous materials and strongly recommends that you use these chemicals sparingly.

HOW TO INSTALL A CEDAR CLOSET

Lining a closet with aromatic red cedar creates an ideal environment to protect your clothes. To convert a newly built or old closet into a cedar closet, simply line the walls with either cedar paneling or cedar particle-board. Many hardware stores sell tongue-in-groove paneling kits that make this task easy.

To install the paneling or particleboard, you will need a stud finder and pencil, measuring tape, a circular saw or hacksaw, and a hammer and nails. First, use the stud finder to find and mark the studs in your closet. Measure the height and width of the walls and cut the paneling or particle-board to fit. Next, nail the lining into the walls along the stud marks. If using particleboard, make sure to leave an $\frac{1}{8}$-inch gap between pieces, to allow for the board to expand and contract.

If using the tongue-in-groove panels, place the panels tongue-side down, starting at the bottom of the closet and working your way up the wall.

If you have a cedar-lined closet that has lost its scent, it probably means that sunlight, air, and dust have worked together to clog the cedar pores, turning the wood brown and keeping it from releasing its aromatic oil. You can restore the cedar's scent—and effectiveness—by sanding down the walls with coarse sandpaper until the aroma is refreshed and the wood turns red again. Never put any kind of finish on the wood, as it will clog the pores.

HOW TO CARE FOR SHOES

If space permits, put your shoes on shelves or in custom-built cubbies. Otherwise, hang a shoe bag with many pockets on the back of a door or put shoe racks or shelves on the floor of the closet. If you keep shoes in their original boxes, label them, or better yet, affix a photo to the box for easy identification.

PREVENTIVE CARE

Wipe shoes clean of dirt or salt, and stuff with tissue paper before putting them away. Well-made shoes with stitched soles and uppers can be repaired over and over, although complicated cobbling on delicate shoes will be apparent. Protective rubber taps do a good job of protecting pointed toes, and should be installed, if possible, before new shoes are worn. Apply silicone protector on every pair of new shoes, following manufacturer's instructions; test in an inconspicuous spot first. Leather soles wear out faster than rubber ones. If rubber soles do not detract from the look of the shoe, it is worth lining the leather with rubber. Finally, wooden shoe stretchers help supple leather shoes keep their shape.

SHOE-CARE KIT

Before you place shoes into their proper storage containers, make sure they are clean.
Stock a shoe kit with everything you'll need for regular maintenance. All of the supplies
noted below are available at shoe repair shops, variety stores, and large pharmacies.

☐ Suede soap or leather cleaner for cleaning shoes

☐ Shoe cream and polish in the most common colors of your leather shoes, plus a neutral for hard-to-match colors

☐ A suede brush and suede shampoo or cleaning liquid

☐ A small application brush for every different color of polish or cream

☐ Two horsehair buffing brushes (one for dark colors, one for light)

☐ Several soft flannel or cotton cloths for the final buffing

HOW TO REVITALIZE LEATHER

1 The first step in revitalizing leather is to work shoe cream into the surface. Make sure the shoes are completely clean and dry before applying cream, or the leather will not absorb the cream. Use cream the color of the shoe, and apply it with a soft cloth or an applicator brush.

2 After applying the cream with a brush, allow it to soak into the surface overnight. This will condition the leather.

3 Next, lightly apply a wax polish with a cotton cloth or an application brush, using a circular motion. Allow the wax to air-dry (never place leather shoes in front of a radiator or other heat source to dry). The wax will protect the shoes.

4 Use a horsehair brush to buff shoes to a shine. For a high shine, or "spit shine," mist a clean cloth lightly with water and buff the shoe: Hold the cloth from both ends and pull it rapidly back and forth over the shoe.

HOW TO CARE FOR PATENT LEATHER

Patent leather's high-gloss finish—the result of several coats of polyurethane—is particularly susceptible to cracking, so take special care not to allow it to get wet.

1. Clean with a soft cloth and a solution of vinegar and water; this also prevents cracking.

2. If cracks appear, stretch the shoe on a wooden shoe tree or cushion-type shoe shaper, and treat the cracks with leather conditioner. If the cracks are still very noticeable, the shoes may not be worth salvaging, and you might consider throwing them away.

3. Always dry patent leather away from heat sources, and take care not to scratch it.

HOW TO POLISH SMOOTH LEATHER SHOES

1. Before you apply any creams or polishes, you must first clean your shoes. To remove mud, use a soft brush.

2. Wipe the shoe with a damp sponge, stuff it with newspaper, and allow it to dry completely. (You should repeat this process after exposure to rain or snow.)

3. Apply a fresh coat of polish, and buff to a shine with a shoe brush.

HOW TO CARE FOR SUEDE

Suede cannot be polished, of course, but the color can fade and become dusty-looking in spots, and the nap can become shiny from wear. Because suede is a porous material, suede shoes are best worn on dry days.

1. Sponge very lightly and gently with a shampoo formulated especially for suede.

2. To raise the nap of the shoe, brush gently with a rubber, nylon, or brass-wire brush made for this purpose. This will also remove dirt and mud.

3. Suede conditioner, available at shoe repair shops, will rejuvenate color.

HOW TO CARE FOR CANVAS

Wash canvas sneakers and sport shoes by hand; machine washing is inadvisable because it can weaken the support structures in the sole.

1. Wash canvas shoes with a specialty cleanser such as Lincoln EZ Cleaner.

2. Use a nailbrush to gently remove stubborn spots, and use a whitener, such as oxygen bleach, if appropriate.

3. Wash rubber-soled shoes only on the outside; don't soak them in water.

4. Sneakers should air dry naturally, but out of harsh, direct sunlight.

STORING ACCESSORIES

In general, hooks and other closet hardware work well for accessories. You might also consider installing a section of Peg-Board on a closet wall. The board is sold in large sheets; have it cut to size, or use a circular saw or jigsaw. Place furring strips (thin pieces of wood) between the board and the wall, so you'll have room for the backs of hooks, which you can then use to hang belts, handbags, hats, and scarves.

BELTS

If you install pullout drawers in your closet system, consider placing belts in drawer dividers (look for them at housewares and organizing stores) or smaller, shallow boxes. Then you can loosely coil your belts and put them into the containers in a single layer; they won't have room to spring to life. An alternative is to hang the belts from hooks—the back of the closet door or a closet wall works well—or on belt carousels.

TIPS If a garment comes with its own belt, it is best to remove it before you hang up the garment; otherwise the belt could pull the fabric out of shape. Hang the belt from the same hanger as the garment, so the two are always stored together.

HANDBAGS

For short-term storage, you may hang handbags from a hook, but after a few days, this begins to put too much strain on the straps or handles. Cubbies built into your closet provide ideal storage for handbags, but you can improvise by making room on accessible closet shelves or in spacious drawers. Use boxes, baskets, or bins made of plastic-coated wire to keep bags neat; stand them upright or lay them on their sides according to their shapes, and don't crowd them. Leather and natural fibers need ventilation, so avoid airtight plastic boxes or bags.

TIPS Always empty a handbag before storing it—empty all the pockets, and shake it gently to remove dust and debris. Fill the bag loosely with balls of tissue paper; flat, envelope-style bags and very stiff bags need not be stuffed, since doing so could distort their shape. Some bags come with storage bags; if so, use them, since they protect bags from both dust and abrasions. Most do not have storage bags, however, but it's easy to sew storage bags yourself, and well worth it, especially for your best handbags. Use natural muslin or flannel to make a roomy drawstring sack for each bag. If you have a large collection of handbags, organize them according to season, size, or use.

HATS

Hatboxes are ideal for storage, since they guard against damage and dust. When storing winter woolens in the off-season, take precautionary measures to avoid damage by moths. (See Mothproofing Tips, page 348.)

TIPS Don't stack crushable hats or those with decoration. Inexpensive hats, such as straw gardening hats, can be slung over a hook, but more valuable hats should be stowed horizontally on a shelf.

THE LINEN CLOSET

ORGANIZING BASICS

The same rules that apply to a clothes closet also apply to a linen closet: Find an organizational system that works for you—and for your linens. Begin by getting rid of things you no longer use. Depending on their condition, donate them to charity, or reserve old sheets for drop cloths, and old towels for cleaning or for drying off pets after a bath; keep these in the

LINEN-CLOSET SHELF CLEARANCES

Sheets
Space shelves about 10 inches apart

Towels
Space shelves about 12 to 16 inches apart

Comforters, blankets, and pillows
Allow 18 inches or more between shelves

STORING SHEET SETS
TOGETHER IN ONE
PILLOWCASE MAKES IT
EASY TO FIND
WHAT YOU NEED WHEN
MAKING A BED.

garage, basement, or utility closet. If you don't have a large hallway closet for linen storage, an armoire will substitute nicely.

Keep anything you won't be using for months at a time in protective zippered bedding bags. Often, your dry cleaner can supply mothproof bags for storage, in particular for wool. They are also available from online retailers; search for "mothproof bags." Line shelves with acid-free paper. Over time, wood can stain fabrics. Once shelves are positioned correctly and lined, you can begin organizing linens.

Sort linens into piles: sheets, towels, comforters, blankets, and table linens. Then divide again, as follows:

SHEETS

Place each set of sheets inside one of its pillowcases. Group by bedroom and stack on shelves. Always use the set on the top and put clean sets, fresh from the wash, on the bottom. This rotation will ensure sheets wear evenly over time.

TOWELS

Group by bathroom, then by size (all master bath towels together; all master bath washcloths together). Stack on shelves. Always use the towel on the top of any given pile and put clean towels on the bottom to ensure even wear.

COMFORTERS

Keep them fluffy and dust-free by storing on a roomy shelf in a loose bag that allows air to circulate. Do not compress them or store them under heavy items. Don't use cedar or camphor—the down absorbs the smell.

BLANKETS

Group by bedroom, then by season, with the heaviest blankets on the bottom and the lightweight ones on top.

TABLE LINENS

Group by size—all tablecloths together, all napkins together. You can further group them by season (all holiday items together) or formality (casual linens on top, formal linens underneath). For more on storing both, turn to page 158 in the dining room chapter.

Spending a few minutes putting identification labels on the edges of the shelves will also save you a lot of time and refolding later, especially when the white fitted queen-size sheet you wanted turns out to be a white flat sheet for a double bed. If you store extra toiletries in the linen closet, put them in bins or place them on a separate shelf, to prevent stains in case of leakages.

TALK TO ANY REALTOR
AND YOU WILL HEAR THIS OVER
AND OVER: CLOSETS
ARE THE NEW MASTER BATHS.
STORAGE IS NOW MORE
IMPORTANT TO HOME BUYERS
THAN GIANT BATHROOMS.
THE CLOSETS NEED TO
BE BIG WITH SENSIBLE AND
USEFUL DESIGN.

LINEN CLOSET AT SKYLANDS

THE UTILITY CLOSET

ORGANIZING BASICS

Ideally, there is a closet in your home that you can designate as the general repository of all cleaning and utility items, including mops, brooms, the vacuum and all its attachments, flashlights, lightbulbs, and all cleaning supplies and polishes. Shelving should be deep and plentiful, and the inside doors of the closets should be outfitted with hooks to accommodate handled brooms and dusters, a snaked vacuum hose, even small tools and spare

ALTERNATIVE STORAGE SPACES

If space is tight in the utility closet—or you don't have a dedicated closet—consider creating satellite storage areas in the kitchen and bathroom, or convert an alcove or space under the stairs. If there's no risk of children or pets getting into them, scouring agents, cleaners, metal polishes, brushes, paper towels, and sponges can all be stowed under the kitchen sink. Likewise, keep an all-purpose cleaner and a roll of paper towels beneath the bathroom sink for touchups to the sink and mirror.

keys. Your cleaning-supplies closet will be much neater and easier to navigate if you keep long-handled brooms and mops off the floor. Most important, don't try to combine your coat closet with your cleaning closet. One sign of a well-kept home is a utility closet that doesn't spill its contents when its door is opened.

Regardless of how many different cleaning supplies your closet holds, keep storage solutions simple. You can group items according to the room in which they're used or store cleansers and supplies in a lightweight bucket, so they are easy to transport from room to room. A modified canvas tool belt can also be used to store and carry cleaning supplies.

Hooks and clips can keep mops and brooms tidy, and other tools at hand. Screw hooks and spring-loaded clips inside the back of a closet door and use them to hold brooms, a dustpan, mop, and duster.

Keep the most frequently used items between waist and eye level to reduce strain on the back and legs when you reach for them. Infrequently used or heavy items should be stored below waist level; rarely used items, on higher shelves. Adjustable shelving can be a good alternative to custom shelving, but you may need to secure modular shelving to the wall for stability.

UTILITY CLOSET CHECKLIST

For more information on specific cleaning tools and equipment,
turn to the Throughout the House section, beginning on page 478.

- ☐ Vacuum cleaner and attachments
- ☐ Stick and handheld vacuum
- ☐ Mops: floor mop, dust mop
- ☐ Brooms: corn broom for sweeping rough surfaces; angled broom for most indoor floors; whisk broom for areas the vacuum can't reach, such as carpet edges, stair corners, and beside the toilet

- ☐ Dustpan
- ☐ Dusters: ostrich feather; lamb's wool; large, soft paintbrush for dusting delicate lamp shades, carved woodwork, and books
- ☐ Bucket
- ☐ Rubber gloves
- ☐ Glass cleaner
- ☐ All-purpose household cleaners
- ☐ Mildly abrasive cleaner

- ☐ Assorted brushes: scrub brush; utility brush; grout brush; toothbrush for cleaning the area around faucets, light switches, knobs, runners on shower doors, and carpet stains; counter brush (or shop brush) for sweeping off windowsills, countertops, and desks; grill brush for cleaning the barbecue
- ☐ Floor and furniture wax

- ☐ Metal polishes
- ☐ Dust cloths
- ☐ Polishing cloths
- ☐ Cleaning cloths
- ☐ Cheesecloth
- ☐ Batteries
- ☐ Flashlights
- ☐ A key rack, with hooks and key fobs neatly labeled, inside the door

THE LAUNDRY ROOM
AT LILY POND LANE

LAUNDRY ROOM

THE ASSEMBLY-LINE SEQUENCE of sorting, soaking, washing, drying, folding, and ironing can be performed just about anywhere in the house—in a spacious laundry room or a hallway laundry nook—as long as all the things you need can be easily stashed away, ready for use at any time. Even the smallest laundry space should be well lit and well ventilated. It should be cheerful and organized, with a fresh coat of paint and a clean, water-resistant floor.

When I was renovating my house in East Hampton, I decided to put the laundry room in a small room off the kitchen; it has a window, and is convenient to everywhere in the house. A small curtain keeps the supplies on the shelves out of sight. When my daughter, Alexis, was renovating her farmhouse nearby, she took an out-of-sight, out-of-mind approach to the laundry room; she situated it in the basement, and created an immaculate space with pure white surfaces. At Skylands, in Maine, I am very lucky to have the ultimate laundry room. It is spacious and bright, situated in the basement, with a wall of windows. It was originally designed in the early twentieth century to be used by a large household staff—it still has several stationary ironing boards at different heights,

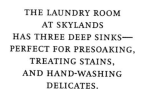

THE LAUNDRY ROOM
AT SKYLANDS
HAS THREE DEEP SINKS—
PERFECT FOR PRESOAKING,
TREATING STAINS,
AND HAND-WASHING
DELICATES.

for laundresses of different heights, soaking tubs, and an "extrata," an early version of the dryer. I love cleaning clothes there.

Some steps in the laundry process can be carried out elsewhere in the house. If you are ironing a tablecloth to put directly on a table, you can save the step of folding it (and, in the process, creasing it) by ironing it on the ironing board right next to the table, sliding it immediately onto the table surface after. Your comfort is important, too. If your laundry room is tiny, perhaps you would prefer to fold clothes on a big bed or in the den if the rest of the family is gathered there, setting up a rack right there to hang the freshly pressed clothing. Streamline your system, and you will streamline the task.

How you organize your laundry room depends on how you use it. If you have young children, your stain kit probably gets more use than your spray starch, so that should be most easily accessible. Organize, too, for ease in using your products. If you buy laundry detergent in bulk, decant it into smaller, unbreakable bottles or airtight containers that will be easier to handle.

How you organize your laundry room depends on how you use it.

When I was young, Monday was always laundry day for my mother, but today, most of us don't have a ritual wash day. You may run a load before work, or after, or before you go to bed. In any case, laundering as you go is the best policy. If you let laundry pile up, you may come to dread tackling the task. But do it a little at a time, and you'll likely share my feeling that doing laundry is satisfying and enjoyable work.

LAYOUT BASICS

Laundry was once the most labor intensive and time consuming of household chores. "For the family wash, good water and good soap are indispensable," wrote Mrs. M. H. Cornelius in her 1871 book, *Young Housekeeper's Friend.* Collecting rainwater was only the beginning. Doing laundry in Mrs. Cornelius's day was such arduous work that she recommended spreading it out over the week: washing on Tuesday, folding on Wednesday, ironing on Thursday. Thankfully, it's no longer necessary to devote three whole days to doing laundry. Keeping a family in clean clothes is still work, but in a well-organized laundry center, the chore will seem less like the "severe labor" that Mrs. Cornelius described.

A laundry area should be clean, simple, and functional, wherever it happens to be located—whether it's in a makeshift setup in the basement, a spacious utility area on the main floor, or near the bedrooms on the second floor. And wherever you do the laundry, you'll need more than just a washer and dryer. The elements listed below can actually fit into a surprisingly small or awkward space—with a little planning, the ideal laundry center is attainable even if you don't have a whole room to devote to it:

- ☐ Bins or baskets for sorting clothes, and, ideally, a deep sink for presoaking and treating stains.
- ☐ Shelves or a cabinet for detergents, whiteners, brighteners, stain removers, starches, and a mending kit.
- ☐ A drying rack or rod for hanging delicates to dry.
- ☐ A table for folding and drying sweaters.
- ☐ An iron, ironing board, and a steamer.

BINS AND BASKETS

Sorting clothes before washing is essential, and it's best to do it as laundry accumulates by encouraging family members to bring their clothes to the laundry room daily. Two bins are the minimum—one for whites, one for darks—but you may want to add others for hand-washables, bright colors, towels, or dry cleaning. Devise a system that works for your household. Wicker baskets with removable, washable liners are attractive, but they can take up a lot of space. Rolling carts make transporting the laundry easy; those with separate compartments are even more space efficient. Clearly label whatever type of container you choose so everyone in the family can sort their clothing correctly.

I LOVE THE LOOK OF THESE HANDWOVEN WICKER BASKETS, AND EACH IS ROOMY ENOUGH TO HOLD A FULL WASH LOAD.

A ROLLING CART—WITH WELL-LABELED COMPARTMENTS FOR SORTING CLOTHES— EASILY MOVES THE LAUNDRY FROM ONE SPOT TO ANOTHER.

SHELVES AND STORAGE

A simple shelf or two stretching above the washer and dryer may well provide enough space for your laundry supplies. Organize items according to how you use them. Anything you use regularly should be within easy reach; extras and incidentals can go on a high shelf, or with bulk storage items in the garage or basement. If you buy those large, economical, but unwieldy containers of powdered detergent, decant it into smaller, well-labeled airtight containers. Shelves shouldn't be a jumble of half-filled bottles covered with messy drips (do keep rags on hand for spills). Keep items tidy by storing small supplies in baskets or bins. Gather stain-removal products in one and mending equipment in another.

RODS AND RACKS

Install a rod for hanging clothes you intend to drip-dry and those you pull from the dryer while still damp (that way, they'll need only a light ironing or none at all). You can build in a wooden or metal rod or simply stretch a curtain or shower tension rod between two walls. If there's no space for a rod, use a collapsible wooden or plastic-coated wire drying rack. They come in several different sizes and fold flat for easy storage.

FOLDING AND IRONING

If you don't have room for a table to fold clothes on, install a fold-down shelf at countertop height (36 inches from the floor) or use a wooden board that fits over a utility sink (when it's not in use, hang it above the sink on hooks). When it comes to ironing, a wall-mounted fold-down board is compact, but often not very comfortable. A space-saving alternative is to install an ironing board hanger that also stows the iron. These plastic or metal hangers are designed to be wall mounted or to fit over a door. Make sure the hanger is heat resistant, so you can put the iron away before it cools. A sturdy wall-mounted or over-the-door hook is useful for hanging clothes to steam.

WASHING MACHINES

TOP-LOADING WASHERS

These machines dominate the American market. The basic design has changed little since the automatic washer was first introduced: Clothes, water, and detergent are agitated around a central column, which loosens dirt. After anywhere from two to fourteen minutes (depending on the setting), the water is pumped out of the washer and the clothes are spun to extract moisture. Fresh water is then added to rinse the clothes and they are spun once again. Keep in mind that routinely choosing a long wash cycle will only wear out your clothing; according to experts, a wash time of just six minutes is sufficient for all but the dirtiest clothes. Top-loading washers hold between 12 and 16 pounds of laundry per load and generally measure 27 to 29 inches wide; compact models are typically about 24 inches wide.

FRONT-LOADING WASHERS

Commonplace in Europe for many years, front-loading washers are steadily gaining popularity in the United States. Also known as high-efficiency washers, front loaders offer several benefits over top loaders. Instead of agitating clothes, they tumble them, similar to the way dryers work: As the drum rotates, the clothes are lifted up, then dropped into a shallow pool of water. This action loosens dirt by forcing water and detergent through the fabric.

EVERY LAUNDRY ROOM SHOULD HAVE AT LEAST ONE COLLAPSIBLE WOODEN RACK (TOP), FOR AIR DRYING HAND WASHABLES AND SMALL LOADS. A SIMPLE FOLDAWAY RACK (BOTTOM) MAKES AN INGENIOUS USE OF WALL SPACE IN A SMALL ROOM.

**A NOTE ABOUT
SAVING ENERGY**
The majority of the
power used by a washing
machine is devoted
to heating the water. You
can significantly cut
energy consumption by
reserving hot water for
only very dirty loads and
always rinsing clothes
in cold water.

Front loaders tend to be gentler on clothing because there is no agitator rubbing against fabric. They also use a third to half as much water as top loaders, and require up to 68 percent less energy to heat the water, thereby helping to reduce your energy bills. Many models have internal water heaters, which heat wash water to 205 degrees, which is nearly boiling, eliminating the need for bleach or other whiteners. Clothes are spun at more than 1,000 revolutions per minute (rpm), versus 600 to 700 rpm for top loaders, so clothes emerge drier, thereby requiring less time in the dryer, which saves even more energy. The tumbling action causes regular laundry detergents to produce an excessive amount of suds, so these machines require a product specifically formulated for front loaders, which is available at supermarkets (for more on detergents, turn to page 378). Front loaders can accommodate 12 to 20 pounds of laundry per load and generally measure 27 to 29 inches wide; stacking units come in 24- and 27-inch widths.

To alleviate bending to load and unload these machines, manufacturers offer elevated pedestals to raise the washer and dryer 8 to 13 inches above the floor. (Pedestals are also a boon if your basement is prone to flooding, but they must be raised 12 inches above the projected flood elevation, and should be made of masonry or pressure-treated lumber.) Some commercial pedestals are even outfitted with drawers, which can conveniently stow laundry supplies.

Despite the benefits of front loaders, traditional top loaders still offer a few advantages: They are less expensive (though this must be weighed against the energy-cost savings offered by front loaders over the life of the washer), they complete a cycle more quickly, and they allow you to stop the washer midcycle to soak clothes, add clothes, or remove them. (You can't soak clothes in a front loader unless the washer has a soak feature.)

CYCLES

There are three basic cycles on every washing machine—Regular, Permanent Press, and Delicate (or Gentle). The more expensive the washer, the more cycle choices you'll have, including options for Prewashing, Soaking, and Extra Rinsing; some even allow you to create your own custom cycles. Understanding these three basic cycles, however, will help you get the most from your washer (and get your laundry cleaner in the process).

THE REGULAR CYCLE

This setting is suitable for most cottons, household linens, and children's play clothes with a moderate to heavy level of soil. The wash water is either hot, warm, or cold; rinse water is warm or cold. The machine agitates or tumbles and spins at a normal level. The Wash cycle generally runs for ten to fourteen minutes on the regular cycle setting.

THE DELICATE (OR GENTLE) CYCLE

For knits and lightweight, sheer, lacy, or loosely woven garments, and any other fabrics that need extra care, choose this cycle. It agitates and spins slowly, mimicking hand-washing. The Wash cycle is warm or cold, with a cold rinse. The Wash cycle generally lasts for two to eight minutes on the delicate or gentle cycle setting.

THE PERMANENT PRESS CYCLE

Because it is a little easier on clothes in general, this cycle is the right choice for loads of shirts, blouses, dresses, trousers, and knits that are lightly or moderately soiled. The wash water is either warm or hot, with an extended cool-down rinse. Cooling the clothes with cold water before they spin minimizes creases in wrinkle-resistant, or permanent-press, cottons and synthetics. The Wash cycle generally runs for four to twelve minutes on the permanent press cycle setting.

A NOTE ABOUT WATER TEMPERATURES

Hot water (110–130°F)
Use it to keep whites white and effectively clean very dirty, color-fast clothes. It will, however, cause colors to fade more quickly than warm water.

Warm water (90–110°F)
This is appropriate for most average loads.

Cold water (below 85°F)
Cold is a wise choice for bright colors that are likely to fade, and for delicates. Warm or cold water is also best for pre-treated stains because it will keep them from setting. Use only cold water for woolens and silks to prevent shrinking. Keep in mind that detergents are less effective in water below 65°F.

WASH CYCLES

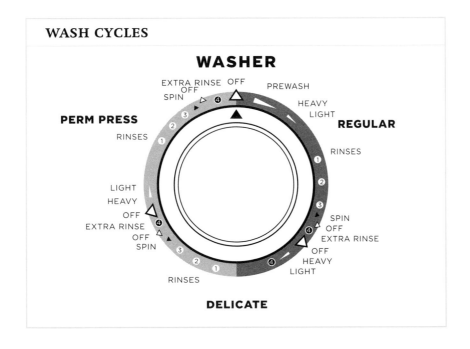

HOW TO CARE FOR YOUR WASHING MACHINE

☐ Wipe up any spills promptly with a soft, damp cloth or paper towel. Most washer (and dryer) tops are porcelain enamel or synthetic enamel, which will not stand up to repeated exposure to ammonia, chlorine bleach, abrasive cleaners, or household solvents.

☐ Protect the top of the washing machine (or dryer) with a folded towel when using it as a work surface to treat stains. Keep stain and laundry products well away from electronic control panels as they can damage the finish.

☐ Leave the lid open after every load to allow moisture to evaporate.

☐ Once a week, wipe down the outside of the machine with a cloth dampened with mild dishwashing liquid and water; rinse with plain water and wipe dry. Wipe the inside of the machine with a damp cloth to remove lint, debris, or soapy residue.

☐ If it seems your clothes are not getting as clean as they should, it's time for a deep cleaning of the machine. Run a short, hot Wash cycle with detergent, then rinse with plain water. If the machine is exceptionally dirty or requires sanitizing, add ¾ cup bleach and 1 tablespoon powdered laundry detergent, fill the washer with warm water, and let it sit in the machine for a few minutes. Then drain and rinse a few times with plain water to eliminate any traces of dirt or bleach.

☐ Consult your product manual for instructions on how to clean fabric softener dispensers and other removable parts. Do not use detergent to clean fabric softener dispensers; if detergent residue mixes with softener, it can stain clothing.

☐ Before going on vacation, shut off the water supply at the faucet. (For more information, turn to page 595.)

☐ Drain water from the hoses if the weather is going to dip below freezing.

☐ Examine hoses periodically to ensure they aren't bent or kinked, and replace them every five years. Many household floods are caused by leaky washing machine hoses.

FIGHTING WASHER MILDEW

It's not uncommon for both top- and front-loading washing machines to develop a ring of mildew around the rubber door seal. This is more likely if you live in a humid climate or have a laundry room that is poorly ventilated, conditions that mildew requires to thrive. Likewise, if you wash with only cold water—which does not kill mildew-causing bacteria—or leave damp clothes in the washing machine for extended periods of time, you may also be encouraging the development of mildew. (It's always a good idea to dry clothes promptly after washing to keep them as fresh as possible.)

To remove mildew and discourage further growth, clean the rubber seal with a solution of 1 cup chlorine bleach to 2 cups warm water. Wearing protective gloves, first wipe the lower portion of the door seal—where water and, thus, bacteria will be most concentrated—with a soft cloth soaked in the bleach solution. Then follow up by wiping down the entire seal. Finally, fill the bleach dispenser with bleach and run the washer (without any laundry) through a complete cycle using hot water. Repeat this process every two to four months to keep mildew in check.

DRYERS

A dryer consists of a perforated rotating drum, through which heated air flows. As laundry tumbles in the drum, the hot air heats the clothes and the moisture in them, causing the moisture to evaporate. Most models vent the moist air outdoors through a duct. Ventless dryers, designed for apartments or areas of the house where outdoor ducting would be impossible, are also available, though much less common. With these models, the condensed water is pumped into a sink or drain or collects in a reservoir, which is built into the dryer, and must be periodically emptied. Dryers are powered by gas (natural, propane, or butane) or electricity. Gas models typically cost more than electric ones, but are less expensive to operate.

Full-size dryers usually measure between 25 and 29 inches wide; space-saving models are typically 24 inches wide. Most manufacturers describe capacity in terms such as "extra large," "super," and "super plus"; suffice it to say that most full-size dryers have plenty of space for a typical load of laundry. Compact models generally have half the capacity of their regular-sized counterparts. It's important that the capacity of washer and dryer coordinate. The dryer should have twice as much capacity as the washer. So if you have a 3.3- or 3.5-cubic-foot washer, you will need a 7-cubic-foot dryer. (The additional dryer space is necessary to allow air to circulate around laundry.)

SETTINGS

All dryers offer three basic settings: Cotton (or Regular), Permanent Press, and Air Fluff. Each is designed for a specific type of fabric, and using the correct settings will keep clothes looking good longer and minimize wrinkles. Dryers are also programmed to shut off in one of two ways: with a thermostat or with a moisture sensor. The majority of dryers on the market today have sensors; thermostats are generally found only on entry-level models. As with washers, the more expensive the model, the greater the number of settings. Here's how the settings work:

THE COTTON (OR REGULAR) SETTING

The cotton setting is designed for cottons and most household linens.

THE AIR FLUFF SETTING

This setting circulates air without heat, which is useful for freshening pillows or clean clothes that are stale but not in need of washing.

THE PERMANENT PRESS SETTING

Designed for wrinkle-free items, the permanent press setting has a Cool-Down cycle at the end. This is because permanent-press garments have a

HOW TO SPOT CLEAN THE DRYER

Felt-tip and ballpoint ink
Apply an all-purpose cleaner to a cloth, then wipe down the drum until the ink is gone. Rinse with clean, damp cloths. Leave the dryer door open, and do not use it for at least several hours, to give the fumes time to evaporate.

Spots on the drum (caused by starched or tinted items)
If you see discolorations, wipe the drum with a sponge or cloth moistened with a solution of bleach and water (10 parts bleach to 1 part water). Rinse off the bleach solution with a clean cloth dampened with a little detergent. Rinse well, then dry.

Melted crayon
Use an all-purpose, nonflammable household cleaner applied directly to a cloth or sponge (do not spray cleaners directly onto the drum). Clean off as much crayon as you can. Wipe dry. Tumble dry some wet rags to absorb as much of the remaining residue as possible. Repeat until no residue appears on the rags (a faint stain may be left behind on the drum; it should not affect subsequent loads).

tendency to crease if left to sit in a warm dryer. It is sometimes called the Easy Care setting.

THE COOL-DOWN SETTING

This setting keeps clothes spinning continuously for a preset amount of time after they are dry to minimize wrinkling.

ELECTRONIC MOISTURE SENSOR

The electronic moisture sensor allows you to choose how dry you want your laundry to be—More Dry, Dry, Less Dry, or Damp—rather than how many minutes you want it to dry. Moisture sensors turn the dryer off when the moisture level in the drum falls below the preset level. A damp setting will leave laundry moist and ready for ironing, which is good for table linens and cotton trousers and shirts. Moisture sensors keep clothes from over-drying, which prevents shrinking, wrinkling, and the overall weakening of fibers caused by too much heat.

THE EXTENDED TUMBLING SETTING

The extended tumbling setting tumbles a dry load of laundry without heat every few minutes to keep wrinkling at bay.

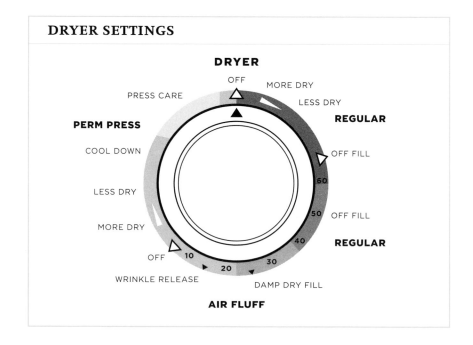

DRYER SETTINGS

THE TIMER SETTING

The timer setting allows you to set how many minutes you want something to dry for. This is less energy efficient than an automated moisture sensor and can be harder on your clothes because it may continue heating your washables long after they have dried.

HOW TO CARE FOR YOUR DRYER

1. Clean the lint screen before every load. This will keep the dryer's airflow clear, and prevent the dryer from overheating. Every machine has a slightly different kind of filter, so consult your owner's manual for instructions.

2. Once a week, wipe down the outside of the machine with mild dishwashing liquid and a damp cloth; rinse with plain water and wipe dry.

3. After drying wet or damp items that were not freshly laundered (beach towels, for example), wipe the drum with a clean, soft cloth dampened with mild dishwashing liquid; rinse thoroughly and wipe dry.

4. Check the exhaust ducting at least once a year. Any obstructions will restrict airflow and result in longer drying times. It is best to have a qualified technician remove any blockages.

BEFORE YOU WASH

READING CARE LABELS

The most important thing you can do to preserve your wardrobe is read care labels carefully. The Federal Trade Commission requires manufacturers to include them in every garment. They offer in words or symbols at least one safe cleaning method. But it may not be the only way—a label does not have to list *all* safe methods. Dare you defy the care label that says Dry-clean? In fact, unless the label reads Dry-clean Only, which means the garment can be cleaned only with a commercial solvent, you can probably wash it. Manufacturers often put the Dry-clean label on garments made of wool (and related fibers, including cashmere), silk, and rayon. But by following the instructions on page 391, you will likely be able to wash them successfully at home. The following criteria can also help you decide whether you can safely disregard the Dry-clean label.

A garment suitable for machine- or hand-washing must be:

☐ Colorfast (test by dampening the fabric in a discreet spot, such as an inside seam, wait a minute or two, and blot with a white cloth to see if color appears)

☐ Made of single material (no lining, beading, or trim)

☐ Constructed simply, so it won't collapse when wet

SORTING

Anyone who has ever had the misfortune of having an errant red sock find its way into a load of whites will appreciate the importance of sorting laundry—it's an essential step that will keep your clothing looking good longer. Each time you wash your clothing, some dye is released into the water. Dyes such as indigo, for example, which colors your favorite blue jeans, are actually intended to fade and will do so throughout the life of the garment. Unless you take care to wash like colors together, your laundry will become dingy in short order. Besides the obvious—separating light-colored clothes from dark and brightly colored ones—you should sort by soil level, fabric type, and lint properties.

CARE LABEL SYMBOLS

WASH		BLEACH	DRY			IRON	DRY-CLEAN
regular	hot	any bleach	normal	any heat	line dry	high temperature	dry-clean
permanent	warm	only non-chlorine bleach	permanent press	high heat	drip-dry	medium temperature	do not dry-clean
gentle	cold	do not bleach	gentle/delicate	medium heat	dry flat	low temperature	
hand wash			do not dry	low heat	do not wring	no steam	
do not wash				no heat/air		do not iron	

SORT BY SOIL LEVEL

Extradirty items, such as children's clothing, aprons, or gardening gear, should be washed separately from lightly or moderately soiled clothing.

SORT BY FABRIC TYPE

Don't mix sturdy cottons with more delicate fabrics—such as cotton knits— which might pill or snag as a result.

SEPARATE LINT-PRODUCING AND LINT-ATTRACTING FABRICS

Washing towels, flannel sheets, and other fabrics that shed lint alone will keep them from depositing fuzz on everything else, particularly dark colors and napped fabrics such as velveteen and corduroy.

WHAT CARE LABELS MEAN

WASHING

Wash by hand means no agitation, just soaking and squeezing.

Machine-wash means agitation is fine. If there is no mention of temperature, water may be as hot as 130°F. Otherwise, the label must say warm or cold.

Wash with like colors or "wash separately" are tip-offs that colors might run.

DRYING

Tumble dry with no mention of a heat setting means that machine drying at any temperature is safe. Otherwise, the label must state a setting.

Dry flat means you should lay the item horizontally to dry; it would stretch if hung when still wet.

Drip-dry means to hang the item dripping wet. Smooth with hands, if desired. Do not wring or spin.

No heat means you can use the dryer's Air Fluff setting to freshen clothes, but you should not tumble dry them.

BLEACHING

No mention of bleach implies all kinds are okay to use.

Only nonchlorine bleach, when needed means just that. These bleaches, however, work best when you use them regularly.

Do not bleach means no bleach is safe.

DRY CLEANING

Dry-clean means that cleaning with a commercial solvent is safe. The label must name one type of solvent (unless all are acceptable) and any other standard factors that should be modified. This doesn't necessarily mean you can't wash the item. If it is unstructured, sturdy, and colorfast, you may be able to—but at your own risk.

Dry-clean only means washing at home is not safe.

IRONING

No mention of ironing means this step isn't necessary for routine care, but occasional touch-ups are fine.

Iron implies you'll need to iron regularly and can use a hot iron. Otherwise, the label must list the temperature setting.

Do not iron means you should not even touch up, as damage may result.

TREATING STAINS

After you've sorted laundry into like piles, you're ready to tackle stains. Stain removal is part art, part science. There is no single technique or product that takes care of every spot and spill. If a garment isn't washable, the safest thing to do is take it to a dry cleaner (the same goes for particularly valuable or delicate pieces of clothing). If a garment is washable, you can tackle the stain yourself, following the guidelines on pages 376–377.

GOLDEN RULES OF STAIN REMOVAL

1. Act quickly. The sooner you get to the stain, the more likely you are to get it out.

2. Always blot liquids with a white cloth (to prevent dye transference onto the item you're treating). Work from the outside in so you don't spread the stain.

3. Scoop up solids, like a dollop of ketchup, with a dull-edged knife before blotting.

4. Sprinkle an oily stain with cornstarch. Wait ten to fifteen minutes, then scrape it off.

5. Dab stains (don't rub or press hard) with cool water, which will lighten most spots and remove others altogether.

HANG A LAMINATED COPY OF THE STAIN-REMOVAL CHART IN A CONVENIENT SPOT IN THE LAUNDRY ROOM, WITH A STAIN-REMOVAL KIT CLOSE AT HAND.

If, after performing this first aid, the stain remains, it's time to move on to more specialized treatments. Generally speaking, stains are either water soluble, solvent soluble, or a combination of both. Most water-soluble stains fall into two categories: protein stains (from human and animal substances, such as egg yolk, milk, blood, vomit, and perspiration) and tannin stains (from plant substances, such as tea, grass, coffee, fruit juice, and red wine). Solvent-soluble stains are generally greasy, from substances such as butter, mayonnaise, or lipstick. Combination stains are the result of two or more of these substances mixing together, such as tea and milk. They are especially challenging and may require multiple steps to treat effectively.

If possible, test stain-removal techniques on a hidden area of the garment, like an inside seam, to see if the fabric will withstand the treatment. After applying the treatment, wash the garment as you normally would, but don't put it in the dryer afterward if any evidence of the stain remains (the heat will set it). Repeat the treatment as necessary, or try another.

STAIN-REMOVAL KIT

SOLVENTS AND CLEANERS

- [ ] Acetone
- [ ] Ammonia
- [ ] Cornstarch
- [ ] Combination stain remover, such as Shout or Spray 'n Wash
- [ ] Digestive-enzyme tablets

- [ ] Commercial dry-cleaning spot remover, such as K2r or Afta
- [ ] Mild dishwashing liquid
- [ ] Enzyme detergent, such as Wisk, ERA Plus, or Biz
- [ ] Hydrogen peroxide (3%)

- [ ] Isopropyl alcohol
- [ ] Mineral spirits
- [ ] Nonchlorinated color-safe bleach, such as Clorox 2
- [ ] Petroleum jelly
- [ ] Shampoo
- [ ] White vinegar

STAIN-REMOVAL TOOLS

- [ ] White cotton cloths, for blotting
- [ ] Cotton swabs, for applying solvents and other cleaners
- [ ] Dull-edged knife, for scooping up spills

- [ ] Embroidery hoop, for isolating stains
- [ ] Eyedropper, for applying solvents and other cleaners
- [ ] Soaking tub, for presoaking stains

- [ ] Soft-bristled brush, for working in solvents and other cleaners
- [ ] Spray bottles, for applying cleaners
- [ ] Cheesecloth

STAIN-REMOVAL GUIDE

This chart is for washable items only. The diluted dishwashing solution called for below is made with 1 tablespoon of fragrance- and dye-free liquid soap (containing sodium laurel sulfate, or sodium laureth sulfate) and 10 ounces of water. Pour it into a small spray bottle. Do not use the enzyme detergent mentioned on protein fibers, such as silk, wool, cashmere, or angora. Always launder garments after using a dry solvent (such as mineral spirits or acetone), and do not use acetone on acetate.

BALLPOINT INK	Build a "dam" around the stain with petroleum jelly. Always work within the confines of the dam. Using an eyedropper, treat the area with isopropyl alcohol. Remove any remaining pigment with a dry solvent (such as mineral spirits or acetone) in a well-ventilated room; let dry. Rinse with the diluted dishwashing-soap solution, then launder with enzyme detergent in warm water.
CHOCOLATE	Gently scrape off excess chocolate, and spray the area with the diluted dishwashing-soap solution. Follow up with an enzyme detergent to remove residue before washing.
COFFEE OR TEA	Using an eyedropper, flush the area with vinegar or lemon juice to remove color. Then treat with a stronger bleach, if necessary. To remove sugar or milk, spray with the diluted dishwashing-soap solution; launder with an enzyme detergent.
FELT-TIP INK	Build a "dam" around the stain with petroleum jelly. Always work within the confines of the dam. Test the ink with a cotton swab saturated with water and another one saturated with isopropyl alcohol to determine whether the ink is oil based (ballpoint ink) or water based. If isopropyl alcohol pulls more pigment out of the stain, follow the steps for ballpoint-ink stains, above. If water is more effective, spray the stain with the diluted dishwashing-soap solution, and flush with cold water.
FRUITS AND VEGETABLES (JAMS, JUICES)	Spray the diluted dishwashing-soap solution on the stain to remove the sugars. Using an eyedropper, flush the area with vinegar and then hydrogen peroxide to remove any remaining color. Follow up with an enzyme detergent to remove residue before laundering.
GRASS	Treat the area with a dry solvent (such as mineral spirits or acetone) in a well-ventilated room. Press with cheesecloth; tamp with a soft-bristled brush. Repeat to remove as much pigment as possible. Flush the area with isopropyl alcohol, tamp, and let dry. Treat the area with an enzyme detergent before laundering.
GREASE (BUTTER, OIL, MAYONNAISE)	Begin by treating the area with a dry solvent (such as mineral spirits or acetone). Using an eyedropper, rinse with isopropyl alcohol; dry well. Spray the diluted dishwashing-soap solution on any remaining residue, and soak the item in an enzyme detergent before laundering.
LIPSTICK	Use a dull-edged knife to remove excess lipstick. Using an eyedropper, apply a dry solvent (such as mineral spirits or acetone) to the stain in a well-ventilated area; tamp with a soft-bristled brush. Apply isopropyl alcohol to flush the area, and tamp. Repeat until all color is removed, and let dry. Spray on diluted dishwashing-soap solution. Treat with an enzyme detergent before laundering.

MUD	If the stain is a combination of mud and grass, treat the grass stain first (see Grass, opposite). Shake or scrape off residue; pretreat the stain with the diluted dishwashing-soap mixture, and soak. Then treat with an enzyme detergent before laundering.
MUSTARD	Using an eyedropper, flush the stain with vinegar; then wash with dishwashing-soap solution.
PERSPIRATION	Saturate fresh stains with shampoo, then launder as usual. For old stains, treat with an enzyme paste. Buy digestive-enzyme tablets at a natural-foods store; grind four tablets and add equal parts water to make a damp paste. Gently rub onto the stain. Let sit for one hour. Launder as usual. Whites can be soaked overnight in hot water and oxygen bleach (follow label directions). Launder as usual.
PROTEIN (BLOOD, EGG YOLK, MILK, VOMIT)	Spray the diluted dishwashing-soap solution on the stain, and let it sit; rinse in tepid water. If visible staining remains, treat the area with enzyme detergent and launder according to label instructions.
RED WINE	Spray the diluted dishwashing-soap solution on the stain; tamp with a soft-bristled brush. Flush with water, apply vinegar, and tamp; let stand for several minutes, and flush again. If the stain remains, apply hydrogen peroxide and let stand. If the stain persists, apply 1 or 2 drops of ammonia to wetted area. Flush with water. Treat with an enzyme detergent; launder. If color remains after washing, apply a powdered nonchlorinated color-safe bleach such as sodium percarbonate; and rewash.
SOY SAUCE	Treat the stain the same as Red Wine (see treatment, above).
TOMATO-BASED SAUCES (BARBECUE, KETCHUP, TOMATO)	Scrape off the sauce; spray the area with the diluted dishwashing-soap solution. Soak in tepid water. Remove any remaining color using an eyedropper filled with white vinegar. Treat with an enzyme detergent, then launder. If color persists, apply several drops of hydrogen peroxide. Let sit, rinse, and treat again with an enzyme detergent before laundering.
VINAIGRETTE	First, treat the stain as a grease stain (see Grease, opposite). Then flush with white vinegar to remove any remaining color. Follow up with an enzyme detergent to remove residue before laundering.
WAX OR GUM	Use ice to freeze the wax or gum, or place the item in the freezer; scrape or crack off as much as you can, then use mineral spirits to remove residue. Rinse with isopropyl alcohol, let dry, and launder with an enzyme detergent.
WHITE WINE	Flush the stain with cold water, and spray with the diluted dishwashing-soap solution. Treat the area with an enzyme detergent before laundering.

DETERGENTS

The key to getting the best performance from a laundry detergent is a simple one: Read the directions on the label, and follow them. In general, label instructions assume that you're washing a load weighing 5 to 7 pounds, that clothing is moderately soiled, that you have moderately hard water (more than 85 percent of U.S. households have hard water), and that you're using an average amount of water—17 gallons for a top loader and 4 to 8 gallons for a front loader.

If you're washing a small or lightly soiled load, you can try using less than the recommended amount of detergent. It's best, however, not to use more. The extra residue that's left behind will attract dirt to clothes. Instead, treat stains before laundering or use one of the whiteners or brighteners shown opposite to boost the effectiveness of your detergent. Different types of detergents each offer specific benefits as outlined below:

TYPES OF DETERGENT

GENERAL PURPOSE
Liquids
Suitable for all washable fabrics. Especially effective on oily dirt. Also good for pretreating spots and stains before washing.

Powders
Suitable for all washable fabrics. Especially effective on clay and ground-in dirt.

CONCENTRATED
(ALSO KNOWN AS ULTRA)
Liquids and powders
These detergents come in smaller packages yet deliver the same cleaning power so you can use less detergent per wash.

COMBINATION
Liquids and powders
A detergent that does double-duty—with a built-in fabric softener or color-safe bleach.

LIGHT DUTY
Liquids and powders
Designed to clean delicates, baby clothes, and other washable fabrics that require gentle treatment. Can be used for hand-washing or in the machine. Includes brands such as Woolite and Ivory Snow.

HIGH EFFICIENCY
Liquids and powders
Designed for front-loading machines, which use less water than top loaders.

A NOTE ABOUT ENVIRONMENTALLY FRIENDLY LAUNDRY DETERGENTS

Manufacturers of detergents with plant-based, rather than the more common petroleum-based, ingredients have made major strides in recent years to achieve the strengths of conventional cleaners, without sacrificing responsibility to the environment. In general, these detergents minimize pollution by using renewable plant resources: Rather than tapping crude oil, their surfactants (the chemicals that give a detergent its cleaning power) come from vegetable oils, often from coconut. When shopping for plant-based detergents, look for labels that state the origin of their surfactants and scents: "coconut-oil-based surfactant," for instance, instead of "cleaning agents," and "fragrance derived from lavender oil" rather than "fragance."

WHITENERS AND BRIGHTENERS

- ☐ Baking Soda
- ☐ Bluing
- ☐ Lemon

- ☐ Borax
- ☐ Chlorine or oxygen bleach
- ☐ Enzyme presoaks

- ☐ Washing soda or sodium carbonate
- ☐ White vinegar

DETERGENT VS. SOAP

The term "detergent" commonly refers to a synthetic product, while soap is made from natural ingredients (either plant- or animal-based ones). Household detergents became widely available in the United States in the 1940s as a result of wartime shortages of the fats and oils needed for soap production (synthetic detergents were developed in Germany in 1916 in response to World War I–related shortages). By 1953, sales of detergents had surpassed those of soap; today, detergents have all but replaced soap-based laundry products, according to the Soap and Detergent Association.

HOW TO WHITEN WITH LEMON

White damask napkins, linens, even socks can be whitened on the stove: fill a pot with water and a few slices of fresh lemon; bring the water to a boil. Turn off heat, add linens, and let soak for up to an hour; launder as usual. For extra brightening, spread them out in the sunlight to dry.

WHITENERS AND BRIGHTENERS

Available in powder or liquid form, these laundry aids can brighten, deodorize, and soften laundry:

BAKING SODA

An effective cleaner, deodorizer, and fabric softener. Apply a paste (mix 4 tablespoons baking soda and an equal amount of water) to stains to absorb odors and help break down grease, or presoak new clothes (¼ cup baking soda to 1 gallon water) to eliminate factory residue.

BLUING

A liquid added to laundry during the Wash or Rinse cycle to combat the yellowing of whites. Its blue (usually ultramarine) pigment adds a subtle tint to fabrics, which makes them appear whiter (but doesn't actually whiten them), because a "blue" white appears brighter and cleaner than a "yellow" white or a "red" white. Bluing must be diluted with water before it's added to the washer. You can still find bluing in some supermarkets, but it is no longer a staple of the laundry room, since today's detergents—which often contain optical brighteners, dyes that make whites appear brighter—do a much better job of cleaning clothes and don't cause them to weaken the way chlorine bleach does.

BORAX

Available at most supermarkets, borax is a naturally occurring mineral. It has antiseptic, antibacterial, water-softening, and whitening properties, and boosts the cleaning power of detergents. It is a useful additive when washing cloth diapers because it whitens and neutralizes the ammonia odors found in urine. Add ½ cup to the wash.

BLEACH

There are two types of bleach: sodium hypochlorite (commonly known as chlorine or liquid household bleach) and oxygen (also called color-safe or nonchlorine). Chlorine and oxygen bleaches should not be used together—chlorine bleach will deactivate any oxygen bleach already in the laundry detergent. A fabric care label that doesn't mention bleach implies that you can use any type safely; it's best to avoid both types when washing anything with a "no bleach" label.

CHLORINE BLEACH is most often used in liquid form, although it is also found in dry form. It is safe only on whites. It can lift stains and maintain whiteness, but can't restore clothing to brand-new whiteness (nothing can). It also deodorizes laundry. The bleaching action of liquid chlorine bleach takes about five minutes after adding it to the wash (although it may occur more quickly in hot water and more slowly in cold). Chlorine bleach also acts as a disinfectant, since it kills bacteria. Always use caution when using chlorine bleach: It can weaken fabrics and even a tiny drop will spot or discolor a colored fabric. Always wear gloves and old clothes or an apron when you use chlorine bleach, and work in a well-ventilated area. Never add chlorine bleach full strength—always dilute it first in water and add it to the wash about five minutes into the washing cycle. (Most machines have a bleach dispenser. Follow the instructions in your user's manual.) Also, *never* mix chlorine bleach with either ammonia or vinegar; these combinations will result in the release of highly poisonous gases. Do not use chlorine bleach on vintage linens, baby clothes, silk, wool, mohair, or any synthetic fabric. Avoid chlorine bleach if your water is high in iron (as well water often is); it may cause yellowing.

OXYGEN BLEACHES are available in both powders and liquids. They are gentler, less toxic alternatives to chlorine beach, which relies on hydrogen peroxide for its cleaning power. Oxygen bleaches maintain colors and help keep whites white (but will not make them whiter). They are safe to use on colored cotton, wool, silk, and synthetic fabrics. Oxygen bleach is added to the wash at the same time as the detergent. It is especially effective with hot water, but will work well at temperatures below 130° F if you increase the exposure time. For dingy whites, presoak the laundry with oxygen bleach overnight before washing (always follow label directions).

KEEP LIQUID DETERGENTS AND BLEACHES ON A LIGHTWEIGHT TRAY WHILE YOU TREAT LAUNDRY, TO ELIMINATE DRIPS AND SPILLS ON THE MACHINE.

ENZYME PRESOAKS

These products are formulated to work on tough stains, especially hard-to-remove stains like perspiration and blood, but they can also be added to a load of wash to boost the effectiveness of regular laundry detergents. Enzyme presoaks consist of a number of active ingredients, including enzymes, which break down stains; builders, which enhance cleaning efficiency; surfactants, which loosen and remove soil; and bluing agents and optical brighteners, to make whites appear whiter. Some enzyme presoaks also contain an oxygen bleach.

WASHING SODA (OR SODIUM CARBONATE)

Available in supermarkets, this mineral has strong cleaning and degreasing properties. Add 2 tablespoons to laundry detergent to make it more effective, or mix it with a small amount of water to form a paste to remove greasy stains.

WHITE VINEGAR

Naturally acidic, white vinegar cuts grease, softens water, and whitens fabrics when added to the rinse water. Add it to the first rinse so it can be washed out by the second rinse. Depending on the size of the load, add anywhere from ⅛ cup to ½ cup. Although it was long thought to be a good idea to add vinegar or salt to wash water to help "set" dyes, this is of doubtful value. These household staples may indeed help to counteract dye loss by reducing the alkalinity of the wash water, but they will also inhibit the detergent's ability to clean your clothes. In any case, the quantities used would have to be extremely large to be effective.

FABRIC SOFTENERS

When used properly, fabric softeners can leave clothes feeling soft and smooth, and cut down on wrinkles (eliminating the need to iron, in some cases). Many people also choose to use them for their ability to reduce static cling. Fabric softeners are by no means necessary, however, and should be used with caution for the sake of your clothes and your dryer, as described below.

There are three different kinds of softeners: liquids, which are added to the machine during the final Rinse cycle; sheets, which are used in the dryer; and liquid and powder detergents that contain softeners. The first two are generally the most effective because they aren't rinsed out in the Wash cycle. However, fabric softener sheets can be hazardous in certain dryers: They leave behind residue that can build up on lint screens, blocking airflow, or on moisture sensors. Always check your dryer manual; some manufacturers recommend specific brands of dryer sheets and some recommend you do not use them at all. Be sure to remove the sheets from the dryer at the end of each cycle and clean the lint screen thoroughly. Here are other considerations to keep in mind:

☐ Follow label directions. Liquid fabric softeners can actually cause oily-looking stains on clothes if used in greater amounts than recommended. If spots appear, pretreat with your regular detergent and wash again.

☐ Never pour softener directly onto fabrics.

☐ Don't use fabric softener every time you wash your clothes. Softeners can build up on the fabric, causing a dingy, yellowed appearance and slippery texture. Fabric softeners may also reduce the flame resistance of some fabrics. Use softeners every few washes instead.

☐ Don't use fabric softeners on cotton towels, baby clothes, diapers, athletic apparel, or any other item designed to be absorbent.

☐ Some fabrics, such as spandex and polyester, are especially prone to spotting when treated with fabric softener sheets. Choose liquid fabric softeners, which distribute themselves evenly in the washer's rinse water, for these fabrics instead.

A NOTE ABOUT WASHING DENIM

To keep jeans and other denim garments from fading too quickly, turn them inside out before you wash them.

☐ Store dryer sheets in a cool, dry area away from heat sources (such as the dryer itself). The softeners in the dryer sheets are sensitive to heat and may clump together when warm.

SEPTIC SYSTEMS AND LAUNDRY

One of the biggest problems involving washing machines and septic tanks is overloading the system with too much water and lint from clothing. If you flood your septic tank by doing ten loads of laundry on a Saturday, you could stir up and flush solids in the tank into the drain field. It's best to have an even flow of water through the tank during the week by doing a load or two every day, rather than doing ten loads in one day. Because lint does not settle in the "sludge" at the bottom of the tank, an overload of it can clog the pores of the soil bed. In addition, lint from synthetic clothing (polyester and nylon) won't biodegrade or break down in the septic system. Installing a reusable, inline filter attached to the washing machine discharge hose will fix this problem.

In terms of laundering supplies, it's best to use a liquid detergent, as powdered detergents can clog the drain field. If you must use powdered detergents, use a highly biodegradable variety. It's also preferable to use a nonphosphate detergent, to prevent the system's runoff causing nearby waterways to become overenriched with nutrients, which can result in depleted oxygen levels. A small amount of chlorine bleach (up to 5 loads per week, say) is okay to use, but too much bleach will harm the microorganisms that help break down the waste in the tank.

A NOTE ABOUT MENDING

It's important to fix tears or ripped hems before laundering clothes. The washer's agitating and tumbling action can make them worse. With a few tools and knowledge of the basic stitches (along with a little patience), you can tackle a host of repairs. See pages 438–444 for simple sewing techniques for fixing ripped seams and hems.

HOW TO PREPARE CLOTHES FOR THE WASHER

1. Remove pins or buckles, zip zippers, close snaps and hooks, and secure Velcro to prevent snags and abrasion (do not fasten buttons, however, which can cause stress on the buttons and buttonholes).

2. Empty pockets and turn them inside out, unfurl socks, and unroll cuffs.

3. Tie sashes and strings to prevent tangling.

4. Place delicate items like bras, stockings, and fine knitwear in zippered mesh bags.

5. Turn delicate items, sweaters, and cotton T-shirts inside out to prevent pilling.

6. Turn dark, fade-prone clothes inside out, as abrasion from rubbing against other clothes can cause fibers to fray, making clothes look faded.

7. Open up button-down collars to reduce wear along folds.

HOW TO MACHINE-WASH

Once you have sorted your laundry into like piles, treated stains, and selected the appropriate detergents and additives, you're ready to wash.

For top loaders, add the detergent while the washer is filling (use only the recommended amount). Wait until the washer is full of water to add clothes. Distribute laundry evenly and loosely. Don't overload or pack the washer, and don't wrap items around the agitator. Even the largest loads shouldn't fill more than three-quarters of the tub. Otherwise, clothes will not get clean; they will also wrinkle, tangle, and retain soap from the Wash cycle. Similarly, do not overstuff a front loader.

PRESOAKING

Water is enough to remove many spots, especially light ones, if you get them when they're fresh. Even stains that have had time to set will loosen somewhat while they soak. Presoak laundry from the "very dirty" basket or clothing with perspiration odor for an hour in an enzyme detergent dissolved in water before running the regular cycle. You can soak laundry in the washer, a large bucket, or a utility sink.

HOW TO KEEP WHITES WHITE

Whites will gradually become dingy if not laundered properly. Always wash whites together (never with colored clothing) using the hottest water appropriate for the fabric (check the care label). Regular use of oxygen bleach can help keep whites white. Soaking whites in oxygen bleach overnight is probably the most effective way to remove yellow perspiration stains and overall dinginess. Sunlight is also an effective whitener—whenever possi-

A NOTE ABOUT SAVING WATER
Before starting every load, adjust the load-size setting. Filling the washer to capacity for a small load is wasteful.

HOW TO ELIMINATE STATIC CLING

1. Remove clothes from the dryer while still slightly damp (allow to air-dry before folding and putting away).

2. Stop the electrical charges from building up in the first place by using a humidifier to put moisture into the air in your home.

3. When purchasing clothing, keep in mind that natural fabrics (such as cotton, linen, and wool) are less likely than synthetic fibers (such as rayon, polyester, and nylon) to produce static.

4. If clothes you're wearing are clinging, mist the air with water from a spray bottle, then walk through it to discharge the static. You can also mist clothing with an antistatic spray, which coats the surface of the fabric with salts that absorb moisture in the air.

5. Use a quarter of a dryer sheet (instead of a whole one) or rub 1 teaspoon of liquid softener into a damp washcloth and place it in the dryer with clothes. Dryer sheets tend to be better static inhibitors than liquid softeners.

ble, hang white clothes in the sun to dry. However, even with these precautions, whites will eventually lose their brand-new brightness, and once it's gone, it can't be restored. During manufacture, whites are often treated with optical brighteners (also known as fluorescent brighteners), which are dyes that give fabrics a blue tint, making them appear whiter. These dyes are washed away as easily as they were added, leaving clothes a bit duller.

HOW TO KEEP DARKS FROM FADING

If you launder your favorite black shirt again and again, it will eventually turn a disappointing shade of gray. Many of the dyes used in clothing production are not truly colorfast. But dyes also fade because of factors such as hot water, oversoaking, sunlight, and abrasion. (You can probably see the results of abrasion on the knees or seat of your jeans, where the fabric is a few shades lighter than on surrounding areas.) Chlorine in tap water may also cause your clothes to fade faster than they should. Detergents specially designed for dark colors may help. Some work to counteract the chlorine in the wash water, while others "lock in" the color to inhibit dye transfer during the Wash cycle, preventing bleeding. As with any laundry product, follow the label directions to ensure good results. Choosing a warm, rather than hot, wash and a cold, rather than warm, rinse may also help.

HOW TO WASH LINGERIE

Set the machine to the Gentle cycle, which mimics the motion of handwashing. If your machine has an agitator, use a lingerie bag for garments with straps and ribbons, as well as panty hose. This bag, available at department or lingerie stores, ensures those items won't get snagged in the machine. Line dry all lingerie to prolong its life. Depending on how often it is worn, the life span of a bra is anywhere from six months to two years. A good way to extend it is to rotate bras—don't wear the same one twice in a row. Alternating bras lets each one return to its original elasticity.

LINGERIE REQUIRES GENTLE HANDLING—USE ZIPPERED MESH BAGS WHEN WASHING IT IN THE MACHINE, AND ALWAYS ALLOW ITEMS TO AIR DRY.

HOW TO WASH BABY CLOTHES

A newborn's skin is too sensitive for many detergents, chlorine bleach, and dry-cleaning chemicals. Gentle detergents designed specifically for baby clothes, such as Ivory Snow and Dreft, are formulated to leave fabric soft, and they contain fewer additives that can cause irritation. (All baby clothes should be washed prior to the first wearing.) However, they often don't have strong cleaning properties, so treat stains before washing to keep baby garments pristine. (Look for stain treatments formulated especially for baby clothes.) Avoid products with dyes and perfumes, and keep an eye out for signs of an allergic reaction. Adding an extra Rinse cycle can help eliminate detergent residue.

GOLDEN RULES OF WASHING BABY CLOTHES

1. Before washing any garment for the first time, read the care label. Infants' and children's sleepwear often requires special care because it is treated with flame-resistant chemicals; some detergents (especially those with built-in fabric softeners) can reduce that resistance.

2. It is not necessary to wash infant clothes separately, so long as you use mild, unscented detergent.

3. Presoak stains in cool water as soon as they appear. Water is enough to remove many spots if you get them when they're fresh. Stains that have had time to set will loosen somewhat while they soak.

4. Choose a stain removal treatment formulated for baby clothes, or use a soft-bristle nylon brush and a small amount of mild detergent to gently work out a spot, but don't scrub or you'll risk damaging the fabric. After using a stain-removal method, always check for any leftover traces before tumble drying (heat will set the stain). If the mark remains, repeat the process over again, or try something stronger.

5. When treating stains, remember that a baby's skin is sensitive. Rinse the clothing thoroughly after treatment, and skip the treatments on any clothes that will be rubbing against a baby's skin, such as cloth diapers and undershirts.

STAIN-REMOVAL GUIDE FOR BABY CLOTHES

FRUIT AND VEGETABLE STAINS
(PUREED FOODS, JUICE, BERRIES)
Flush with cool water; soak in a mixture of half rubbing alcohol and half water. If the stain loosens, launder as usual. If not, apply an enzyme-based stain remover, then wash. For a very stubborn stain, lightly bleach the area by soaking in a mixture of equal parts white vinegar and water.

LEAKY DIAPER STAINS
Bowel-movement stains should be treated in the same way as protein stains, below left. For urine stains, pretreat the area with a tablespoon of ammonia diluted in 1 cup water. Follow with an enzyme-based stain remover. Launder as usual. (Do not use these treatments on the diapers themselves, as they could result in skin irritation.)

PROTEIN STAINS
(BREAST MILK, FORMULA,
FOOD STAINS, SPIT-UP, BLOOD)
Soak in plain water first, then add an enzyme detergent. If the stain remains, apply an enzyme-based stain remover, then launder.

OILY, GREASY STAINS
(BABY OIL, CREAMS, PETROLEUM JELLY)
If fresh, remove any excess, and cover the area with cornstarch or talcum powder to absorb oil; scrape off after ten to fifteen minutes. Apply an enzyme-based stain remover, then launder.

AIRING DOWN-FILLED
PILLOWS AND
COMFORTERS ON A
CLOTHESLINE SEVERAL
TIMES PER
YEAR CAN KEEP THEM
SMELLING FRESH
AND MINIMIZE THE NEED
FOR LAUNDERING.

HOW TO WASH DOWN ITEMS

Although it's exceptionally durable, down requires some special care. Following a few simple guidelines for regular maintenance, and knowing how to treat spills and stains, will help keep down-filled pieces looking like new. (For information on selecting down, turn to page 281.)

Guard your comforter from stains and spills with a fabric cover that buttons for easy changing and washing. Protect pillows with zippered pillow protectors, and, of course, pillowcases. Down-filled sleeping bags and down clothing, such as parkas and vests, are more prone to stains and dirt, but their outer fabric coverings often come treated with water repellents specially formulated to allow the down inside to breathe.

If garments or bedding become soiled, spot treat them promptly with a mild detergent to prevent staining. Push the down away from the area to be cleaned so the feathers won't get wet during the cleaning. Apply warm water with an eyedropper to the area; then apply a small amount of mild detergent or baby shampoo with a soft, clean toothbrush; sponge the area thoroughly with warm water; and blot dry with a clean, color-safe towel. Hang to dry in a warm, airy location, preferably outside on a clothesline.

Although some experts recommend professional dry cleaning for all down items, it is generally safe to wash them, either in the machine, on the gentle cycle, or by hand.

WASHING DOWN IN THE WASHER

Use a front-loading machine that is large enough to hold dry articles without crowding (the jerking action of the agitator in a top-load washer may cause damage by packing the down). If you don't have a front loader, you can take the item to a self-service laundry. (See directions below for drying.)

WASHING DOWN BY HAND

Fill a bathtub with lukewarm water and add detergent. To determine the amount, follow the label directions for hand-washing loads—use the minimum amount recommended (there should not be a mountain of suds). Gently squeeze the soapy water through the down-filled article, then drain the wash water. Rinse with fresh cool water, refilling the tub as necessary.

HOW TO DRY DOWN

After rinsing items completely—either by hand or machine—press out the water by hand, or use a washing machine's Spin cycle (a top-loading machine is fine since it won't agitate while spinning). Do not wring. Tumble dry on low heat for a few hours, until completely dry. Adding several clean, dry towels will absorb moisture and speed the drying process; a few clean tennis balls stuffed in clean cotton socks, or clean canvas tennis shoes, added to the dryer will help break up any clumps of filling that form.

After the cycle finishes, take the items out to fluff. If they're still damp, repeat.

HOW TO WASH PILLOWS

Whether made of natural fibers (such as down) or synthetic materials (often polyester), most pillows can be washed in the machine. (For information on selecting pillows, turn to page 278.) They should be cleaned every three to six months to remove mold, bacteria, and odors. Read instructions on the tag to make sure the pillow is not Dry-clean Only. (Down pillows that were manufactured before washable ones became common often carry this caveat.)

It's best to use a front-loading washer, since pillows tend to float and stay dry in spots in a top-loading machine. If you don't have such an appliance, consider going to a self-service laundry. Set the machine on its gentlest cycle, using warm water; add a small amount of a mild liquid detergent, such as Ivory Snow or Dreft (powder detergent may leave a residue), then fill the tub loosely with your pillows. Repeat the Rinse cycle a second time to remove detergent completely. For pillows that shouldn't go in the dryer (usually the foam kind, which can melt), dry them on a rack (secure with clothespins) or a clothesline.

HOW TO HAND-WASH

Hand-washing is appropriate to any delicate fabric, such as wool or silk, as well as lingerie and vintage clothing or linens. The basic technique described for hand-washing a sweater on pages 390–391 works well for most any article. Special handling techniques follow.

SILK

Washing can damage poor-quality silk, but most silk garments can be washed safely. To test silk quality, crush the fabric in your hand, then let go. If it feels full and "liquid" and smooths out quickly, it probably can be hand-washed. If it holds the wrinkles, have the garment dry-cleaned. Before washing colored silk, test for colorfastness. Dampen the fabric inside a seam and wait a few minutes. Then dab the spot with a white cloth. If the color comes off, the dye will run when washed, and you must dry-clean the garment.

Wash white and colorfast silks in tepid water—no warmer than your skin—with mild detergent. Add ¼ cup of white vinegar in the first rinse to remove soap residue and restore luster to the fabric. Then rinse thoroughly with water one final time. If the label on the garment says it's safe to iron, do so. Iron while the item is still damp for the best results, with a cool iron, on the wrong side, and finish drying on a padded hanger.

WOOL

The term "wool" refers to the curly undercoat of various hairy mammals, including lambs, sheep, Kashmir goats, Angora goats, camels, llamas, alpacas, and vicuñas. Wool from sheep is the most common—lamb's wool is shorn from sheep less than eight months old, and merino wool is from a specific breed that yields the finest and softest sheep wool.

Wool has some amazing qualities: It can last for decades and keeps you toasty when the weather's cold; even when the fiber is wet, it can keep you warm. But it does require special care, and unfortunately, once wool shrinks, the damage is irreversible. Each wool fiber is covered with tiny overlapping scales, much like the tiles on a roof, which repel water. Once fibers are spun into yarn and woven into fabric, the scales play a role in shrinkage: As the washing machine twists, turns, and churns a wool sweater, the scales catch on one another and wind up permanently locked together. The result is an item that has become felted, meaning it is thick and matted—and smaller by a size or two. Rewashing and stretching are likely to be in vain; the fabric will only spring back to its newly smaller self.

To keep from suffering the disappointment of a ruined garment, always check care labels. Some will indicate that the clothing has been

CONTINUED ON PAGE 392 >>

HOW TO WASH A SWEATER

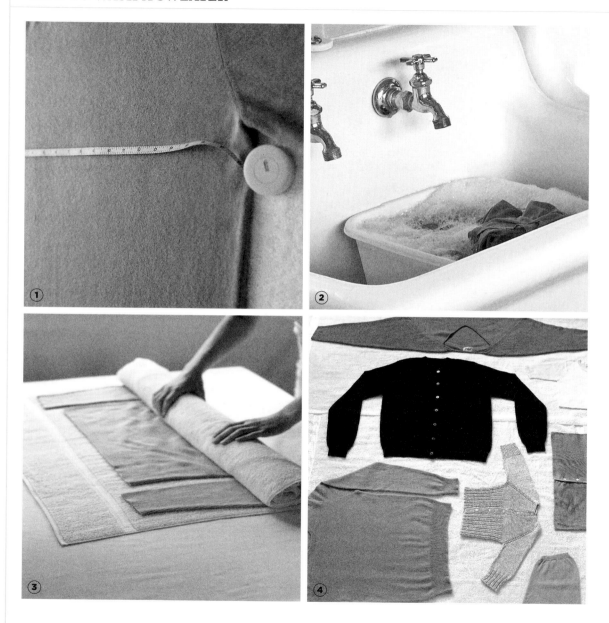

1. Before washing any stretchable knit, measure in four places (shoulder to shoulder, across the bottom, and along the outside of each arm) so that you can restore it to its correct shape (also known as blocking) before drying. For more precise shaping, trace the outline of the article while dry on a piece of kraft paper; use the outline as a reference for reshaping.

2. Use a detergent designed for hand-washables or a mild dishwashing liquid. Dissolve the detergent in a sink or basin with cool water. Use the amount suggested on the label, or just enough to create suds that cover the surface of the water (but not enough to overflow the basin). Dissolve detergent in water completely before adding clothes. Immerse the article in the sudsy water. Swish it about, and gently squeeze the suds through the fabric. Do not wring or twist. Let it soak for several minutes, gently squeezing, then gently lift the item over the basin and drain the water. Run fresh water into the basin to rinse. Repeat until the water runs clear. Gently squeeze over the basin to remove excess water.

3. Carefully transfer the item to a clean, dry, white towel on a flat surface. Support the weight of the fabric as you lift so that it does not stretch. Reshape the article on the towel, then roll the article and towel together, pressing as you go to remove water. Repeat with a second towel, if necessary.

4. Hang lightweight items that will not stretch on a rack or the clothesline. Dry heavy items flat on a mesh sweater dryer on a dry towel. You will need to replace towels as they get wet. It's also a good idea to place a hand towel inside the sweater, between the front and back, to help it dry faster. Reshape according to the measurements you took before washing.

5. Once the sweater is dry, run a handheld steamer over it to remove any wrinkles, if necessary. Lay the sweater on a flat surface and gently hold it in place with one hand while running a depilling sweater comb from one end to the other in a straight line. When you've finished one side, turn the sweater over and repeat. If you don't have a depiller, or if the item is fragile and you'd rather not use a blade, try a fine-toothed comb instead.

treated so it can, in fact, be cleaned in a washing machine on the Gentle cycle; the fibers in such pieces are coated with a resin that keeps the scales from interlocking. Others will be marked Dry-clean Only and should not be washed (jackets, felted wool garments, trousers, dresses, and coats fall into this category). But the best way to wash wool sweaters and unlined mittens and gloves (which may be marked Dry-clean) is by hand. Just remember to always use cool water and follow the hand-washing guidelines on pages 390–391.

HOW TO WASH BLANKETS

Most cotton blankets and those made of synthetics and blends can be washed in the machine; see the label for instructions. Many other blankets can be washed safely by hand at home, even wool, cashmere, and mohair. However, if the blanket is very expensive, an heirloom, or a vintage piece, dry-clean it.

1. Shake the blanket outdoors before washing to remove any dust and loose dirt.

2. If the blanket has not been washed before, test for colorfastness. Use a wet cotton swab to moisten a small section near the edge of the blanket; blot the spot with a clean white cloth. If the color does not bleed onto the cloth, the blanket is safe to wash.

3. Fill a tub or deep sink with cool water and mild detergent. Then add the blanket, swishing it through the water. Do not use hot water on a wool blanket, or the weave might shrink or warp, causing a wavy surface. Soak the blanket for up to thirty minutes if very soiled. Drain the water and gently press out excess sudsy water. Fill the tub or sink with cool water. Swish the blanket around. Drain, rinse again, and repeat until all the soap is gone and the water is clear.

4. Do not wring. Instead, press out excess water, then roll the blanket between clean, dry towels to remove as much water as possible. Replace the towels often as they become wet and turn the blanket over frequently.

5. Smooth the blanket onto clean, dry towels. Don't hang it, as this could loosen the weave.

HOW TO WASH VINTAGE CLOTHING

First, determine whether the fabric is strong enough to wash. If the fabric smells of must or mildew, or if it feels dry and brittle, it may not stand up to submersion in water and should be taken to a professional cleaner. Otherwise, follow these steps:

1. Place the garment on a piece of nylon net to support the delicate fibers, then soak it in cool water.

2. Choose a mild detergent such as Orvus Paste, which is available at many sewing and art supply stores. It has cleaning and whitening properties but is gentle on fabric.

3. With delicate fabrics, do not try to remove small stains, but if the fabric is sturdy, you can try a detergent that contains a color-safe bleach. This will help to lighten yellow age marks on fabric and brighten whites that haven't been laundered for many years.

4. Rinse well to remove all traces of detergent.

5. Always air-dry vintage clothing.

HOW TO WASH VINTAGE LINENS

Cleaning vintage linens can be easier than you might think. Many vintage pieces are made from cotton or linen, which are durable fibers. Unless a piece is particularly valuable—in which case you should take it to a professional textile cleaner or restorer—you can launder it at home. Here's how:

1. Soak overnight in plain, tepid water (keeping like colors together, if you're washing more than one item at a time). Soaking will begin to remove dirt and old detergent, and will rehydrate the fabric. If linens are yellowed, add ½ cup oxygen bleach to 2 to 3 gallons of water (do not use chlorine bleach, which can weaken fibers). Gently agitate by hand, then let soak until the cloth appears white (this may take several hours). Rinse with cold water.

2. Treat stains on vintage fabrics using the chart on pages 376–377, although it may take some guesswork to determine the cause.

3. After dealing with stains, put linens into a tub of warm water with a mild detergent, such as Ivory Snow (follow label directions for hand-washing). Agitate gently; don't wring or rub hard. Drain off the dirty water, and rinse with fresh warm water. Don't run the water directly onto the fabric. Repeat until the rinse water runs clear. Don't wring or twist.

4. Roll up the article in a clean, white towel and blot excess water.

5. Dry on a line or rack.

6. Iron while still slightly damp with a dry iron.

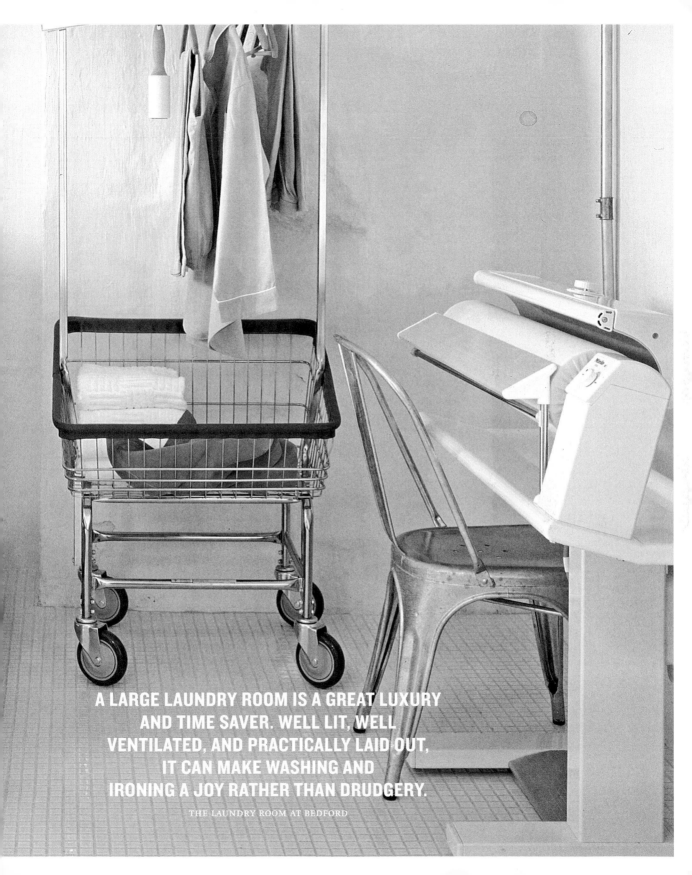

A LARGE LAUNDRY ROOM IS A GREAT LUXURY AND TIME SAVER. WELL LIT, WELL VENTILATED, AND PRACTICALLY LAID OUT, IT CAN MAKE WASHING AND IRONING A JOY RATHER THAN DRUDGERY.

THE LAUNDRY ROOM AT BEDFORD

HOW TO DRY LAUNDRY

TUMBLE DRYING

A dryer is a wonderful convenience, but you can maintain your clothing much longer by line drying it. The tumbling action of the dryer rubs clothes against one another and against the dryer drum, abrading the fibers. Dryer lint is actually bits of worn-away fabric. Although line drying everything may not be practical for a large family, at the minimum, line dry fine washables, and garments that contain elastic or spandex, which shrinks and breaks down in the dryer.

For those items that may be safely tumble dried (always check care labels for guidance), follow these tips:

☐ Don't overload the dryer. This makes it work harder, consuming more energy. It also encourages wrinkling.

☐ Don't overdry laundry. This leads to static cling, stubborn wrinkles, and shrinkage (when clothes overdry, they heat up, which is what causes shrinkage). Remove laundry when it is just dry, or better yet, still damp, especially if you're going to iron it right away. (Be sure items are completely dry before putting them away.)

☐ To minimize wrinkling, remove clothing as soon as possible once the dryer shuts off, then fold them or hang them up.

☐ Do not tumble dry items containing rubber, plastic, or foam (such as rubber-backed bath mats or padded bras), which can create a fire hazard.

☐ If you find paper bits on clothes after a wash (evidence of a forgotten note in a pocket), dry half the load at a time to remove the bits effectively; clean the filter midway through the cycle if there's a lot of paper.

☐ Items marked Wash Separately are likely to bleed, at least for the first few washes. Dye transference can happen in the dryer as well as the washer, so it's best to not only wash such items with like colors or alone but to tumble dry them the same way—or even line dry them. If you choose to tumble dry them, check the dryer after removing such items, as a residue may remain, which could then transfer to the next load. If so, wipe the drum with a cloth dampened with water and mild dishwashing liquid until no color comes off. Rinse thoroughly with a clean damp cloth.

LINE DRYING

Anything that can be tumble dried can also be dried on a clothesline or drying rack. If weather and space permit, outdoor drying is best: It offers the benefits of the whitening effects of the sun (which means you'll use less bleach) and the fresh scent of the air. But for apartment living, during the cold, wet months, and for items that might fade in direct sunlight, the basement (if it's not too damp), attic, utility room, or in a pinch, the bathroom are all appropriate places for air drying laundry. Store-bought wooden or plastic-coated wire racks are handy for this purpose. You also can make a simple foldaway rack like the one pictured on page 365. Wherever you dry clothes, you'll minimize wrinkling by folding directly from the line or rack and placing the laundry in a large basket or tub before putting it away.

Outdoor clotheslines should be hung near the laundry room in a space with a 4-foot allowance on either side to keep clothes from rubbing against fences, plants, and walls. Clotheslines should be long enough to accommodate at least one load of wash—about 35 feet is optimal—but not much longer, or the weight of your wet laundry may bring the load sagging to the ground (any clothesline will stretch out after a few uses, so you'll occasionally have to untie it and pull it tight again). A spot that gets generous sun, tempered by a period of shade (for light-sensitive delicate fabrics), is ideal.

The most common types of clotheslines are plastic, nylon, and cotton rope. All will need to be changed if they develop mold or mildew.

PLASTIC CLOTHESLINES

Plastic clotheslines with wire and fiber reinforcement are stretch-resistant, waterproof, inexpensive, and easy to clean. However, they are thin, which makes it more difficult for the clothespin to hold laundry tightly. Also, dirt clings to these lines, so they need to be wiped weekly with a damp cloth.

NYLON CLOTHESLINES

Nylon lines are lightweight, water-resistant, mildew-resistant, and strong, but clothespins slip off its slick surface and knots don't hold well. They should also be wiped weekly with a damp cloth.

COTTON ROPE

Cotton rope is not as strong as plastic or nylon, but can still support a load of wet laundry. It provides a good gripping surface and diameter for clothespins and it ties well. To clean it, take it down, wrap it around a wooden board, and scrub it with a brush and detergent. Unfortunately, cotton fiber will inevitably mildew. Once that happens, the clothesline cannot be saved; simply replace it. To minimize stretching of new cotton line, boil it in a large stockpot for a few minutes and allow it to dry in the sun before installing it.

LINE-DRYING TECHNIQUES

Laundry will dry faster and with fewer wrinkles if a breeze can pass through it, thanks to strategic hanging. There are two basic kinds of clothespins. One is simply a split piece of wood that slides over the fabric and line. The other type works like a pair of scissors, with a hinge that allows it to "pinch" the fabric and line together. Which type you use depends on your own preference. Here's how to hang laundry effectively:

HOW TO HANG CLOTHING

Hang upside down to avoid stretching the material where it might be most noticeable (such as the shoulders). To avoid leaving marks on a cotton sweater, thread panty-hose legs through its sleeves and pull the waist of the hose out the sweater's neck; then pin the waist and feet of the hose to the line, so the sweater's arms are horizontal and its body hangs free. Turn colored items inside out and hang them out of direct sunlight. A few hours in the sun probably won't damage them, but they can fade if they're left on the line for a full day.

HOW TO HANG SHEETS AND TABLECLOTHS

Instead of draping them over the clothesline, fold these large items in half, and pin the corners of the hem edges to the line, allowing the fold to hang open at the bottom. Then, in between those corners, pin each hem to the line separately, creating gaps at the top to catch the breeze.

HOW TO HANG TOWELS

Drape the short end over the line so it overlaps by 3 inches, then clip. You can reduce the stiff texture towels acquire on the line by giving them a sharp snap just before pinning them to the line and once again before taking them down. You can also remove them from the line while still slightly damp and tumble them in the dryer or add ¼ cup of white vinegar or baking soda along with your laundry detergent during the Wash cycle.

HOW TO INSTALL AN OUTDOOR CLOTHESLINE

The height of the clothesline depends on how tall you are; extend your arms above your head, and use that height as your guide. Seven to eight feet above the ground is the general rule, but just make sure the line is comfortable for you to reach, and high enough that your laundry won't touch the ground. The length of the line depends on the size of your backyard, but 20 to 35 feet is average. You'll need two strong supports, such as trees or a post of the porch. Choose an area of the yard where the clothesline won't get in anyone's way.

You'll need a drill; a screwdriver; a heavy-duty hook; a metal eye hook; a cleat, a small metal fitting that you'll wrap the rope around to anchor it (if you're not sure what a cleat looks like, imagine the device you use to secure a rope on a flagpole); and a metal ring. (All of the supplies should be available at any hardware store.)

Start by marking the height you want the line to be on each support. On one support, screw in the hook at the point you marked; start the hole with a drill. On the other, screw in the eye hook. Twelve inches below the eye hook, install a cleat. Using a tight knot, tie one end of the rope to the ring. Loop the ring over the hook, and walk the rope over to the other support; thread the other end through the eye hook, pull it tight, and wind it around the cleat to secure.

IRONING

Before the advent of the automatic washer and dryer, so strenuous was ironing the laundry that it often took up an entire day—especially for large families. The freshly washed laundry might be dried outdoors on a line and then stored, slightly damp, overnight so that it was just right for ironing the next morning. Today, because of the prevalence of chemical resin treatments on clothing and household linens that minimize wrinkling and give them a smooth appearance, ironing is no longer the essential task it once was. Permanent press, often labeled No Iron or Wrinkle Resistant, clothing has been around since the late 1960s, but recent refinements in the chemical process have resulted in fabrics—including 100 percent cotton—that look and feel more natural.

There are still many instances, however, when there's no substitute for a good pressing. Having the tools at the ready and knowing a few simple techniques will guarantee success.

Start by outfitting your laundry areas with the necessary tools and equipment and putting together a kit of ironing aids (see the list on pages 408–411) in a bin or basket.

IRONING BOARDS

Ironing boards typically range from 49 to 59 inches long and 13 to 19 inches wide. The larger the work surface, the easier the task, especially when it comes to ironing table and bed linens. An ironing board should be sturdy, for obvious safety reasons, and adjust up and down for the comfort of users of different heights. Ironing boards should be covered with two separate layers: a pad, to provide a smooth, cushioned surface, and a cover that fits securely over the pad. Covers are often treated with a coating such as Teflon or silicone for scorch and stain resistance (before washing a coated cover, check for a care label; laundering can damage this protective finish). A sleeve board—a padded mini board for ironing the sleeves of blouses, shirts, and jackets—is a useful accessory. Another convenience: an iron rest, a steel iron-shaped plate or clamp-on rack that attaches to your ironing board, which allows you to rest the iron flat without scorching while you're not handling it.

If you iron a lot of large items, a standard-size ironing board might be inadequate. A good way to deal with this is to pad the top of a table to create an oversized ironing surface. Cover a tabletop with three layers of blankets, then top with a sheet. You can also use the protective pad you place under your tablecloth in lieu of blankets; add a layer of toweling for extra cushioning, then drape with a sheet.

A WELL-EQUIPPED IRONING BOARD INCLUDES A SHELF FOR FOLDED ITEMS, AND A SLEEVE BOARD FOR SHIRTS AND BLOUSES.

TYPES OF IRONS

Irons with specialty features abound, but these days even some of the most basic irons available include options such as automatic shutoff, clog-preventing water filters (particularly useful in areas with hard water), vertical steaming ability, and multiple steam settings. Many new irons are also self-cleaning.

THE IRON

Your most important tool, of course, is the iron itself. Invest in a high-quality model, which should last for years, and choose one that suits your ironing needs. Irons generally weigh between 2 and 4 pounds—the heavier the iron, the better it will remove wrinkles, since weight is what gives it pressing power. Heavy irons can be difficult to hold, however, and can quickly cause fatigue or cramping. Lighter irons require less effort to move across the fabric, but they also require more passes back and forth in order to be effective, which can also be tiring. The right one for you is one that is comfortable to handle and easy to maneuver. Consider the construction of the soleplate (the flat part of the iron that heats up) as well, since that can determine the amount of glide, or friction, between it and the fabric being pressed. The soleplate can be made of slick stainless steel or aluminum; on some models, the soleplate's surface is made of one metal, and the core, or heating element, of another. Its surface is usually covered with a series of channels to help it glide smoothly and evenly, and may also be coated with a nonstick substance that makes it easy to clean. If you regularly iron with spray starch, or use bondable interfacing as part of sewing and other craft projects, an iron with an easy-to-clean, nonstick soleplate is essential. (Irons without a shutoff feature are also useful for sewers and crafters.)

HOW TO IRON A MONOGRAM

To keep an embroidered design or monogram crisp and clear, iron the design facedown against a towel. The soft texture of the towel will prevent the pattern from being flattened. Finish by turning the cloth right side up and ironing gently around the design. Starch also helps keep shape: You can use spray starch alone, or for more crispness, add starch to your wash. (For instructions, turn to pages 408–410.)

STEAM IRONS

If you've ever pulled a wrinkled pair of pants from a suitcase and hung them in the bathroom while the shower is running, you know how steam can eliminate wrinkles. When choosing a steam iron, look for these features:

☐ A large water tank or reservoir. A bigger tank means you won't have to stop in the middle of a big load of ironing to refill it with water, then wait for the water to heat up. Opt for a see-through, removable tank, so that you can track the water level as you iron, and bring the tank directly to the sink and back for refilling and emptying.

☐ Two parallel rows of steam holes, which spread the steam out over a bigger area than a single row of holes can.

☐ Variable steam settings. These allow you to set the amount of steam according to the fabric you are ironing—synthetic, cotton, or wool.

☐ Vertical steaming. This allows you to mimic a handheld steamer, by holding the iron upright to steam garments while they hang. It's also practical for steaming curtains while in place.

☐ An antidrip system. Sometimes ironing on low temperatures can cause the water to spit or hiss rather than steam; an antidrip system is designed to prevent that.

☐ A burst of steam. This feature provides an extra boost of steaming action, for tackling particularly deep-set wrinkles, or setting crisp creases.

HOW TO IRON

There are two important laws of ironing: First, use as much moisture as a fabric can stand. Second, use a damp pressing cloth—a clean cotton or linen handkerchief—on all dark fabrics and anything with a lining, to keep the "skeleton," the seams and pockets, from showing through. A pressing cloth will also guard against glazing, which is when the top layers of a fabric melt, forming a smooth surface. In addition, follow these basic guidelines:

☐ Read care labels and follow them (the chart on page 373 will help you decipher them).

☐ Iron fabrics requiring the lowest temperature first.

☐ With mixed fibers, iron on the temperature for the most delicate fiber.

☐ Test delicate fabrics on an inside seam before ironing.

☐ Iron cotton and linen fabrics damp out of the dryer.

☐ Always move the iron back and forth with the grain of the fabric; ironing in a circular motion can stretch fabric.

☐ Keep the iron moving, but don't rush. After finishing one area, wait about ten seconds before moving on, to set the press.

☐ Never iron velvet or any other fabric with a nap (or pile); the heat and weight of the iron can cause shine and damage the pile. Steam it instead.

☐ To prevent scratching the soleplate, don't iron over zippers, hooks, snaps, or buttons.

IRONING CREASES

Crisp creases make trousers look fresh and neat. As a general guideline, creases start a few inches below the waistline and run right down the center of each leg, in front and in back. On pleated pants, the crease starts where the pleat ends; with flat-front pants, the top of the crease should fall somewhere between the crotch of the pants and the midpoint of the fly.

The technique below makes much more sense than working on one pant leg while the other dangles from the board, and moving efficiently from the inside to the outside keeps the pants as crisp as possible. Be sure to hang the trousers in the same manner that you laid them down on the ironing board—with seams together—to preserve the creases. You should use a good-quality wood clamp hanger, which grips the trouser bottoms, or drape the pants neatly over a trouser hanger.

HOW TO IRON CREASES INTO TROUSERS

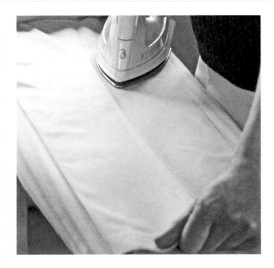

1 Lay the pant legs lengthwise along the ironing board with all four seams aligned so that they are in the middle of the legs; this will put creases in just the right spot.

2 Fold the top leg back, and iron the exposed part of the bottom leg; go right up to the center seam, but don't iron over it. Fold the top leg back down, and flip the pants over (keeping the legs together); now fold back the already-ironed leg, and press the exposed part of the second leg. Bring that leg back down.

3 With both legs together again, iron the top, flip the pants, and, finally, iron the top of the other leg.

HOW TO IRON TROUSERS

1. If you are pressing wool trousers, you must use a pressing cloth to prevent shine.

2. Iron the inside of the waistband.

3. Turn the back pockets inside out. Iron the pockets so they will lie flat. With the pocket still inside out, iron the outside of the pants where the pockets will lie. Tuck the pockets back into place. Direct the tip of the iron into each pocket. Then iron between, above, and around pockets.

4. Repeat with front pockets, pulling pockets inside out, then ironing into the pockets. Iron in pleats, and touch up the rest of the front.

5. To iron creases in, match up all four seams in the pant legs, and lay the trousers along the ironing board. Fold back the leg that's on top, and iron the inside of the leg that's exposed; iron right up to the seam, but not over it. Fold the top leg back down, and flip the trousers over. Now fold back the already-ironed leg, and iron the inside of the second leg.

6. Lay the folded leg back down, so both legs are together. Iron the outside of the top leg lightly, flip the trousers over, and finish by ironing the outside of the other leg lightly. Hang from a clamp hanger.

HOW TO IRON RUFFLES AND PLEATS

To press both ruffles and pleats, always use a steam iron set at the hottest temperature appropriate for the fabric, and lay the fabric on a thick towel.

TO IRON RUFFLES

1. Iron fabric on the wrong side to prevent damage.

2. Press the nose of the iron into the top of the gather, and gently iron downward.

TO IRON BOX PLEATS

1. Lay fabric flat and press on the right side.

2. Cover the pleats with a pressing cloth to prevent shiny spots, and iron section by section.

HOW TO IRON A SHIRT

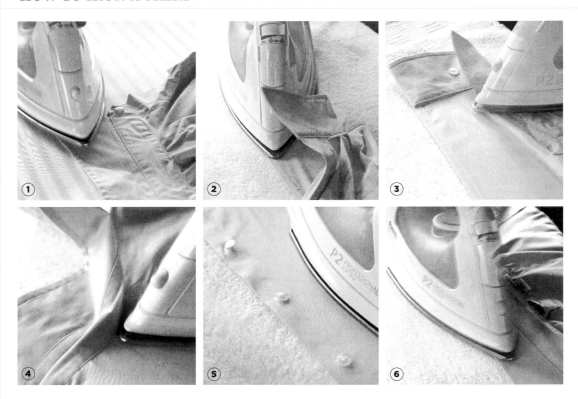

1. Begin with a shirt still damp from the dryer, or sprinkle a dry shirt until thoroughly damp (see page 410 for a note about laundry sprinklers). Start with the underside of the collar; gently pull and stretch the fabric away from the iron to prevent puckering.

2. Iron the inside of the cuffs.

3. Move on to the inside of the sleeve fronts and placket. Slip a towel under the face-down buttons to cushion them as you iron. Iron the outside of the sleeves, using a sleeve board, if possible—it's the only way to avoid a crease. Iron the outside of the cuffs after each sleeve.

4. Iron the inside of the yoke, the part of the shirt that rests on your shoulders, then iron the back of the shirt. Iron the outside of the yoke and the back.

5. Iron the outsides of the shirt fronts; always iron around the buttons, not over them.

6. Finish ironing with the outside of the shirt collar. Hang the shirt on a wooden hanger, and fasten the top button.

HOW TO IRON A ROUND OR OVAL TABLECLOTH

1. If you are planning to put the cloth directly on a table, set the ironing board up right next to the table, to save the step of folding it (and creasing it). Lay a clean sheet on the floor under the board to keep the ends of the cloth from getting dirty.

2. Iron the cloth while still damp, just out of the dryer, or sprinkle to dampen.

3. Lay the cloth across the board and press all around the edges, turning the cloth as you iron.

4. After the edges are done, iron the center of the cloth.

5. Unless the cloth is going straight onto the table, roll it on a cardboard tube for storage, following the instructions on page 158.

6. If folding for storage, fold the cloth in half, wrong sides together, forming a semicircle. Fold again into quarters. Lay the cloth across the board; bring the edges together to fold crosswise two more times until you have a pie-shaped folded cloth. Store the folded cloth on a hanger draped with acid-free tissue paper. Or bring the point down, fold once more, and store flat.

HOW TO IRON A RECTANGULAR TABLECLOTH

1. If you are planning to put the cloth directly on a table, set the ironing board up right next to the table, to save the step of folding it (and creasing it). Lay a clean sheet on the floor under the board to keep the ends of the cloth from getting dirty.

2. Iron the cloth damp out of the dryer or sprinkle to dampen.

3. Iron the wrong side first, pushing the cloth over the board as you work, then finish on the right side (for delicate fabric, or to avoid a sheen, use a lower setting and press wrong side only). If you have a large or unwieldy cloth, try this alternative method: Fold in half lengthwise, right sides together, and press; refold wrong sides together, and iron until dry. Erase any unwanted center crease by folding the cloth loosely into thirds, and gently ironing down the middle.

4. Unless the cloth is going straight onto the table, store it on a cardboard tube, following the instructions on page 158. Or, fold in half lengthwise, wrong sides together. Smooth or re-iron, and fold again to form a long rectangle. Bring top and bottom ends together, folding in half crosswise. Fold the bottom end toward the center. Bring the top ends to cover the already folded portion. Store on a hanger draped with acid-free tissue; or fold in half a final time, and store flat.

A NOTE ABOUT ROTARY IRONS

A rotary ironing machine, also known as a mangle, can be a valuable investment for a household with a lot of linens to care for. It quickly and perfectly presses large, flat items such as tablecloths, napkins, bed sheets, and pillowcases. (The model pictured above is very large, but there are more compact styles available.) Dampened linens are passed between a cloth-covered roller and heater plate; a foot pedal presses the heater plate onto the roller, which rotates, pulling the fabric through. The machine establishes a perfect balance of heat and weight, so that most items need to be passed through just once to come out crisp and wrinkle-free. The results are unmatched by hand-ironing—and achieved in far less time.

HOW TO CLEAN AN IRON

To clean mineral deposits from steam irons, homemakers used to run vinegar and water through them. Today, some manufacturers warn against that procedure because it may result in a brown substance oozing from the holes. Instead, they recommend cleaning an iron with its own steam. Use the Steam Clean setting if there is one. Or place the iron on a metal cooling rack over a surface that won't be harmed by heat or water; turn the setting to steam and maximum heat, and let steam and water jet through the holes.

If an iron drags, the soleplate needs cleaning. Every time you use your iron, products such as spray starch, detergent, and fabric softeners adhere to the soleplate. This buildup must be removed periodically in order for your iron to function effectively. Buy a hot-iron cleaner, which comes in a tube (like toothpaste) and is sold in most hardware stores and from many iron retailers. Put a dab on a scrap of an old terry-cloth towel, and run the hot iron over it. Remove residue by ironing a clean terry-cloth rag. If residue lingers in steam holes, repeat the process, or wad up the cloth so you can rub the buildup out of the holes without burning your fingers. Never use steel wool or other abrasive cleansers or tools, all of which will scratch the soleplate's surface.

IRONING AIDS

SPRAY STARCH

In addition to giving a fabric body, starch penetrates the fabric, providing a barrier against stains and dirt. Starch is most effective on cotton and cotton-blend fabrics. Keep in mind that items ironed with starch can develop mold and attract insects, so it's important to starch only before use rather than before storing.

Commercial starching agents were traditionally added to the Wash cycle, and you can still find starch that's added to the Final Rinse, but it is challenging to use (garments can emerge as stiff as boards if you use too much), and leaves a sticky residue in the machine. (Cornstarch is gentler; see instructions for using it on page 410.) Fortunately, spray starch is easy to use, provided you follow a few guidelines:

☐ Use spray starch on washable garments only. Spray starch contains water, which may cause spots or stains on some fabrics marked Dry-clean Only.

☐ Spray starch can be used with a dry iron or with steam.

☐ Allow time for the spray starch to penetrate the fabric. The less porous the fabric, the longer it will take for the starch to soak in. If you are doing a lot of ironing, spray the garments thoroughly, roll them up, and let

IRONING AIDS

- ☐ Pressing cloths
- ☐ Spray bottle
- ☐ Sprinkle bottle
- ☐ Spray starch
- ☐ Cornstarch
- ☐ Sizing

A NOTE ABOUT SPRINKLING LAUNDRY

Before steam irons were common, sprinkling clothes and household linens to make ironing easier was an integral part of the laundry routine. It's still a useful technique, especially when ironing stubborn cottons and linens. Fill a sprinkle-top bottle with water (you can also use a bottle without a top and simply control the flow by placing your finger over the opening). Dampen the fabric well, and allow moisture to penetrate. Roll the article into a tight bundle. Place the roll in a plastic bag for fifteen minutes to a few hours. If you can't get to it right away, put it in the refrigerator for up to twenty-four hours.

them sit for several minutes before you begin to iron. The problems most commonly encountered with spray starch—flaking, scorching, sticking— result when the starch has not had time to soak into the fabric.

☐ Do not use starch on synthetic fabrics; it won't penetrate. Synthetic fabrics respond better to spray sizing instead (see opposite page).

☐ If wayward spray finds its way onto floors or walls, remove it using mild dishwashing liquid and warm water, reapplying as necessary until all traces are gone.

☐ Do not store starch in the refrigerator or freezer, or near any heat source, such as the dryer. Starch will stay fresh when temperatures do not exceed 120°F or fall below 50°F.

☐ Canned spray starch doesn't spoil, but it begins to lose its potency after one year. Check the date of manufacture on the bottom of the can and replace it after a year.

☐ To prevent a clogged nozzle, take it off the can after each use and rinse it under warm water.

☐ If the nozzle is already clogged, do not try to open it by inserting a pin, which will only embed the clog more deeply. Instead, soak the nozzle in warm water until the clog dissolves.

☐ After ironing with starch, wipe the soleplate after it cools with a damp cloth. If there's heavy buildup, clean using the technique on page 408.

CORNSTARCH

Adding cornstarch to the Rinse cycle is a convenient way to add body and crispness to a large batch of table linens or shirts (without leaving the sticky residue that old-fashioned liquid starch can). Here's how it works:

☐ Launder clothes as usual.

☐ When the entire cycle is finished, reset the washer to the beginning of a Rinse cycle, and allow the machine to refill.

☐ Add 2 tablespoons of cornstarch dissolved in 1 cup of cold water. Stir it into the rinse water with your hands or the end of a broomstick. If you have a front-loading machine, add the cornstarch-and-water solution to the fabric-softener compartment. Start the Rinse cycle.

☐ After the Spin cycle is complete, tumble the laundry in the dryer for about twenty minutes, then iron while damp. If the laundry becomes dry, mist it with water before continuing to iron.

SIZING

Sizing should not be used on natural fibers; it is designed to be used only on synthetic fabrics and synthetic blends. Like spray starch, sizing gives fabrics body and makes them smoother to iron. Sizing does not make fabrics crisp in the same way that spray starch does, however, and it does not flake or become gummy; it helps to eliminate static cling.

Many commercial fabrics are treated with sizing, which is made of cotton and cellulose gum, to add luster; it readily washes off with repeated washing. Sizing is generally available wherever spray starch is sold. Follow these tips when using it:

☐ Use sizing only on washable fabrics; do not use on items marked Dry-clean Only because water in the composition might cause spots or stains.

☐ Use with or without steam.

☐ Store cans of sizing as you would spray starch, at room temperature, below 120°F and above 50°F. As with spray starch, sizing is best used in the first year after it was manufactured. Check on the bottom of the can for the date of manufacture.

STEAMERS

A hot iron has the potential to compromise fabrics, adding unwanted shine to napped materials such as corduroy and velvet and singeing delicate fabrics such as silk. But steam is generally safe for any fabric. Steaming does not disturb fibers the way that a hot iron does, and it eliminates the risk of scorching. It's also quicker than ironing, and in the long run, clothes are likely to last longer if they are steamed regularly rather than ironed.

The size of the fill tank determines the length of a steamer's cycle: A professional-style standing steamer can generally operate for an hour or so before it needs to be refilled; smaller models, including handhelds, may need to be refilled every several minutes. With either type, it's important to test on an inside seam before steaming the entire garment, to make sure you won't cause puckering or spotting.

As long as you are not steaming fragile materials such as silk or velvet, it's okay to let the steamer head touch the fabric directly while you work; a quick, light touch is best. To protect the pile of velvet fabrics, you can steam the reverse side of the fabric.

A STANDING STEAMER MAKES IT A SNAP TO REFRESH CLOTHES BETWEEN WASHINGS.

FOLDING

Once your laundry has been washed and ironed, it needs to be folded. Taking care during this final step will ensure that you can pull clothing from drawers and cupboards secure in the knowledge that they'll be wrinkle-free and ready to wear.

The best way to reduce wrinkling is to remove clothes from the dryer and fold or hang them as soon as possible after the cycle ends. If you must put off folding or hanging, and garments linger in the dryer, slightly dampen a cloth, add it to the load, then restart the dryer and run it for a few minutes. The moisture and heat will help the wrinkles fall out.

HOW TO FOLD A SWEATER

The instructions below are designed for freehand folding, but you can also use an 8½ by 11-inch cutting board to make easy work of evenly folding sweaters so they stack neatly. When the sweater is lying flat, facedown, place board vertically, aligning it with the collar and top edge. Fold sides and arms over the board, slip it out, and fold sweater in half.

1. Lay flat, facedown. Fold one sleeve straight across, toward the opposite shoulder, then the other.

2. Fold one side in so corner of sleeve is at the center of sweater. Repeat with other side of sweater.

3. Fold sweater from the bottom up, once or twice depending on length of sweater. Store sweaters on wide, well-spaced shelves, or in deep drawers, with cedar blocks placed among them.

HOW TO FOLD A BUTTON-DOWN SHIRT

1. Button the shirt (except for cuffs), and place it facedown on a flat surface, arms out to the sides.

2. Take one arm, and fold it over the back, bringing half the body of the shirt over, too.

3. Fold the arm back on itself and down at an angle, so it lines up with the vertical edge of the body. Repeat on the other side.

4. Bring the shirttail halfway up the back, then fold the bottom half once more, to meet the shoulders.

5. Flip the shirt over, and smooth down any creases.

HOW TO FOLD A TOWEL

As with sheets, there's a right way to fold a towel, so that the edges are hidden and the towel looks fluffy and neat.

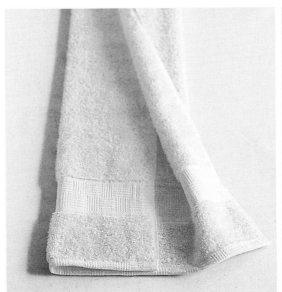

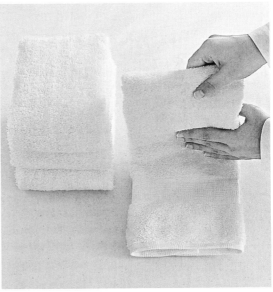

1. Fold the towel in thirds lengthwise. This is the way it should be folded to be hung over a towel rod; if there's a monogram, it will be centered and visible.

2. Fold the towel in one-third from the top, then fold that portion over onto the bottom third, to form a rectangle.

HOW TO FOLD A FITTED SHEET

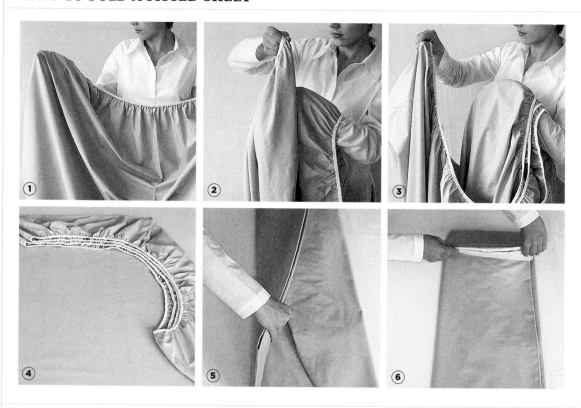

1. With the sheet inside out, place one hand in each of two adjacent corners.

2. Bring your right hand to your left, and fold the corner in your right hand over the one in your left, so the corner on the top is right side out. Next, reach down and pick up the corner that is adjacent to the one that was in your right hand (it will be hanging in front), and fold it over the other two; this third corner will be inside out.

3. Bring the last corner up, and fold it over the others so it is right side out.

4. Lay the sheet on a flat surface, and straighten it into the shape shown above.

5. Fold in two edges, folding the edge with elastic in first, so all elastic is hidden.

6. Fold the strip into a smaller rectangle. Continue folding until the rectangle is the size that will fit on your shelf.

ABOUT DRY CLEANING

The process of dry cleaning, also known as French cleaning, has been around since 1849, when a French tailor, Monsieur Jolly-Bollin, discovered that a chemical solvent could remove dirt and grease from fabrics that could not be laundered with soap and water.

Perchloroethylene, or perc for short, is the degreasing solvent that has been used for decades by most dry cleaners. Perc breaks down oil-based stains such as lipstick or grease by isolating dirt from the oily part of the stain, then dissolving the oil. Dry cleaners use perc in combination with a product called oily type paint remover, or OTPR. Usually, oil-based stains are pretreated with OTPR to loosen the dirt from the fabric before cleaning in perc. The perc also flushes the OTPR from the garment.

Today, most dry cleaners use what looks like a front-loading washing machine to soak clothes in perc and detergent and then spin them dry. There's a Rinse cycle where the clothes are flushed with clean perc, and, finally, they are spun again. Then they are dried, still in the same machine, with hot air, usually at about 140°F. The process takes about fifty minutes.

It is a good idea to interview a dry cleaner thoroughly, finding out what steps he or she takes to protect the clothing. Does she remove, or at least cover, buttons and decorations? Buttons made of plastic, wood, or bone, for example, should always be wrapped in foil during cleaning and pressing. Fine ornamental buttons, such as mother-of-pearl, are best removed before cleaning and pressing, and then sewn back on. Garment by garment, does she check fabrics and construction methods to make sure that the chemicals used will not damage them? Will she consult with you if she wants to handle the garment in a way not recommended on the label?

Do not assume the cleaner will check for stains before she cleans the article. Point out all stains to the cleaner, even unnoticeable ones such as white wine.

Once garments are home, remove plastic immediately and thoroughly air out the items prior to use and storage (to ensure that all traces of chemicals have disappeared).

As a rule, tailored clothing, such as wool trousers and jackets, should be dry-cleaned (which will also maintain their shape). But any unlined garments made of cotton, silk, or linen—so long as they do not have a complicated structure—can almost certainly be washed in cold water (see pages 390–391 for hand-washing techniques). Exceptions to this rule are very dark garments, where there is a risk of the dye bleeding. The challenge, of course, is the pressing after washing. A dry cleaner uses a steam machine, and it is difficult to get the same pressed look with home ironing.

A SAFETY NOTE ABOUT USING PERC
Cleaning with perc at home is not recommended. Accidental ingestion or inhalation can cause permanent damage to the central nervous system. For this reason, keeping perc in your home is inadvisable; in many states, it's illegal for home use.

UTILITY SPACES

GOING "BACKSTAGE" IN ANY HOUSE—into the garage or basement or attic—reveals a great deal about that home's inhabitants. These are the places in which you can visit the past through what is "archived" there and, where remodeling is a possibility, anticipate the future.

When they are properly organized and used, utility spaces free up storage areas elsewhere. But utility spaces can also be pleasant all on their own. It's worth a little investment of time and money to make utility spaces as nice as they can be—just imagine the difference between a finished basement and one with rough cement floors and old cinder-block walls. For many years, I took pride in my well-organized attic at Turkey Hill, and these days I actually like going down to my basement at Bedford. It's clean, with a fresh coat of white paint on the wall and a new white tile floor. I've outfitted it with open industrial shelving units on casters; the shelves keep everything off the floor and out of bins, and I can rearrange them as I like. They hold all kinds of things: sets of dishes and glassware, extra bottled water and other pantry supplies, paint cans and tools and hardware. I also have a gift-wrapping station there, which would be easy to squeeze into just about any basement, and, in an extra-cool area closed off with a door, my wine cellar.

In fact, you can carve out a little space in a utility area for any number of hobbies or household tasks. The tiniest closet or alcove can become a workroom. Why not make a flower-arranging station or a crafts corner or a sewing nook? Take advantage of the hidden potential of simple utility spaces, and you will expand the possibilities for every other room in the house—and perhaps for your own creativity as well.

LAYOUT BASICS

Take a little time now to create an efficient utility space, and you'll save yourself time later searching for an elusive can of paint or spool of thread. Creating a well-organized area is a matter of following a few simple guidelines.

☐ Paint the walls in light colors and install adequate lighting so that you can see what you're looking for and storing. If you use your utility spaces for hobbies and home projects, you'll need to provide task lighting over those work areas.

☐ Before reorganizing the items in a room, sort and discard possessions using the same four-pile method described on page 339: keep, repair, give away, and discard.

☐ Take inventory before customizing storage. Measure and count what you're going to put away before you block out space and shelving. Put the necessary tools and equipment for crafts and hobbies into portable containers, if possible, so you can easily transport them to other areas as needed.

☐ Create zones with similar items grouped together, and redistribute possessions as necessary, to make it easy to access things when you need them. For instance, if you play golf only once or twice a year, free up space in the garage by storing clubs in the basement. If bringing the Christmas tree ornaments down from the attic is perilous, consider putting them on a shelf in the garage.

☐ Stash the things you need most often at the middle or lowest level of shelves, and place the less-in-demand paraphernalia on the higher tiers.

☐ Investigate heating and cooling options for a basement, attic, or garage hobby area by talking to a heating-system professional about installing extra ductwork, or consider purchasing a space heater.

☐ Keep cleaning of your utility spaces to a minimum by remembering these two rules: sweep monthly, purge yearly. A push broom is the best bet for maintaining hard floors. A shop vacuum is also handy; avoid using the regular vacuum in areas subject to lots of dust and dirt as the brushes will quickly become grimy.

HOW TO ORGANIZE BULK SHELVING

Set up shelving for bulk items—food and household products—near the door or the stairs, where the items will be the most accessible.

Stack heavier items on the bottom shelves, for stability.

Stretch bungee cords across the front and sides of open shelves to secure items that might slide or tip over.

Tuck a step stool underneath so you can reach items at the top.

Use S-hooks to hold an inventory list and keep necessities handy: scissors or a box cutter for packages, a funnel for decanting liquids, and a scoop for dry goods.

THE ATTIC

Since an attic typically stays drier and cleaner than a basement, it's often chock-full of family treasures. Make sure yours is well-ventilated (see sidebar, right). Even with good ventilation, however, there are some things that won't do well in an attic—candles, for instance. The space should be accessible, with stairs that are navigable for a person laden with boxes and packages. Here are a few other considerations when it comes to outfitting the attic:

☐ Avoid covering the attic walls or insulation with plastic, which traps heat and moisture.

☐ Line an unfinished floor with plywood to provide solid footing.

☐ Divide the attic into two zones: one for items you'll likely need to retrieve in the next six months, such as clothes or linens, and the other for objects that may be there for years, such as furniture. Install separate shelves and bins for items in each category, and clearly label everything. (For information on how to store specific items, turn to page 422.)

CLIMATE CONTROL

The attic can account for the greatest heat loss in the house, so make sure it is adequately insulated. To determine whether you need to install more insulation, log on to the Department of Energy's website, www.ornl.gov/sci/roofs+walls/insulation, which includes information to help you determine how much R-value the insulation in your attic is providing. R-value refers to how resistant a material is to heat flow—the higher a material's R-value, the greater its ability to insulate. On the low end, loose-fill fiberglass has an R-value ranging between 2.3 and 2.7 per inch of thickness; on the higher end, spray polyurethane foam has an R-value ranging from 5.6 to 6.3 per inch of thickness. Where your home is located, how it's heated, and whether you're putting insulation into a new house or adding more to a preexisting home will determine the R-value you need. The Department of Energy, for instance, recommends that a house in St. Paul, Minnesota, with a gas furnace have attic-floor insulation with an R-value of 38. If the existing insulation provides an R-value of 11, the homeowner would need to install additional insulation with a combined R-value of 27.

A NOTE ABOUT ATTIC VENTILATION

Attic fans—also referred to as vents—help ventilate hot air that can become trapped in the attic. You can purchase a roof- or gable-mounted vent at home centers and hardware stores; have a contractor install it. Another option is a whole-house fan, which draws cool air in through the windows throughout the house and expels hot air through a vent mounted on the roof. These fans can be used instead of, or as a supplement to, air-conditioning. For more information about fans, turn to page 561.

THE BASEMENT

A basement provides a wonderful opportunity for storage. Plan well, and you'll have an abundance of space for your extras. Divide the basement into zones for different types of items and activities: bulk, short-, and long-term storage; laundry; and a work area for building projects or crafts. Short- and long-term storage can be combined on the same shelving; stow short-term items, such as sports equipment, on the bottom or middle shelves, where they're easy to reach, in waterproof plastic utility crates. Items that will be stored for the long haul can be placed on the top shelves, since you won't need to access them often. Choose freestanding, heavy-duty metal shelves that can be moved or reconfigured as your needs change. Make sure that the areas around mechanical systems such as the furnace and hot-water heater are kept clutter-free. Use yellow paint or colored tape to mark off an 18-inch perimeter.

CLIMATE CONTROL

Basements are often humid and damp. Pores in concrete floors and walls draw in moisture, and pipes and boilers mean leaks are common. All of this moisture can undermine a home's foundation and contribute to the growth of mold and mildew (for information on mold, mildew, and humidity, turn to Air Quality, beginning on page 560).

HOW TO PREVENT WATER DAMAGE

Anything stored in the basement—especially for the long term—will benefit from the following precautions:

ELEVATE ITEMS
Use concrete blocks, wooden or plastic pallets, or 2-by-6 pieces of wood to keep objects off the ground. Manufacturers of washers and dryers make elevated pedestals to protect the machines and prevent electrical shock in the event of flooding; they also eliminate the need for stooping when doing laundry (for more information on pedestals, turn to Laundry, page 366).

REMOVE RUGS
A carpet in a humid basement will quickly become moldy; opt for bare floors instead.

USE AIRTIGHT PLASTIC BINS
Place anything stored on low shelves in waterproof, see-through plastic bins.

CONTROL HUMIDITY
Desiccants reduce humidity in small spaces; for more information, turn to page 347 in Closets.

HOW TO PROVIDE EXTERIOR DRAINAGE

The first step in keeping moisture at bay is making sure outside drainage is adequate; rain and groundwater should flow away from the foundation. A few measures will ensure that items in your basement stay dry, even in an area of high humidity or in a region prone to flooding.

UNCLOG ROOF GUTTERS
Gutters stopped up with leaves and other debris can result in rainwater overflow and gutter leakage. Clean the gutters monthly in spring or fall, or after a rain- or windstorm.

INSTALL A SPLASH BLOCK
Downspouts empty rainwater from the roof onto the ground, where it can pool next to the foundation. The solution: Place a splash block—a 2-foot-long concrete or plastic trough available at hardware stores—to direct water away from the house.

AVOID OVERWATERING
Don't excessively water shrubbery and flowers planted next to the house.

HOW TO COMBAT MOISTURE IN BASEMENT WALLS AND FLOORS

Controlling basement dampness in your home is an ongoing process that begins as soon as you move in. At least once a season, check basement walls and floors, and the foundation, for signs of trouble, and treat the situation accordingly.

SEAL
Seal concrete or masonry walls and floors. If you're treating the walls and floor of a new house, let the concrete or cinder blocks dry for three months, then apply latex or oil-based paints or sealants. Choose paints with mold and mildew-inhibiting chemicals designed specifically for damp spaces such as basements (the label will indicate that information). For an existing house, clean the walls and floor with a solution of 1 part chlorine bleach to 10 parts water. Let dry. Next, fill large pores and gouges with grout or resin filler, available at hardware stores. Finally, apply a latex or oil-based paint or a sealant with mildew inhibitors.

INSULATE
Condensation forms when warm, moist air comes in contact with a cooler surface. A good way to prevent moisture from collecting is to install storm windows, which can reduce the temperature differential. That's also why insulating walls is wise. Rigid foam insulation board reduces the passage of water vapor without requiring an additional vapor-retarder treatment as does blanket-type insulation (vapor retarders are treated papers, paints, plastic sheets, and foils that reduce moisture diffusion through walls, ceilings, and windows). Walls must be dry before insulation can be installed, and leaks must be repaired. Wrap pipes with insulation to avoid heat loss during the winter and to minimize water damage from cold pipes "sweating" in the summer.

REPAIR
After a heavy rain, check the walls and floor for leaking water. If there are cracks, fill them with hydraulic cement, which is used for plugging leaks in concrete and masonry. Hydraulic cement mixtures are available at hardware stores; look for those that are sold premixed rather than powdered.

HOW TO PACK ITEMS FOR LONG-TERM STORAGE

Here are guidelines for how to store everything from clothing to china. Keep in mind that antiques and valuable pieces should not be stored in areas with dramatic fluctuations in temperature or humidity. (For more on storing specialty materials, turn to the Materials Guide, starting on page 690.)

ARTWORK AND MIRRORS
How to Pack
Take a picture of each framed piece, so that you can identify it once it's wrapped. Wrap entirely in acid-free tissue paper and sandwich the item between two layers of $\frac{1}{4}$-inch foam board, cut slightly larger than the frame. Secure the corners with small strips of foam board and tape. Cover this bundle with Kraft paper, tie or tape closed, and tape the photo to the front.

Special Considerations
Never store artwork or mirrors flat; set wrapped pieces vertically on a shelf. Unframed works on paper should never be stored in an attic, as low humidity can cause the paper to become brittle. Store instead in a stable environment, in a heavy acid-free box with a lid.

CHINA AND GLASSWARE
How to Pack
Make your own storage containers by padding the bottom of a small, rigid cardboard box with cushioning material such as Bubble Wrap or tissue paper. Wrap each piece of china separately in Bubble Wrap or paper before storing. For glassware, cut cardboard dividers or use the crisscrossed inserts from liquor boxes. Wrap glasses in Bubble Wrap or tissue paper, and place in slots. Attach a photo or write a detailed description of the contents on the outside of the box.

Special Considerations
To avoid breakage, don't stack more than four or five plates in any one box. Always put plates that have been repaired on top. Do not stack boxes containing china or glassware on top of one another and don't place heavy objects on top of boxes.

CURTAINS AND TABLE LINENS
How to Pack
Launder or dry-clean all fabrics before storing them. Wrap one or two cotton hand towels around the bar of a cedar suit hanger, drape a layer of acid-free tissue paper over that, and then hang the fabric. Cover with a fabric dust cover: Cut a hole in an old sheet or pillowcase, reinforce it with a grommet, and slide it over the hanger. Place curtain hardware in a small drawstring bag and attach it to the hanger.

Special Considerations
Iron table linens before storing them, but do not iron in folds, which can weaken fibers. Every so often, refold linens and curtains to prevent discoloration at the creases. Avoid draping fabric with plastic; it can trap moisture and encourage mold.

LUGGAGE
How to Pack
Simply store upright on the floor.

Special Considerations
Suitcases can double as handy storage bins for clothes, jewelry, and, if well wrapped, fragile items. Hat boxes also work well.

PAINT
How to Pack
Tightly seal the can and store it upside down so that the paint will form an airtight seal around the lid.

Special Considerations
If you keep latex paint in the garage, where it might freeze, you will need to throw it out if it has been frozen and thawed three or more times.

FURNITURE
How to Pack

Cover furniture and other large, unboxed items to protect surfaces from dust and light. Wrap furniture in tightly woven, unbleached drop cloths, available at hardware stores. Spread a cloth out on a clean section of the floor, and set a piece of furniture in the middle. Gather up the edges, and wrap it like a present, securing the openings with twine or duct tape.

Special Considerations

Cover any exposed fabric with acid-free tissue paper to help preserve the color.

WOOLENS
How to Pack

Wash or dry-clean before storing in zippered sweater or blanket bags, which are available at stores that sell organizing and closet supplies.

Special Considerations

For more information on wool storage, turn to page 348 of Closets.

HOLIDAY DECORATIONS
How to Pack

Compartmentalized boxes, which are available at stores that sell organizing and closet supplies, are best for ornaments. Wrap garlands and strings of lights around rectangles of sturdy cardboard. Wrap large decorations like wreaths in tissue paper and pack them in padded boxes.

Special Considerations

Always use acid-free white tissue paper, which won't bleed or harm delicate finishes, when wrapping decorations. If using a plastic storage box for ornaments, include a desiccant, such as a packet of silica gel, to absorb any moisture, which can become trapped in the airtight environment. Moisture, along with extremes in temperature, can damage ornaments.

RUGS AND CARPETS
How to Pack

First, clean the fabric. Cotton rugs can often be run through a washing machine and dried on a line, if they aren't too large or heavy; some smaller carpets can be washed by hand. Have valuable handwoven rugs cleaned professionally. Once the rug is clean, roll it around an acid-free tube, available at storage-supply stores, rolling in the direction of the pile. Roll delicate rugs (such as silk) with the pile facing in; if the foundation of the rug is frail or brittle, cracked, or has an extra lining sewn on, roll with the pile out. Wrap the rolled rug in a clean sheet of cotton, muslin, or polyethylene that is slightly wider than the length of the rolled carpet. Secure the sheet with fabric twill tape. Write a description of the rug, or tape a photograph of it, noting its size, on the outside.

Special Considerations

Store the rug upright and, if possible, on a surface that's metal rather than wood, to reduce the risk of insect infestation. Choose a cool, dry spot, and unroll the rug every six months to check for pests (if it is infested, bring it to a dry cleaner). Spring and fall cleanings are ideal because you can lay the rug out on a tarp on the driveway, vacuum it if necessary, and let it air out before returning it to storage.

A NOTE ABOUT ROLLING CARTS

If your garage lacks space for an entire workbench, a rolling cart fitted with Peg-Board on either end can hold the most-in-demand tools, such as hammers or drills. The wheels allow you to roll the cart out onto the driveway should you need to work on a project outdoors. Place the cart next to a Peg-Board-covered wall, and install cupboards and shelves above. Screw the lids of glass jars into the underside of the bottom shelf to organize nails, screws, and other hardware.

HOW TO PARK THE CAR

Take the guesswork out of parking in a tight space. So that you don't pull too far into the garage and bump into walls, set up a marker that will indicate when to stop. Position the car in the ideal spot, then hang a tennis ball on a string from the ceiling so it just touches the windshield. When you pull in, you'll know to stop at that point.

THE GARAGE

A garage is not just a home for your car. It tends to collect many of life's accessories: bicycles and beach chairs, mowers and grills, old tires and abandoned wires. Organize it, and you'll have a storage center, workshop, and parking space all in one. As with all of your utility spaces, organize the garage into zones. Think about what you use in the garage, whether it's tools, gardening supplies, or sporting equipment, and designate an area for each. Make sure you install adequate lighting and electricity in the garage, especially if you will use it to set up a workbench or laundry area, or to install an extra refrigerator or freezer for food storage.

MAXIMIZE WALL SPACE

There's plenty of space along the perimeter of a garage with storage potential. One of the simplest ways to take advantage of that space is to install Peg-Board. This hardware-store staple is a grid of pinholes and can be screwed into the studs along any expanse of wall and outfitted with hooks for hanging everything from small items like keys and flashlights to large rakes and push brooms. Here's how to customize Peg-Board:

☐ Hook brackets into the board to hold adjustable shelving.

☐ Place containers—glass jars for hardware, mini drawers, or clear plastic bins—on the shelves, and then organize items on the shelves by type (painting supplies, gardening tools, holiday decorations).

☐ To get the most of vertical space, you can install the board from floor to ceiling on at least one wall. Leave the two walls bare so you can exploit the space between the studs (assuming they are exposed). Anything that can stand or lean, like a shovel, can be placed there. Stretch a couple of bungee cords across tall, light objects that might teeter over, like gardening stakes, and hook the cords onto screws in the studs.

☐ Choose ladder hooks for big, bulky items like lawn furniture, bikes, ladders, and garden hoses. Like Peg-Board, these sturdy, rubber-coated hooks are widely available at hardware stores and in a range of shapes and sizes.

☐ A wall-hung clipboard with a notepad is handy for reminders about oil changes, lawn fertilizing, watering, or planting schedules.

PAINTING THE FLOOR

If you choose to paint a concrete garage floor, choose an epoxy acrylic paint, which will withstand the heat of rubber tires and is resistant to chemicals, oil, and gasoline spills. Epoxy will also hold up to moisture vapor rising from the ground (in newer garages, there's often a vapor barrier beneath the concrete, to prevent this). With nonepoxy paints, moisture vapor can loosen the coating's bond with the concrete. To keep the floor in good condition, place a pan of sand underneath the car to catch drips.

OUTLINING THE SHAPES OF YOUR TOOLS WITH A MARKER ON THE WALL MAKES IT EASY TO DESIGNATE A PERMANENT PLACE FOR EACH.

CAR TRUNK KITS

A box or plastic bin of safety and repair essentials for your car will ensure that you're prepared during a snowstorm or breakdown (for more information about being prepared for emergencies, turn to page 636).

COLD-WEATHER KIT

☐ Coffee can and candle, to act as a heater

☐ Ice scraper

☐ Sand or nonclumping cat litter, for generating traction

☐ Small shovel

☐ Snow brush

☐ Spray deicer

EMERGENCY KIT

☐ Blanket

☐ Bottled water

☐ Fire extinguisher

☐ First-aid kit

☐ Flare or reflector triangle

☐ Flashlight and extra batteries

☐ Jumper cables

☐ Tire jack

☐ Windshield washer fluid

☐ Work gloves

GARBAGE AND RECYCLING

Set up trash and recycling near the door to the house and the opening onto the street. Hang a copy of the local trash and recycling rules nearby.

☐ Wide bins with open faces like the ones pictured above make it easy to sort recycling. Screw metal label holders to the front of each bin; attach the bottom bin to a dolly with utility-drawer latches, which are available at hardware stores. The whole unit can be rolled to the curb and unstacked with minimal effort.

☐ Another portable option is to stack large translucent containers atop a custom-built dolly, and secure them with a tight-fitting bungee cord. Label the containers and attach handles to each bin with stove bolts. The handles allow you to unstack the containers and line them up to be emptied, and the dolly lets you roll all your recyclables to the curb without spills.

SPECIALTY UTILITY AREAS

Depending on your favorite pastimes and hobbies, you may want to create an area that makes it easy and welcoming for you to do what you love, whether it's sewing, woodworking, or flower arranging. Of course, even if you're not a sewing enthusiast, it's still useful to have a needle and thread on hand for mending hems and replacing buttons. In each of the following sections, there are checklists of basic items everyone needs (such as a hammer or a needle and thread) and, in some cases, specialized tools for the more serious hobbyist.

BASIC HAND TOOLS

Every home needs a well-stocked toolbox—it will be much easier to conquer household projects armed with one. As specific projects arise, more tools can be added. Keep the following in mind:

☐ With hand tools, price does matter. Better-quality tools are going to cost more, but will make the job easier and safer since they are better balanced, have more comfortable grips, and are less likely to slip or break under pressure. They will last longer than inexpensive ones.

☐ Handle tools in the store before making a purchase, and select those that are right for the job and for you. A powerful drill becomes dangerous if it's too heavy to hold steady. Most women should look for smaller grips and lighter-weight tools: a 10-ounce hammer might be more comfortable than a 16-ounce one, for example.

☐ When purchasing a toolbox, look for features that keep small items organized, such as removable trays with compartments and a case on the exterior for drill bits. Make sure to allow enough room for future acquisitions. The most versatile toolboxes are large enough to hold many tools but light enough to carry from room to room. A durable plastic version is preferable to metal, since it won't corrode.

☐ Where you put your tools depends on how many you have and where you'll be working. The three best areas? The garage, the basement, and a toolshed.

☐ A workbench is a wonderful addition to any workshop, especially for cutting wood. Attach a vise to the workbench to hold tools, axes, saws, and chisels in place while sharpening them.

BASIC TOOL KIT COMPONENTS

CLAMPS
These tools secure items to each other while they are being glued or nailed together. C-clamps hold items steady by securing them to a workbench and offer the firmest grip; spring clamps work like clothespins and are good for jobs with smaller items.

HARDWARE
Stock up on nails, screws, eye and cup hooks, bolts, wingnuts, plastic anchors, screw eyes, wall anchors, thumbtacks, and picture-hanging wire. Keep each separate, sorted in an organizer with small compartments.

CORDLESS DRILL
For most tasks, 9.6 volts will do; for heavy-duty jobs, such as drilling into brick, choose a 12-volt model. A keyless chuck (the mechanism that allows for changing bits) is convenient. One downside to a cordless drill is that it's heavier than a corded model.

LEVEL
This tool tells you when something is perfectly straight. Move it around until the bubbles balance inside; that's how you know where the straight line lies. A carpenters' level can identify 45-degree angles, but a torpedo is tiny enough to fit in small spaces.

CUTTERS
Dedicate a pair of standard scissors to the toolbox so you won't ruin the household pair. For more detailed jobs, use a utility knife with a retractable blade; choose one that can be locked, so it won't be likely to pop out of place while you are in the middle of cutting.

MEASURING TOOLS
The best material for a straightedge is metal, because wood and plastic tend to get nicked by cutting blades and are more easily scratched. Use a 25-foot-long measuring tape to calculate longer distances.

HAMMER
Model weights vary, but a 16-ounce hammer is the standard option. If your hammer is too heavy, you might bend nails; too light, and you might have to use extra strokes to drive them in. For comfort and a good grip, look for a style with a rubber handle.

PLIERS
Use slip-joint pliers for tightening and loosening nuts and bolts (a too-tight nut, however, calls for a wrench). You'll also need a needlenose pair, perfect for twisting wire. In addition, the thin tips on the pincers are useful for working in a cramped space.

PUTTY KNIFE
The primary purpose of this tool is for smoothing over putty, mending plaster, and the like. However, it can also function as a scraper, for peeling away loose paint and caked-on glue. Opt for one that has a 1½- to 3-inch-long blade.

SCREWDRIVER
A multihead tool has interchangeable tips, which saves space. One with "ratchet action" means that you won't have to reset the tool after each turn. Four regular screwdrivers are also adequate: a small and a large each of the flathead and Phillips models.

SAFETY EQUIPMENT
Wear protective glasses when working with harmful chemicals or sawing. Leather gloves prevent blisters and injury, and also improve your grip for jobs such as carrying firewood; latex gloves are handy when working with paint or grease.

STAPLE GUN
Use this versatile tool to install screens, attach upholstery, and cover objects with fabric (such as a bulletin board). Pick a small- or medium-size version; it will fit well in a toolbox and is easier to handle than larger models.

SAW
One with a 15-inch steel blade is long enough for a variety of tasks and short enough to fit in many tool kits. Look for "general purpose" on the label, which means the saw cuts both with and against the grain.

WRENCH
There's no need to purchase an entire wrench set when you've got an adjustable one, with a movable lower jaw that can be adapted for almost any job. Use it to loosen bolts that are too tight (pliers tend to strip them) and to assemble furniture, toys, and bikes.

MISCELLANY
Add these items to your tool kit: a pencil; a flashlight, for repairs in dark spaces; a selection of sandpaper, for smoothing edges; felt pads, for preventing scratches underneath items; and a bottle of adhesive remover, for eliminating tape and glue residue.

Keep carpenter's glue on hand for wood and paper. Tapes in 1- to 2-inch widths are invaluable as well, including masking; painter's; duct, for holding items together temporarily; and electrical, for wrapping wires and cables.

SPECIALTY HAND TOOLS

For the fix-it type—or if you are inspired by using the basic tool kit—an advanced tool kit is a smart idea. Here are some guidelines on what to include.

AWL
Use it to pierce holes in leather or start a hole in wood for a screw or a drill bit.

PRY BAR
Use it to pull out nails.

SPADE DRILL BIT
A spade drill bores a wide, clean hole through wood.

CHISELS
A selection of chisels will allow you to chip, carve, and gouge wood.

SAWS
A circular saw is a powerful tool for cutting thick planks; a jigsaw features a narrow, vertical-action blade that pivots to cut curvilinear patterns in wood or thin metal; and a hacksaw blade is slim and small toothed, for use on metal.

TRIANGLE
Also known as a speed square, this tool ensures perfect right angles.

ORBITAL OR PALM-GRIP SANDER
Choose a power sander such as this to finish and polish wood.

WIRE BRUSHES
For cleaning encrusted surfaces.

PAINTBRUSHES, NATURAL AND SYNTHETIC
Natural-bristle brushes are best for applying resin varnishes. Synthetic bristles are fine for most other jobs.

GROMMET KIT
Use the parts to punch neat holes in heavyweight fabrics; the holes are then sealed with metal (usually brass) rings.

WIRE STRIPPER
This tool allows you to strip insulation from electrical wires.

CRAFTS

Doing crafts projects is more enjoyable and successful if you've got a designated area in which to work. A closet, an armoire, or a cupboard can easily be converted into a craft "room" with the addition of a few shelves and some dowels on the door. Since you'll be hanging tools and materials from the dowels, cut the shelves a little narrower than the depth of the cupboard so that the door will close. Another option is to set up your supplies on a rolling cart with shelving, so that you can work anywhere in the house. From basic tape to colorful pipe cleaners, the checklists on the opposite page will ensure you're well stocked for every project, all year long. The glossaries of craft glues and paints on the pages that follow are meant as suggestions for materials you might wish to add to your craft supply closet depending on the kinds of craft projects you like to do.

TAPE CHECKLIST

- [ ] Masking tape, for general-purpose jobs
- [ ] Blue painter's tape, for painting
- [ ] Double-sided tape, for decorating cards and other paper crafts
- [ ] Transparent tape, for wrapping gifts

DECORATIVE CHECKLIST

- [ ] Ribbons in various widths, colors, and patterns
- [ ] Chenille stems (pipe cleaners)
- [ ] Craft papers
- [ ] Felt
- [ ] Glitter
- [ ] Seam binding
- [ ] String
- [ ] Twine (including waxed)
- [ ] Yarn

UTILITY TOOLS CHECKLIST

- [ ] Extension cord
- [ ] Labeling machine
- [ ] Laminating machine
- [ ] Rubber gloves
- [ ] Small spring clamps

MEASURING TOOLS CHECKLIST

- [ ] Clear grids
- [ ] Compass, for making circles
- [ ] Ruler
- [ ] Tape measure

CUTTING TOOLS CHECKLIST

- [ ] Heavy-duty craft scissors
- [ ] Patterned paper edges
- [ ] Pinking shears
- [ ] Pointed trimmers
- [ ] Rotary cutter
- [ ] Rotary tool, such as a Dremel, for making holes in pumpkins and other craft items
- [ ] Self-healing rubber mat and a heavier knife mat
- [ ] Small scissors
- [ ] Utility knife
- [ ] Wire cutters

MARKING TOOLS CHECKLIST

- [ ] Permanent markers
- [ ] White pencil or fabric chalk
- [ ] Craft sponges
- [ ] Erasers

FINISHING TOOLS CHECKLIST

- [ ] Awl
- [ ] Bone folder
- [ ] Emery board
- [ ] Hole punch
- [ ] Sanding attachment for rotary tool

CRAFT GLUE GLOSSARY

ARCHIVAL PASTE

Acid-free archival paste glue is good for papers (especially ones as fine as tissue), photographs, and scrapbooking. Coccoina paste from Italy includes a metal-handled applicator brush inside the container. This glue is nontoxic.

FABRIC GLUE

These glues, such as Unique Stitch, set in twenty-four hours and remain flexible. Joined fabrics can be washed, but not dry-cleaned. Keep out of reach of children.

CHINA AND GLASS CEMENT

This adhesive is specially designed for semiporous materials such as china, ceramics, and crystal. Excess glue cleans up easily with a damp cloth. It is dishwasher-safe and nontoxic.

GLUE STICK

A quick-drying, acid-free, nontoxic stick, such as UHU Stic, is good for all papers, including thin ones. The glue won't deteriorate or stain materials over time.

HOT GLUE

Applied with a glue gun, this adhesive provides an immediate, but not particularly strong, bond. It joins porous and nonporous materials, and can be peeled off the latter. Fresh glue and applicator tip can burn; keep out of reach of children.

CRAFT

A nontoxic glue, such as Sobo, is used for paper, cardboard, fabric, felt, burlap, and glitter. When diluted, it stops the fraying edges on fabric. Aleen's Original Tacky Glue has a thick consistency that makes it good for heavier items such as buttons and beads. Craft glue can be used as a cool, safe alternative to a hot-glue gun for many projects.

INSTANT ADHESIVE

Brands such as Hot Stuff, Krazy Glue, and Super Glue work on all nonporous materials, including metal, vinyl, and plastic. Use just a tiny amount, and be careful, since this substance bonds strongly to skin. You can remove it with acetone (nail-polish remover).

METHYLCELLULOSE
This archival glue is used primarily in bookbinding. Its long drying time (twelve hours) allows adjusting of surfaces. It also remains flexible when dry. You need to mix glue powder, which is nontoxic, with cold water before using.

MUCILAGE
This nontoxic substance works well for lightweight paper projects, like sealing envelopes. It is recommended for children's use, but it may stain paper and photographs over time.

TWO-PART EPOXY
These glues are excellent for joining anything to nonporous materials. They prove just about the strongest bond you can get. Clean up excess with acetone (nail-polish remover). Use two-part epoxy in a well-ventilated area, and keep out of reach of children.

RUBBER CEMENT
Works well on paper projects that must be done cleanly, since excess can be rolled off when dry. Use it in well-ventilated area, keep away from children, and don't put on photos.

WHITE
Multipurpose white glues, such as Elmer's Glue-All, are best for paper or other lightweight materials, and good for children's projects because they're nontoxic.

SPRAY ADHESIVE
This product works best for thin materials and large surfaces, as well as porous and nonporous materials. Use it in a well-ventilated area, and keep out of reach of children.

WOOD
Wood glue is odorless, nontoxic, and can be sanded and filed when dry. Use it for both hard and soft woods on interior projects that will not be exposed to high moisture levels.

CRAFT PAINT CHECKLIST

ACRYLIC
Use this water-based artist's paint on paper, canvas, cardboard, and wood. Clean it immediately with soap and water. Acrylic dries in fifteen minutes.

FABRIC
Best on prewashed natural fibers, not water-repellent fabrics. Apply this water-based paint with a brush or rubber stamp. Set by ironing on the wrong side with a hot iron. Fabric paint is fast drying.

BLOCK PRINTING INK
Comes in both oil- and water-based, nontoxic versions. For printing images cut into wood, linoleum, cardboard, polystyrene, and erasers. Apply with a rubber roller. It is fast drying.

GLASS
Water or oil based; translucent colors can be combined but shouldn't be thinned. Best on frosted or etched glass; may be used with spray-on etching solution. Drying times vary.

CERAMIC/PORCELAIN PAINT
Water-based types come in a narrow range of colors; solvent-based types offer a wider spectrum. These paints may be toxic; check label regarding suitability for tableware. Drying times vary.

GLOW-IN-THE-DARK ACRYLIC
Water-based, phosphorescent pigments absorb natural light. Mixing them with other paints dramatically diminishes their luminosity, however. The thicker the application, the longer the glow. This paint dries in fifteen minutes.

ENAMEL
This paint is made up of highly concentrated pigments in an oil or water base. It has an opaque finish, high gloss or flat. It is heat-proof and can be toxic; use with adequate ventilation. Cleanup may require solvent. Drying times vary.

GOUACHE
Gouache paints are opaque watercolors with strong colors and a velvety finish. Use on cardboard, art paper, wood; they are excellent for posters. Scrub the paint for softer effects. It is nontoxic and fast drying.

LATEX HOUSEPAINT

Water-based latex is available in finishes from matte to glossy. It is suitable for small craft projects. On walls apply latex primer before painting with a brush, roller, or spray gun. Clean with soap and water. It dries in one hour.

POSTER

A water-based paint that's sometimes called tempera (not to be confused with egg tempera), poster paint is excellent for paper crafts and has a matte finish. It is fast drying, and comes in a nontoxic, washable form for children.

LATEX PRIMER

This water-based paint is appropriate for walls, trim, and a wide range of craft projects using wood. It can also be used before layering light color over dark. Use soap and water for cleanup. It dries in one hour.

SPRAY ENAMEL

For interior or exterior wood, metal, and other paintable surfaces. New metal must be primed. Spray enamel inhibits rust. Apply multiple thin coats and use with adequate ventilation. It dries in one hour.

METALLIC ACRYLIC

This water-based paint is colored with metallic pigments, such as copper bronze (for gold) and aluminum (for silver). Its brightness depends on the purity of the metallic ingredients. The paint dries in fifteen minutes.

VINYL

Water-based matte vinyl-acrylic paint such as Flashe is insoluble once dry. Saturated color. "High-hiding" property useful in masking other tones. Dries in fifteen minutes.

OIL

Use oil paints on wood, primed canvas, cardboard, heavy art paper, and fiberboard. Clean it with turpentine. The drying time varies from days to weeks, depending on color and thickness.

WATERCOLOR

This transparent paint works best with textured watercolor paper or other art stock; ideal for handmade projects. Watercolor paints are fast drying.

GIFT WRAPPING

Keeping all your gift-wrapping supplies together and ready for use makes it much easier to give and send artfully packaged presents in a pinch—not to mention during the busy holiday seasons.

☐ Store rolls of wrapping paper flat in wide bins or a wide drawer, or vertically inside a high-sided wastebasket.

☐ Flat files—large, shallow drawers available at art supply stores—are specially made to store papers that can't be folded. Alternatively, drape individual sheets of paper over horizontal dowels supported by curtain hardware mounted on a door or wall of a craft closet or armoire.

☐ For loose ribbon, gift cards, and scissors, opt for see-through storage containers such as glass jars or stackable plastic or metal bins—or a sturdy tool chest with dividers or drawers; organize the supplies into categories and label the bins accordingly.

☐ If you have a full-service wrapping station with spools of ribbon, cord, and twine, use a dowel or metal rod to hold the spools for easy cutting; hang a pair of scissors from a length of string on one end. Place seam binding in a cardboard box with grommet-reinforced holes.

SEWING

With a few basic tools and good lighting you can sew by hand anywhere. But setting up a sewing station keeps things organized and functional. You don't need a lot of space to set one up; an extra closet is a great option. Install shelves to hold fabrics and notions. Cover a table with a measuring grid to create a workstation. If you sew a lot, you'll also need a sewing machine, a cutting surface, such as a self-healing mat, and an iron. Many sewing machines feature compartments for stowing a small supply of needles, presser feet, and small tools. Other storage ideas include:

☐ A lidded bin with dividers is ideal for holding hand-sewing supplies, but multiple spools of thread, collections of buttons, and assorted pins and needles may demand larger quarters. Use plastic or metal boxes; small porcelain dishes can organize odds and ends in a drawer.

☐ A "button book" can hold loose buttons: Attach button envelopes and thread cards to blank sheets of paper (use double-sided tape so you can open the envelopes without removing them from the page), or slide them into plastic sleeves, and store in a ring binder. Write a note alongside each button to remind you which article of clothing it belongs to.

CARING FOR SCISSORS

Good scissors can serve you well for years if you use and treat them with care. Most scissors simply need to be wiped with a soft cloth after use to remove any dust and grit that accumulate on and between the blades. Designate specific pairs for specific tasks—such as cutting paper, sewing, and flower arranging—and don't substitute one for the other. Use paint thinner (in a well-ventilated area) to remove any sticky residue or other stubborn dirt from the blades of scissors used for crafts or gardening. For maintenance, apply a little lubricating oil with a soft cloth to the screw area every few months. This keeps the blades moving smoothly, without friction. Rub off the excess oil before using the scissors again. If you have a problem with the oil staining the next fabric you cut, switch to a Teflon-based lubricant, which can be found in hardware stores.

GIFT-WRAPPING STATIONS, WINE CELLARS, CRAFT ROOMS—THESE ARE BECOMING MORE COMMON AS WE ALLOCATE AREAS FOR HOBBIES.

A CORNER OF THE GIFT-WRAPPING STATION AT BEDFORD

SIMPLE SEWING REPAIRS

HAND STITCHES

Four hand stitches—the slip stitch, the catch stitch, the backstitch, and the running stitch—will get you through just about any hand sewing task. Start by threading a needle with a 24-inch length of thread; knot the end. After you're done stitching, take a tiny stitch on the wrong (back) side of the fabric; before pulling the thread all the way through, send the needle through the loop of thread. Pull the thread until a second small loop forms, send the needle through that loop, and then pull taut.

SLIP STITCH

Use for hemming. This stitch is virtually invisible and very durable—the thread is hidden inside the fold of the fabric, where it's not subject to wear and tear. Make a small fold in the fabric, just enough to encase the raw fabric edge; press. Make another fold the size you want the hem to be. Put the needle inside the fold, push it through to the front layer of fabric, and pick up just a thread or two of the fabric. Send the needle back into the fold, and repeat.

CATCH STITCH

Use for hemming. This stitch allows a little bit of movement between the hem and garment. Just above the hem, insert the needle through the fabric from right to left. Make the smallest possible stitch; it will show on the right side of the fabric. Bring the thread down and to the right on the diagonal, and make a stitch in the hem, piercing only the top layer of fabric, again pushing the needle from right to left. Inserting the needle from right to left will create tiny Xs. Repeat.

BACKSTITCH

Approximates the straight stitch on the sewing machine. It is a strong stitch that's perfect for mending a seam. With right (front) sides of the fabric together, bring the needle through the two layers of fabric. Insert the needle back down through the fabric about ⅛ inch to the right; bring it back up ⅛ inch to the left of where you started (so each stitch will overlap the last by ⅛ inch). Repeat.

RUNNING STITCH

Also called basting, this type of stitch joins pieces of fabric together temporarily. Novices may want to baste before sewing to hold fabric in place. Insert the needle at evenly spaced intervals into the fabric several times, then pull needle and thread through. Repeat.

SEWING TIPS

To ease you through the process of even the most basic repair, remember the following:

Cut thread off the spool on an angle with sharp scissors so you can thread a needle quickly.

Keep the length of the thread for each repair no longer than a foot to minimize tangles.

Tape down the ends of threads on spools, so they won't unwind when not in use.

Always sew in good light, and keep your sewing kit neat and accessible.

ESSENTIAL SEWING SUPPLIES

MERCERIZED-COTTON THREAD
Because it is processed for strength and luster, this thread works well on most cotton, rayon, and linen; size 50, a medium thickness, is good for general sewing.

BUTTON TWIST THREAD
This thick thread, size 16, is good for repairs on heavy clothing like coats.

HEAVY-DUTY THREAD
You'll need this for reattaching coat buttons.

BEESWAX
Use this disk to stiffen thread, which makes it easier to push through a needle's eye, and helps prevent tangling; run a length of thread over the disk to coat it with wax.

MARKING PENCIL
For accuracy in any sewing project—even hems.

SIX-INCH RULER
A transparent tool lets you see from one marked measure to another.

NEEDLES
Needles vary in type, length, eye shape, point, and width. They are categorized by name and number—the larger the number, the shorter and finer the needle. Choose a needle fine enough to pass through your chosen fabric easily yet sturdy enough not to bend or break. Pictured here are sharps (medium-length needles for general sewing) and betweens (similar to sharps but shorter, for fine stitching and tailoring).

THIMBLE
This protects the middle finger of your dominant hand during sewing.

PINS
Available in different lengths and gauges; medium-gauge, or dressmaker, pins are fine for general sewing.

EMBROIDERY SCISSORS
Have two pairs of scissors to use solely for sewing—the larger for trimming fabric, the smaller for snipping threads.

SEWING ON A BUTTON

There are two methods that will help keep a button in place longer, with a minimum of tangled thread and wrinkled fabric: the shank technique, which is better suited to heavier textiles, and the flat technique, preferable for thin or delicate fabrics.

SHANK TECHNIQUE

A shank is a short length of thread that creates slack between the button and the fabric to make the button more movable. To attach a button using this method, first measure for accurate button placement. Thread the needle, knot the end of the thread, and push the needle through the fabric from back to front. Pull the needle and thread through the button's holes three times, matching the pattern of the other buttons—either stitching in a crisscross pattern or with two parallel stitches—and leaving ⅛ inch between the button and the fabric (wedge your finger between the button and the fabric to create space or place a toothpick or wooden matchstick over the button, then stitch down over it). Then, lift up the button and wind the thread around the exposed threads between the button and the fabric six or seven times to create the shank. Push the needle through the shank two times, then tie off the thread. Cut off the excess close to the knot.

FLAT TECHNIQUE

Thread the needle, knot the end of the thread, and push the needle through the fabric from front to back so that the knot is between the button and the fabric's exterior (this will help prevent bunching and won't show through on the inside of the garment). Bring the needle through the front of the fabric and through one of the button's holes. Continue as you would for the shank technique, but don't wrap the thread around the underside of the button. Remember that you don't need to pull tightly; keeping the sewing loose will help prevent pulling and wrinkling.

HOW TO FIX A PULLED HEM

The catch stitch (also called the cross-stitch) was used to mend these cotton-Lycra pants, and mercerized-cotton thread in a contrasting color was used to illustrate (your thread and fabric should match).

1. Turn the pant leg inside out. Start and end your repair about ½ inch on either side of the rip. You don't have to knot your thread for this task; to secure it in the fabric, use a short backstitch: Piercing only the folded inner edge of the fabric, insert the needle in the hem, below the seam, and pull it out to make an ⅛-inch stitch. Reinsert the needle through the same stitch, and repeat once more to secure.

2. Just above the hem, insert needle through the fabric from right to left. Make the smallest possible stitch; it will show on the right side of the fabric. Bring the thread down and to the right on the diagonal, and make a stitch in the hem, piercing only the top layer of fabric, again pushing the needle from right to left. Draw the thread up and take another stitch above the hem, about ½ inch to the right of the previous stitch, again inserting the needle from right to left. Repeat.

3. Continue stitching up and down the hemline until the rip is closed. As you sew, keep the tension of the thread slightly loose; pulling it too tight could break it or pucker the fabric. Secure your work with a short backstitch, as at the start.

HOW TO PATCH A HOLE IN A SHIRT

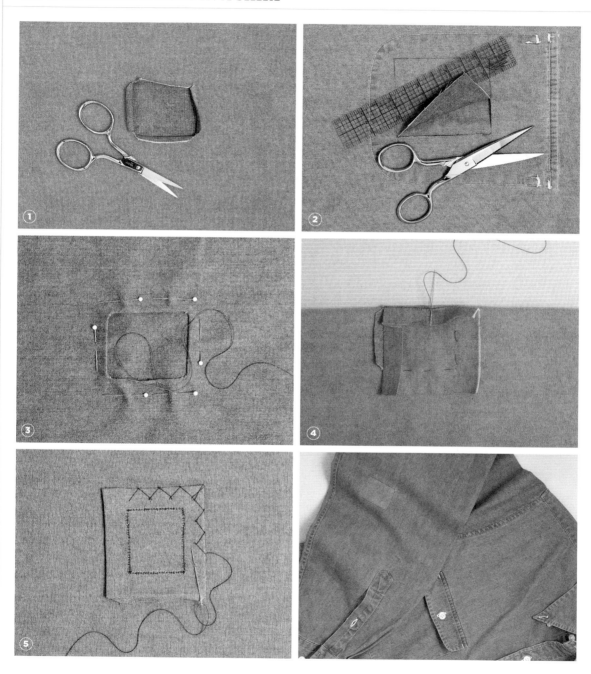

1. With small scissors, cut the hole into a clean square or rectangle. This will make the repair neater and easier. Trim any loose threads. At each corner of the square hole, cut a ¼-inch notch at a 45-degree angle. Turn material inside out, fold the square's ¼-inch edges onto material's wrong side, and press them flat.

2. With larger scissors, cut out the patch material; this patch was cut from the back of the shirt's pocket (the hole left behind can be patched later with another material, since it won't be visible). Measure, mark, and cut out a square that's ½ inch bigger all around than the hole you're repairing.

3. With the shirt still inside out, position the patch on top of the hole, right (front) side down. If using a material with obvious grain, like denim, be sure to match up the patch and shirt so the grains run the same way. Turn the material right side out, and pin the patch in place. Now baste the patch from the outside of the shirt: Starting anywhere on the square, make a ¼-inch stitch down through the patch; push the needle up and out, catching the folded edge of the hole. Continue all around the hole, and remove pins.

4. Turn the shirt inside out. Next, perform the overhand stitch, simply a tighter version of the overcast stitch described on page 444: Fold back the ½ inch excess of patch fabric, so it's flush with the folded edge of the hole. Insert the needle down through the folded edge of the patch (only one layer of fabric) and then stitch up diagonally through the folded edge of the shirt, joining the two fabrics. Continue this stitch in a uniform manner all around the square. Make several short backstitches at each corner to further secure the patch to the fabric. The overcast stitch will be slightly visible on the front of the shirt. Snip and pull out the basting thread.

5. To finish the edges of the patch inside the shirt, use the catch stitch described on page 438. Cut off the tips of the four corners of the patch at 45-degree angles. Fold back each edge ¼ inch. Catch-stitch the edges to the shirt, picking up only one or two threads with each stitch. Press the patch when finished.

HOW TO MEND A RIPPED SEAM

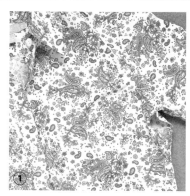
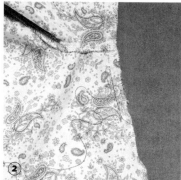
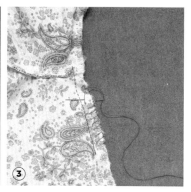

The seam on this cotton shirt was mended using mercerized-cotton thread
(in a contrasting color to illustrate; you should use thread that matches your
fabric) and the even backstitch, one of the strongest hand stitches.

① Turn the shirt inside out. Tie off the loose machine-stitched threads around the tear. To follow the original stitch line, draw a guideline with a marking pencil. To secure the thread, make a short backstitch about ½ inch before the rip, as described in "How to Fix a Pulled Hem" on page 411. This time, take the stitch through both layers of the fabric.

② Close the rip with the backstitch: With right (front) sides of the fabric together, bring the needle through the two layers of fabric. Insert the needle back down through the fabric about ⅛ inch to the right; bring it back up ⅛ inch to the left of where you started (so each stitch will overlap the last by ⅛ inch). Repeat.

③ Now, depending on the garment's original seam finish, you can open the seam and press it flat, or finish the seam with an overcast stitch: From underneath, pull needle and thread through both pieces of fabric; then come up and over the seam allowance, on a slight diagonal, and reinsert the needle and thread, being careful not to pull the thread too taut. Repeat until the repaired area is covered. Secure stitches with a short backstitch. Press seam.

FLOWER ARRANGING

A beautiful display of fresh blooms is one of the easiest ways to brighten a room. If you love arranging flowers, set up an area specifically for that purpose in a small section of your home. A utility sink, the potting shed, and the garden-supply area of the garage are all smart choices.

FLORAL SUPPLY CHECKLIST

FLORAL TAPE
This green, only slightly sticky tape is used to wrap stems to hold them together.

FLOWER FOOD
To lengthen the life of blooms and foliage.

FLOWER FROGS
These charming bloom holders can be made of wire, glass, or ceramic; they sit at the bottom of a vase to anchor and direct the stems.

FLORIST'S CLAY OR GUM
A sticky adhesive for securing flower frogs to vessels.

LINERS FOR DELICATE VASES
Plastic liners protect fragile or antique vases.

FLORAL FOAM
This green, porous material (Oasis is a common brand) keeps stems in place and is usually trimmed and soaked before being placed in a vase.

PRUNING SHEARS AND CLIPPERS
To cut woody stalks and stems.

RUBBER BANDS
For keeping stems together.

HOW TO CONDITION CUT FLOWERS

Whenever you pick flowers from your garden or buy a growers' bunch at a farm stand, follow these simple steps to keep them in good shape for a week or longer.

☐ Cut flowers from the garden early in the morning (after a cool night has restored their strength) or at the end of the day (when they are filled with food).

☐ Carry a bucket of water with you when cutting from your garden. If you cut a stem and leave it exposed to the air, the cut will begin to heal and seal, and the flowers will wilt.

☐ Never pull or break stems by hand. Use sharp clippers or pruning shears to cut woody stalks and sharp scissors to cut stems, which will ensure clean cuts and reduce the risk of bruising or tearing delicate stems.

☐ Once you bring the flowers indoors, recut the stems again under water. Cut all green and woody stems at a 45-degree angle. This prevents stems from sitting flat in the vase and creates a large surface area, ensuring maximum water absorption.

THE FLOWER ROOM
AT SKYLANDS CONTAINS
AN ASSORTMENT OF
VASES AND ALL THE
NECESSARY SUPPLIES FOR
FLORAL ARRANGEMENTS.

FLORAL STEM VARIETIES AND HOW TO CARE FOR THEM

Stem Type	Examples	How to Cut	Special Considerations
BULB	☐ Tulips ☐ Daffodils ☐ Crocus	Snip off the white part at the bottom of the stem before submerging it in water.	These flowers have trouble drawing water through the thickened tissue at the bottom, which is why it's best to snip it off.
HOLLOW	☐ Amaryllis ☐ Lupine ☐ Delphinium	Cut at a 45-degree angle.	Hollow stems need to stay full of water; after pouring water into the stem, put your finger over the bottom, put the flower in a vase, and then remove your finger when the stem is underwater.
MILKY	☐ Poppy ☐ Sunflower ☐ Zinnia	After cutting, dip the stem in boiling water for about thirty seconds, or sear it with a match, to keep the flower from losing its nutrients.	These blooms will take in water through the stem.
NODAL	☐ Carnations	Make your cut between the nodes of the stalk so that it can more easily draw the water it needs.	The nodes are the points on the stem where leaves are attached.
THORNY	☐ Rose	At home, pare thorns from stems with a sharp knife, working from the top down (to put less stress on the stem).	Wear gloves to protect your hands.
WOODY	☐ Lilac ☐ Forsythia ☐ Dogwood	Use clippers or shears.	If the stems are thick, smash the bottom with a hammer until it is frayed.

HOW TO DISPLAY FLOWERS

Before putting together a flower arrangement, make certain your vase is clean. Scrub it well, and fill it with tepid water.

For all flowers, remove any leaves that sit under the waterline in the vase; leaves rot when submerged, encouraging algae and bacteria and shortening the life of the blooms. While you can lengthen the life of flowers by putting them in the refrigerator overnight, do so only if you don't have any fruit in the refrigerator; ethylene gas, emitted from rotting fruit, will cause flowers to deteriorate faster. (Vegetables will not affect flowers.)

Cut flowers need sugar for nourishment, and an acidic ingredient, such as aspirin or lemon juice, to help them absorb water. Cut-flower food provides all the nutrition stems need, but you can also use this formula: For every quart of water, add two aspirins or the juice of half a lemon, a teaspoon of sugar, and a few drops of chlorine bleach (to reduce bacteria). Check the water level frequently to make sure stem ends are covered; change the water and recut the stems every five days. If the water begins to look cloudy, pour it out and recut the stems before refilling the vase.

A FEW COMMON HOUSEHOLD INGREDIENTS—INCLUDING SUGAR, LEMON JUICE, AND CHLORINE BLEACH— CAN HELP KEEP FRESH BOUQUETS BLOOMING LONGER.

THE PORCH AT BEDFORD

OUTDOOR SPACES

THE TENETS OF GOOD HOMEKEEPING reach beyond the walls of a home, into all of our outdoor spaces. Porches, pergolas, arbors, garden rooms, patios, balconies, decks, and terraces can all be thoughtfully planned, furnished, and maintained, in the same manner as indoor rooms.

An outdoor living room is easily conceived and achieved. A weather-resistant sofa, chair, and table, and some shade, whether provided by an awning, an umbrella, or a covered porch, are the necessities. At Bedford, I have a porch that overlooks the property. On it, I have wooden furniture that I've stained the same color as the house—Bedford Grey. It feels like a true extension of the home, and I love entertaining there. In East Hampton, my porch is wide, like what would be called a verandah in the South, with room for full seating areas. There are electrical outlets, floor lamps, and a sisal carpet—the idea of a "real" living room comes to mind. Fresh flowers in a vase, a newspaper set on the side table, music wafting from an open window...one is ready to relax and entertain.

Outdoor furnishings encompass everything from birdbaths, to sofas with plump outdoor cushions, to sleek chaise longues by a pool. All of these require maintenance. Damp cushions, dirty birdbaths (so unhealthy for the birds!), and even swing sets with tattered seats discourage use. Our outdoor spaces and their furnishings should be prepared for the season every spring. In summer, dew and dampness should be wiped away daily, and stray leaves and pollen cleaned off every couple of days, to keep these spaces ready for use at any time. Glass-topped tables need a daily wiping, and stone and brick terraces should be swept clean.

If you live in a climate that is warm all year, the rituals of maintaining outdoor living spaces should be just as consistent as indoor routines. If you live farther north, you will have to adjust your rituals to the season. Perhaps that outdoor dining area just outside the kitchen door becomes, in winter, the place where you store firewood. In any case, summer furnishings should be stored away during the winter, for protection.

At Bedford, I decorate the porch every season. Whether it's hanging baskets of flowers or ferns in spring and summer, arranging gorgeous gourds in the fall on the porch tables, or hanging wreaths and garlands in winter, the natural decorations always welcome guests graciously.

THE DECK AT SKYLANDS IS
AN INVITING SPOT
TO RELAX OR ENTERTAIN.

PORCHES

No other part of a house stirs the romantic—or nostalgic—in us so much as a porch. Its prime was the late nineteenth century, when the advances brought about by the Industrial Revolution allowed Americans more leisure time to enjoy the outdoors. It's been estimated that more than 90 percent of houses built in the United States before the 1930s had porches. But by the 1950s, with the advent of air conditioning, demand for porches diminished, though they did not disappear entirely.

Over the years, porches became more commodious, adapting to different functions and blossoming from all parts of the house: screened-in sun parlors off the living room; back service porches off kitchens; porte

THE PORCH AT LILY POND
LANE IS TRULY AN
OUTDOOR LIVING ROOM.

cocheres, roofed structures extending from the entrance of a building, under which carriages (and cars) could unload; sleeping porches off bedrooms. But the front porch has always been the grandest of them all. It's an outdoor living room, a place to socialize, drink a glass of iced tea, and enjoy a swing on a hot summer day.

Porches require even more regular maintenance than indoor spaces. Neglect them, and dirt and debris can quickly build up.

ROUTINE CARE

☐ Every week, sweep the floors with an outdoor push broom; dust the windowsills, door frames, and ceiling-fan blades using a counter brush.

☐ Every month, wash light fixture covers. Because insects tend to collect in them, always remove covers to clean them. Rinse and dry thoroughly before replacing them.

SEASONAL MAINTENANCE

☐ Sweep away cobwebs and debris from walls and ceilings with a corn broom, and wash down the walls with a solution of all-purpose cleaner and water using a large polyester sponge.

☐ After thoroughly sweeping the floor with an outdoor push broom, scrub away grime with a long-handled deck brush and a solution of all-purpose cleaner and hot water.

☐ If you notice an accumulation of mildew on the floor, scrub with a solution of 1 part oxygen bleach to 3 parts water using a deck brush. (Wear protective gloves and goggles.)

☐ Clean porch screens with warm water and a nonammoniated all-purpose cleaner using a scrub or utility brush, washing the mesh as well as the frame. Rinse the screens thoroughly with a garden hose, and allow them to air dry. Between deep cleanings, whisk away dust and dirt with a hand-held vacuum or a soft counter brush.

☐ Wooden porch floors and steps look best and last longer if they are painted. Paints formulated specifically for porches and floors are latex or oil-based, self-priming, and are durable enough to withstand the elements. Painting a porch floor is no different from painting any other surface; you must clean and sand first. Because porch floors are usually made from inexpensive wood, however, it is generally not worth investing too much time in meticulous preparation; priming, for example, is not necessary. Sand to roughen existing paint. Sweep away any debris, clean the floor and steps well with water and an all-purpose cleaner, rinse, and wait until surfaces are thoroughly dry before applying paint.

A STURDY CORN BROOM IS IDEAL FOR SWEEPING LEAVES FROM TEXTURED SURFACES.

DECKS

A deck, which is a roofless extension of your home, can be a wonderful gathering spot in beautiful weather. Decks are ideal for lounging, eating, or grilling—or simply as a vantage from which to enjoy your landscape. Most new decks are made of pressure-treated lumber—wood that has been processed with chemicals to make it more resistant to moisture and insects.

ROUTINE CARE

☐ Every week, sweep deck floors and thresholds with an outdoor push broom (or more frequently, if necessary) to remove leaves and other debris. Dust railings and windowsills with a counter brush.

☐ Always shovel your deck after snowstorms. The weight of snow can damage the deck and the excess moisture can harm untreated wood.

SEASONAL MAINTENANCE

☐ To wash a deck by hand, first sweep thoroughly with an outdoor push broom and use an old saw blade or putty knife to remove any debris caught between the boards. Next, hose down the deck and scrub the surface with a long-handled deck brush and a solution of all-purpose cleaner and water. Work in strokes that run parallel to the grain of the boards. Remove mildew by scrubbing with oxygen bleach and water (follow label directions). For tough stains, use a commercial deck brightener or oxalic acid (both of which are available at home centers and hardware stores), which lighten dingy, gray wood.

☐ If you have a large deck or porch, a power washer saves time. This machine uses high-pressured water to blast away any dirt, mildew, and some stains. However, power washers can open the pores in untreated wood surfaces, exposing the surface to the elements and decreasing the life span of your deck. Because a power washer, if the pressure is high enough, can actually take off some of the wood itself, including loose decking or siding, and break windows, use extreme caution. Test in a small unobtrusive corner of the deck to know if you should proceed with the entire surface. The blast from the water is very powerful, so make sure people and pets are well out of its reach. Follow the instructions that come with the machine, and be careful where you point the nozzle. Wear as much protection as possible, such as rubber boots, a raincoat, and safety goggles, and place a drop cloth on any nearby shrubbery. You can buy a power washer, or rent one from a tool-rental outlet (look in the Yellow Pages under "Tools—Renting") or some home centers.

☐ Once the deck is clean, check for wobbly nails that may have come loose over the winter. Remove them, and replace with galvanized, all-purpose deck screws, which are less likely to pop out of wood than nails are; screw these in close to the old nail holes. Fill those holes with wood filler, and sand smooth if necessary. Carry out any other repairs, such as replacing a splintered or warped board, before the damage worsens. Splintered areas should be lightly sanded until smooth, while larger splints should be glued with epoxy. Check for rotted areas as well, and replace as necessary, or call a deck specialist if the damage is extensive.

☐ Once a year (or when drops of water no longer bead on the surface but are absorbed into the wood), coat the deck with a water-based waterproofing sealer. This will help preserve the natural beauty of the wood and prevent the growth of mold and mildew. Choose a sealer that contains a UV protector to help block the sun's damaging ultraviolet rays, which can attack wood-cell molecules and turn the wood gray. Strip off old sealer using a commercial stripper or by sanding before resealing, or it will not last well and the color won't be even. Make certain that the deck is clean (follow directions for how to wash a deck by hand on page 453) and dry before resealing using a paint roller with an extension handle. Begin applying the sealer on the area of the deck nearest the house, and work your way toward the stairs. But before you seal your deck, check the weather forecast; it's important that it not rain two days before and after application, so the wood is completely dry when you seal it. Otherwise the sealer will not cure properly and may peel.

FURNITURE CARE

Outdoor tables, chairs, and lawn chaises are built from materials that are generally tough enough to withstand sun, rain, and wind. Day to day, they require little more than frequent hosing off. Specialized care is required, however, when stains, scuffs, and scrapes appear. In many cases, cleaners and waxes designed for the care of cars, boats, and decks are appropriate for use on outdoor furnishings. At the end of the season, cover outdoor furnishings with canvas or cotton sheeting to keep them free of dust and protected from moisture. Store the furniture in a shed, a garage, or on a covered porch. Or, if it can't be kept in a protected area, wrap it well in waterproof tarps designed for outdoor storage of furniture (such coverings are available at home centers).

RESTORING METAL FURNITURE

Metal outdoor furniture is made of iron (cast or wrought), steel (sheet or tubular), and aluminum. When exposed to air, iron and steel oxidize from moisture in the air and rust. It is best to keep all metal furniture well protected with paint or a finish.

Before you start to restore an outdoor table or chair, determine if the particular piece of furniture is worth your effort. Restoring metal furniture is hard work and will take many hours, so decide whether the furniture is pleasing to you aesthetically or if it is of value otherwise (for example, an antique). Make sure it is structurally sound, that there are no weak spots or suspect welded joints (old iron can break repeatedly in the same spot). Next, find out what the furniture is made of. Tubular steel, which was mass produced and spread across suburbia in the fifties and sixties, often has arms and legs made of hollow tubes and seats and backs made of sheet steel. Aluminum outdoor furniture is lightweight and doesn't rust. A magnet will not stick to aluminum the way it will to iron or steel. Finally, there is cast- and wrought-iron garden furniture, which you can recognize by its heavy weight (cast iron is chunky and looks sand-cast, and wrought iron is usually bent or twisted). Victorian garden furniture is generally cast iron.

Once you've determined which metal the piece of furniture is made of and whether or not it's structurally sound, you can begin stripping the paint off of it. If the job is large, consider hiring a professional. Otherwise, the best approach is to use a combination of techniques, including chemical or mechanical stripping.

Chemical paint strippers generally contain methylene chloride and solvents that can irritate the skin and cause nausea and dizziness. Yet they make the job easier because they dissolve the paint quickly and efficiently. Look for water-based strippers (like 3M Safest Stripper) that contain dibasic esters (DBEs), which aren't as volatile and hazardous as methylene chloride. However, they take longer to work because the chemicals aren't as strong. Whichever stripper you choose, you must read the label carefully. Always work outdoors or in a room with good ventilation, and wear gloves and a respirator to protect yourself. Respirators, available at hardware stores, should have a HEPA (high-efficiency particulate air) filter. Use an inexpensive paintbrush to apply the stripper. You may need several applications, depending on how many layers of paint you must remove. Remove the paint using a paint scraper according to the instructions on the stripper. If any paint remains, reapply the stripper and scrape again. (If your furniture was made before the 1960s, there's a good chance its paint is lead-based, in which case you want to take special precautions as you remove it, especially if you have children. Use a drop cloth to collect any paint chips or debris and consult your local sanitation department for disposal regulations.)

Once the furniture is stripped, wash it thoroughly with water and mild dishwashing liquid to remove all traces of stripper. Dry with a clean cloth as quickly as possible; any moisture left on bare steel or iron will immediately cause rust to form, which will eat away at the metal.

If you choose not to use a chemical stripper, you can remove paint with a wire brush or wheel. Even if you've used chemicals, you'll probably need an abrasive to get all the paint off. Use a handheld steel brush if the job is small, or attach a wire wheel to a drill for larger jobs. Go back and forth in a fluid motion, so as not to stop too long in one area, which will wear away the metal. Always wear safety goggles and a respirator when you use a steel brush or wheel, because pieces of steel and old paint will break off while you're working. If you're removing lead paint, mist debris and dust with plain water before sweeping it up. Dispose of the cleaning materials and dust according to local regulations.

Use a steel-wool pad and a small amount of paint thinner to remove any small flecks of paint that cling to the metal in corners and small places. If you want to bring the furniture down to the metal and seal it instead of painting it, be careful not to scratch the metal. For a smooth finish, use fine steel wool (00 or 000) or sandpaper (600 grit).

Once the furniture is free of old paint and stripper and completely dry, you're ready to seal or paint. You can simply cover the stripped piece with a clear sealer such as polyurethane. You can also use linseed oil, or liquid or paste car wax, although they both require reapplication several times a year. But a clear sealer alone will not preserve the furniture as well as paint.

If you decide to paint, start with a primer made specifically for metal. It's usually red or gray and contains zinc oxide, which inhibits rust. Paint or spray on the primer, and let the furniture dry (the manufacturer's label will tell you for how long). When dry, apply an exterior-grade paint.

If the piece of furniture has only a rust problem, your job is a little easier than if you have to strip the entire thing. Use paint thinner and a little steel wool to remove the rust. If the rust is stubborn, you may have to employ a product such as Rust Reformer or Naval Jelly (available at hardware stores and home centers), both of which are designed to dissolve rust. When the piece is dry, sand and paint the patches as described above.

HOW TO STRIP AND REPAINT A METAL CHAIR

1. Before stripping a chair, determine whether it is structurally sound. If so, apply a paint stripper in one direction with a clean paintbrush. Work outdoors, or in a well-ventilated area, and wear gloves and a respirator for protection.

2. After letting the stripper sit according to label directions, remove flaking and bubbled-up paint with a scraper.

3. Wash the stripped chair with mild dishwashing liquid and water to remove residue.

4. Use fine steel wool to remove encrusted paint from hard-to-reach areas.

5. Coat the entire chair with a rust-inhibiting metal primer.

6. When the primer is dry, brush on a metal paint rated for exterior use.

HOW TO CARE FOR OUTDOOR FURNITURE, BY MATERIAL

IRON AND STEEL

When exposed to moisture in the air, iron and steel oxidize and rust. In the winter, cover furniture as described on page 454 and store it in a dry place, especially if you live near the ocean (sea salts will quickly erode both metals). Otherwise, regular attention is required to prevent rust, which will eat through the metal if left unchecked. Inspect furniture frequently, especially at welded joints. If paint is peeling or if reddish rust stains appear, sand the problem area down with steel wool dampened with a little paint thinner, a wire brush, or fine, 600-grade sandpaper until metal is exposed. For heavy rust, treat with Naval Jelly (available at hardware stores) as directed. Apply a metal primer, then coat with a rust-inhibiting metal paint rated for exterior use. Follow up with liquid or paste car wax; if the furniture has an ornate design, use a spray car wax.

ALUMINUM

Manufacturers coat aluminum with paint or a clear finish to prevent corrosion, which can pit the surface. Prolong either coating's life by cleaning it with a solution of mild dishwashing liquid and water and treating it with liquid or paste car wax. (Never use alkaline products, such as ammonia, or ammoniated all-purpose or window cleaners, which will discolor aluminum.) If scratches appear in a painted surface, recoat the surface promptly with exterior metal paint. Furniture that has a "powder coat" (applied by spraying electrically charged dry paint onto grounded metal, and then baking it) requires specific touch-up paint, available from the furniture manufacturer.

RESIN (PLASTIC)

Furniture plastic is porous. Apply car wax to prevent stains from setting. If stained, scrub with a mild dishwashing liquid and water using a soft-bristled brush. If that doesn't work, try a solution of 1 part bleach or vinegar to 10 parts water, or use a resin-furniture cleaner or a deck wash with phosphoric acid (both are available at hardware stores or home centers). Nonabrasive household cleaners may also help. Keep clean surfaces polished with liquid or paste car wax.

TEAK

Teak has a high oil content; the oil acts like a sealant, making the wood water-resistant. If left outside unfinished, the furniture will develop an attractive silver-gray patina. (Other wood furniture should not be left outdoors year-round.) The rot-resistant wood needs only periodic cleaning if you accept its naturally weathered look— gray with small surface checks. Retaining the original amber color requires applying a teak sealer or teak oil (both found at outdoor-furniture, hardware, and marine-supply stores) once or twice a year before the color begins to change. Before applying a sealer or oil, wash new teak with warm soapy water. When dry, apply a light, even coat of teak sealer with a clean cloth or paintbrush. This will help block some of the sun's ultraviolet rays. Then, whenever the wood looks parched, scrub with a teak cleaner and rinse. Follow with a commercial deck brightener or oxalic acid (available at home centers and hardware stores) to restore the wood's color. Finally, when dry, apply more sealer.

WICKER

Furniture woven of a range of materials is called wicker. Traditionally, plant fibers, such as rattan, or coated paper are used. "Outdoor" or "all-weather" wicker is generally woven of resin or vinyl, which is much more durable. The chief challenge with all wicker is cleaning the textured surface. To remove dust, vacuum or use a counter brush. Take care of spills immediately, before they harden or stain. For deeper cleaning, scrub with a solution of mild dishwashing liquid and water. Avoid using too much water on traditional wicker as it can weaken or loosen the fibers. If the wicker incorporates wood, wipe it separately with a damp cloth. Place the entire piece in the sun to dry, and dry completely before reusing to prevent distorting the shape. To prevent traditional wicker from drying out and cracking, apply boiled linseed oil with a rag, then wipe dry. (The used rags are flammable; soak them in water and wrap tightly in plastic before disposing.) To repair traditional wicker, apply a damp towel to any loose strands until they become flexible enough to reweave (this should take about an hour). If necessary, tack a loose strand with an exterior brad to secure.

WOOD (PAINTED OR STAINED, NONTEAK)

Clean painted or stained wood with mild dishwashing liquid and water. If repainting is necessary, scrape off loose paint, and sand lightly to smooth edges of paint on remaining areas. Prime, let dry, and repaint. If stained furniture has not been sealed with a clear coating, deep clean by scrubbing with deck brightener or oxalic acid (available at home centers and hardware stores). To restore stained furniture, sand off any protective coatings and restain in a tone that matches the existing color. To preserve the wood, apply a protective clear coating, such as polyurethane, or choose a one-step stain product that adds both color and a finish.

FABRIC

Outdoor woven fabrics generally undergo a chemical treatment during manufacturing to increase stain and moisture resistance, regardless of whether they are made from synthetic fibers, such as vinyl-coated polyester or acrylic, or from cotton blends. Even treated fabric can grow mildew, however, so it's important to keep these fabrics clean and dry.

Once a week, hose fabrics down to remove dust, dirt, and body oils, which can all support mold growth. To clean, scrub with a utility brush and a solution of mild soap, such as Dr. Bronner's, and lukewarm water. Avoid detergents and hot water, which can strip the protective coating off outdoor fabrics. If fabrics are badly stained or mildewed, scrub with a solution of 1/2 cup oxygen bleach and 5 gallons of warm water. Check the manufacturer's care label to determine how often the fabric should be re-treated with a commercial fabric protector (available from outdoor furni-

ture retailers). If there's no label, test the fabric by sprinkling it with a few drops of water. If the water does not bead up and roll off, it's time to re-treat. Before re-treating fabric, wash it thoroughly and rinse well to remove all traces of soap residue so the chemicals in the fabric protector adhere well. Once the fabric is dry (do not machine dry, as it can cause fibers to melt), apply the fabric protector, following the instructions on the label.

CUSHIONS

Store all outdoor cushions in a covered area to protect them from rain. If cushions become wet, stand them on end to expedite drying.

UMBRELLAS

Rinse regularly with a spray hose throughout the outdoor season, or all year if you live in a warm climate or humid environment. If mildew is present, remove the cover from the frame, if possible, and brush away any mildew. If the label says "machine-washable," place it in a washing machine filled with cold water and a cup of oxygen bleach. Agitate to mix and let the cover sit overnight. Next, drain the water and spin, then launder the cover in cold water using mild soap, such as Dr. Bronner's. Return it to the frame, in the open position, to dry in the sun. If the cover can't be laundered, follow the cleaning directions for awnings, below. For a professional cleaning, look for a company that specializes in awnings; they will often clean um-brellas as well. (Look up "Awnings" in the Yellow Pages.) Prevent mildew growth during storage by making sure the umbrella is completely dry when taken down; never close it while it is still wet.

AWNINGS

Rinse regularly with a spray hose throughout the outdoor season, or all year long if you live in a warm climate or humid environment. Allow the awning to air-dry thoroughly after cleaning; similarly, always open awnings after rain to let them dry thoroughly. For a deep cleaning, first rinse the awning, then use a long-handled brush to apply a solution of water and mild soap, such as Dr. Bronner's. Rinse again. Clean awnings thoroughly and let them dry completely before storing. Follow the manufacturer's instructions to take them down and then store them in bags that will allow for ventilation (do not use plastic, which encourages mildew). Store awnings off the ground to lessen the chance that they will become winter homes for rodents. If awnings are extremely dirty or stained, look up "Awnings" in the Yellow Pages to find a professional cleaning service in your area.

GRILLS

When you have an outdoor area where people like to congregate, it's wonderful to set up a grill. There's nothing like the taste of grilled food, and being able to cook outside in nice weather is a treat in itself, particularly when others are gathered around. Whether you burn charcoal, gas, or wood, if cared for properly, your grill can serve you well for as many as fifteen years, or longer. Before using it the first time, familiarize yourself with a new grill by reading the instruction manual. Keep the manual in a convenient spot where it will be handy every time you grill.

Set up your grill safely, following these guidelines:

☐ Place the grill (gas or charcoal) on a level surface away from the house, other structures, or frequently traveled paths.

☐ Keep the grill away from children's and pets' play areas.

☐ Keep the grill away from combustible materials.

IT'S EASIEST TO CLEAN A GRILL RIGHT AFTER COOKING, WHILE IT'S STILL HOT (WEAR A BARBECUE MITT TO PROTECT SKIN).

ROUTINE CARE

☐ Oil the cooking grate before every use of the grill to prevent food from sticking. Brush it lightly with cooking oil that can withstand high temperatures, such as safflower or grapeseed oil.

☐ After grilling, remove cooked food and close the lid (if using gas, turn the heat to high); after fifteen to twenty minutes, shut off the gas or extinguish flames. Rub the heated grate with balled foil, or brush the grates with a tight-bristled brass or stainless-steel grill brush (wear long-cuffed gloves to protect hands and forearms if cleaning a charcoal grill). To loosen burned-on food from a grate, sandwich it between wet newspapers, cover it with plastic, and leave it outdoors overnight, then scrub.

GAS GRILL GUIDELINES

CARE

☐ Wash the exterior of the grill with mild dishwashing liquid and water. Rinse thoroughly; burning detergent residue gives off an unappetizing odor and can affect the taste of your food.

☐ When burner holes are blocked with food debris, cooking temperatures may become uneven. Go over the burners with a grill brush, and clear clogged holes with a pipe cleaner or a sewing needle.

☐ If lava rocks, ceramic blocks, or metal heat diffusers are dirty, heat will be uneven. Clean by turning them over and running the burners on high for at least thirty minutes.

☐ Once a year, spray the cooking grate with a grease-cutting solution of 1 part distilled white vinegar to 1 part water. Close the lid, and let the solution work for at least an hour. Scrape the grill gently with a putty knife.

SAFETY

☐ To detect a leak on a gas-hose connection, brush soapy water over hoses and hose connections. If bubbles emerge, shut off the gas valve, and disconnect the tank from the grill; contact the manufacturer for information on finding a qualified repairperson.

☐ Always open the lid well before lighting any cooking fire, to avoid a concentration of gas or fumes, which may explode when lit. Don't assume that lowering the lid will extinguish flames, since vents may still admit air.

☐ Shut off the gas valve before starting any maintenance procedure.

☐ Disconnect gas tanks in off-seasons, and never store tanks in the house, garage, basement, or any other enclosed space.

HOW TO SEASON A NEW CAST-IRON GRATE

Wash and dry the grate, brush cooking oil onto the surfaces, start a charcoal fire, and cover with the lid (keep the vent open). After an hour, close the vent. When the grate has cooled, it's seasoned.

HOW TO LIGHT A CHARCOAL GRILL

Make sure you use a good, dry charcoal (avoid using brands that have fillers; they don't provide even heat and won't burn as long). Consider using a lighter cube instead of lighter fluid, which some people believe adds a chemical flavor to food. A chimney starter is a useful tool that holds coals in a cylinder while heating. The small, contained space allows the coals to light faster and heat more quickly than lighting them in the grill itself. Once the coals have a coating of gray ash (in about twenty-five to thirty minutes), they can be poured from the chimney into the grill and arranged with long-handled tongs.

CHARCOAL GRILL GUIDELINES

CARE

☐ Over time, high temperatures can stress the bottom of the charcoal grill, but a $\frac{1}{2}$-inch layer of sand in the grill bed will absorb the heat of falling embers and prolong the life of the kettle. The ash pan under the kettle will catch any sand that falls through the bottom vent.

☐ To clean the kettle, first gently loosen grease and carbon with a putty knife. Scrub lightly with mild dishwashing liquid and hot water, using abrasive nylon or steel-wool pads. Cut stubborn grease with 1 part distilled white vinegar mixed with water.

SAFETY

☐ Dousing a flaring grill with water tends to spread cooking-grease fires. Extinguish a flare-up instead by spraying it with a class-ABC fire extinguisher, or smother the fire with dry sand (keep a potful of sand nearby).

☐ To dispose of ashes, wait at least twenty-four hours after cooking to be sure the ash has cooled. Even tiny embers can spark a fire if swept into a trash receptacle while they are hot.

CHOOSING A CHARCOAL GRILL

Although they take longer to light than gas grills, charcoal grills burn hotter and the charcoal adds a distinct flavor. At a minimum a grill should have:

☐ Sturdy legs
☐ Heavy metal kettle with a tight-fitting lid
☐ Wooden or heat-proof handles
☐ Air vents on top and bottom
  for temperature and smoke control
☐ Sturdy grate at the bottom of the kettle
  to hold the charcoal
☐ Solid cooking grate with handles
  for easy rotation
☐ Ash catcher

CHOOSING A GAS GRILL

Gas grills are more convenient and easier to control than charcoal grills, providing a steady, even heat. Grill enthusiasts might consider a few of the added features available on top-of-the-line models, such as built-in smoker boxes, warming racks, and side burners for sauces, but the following basic features should suffice for everyone else:

☐ Sturdy construction
☐ Thick firebox and a tight-fitting lid
☐ Push-button ignition
☐ Separate heating zones and burners
☐ Adjustable controls for each heating zone
☐ Easy-to-read gas gauge
☐ Large cooking surface
☐ Built-in thermometer
☐ Drip pan

TOOLS FOR THE GRILL

BASIC TOOLS

- [ ] Long-handled fork
- [ ] Basting brush (choose one made of silicone; it will withstand high heat and is easy to clean)
- [ ] Spring-loaded, long-handled tongs
- [ ] Large off-set spatula
- [ ] Wire brush for cleaning the grill
- [ ] Long-cuffed barbecue mitts

SPECIALTY TOOLS

- [ ] Digital thermometer with a remote control—this will alert you when meats have reached a preset temperature
- [ ] Grilling basket for fish, shellfish, vegetables, and other small items that can slip through the grate
- [ ] Skewers for making kebabs (metal or bamboo, the latter of which have to be soaked for twenty minutes or so before grilling)
- [ ] Long-handled lighter
- [ ] Chimney starter for charcoal grills

CHARCOAL FUELS AND FLAVORINGS

CHARCOAL AND HARDWOOD

Using charcoal or hardwoods (woods that come from deciduous, broad-leafed trees) imparts a smoky flavor to grilled food.

- [ ] Charcoal briquettes are typically made of compressed charcoal with clay or another additive as a binder. They light quickly and provide long-lasting heat. Compare brands and choose those with the fewest additives; besides altering flavor and providing uneven cooking temperatures, chemical binders may be unhealthy.
- [ ] Lump charcoal is pure, uncompressed charred wood, although it is used in the same manner as briquettes. Lump charcoal tends to spark.
- [ ] Hardwood, the original grilling fuel, takes longer to start burning but emits the most flavorful smoke.

FLAVORINGS FOR SMOKING

For materials to smoke, rather than burn, they should be soaked in water for at least two hours before grilling. Wrap soaked wood chips, vines, or herbs in foil packets, poke holes in the foil, and lay the packets on the charcoal or other heat source before putting food on the grate.

- [ ] Vine stems and herbs such as rosemary or thyme help enhance the flavor of grilled foods by scenting the smoke that envelops them.
- [ ] Fruitwoods such as apple or cherry wood impart sweet flavors, whereas the flavors from hardwoods (mesquite is one example) are generally savory.
- [ ] Wood chips provide quick bursts of smoke, which is ideal when you won't be smoking food for an extended period or you don't want a strong smoky flavor. Some smokers can use only wood chips.

PETROLEUM-FREE STARTERS

Because petroleum-based lighting fluids can flare up as well as impart an acrid taste to food, use an odorless wax or paraffin-based starter instead. When placed at the base of a pyramid of charcoal, these starters will produce a steady flame.

- [ ] Wax "ice cubes" and wax-and-sawdust rings make good starters when topped with dry kindling under the charcoal.
- [ ] Wax-impregnated sticks double as starter and kindling.
- [ ] Newspaper is a good starter under kindling by itself or in combination with other starters.

Outdoor lighting can provide for safe navigation while also enhancing the look of a landscape, driveway, or pathway. Hardware stores and home superstores sell packages of low-voltage lighting equipment that can simply be plugged into an exterior outlet. Outdoor lighting can also be hardwired to the power supply of the house. This should be installed by a licensed electrician, to ensure that the wiring meets electrical codes. And make sure any lighting designer you hire is experienced with outdoor installations; an electrician or interior lighting designer may not necessarily know enough about positioning units in trees and among plants.

LOW-VOLTAGE LIGHTING

When installing low-voltage lighting, a power pack (or transformer) plugs into a standard outlet to reduce the regular household current from 120 volts to 12 volts. These transformers often have an automatic timer built in, allowing the lights to turn on and off at preset times. Low-voltage exterior lighting systems are an inexpensive way to both accent your property and make your home safer. Installing them makes for an easy project; no special tools are needed and installation can usually be completed in less than an hour. And because it's low voltage and there's little danger of electrical shock, it's safe for use around children and pets.

HARDWIRED LIGHTING

This permanent lighting uses a 120-volt electrical system, which is the same voltage that powers your home. Therefore, it is subject to the same regulations as house wiring and requires professional installation, which can be costly. Not only will it need to be installed according to code, but it could even require a buried conduit. Unlike low-voltage systems which can be easily repositioned, once installed, hardwired systems are fixed.

SOLAR-POWERED LIGHTING

Solar panels (also known as photovoltaic cells) located on top of outdoor light fixtures produce (and store) power when sunlight shines on them. Installing solar-powered outdoor lighting is easy and doesn't require any special skills or wiring (all you need to do is push each fixture into the ground). Usually you can finish in less than an hour. Solar energy is free; it is also safe as there is no risk of shock. Make sure, however, that the light fixtures are placed in areas where they will receive regular sun; most units will not work if they go more than a few days without it.

A TERRACE WHERE A TABLE
CAN BE SET UP FOR ALFRESCO DINING
IS A BEAUTIFUL AND
USEFUL EXTENSION OF THE HOME.

THE PERGOLA AT LILY POND LANE

LIGHTING INSTALLATION AND DESIGN TIPS

DO

☐ Purchase only lights that are Underwriters Laboratories (UL) approved.

☐ Make sure lights are rated for outdoor use.

☐ Keep plug connections dry.

☐ Experiment with backlighting. Lighted trees in the background of a forested area create picturesque silhouettes in the foreground. An up-lighted hedge behind a shrub or tree will do the same.

☐ Create a different look for your property after dark. The night view will often be more dramatic than the day view.

☐ Take advantage of the many lenses, diffusers, and mounts available so that your outdoor fixtures are tailored to your needs.

☐ Conceal the light fixture, either with a covering on the fixture or by tucking it behind a shrub, large branch, wall, or rock.

DON'T

☐ Don't install fixtures in undergrowth or among low shrubs or tall grasses. The beam of light needs unimpeded passage from the fixture to the focal point so there are no distracting reflections or shadows (unless you want a shadowy effect, in which case the opposite applies).

☐ Don't overlight a particular area or your property in general—bright illumination tends to create a garish, theatrical look.

☐ Don't illuminate every surface. Shadows work to define lighted areas.

HOLIDAY LIGHTING SAFETY TIPS

Make holidays merry—and safe—by observing a few guidelines when installing outdoor lights.

☐ A standard strand of outdoor holiday lights can accommodate a great variety of bulb wattages and sizes without hazard. Provided the bulbs fit the sockets on the strand, almost any bulb choice is possible. But though the wattages don't need to conform to one another along a single strand, the total wattage of the bulbs being used must not exceed the wattage of the strand itself. Bulbs range from 3 to 15 watts. Standard strands are rated at 600 watts.

☐ Use only heavy-duty exterior-use extension cords to run electricity from the house to the lighting.

☐ Because there is nothing inside them to expand or contract, bulbs rated for outdoor use won't freeze and shatter. The greater concern is the connection between strands, where one plugs into the next. As a precaution, wrap the connections securely in wide electrical tape and do not link more than three strands together.

☐ The average outlet is generally wired to accommodate about 1,800 watts. Plug in more than that and you risk tripping the circuit. If possible, put the lights on their own circuit, so that if the circuit does trip, it won't affect anything indoors.

OUTDOOR ENTERTAINING CHECKLIST

Whether you're hosting a garden party, cookout, or backyard picnic, be sure to assemble all your supplies a few days in advance of the party to save yourself from having to rush around during the event. Rent or buy the basics, and use as many lightweight and waterproof items as possible.

☐ Aprons

☐ Bar towels

☐ Blender, if making blended drinks; you'll also need a power source or an extension cord

☐ Corkscrew and bottle opener

☐ Table, chairs, ground cloth, cushions

☐ Tablecloths and napkins

☐ Dinnerware, glassware, flatware, serving bowls, utensils, and trays

☐ Food protectors: Mesh fly covers will keep pests away from food; beverages can be covered with weighted handkerchiefs or napkins.

☐ Cooler, ice bucket, ice, tongs

☐ Lighting, which could include votive candles, torches, kerosene lamps, or string lights, and extras of each; glass hurricanes protect a candle's flame from wind. Low-wattage bulbs are less likely to attract bugs.

☐ Grill and grilling equipment (see checklist on page 465)

☐ Paper towels, damp cloths or sponges, garbage bags and garbage receptacles

☐ Music: Again, you'll need either a power source or plenty of batteries.

☐ Hypoallergenic insect repellent and citronella candles to repel insects

☐ Sweaters, shawls, portable heaters

DRIVEWAYS, WALKS, AND PATIOS

Although driveways and walks are utilitarian, they are extensions of the home, and one of the first things people see when entering your property. Regular care of these areas will prevent them from becoming damaged or unsightly. Sweep surfaces weekly with an outdoor push or corn broom or rinse with a hose to keep them clean.

CLEANING OUTDOOR SURFACES, BY MATERIAL

ASPHALT

A deck brush along with water and an asphalt cleaner (available at home centers and hardware stores) usually works on many spots. Stains from petroleum-based products, such as engine and transmission fluids, paints, and solvents, are stubborn. These spills must be treated with a petroleum neutralizer, a chemical available from hardware stores. To protect your asphalt against decay and the elements, seal it every two to three years with an outdoor sealant. Ask your hardware store to recommend a brand for your region, and follow the manufacturer's instructions. Small cracks (up to 1/2 inch wide) can be repaired with blacktop crack filler, applied with a caulking gun.

CONCRETE

Protect concrete, which stains easily, with an exterior-grade concrete sealer. Wash stained concrete with a commercial concrete cleaner (available at home centers and hardware stores) following label directions. Prevent grease stains on a concrete garage floor by placing shallow metal pans filled with a layer of an absorbent material (such as sawdust or sand) under parked cars to catch dripping oil. Replace the absorbent material as necessary.

GRAVEL

Raking gravel drives and paths will even out the surface and keep the top layers circulating among the lower layers; turning the stones over will hide motor oil stains and disperse dirt so it is less obvious. Weed the edges of gravel drives and walks regularly, and rake gravel every few weeks, or whenever it begins to look untidy. Over time and with use, gravel will sink into the ground. Replenish every two years with a layer of fresh gravel.

STONE AND BRICK

When stone and brick areas (around a pool, near pumps and air-conditioning units) become green from mildew, scrub them clean with a long-handled deck brush and 1 part chlorine bleach to 10 parts hot water. Do not let moss gather on a brick terrace, patio, or porch; in rainy weather, the moss can easily become slick and dangerous. To remove it, use a moss-removing product (available in garden centers). To use, first wet the surface of the brick with a garden hose, then spray liberally with the product. It will require a few days to work, so try to do this when no heavy rain is forecast.
You can also try garden lime in the cracks between bricks; by making the soil more alkaline, this will eradicate moss, which likes acidic conditions.
Always wear gloves and a mask when handling lime. Sprinkle the lime heavily over the moss, allow a few days for the moss to dry up and die, then simply sweep it away.

PAVING STONE MATERIALS

Paving is usually mortared in concrete, which is stable and permanent. It can also be
"dry-laid" on a bed of sand, which allows for design flexibility and appears more informal
and relaxed over the years as it settles and vegetation grows around the cracks.

BELGIAN BLOCK
This type of paving stone is
typically cut from granite or
other durable stone. These
roughly cut 4-by-7-by-11-inch
stones have been laid in an
overlapping "running bond"
pattern, which is emphasized by
the contrast of darker rock
dust swept between the blocks.

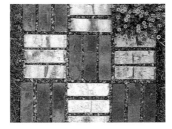

BRICK
This conventional basket-weave
pattern looks fresh when
composed of hard-fired paving
bricks in contrasting colors.
The spaces between the 4-by-8-
inch bricks are filled with
³/₈-inch washed stone. Although
brick can become cracked or
dislodged, it is easy to repair.

CONCRETE AND BRICK
Subtle patterns result from the
combination of 4-inch-square
concrete blocks (tumbled to
soften their edges) with a double
border of 8-inch-long paving
bricks, all held in place by
coarse sand. Concrete blocks
will crack, but they can be lifted
out and replaced.

PATIO BLOCK
Cast-concrete patio blocks lend
themselves to graphic, modern
patterns. Here, gray threshold
pavers flank 4-by-8-inch "flash
red" (red flecked with black)
pavers and gray ⁵/₈-inch stones.

RIVER STONE
There's a soothing quality to
this pairing of opposites: dark,
rounded Mexican river stones
between pale 8-by-16-inch patio
blocks. The stones were pushed
edgewise into a shallow bed
of rock dust. River stones can
settle over time and may
need to be relaid periodically.

SANDSTONE
Irregularly shaped slabs of
Colorado sandstone, which won't
show wear patterns, are loosely
fitted in a random arrangement.
The spaces between slabs,
filled with washed stones, have
been planted with tufts of
woolly thyme and pearlwort.

FIREWOOD

Before ordering firewood, it helps to understand some of the basics. Wood is usually classified into two broad categories: hardwood and softwood. Hardwoods come from deciduous, broad-leafed trees; softwoods come from needle-bearing coniferous trees. Hardwood makes the best firewood because it is usually denser and less resinous than softwood, and therefore burns more efficiently. Softwood is generally better as kindling for starting fires. Hickory, white oak, and sugar maple provide some of the best fuel for winter fires, along with red oak, beech, and yellow birch.

No wood, regardless of its density, will burn unless it has been properly seasoned. Once cut into logs and split into pieces for the fireplace, wood must be stacked outdoors to dry for six months to a year. When the moisture content of the wood has dropped from about 45 percent to 20 percent, the wood will burn efficiently. Most wood sold and delivered to homes as firewood has already been seasoned. Before accepting a delivery, examine it for sufficient seasoning. Cracks should radiate from the center of the logs, a sign that a substantial amount of moisture has left the wood. Also look for loose bark and a dull color.

For information on how to build a fireplace fire, turn to page 206.

STACKING WOOD

Use care when stacking a woodpile. *The Old Farmer's Almanac* specifies that the space between each log should be "large enough for a mouse to run through, but tight enough to prevent a cat from chasing it." A well-stacked pile protects the wood from the effects of foul weather, including excess dampness and mold, and insects.

Choose a protected, sunny spot with good ventilation that will accommodate the logs and help season the wood. Wood should be stacked outside from six months to a year to dry thoroughly.

Stack wood on a supporting base at least 3 inches off the ground to keep wood from direct contact with the ground; otherwise, insects, dirt, and moisture will accumulate. The base should be made of pressure-treated 4-by-4s or cinder blocks. The best way to stack logs is by crisscrossing layers, alternating the direction of each. This method creates a sturdy pile and allows for ample ventilation.

During damp or snowy weather, cover the top of the woodpile with tarps. Ideally, the tarp should not come in direct contact with the logs (lay a few rocks or bricks on top of the wood to keep the tarp elevated), because it can trap moisture. Remove tarps on sunny days to allow the wood to dry out.

STACK FIREWOOD ON
A SUPPORTING BASE.

THE BEST FIREWOODS

Hardwoods are not all the same. Hickory varieties are the highest quality, followed by oak, maple, beech, birch, ash, and cherry.

ASH
Native Americans once made a dark, bitter sugar from the sap of the ash. Deer nibble at its branches, and bees extract nectar from its small flowers. White ash produces few sparks, and releases a subtle fragrance.

BEECH
At one time, vast groves of American beech were the habitat of huge flocks of the now extinct passenger pigeon. The beech burns well but produces only a slight fragrance. Unlike most trees, its bark remains smooth as it ages.

BIRCH
Birch bark has played a significant role in the history of American crafts. Native Americans used it to make canoe and wigwam coverings, as well as makeshift shoes. The yellow birch is rated among the best fuels for fire, along with the white birch.

CHERRY
There are many kinds of cherry trees, but not all of them bear the sweet cherry fruit used in pies. The chokecherry produces the tart cherries used in baking and cooking. The black cherry's main uses are as lumber, firewood, and fine furniture. Black cherry releases a potent fragrance when it burns.

HICKORY
Hickory is the densest of firewoods, burning for long periods and providing lasting heat.

MAPLE
The sugar maple is known for its sap, which is used to make maple syrup, while the tree itself is among the densest of hardwoods. Although sugar-maple firewood does not light easily, it burns very efficiently and gives off a strong fragrance.

OAK
Aside from being one of the finest firewoods, white oak is widely used to make furniture and the barrels in which whiskey is aged. Red oak's slightly reddish wood burns a little less efficiently than white oak, but its fragrance is more pronounced.

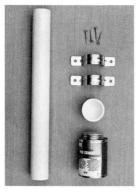

GARDEN-STAKE HOLDER

A simple PVC pipe can be turned into the ideal holder for long, thin objects, such as garden stakes (shown opposite). Here's how:

Apply PVC cement to the inside of a 1½-inch PVC pipe cap, and attach the cap to one end of a PVC pipe 1½ inches in diameter cut to desired length. Let dry until set, about thirty minutes.

Position the pipe, cap side down, against a crosspiece (or a piece of 1-by-6 attached to the wall or door) so the bottom overhangs by an inch.

Place two metal conduit straps over the pipe at the top and bottom of the crosspiece; drill pilot holes using a 5/64-inch bit, and screw into place with 1-inch wood screws.

POTTING SHEDS

A wooden cupboard is all that's needed to create storage for gardening supplies. When placed in a location convenient to both the house and the garden, a potting shed will serve as a useful way station. Fill it with pots, bulbs, seeds, fertilizer and potting soil, a hose, and other gardening essentials.

A disorganized toolshed defeats the purpose of having useful specialized tools. When they are difficult to find, you won't use them. But if everything has a designated place, your tools will be easy to take out and to put away, and won't be at risk of getting damaged. The following are simple additions you can make to any shed in order to create just the right kind of storage space for gardening supplies and tools.

SHELVING

Maintain order with a large shelf unit; install smaller ledges up high for infrequently used items.

CLAMPS AND HOOKS

Mount metal spring clamps and rubber-coated utility hooks to the crosspieces inside the shed door so you can hang those tools you reach for the most. If you don't have a crosspiece, you can attach a 1-by-6 to the door with 1½-inch screws. Attach hooks to the shed itself to hang long-handled tools. The space above shelves needn't go to waste either—add hooks to hang equipment horizontally.

RAMP

If the door to your shed is slightly higher than the ground, you will need a ramp that you can put down to make it easier to wheel out large items such as lawn mowers and wheelbarrows.

COVERED STORAGE

A store-bought wooden box with a fitted lid corrals bags of potting soil, fertilizer, or charcoal for the grill. Insert a divider cut ⅛ inch smaller than the depth and width of the box; this will help keep the bags upright and divide a large box into two. If your lid doesn't have a handle, screw in a metal one yourself. Store the box on the floor, under the shelves.

PROTECTIVE RACKS FOR SAWS AND SHEARS

To prevent tools from getting jostled around and scratching each other, put them in a wall or door rack that holds each tool snugly. You can make one using two 1-by-6 pieces of wood; attach 2-inch wood blocks between the boards at different intervals to hold each tool firmly in place.

PEG HOLDER

Small tools such as trowels, hand cultivators, and pruners can easily get lost on shelves or in bins. Keep them on the inside of your shed door and you'll always know where to find them. Drill ¼-inch holes into the door's crosspiece or into a 1-by-6 attached to the wall; cover the bottom half of ¼-inch pegs with wood glue, and insert them into the holes. Let the glue set before hanging up items. To hang a tool with a handle but no strap, install two pegs: Drill two holes, spaced to accommodate the thickness of the handle, then proceed with glue and pegs.

AN ORGANIZED POTTING SHED

COMPOSTING

Compost, a valuable soil amendment, is decomposed organic matter. Also known as humus, it helps soil hold water, allows for airflow, controls erosion, protects plants against disease, snags airborne nitrogen, lures soil-enriching earthworms, and ferries minerals from the subsoil. Compost comes from leaves, branches, and fallen fruit; from the remains of the garden's harvest; from lawn mowers; kitchen tables; a stable; a henhouse; and the fireplace. From all of these sources, you can start your own compost heap, which is a series of layers of these ingredients in a proper bin.

If you compost, feed the compost heap every day, rather than letting all your cuttings and coffee grounds pile up in the house. You can do it every time you prepare a meal. Keep a stainless-steel bowl on the kitchen counter, then throw all your compost ingredients—including tea leaves and coffee grounds—into it. Cut scraps into small pieces if you want the pile to break down quickly. As the meal is cooking, empty the bowl onto the compost heap. This eliminates the need to keep a compost bucket indoors.

Wire-mesh or cinder block can be used to construct compost bins, but the best bins have timber frames, which can be easily disassembled and moved. Sink four 5-foot-high, 4-by-4-inch corner posts into the ground to form a 4-by-4-foot square. (Smaller bins lose heat too fast.) Build sides by bolting 4-foot-long, 2-by-6-inch boards to the posts, leaving space for air between the boards. There are also many types of premade compost bins available at home stores if you would prefer not to build your own. Some towns even promote the practice of composting and will offer bins to interested citizens; check with your township.

BUILDING A COMPOST HEAP

☐ Choose a location for your bin that has good drainage and at least partial sunlight. Place the bin 8 to 12 inches away from fences, decks, and buildings to discourage pests.

☐ Line the bottom of the bin with 6 inches of cornstalks, coarse twigs, or chopped brush. Add a few inches of "green," then twice as much "brown" material (see the chart, opposite). Sprinkle with well-rotted farm-animal manure or garden soil. Continue building in layers, poking holes for aeration and keeping the top slightly concave to catch rain.

☐ Always cover exposed food matter with a layer of dried leaves or grass clippings. This will help reduce any odors that may attract pests.

☐ As compost "cooks" and reduces, turn the pile with a compost fork every few days, and keep adding more layers.

☐ The pile should always be about as moist as a wrung-out sponge. Too much or too little water can slow down or even stop the composting process. Water the pile with a hose or cover with a tarp during heavy rain, as necessary.

☐ Never compost meats, fish, animal products, oils, bones, fatty foods such as peanut butter, or pet manure. Although they will decompose eventually, they will cause a foul odor and attract pests.

☐ You can compost year-round, although during the winter months you will be generating more food waste than yard waste. To maintain a proper carbon/nitrogen balance, you need to find a constant source of carbon to mix with the food waste.

COMPOST INGREDIENTS

The best ratio of materials for the compost heap is one-third nitrogen-rich to two-thirds carbon-rich. Think "green" for nitrogen, "brown" for carbon. To get the decomposition process started, you'll need inocula, or microbial colonies. And to speed up the process of decomposition, add earthworms; they'll also mix materials and aerate the heap.

GREENS (NITROGEN)
- ☐ Fruit and vegetable scraps (though no leftover greens or vegetables with any kind of salad dressing or other oil)
- ☐ Grass clippings (dry and free of weed killer and pesticides)
- ☐ Houseplant trimmings
- ☐ Soft prunings
- ☐ Eggshells
- ☐ Tea leaves and bags
- ☐ Coffee grounds and filters
- ☐ Farm-animal manure
- ☐ Flowers
- ☐ Hair

BROWNS (CARBON)
- ☐ Fallen leaves (and mulch from rain gutters)
- ☐ Pine needles
- ☐ Cornstalks
- ☐ Twigs and branches
- ☐ Paper egg cartons
- ☐ Wood ashes
- ☐ Straw
- ☐ Wood chips and shavings
- ☐ Sawdust
- ☐ Dryer lint
- ☐ Finely shredded newsprint

INOCULA SOURCES
- ☐ Rich topsoil
- ☐ Well-rotted manure
- ☐ Partially decayed compost

THINGS TO AVOID
- ☐ Anything treated with pesticides and herbicides
- ☐ Animal and dairy products
- ☐ Stones
- ☐ Diseased plants
- ☐ Weeds
- ☐ Wood chips from pressure-treated lumber, which can contain toxic chemicals
- ☐ Eucalyptus, black walnut, poison oak, poison ivy, and sumac

3 THROUGHOUT THE HOUSE

ANYTHING WORTH DOING IS WORTH DOING WELL, so the saying goes.
When it comes to homekeeping, doing well is simply a matter
of mastering a few easy cleaning techniques. Many years ago, when
homekeeping was a woman's primary occupation, these techniques
were passed down from generation to generation. Every homekeeper learned how best to accomplish the tasks that made up the
weekly routine as well as the thorough cleaning traditionally
undertaken in spring—whether it was sweeping a floor or waxing
a table. Times have changed. Homekeepers today have access
to many more time-saving tools and products, but they may not be
taught the techniques to use them. Learn the methods (anyone
can) and you will be able to confidently clean surfaces throughout
the house.

There are five basic cleaning techniques essential to the
weekly routine: dusting, wiping up, sweeping, vacuuming,
and mopping. Along with proper technique, the right tools are
essential to a successful outcome and can greatly reduce the
amount of effort you'll need to expend. Think of cleaning tools as
an investment and care for them well so you'll be able to rely
on them for years to come.

Periodically, you will need to go beyond your weekly routine
in order to keep the surfaces and furnishings throughout the house

in like-new condition. Carpets need to be shampooed, window treatments need to be washed, and ceilings need to be cleaned. Like your regular routine, this periodic maintenance—generally undertaken in the spring and fall or whenever something has been damaged or badly stained—will make your rooms more beautiful and functional, as well as make cleaning during the rest of the year easier. Windows that are washed twice a year, for example, will never accumulate a stubborn layer of grime that will require hours of painstaking scrubbing. More important, this periodic maintenance will add years to the life of most everything in your home.

Finally, keep in mind that the most important technique of all is prevention—taking steps to ensure your belongings don't become dirty or damaged in the first place. The list opposite includes fifteen simple measures that can save you countless hours of cleaning.

PREVENTIVE CARE

PROTECT FLOORS

☐ Place doormats inside and outside of every door that leads outside or into the garage. Use coarse coir mats outside to trap mud and grit, and cotton indoors to absorb water.

☐ Institute a no-shoes policy. Shoes track in all kinds of grime and abrade hard surfaces. Add years to the life of your floor by asking all household members to remove their shoes before entering the house.

☐ To prevent scratches, attach self-adhesive felt pads to the bottoms of furniture legs and always lift, rather than drag or roll, furniture when moving it.

☐ To protect carpets from dents, support heavy furniture on plastic or rubber floor protectors that are at least an inch in diameter. The heavier the piece of furniture, the larger the floor protector should be.

MINIMIZE DUST

☐ Install door sweeps on the bottoms of doors that lead outside. These strips, which have either a vinyl flap or a polyester brush attached to them, are generally installed on the interior of the door. They block the gap between the door and threshold, keeping out dirt (and pests).

☐ Apply weather stripping to drafty doors and windows. Not only do gaps let precious heating or cool air out, but they let drafts—along with plenty of dust—in.

☐ Use high-efficiency furnace filters and room air filters.

☐ Install window screens to keep out large particles and flying insects.

GUARD AGAINST FADING

☐ Draw blinds when windows get direct sun to protect furniture, carpeting, and artwork.

☐ Rearrange furniture and rotate carpets, lamp shades, and artwork every six months to ensure that no one area gets more exposure to light and sun than another.

☐ Cover windows or skylights that get intense exposure with film (available from professional installers; check the Yellow Pages under "Windows—Installation") designed to block ultraviolet light.

PRESERVE SURFACES

☐ Use trivets, cutting boards, and coasters to prevent scratches, rings, and burn marks.

☐ Attach rubber disks or felt to the bottoms of vases, candlesticks, and collectibles to protect furniture from scratches. Add felt glides to the bottom of small countertop appliances like coffeemakers and blenders.

☐ Seal stone surfaces and grout to guard against stains.

☐ Install doorstops to prevent doors from denting walls.

DUSTING

SOME FORTY POUNDS OF DUST waft into the average house each year. It's composed of things such as rock, sawdust, and pollen. If you were to look at dust under a microscope, you would also find strands of hair, flakes of dead skin, and tiny insect bodies— no wonder we should get rid of it. And if you think it's hard to stay ahead of dust, you're right. As soon as you clean, more will be on its way: People and pets track it in from outdoors (and also generate it themselves), and it seeps through loose windows and doors. Eliminating drafts will go a long way toward reducing dust, so ensure your home is weather-stripped. Placing doormats inside and out and vacuuming them as needed will also help. Beyond those basics, there are ways to clean more efficiently and effectively, using the right tools and techniques.

DUSTING TOOLS

Dusting tools should pick up rather than disperse dust. Some tools, such as electrostatic cloths, are designed or treated to do just this. Plain cotton cloths should always be dampened slightly so dust clings.

VACUUM CLEANER

Using a vacuum cleaner with a good filtration system is the best way to dust many areas and objects, as it collects and contains the dust, rather than merely moving it around. And it's not just for floors. Use the dust-brush attachment to dust blinds, ceilings, and walls; the crevice tool for corners by baseboards or any tight spot; and the upholstery tool for sofas, throw pillows, chairs, and beds. (For more on vacuuming, turn to page 496.)

VACUUM CLEANER

FEATHER DUSTER

This classic tool is useful and versatile; though it doesn't hold dust as well as some products, it can reach into small crevices or sweep across large surfaces. Use it for general dusting, on end tables, bookshelves, lamps, and more. If you are partial to a feather duster, it's worth investing in a good-quality one made of ostrich feathers. This will be less likely to scratch and lose feathers, and it will hold dust better. Release the dust by shaking the tool outside, or gently tap the duster on your ankle to release the dust onto the floor, then vacuum it up. Do not use a feather duster on rough wood or masonry surfaces; it can catch and tear.

FEATHER DUSTER

LAMB'S-WOOL DUSTER

The natural lanolin oils in this type of duster combine with static electricity to attract and hold dust. Use it the same way as a feather duster, described above. Look for dusters with attachable, extendable handles for reaching ceilings and other high spots.

LAMB'S-WOOL DUSTER

ELECTROSTATIC DUSTER

These popular products, available at any grocery store, don't just pick up surface dust; they use static electricity to attract and hold tiny airborne particles. Electrostatic dusters allow you to dust without moistening the cloth first, and they keep dust from getting kicked back into the room. You'll find this fabriclike material in different forms: plain dusting cloths, dusters designed to get into crevices, mitts to wear as you work, and covers for floor sweepers. Use for general dusting on wood furniture and floors, decorative accessories, and more. Most electrostatic dusters are disposable, which makes them less economical but easy to use, since you don't have

ELECTROSTATIC DUSTER

to clean them. You can also find machine-washable ones at hardware stores and home centers. Because these cloths hold on to tiny particles that might otherwise become airborne while dusting, they are especially good for people with allergies.

MICROFIBER CLOTH

MICROFIBER CLOTH

These soft cloths, woven from superfine synthetic fibers, are gentle on surfaces prone to scratching, such as computer screens and stainless-steel surfaces. Use them dry or barely damp (they do not require cleaning solution).

COTTON CLOTH

COTTON CLOTH

A soft cotton cloth, such as one made of flannel, can be used on almost any surface. Boost its dust-attracting ability by misting it with water. Or treat it with a mixture of mild laundry flakes, ammonia, and linseed oil: Combine 1 tablespoon flakes, 1 tablespoon ammonia, 2 tablespoons linseed oil, and 1 quart of warm water. Soak the cloth for several minutes, wring it out, and hang it up to dry before using. When not in use, store in a covered container. These dust cloths can be used several times before they need to be washed. Once you wash a dust cloth, it will need to be treated again. Do not use fabric softener when washing a dust cloth.

DUST MOP

DUST MOP

A dust mop is better than a broom at picking up fine dust on hardwood floors. But an electrostatic floor duster (see electrostatic cloths, page 483) is better still, and doesn't have to be shaken out after use. If you like to use a traditional dust mop, shake excess dust into a moistened bag after each use, or vacuum the mop thoroughly. When necessary, wash your dust mop in hot, sudsy water, rinse, then hang it to dry (or place the mop head in a mesh bag and put it in the washing machine).

HOW OFTEN TO DUST

Frequency depends partially on where you live and the season. Some climates generate more dust, and more of it will come into your home when you have your windows open. Generally, a major dusting should be done once or twice a month, with touch-ups weekly. High-use areas, such as kitchen counters and floors, should be wiped or swept daily, which will keep them free of dust.

HOW TO DUST A CEILING FAN

Once a month, clean fans using a long-handled pole with a dusting attachment that either bends or is shaped specifically for ceiling-fan blades. You should be able to find products like this at hardware stores.

PAINTBRUSH

A soft, clean, natural-bristle paintbrush is an ideal dusting tool; it's easy to control and has a light touch. Use on fragile items like lamp shades or things with intricate designs, or to reach into tight spaces. Try one on the pleats of a fabric lamp shade or the crevices of carved woodwork. Sable brushes (available at art supply stores) are costly but best for the most delicate surfaces, such as paintings and gold leaf. Keep paintbrushes used for dusting separate from those used for paint touch-ups.

PAINTBRUSH

COTTON SWAB

Use a cotton swab to reach detailed areas of very fragile or intricate objects and surfaces, such as a carved picture frame. Cotton swabs can leave behind lint, however, so moisten them lightly.

COTTON SWABS

COMPRESSED AIR

A can of compressed air is great for cleaning computer keyboards and piano keys and other small, hard-to-reach spots. The air blows the dust away without leaving behind any residue. It is ideal for objects that can't tolerate moisture. Cans are available at office supply stores.

COMPRESSED AIR

GOLDEN RULES OF DUSTING

1. Always work from the top down, and then vacuum the dust that settles to the floor.

2. Don't just dust the places you can see but the places you can't. When doing a thorough cleaning, include the tops of doors, walls, molding, ceiling fans, window treatments, and even lightbulbs (when lights are off and the bulbs are cool).

3. Instead of dusting around items such as collectibles, books, and telephones, move them aside and get underneath.

4. When dusting a flat surface, move the cloth smoothly from one end to the other, stopping at the end. Don't flick the cloth, or dust will merely be released back into the air before settling on the floor, instead of getting trapped by your cloth.

5. Avoid dusting sprays, or use them sparingly. They contain oily substances that actually attract more dust. They also build up over time, and can damage a finish.

6. On wood, dust in the direction of the grain.

7. If using dusting cloths, have several on hand. Turn the cloth frequently, presenting a clean surface to the object with each pass, and start fresh with a new one as necessary.

8. Finishes that are unstable (flaking, cracking, or with lifting edges) or are splintered should not be dusted with a cloth; fabric from a dust cloth can easily snag. Use a soft paintbrush instead.

WIPING UP

IN BUSY HOUSEHOLDS, it can sometimes seem that fingerprints and paw prints accumulate faster than you can wipe them. This most ordinary of household chores is indeed a regular and essential part of every cleaning routine. It's so basic that, often, we don't think much about the tools we use. But choosing the correct sponge or cloth can make the tasks of wiping and washing much easier—and the results much more satisfying. Unlike dusting, which is essentially a dry process involving few or no cleaning products, washing surfaces requires water and cleaning products appropriate to the surface you're tackling.

SPONGES

There are many types of sponges sold for use around the house, but each works in a slightly different way, with a different level of effectiveness. The type most of us use for day-to-day cleaning comes in bright colors and is made of cellulose, a material derived from wood pulp. But natural sponges, the fluffy puffs that show up in bathtubs and painters' toolboxes, are the prototype for those and all others.

TYPES OF SPONGES

POLYESTER

NATURAL

POP-UP

PLAIN CELLULOSE

ABRASIVE CELLULOSE

CELLULOSE WIPE

PLAIN CELLULOSE SPONGE

Cellulose sponges harden when dry so they are often impregnated with soap and biocide to keep them soft in the package and to inhibit bacteria and mildew growth. (The biocide does not, however, prevent germ transfer from one surface to another.) Holes created in the manufacturing process help the sponge absorb liquid. Cellulose sponges don't discharge liquid completely, so debris collects with repeated use. However, they are inexpensive, absorbent, and durable, and best for most routine cleaning jobs. Use them for washing dishes, wiping countertops, cleaning bathrooms, and blotting spills. These sponges are sold in a range of shapes, sizes, and colors so you can buy a variety to suit your needs. Cutting a large one down to a

A NOTE ABOUT DISINFECTING SPONGES

Putting sponges in the microwave to disinfect them is a bad idea. Although it may kill bacteria, it can also cause a fire. Replace sponges every two weeks or use dish cloths you can launder every couple of days.

more manageable size with scissors can be economical. Always rinse sponges after use, and squeeze them out well. Keep them in an open dish where air can circulate so they dry thoroughly. Kitchen sponges should be discarded after about two weeks of use. Don't use them for wiping up raw-meat juices; use a paper towel instead.

CELLULOSE WIPE

A thin sheet of cellulose sponge. Made with very fine pores and virtually lint-free, the cellulose wipe is an excellent dusting cloth and polishing rag. It is more absorbent than cloth, so it rarely leaves behind streaks of moisture. Use the wipes for dusting furniture, wiping up food spills, and shining stainless-steel appliances. Look for these where regular cellulose sponges are sold, and care for them in the same manner. They are a smart alternative to paper towels for many tasks, since they are reusable and long lasting. And because they're thin enough to dry between uses, they are more sanitary in kitchens than thicker sponges.

POP-UP SPONGE

A cellulose sponge that has been compressed, the pop up is sold in a compact, flattened form—sometimes cut into novelty shapes—and expands substantially when it gets wet for the first time. Once it expands, it can't be flattened again. Use for the same jobs as cellulose sponges (see page 487). Pop-up sponges cost a bit more than plain cellulose but are a good choice if you don't want the soaps or chemicals found on those sponges.

ABRASIVE SPONGE

A cellulose sponge with an abrasive material attached, often to just one side, or a thin, abrasive pad alone. Choose this option when you need extra scrubbing power. Use for cleaning stuck-on food from cookware, scouring outdoor grills, and removing scuff marks from floors. Pads are color coded according to abrasiveness. Colors don't always mean the same thing, even within the same brand, but white generally is for delicate surfaces, such as glazed tile, some plastics, and glass. Green is usually much more abrasive, and maroon, tougher yet. Some blue pads are mild, but others are so coarse you can use them on outdoor grills. Care for them the same way you would a plain cellulose sponge (see page 487).

NATURAL SPONGE

A sea sponge is harvested from the ocean floor. Each sponge has a structure of channels that allows it to draw in a great amount of water, hold it, then release it completely when squeezed. Use for sopping up big spills, bailing water, and soaping windows. Look in home or paint supply stores

KITCHEN SPONGE SAFETY

As a sponge soaks up iquid, it also takes in whatever's mixed with it. When that includes nasty microorganisms, the sponge becomes a breeding ground for bacteria. To avoid contaminating surfaces, thoroughly rinse and squeeze out the sponge after each use, and store it where it can dry; bacteria usually die without moisture and food. Purchase several sponges and rotate them so they can dry completely between uses. Also, designate a separate sponge for each task. Never wipe up the floor, rinse the sponge, and then wipe off a dish rack, for example. You can sterilize a sponge by soaking it for a minute in 1 cup water mixed with 2 teaspoons chlorine bleach, then rinse thoroughly before drying.

for the types called sheepswool or wool; they are the strongest and most absorbent. Beige ones are often sturdier than yellow. After use, wash in hot soapy water, rinse, squeeze out, and let dry. Because it won't trap debris, a good-quality natural sponge can last a year or more.

POLYESTER SPONGE

A sponge made of chemically produced foam that is soft even when dry. An ordinary polyester sponge won't hold a lot of water; one marked "hydrophilic" or "reticulated," however, will be more absorbent. It functions like a natural sea sponge, but is less expensive; it is good for transferring liquid. Use for touching up paint jobs, washing the car, wiping down walls, and when installing wallpaper. Plain polyester sponges are often sold on sticks or rollers as touch-up painting tools. For the hydrophilic type, select one with large pores to wash down surfaces and one with fine pores to wipe away moisture without leaving a trail. Wash in warm water before and after each use, wring out, and let dry thoroughly.

DRY SPONGE

Rubber foam with a small amount of soap added to make the material stickier. Also called a dry cleaning sponge, it is used completely dry, making it ideal for delicate surfaces or any that would be damaged by moisture. Companies that clean up after fires use them to remove soot from walls. Use for whisking dust from lamp shades, gently cleaning papered walls, and wiping fabric window blinds. Not as readily available as other types, these are worth seeking out in hardware and home-supply stores, or on the Internet (search for "dry cleaning sponge"). Store in tightly sealed plastic bags to prevent hardening. Heavily soiled sponges can be rinsed well in warm water (let the sponge dry completely before reusing). Alternatively, sand the surface; the exposed area will be as good as new.

TYPES OF CLOTHS

Not all cleaning cloths are created equal. Depending on the task at hand, you might reach for a terry-cloth towel, a microfiber cloth, or even an old T-shirt. Here are cloths suited to the most common household chores:

TERRY CLOTH

A cotton cloth with thousands of raised, woven loops on the surface that absorb a lot of liquid. Use for blotting surface stains on carpets and upholstery and for soaking up big spills. White towels are best so there's no chance of dye transfer when blotting spills. Look for inexpensive bar mops, the classic white towels used in restaurant kitchens and bars, at kitchen-supply stores. Machine-wash and dry after a couple of uses.

HOW TO CLEAN SWITCH PLATES

The oils in skin leave behind a residue every time you switch on or off lights, which attracts dust and grime to switch plates. Clean them with a cloth dampened with warm water and mild dishwashing liquid. Wring the cloth well before using. To avoid damaging the switch, never spray cleaner directly on the plate. To clean very dirty plates, remove them from the wall and wash them in warm, soapy water. Rinse and dry thoroughly.

DRY SPONGE

TERRY CLOTH

PAPER TOWELS

MICROFIBER

LINT-FREE COTTON

POLISHING CLOTH

PAPER TOWELS

Made of wood pulp and generally treated with chlorine bleach (harmful to humans, marine life, and wildlife) to whiten the brown pulp and remove lignin (a gluelike substance that holds wood fibers together). For the sake of the environment and your budget, reserve paper towels for minor messes (puddle-size spills can use as much as half a roll), spills that stain, such as red wine, and bacteria-laden spills, such as poultry and meat juices. Unbleached or non-chlorine-bleached recycled paper towels with at least 40 percent postconsumer material (paper waste generated by consumers and diverted from landfill) are the most eco-friendly choice. Avoid patterned paper towels; the dyes can run when they come in contact with cleaning products and stain the surface you're cleaning.

MICROFIBER CLOTHS

Woven from superfine synthetic fibers. Millions of tiny loops on the surface of the cloth create pockets that collect and trap dirt. Use on surfaces prone to scratching, such as computer and television screens and stainless-steel appliances. Cloths come in different weights and with different loop sizes for specific purposes (fine, light cloths for computer screens and thicker ones, with more pronounced loops, for stainless steel, for example). Use a dry one to rub out small smudges, or a damp one for more stubborn marks, such as fingerprints. Because they are so effective, there's no need to use cleaning solutions. Machine-wash after use; hang to dry.

LINT-FREE LINEN OR COTTON

Thin, plain-woven towels (without nap or loops). Use for wiping mirrors and on any other surface where lint will be a nuisance. Flour-sack and huck towels, diapers, and cut-up old white cotton T-shirts all make excellent lint-free cloths. Machine-wash and dry after several uses.

POLISHING CLOTH

Soft, napped cloths that distribute polish evenly. Use for polishing silver or other metals. Choose untreated 100-percent-cotton flannel, which is softer than plain cotton. Even with these gentle cloths, however, you should not polish silver-plated items too aggressively or too often (once a year should do the trick) because the coating can wear away. Machine-wash and dry.

CHAMOIS

Natural chamois is made from the skin of the chamois, a small, goatlike antelope, or from sheepskin. Use chamois for wiping down large surfaces, drying wet lawn furniture, and drying the car. Imitation chamois, which is much less expensive, is made of cotton or synthetic fibers woven to approximate the suede texture of natural chamois. Both are lint-free and can absorb many times their weight in water, and then be wrung nearly dry. Natural and imitation chamois are very soft, so they're safe for delicate surfaces. Rinse and wring chamois well before use; chamois must be damp (but not wet) to work. After use, hand-wash natural chamois well in lukewarm water and a mild dishwashing liquid; rinse and hang to dry out of direct sunlight. Imitation chamois can be machine washed; hang to dry.

CHAMOIS

CLOTH CARE

If you can't launder cleaning cloths right after use, let them dry on a rack before throwing them in the laundry basket. This will prevent them from acquiring a sour smell. Do not use fabric softener or dryer sheets on cleaning cloths. Softeners reduce absorbency and can leave behind a residue.

HOW OFTEN TO WIPE UP

Heavily used surfaces, such as kitchen counters, will need to be wiped several times a day, while most others, such as the bathtub, will need to be wiped weekly.

GOLDEN RULES OF WIPING UP

Wiping up hard surfaces around the house is a basic part of the weekly cleaning routine. Any surface that is moisture tolerant can be wiped using these guidelines.

1. Always start with the mildest cleaning product before moving on to stronger products or stronger concentrations of a cleaning solution.

2. Some cleaning products are designed to be used full strength, while others are meant to be diluted. Always read and follow label directions. Use only the recommended amount; more will not guarantee a cleaner surface—it will only leave behind residue that can actually attract dirt and grime.

3. Most detergents work best in warm to hot water, but be sure to read the manufacturer's instructions on the product label. If you're cleaning a surface you have treated with wax, use tepid water.

4. When using a spray cleaner, always apply the spray to the cloth rather than to the surface being cleaned. This prevents drips and will keep the spray off areas where it doesn't belong.

5. Don't overwet surfaces. With the exception of bathtubs, bathtub surrounds, showers, and outdoor surfaces such as decks and patios, all of which are designed to withstand moisture, you should wipe surfaces with well-wrung cloths. Cleaning with excessive amounts of water can cause finishes to fail and surfaces to warp.

6. Rinse surfaces with a clean, damp cloth and polish them dry with another clean cloth.

SWEEPING

BROOMS HAVE BEEN USED for centuries in America. Colonists tied tree branches, twigs, cornhusks, or long splinters of wood to sticks or handles and used them to sweep floors and clean ashes from fireplaces. While there are more high-tech tools available today, an old-fashioned broom is sometimes still the best one for the job. You can use one to sweep up crumbs in a jiffy, or whisk away leaves from a walkway. Matching the broom to the task helps you work efficiently. Soft bristles gather fine dust or dirt on a smooth surface, such as a wood floor. Stiff, coarse bristles reach into crevices, lifting dirt from a rough surface, such as a concrete floor or outdoor path. If you find yourself pressing hard as you clean, you probably need a brush with stiffer bristles.

TYPES OF BROOMS

ANGLED BROOM

A synthetic broom with angled bristles is the tool you'll reach for almost every day, to sweep up after dinner or to give the entryway a quick cleaning. This broom often has split (or flagged) tips, packed close together, which allow the broom to get into tight spaces and pick up more debris than other brooms. Blunt tips won't clump when debris is damp.

ANGLED BROOM

CORN BROOM

This traditional cleaning tool is made from the stiff stems of a plant called broomcorn, a variety of the upright grass *Sorghum vulgare.* The stems are harvested and dried, then processed and bound to form broom heads and brushes. Corn brooms are best for rough surfaces, such as a garage floor, driveway, or sidewalk. They will scrape up debris such as leaves and gravel but won't pick up fine dirt. Look for a nonslip handle that is comfortable to hold—thicker handles cause less strain. This is true for any broom you use for anything more than a quick sweep.

CORN BROOM

OUTDOOR PUSH BROOM

This heavy-duty tool is best for large, open outdoor spaces, such as a driveway or patio. Look for a push broom with a head that is at least 18 inches wide, with stiff center fibers and flexible, split-tipped outer ones to both dislodge debris and pick up dirt. Two holes in the broom's head let you switch the handle from side to side for even wear.

INDOOR PUSH BROOM

This wide broom with soft natural or synthetic bristles is good for large indoor areas, such as a hallway or kitchen. An angled handle allows you to maneuver easily. To keep dust under control, push in long, smooth strokes, keeping the bristles on the floor as much as possible.

OUTDOOR AND INDOOR
PUSH BROOMS

WHISK BROOM

Use this small handheld broom and a dustpan to pick up the dirt and debris you've swept into a pile with a larger broom. You can also use it wherever the vacuum cleaner can't reach: on the edges of carpeting, at the base of the refrigerator, in stair corners, beside the toilet. A whisk broom with synthetic bristles and a plastic handle is ideal for many household tasks. Whisk brooms with corn bristles are better for coarse debris, such as dirt in a mudroom or on outdoor surfaces, such as patios and porches.

WHISK BROOM

TYPES OF BROOMS

HEARTH BROOM

COUNTER BRUSH

A NOTE ABOUT ELECTROSTATIC SWEEPERS

These days, many people prefer this cleaning tool, which is similar to a dust mop but with a replaceable electrostatic cover that attracts and holds dust. It does a great job picking up dust and hair on wood and other smooth floors. But it can't corral coarse debris, such as crumbs, so you'll still need a broom.

HEARTH BROOM

Similar in appearance to a whisk broom but longer (about 24 inches), this tool is best for sweeping up ashes. Sturdier than those often sold with fireplace tools, this is a good choice if you use your fireplace frequently. Some companies make these in black, a sensible option when dealing with soot.

COUNTER BRUSH

Also called a shop brush, this tool has shorter bristles than a broom, a long head, and a short handle. It can do many of the same jobs as a whisk broom, and more: Use it on windowsills, shelves, desks, and work surfaces in the garage, garden shed, or basement. You can find counter brushes with medium-soft natural or synthetic bristles.

DUSTPANS

Dustpans are made of plastic or metal, with either a flat or a sloped edge. Sometimes dustpans and brushes are sold in sets, which is convenient for quick touch-ups. A dustpan with a thin rubber lip is preferable because it catches more dirt, doesn't allow dust to slip underneath the dustpan, and won't scratch floors. Replace the dustpan if it becomes warped; an even seal is essential for a clean sweep. Look for a long-handled dustpan so you can stand up straight as you work. Always use a metal dustpan to collect fireplace ashes; a plastic one could melt if there are any stray embers.

HOW TO SWEEP

To avoid kicking up dust, hold the broom at an angle so the bristles sit flat on the floor (if you're right-handed, the bristles should be on your left; if you're left-handed, they will be on your right). Start in one corner and sweep outward without lifting the broom from the floor, being sure to run the broom close to baseboards. Work toward the center of the room, sweeping away from your body, pushing dirt into a pile (or several).

HOW OFTEN TO SWEEP

Unlike with other cleaning tasks, there's no set schedule for sweeping. You might use a broom every day for sweeping up crumbs after dinner, and an electrostatic sweeper for picking up dog hair in the living room. You'll also reach for a broom when you need a low-tech, quick fix for a small mess, such as spilled nails in the garage or flour in the kitchen. For your more thorough house cleaning, a vacuum cleaner is more effective and efficient. Outdoors, too, use a broom as needed: when a few leaves start to scatter across the patio, or when the walkway seems particularly dirty.

CARING FOR BROOMS

Avoid standing a broom or any kind of cleaning brush on its bristles, as this can make them bend and break. Storing a broom upside down is one solution; special clips for that purpose are available at hardware stores. Many brooms have a loop at the end of the handle, and hanging them right side up from a hook is just as effective.

To release dirt from a broom's bristles, shake them out or run them along a stiff edge, such as a deck stair for an outdoor corn broom. Replace your broom once the bristles are splayed or have become shorter or show evidence of breakage.

VACUUMING

UP UNTIL THE MID-NINETEENTH CENTURY, when the vacuum cleaner was invented, there was really no way to gather dust. Sweeping would collect some of it but would also rerelease it into the air. The first vacuum cleaners were pumped by hand; they drew the dust inside, like a bellows in reverse. Electric vacuum cleaners were introduced early in the twentieth century and have been continually improved upon; today, the really good ones can draw in up to 99 percent of the dust and dirt in an area—a boon to neatness as well as healthy living. They have also become expensive appliances with multiple attachments and features, so it's well worth doing some research before you buy, and making sure you understand how to use and care for a vacuum properly when you get one home.

TYPES OF VACUUMS

CENTRAL VACUUMING SYSTEM

If your home has this feature, you need never lug a vacuum cleaner from room to room again. A central vacuuming system is set up in a home through a series of tubes in the walls that feed to a central receptacle in a garage or basement. There are discreet inlet holes (about the size of an electrical outlet) placed throughout the home where a lightweight hose and power brush unit are plugged in, allowing for instant vacuuming.

This system isn't just a matter of convenience. Central vacuums have three to five times more power than a traditional vacuum because the motor doesn't have to be mobile (and they are quieter, too, since the motor is not following you). They also eliminate the recirculation of dirty air because the dust and debris are carried through the tubes to the receptacle, all of which makes these machines ideal for people with allergies to dust and dust mites. As an added convenience, you can also have automatic dust-pans installed that allow you to sweep straight into a vent in the wall. These systems can be built into a new home or installed in an existing home. They are not inexpensive, but they can increase the value of your home.

UPRIGHT VACUUM CLEANER

The upright was originally made primarily for removing dirt from pile carpeting, and if you have a lot of carpeting in your home, it is still most likely the best choice. The machine's head has a beater bar, a rotating brush also known as a power brush or turbo brush, which stirs debris from the bottom of the pile to the surface so the suction can whisk it away. Most machines available now are more versatile, allowing you to raise or turn off the beater bar so you can vacuum bare floors. Upright vacuums are easy to manage and powerful—especially on carpets—but they do not always provide strong suction when attachments are used, and are not the best for edges and corners.

UPRIGHT VACUUM
CLEANER

CANISTER VACUUM CLEANER

This machine, with a flexible hose attached to a "canister," where the motor is housed, was designed primarily for hard floors, which should not be cleaned with the beater bar that's standard in an upright vacuum. These days, canisters also come with a beater-bar attachment, however, so you can use them on pile carpeting as well. The hose makes a canister good for reaching into tight spots, cleaning stairs and curtains, and pulling cobwebs from ceilings. If you find the canister clumsy, try carrying it, which prevents the machine from knocking into furniture.

CANISTER VACUUM
CLEANER

STICK VACUUM CLEANER

HAND-HELD
VACUUM CLEANER

WET/DRY VACUUM
CLEANER

CARPET SWEEPER

ROBOTIC VACUUM CLEANER

This clever machine makes its way around a room on its own. Its works best in open areas clear of clutter. It can help keep a room cleaner in between regular vacuumings but doesn't work as well as a standard upright or canister vacuum. It tends to miss corners and edges.

STICK VACUUM CLEANER

This lightweight, less-powerful version of an upright vacuum cleaner is handy to have around. It's small enough to stash in any closet and easy to pull out and use every day, if necessary, for high-traffic areas, such as the mudroom, front hall, or kitchen. Look for one with a beater bar, so it can be used on carpet as well as hard floors. Unless you live in a very small space or have trouble maneuvering a full-size vacuum cleaner, this tool is usually a supplement to a full-size machine rather than a replacement for it.

HAND-HELD VACUUM CLEANER

This portable tool is a convenient, compact machine, ideal for quick cleanups, such as spilled sugar or tracked-in dirt. It is also good for cleaning upholstery when you have pets (a motorized beater-bar attachment works best).

WET/DRY VACUUM CLEANER

Also known as a Shop-Vac, this machine can extract all the things that would ruin your everyday vacuum cleaner, such as water, paint chips, and sawdust. As useful as a wet/dry vacuum cleaner is, however, it should not be your primary vacuum cleaner. Its filtration system is less effective, so it may pull up the dirt but blow some particulates back into the room. Never try to use a wet/dry vacuum to steam clean a carpet; although it can vacuum wet surfaces, it cannot be filled with water and used to steam carpets. (Turn to page 534 for information on renting a hot-water extraction unit to steam your carpets at home or hiring a professional to do it for you.)

CARPET SWEEPER

This machine is perfect for small jobs, such as sweeping up crumbs. Use it whenever you need to clean up quickly and easily, without having to pull out a heavier vacuum cleaner. Its handle lies flat, allowing an easy reach beneath tables and chairs, and making storage convenient. Cordless, motorless sweepers are often used in restaurants and hotels, or anywhere where noise might be a problem. They are usually made of metal, but have plastic or rubber bumpers to prevent damage to furniture.

ABOUT FILTRATION SYSTEMS

Vacuum cleaners vacuum up dust and dirt—but some models send quite a bit of both right back out into the air. If anyone in your household suffers from allergies or asthma, consider buying a vacuum cleaner with a high-efficiency particulate air (HEPA) filter. This type of filter removes a minimum of 99.7 percent of contaminants as small as 0.3 microns in size, which helps capture both dust mites and their by-products, both of which are very common allergens that contribute to asthma. (For size comparison, a human hair is about 60 to 75 microns; particles below 35 microns in size can't be seen with the naked eye.) Particles below 5 microns in size are the most troubling for asthmatics. Though HEPA filters trap tiny particles better than other filters do, all vacuum cleaners tend to stir up particles during vacuuming, so some amount of contamination in the air is unavoidable.

As a less-costly (and less-effective) option, you may be able to purchase high-filtration bags to use with an ordinary vacuum cleaner. These bags consist of multiple layers of special filter media. They come in different sizes and will list what models they fit. The size of the bag is as important as the filtering capability; a larger bag decreases the resistance to airflow, which means that the vacuum is less likely to clog and lose suction.

Some machines have water-filtration systems, which trap dust by pulling the dirty air through water. After vacuuming, the dirty water is poured from the tank, and the tank is rinsed.

CARPETING

Vacuuming your carpets will not only keep them clean but make them last longer by removing the dirt that can grind away at the yarn fibers. One pass with the vacuum isn't enough; to pick up as much dirt as possible, try twelve passes by doorways, eight passes in high-traffic areas, and four passes in low-traffic areas. Occasionally changing the vacuum direction will help the pile stand upright, which will reduce matting.

A NOTE ABOUT CYCLONIC VACUUMS

Cyclonic vacuums don't use a vacuum bag to retain the dirt they pick up. Instead, they rely on the centrifugal force of a "cyclone" to whip the air and dirt through various cylinders. This force separates the dirt from the air, and once separated, it falls to the bottom of a canister, which can be taken out and emptied. Many of these vacuums can also be fitted with a HEPA filter.

VACUUMING FIREPLACE SCREENS

Vacuum fireplace screens on both sides with a dust-brush attachment to remove soot and ash. You'll want to have an extra attachment just for this chore so you don't transfer the soot to other surfaces. Never use a standard vacuum cleaner to remove ashes from the fireplace, however, as they can damage the machine. Sweep them out or use a wet/dry vacuum instead. (For more on cleaning out the fireplace, turn to page 203.)

VACUUM CLEANER TOOLS AND ATTACHMENTS

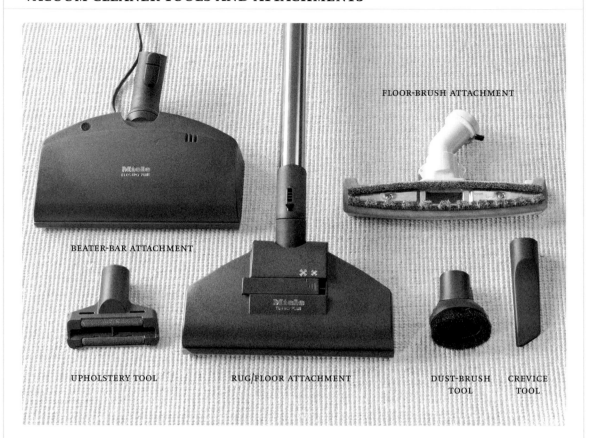

FLOOR-BRUSH ATTACHMENT

BEATER-BAR ATTACHMENT

UPHOLSTERY TOOL

RUG/FLOOR ATTACHMENT

DUST-BRUSH TOOL

CREVICE TOOL

BEATER-BAR ATTACHMENT
A rotating brush used with canister vacuums. Also known as a power brush or turbo brush, it stirs debris from the bottom of pile carpeting so the suction can whisk it away.

UPHOLSTERY TOOL
This small, flat head removes dust from furniture and mattresses, which should be vacuumed thoroughly every three months.

RUG/FLOOR ATTACHMENT
This nozzle, which is often smooth with no brushes, comes with some canister vacuums. Use it instead of the beater bar on delicate carpets, such as antique ones.

CREVICE TOOL
Use this narrow nozzle for tight areas, such as next to and under the refrigerator and other large appliances and along baseboards. This tool will also draw out dust from hard-to-reach heating vents and between the flanges of a radiator.

FLOOR-BRUSH ATTACHMENT
This is best for wood floors; the brush around the edge of its thin, rectangular opening prevents scratching. It is also used for wide stair treads and for brick, stone, and tile flooring.

DUST-BRUSH TOOL
With its soft brush edge, this attachment is ideal for windowsills, shelves, and chair legs; it picks up dust without scratching. It is also the tool to use on the slats of window blinds.

GOLDEN RULES OF VACUUMING

1. When doing your thorough cleaning, dust the room before vacuuming so you can vacuum up the particles that float into the air as you work and settle on the floor.

2. Move furniture out of your way before you begin vacuuming (both so you don't bump into it and so you do a thorough job of cleaning under and around it). Never vacuum between the legs of a fine chair, for example. Be especially careful around baseboards to avoid marring them. If you use a canister-style vacuum cleaner, you might find it's easier to control if you carry it rather than drag it behind you.

3. When vacuuming the floor, start inside a room and vacuum your way out of it.

4. Vacuum in long, slow, overlapping strokes, bending down to pick or sweep up any small objects that lie in your path, such as pine needles, leaves of houseplants, paint chips, or cat litter, as they might present a danger to the vacuum's motor.

5. Don't let the vacuum bag get too full. For maximum efficiency, always change it when it's half to three-quarters full.

USING THE BEATER BAR

Wall-to-wall carpeting and other durable cut-pile carpeting should be cleaned with the rotating brush known as a beater bar. It agitates the carpet pile and loosens dirt. But there are some exceptions, and in those cases, using the floor setting on an upright, which turns the beater bar off, or the rug/floor tool on a canister, which doesn't have a brush, is better.

AREA RUGS
As long as they're not too large, these can be rolled up and taken outdoors. Shake and beat them with a broom or tennis racket, then bring them back indoors and vacuum with the beater bar on both sides.

LOOP-PILE CARPET
Carpet with thick loop pile construction (particularly wool and wool blends) may gradually be damaged by the vigorous brushing action of the beater bar. For this, use a floor setting or rug/floor attachment.

DELICATE AND VALUABLE RUGS
For silk rugs or Orientals, use a "floor" setting or rug/floor attachment. If the rug is not too large, vacuum both sides.

SISAL AND OTHER NATURAL-FIBER CARPET
Use a floor setting or rug/floor attachment so you don't abrade the fibers.

FRINGE
To clean the fringe on the edge of an area rug using an upright vacuum, use the floor setting, tip up the front slightly, and push it over the fringe and off the carpet. With a canister vacuum, use the rug/floor attachment. If you cannot turn off your beater bar, use a hose and lower the suction.

HOW TO VACUUM ANY SURFACE

CARPETING
How to For most carpets, use the beater bar. For delicate materials or constructions, use the floor setting or a rug/floor attachment. (Turn to page 501 for more information.)

How often High-traffic areas, such as by the door, benefit from frequent vacuuming, as often as every day but at least twice a week. Other areas should be vacuumed once a week.

HARD FLOORS
How to Use a floor brush or the floor setting.

How often High-traffic areas, such as by the door, benefit from frequent cleaning, as often as every day but at least twice a week. Hard floors can be swept instead of vacuumed for these quick cleanups. In general, all floors should be vacuumed once a week.

STAIRS
How to Upright and canister vacuums can be difficult to maneuver on stairs. A stick vacuum or a handheld vacuum with a motorized beater-bar attachment are more convenient.

How often Vacuum high-traffic stairs twice a week, or as needed, and others once a week. Once a month, do a more thorough job, making sure you vacuum corners and edges well.

WALLS AND CEILINGS
How to Start with the ceiling and work your way down by vacuuming with the dust-brush tool; add an additional pipe section to extend the length so you can reach. Vacuuming walls regularly with the brush tool is especially important for flocked and fabric wallpaper, which collect dust easily and are more difficult to clean than a painted wall. (If, even after vacuuming, wallpaper begins to look dingy, turn to page 542 for cleaning instructions.)

How often Vacuum painted ceilings and walls once or twice a year. Vacuum flocked wallpaper once a month.

WINDOWSILLS AND BOOKSHELVES
How to Use the dust-brush tool or the crevice tool, if necessary, to reach into a tight spot.

How often Weekly.

UPHOLSTERED FURNITURE AND BEDS
How to Use the upholstery tool on fabric furniture and mattresses, or the crevice tool to reach into tight spots. Reduce suction when cleaning delicate fabrics. Use the dust-brush tool on leather furniture.

How often Weekly.

BASEBOARDS, CURTAINS, AND BLINDS
How to For baseboards, use the dust-brush tool. On curtains, reduce suction and use the upholstery tool, working from the top down. For blinds, close them (so they lie flat) and use the dust-brush tool. Then reverse them, so they close the other way, and repeat.

How often Monthly.

VENTS IN FLOORS, WALLS, AND CEILINGS
How to Use the dust-brush tool or the crevice tool.

How often Vacuum weekly during heating and cooling seasons.

ABOUT CARPET FIBERS

COIR	Coir is the fiber taken from the hairy husk of coconuts. It is durable, wiry, and mildew-resistant—ideal for doormats.
COTTON	Cotton carpet, like cotton clothing, wears well and feels good. It is a magnet for dust and dirt, however, and should not be used in high-traffic areas unless it is washable.
JUTE	Jute comes from the jute plant, which is also used to make burlap and twine. Jute is softer than sisal but also less durable. Like sisal, it can be easily damaged by sunlight and liquids. Stains generally can't be removed.
LINEN	Linen, made of flax, is lustrous. But it is more expensive than many other carpet fibers and, with age, linen carpet will reveal traffic patterns.
NYLON	Nylon, a synthetic, is the most popular carpet fiber in the United States. It is durable, resilient, and stain-resistant.
OLEFIN	Olefin is a glossy synthetic that is water- and stain-resistant, and often used outdoors. However, it crushes easily.
POLYESTER	Polyester has a wool-like appearance and is often used for cut-pile carpets. It is soft and affordable, but may mat down in a short period.
SEA GRASS	Sea grass is made from a variety of reedy plants. It should not be used in a moist or humid room. Sea grass costs less than sisal and jute, and it is more stain-resistant.
SILK	Silk carpets are soft and luxurious. Silk takes dyes beautifully and is durable. Because of its high cost, it is often blended with wool in carpet construction.
SISAL	Sisal comes from the agave plant. It is strong but particularly prone to fading and can be stained very easily, even by water. Stains generally can't be removed.
WOOL	Wool is strong, static-resistant, and pleasing to the touch. It is also resilient and naturally stain-resistant and flame-retardant. It is more costly than many other fibers.

CARING FOR A VACUUM CLEANER

1. Make sure the vacuum cleaner is unplugged before cleaning it. Once a month, use a damp cloth and mild detergent to wipe off any dirt from the casing, hoses, and attachments. After each use, vacuum the rug/floor attachment with the crevice tool or hose before putting away the machine.

2. When blockages occur, unplug the unit and inspect the wand, hose, and beater bar, as well as the intake and exhaust ports to ensure that they are free of obstructions.

3. If the roller on the beater bar gets wound tightly with threads or clogged with fibers, cut them away with scissors or a seam ripper. Again, ensure the unit is unplugged before removing any obstruction.

4. Empty or change vacuum bags every week or as often as needed. Air travels through the bag, and as it fills, airflow and suction are significantly reduced. Do not trust a bag-full indicator light. Check the bag frequently, and do not let it get more than three-quarters full.

5. Change and empty cloth bags outdoors, or inside a large garbage bag if you must do it indoors. To minimize the spread of dust, you can place the vacuum bag inside of a large garbage bag, then hold the garbage bag closed with one hand while you shake the vacuum bag clean with your other hand.

6. If your vacuum has a bin, empty it and then rinse it with plain water only (never add detergent) and dry it thoroughly before replacing it. The inner cyclone, shroud, and cone should never get damp or wet. To remove lint buildup on the shroud, clean it with a dry cloth or brush.

7. If your vacuum uses a replaceable paper filter, check it every week when you check the bag. Many filters can be rinsed clean, dried, and reused. A filter that is torn or very dirty should be replaced. A blocked filter will also prevent the free flow of air through the vacuum. Never use the vacuum without the filter. For HEPA filters, follow the manufacturer's instructions.

8. When you notice that you need to go over the same area two or three times, it may be because the motor's belt has stretched. With most models, you can replace it yourself by buying a new belt from your vacuum's manufacturer and following the instructions on the package.

9. To maintain the belt, wipe it with a paper towel or cloth. Because it could shrink, the belt should never be near water. Always store your vacuum in a temperate place so the belt doesn't become brittle and crack.

10. Once every one to two years, take your vacuum to a dealership or reliable repair shop for a professional cleaning and to have damaged parts replaced. With this preventive treatment, a good, properly maintained vacuum can last for up to twenty years.

BUYING A NEW VACUUM CLEANER

☐ It's worth spending more on a high-quality machine. Although a lower-quality vacuum cleaner will remove surface dirt, it won't effectively remove the dirt and particles embedded in carpet pile.

☐ Shop at a store with knowledgeable salespeople. Always ask for a demonstration, and inquire about the warranty and return policy in case you are not satisfied with your vacuum cleaner after you get it home.

☐ Look for signs of durable construction, in both the machine and the cord. The machine should feel sturdy, solid, and weighted (but not too heavy to carry). Check the wheel axle. A steel axle will endure much more wear than a plastic one. Ask the salesperson what kind of belt the motor has. A geared belt will far outlive an elastic rubber belt.

☐ Choose a vacuum cleaner with good suction power. Many manufacturers indicate the power in amps, which signifies the total amount of energy the machine draws from the power source. This is usually between 7 and 12 amps, although the number can be misleading. In theory, the higher the amperage, the more powerful the motor and thus the stronger the suction. In reality, though, if a machine is not well constructed or if it has lots of extra features like lights and switches, it will take more power to operate with less efficiency, and less suction. Take this figure into consideration, but do not make your decision based on power alone. Ask to try out the machine in the store, so you can feel the suction.

☐ Consider the filtration system, and get the right one for your needs. (For more information on filtration systems, turn to page 499.)

☐ Look for a vacuum cleaner that's been given the Carpet and Rug Institute's Green Label. This industry group performs rigorous testing on vacuum cleaners. The ones that qualify for the Green Label are superior in soil removal, dust containment, and carpet appearance retention, meaning that the carpet stays looking good even after it has been vacuumed repeatedly.

VACUUM CLEANER SAFETY

1 Keep hair, loose clothing, and body parts away from openings, rotating brushes, and other moving parts of the vacuum cleaner.

2 Do not use a vacuum designed for household use outdoors or on a wet surface.

3 Do not pick up anything that is burning or smoking, such as cigarettes, matches, or hot ashes from the fireplace.

4 Turn off the vacuum before plugging it in or unplugging it.

5 Avoid picking up hard, sharp objects.

6 Turn off the appliance before connecting or disconnecting the hose.

7 Do not pull or carry a vacuum by the cord, use the cord as a handle, or use the appliance if the cord or plug is damaged.

8 Use an extension cord with the proper wattage or amp rating. Many typical thin cords are not appropriate for powerful vacuums and can pose a fire hazard.

MOPPING

IN MANY CULTURES, it is a common practice for homeowners and guests alike to shed their shoes at the door. Were this habit more widespread in the United States, our floors would certainly thank us. Mud, sand, and water, not to mention a host of pollutants, including pesticides, fertilizers, and pollen, would never make it over the threshold. If a no-shoes policy isn't practical in your household, doormats, both inside and outside the door, are the next best line of defense. This alone can add years to your floors. Even with the best precautions, however, some dirt will get in, and once it does, the best remedy is a good mopping. Cleaning is an endless cycle, and floor care may be the most relentless, but a little vigilance goes a long way.

TYPES OF MOPS

The sturdier the mop, the better. The particular type you use—all-in-one, sponge mop, or rag mop—is a matter of personal preference. Choose one that is both convenient and effective.

ALL-IN-ONE MOP

These are especially convenient for quick touch-ups. They consist of a replaceable or refillable reservoir attached to the mop handle and a spray nozzle attached to the head. By pressing a button on the handle, you release a mist of cleaning fluid onto the floor, eliminating the need for a bucket. Most all-in-one mops come with disposable cleaning pads, though you can often just as easily attach a washable cotton or microfiber cloth instead. When mopping a large floor, you may need to change pads or rinse out the cloth several times. Most are also designed for use only with a specific brand of cleaning solution, although Leifheit brand makes an all-in-one mop (called the Mr. Mister Pico Spray Mop) you can fill with the cleaner of your choice.

ALL-IN-ONE MOP

SPONGE MOP

These convenient mops have a wringer lever halfway up the handle, which allows the user to wring out the mop head without bending or stooping. Some brands also have a mop head with an abrasive strip for removing scuffs. Mop head sponges can be made of lightweight synthetic foam; PVA foam, a rigid synthetic substance that becomes soft and extremely absorbent when wet; or cellulose, a porous plant material. Sponge mops can also be used for applying wax and other surface sealers.

SPONGE MOP

RAG OR STRING MOP

This old-fashioned kind is best for absorbing big spills immediately. It covers a lot of surface area, so is also particularly good for mopping large rooms. Its durability makes it effective on textured surfaces, such as concrete and brick, which can snag and tear sponge mops. Look for mop handles that are self-wringing (they often have a twisting mechanism), or choose a bucket with a wringer attachment. Most rag heads are made of a cotton-rayon blend, which dry more quickly than all-cotton mops. Mops with looped ends will last longest, since they resist fraying. Some manufacturers now make synthetic microfiber rag mops.

STRING MOP

MOPPING TOOLS

PLASTIC BUCKETS

Plastic buckets with handles are easier to maneuver and gentler on floors than metal ones; wheeled plastic buckets are useful if you have very large rooms. Buckets with measurement markings can make portioning cleaning products easier. For convenience, choose a bucket that is suited to your mop—round buckets may be the most common, but a rectangular one will better accommodate a typical sponge mop.

RUBBER GLOVES

Rubber gloves protect your hands from dirty water and soiled mop heads.

LIGHT-DUTY NYLON SCRUBBING PAD

These are useful for removing scuff marks the mop can't budge.

HOW TO USE A DUST MOP

Dust mops, also known as dry mops, are designed to pick dust off hard surfaces. They are used in place of a vacuum or broom. Traditional dust mops are made of looped cotton or synthetic fibers. They are often treated to collect rather than spread dust. If they're not treated, mist them lightly with water before use. The new generation of dust mops uses an electrostatic disposable cloth instead. Before dust mopping with either type of mop, dry any wet spots and wipe any sticky patches. Start in one corner and, to avoid redepositing dust and grime back onto the floor, do not lift the mop off the floor once you've started. Use the swivel action of the mop to change direction. When you're finished, shake dust from a traditional mop into a moistened bag or vacuum the mop; throw electrostatic cloths in the trash.

HOW OFTEN TO MOP

High-traffic areas such as the kitchen, baths, hallways, and entranceways require weekly mopping. Infrequently used rooms, such as formal living areas or guest rooms, can be mopped every other week, or even once a month, as long as they're vacuumed weekly, which will remove dust and grit. An all-in-one mop is an easy way to touch up floors in between moppings. It will allow you to whisk away kitchen spills or muddy foot- or paw prints without going to the trouble of dragging out a bucket.

CARING FOR MOPS

Keeping a mop impeccably clean is essential—not only will this ensure cleaner floors, but even a little bit of leftover soil can result in a sour smell. After washing the floor, rinse the mop head thoroughly in a bucket of clean, hot (but not boiling) water. If the mop head is easily detachable, you can rinse it in a utility sink instead (to avoid spreading germs, never rinse mop heads or other tools used for cleaning in the kitchen sink).

Hang the mop to dry in a well-ventilated area. Do not set mops on the floor or put them in closets while damp. The more quickly the mop dries, the less likely it is to become malodorous. Replace the mop head when it becomes stained or has an odor that rinsing well will not remove. When buying a new mop head, be sure to choose one that's labeled Machine-washable and launder it about once a month.

CREATING YOUR OWN MACHINE-WASHABLE MOP HEAD

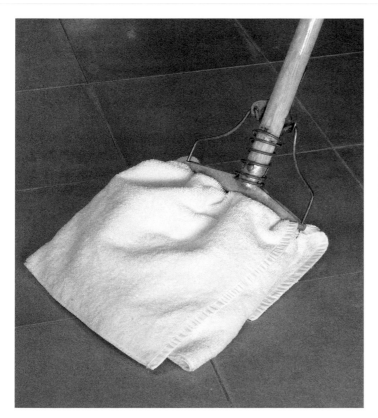

To create a homemade machine-washable mop head, try this technique: Fold and clamp an old bath or hand towel onto a sponge mop head. Thicker towels work best. White or light-colored towels are also preferable because you can see the dirt as you mop. Wring out the towel or replace it with a clean one as it becomes dirty. When you're finished, toss the towels in the washing machine and rinse the sponge head in hot water.

HOW TO MOP

1. Before mopping any floor, sweep or vacuum it well to remove grit, hair, and other large particles (for more on sweeping and vacuuming, see pages 492 and 496). Removing the everyday accumulation of dirt makes the task of mopping less arduous. Be sure to blot dry any wet areas before sweeping or vacuuming; otherwise, you'll dirty the floor further by spreading the grime.

2. Fill a bucket with warm water (unless floors are waxed, in which case you should use tepid water) and a small amount of cleaner—generally a squirt or two is sufficient. Using too much cleaner can leave behind a residue, which will make floors look dull. For specific information on what cleaners are best for what surfaces, see the chart, opposite.

3. Start in the farthest corner from the entrance and work your way backward, toward the door. Keep the bucket on an unwashed portion of the floor. Immerse the mop in the bucket, remove it, and wring it out well. No floor benefits from copious amounts of water, which can seep between cracks and under baseboards, causing serious damage. A mop that's too wet will also merely swish the dirt around instead of lifting it off the floor and will leave water marks as it dries. You'll know you've wrung the mop sufficiently if the mopped areas dry almost immediately.

4. Begin mopping along the edge of the baseboard in back-and-forth strokes. Move to the open area of the floor, overlapping the back-and-forth strokes as you work. Make two passes over each area—once to wet and to spread the solution and again to remove it. If you don't pass a second time, detergent may remain, leaving the floor sticky and cloudy. Remove any tough scuff marks with a light-duty nylon pad (be sure to keep separate pads for floors and dishes). If you can't get into tight corners without hitting baseboards, wipe them by hand with a damp cloth.

5. After several passes, immerse the mop in the bucket, wring it out, and continue. If you're working with a two-sided sponge mop or a string mop, turn it frequently to avoid redepositing soil onto floors. As soon as the water becomes murky, replace it with fresh (never dump dirty water down sinks, where it can spread germs and contribute to clogs; flush it down the toilet instead). When you've finished, mop again with clear water to remove any cleaning-solution residue. If the room is very large, mop and rinse the floor in sections.

6. You should have to get on your hands and knees to scrub a floor with a brush only if it has been neglected for some time. Frequent mopping will make this unnecessary.

MOPPING BY FLOOR TYPES

Each floor material has specific care requirements. All look best with regular, gentle maintenance. To prevent scratches, never use steel wool, metal-bristled brushes, or other strong abrasives on floors. Use only a light-duty nylon pad to remove scuff marks or sticky residue.

BAMBOO

Bamboo is the only woody member of the grass family. Because it grows fast and rejuvenates quickly (usually in about four years, as opposed to decades for trees), it is an environmentally friendly alternative to wood (it is usually shipped from Asia, however, which requires a great deal of fossil fuel). Bamboo is widely used in Asia for decorative items, including furniture, window blinds, and utensils, and is also becoming an increasingly popular choice for floors in the United States. Like wood, bamboo floors are generally coated with a polyurethane finish during manufacture or at the time of installation.

Cleaning solution Follow instructions for Wood Sealed with Polyurethane on page 513.

BRICK

Like other masonry flooring materials, bricks have a spongelike tendency to absorb spills and stain easily. Indoor brick floors must be sealed with a masonry-floor sealer (available at hardware and flooring stores). Sealed brick floors can also benefit from an additional coat of protective paste wax (for more on waxing floors, turn to page 522). Outdoor brick floors, terraces, and patios do not require the same meticulous care as indoor floors and do not need to be sealed.

Cleaning solution Warm water and a pH-neutral all-purpose cleaner.

CONCRETE

When used indoors, this porous material, which is especially prone to staining, should be sealed at the time of installation with a concrete sealer and can benefit from an additional layer of protective paste wax (for more on waxing floors, turn to page 000). Outdoor concrete does not require the same meticulous care as indoor surfaces, but should be sealed with a penetrating sealer as well.

Cleaning solution Warm water and a pH-neutral all-purpose cleaner. For waxed concrete, follow directions for Wood Finished with Wax on page 513.

CORK

Like wood, cork is generally sealed with a synthetic plasticlike finish at the time of manufacture or during installation. Never let water stand on the floor; it can seep around the edges of tiles and cause the cork to swell. Wring mops well (until almost dry) and wipe spills as soon as they hit the floor. If the cork has a wax finish, wax and buff once or twice a year (for more on waxing, turn to page 520).

Cleaning solution Warm water and pH-neutral all-purpose cleaner. If cork is waxed, follow directions for Wood Finished with Wax on page 513.

MOPPING BY FLOOR TYPES (CONTINUED)

GLAZED CERAMIC TILE

This durable surface is easy to keep clean but stains can set in grout, which should be sealed with a penetrating grout sealer several times a year. Always rinse ceramic tile and grout well, as grout can absorb cleaners, which will attract dirt.

Cleaning solution Warm water and an all-purpose cleaner. Do not use oil-based cleaners, which will leave an oily or waxy buildup that can attract grime to grout. Avoid regular use of acidic cleaners (such as distilled white vinegar or citrus cleaners), which can etch glazed surfaces and damage grout, and ammonia, which can discolor grout. Use caution with chlorine bleach as it can lighten colored grout.

LINOLEUM

This venerable flooring material has made a comeback in the United States, after being out of production here for several decades. It's often confused with vinyl, but linoleum is made from natural ingredients (including cork, limestone, wood flour, resin, linseed oil, and jute). Linoleum can be waxed with a product designed specifically to give it shine and make it easier to clean. (For more on how to wax floors, turn to page 522.)

Cleaning solution For unwaxed linoleum, use a pH-neutral all-purpose cleaner and warm water. For waxed linoleum, follow directions for Wood Finished with Wax, opposite. Never use strongly alkaline cleaners, such as ammonia, on linoleum or alkaline wax strippers. Both can damage and discolor it.

LAMINATE

Made of sheets of fiberboard coated with a layer of melamine, laminate floors mimic wood or stone. Floors, which come in planks or tiles, are manufactured with a clear wear layer that resists scuffs, scratches, and stains.

Cleaning solution Use 1 cup white vinegar to 1 gallon of water. Do not use detergents, all-purpose cleaners, waxes, or polishes, all of which can leave behind a dull film. Tough stains can be treated with acetone or denatured alcohol and a soft cloth.

STONE

When used indoors as flooring, all stone surfaces should be sealed with a penetrating stone sealer (available at hardware and flooring stores). In addition, grout, which is very porous and prone to staining, should be sealed with a penetrating grout sealer (available at hardware stores and home centers).

Cleaning solution Warm water and a pH-neutral all-purpose cleaner. Acidic or citrus-based cleaners will etch marble and limestone floors. Such cleaners can also damage the grout of all stone floors over time. Use stone poultices to remove deep-set stains. (For instructions, turn to page 55.)

TERRAZZO

Made from small chips of marble embedded in a cement binder, terrazzo is polished to a sheen at installation. After polishing, these floors are almost always coated with a penetrating sealer made especially for terrazzo (water-based acrylic products are best). Such sealers offer some stain protection but spills still must be wiped up immediately.

Cleaning solution Warm water and pH-neutral cleaner. Do not wax terrazzo or use an all-purpose sealer; both can make terrazzo dangerously slippery.

UNGLAZED TILE

Unglazed tile, such as terra cotta, is extremely porous if left unsealed; even water drops can cause permanent stains. It should be sealed at the time of installation with a penetrating sealer (available at hardware and flooring stores), and can benefit from an additional layer of protective paste wax. (For more on waxing floors, turn to page 522.) Grout should likewise be sealed with a penetrating sealer, which should be reapplied several times a year.

Cleaning solution Follow directions for Glazed Ceramic Tile, opposite; for waxed tile, follow directions for Wood Finished with Wax, below right.

VINYL

Often mistakenly referred to as linoleum, vinyl is a synthetic sheet or tile flooring that replaced linoleum in the 1950s as the preferred covering in homes because it was much less expensive to manufacture. If your house was built in the 1950s or later and you have resilient flooring, it's likely vinyl. If you've had a vinyl floor installed since about 1970, it's probably no-wax vinyl. This kind of floor is covered with a plasticlike coating that lends shine and protection and should, as a rule, not be stripped or polished. Over time, this protective layer will dull, however. When that happens, you can apply a polish designed specifically to revive no-wax vinyl, which you'll find at flooring stores. Older vinyl without a wear layer should be waxed with a wax formulated especially for vinyl floors. It should be stripped after every six to eight applications.

Cleaning solution For no-wax vinyl, use a pH-neutral cleaner and warm water. For waxed vinyl, use plain water or, for very grimy floors, a cleaner formulated specifically for waxed vinyl floors. Use a well-wrung (almost dry) mop on vinyl tile so water does not seep into the seams.

WOOD SEALED WITH POLYURETHANE

The majority of wood floors today are sealed with polyurethane, which is a durable, plasticlike coating. It needs little care beyond regular vacuuming to remove grit, which can cause scratches, and occasional damp mopping. Water should never be allowed to saturate the surface, as it can seep into cracks and under baseboards, causing wood to expand and contract.

Cleaning solution Use ¼ cup white vinegar to 1 quart warm water or a commercial cleaner specifically formulated for polyurethane. Avoid oil soaps, which create a film that keeps floors from looking their best and can leave a residue that traps dust, which will actually cause the floor to become dirty more quickly.

WOOD FINISHED WITH WAX

This surface is both more generous and less forgiving than polyurethane. Small surface scratches can be buffed away, but the wax surface is not watertight and liquid can damage it. Spills should be wiped up as soon as they hit the floor (use a damp cloth for sticky spills) and the area buffed with a soft cloth. Whenever floors are covered with dust or footprints that a vacuum can't remove, wash gently, using a mop that is only very slightly damp (almost dry). (For more on waxing floors, turn to page 522.)

Cleaning solution Plain, tepid water.

SCRUBBING

MANY PEOPLE BELIEVE THAT keeping an immaculate house involves many tedious hours spent scrubbing on hands and knees. In fact, scrubbing—whether a floor or a tub or a countertop—is rarely necessary and certainly not an essential part of a regular routine. Aside from the kitchen, where scrubbing pots and pans is a fact of life, other surfaces throughout the house will rarely need to be subjected to the rigors of brushes or abrasive pads unless they've been neglected for some time or have been damaged. If you do have to bring out the heavy artillery as a last resort, use the right tools and techniques to get the job done.

BRUSHES

Prickly as a porcupine or soft as a feather, there's nothing fancy about scrub brushes, which consist of bristles—either natural, plastic, or metal—inserted into a block or onto a handle—either wood, plastic, or metal. They're not high-tech, and they're rarely described as "new and improved." Yet with the staggering selection available, how do you choose?

The main consideration is whether the bristles are appropriate for the surface you're cleaning. Stiff, coarse bristles reach into crevices, lifting dirt from a rough surface, like a concrete floor; they're generally too rough for indoor surfaces. Soft bristles gather fine dust or dirt on a smooth surface, like a lamp shade. Medium bristles are for everything in between: They will dislodge dirt from a textured or flat surface, like tile and grout or pots and pans. The tips of the bristles are what provide the cleaning power; if you find yourself pressing hard as you clean, you probably need a brush with stiffer bristles (before vigorously attacking any polished or delicate surface, test the brush to ensure it won't leave behind fine scratches).

The degree of stiffness is, zin fact, more important than the material the brush is made of. Both synthetic and natural-fiber bristles can range from soft to stiff and work equally well. Natural bristles get softer when wet; synthetics are generally more durable and last longer.

Consider the size of the brush, too. To find the right one for the job, consider the shape of the handle and the size of the surface to be scrubbed. For an expansive area with indentations, such as tile and grout or textured flooring, you'll want a large brush with bristles stiff enough to reach into the grooves. Brushes with long handles should also help keep you from having to stoop or get on your hands and knees while cleaning.

Here are brush types you're most likely to need. Although most are available at home supply stores, janitorial supply stores and online retailers are also excellent sources for more specialized types. Be sure to keep brushes used at the kitchen sink separate from those used for cleaning.

SCRUB BRUSH

Bristles are inserted into a rectangular block, a block with pointed ends, or into a block with a handle that resembles the handle on an iron. The block is generally about 6 inches long. Use it for scrubbing floors, countertops, and walls. Iron-handled versions provide the most convenient grip.

SCRUB BRUSH

UTILITY BRUSH

GROUT BRUSH

TOOTHBRUSH

TOILET BRUSH

POT SCRUBBER

DISH BRUSH

BOTTLE AND JAR BRUSHES

UTILITY

A brush with a square or rectangular face that is 5 to 6 inches wide and a handle that is 5 to 6 inches long. Designed to scrub larger surfaces both indoors and out, this all-purpose brush can be used on floors and other hard surfaces, particularly tile walls in the bathroom.

GROUT

A narrow row of stiff bristles on a 5- to 6-inch handle. Use it to scrub grout between ceramic, stone, brick, and other tiles as well as for reaching grime in shower-door and window tracks.

TOOTHBRUSH

Old toothbrushes can be recycled for use in the bath, kitchen, and all around the house. Use them to reach otherwise-inaccessible spots, such as corners, and to remove grime from around faucets, light switches, and cabinet hardware. There are also "toothbrushes" designed specifically for cleaning; the bristles are often stiffer than those in regular toothbrushes.

TOILET

A cylindrical brush on a 15-inch handle for scrubbing the inside of the toilet bowl. Avoid brushes with exposed metal wire, which can rust and can scratch the porcelain. Some brushes come with a caddy, which makes storage more convenient.

POT SCRUBBER

Stiff bristles on a squat, round block or an 8- to 10-inch handle (good for keeping hands out of greasy water). The compact face—generally 2 to 3 inches across—allows you to easily maneuver inside pots and pans. Do not use pot scrubbers, even soft ones, on nonstick cookware, which scratches easily.

DISH

Stiff bristles on an 8- to 10-inch handle. The bristle head is angled so you can scrub food from plates while they're lying flat in the sink. The handles of some models can be filled with dishwashing liquid, which is released as you apply pressure to the brush head. You can cut down on the amount of dishwashing liquid you use by diluting it with water before filling the handle.

BOTTLE, JAR

Long-handled, narrow cylindrical brush for use in bottles, jars, teapot spouts, and vases. A soft cotton or lamb's-wool tip will ensure the bottle brush is safe for even delicate surfaces. Before attempting to clean particularly dirty bottles, soak them overnight with water and denture tablets.

DRYER VENT

A cylindrical brush mounted on a 10-foot-long flexible rod. Use it dry to remove lint from your dryer vent (the hose at the back of the dryer that vents air outdoors). Clean the hose yearly to improve dryer efficiency and reduce the possibility of lint catching fire.

DRYER VENT BRUSH

REFRIGERATOR COIL

A thin, cylindrical brush measuring about 25 inches long. Use it dry to gently remove dust and lint from refrigerator coils at least twice a year (more often if you have pets) in order to keep the refrigerator running at peak performance. (For more on cleaning coils, turn to page 91.) You can also use it to clean steam and hot-water radiators.

REFRIGERATOR COIL BRUSH

DECK

A stiff-bristled brush on a 10- to 12-inch-long rectangular block that has a threaded hole for a long handle. Designed for use outdoors, to scrub decks and other hard surfaces, such as patios or walkways.

DECK BRUSH

GRILL

Sturdy, wire-bristled brush on a 15- to 18-inch-long handle for scraping and removing charred bits of food from the grill. Look for bristles made of a metal that won't rust, such as stainless steel, and with a scraper attached to the end of the brush to remove stubborn particles of food.

GRILL BRUSH

ABRASIVES

Scrubbing pads can be made of metal, such as copper or soap-infused steel wool; plastic; or nylon. They are designed to be used wet. The majority of such pads are too harsh for many household surfaces.

Round plastic pads, which are relatively gentle, are useful for scrubbing baked food off of pots and pans but are often too loosely constructed to be useful on other surfaces with finer accumulations of soil. For most jobs where extra scrubbing is essential, thin, rectangular nylon pads are the best choice. They are color coded to indicate their level of abrasiveness, although there is little consistency from brand to brand or even within a brand. In general, however, white pads are the gentlest. Always read labels carefully before buying them and choose pads labeled "nonabrasive," "mildly abrasive," or "light duty." Before using an abrasive pad, test it first to make sure it won't scratch. Never use any type of abrasive on mirrored or reflective surfaces such as chrome; on any type of plastic, including fiberglass or acrylic tubs; or on nonstick cookware.

A NOTE ABOUT ABRASIVE CLEANSERS

Although many people use scouring powders every time they clean the bathroom or the kitchen sink, these products can do more harm than good when used regularly. Scouring powders contain abrasives designed to wear away dirt and grease—and in the process can wear away the surface you're trying to maintain. They may also contain chlorine bleach to lift stains, which can further damage surfaces. To minimize wear, reserve cleansers, even liquid cleansers, which are gentler than powdered ones, for stubborn stains or buildup. If you choose to use an abrasive cleanser, purchase one labeled "mildly abrasive" or "safe for acrylics or fiberglass" and "chlorine free," which will help ensure they are gentle. Mildest of all is plain baking soda mixed with water.

HOW TO SCRUB SURFACES

Unlike wiping up surfaces around the house, scrubbing involves a great deal of water. Only surfaces that can stand up to lots of moisture should be scrubbed. Wood floors and ungrouted tile (such as vinyl or linoleum), for example, should never be scrubbed.

GOLDEN RULES OF SCRUBBING

1. Always start with the mildest cleaning product before moving on to stronger products or stronger concentrations of cleaning solution.

2. Some cleaning products are designed to be used full strength, while others are meant to be diluted. Always read and follow label directions. Use only the recommended amount; more will not guarantee a cleaner surface—it will only leave behind residue that can attract dirt and grime.

3. Most detergents work best in warm to hot water, but be sure to read the label instructions.

4. Use a scrub brush or a nylon scrub pad to agitate the cleaning solution on the surface you're tending to. If the brush drags, add more solution.

5. Agitate in circular motions using light pressure. If you find yourself pressing hard as you clean, you probably need a brush with stiffer bristles or a more abrasive pad.

6. After scrubbing, let the cleaning solution sit for a few minutes to emulsify, or dissolve, stubborn dirt.

7. Rinse the surface well with a clean, damp cloth and dry it with another clean cloth.

CARING FOR SCRUB BRUSHES

After each use, rinse brushes thoroughly to remove any particles of food or dirt. Do not soak brushes to clean them; doing so can weaken or dislodge bristles. To prevent them from becoming moldy or sour, allow brushes to air dry before storing them. Dry them bristle side up or hanging from a hook to prevent the bristles from warping.

WAXING AND POLISHING

WAXING MAY SEEM LIKE FUSSY housekeeping from another era, but it's actually a shortcut to cleanliness. Both paste and liquid wax (sometimes called polish) repel dust and water, shielding surfaces from dirt and spills, while also adding a soft luster that helps preserve almost any material, from plastic and fiberglass to silver and concrete. Since pure waxes cannot be spread, they contain other ingredients, although pastes have a higher percentage of wax than liquids. Most waxes are suitable for more than one job, but none works on every surface. Before choosing a wax, read the label carefully to ensure it will work with the surface you are waxing. It's wise to do the same with metal polishes, which are each formulated to restore the luster to specific materials.

WOOD FURNITURE

Most commercially manufactured furniture made since the 1930s is finished with clear lacquer, which is a hard, durable, and flexible coating that is scratch-resistant and impervious to most household cleaners and spills. Furniture coated with lacquer does not need to be waxed. Vintage and antique pieces, which are often finished with varnish, oil, or shellac, all of which are less durable than clear lacquer, benefit from a yearly coat of paste wax. This protective coating, which will not darken or harden over time, not only lends furniture a warm glow but also forms a sleek barrier between the finish, applied by the original furniture maker or restorer to seal the raw wood, and abusive elements. According to some conservators, it's best to avoid cream or liquid furniture waxes (sometimes called polishes). Although they are easier to apply, they sometimes contain unnecessary ingredients that can damage finishes.

HOW TO WAX WOOD FURNITURE

1. Wipe wood surfaces with a soft cloth dampened with water and mild dishwashing liquid. If a piece is especially dirty, use a mild solvent like mineral spirits or odorless paint thinner. Test an inconspicuous area to make sure it doesn't damage the finish. (Be cautious: Solvent-soaked rags are flammable; store them in an airtight metal container and consult your sanitation department for disposal guidelines.) If the finish is unchanged, dampen a soft cloth with the solvent—use it straight, but sparingly—and rub it over the wood.

2. Apply a paste wax, such as Butcher's Wax, which is available in hardware stores and many supermarkets, with a cotton rag folded into a square pad. Paste wax, which is solid and comes in a tin, contains a blend of waxes (often carnauba and beeswax) and a mild solvent (like mineral spirits or turpentine) to soften the wax. Natural (clear) wax can be used on any wood, but dark woods may benefit from a tinted wax; it will mask tiny scratches. Apply a thin, even coat to a few square feet at a time, covering every inch of wood.

3. If the piece has carved or detailed molding, apply the wax to those areas with an old toothbrush using circular motions.

4. Allow the wax to dry for ten to twenty-five minutes. If you don't wait long enough, you'll wipe the wax right off. If you wait too long, it will be difficult to buff out. In that case, simply add more wax to soften the existing coat.

5. Buff with a clean cloth, turning it frequently, and try to remove all the wax. When the rag slides easily rather than drags, you're all done.

FLOORS

WOOD

Wood floors installed since the 1970s are generally finished with polyurethane, which is a durable, plasticlike coating that protects against scuffs, scratches, and spills. Wood floors coated with polyurethane do not need an additional protective layer of wax. Unfinished wood floors or floors finished with varnish or shellac—rarely found these days, unless your floors haven't been refinished since the mid-1960s—should be waxed once or twice a year to add protection.

STONE, CONCRETE, BRICK, UNGLAZED TILE

These floors all benefit from regular sealing to help them resist stains (for more on sealing these surfaces, turn to page 531). In addition, a yearly coat of wax can offer another layer of protection to these porous surfaces as well as lend them shine. Polished stone floors should not be waxed, however, as they will become dangerously slippery.

HOW TO WAX A WOOD, STONE, MASONRY, OR TILE FLOOR

All of these floors can be waxed with either a paste or liquid wax. Read labels to ensure the wax is designed for the specific material you're treating. Do not use acrylic wax formulated for vinyl floors on these surfaces.

1. On your hands and knees, apply paste wax using fine-grade (0000) steel wool or a soft cotton cloth (such as an old T-shirt or cheesecloth). Smooth a thin coating over a square yard or so of flooring. Or, apply liquid wax using a wax applicator, which looks like a sponge mop but has a lamb's-wool head (available at hardware stores).

2. When the wax starts to dry and harden, buff with a residential rotary electric buffer (which can be purchased or rented at hardware stores).

3. Buff with a rotary buffing machine monthly to revive the shine. Once buffing fails to do the trick, it's time to rewax the areas that need it, such as high-traffic spots. There's no need to strip wax first, as it just wears away gradually under your feet.

HOW TO BUFF WAXED FLOORS

Using an electric rotary buffing machine is the only way to bring out wax's luster, give it an even finish, and keep floors from becoming too slick. The heart of the buffer is the large, soft-bristled pad; as it begins to spin, the heavy machine appears to hover above the floor. The buffer should be guided in a side-to-side motion. Waxed floors can be buffed as often as weekly, but will remain beautiful with monthly buffing. (Keep in mind that acrylic waxes designed for vinyl floors do not need to be buffed.)

DETERMINING THE FINISH ON WOOD FLOORS

Floors in older houses that have not been remodeled since the mid-1960s may be finished with shellac or varnish rather than polyurethane. Here's how to tell:

1. Scratch the surface of the floor in an inconspicuous place with a dime. If the finish flakes, it's probably shellac or varnish.

2. Sprinkle a few drops of water on the floor in an inconspicuous place. Wait ten minutes. If white spots appear, there is wax on the floor. (You can remove the spots by buffing with some fresh paste wax.)

3. If the finish neither flakes nor spots, the floor is coated with polyurethane.

HOW TO WAX A VINYL OR LINOLEUM FLOOR

Vinyl floors without a no-wax finish or no-wax floors that have lost their shine should be waxed with a polish designed especially for vinyl floors (it will specify this on the label). These products, which are often called acrylic or polymer wax or polish, are generally also suitable for linoleum floors (to learn more about vinyl and linoleum, turn to pages 512 and 513). Wax should be reapplied when floors begin to look dull and mopping no longer removes grime, generally every six months.

1. On a clean floor, spread polish with a clean sponge mop or wax applicator and let it dry for twenty to thirty minutes.

2. For extra shine, apply a second coat. You do not need to buff polishes designed for vinyl; they will dry to a high shine.

3. Reapply polish when the floor becomes dull, and strip all the wax after six to eight applications with a commercial floor-wax stripper. Apply the stripper, let it sit for three to five minutes, then scrub the floor with a plastic-bristled brush. Wash the floor with an all-purpose cleaner and let it dry before applying a fresh coat of wax.

BASIC WAXING TECHNIQUE FOR HOUSEHOLD OBJECTS

Although buffing a living room floor may seem daunting, waxing household articles—such as a patinated copper planter, Lucite lamp base, or a tole tray—doesn't require as much elbow grease and provides the same long-lasting protection and shine.

1. Start with a clean, dry surface.

2. Wipe a clean, soft, lint-free cotton cloth, such as a diaper or T-shirt, against the wax to pick up a small amount.

3. Rub on a thin layer of wax in a circular motion, or with the grain, covering an area no larger than several square feet.

4. Let the wax stand until it no longer looks wet, about five minutes, then use another soft, clean cloth to buff it—in the direction of the grain, if there is one—until the surface isn't sticky. If you feel any drag on the cloth, or if your finger leaves a trail, there's too much wax left and you should continue to buff.

5. After you have finished buffing one section, repeat the process on the adjoining areas until the entire surface gleams.

THE RIGHT WAX FOR THE JOB

When buffing no longer restores a shine to a waxed surface, it's time to rewax. Solvent-based waxes will not build up and rarely need to be stripped. Solvents in the wax soften the previous layers, so you remove any excess as you buff. However, if the old wax is heavily soiled, you should strip it. Wear rubber gloves and open the windows to allow for ventilation; then rub off the old wax with mineral spirits or wax remover. As the wax dissolves, so will the grime. Waxes designed for vinyl do build up and will need to be stripped after successive applications when the wax becomes yellow or looks grimy. Here's how to choose the correct type of wax:

UNFINISHED, SHELLACKED, OILED, AND VARNISHED WOOD
Solvent-based paste wax or microcrystalline wax

PAINTED AND BARE METAL, PLASTIC, LAWN FURNITURE, GLASS
Paste car wax

STONE, CONCRETE, BRICK, POROUS TILE (TERRA COTTA)
Solvent-based paste wax; avoid waxing irregular surfaces where trapped wax will attract grime and do not wax glazed ceramic tile. All these materials should be sealed before waxing (for more on sealing, turn to page 531).

VINYL SHEET AND TILE FLOORS WITHOUT A NO-WAX FINISH, LINOLEUM
Acrylic or polymer wax designed specifically for such floors

APPLIANCES
Paste car wax

POLISHING METAL

It is surprising just how vulnerable a metal is to its environment. Oils and acids from your hands attack the surface of metal objects every time you touch them. Sulfur compounds in foods such as eggs and Brussels sprouts do the same. Similar threats lurk within cupboards and drawers, where bare wood, many paints, and fabric drawer linings release organic chemicals that dull the finish of silver and pewter. Metal items left out in the open are no safer. The summer sun affects silver, copper, and brass, as does smoke from the fireplace in winter. Simple dust draws water from the air, which causes trouble, namely rust, year-round. Washing and polishing each item will remove the tarnish, whatever its cause, and regular dusting will help retard it. But if you leave behind any traces of detergent or polishing compound, they'll attract moisture faster than dust, doing more harm than good to the finish and necessitating another cleaning.

Although tarnish is inevitable, you can learn to live with it. Tarnish is not dirt. Nor is tarnish particularly harmful to metal; it does not penetrate beyond the surface. It is simply a dull or discolored look that metal acquires as a result of exposure to air. You may want to consider the value of tarnish as patina—antiques dealers and conservators regularly advise owners simply to leave their objects alone. Patina contributes to the beauty and value of many pieces, providing shading to engraved designs and giving any piece a sense of age. Hardware that may have been meant to shine origi-

A NOTE ABOUT FIRESCALE
A purplish stain of oxidized copper, called firescale, may remain even after you finish cleaning silver. Don't mistake it for tarnish or try to remove it. The stain results from years of polishing antique sterling and coin silver manufactured during the eighteenth and nineteenth centuries.

HOW TO POLISH METAL OBJECTS

1. Work in a well-lighted area on a non-porous surface. To prevent making any dents and scratches, pad your work area with an old towel.

2. Protect your hands with white cotton gloves, which will also protect the silver you're polishing from the oils and acids on your skin.

3. Before applying polish, inspect the piece for a previous polishing pattern. This is usually circular on hollowware and lengthwise on flatware. Polish in that pattern with a light touch, following the manufacturer's instructions and avoiding areas where different materials meet.

4. Start with a polish-imbued cloth or liquid polish designed specifically for the metal you're polishing. If this proves inadequate, move on to a paste or cream. Apply with a 100-percent cotton flannel cloth. Use a soft toothbrush or wooden cuticle stick wrapped in cotton on monograms and areas with ornate design.

5. Wash the piece when you're finished, being sure to remove all of the polishing compound, then dry it with a soft cotton cloth.

nally, such as the pulls on a time-mellowed antique cabinet, will seem out of place glowing brightly. Even objects that receive occasional polishing—no one wants to set a table with heavily tarnished silver flatware, for example—require a light touch. If you remove the tarnish from every etched line in the handles of your knives, forks, and spoons, you're reducing the contrasts of light and dark that bring out flatware patterns.

Commercial metal polishes are composed primarily of abrasives and cleaners and/or acids. Choose a polish formulated specifically for the metal you're treating because each one has a different level of abrasiveness. Relatively soft metals, such as silver and pewter, require gentler abrasives than harder metals, such as copper or brass.

In general, liquids and polish-impregnated cloths work well for medium tarnish; pastes and creams are better for heavier work. Metal is sturdy, but it scratches easily and is worn away a bit with every polishing. Test any polish first on an inconspicuous spot, and start with a gentle product. If it doesn't remove tarnish, upgrade to something stronger.

The best advice for dealing with stubborn tarnish is not to put off polishing too long. Don't be tempted to use commercially available acid baths, called silver dips, for heavily tarnished pieces. They remove a layer of metal and are much too harsh.

COMMON METAL FINISHES

BRUSHED, OR BUTLER
A soft finish achieved with a scratch-brush wheel and water that looks almost hand rubbed. This finish is typical for silver serving pieces. Old silver can acquire this finish over time, after many polishings.

BURNISHED FRENCH GOLD PLATING
An increasingly rare French technique, performed by hand, of raising highlights on gold plating by pressing against it with a steel-burnishing tool dipped in stale beer.

DULL OR MATTE
A finish in which the shine has been almost completely removed with a polishing wheel, pumice, and water.

POLISHED
A bright, mirrorlike finish achieved with a polishing wheel and a compound called rouge. Flatware and many serving pieces get this treatment, which makes even century-old pieces look new.

LACQUER
A clear protective coating that keeps metal from oxidizing. Lacquer is fragile and should not be used on objects that are handled often; if it's nicked, the metal beneath can discolor. It is also poisonous and should not be used on pieces that come into contact with food.

SATIN
A semi-matte, directional finish, meaning you can see a grain. A polishing machine fitted with a cotton-covered wheel rubs a compound of glass and glue into the surface. Common on pewter and nickel hardware, especially on restorations or reproductions of Art Deco pieces.

I TAKE A CERTAIN PRIDE IN HAVING FRESH AND LOVELY SPACES—AND IN SHINING POTS AND SPARKLING GLASSWARE AND WELL-ORGANIZED CUPBOARDS.

THE KITCHEN AT TURKEY HILL

FLOORS AND FLOOR COVERINGS

WE ASK A LOT OF OUR FLOORS and floor coverings, both functionally and aesthetically. We want years of durable service, yet expect hard floors to shine as they did on the day they were installed. We expect carpets to wear evenly, despite the fact that the traffic over them is uneven. In most households, dirt is tracked indoors perhaps dozens of times a day by family members (and pets), subjecting floors to more wear and tear than most any surface in the house. Even with regular sweeping, vacuuming, and mopping, additional maintenance is critical to keep floors looking their best. From camouflaging nicks in wood to sealing stone to shampooing carpets and rugs, you'll enjoy the benefits of periodic maintenance with every step you take.

WOOD FLOORS

Wood floors are valued for their beauty and longevity. They can last for generations if properly cared for. Though extremely durable, polyurethane finishes are difficult to repair if damaged. Blemishes can be spot-repaired, but when the finish has worn thin, is uneven, or is badly scratched, the entire floor needs to be sanded and a new coat of finish needs to be applied. If you lay a new coat of polyurethane on top of an existing one without sanding, the top coat will eventually peel.

SCREENING

This process refreshes the existing finish, without the effort and expense of refinishing. It is appropriate for floors that are dull but not badly damaged. Screening will also remedy minor scratches that have not penetrated the wood itself. The existing finish is abraded with a mesh screen that's attached to a rotary buffing machine, which prepares the surface for a new coat of finish. To adhere properly, the new finish must be compatible with the old one. If you choose to do this job yourself, consult a wood-flooring professional to find the polyurethane best suited to your floor.

REFINISHING

Floors with stains, gouges, or deep scratches should be refinished. This involves sanding down the surface to bare wood with a drum or belt sander, staining (to enhance or change the color of the wood), and then coating with several layers of polyurethane. This is a messy, strenuous job best left to a wood-flooring professional.

HOW TO SPOT-REPAIR POLYURETHANE-TREATED WOOD FLOORS

SANDING

First, gently rub the damaged area with fine (220-grit) sandpaper. Don't cut into the wood itself. Going too deep makes color matching difficult: It strips off wood fibers that have changed color with age or stain.

CLEANING

After sanding, wipe away dust that could become trapped in the touch-up coat. Wipe well with a commercial cleaner formulated for polyurethane; these products contain ingredients that evaporate quickly so the moisture won't affect the floor.

REAPPLYING THE FINISH COAT

Brush on the polyurethane (use the same finish that's already on the floor) with a foam paint pad, and then thin out the edges with a dry brush. Work outward from the center. Where the old surface wasn't sufficiently sanded, some new finish may peel. A water-based finish will dry clear while an oil-based polyurethane will appear lighter than its surroundings at first but will darken with age. If the floor was stained, you will have to restain the sanded patch before applying polyurethane.

REPAIRING WOOD FLOORS

Problem	Polyurethane Finish	Wax Finish
LIGHT SCRATCHES	Camouflage with wax sticks, available at hardware stores. These are similar to crayons, and come in many shades common to wood and bamboo floors. Alternatively, wood stain markers, also available at hardware stores, may be used to touch up scratches.	Scratches on waxed wood can be eliminated rather than simply camouflaged. Rub with extrafine (000) steel wool and reapply paste wax. To fix divots where heavy furniture has compressed wood fibers, lay a damp flannel cloth over the area and heat it briefly with an iron. This will cause the wood fibers to swell and spring back into shape.
WHITE SPOTS	Spots are probably dried spills. Rub with a slightly damp cloth, or use a commercial cleaner formulated for polyurethane.	Rub the spot with extrafine (000) steel wool, and then reapply wax. Let the wax dry, then buff with a cotton cloth.
DARK SPOTS (INK, PET STAINS, AND WATER)	For minor stains, rub with fine steel wool (00). To erase deeper water stains, use oxalic acid (a common ingredient in deck brighteners), which is available at hardware stores. Mix with water to make a paste, leave on for five to ten minutes, then wipe off with a damp cloth. Refer to the box on page 529 for instructions on repairing the finish.	Rub with fine steel wool (00). On deep water stains, apply a paste made from water and oxalic acid. Leave on for five to ten minutes, then wipe off (don't use a damp cloth). Rub on wax, and buff with a cloth.
CHEWING GUM, CRAYON, AND CANDLE WAX	Cover the area for five minutes with a plastic bag filled with ice, and then scrape with a spoon or credit card. Follow with a commercial cleaner made specifically for polyurethane.	For gum, cover the area for five minutes with a plastic bag filled with ice, and then scrape with a spoon or credit card. For candle wax or crayon, try the ice method or soften with a blow-dryer set on warm. Scrape with a credit card or spoon. Buff with a dry cotton cloth.
OIL OR GREASE	Wipe the area with a cloth dampened with a commercial cleaner formulated for polyurethane.	Dampen a cloth with odor-free mineral spirits (less toxic than standard mineral spirits, because benzene and other aromatic hydrocarbons have been stripped out). Wipe the area dry, rewax, and buff with a cotton cloth.
BURNS	Gently scrape away char with a putty knife, then follow the instructions in the box on page 529. If the floor has been stained, the patch will be noticeable.	Lightly scrape away char with a putty knife. Rewax and buff with a soft cloth.

STONE, BRICK, AND UNGLAZED TILE

Stone and brick are durable, beautiful flooring surfaces, but they are porous and vulnerable to staining. All brick, unglazed tile, and almost all stone should be sealed at least once a year to guard against grime and dirt.

The best way to improve these materials' stain resistance is to apply a penetrating sealer, also known as an impregnator. Unlike waxes or other coatings, these sealers go below the surface and protect the materials from within. And sealing is easy to do on your own. A stone dealer or specialty flooring retailer can suggest the appropriate sealer for your flooring material.

First, though, you must determine whether or not the surface needs to be sealed. Begin with this simple test: Place a drop of water on the surface. If after several minutes the area below the water becomes dark, your flooring is porous and requires a protective sealant; if the color remains the same, then sealing is optional (though most flooring professionals still recommend it). To be safe, you should conduct a few tests with the sealant in different (inconspicuous) spots on the floor or counter, and wait twenty-four hours before you begin treatment, to ensure test areas are dry. (Water spots must dry completely before sealing the surface or they will become permanent.)

To prepare the stone or brick for sealing, clean the surface thoroughly with a pH-balanced detergent and water; wipe with a clean cloth and let dry completely, which will likely take several hours. Tape off adjacent areas you don't want to treat in order to protect them from splashes. Using a clean white towel or a clean sponge or rag mop, apply sealant evenly to the surface, saturating it thoroughly. Take care to keep the sealer from getting into any open joints. Following the manufacturer's instructions, let the sealer stand for several minutes before removing excess with a clean, dry towel. The sealed stone or brick will not be stain-proof, but the sealer will have filled in the pores, slowing down the time that it takes a stain to set (thereby giving you more time to wipe up a spill after it happens).

HOW TO SEAL GROUT
Grout, used to fill the gaps between ceramic tile, stone tile, and masonry, is made of a mixture of cement, sand, and water. It is extremely porous and stains easily. Seal it twice a year with a penetrating grout sealer, available from home centers or hardware stores, following the label directions. It's best to apply the sealer to the grout with a small foam brush; excess can be buffed off the tile and will not leave any lasting residue.

HOW TO WAX FLOORS
For step-by-step instructions on how to wax a wood, stone, masonry, or tile floor, turn to page 522.

CARPETS AND RUGS

About once a year or so, or when vacuuming fails to restore the fresh look of carpets, it's time for a deep cleaning. Wall-to-wall carpeting can be cleaned either by a professional carpet cleaner or with a rented rotary shampoo machine and hot-water extraction machine, as can area rugs that have waterproof backings (such as those made of latex or rubber). Area rugs without backings, such as most Oriental rugs, can't be cleaned at home and must be sent out to a carpet-cleaning facility.

STAIN REMOVAL

Spills should be attended to as soon as you notice them. Blot up liquid spills with clean, white cotton towels or with white paper towels—colored towels can make the problem worse, if their dye bleeds into the rug. White towels also allow you to gauge when the stain stops pulling away. Never rub. Doing so will push the spill into the pile and cause fibers to mat. Continue blotting (press down with the heel of your hand or with your foot) with dry towels until the area is nearly dry.

Mix your own spot-cleaning solution by diluting a few drops of clear (not creamy looking) dishwashing liquid in water. Use about ¼ teaspoon per quart. Apply to the stain, being careful not to saturate the carpet. Blot gently, as above, then rinse with clean water and blot again. If there's a stain left behind after blotting a spill well with plain water and treating the area with the soapy water solution, try the techniques on the opposite page. Some commercial carpet spot removers take off the protective coatings or break down dyes that are found on most carpets, but the remedies listed there do not.

HOW TO ELIMINATE CARPET GHOSTS

To remove the indentations left by furniture in pile carpet, place ice cubes where the pile has been crushed or matted. The fibers will swell as they absorb the water. Afterward, blot the area with a dry towel; then vacuum the carpet to straighten the fibers.

TREATING PET STAINS

The sooner you can get to a pet stain, the better. Pet urine left on carpets can permanently alter the dyes in carpet fibers, especially beige ones.

Blot fresh stains as soon as you detect them with a clean, white cloth. After absorbing as much moisture as possible, apply a solution of ¼ teaspoon clear dishwashing liquid mixed with 1 cup tepid water; blot with another clean, dry towel. Rinse by blotting with a towel dampened with tepid water. Continue alternating with a soapy towel and a clean, damp towel until the stain is gone. Follow

up with an enzymatic product designed for pet stains, such as Nature's Miracle. The enzymes break down stains and remove odors that might be undetectable to you but that can attract your pet to the same area again.

For stale stains, treat with the enzymatic cleaner. If odor persists, call a professional carpet cleaner to treat the carpet. In extreme cases, the carpet and padding underneath (and sometimes even the subfloor) will need to be replaced.

CARPET CLEANING

Carpet Type	How to Handle Spills	How to Deep Clean
SYNTHETIC	Clean promptly, using blot technique described in Stain Removal, opposite. If the area discolors, there's probably a sticky spill residue that has trapped soil. Clean by misting the area with warm water and blotting with a clean, white cloth.	Shampooing and hot-water extraction cleaning (also known as steam cleaning) work best on wall-to-wall carpeting. If you want to do it by yourself, vacuum thoroughly, then use shampooing and extraction machines from a rental company (supermarket models are less powerful and may leave carpets too wet). Area rugs with waterproof backings, such as latex, can be cleaned using the same methods. For do-it-yourself instructions, turn to page 534.
WOOL	Clean by misting with tepid water and blotting, using the technique described in Stain Removal, opposite. Never use ammonia or any other highly alkaline cleaner, which can damage wool.	For both area rugs and wall-to-wall carpets, professional cleaning is recommended. Rental extraction units can leave too much water in carpets, making them vulnerable to damage. Plus, a lot of commercial cleaning solutions are too alkaline for wool. Many of today's carpets, however, even Oriental-style ones, are actually made from synthetic fibers that look like wool. To test for wool, snip a strand, and hold a lit match to it; burning wool smells like burned hair.
PLANT INCLUDING ABACA, COIR, HEMP, JUTE, RUSH, SEA GRASS, AND SISAL	Blot spills promptly; plant fibers are less stain-resistant than synthetics or wool, even if they have been treated with a water repellent, so blot spills promptly, following instructions in Stain Removal, opposite. Make sure damp areas dry quickly by using a fan or a hair dryer set on low heat.	Manufacturers recommend the use of dry-extraction cleaning methods only. Leave that to a carpet-cleaning professional. Because plant-based carpets are hard to keep clean (most stains simply can't be removed), they should be placed in low-traffic, dry areas of the house.

SHAMPOOING AND HOT WATER EXTRACTION

The two main methods for deep cleaning carpeting are rotary shampooing and hot-water extraction (which is often mistakenly called steam cleaning). Each has advantages and disadvantages. (It is very important that before undertaking any cleaning process more aggressive than vacuuming on a new carpet, you refer to the manufacturer's recommendations; ignoring this advice could invalidate the carpet's warranty.)

A rotary shampoo machine releases a soapy solution, then works it into the carpet with rotating round brushes that lift dirt from the bottom of the pile. The shampoo is left to dry, then vacuumed up along with the dirt; however, some soap always remains in the carpet fibers, and when you and your family walk on the carpet, it will take the dirt off the bottoms of your shoes, making the carpet dingy again.

An extractor sends hot sudsy water into the carpet, then sucks it right back up; it cleans well, but may not reach ground-in dirt. Although the grit at the bottom of the pile isn't as visible, it gnaws away at the fibers whenever you walk on it, damaging the carpet. Some people prefer shampooing, while others swear by extraction, but a combination of the two is most effective: First, shampoo to clean the fibers and stir up the dirt, then extract with clean hot water, rinsing and removing dirt and soap. These methods can generally be used on both synthetic and wool wall-to-wall carpeting.

It is possible to clean synthetic carpeting yourself; wool carpet, however, should always be left to a professional. The natural fibers in wool carpeting can shrink or develop a stain called browning; both of these problems often result from using too much water. A professional carpet cleaner is trained to avoid these problems. He will come to your house with the machines and can either clean all of the carpeting or just the carpeting in one particular room. The cost and time involved will correlate with the amount of carpeting cleaned.

When hiring a professional, the Carpet and Rug Institute recommends that you avoid companies that offer pricing by the room or give quotes over the phone. Instead, ask the carpet cleaning representative to come to your home to check the condition of the carpet, note any difficult stains, and calculate the square footage to be cleaned. Get quotes in writing and read the contract carefully to ensure there are no hidden charges for things such as vacuuming prior to cleaning or removing spots, which should be included as part of the normal cleaning. Ask, too, for a reference or two and check them. A reputable company will be able to offer the names and telephone numbers of satisfied residential clients and businesses.

If you elect to clean carpets yourself, shampooers and extractors can be rented at hardware stores, grocery stores, and janitorial supply stores (less powerful machines, including combination shampooer/extractors, can be purchased for spot cleaning). Grocery-store machines should be avoided, as they are not very powerful and can leave behind too much water.

Although each machine works differently, here are the basics of operation: Fill the shampooer with the soapy solution recommended for that machine (mix it according to package instructions), and the extractor with hot tap water. Each machine should have a trigger on the handle to control the amount of liquid. Release water sparingly at first; do not overwet the carpet. Start by shampooing an area about 4 feet by 6 feet, then go back over it with the extractor. Working in long, overlapping strokes, release water with one stroke, then extract it immediately. Move on to the next area, repeating the process. When you're finished, open the windows or set up fans, and let the carpet dry, which will take about five to seven hours.

HOW TO PATCH A DAMAGED CARPET

1. You will need a remnant of your carpet. Begin by cutting a neat square around the hole or worn spot in your carpet with a utility knife and a straightedge. Cut completely and evenly through the rug's backing, lifting as you go, avoiding any padding as well as the floor surface below.

2. Using the remnant, make a patch identical in shape, size, design, and pile direction to the carpet section you removed. Test to see that the patch fits properly, and trim to make any necessary adjustments.

3. Apply carpet adhesive in a thin layer to the underside of the patch and along each edge and the surrounding carpet.

4. Carefully set patch into hole, then gently brush the pile so that the repaired section blends in seamlessly. Allow several hours for the adhesive to set before vacuuming over the repaired area.

ABOUT CARPET THICKNESS

Plush pile wall-to-wall carpeting (such as the bottom three examples in the photograph) is cut to a smooth, level height. It's higher and less dense than velvet pile (like the top two examples), which is short and uniform, with fibers packed closely together. Deeper-pile carpeting has a more luxurious feel, making it a cozy covering for a bedroom floor, but short pile tends to be easier to care for.

CEILINGS, WALLS, AND WOODWORK

DUST DOESN'T DISCRIMINATE—it clings to vertical surfaces just as well as it does to horizontal ones. It seeps into cracks and crevices in baseboards and moldings and even manages to defy gravity and blanket ceilings. Periodically, these surfaces need to be tended to. Woodwork will benefit from monthly attention; ceilings and walls need no more than yearly cleaning. With a good vacuum cleaner and the right attachments, you can quickly (and easily) whisk dust away. Ceilings, walls, and woodwork will also need small repairs to keep them looking new. Few skills or tools are required. By simply setting aside the time once or twice a year to fill holes and cracks and patch paint and wallpaper, you can prolong the time—maybe even by years—between major overhauls.

PAINTED CEILINGS AND WALLS

Flat latex paint, the most common of interior paints, rarely fares well when it is washed. Stains can be difficult, or even impossible, to remove, and water and detergent can leave streaks and spots (particularly on dark-colored walls) that often look worse than the original problem. Some paint manufacturers do produce latex paints that are scrubbable, and these are an especially good choice for households with children. But if this is not the type of paint you have, limit your cleaning to periodic vacuuming and repaint when scuffs and marks accumulate.

Use the dust-brush attachment of your vacuum (for an illustration, turn to page 500) to go over the ceiling and walls. Start with the ceiling first, inserting an extra length of pipe, if you have one, to allow you to reach ceilings without a ladder. When you've finished with the ceiling, vacuum the walls, starting at the top and working your way down. Periodically remove the dusting brush from the pipe, and vacuum it well to remove dust and grit. This should be sufficient in most rooms.

To test a wall for washability, wipe a small section of the wall in an inconspicuous spot with a sponge dampened with warm water and a couple of drops of all-purpose cleaner, then rinse with another damp sponge, and let dry. If the paint itself comes off, or if a water spot has been left behind, the paint isn't washable. If, however, the paint stays intact and you see no stain or water mark, you can proceed safely.

Always vacuum first to remove any loose dirt, then use a sponge dampened in a diluted solution of all-purpose cleaner and warm water (read the cleaner manufacturer's instructions for proportions) to wipe down walls. Start at the top and work your way down, taking care to wring out the sponge as you go so that excess water doesn't streak the walls. Work on one small area (a few square feet) at a time; go back over the surface with a clean, damp sponge to rinse, then wipe dry with a soft cloth.

Eggshell, semigloss, high-gloss latex, and oil-based paints—most often found on kitchen and bath walls, where spills, splatters, and mildew are common—respond well to washing. Vacuum and wash following the directions above.

HOW TO CLEAN AN UPHOLSTERED WALL
Walls upholstered in fabric can be a challenge to keep clean. Commercial fabrics, which are made specifically for use in high-traffic areas such as offices, are the best choice for such applications, since they are stronger, usually treated to repel stains, and sometimes backed with a lining. But any upholstered surface will collect dust; these surfaces must be vacuumed weekly with the upholstery attachment.

HOW TO REMOVE GREASY KITCHEN RESIDUE

In kitchens, greasy residue from cooking can leave a film on ceilings and walls. Use a solvent-free degreaser to remove this stubborn grime (kitchens are generally painted with washable paint, but test the degreaser in an inconspicuous spot to ensure it won't mar surfaces). Unlike other ceilings in the house, which will probably need only an annual vacuuming, the kitchen ceiling should be tended to several times a year. If the paint does not respond well to damp cleaning, try a dry sponge. These are typically made of foam, and are specifically designed for cleaning surfaces that would be damaged by moisture. Rub the dry sponge across the soiled surface; slice off the dirty portion with a knife (or rub it with sandpaper) to expose clean sponge underneath, and continue cleaning as necessary.

HOW TO CLEAN TEXTURED CEILINGS

If you have popcorn ceilings put up between the 1960s and the early 1980s, they may contain asbestos. Unless you know for certain that yours do not, you should never attempt to clean them or disturb them in any way. To have them tested for asbestos, consult an asbestos professional (look in the Yellow Pages under "Asbestos"); he or she can tell you how to safely collect a sample for analysis in a lab. Popcorn ceilings that do not contain asbestos can be gently vacuumed with the dust-brush tool.

HOW TO CLEAN A CEILING FAN

When cleaning ceilings, be sure to clean ceiling fans thoroughly at the same time. They accumulate an amazing amount of grime (even if they're dusted monthly using a long-handled duster, as explained on page 484), making it impossible to tackle this chore from the ground. The main difficulty when cleaning a fan, of course, is reaching it. You'll need to stand on a ladder or a sturdy chair. The fan needs to be turned off when you clean it, and if a lighting fixture is attached, make sure it's off too. Once you're perched securely on the ladder, use a soft cleaning cloth dampened with an all-purpose cleaner to wipe the blades, light fixture, and casing, being sure to not to get moisture near the motor. Always spray the cloth, not the fan itself.

DRYWALL

Drywall, often called Sheetrock, which is a brand of drywall, is made from gypsum rock sandwiched between two layers of heavy paper. Sheets of drywall are screwed to studs, and seams are concealed with joint tape and joint compound, which is sanded smooth before the drywall is primed and painted. Walls in moist rooms, such as in kitchens and bathrooms, may be made of a more water-resistant board such as "greenboard" or cement board.

It's easy to make small repairs yourself. The supplies noted below and on the following page are available at hardware stores. Working with drywall generates a lot of dust, so whenever repairing damage, seal off the room as best you can, and always wear safety glasses and a dust mask.

REPAIRING BUMPS IN DRYWALL

Occasionally, the nails or screws that fasten new drywall to studs will begin to protrude. This is because as the seasons change and the wood beneath the wall swells and shrinks, the nails or screws are pushed out slightly. To repair these bumps:

1. Gently scrape away the layers of compound over the nail or screw heads.

2. Drive nails and turn screws tightly into the stud—you don't want to break through the drywall, but just slightly dimple it.

3. Using ready-mixed joint or spackling compound, refill and cover the hole.

4. Sand flat, prime, and repaint.

TOUCHING UP PAINTED SURFACES

1. Fill holes with spackling paste using a flexible putty knife. Overfill slightly since compounds will shrink. Let the paste dry completely, then sand, using a medium-grit paper on walls and a coarse-grit paper on wood.

2. Fill cracks between the baseboard—or any trim—and the wall with latex caulk, following the manufacturer's instructions. Smooth caulk immediately after applying it with a damp sponge. Latex caulk can be painted.

3. Mix paint with a wooden stir stick, then pour some into a smaller plastic vessel, filling it about halfway.

4. Dip a 2-inch brush a little more than 1 inch into the paint, then tap it against the sides of the container to remove excess.

5. Apply paint to the affected area, feathering it well when overlapping already-painted areas.

REPAIRING DENTS IN DRYWALL

1. Carefully chip off any flaking paint or finish on the surface, and with a utility knife, trim off any loose or bunched paper around the dent.

2. Sand the area with coarse sandpaper, and brush away any loose particles.

3. With a dampened sponge, moisten the sanded area.

4. Push spackling or joint compound into the area with a putty knife, working from the center to the outside edges, until the patch is slightly higher than the undamaged surface.

5. Using a putty knife wide enough to span the entire patch, stroke across the patch in broad, smooth passes, removing extraneous compound as you go.

6. Allow the patch to dry; if it shrinks up at all, you'll have to apply a second coat.

7. Smooth the patch with a sanding screen, which is least likely to clog up with dust, or fine-grit sandpaper on a sanding block.

8. Pick up dust with a vacuum, then prime and paint.

PLASTER

If your home was built before 1945, chances are your walls are covered in plaster, which was the interior wall composition of choice across America until the advent of drywall, which was less expensive and easier to install. Plaster is a remarkably sturdy material, derived from ground-up and processed gypsum rock. The powdered rock, known as plaster of Paris, is mixed with water for use. The pastelike wet plaster was generally troweled over wood lath (narrow slats nailed horizontally over wall studs) or over plasterboard or wallboard (early types of drywall, which were much more brittle than currently available drywall sheets).

Most experts agree that it's a waste of time and money to repair plaster without first fixing the cause of the trouble. Although it's durable, it's vulnerable to damage from leaking pipes, which can cause it to become crumbly or powdery. If you can't diagnose the problem yourself, consult a home inspector or building contractor. Once the underlying problem has been solved, you can repair the plaster. Major damage—deep wall-to-wall fissures or a vast network of spidery cracks—should be handled by a plaster professional. You can, however, tackle minor damage, such as a small crack or small holes. All the supplies noted opposite are available at hardware stores. Plaster dust can be abrasive: Remove furniture and use a plastic or canvas drop cloth. If the plaster is old, wear safety glasses and a dust mask.

REPAIRING PLASTER WALLS

SANDING BLOCK   MESH FIBER TAPE   SIX-INCH   FIVE-IN-ONE   PROTECTIVE
TAPING KNIFE   TOOL   GLOVES

1. Begin by carefully removing any flaking or chipping plaster or paint; cracks that reopen during season changes should be widened first with the pointed edge of a five-in-one tool, to ensure that they will not widen further after being repaired.

2. Use mesh fiber tape to cover over the cracks; this flexible but strong tape will bear the brunt of the movement when walls swell and contract, thus protecting your patch from new cracks.

3. Fill cracks with lightweight spackling compound, which dries quickly: Using a taping or putty knife, push compound through the mesh of the tape, and build up the surface until it completely covers the gridwork of the tape.

4. Smooth the edges so they are flush with the wall and let the compound dry according to manufacturer's instructions. (You can also use joint compound to fill holes or cracks, but check the label, as drying times will vary.)

5. Using a sanding block and coarse-grit sandpaper, sand the area and if needed, apply another thin layer of plaster over the compound, following the method described above. (You will probably have to mix the plaster yourself, and apply and smooth it quickly, as it dries fast.)

6. After curing completely, prime with an alkaline-resistant primer specially formulated for plaster before painting.

WALLPAPER

Wallpaper can be made of vinyl, paper treated with an acrylic or a wax coating, untreated paper, or natural materials such as grass cloth. Care instructions are generally printed on the back of wallpaper, so it's always wise to keep a remnant. (All wallpaper, however, can be cleaned with the dusting attachment on your vacuum. Follow the instructions on page 537 for vacuuming a painted wall.)

If you do not know whether your wallpaper is washable or not, you should test it first in an inconspicuous area to see if the colors run, bleed, or fade. If this occurs, use a dry sponge (available at hardware stores) or wallpaper dough (found in painting supply stores). Both pick up dirt without using moisture.

Vinyl wallpaper or papers coated with acrylic can be wiped with a sponge or cloth dampened with mild dishwashing liquid. Never use scouring powders or products containing bleach or ammonia. Be very careful not to overwet the wallpaper, and avoid wiping over seams. If water seeps between seams, the paper can peel.

HOW TO SPOT-REPAIR DAMAGED WALLPAPER

To repair a damaged area, you will need a remnant of the original wallpaper (which is why you should always buy an extra roll whenever you install new wallpaper).

1. Cut a piece of wallpaper slightly larger than the damaged spot.

2. Carefully line up the pattern of the new paper with the pattern of the paper on the wall; use masking tape to hold the new paper in place.

3. Using a utility knife and a straightedge, cut a neat square an inch or two larger all the way around the damaged area, making sure to cut through both pieces of paper but not too deep into the wall.

4. Remove the patch and set aside. Dampen the damaged paper with a sponge, then carefully peel back the cut square and remove it. Clean the wall underneath to remove any residue or dirt.

5. Let the wall dry completely before applying adhesive to the patch. Carefully place the patch onto the wall, lining it up with the wallpaper pattern. (Or if the paper is self-adhesive, lightly dampen it before placing it on the wall.)

6. Depending on the size of the patch, you may need to use a seam roller to smooth the paper into place. Remove any excess adhesive by running a lightly dampened sponge over the area.

HOW TO REMOVE WALLPAPER

If you tire of wallpaper or it's damaged, it's always best to remove it
rather than paint over it. Using the proper tools and technique can make
this rather time-consuming job easier.

1. Empty the room of furniture and place a drop cloth (preferably cotton since plastic isn't absorbent) on the floor. Cover the entire floor; wallpaper dyes may run, staining your floor and other surfaces. Protect any electrical sources.

2. Lightly score the walls with a wallpaper scraper, a long-handled knife with an angled head, which you should be able to find in most hardware stores.

3. Dampen the walls with warm water, either by spraying or steaming. A garden pump sprayer is the perfect tool for the former method; or else you can rent a commercial wallpaper steamer from a tool-rental company or a paint store. Vinyl and foil wallpapers are waterproof, so any water sprayed on them will not penetrate. Instead, try using a scraper edge or long-handled wire brush to perforate any waterproof wallpaper, creating a crosshatch of pores that will better allow moisture to permeate. Vinyl paper is often two-ply; the surface layer is vinyl and the layer underneath is paper. In this case, the vinyl layer may be pulled off first, and then the paper backing can be removed with water and a scraper.

4. Try scratching the wet wallpaper—paper that comes off easily is ready to be removed. Otherwise, spray with more water and allow it to soak in. The paper will darken as it absorbs the water. Be careful not to oversoak your walls, however, or water will run all over the floor.

5. Whenever paper becomes dry or difficult to loosen, respray sparingly with water.

6. Use the wallpaper scraper to remove all of the paper, taking care not to scrape too hard or you risk tearing up the drywall. Once you've successfully removed all the paper, spray the bare walls sparingly to loosen the remaining glue.

7. Sponge walls with warm water, rinsing often, until all surfaces are smooth and free of glue.

8. Wherever glue is thick, use the scraper or an old putty knife to gently scrape it off.

9. Finally, blot the walls dry with clean, lint-free cloths.

10. If you are planning on painting after removing wallpaper, let the walls dry for at least twenty-four hours before you begin prepping. Then fill any holes or cracks with spackling compound, and sand lightly to remove any imperfections. Wipe walls with a clean damp towel to remove dust, and prime walls with a primer-sealer. Let walls dry completely before painting.

WOODWORK

The trim throughout your house, also known as molding, is decorative as well as practical. It hides gaps where floors, walls, and ceilings meet and protects walls from scuffs and wear and tear. It must be dusted, wiped, and touched up regularly to keep it looking good. Once a month, wipe the trim around doors, where it's most likely to become soiled from fingerprints, with a cloth dampened with warm water and an all-purpose cleaner.

Twice a year, wipe molding throughout the house, including crown moldings and window moldings, with a cloth dampened with warm water and an all-purpose cleaner or mild dishwashing liquid.

HOW TO CLEAN BASEBOARDS

Vacuum baseboards once a month using the dust-brush attachment. Rather than doing the whole house at once, you may want to do a different room every week during your regular vacuuming routine. Depending on how big your house is, this should suffice.

Twice a year, after vacuuming well, wipe baseboards with a cloth dampened with warm water and an all-purpose cleaner or mild dishwashing liquid. Because baseboards are usually painted with glossy paint or sealed with a protective finish, they can be gently scrubbed. Use a light-duty nylon pad to remove scuff marks. Baseboards in the kitchen and bath, which are subject to moisture and spills, may need to be wiped monthly to keep them looking their best.

If paint on baseboards is chipped, follow the directions on page 540 for touching up painted surfaces.

HOW TO REPAIR A DOOR THAT STICKS

A door can stick for a number of reasons, but most commonly, the frame has shifted or the door has swelled. Unless you have experience hanging doors, most sticky doors require the attention of a professional contractor or handyman, especially if you can't determine the source of the sticking. However, you can try these quick fixes.

☐ If there are obvious drips of paint protruding from the door or frame, remove them with sandpaper—but be careful not to remove all finish from the door; raw wood should never be left exposed.

☐ Check for damp or damaged weather stripping and replace it as necessary.

☐ Oil hinges with a lubricant such as WD-40.

DOORS

Like trim, doors are usually well sealed with a glossy paint or finish and tolerate washing well. Regular, gentle care will keep daily wear and tear from taking a toll.

INTERIOR DOORS

Once a month sweep dust out of the crevices of recessed-panel doors or French doors with a natural-bristle paintbrush. Then wipe down both sides of the door using a cloth dampened with warm water and an all-purpose cleaner or mild dishwashing liquid. Start at the top and work your way down. Your cloth should be wrung well enough so the cleaning solution does not drip down the surface of the door. To remove stubborn fingerprints, which tend to collect around doorknobs, dampen the cloth with undiluted cleaner. Wipe doorknobs well with a damp cloth and buff dry with a clean, soft cloth.

EXTERIOR DOORS

Your front door is the first thing guests see when they visit your home. It should be pristine and welcoming at all times. Once a month, dust the entire surface of the door well with a soft-bristled utility or counter brush to remove cobwebs and loose dirt. Then, wipe using a cloth dampened with warm water and an all-purpose cleaner (dusting the door first will ensure grime won't turn to muddy water when you wipe it). Because exterior doors will be much dirtier than interior ones, particularly during the cold months, you may need to wet the surface thoroughly and let the cleaner sit for a few minutes so it can emulsify the dirt. Tend to any scuff marks or stubborn dirt with a nylon scrubbing pad or plastic-bristled brush, taking care not to scratch the finish. Rinse well using a clean, damp cloth.

All wood or metal exterior doors can be cleaned using this method. For information on cleaning glass doors, follow the instructions for how to wash windows on page 548. Polish any hardware following the directions on page 525.

WINDOWS AND WINDOW TREATMENTS

WINDOWS ADMIT WELCOME BREEZES, let the sun shine in, and frame our vision of the outdoors. They also present one of the biggest homekeeping challenges there is. No matter how you approach this chore, the time and effort required to keep windows sparkling and curtains, drapes, and shades dust-free is considerable. Fortunately, the reward for doing so is considerable, too. Regularly wiping away fingerprints and smudges (this may be a daily task if you have small children or pets) keeps windows tolerably clean most of the time, but at least once a year, it's necessary to pull out a bucket and squeegee (the professionals' time- and effort-saving tool of choice) and wash them inside and out. One weekend's work can yield clear views for the rest of the year.

WINDOW WASHING

A mild, cloudy day is best for window washing (since sun can dry the cleaner more quickly than you can wipe it, causing streaking), so include this task as part of your spring and fall cleaning. A rubber-edged squeegee can make window washing a relatively painless process. A squeegee will also make neater work of the task than newspaper or cloths and is more environmentally sound than paper towels. Like window panes, squeegees come in a variety of sizes; window washers use blades ranging from 8 to 18 inches (a screw-on extension will help you reach tall windows with hardly a stretch). Though 10- and 12-inch blades work best for most windows, it's useful to have a selection—using a small squeegee on a large window will require too many passes.

A straight-edged razor-blade scraper is useful for removing dried paint and other stubborn matter, but use it with extreme care as it can easily scratch glass (and since scratches aren't covered under the warranties of most new windows, you'll have to learn to live with a scratch or buy a new window). A mixture of equal parts white vinegar and hot water is an effective, inexpensive cleaner. It is less toxic than ammonia, which can react with window putty and discolor aluminum window frames. You can also try a few drops of mild dishwashing liquid in hot water; if this solution leaves streaks, use less detergent. Both solutions can be decanted into spray bottles, as well.

CLEANING STORM WINDOWS

Storm windows provide extra protection against drafts and cold, and may be replaced in the summer with screens. They should be thoroughly cleaned twice a year—before they are installed and after they are taken off.

TYPES OF WINDOWS

AWNING Top-hinged windows that open outward.	**DOUBLE-HUNG** Two sashes (frames into which the panes of a window or door are set) slide vertically past each other in a channeled jamb.	**HOPPER** Bottom-hinged windows that open inward.
CASEMENT Side-hinged windows that pivot outward like doors.		**SLIDING** Two sashes slide past each other like double-hung windows, but these windows slide horizontally rather than vertically.

**HOW TO CLEAN
WINDOW HARDWARE**

Window locks, handles, cranks, and knobs should be dusted monthly with a clean cotton cloth; use cotton swabs to clean crevices. Occasionally oil any moving parts, such as window locks, with machine oil such as WD-40 (vacuum first to remove any dirt and dust). If hardware is oxidized and requires polishing, turn to page 525 for instructions.

It's easiest to clean them outdoors, where they can be hosed down. Alternatively, clean them in the garage or basement (be sure to protect floors with a drop cloth).

Keep track of any hardware in plastic bags and add labels so you'll know where everything belongs later. If windows aren't already labeled, use a permanent marker to note the room or position in the room along the thin edge of the frame that's not exposed. This will make installation quicker next season.

Start by vacuuming the glass and the grooves of the window, with a dust-brush tool. A shop vacuum would be best for this task. Clean glass following the directions on the opposite page. If your storm windows are not removable, clean them in place following the same directions. Allow these windows to dry completely before closing them, as moisture trapped between panes can damage frames.

HOW TO CLEAN WINDOW SCREENS

Dirty window screens are a nuisance: They block light and make your windows look dingy even when the glass is sparkling clean. Between major cleanings, you can keep your screens clean by wiping them down with a soft brush, and then whisking away loosened dust and dirt with the vacuum and a dust-brush tool.

If you remove screens for the winter, as is necessary in cold climates where storm windows are used, clean them well after taking them down. If you leave them up year-round, they should still come down once a year, generally in the spring, for deep cleaning.

When removing screens, keep track of any hardware—stash screws or other pieces in a plastic bag (or several plastic bags if you have different kinds of windows and screens in the house) and add labels so you'll know where everything belongs later. Use a permanent-marking pen to note their rooms and positions on inconspicuous parts of their frames.

When cleaning screens, if you don't have a yard to work in, the next best option is a basement or laundry room with a drain in the floor. This is a messy project for indoors, however. Lay screens flat on the ground or lean them up against a wall. Using warm water and a mild dishwashing liquid, go over each screen with a scrub brush, washing the mesh as well as the frame. Rinse thoroughly, preferably with a garden hose, and allow them to dry completely, in the breeze and sun, if possible.

WINDOW-WASHING KIT

Keep all your window-washing tools in one plastic or metal bucket (and use a second bucket to mix cleaning solutions).

- ☐ Soft-bristled counter brush
- ☐ White vinegar (or mild dishwashing liquid)
- ☐ Large polyester or natural sea sponges
- ☐ Squeegees, with extension poles
- ☐ Lint-free cloths (huck cloth or cloth diapers) that have not been washed or dried with fabric softener (which can leave behind a residue that will streak glass)
- ☐ Rubber gloves
- ☐ Straight-edged razor blade
- ☐ Sturdy ladder (with a label indicating it is approved by Underwriters Laboratories).
- ☐ Nonammoniated all-purpose cleaner

WASHING LARGE WINDOWS

For huge picture windows, professionals favor a method called "the snake." Starting in an upper corner, pull the squeegee horizontally across the window. At the opposite corner, turn, lower the squeegee to the water line, then pull it across the window. Work your way down, and touch up edges with a cloth.

HOW TO WASH WINDOWS

1. Choose a time of day when the sun is not shining directly on the windows. The heat from the sun can cause the cleaning fluid to dry, which will result in streaks.

2. Brush the exteriors of windows and frames lightly with a soft-bristled counter brush, dusting away cobwebs and loose dirt. Don't forget the hinges, sills, and tracks.

3. Mix a solution of 1 part white vinegar and 1 part hot water.

4. When using the squeegee indoors, place a towel along the windowsill to catch drips.

5. Using a sponge, wet (but don't drench) the window with the vinegar-and-water solution and rub the dirt away. Keep the solution from touching the window frames.

6. Wet your squeegee; a dry blade will skip.

7. Starting at an upper corner of the pane, draw the squeegee down in a straight, confident stroke. Return to the top and repeat, slightly overlapping the first stroke. After each stroke, wipe the rubber edge of the squeegee with a sponge or lint-free cloth. Finish by pulling the squeegee across the bottom of the window, and dry the sill with a sponge or cloth.

8. Wipe frames with a cloth dampened with a nonammoniated all-purpose cleaner and water. Rinse them thoroughly with a clean, damp cloth to remove cleaning solution and dry immediately by wiping with a clean, dry cloth.

SPECIAL WINDOWS

Be gentle when cleaning leaded, stained, or painted glass. Never clean them with ammonia, ammonia-based commercial cleaners, or vinegar-and-water solutions, all of which can discolor or damage window frames and painted surfaces. Dust surfaces with a soft brush before cleaning.

LEADED WINDOWS

Use a solution of warm water with a squirt of pH-neutral cleaner. Apply the solution to a clean cloth and wring it out—don't spray directly on glass. Be careful not to press too hard; doing so could push panes out of the lead strips, or caming, that hold them in place (since lead is a soft metal, these windows are especially susceptible to this mishap). If necessary, clean crevices between glass and lead with damp cotton swabs. Dry thoroughly with clean cloths. The lead can oxidize if water or cleaning solution gets trapped against it, causing the window to bow or sag.

PAINTED WINDOWS

These windows are very delicate, especially if they're antique (painted details are common on nineteenth-century stained glass). Do not use detergents of any kind. Instead, dip a sponge in warm water and squeeze it out until nearly dry. Rub the window very gently. Dry thoroughly with a soft, lint-free cloth. Cotton swabs, dampened with water, may be used to wipe dust out of small or delicate areas, but follow them with clean cotton swabs to avoid trapped moisture. Soft, dry, clean natural paintbrushes can be used to sweep dust out of crevices.

STAINED GLASS

Decorative stained glass can be washed carefully with warm water and a pH-neutral cleaner, as long as the glass is not painted. Rinse with a clean, damp sponge and dry thoroughly with a lint-free cloth. If your stained-glass window is covered by a storm window, make sure both glass and caming are completely dry before closing the window to avoid oxidizing the lead.

GLASS BRICK

Glass brick is very durable, but it must be treated carefully to protect the porous mortar between the blocks. This mortar should be sealed with a penetrating sealer to protect it from dirt and moisture. (For information on sealing grout, turn to page 531.) To keep grout in good condition, clean glass block with a pH-neutral cleaner and water. Wipe with a cloth dampened with cleaner and water rather than spraying the cleaner directly on the surface.

SKYLIGHTS

Maintenance of skylights should be left to a professional window cleaner. It's wise to have skylights inspected annually to ensure they are tightly sealed.

A NOTE ABOUT BROKEN LOCKS

☐ Replace only locks that have visible and accessible screws, as tampering with locks that are an integral part of the frame can ruin the entire window.

☐ To replace locks with visible screws, unscrew the current lock and screw on a replacement.

☐ If your windows have double-paned glass or vinyl-covered wood frames, consult a window professional—incorrect installation of hardware may permanently damage the window frames or break the insulating seal.

HOW TO REMOVE PAINT FROM WINDOW HARDWARE

Paint-spattered or completely painted hardware should be removed and stripped with paint stripper (always work in a well-ventilated area and wear protective gloves).

① First, use a utility knife to carefully score paint where the hardware engages with the window frame. (When working with a utility knife in this manner, wear heavy gloves, and always point the knife away from you.) Work slowly to avoid marring the surrounding painted surfaces.

② After scoring, scrape off any paint covering screws and dig paint out of grooves in screw heads with a utility knife or awl. As you're cleaning, keep track of which screws go with which hardware—or clean sets together. To release paint from screw holes, remove screws with the appropriate screwdriver, then place an awl at an angle in the screw holes and gently tap the paint out with a small hammer. (Additional scoring with a utility knife may be necessary.)

③ Wearing appropriate skin and face protection, place hardware and screws in a small bowl or can and cover with a low-toxicity paint remover. After stripping, clean hardware thoroughly with mild dishwashing liquid and water and polish if necessary with the appropriate metal polish (for instructions, turn to page 525).

COMMON WINDOW TERMS

Windows add greatly to the beauty of a home, but they can also add greatly to utility bills both in winter and summer. Here are important terms to know if you're considering purchasing new windows.

DOUBLE-PANE
A window composed of two sheets of glass with a gap in between that creates a layer of insulation. The gap is usually filled with a nontoxic gas, either argon or krypton, which reduces heat transfer. Double-pane windows can cut heat loss by half compared with single-pane windows.

LOW-EMITTANCE (LOW-E) COATING
A transparent coating on glass that blocks long-wave radiation (which is heat), but admits short-wave radiation (which is light).

U-FACTOR
Refers to the resistance of window glass and window frames to the transfer of heat. The lower the U-factor, the higher the insulating capability of the window. U-factors generally range from 0.15 for triple-pane windows to 0.20 for single-pane windows.

HOW TO UNSTICK A WINDOW

To make sure nothing is causing an obstruction, use a bristle brush to clean the channels and all surfaces that touch when the sash is in motion. If the channels are not well lubricated, running a candle stub up and down the channels may be all that's needed to restore their easy slide. A window that sticks after a cleaning and lubrication was probably improperly painted: Either it has too little paint on it, which encourages moisture absorption and swelling, or else it has too much, which creates a gluelike bond between the sash and its channels. In the former case, wait for a spell of dry weather, which will allow the wood to shrink a bit, and paint it. For the latter problem, you'll have to strip the old paint and apply new paint. This can involve disassembling the windows and stripping all pieces—consult a contractor if you're unsure how to tackle this repair.

HOW TO REPAIR DAMAGED WINDOW FRAMES

A dented or gouged window frame isn't just an eyesore—it's an invitation to further deterioration. Dents can leave unsealed materials exposed, allowing metal frames to rust and wood frames to warp.

☐ To repair a dent in wood, sand first to remove rough edges. By hand or using a putty knife, fill the dent with a plastic wood filler or putty. Let it harden, sand slightly if the surface is uneven, and add more filler if necessary.

☐ Round holes in wood may be simply filled with plastic wood. Follow the manufacturer's instructions for application and drying times, then reapply the finish.

☐ A dented frame on a vinyl window could mean that the seal on the window is broken. Check for drafts with a lighted candle (if it flickers, outside air is seeping in). When these types of windows are damaged, they must be repaired or replaced by a window professional.

☐ Dented metal frames can be repaired in a similar fashion to wood ones, but with auto-body filler (available at auto-supply stores). This filler adheres well to metal surfaces, and is easily sanded smooth and repainted, if necessary. When using auto-body filler, open as many windows as possible and wear a dust mask; follow all label directions. Sand the area that needs to be repaired first with a coarse-grit paper, 80 to 120 grit, to remove any flakes or splinters of metal and make the surface rough enough to accept filler. Apply filler to the dent, and allow it to dry according to instructions. Sand the dry patch with a medium-grit paper, 150 to 180 grit. If more filler is needed, repeat. Then sand again, finishing up with a fine-grit paper, 220 to 280 grit.

PATCHING A SCREEN

Badly ripped screening should be replaced, but most small tears may be easily repaired.

☐ Fill small holes in nylon or fiberglass screens with a few drops of instant adhesive.

☐ Fill small holes in metal screens with epoxy.

☐ Patch kits are often available at home supply and hardware stores. If using a kit, follow the manufacturer's instructions.

☐ To make your own patch for nylon or fiberglass screens, cut a patch just barely larger than the hole. Apply a thin layer of fast-drying glue along the edges of the patch, and press it in place. To avoid sticking fingers to glue, use low-tack painter's tape to hold the screen together as it dries; cut a piece of tape larger than the patch, gently tape it to the patch, and leave until dry.

☐ To make your own patch for a metal screen, begin by trimming around the tear in the screen to create a small, clean-edged rectangular or square opening. Cut a piece of screen about ½ inch larger than the hole in length and width. Unravel a couple of strands of screen away from each of the piece's four sides until the central woven section is just large enough to cover the hole. Fold the resulting "fingers" away from you at 90 degrees to the patch's surface. Cover the hole with the patch, inserting the fingers into the mesh of the existing screen. To complete, fold and carefully weave the fingers, under and inward onto the patch or outward toward the screen frame, into the surrounding screen.

CLEANING BLINDS

If metal or vinyl blinds are too dirty to wipe easily while they're hanging in the window, you can either take them down to scrub them yourself or hire a professional to perform an ultrasonic cleaning (find a cleaner in the Yellow Pages under "Window Treatments—Cleaning and Repair"). An ultrasonic cleaning will restore slats, cords, and fabric ladders to like-new cleanliness. Fabric blinds can't be scrubbed, but can be professionally cleaned using the dry ultrasonic method. Wood blinds cannot be either scrubbed or ultrasonically cleaned; because the finish on wood blinds is much the same as that found on wood furniture, the blinds have to be gently wiped by hand with a soft, damp cloth.

For do-it-yourself cleaning of metal or vinyl blinds, first remove the blind from the window. Take it outside and lay it on a drop cloth on the ground. Close blinds so they lie flat. Scrub gently with a soft plastic-bristled brush and a solution of hot water and mild dishwashing liquid (just a few drops should do the trick). Turn over the blind and scrub the other side. Rinse both sides with a hose. Hang the blind from a sturdy clothesline, with slats open, and allow it to air dry. Do not use abrasives of any sort to clean blinds; doing so will scratch the finish.

HOW TO CLEAN VALANCES

Valances, which are decorative horizontal panels at the tops of windows, should be dusted as part of your regular monthly window-treatment cleaning. You can blow dust off valances using a can of compressed air (available at office-supply stores) or vacuum them with a handheld vacuum.

CHOOSING WINDOW TREATMENTS

There's more to think about when choosing a window treatment than just color and style. In fact, window treatments can make a room feel more comfortable by keeping heat in during the winter and out in the summer. Honeycomb, or cellular shades, which are composed of horizontal rows of hollow channels, are among the most energy-efficient window treatments available. Their channels provide an effective layer of insulation that manufacturers claim can more than double the energy efficiency of a double-pane window. But even plain vinyl blinds can effectively block the sun's rays, which is one of the most effective ways to keep a room cool. To ensure that they keep rooms warmer in winter, install them as close to window-panes and the sides of the window frame as possible to create an effective air barrier.

HOW TO CLEAN WINDOW TREATMENTS, BY TYPE

Window treatments are not just decorative; they allow you to control the amount of light coming in—essential to avoid the bleaching of furniture or the sun's staining of wooden floors—as well as the degree of privacy. All window treatments should be dusted monthly. Deep-cleaning techniques depend on the material you're treating.

FABRIC SHADES
Monthly Dust using the dust-brush tool on the vacuum (set on low suction).

Once a year Dry clean.

FABRIC VERTICAL BLINDS
Monthly Close blinds so they lie flat. Dust with the dust-brush tool on the vacuum (set on low suction). To spot clean, take down the slat and lay it on a flat surface. Blot the stain with a sponge dampened with mild dishwashing liquid and tepid water. Treat heavy stains with a commercial upholstery cleaner (test on an inconspicuous spot).

Once a year Have a professional clean blinds using a dry ultrasonic technique (look in the Yellow Pages under "Window Treatments—Cleaning and Repair").

HONEYCOMB SHADES
Monthly: Dust with a feather duster or the dust-brush tool of the vacuum (set on low suction). Spot clean with a white cloth dampened with tepid water and mild dishwashing liquid. Blot only; do not rub.

Once a year: Have a professional clean the blinds using the injection/extraction method (check the Yellow Pages under "Window Treatments—Cleaning and Repair").

METAL AND VINYL VENETIAN AND VERTICAL BLINDS
Monthly: Close blinds so they lie flat. Moving from top to bottom, dust with a feather duster, lamb's-wool duster, barely damp soft cloth, or the dust-brush tool on the vacuum (set on low suction). Close them in the opposite direction and repeat.

Twice a year: Wipe each slat individually with a cloth dampened with warm water and mild dishwashing liquid. Never use abrasive cleaners, which will damage the finish. The slats of vertical blinds can be taken down several at a time and laid flat to make wiping easier.

PLEATED SHADES
Monthly: Dust using the dust-brush tool on the vacuum (set suction on low). Regular vacuuming is the only way to clean these shades.

SOLAR SHADES
Monthly: Dust using the dust-brush tool on the vacuum (set on low suction) or wipe with a damp cloth.

Twice a year: Wipe with a cloth dampened with warm water and a mild dishwashing liquid.

DRAPERIES AND CURTAINS
Monthly: Dust using the upholstery tool on the vacuum (set on low suction).

Once a year: If fabric is washable, launder in the machine on the Gentle cycle. Hang to dry and iron while still damp. If fabric is not washable, dry clean. Draperies and curtains in the kitchen or bath or in particularly dusty climates may need to be cleaned more frequently.

WOOD BLINDS AND SHUTTERS
Monthly: Close slats so they lie flat. Working from top to bottom, dust with a feather duster, a lamb's-wool duster, an electrostatic cloth, or the dust-brush tool on the vacuum (set on low suction). Close them in the opposite direction and repeat. Wood blinds and shutters should not be exposed to steam or moisture in a kitchen or bath.

Twice a year: Wipe each slat with a slightly dampened cloth, then dry.

WOVEN WOOD AND BAMBOO SHADES
Monthly: Dust with the dust-brush tool of the vacuum (set on low suction).

Twice a year: Gently wipe with a lightly dampened white cloth.

COMFORT AND SAFETY

THE PRINCIPLES OF GOOD HOMEKEEPING go beyond simply tackling dust and dirt. For a home to be comfortable and safe, all its various components—the ones you can see and the ones you can't—must be in good working order. Pipes need to be free of leaks, the electrical systems must be able to accommodate the requisite appliances and electronics, and the furnace and air conditioner need to keep temperatures throughout the house comfortable year-round.

Learning just how the various mechanical systems in your home function can seem a little daunting, however, and many homeowners are content to leave their care and maintenance to professionals. Although it is often inevitable that a professional will need to undertake a major repair, it is decidedly advantageous to understand how electricity is delivered and dispersed, for example, so you can respond properly to a power outage. And taking a few minutes to study your kitchen faucet and its composite parts will provide you with invaluable information should a leak develop. Getting to know your plumbing, heating and cooling, and electrical systems will allow you to attend to regular upkeep yourself (a great money saver since you'll be able to head off serious problems before they occur), as well as make more-informed decisions when you do have to hire a professional.

Besides prolonging the very life of your house, good homekeeping is also about taking steps to safeguard the well-being of everyone who lives in it. This means ensuring both air and water are clean (which can have a measurable impact on health), putting practical systems in place to deal with natural disasters, and preventing fires, to name a few crucial tasks. Spending time thinking about potential dangers in the home is never a pleasant or welcome occupation, but even a little preparation—whether it's assembling a first-aid kit that's always at the ready or implementing some basic child-proofing measures—can go a long way toward maintaining the well-being of family and friends and eliminating the nagging worry about the what-ifs.

In the end, creating a comfortable, safe home is as easy as taking a few proactive steps. Use the calendar opposite to remind yourself of the essential maintenance tasks that will keep mechanical systems humming. To make sure that your house is indeed a home—the secure cocoon where you long to be at the end of the day—consult the various checklists in the ten chapters that follow, all of which will help you improve the quality of your life and your family's.

MONTHLY MAINTENANCE

- ☐ Inspect water pipes throughout the house for leaks
- ☐ Clean air-conditioner filters (only during the cooling season)
- ☐ Clean the furnace filter (only during the heating season)

FALL MAINTENANCE

- ☐ Have the water heater, heating, ventilation, and air-conditioning systems (HVAC) and gas fireplaces professionally inspected
- ☐ Replace the furnace filters
- ☐ Check to make sure fire extinguishers are pressurized
- ☐ Replace frayed or cracked electrical cords throughout the house
- ☐ Check and replenish first-aid and disaster kits
- ☐ Replace the batteries in all carbon-monoxide detectors and smoke alarms
- ☐ Have septic tank serviced

SPRING MAINTENANCE

- ☐ Have chimneys swept and professionally inspected
- ☐ Replace air-conditioning filters

AIR QUALITY

EVEN IF NO ONE IN YOUR HOME SUFFERS from allergies or asthma, and you do not reside in an unusually polluted area, it is essential that you learn to assess the condition of the air you breathe. The quality of the air in your home goes a long way toward determining your quality of life. Mold, mildew, pet dander, pollen, secondhand smoke, dust mites, and odors all contribute to indoor air pollution. It goes without saying that the cleaner your house, the fresher the air will be—but cleanliness alone might not be enough. You may also need ventilation and filtration systems.

VENTILATION

According to the Environmental Protection Agency (EPA), if too little out-door air enters your home, pollutant levels will increase, potentially causing health problems and discomfort. This is of particular concern in newer homes, which tend to be well insulated and sealed. During winter months, when windows are closed tight, pollutants can accumulate and pose a problem in older houses as well. Signs that your home may not have enough ventilation include condensation on windows or walls, foul-smelling or stuffy air, dirty central-heating and air-cooling vents, and mold in areas where books, shoes, or other items collect. Ventilation levels are measured through the air exchange rate. The American Society of Heating, Refrigerating and Air-Conditioning Engineers (ASHRAE) recommends that the total volume of air changes per hour between indoor and outdoor or filtered air be .35 (a maintenance technician can determine this based on the ventilation systems in your home).

Outside air enters and exits the home through three different processes: infiltration, natural ventilation, and mechanical ventilation.

☐ Infiltrated air flows through openings in your home, such as joints and cracks in walls, floors, and ceilings, as well as around doors and windows.

☐ Natural ventilation occurs when air passes through open windows and doors. Wind and the temperature difference between indoors and outdoors create the current that allows for infiltration and ventilation.

☐ Mechanical ventilation occurs when air is moved by devices such as exhaust fans that vent air outdoors from a single room, commonly a kitchen or bathroom, or fans and ductwork that remove indoor air and distribute filtered outdoor air to the whole house.

If you have an attic, ventilation can play an important role here since heat rises. An exhaust fan installed in a gable or the roof will help draw the hot air up and out of the house, while encouraging cooler air to enter from windows below. Many people choose basic heating, ventilating, and air-conditioning (HVAC) systems as the only methods to warm, cool, and ventilate their homes, not realizing that many of these systems do not bring fresh air indoors. A system of fans—be it tabletop, window, ceiling, or kitchen and bathroom exhaust—should be utilized year-round to augment your HVAC system. Fans facilitate the flow of heat in the winter, circulate air-conditioning in the summer, and disperse humidity.

HOW TO LOWER INDOOR AIR POLLUTANTS

A simple way to lower concentrations of indoor air pollutants is to open windows whenever possible to let in fresh air. To create cross-ventilation, open facing and adjacent windows at the same time. To keep HVAC systems running at peak performance, have a ventilation professional annually inspect, clean, and repair central heating systems (such as furnaces), chimneys, cooling systems, and ventilation systems.

TYPES OF FANS

Fans don't actually cool air but aid the evaporation of moisture in the air. A fan will make air feel cooler, even if the temperature doesn't drop. Once the air feels cooler, you may even be able to raise the thermostat on your air conditioner 5°F in the summer without feeling a change, and obtain substantial savings on your energy bill as a result. Similarly, when you use fans during colder months to distribute heating throughout the house, you can lower the thermostat.

ATTIC

These units are designed to cool off the attic itself in order to reduce the load on the air conditioner.

CEILING

Ceiling fans are comforting year-round. Most have a switch to allow you to change their direction. In the summer, operate them in a counterclockwise direction to circulate cool breezes; and in the winter, clockwise to produce a gentle updraft, which forces warm air near the ceiling down into the room.

EXHAUST

In bathrooms, kitchens, and laundry rooms, it's important to move moist air outdoors to prevent mold. Turn on the exhaust fan whenever you use the shower, heat-generating kitchen appliances, and the clothes dryer (especially if the dryer itself is not vented outdoors) and let them run for at least thirty minutes.

PORTABLE OSCILLATING

Table, floor, and clip-on models are effective for circulating fresh air in individual rooms year-round. In winter months, set them on Low (to avoid creating a draft) and point them directly toward the ceiling to achieve the same benefits provided by a ceiling fan. (Warm air will continuously be circulating and won't be squandered up where you can't feel it.)

WHOLE-HOUSE EXHAUST

Designed to pull air through the house (through vents located in the hallways), these are sized according to a house's cubic feet (the bigger the house, the higher the cubic feet per minute [CFM] rating required). Unfortunately, they can be noisy and are not ideal in regions where there is a lot of dust or pollen, which can be pulled into the house.

WINDOW

These fans are generally small, about 8 to 20 inches in diameter, and are easy to install. Because they sit in a window, they effectively bring outside air in or send indoor air outside. When choosing size, don't base it on the size of your window; instead check the volume of air the fan will move, measured in cubic feet per minute (CFM). If you wanted to cool a room that's 10 by 20 feet with an 8-foot-high ceiling, you would want a CFM of 1600 ($10 \times 20 \times 8$). Some large fans may have the capacity to cool a few rooms. Ideally a fan will have one setting for intake and another for exhaust.

HOW TO CLEAN A FAN

Keep fan blades and screens clean to prevent dust from blowing through the house. Dusting monthly should suffice, but if you notice accumulations between cleanings, dust more frequently. Before you clean any fan, turn off the power source: Unplug portable fans and cut the circuit to ceiling or whole-house fans.

Carefully remove the screens, then wipe each blade with a soft cloth dampened with warm soapy water (use a mild dishwashing liquid). Make sure you do not get the cloth too wet, because you do not want to get water into the fan's motor or gears. Use a soft-bristled brush on the screen to clean crevices. Wait until all parts of the fan are dry before reassembling it and plugging it in. For instructions on how to clean ceiling fans, turn to page 538.

HUMIDITY

Humidity refers to the amount of moisture or water vapor in the air. Relative humidity (RH) is a percentage that indicates the amount of moisture in the air relative to the maximum amount the air can hold at a given temperature. For example, if the air contains half as much moisture as it possibly can (saturation), it is said to be at "50 percent relative humidity." According to the EPA, the ideal relative indoor humidity level is 30 to 50 percent. You can purchase a hygrometer or humidistat (available at hardware stores and home centers) to monitor the humidity in household air. When humidity rises above 50 percent, condensation—excess moisture falling out of the air and onto cold surfaces—develops on pipes, windows, and tile, providing an ideal environment for mold, mildew, and rust. When mold and mildew are present in closets, clothes and linens can absorb a musty odor. Excessive humidity can also warp wood, causing damage to floors and furniture. Too much moisture can even cause labels to slip off bottles— one reason medications should not be stored in a humid bathroom.

Warm air is able to support a much higher volume of water vapor than cold air, which is why the relative humidity drops dramatically when you heat your home in the winter. Very dry household air can make people feel colder and cause a dry nose, throat, lips, and skin, and be uncomfortable for allergy and cold sufferers. It can also cause paint and furniture to crack. Programming thermostats to drop a few degrees at timed intervals will help to keep dry heat from building up, but when conditions become uncomfortable, it's best to use a humidifier.

TIPS FOR DEHUMIDIFYING YOUR HOME

☐ To keep humidity levels down in summer, run air-conditioning and fans together.

☐ Operate exhaust fans in kitchens and bathrooms, and vent clothes dryers to the outdoors, if possible.

☐ Turn off lights and other heat-generating appliances when not in use.

☐ Allow fresh air in when it is cool outside—preferably in the morning and at night—and keep it circulating with fans.

☐ If condensation forms on metal window frames, seal windows tightly, add weather stripping, and install storm windows.

☐ Repair leaky pipes and faucets. As a temporary measure, wrap them in pipe insulation to keep them from dripping.

☐ Remove absorbent materials—rugs, carpets, and pillows—from areas subject to chronic moisture problems, such as bathrooms, basements, and laundry rooms.

☐ In basements, an electronic dehumidifier unit may prove helpful; removing the extra moisture will help control mustiness and odors. But because dehumidifiers emit heat, they're not recommended as a solution to whole-house humidity problems. If you do purchase a dehumidifier, choose one with an Association of Home Appliance Manufacturers seal of approval.

USING DESICCANTS TO CONTROL MOISTURE

Place desiccants in closets, cabinets, drawers, and storage boxes to control moisture. They are available from stores selling closet-organizing products and housewares. These nonmechanical dehumidifiers are made from several different materials:

☐ Silica gel (a nontoxic, non-corrosive form of silicon)

☐ Molecular sieve (a combination of desiccant materials such as zeolite alumino silicates).

☐ Activated clay (a naturally occurring, nonhazardous, sulfur-free substance)

☐ Chalk. Make your own desiccant by fastening a rubber band around a dozen pieces of chalk, and cover the band with ribbon, allowing enough loop to hang over a hook.

HOW TO USE A HUMIDIFIER

☐ Place humidifiers in high-circulation areas but avoid especially humid zones such as kitchens, bathrooms, and laundry rooms.

☐ Use humidifiers only when air feels dry or a hygrometer indicates that relative humidity is below 30 percent. Do not use a humidifier if relative humidity levels rise above 50 percent.

☐ Do not allow a film or scale to build up in your humidifier. If the mineral scale is not removed, the water will not vaporize as efficiently and the unit will eventually stop working.

☐ Empty the water tank daily, and wipe surfaces dry before refilling it with fresh water; use distilled water, if possible, which helps minimize the buildup of mineral scale.

☐ To obtain maximum airflow, do not situate the unit in the corner of a room or near a large piece of furniture.

☐ Drain and thoroughly clean the unit before storing it; bacteria can collect and multiply in stagnant water.

☐ When cleaning or replacing a wick in your humidifier, use only products that have been recommended by the manufacturer.

TYPES OF HUMIDIFIERS

CENTRAL
These humidifiers are built into heating, ventilating, and air-conditioning systems and are therefore able to control the humidity in the whole house.

CONSOLE
These are encased in cabinets that sit on the floor, for use in individual rooms.

PORTABLE
These are smaller, portable appliances that are easy to move around for spot humidifying.

COOL VS. WARM MIST

☐ Cool-mist humidifiers disperse cool moisture, which is most comfortable in rooms that tend to be warm. They generally have a fan that blows air over a wick, which absorbs water from a reservoir. Wicks can become moldy and need to be replaced at least once a season. Humidifiers that use ultrasonic sound vibrations (ultrasonic humidifiers) or high-speed rotating disks (impeller humidifiers) produce a cool mist.

☐ Warm-mist humidifiers heat moisture before it is dispersed; they are useful in rooms that tend to be cold. A heating element boils water, causing steam to rise. These are not the best choice in households with small children, as they can cause burns.

AIR FILTERS

Whether filters reduce allergens or are capable of significantly cleaning the air is a matter of some debate. The EPA has not taken a position for or against their use by consumers. Although a filter may aid in purifying air, it is not a substitute for limiting exposure to pollution and for adequate ventilation. Some types of systems clean only particles in the air; others may also be able to remove some gaseous materials.

Devices are rated not by the percentage of pollutants a filter can remove, but by their ability to deliver a specific amount of filtered air to a room; if a device removes 99 percent of air pollutants but can clean only 10 cubic feet per minute, it will not be very effective in a 1,000-cubic-foot room. The Clean Air Delivery Rate (CADR) notes the number of cubic feet of filtered air a unit delivers per minute. The efficiency rating of air filters refers to their ability to remove respirable particles. At the high end of the efficiency spectrum are high-efficiency particulate air (HEPA) filters. These remove the smallest particles (0.3 microns in size).

TYPES OF FURNACE FILTERS

MECHANICAL FILTERS

Flat filters (also called panel filters) are usually made of coarse glass fibers, animal hair, vegetable fibers, or synthetic fibers often coated with an oily substance to attract large particulates. Flat filters may also be made of permanently charged plastic film or fiber; particles are attracted to the charge. Pleated filters are generally more efficient at capturing particles than flat filters. Because they have a greater surface area, they can be constructed of smaller fibers, which increases efficiency but does not decrease airflow.

ELECTRONIC FILTERS

Electronic air filters are usually referred to as electrostatic precipitators or charged-media filters. These filters are electrified to create a static charge, making them more efficient (and expensive) than mechanical filters.

PORTABLE AIR PURIFIERS

These portable units draw air in using a fan, filter it, and release it back into the room. A mechanical filter absorbs particulates. Some models may also include activated carbon to absorb odors and pre-filters to trap large particles, which protects the main filter, extending its life. (Ion generators use an electrostatic charge to attract dust. There is some concern that these air purifiers generate ozone, which can be damaging to lungs, and they are best avoided.)

Proper placement of portable units is key (as is ensuring that the device is UL listed). Situate it near a specific pollutant source, such as a range or open window, so that clean air will be immediately forced into the area. Routine maintenance is crucial; clean and replace filters per the manufacturer's instructions (each unit will have unique guidelines). Wipe the outside of the unit with a damp cloth weekly.

NATURAL AIR FRESHENERS

Household odors can be separated into two groups: acid odors, such as cigarette smoke, and alkaline odors, such as fish. Baking soda absorbs and neutralizes both types. Lemon (simmering in a pan of water on the stove) is effective at neutralizing alkaline odors. Fresh air alone will eradicate many household odors, but for persistent problems, these natural remedies (preferable to commercial air fresheners, which can contain toxic chemicals) are helpful:

TYPES OF AIR FRESHENERS

EUCALYPTUS
The invigorating aroma of this gum tree is known for its sinus-clearing power. In Australia, where eucalyptus grows, brews of the green, leathery leaves are kept simmering on the stove at the first sign of a sore throat. A sprig of fresh eucalyptus will also scent rooms for about two weeks.

FRESH FLOWERS
A bunch of tulips is more than just pretty to look at; tulips purify air by helping to remove the formaldehyde given off by new kitchen cabinets or furniture made with medium-density fiberboard. Bamboo palms, azaleas, and rubber plants are also believed to have this ability.

LEMON
To eliminate strong odors from cooking fish or vegetables that give off sulfur odors, such as broccoli, cauliflower, or cabbage, simmer half a dozen lemon slices and a handful of cloves in a pan of water for ten minutes.

POMANDERS
Ideal for scenting closets and drawers. These aromatic spheres, once carried by medieval kings, are prepared by studding oranges with whole cloves, spaced evenly and as close together as possible.

POTPOURRI
Dried lavender, rose hips, senna pods, nigella pods, and juniper berries—available from crafts stores and some florists—are pleasing scents for homemade potpourri. Combine generous handfuls of each in a large bowl. Place two scoops of orrisroot powder (available from craft stores, health food stores, and pharmacies) in a small bowl and add a few drops of essential oil, such as lily of the valley or freesia. Blend with a wooden spoon. Sprinkle the orrisroot mixture over the potpourri and gently toss by hand until completely mixed. Potpourri may be refreshed with essential oil once a month or as needed.

ROSE WATER
To make your own, place a few drops of rose oil in a small bowl of water, then add a solubilizer (available in the cosmetics sections of health food stores) one drop at a time, to make the oil and water mix. Float rose petals on top—but change them regularly, since they turn brown within a few days.

VINEGAR
A small dish of vinegar can neutralize cigarette smoke, cooking odors, and musty smells. To get rid of a musty smell in dresser drawers, fill a glass dish with ½ inch of white vinegar and set it in the drawer until the smell goes away. Make sure the dish has high sides to prevent spilling.

ZEOLITE
Sold in hardware stores in pouches or in a shaker can, zeolite is a nontoxic, odorless volcanic rock. It removes smoke, cooking, and pet odors. To eliminate mustiness, hang pouches in a closet or basement, or use the powder to tackle spot odors.

INDOOR AIR POLLUTION

Today's homes are often well sealed to conserve energy. While your heating and cooling bills might be more manageable, pollutants tend to accumulate when the air exchange rate is low. The following pages offer strategies for reducing your exposure to common biological and chemical pollutants.

BIOLOGICAL POLLUTANTS

MOLD

The common name for the more than 100,000 species of fungi that can cause the disintegration of organic matter. Mold flourishes in damp environments, but can grow on virtually any household surface (including drywall, insulation, paint, fabric, carpet, and any household dirt), as long as moisture is present. It commonly appears when there is excessive humidity, water damage, condensation, water infiltration, or leaky plumbing. Besides being an eyesore, mold is destructive and can produce allergens. Ailments include a runny nose, a cough, congestion, as well as asthma in people with weak immune systems, hay fever, or allergies. As mold consumes its food, it produces gases that leak into the air known as volatile organic compounds, or VOCs, which give off a musty odor and can cause irritation to the eyes, nose, and throat. Mold spores become airborne whenever moldy surfaces are disturbed and are then accidentally inhaled. Certain uncommon molds, such as black mold, produce mycotoxins—chemicals that, in large quantities and in rare cases, can provoke severe reactions in people who have allergies and can be dangerous for people with respiratory problems and infants with developing lungs. All molds should be treated in the same manner in terms of prevention and removal. (For more on mold removal, turn to page 570.)

COCKROACHES

Droppings or shed skins can cause allergic reactions, eye, nose, and throat irritations, and skin rashes and can provoke asthma in some people. Cockroach allergens are particularly problematic in urban areas, and throughout parts of the southern United States. Because roaches thrive in damp conditions, humidity levels must be controlled at all times, so repair leaky faucets and any other conditions that can cause increased moisture. Wash dishes immediately after a meal, do not leave food in the garbage, store food in airtight containers, and wipe up crumbs and spills immediately. Because pesticides contain toxic chemicals, try using nontoxic bait traps and boric acid (available at hardware stores and home centers) before resorting to pesticidal sprays (which should not be sprayed near where you store or prepare food, nor near where children play, crawl, or sleep).

BIOLOGICAL POLLUTANTS (CONTINUED)

POLLEN

A fine powderlike material produced in the anthers of flowering plants or the male cones of coniferous plants. An average grain of pollen is usually smaller than the width of an average human hair. Not all pollen causes allergies, however. The pollen of brightly colored flowers, such as roses, which is typically waxy and is carried by bees and other insects, does not cause an allergic reaction in most people. However, many trees, grasses, and low-growing weeds have light, dry pollens that are easily carried on wind currents, and can cause allergic reactions. Pollen is measured in grains per cubic meter of air collected over a twenty-four-hour period. Weeds, grasses, and trees can each have different pollen counts, but generally a pollen count of more than 500 for grasses and weeds and over 1,500 for trees is considered high. Avoid keeping windows open during pollen season, and dust and vacuum regularly using a filter that captures particles to at least 10 microns. Though high pollen counts can cause numerous kinds of reactions, from eye allergies (conjunctivitis) to rashes (dermatitis), the most common ailment is allergic rhinitis, or "hay fever." When the pollen season begins (which varies across the country), people who have any sensitivity start to experience symptoms, especially on warm, dry, breezy days. To determine your region's pollen count, visit www.aaaai.org.

DUST MITES

Dust itself does not generally cause allergies. It is the microscopic creatures called mites that reside in dust—and the residue they leave behind in their droppings and cast-off skin—that are most often the culprits. Exposure to dust mites can cause eye, nose, and throat irritations as well as asthma, particularly in susceptible children. Mites thrive in high humidity and places where human or animal dander is present, including mattresses, pillows, bed linens, carpets, and upholstered furniture. To minimize them, encase mattresses and pillows with washable zippered covers and change and launder sheets weekly. Duvet covers and pillow shams should be washed monthly. Keep humidity levels below 50 percent to prevent dust mites from breeding. If you have pets, groom and bathe them regularly. (For instructions, turn to pages 661–663.) Vacuum weekly with a vacuum that has a HEPA filter and mop wood floors regularly (dry mopping and sweeping can make the allergens airborne).

ANIMAL DANDER

Tiny flakes of skin, hair, or feathers of domestic animals, including dogs, cats, and birds, can trigger asthma and can cause eye, nose, and throat irritations. If possible, keep pets off of upholstered furniture where dander can settle, and groom pets regularly. (Turn to Living with Pets, page 658.) Dust and vacuum weekly with a vacuum that has a HEPA filter.

HOW TO ELIMINATE MOLD

As soon as you notice mold on surfaces, clean it immediately before it has time to spread. The best way to remove mold is with a solution of 1 part chlorine bleach to 10 parts water. Wearing rubber gloves, saturate a clean sponge or cloth with the bleach solution and apply it to the mold. Let the solution soak in for fifteen minutes, then rinse it off. Thoroughly dry the surface and throw away the sponges or rags you used (to avoid spreading mold spores to other surfaces). Increase the proportion of bleach to water and re-treat the area if mold remains.

TIPS FOR PREVENTING MOLD

☐ Wipe surfaces regularly, especially counter-tops, using a few drops of mild dishwashing liquid (or dishwashing liquid added to the bleach solution mentioned above) to remove dirt and oils, which will attract mold.

☐ Monitor areas you've cleaned for signs of mold speedily reappearing. If the area becomes moldy again right away, or if the mold spreads to an adjacent area, you may have a leak that needs repair.

☐ Add insulation to prevent condensation on cold windows, pipes, exterior walls, and other cold surfaces.

☐ If mold is present on insulation or through-out a carpet, discard it immediately; and if mold is a result of flooding, to avoid health risk, it should be managed by a professional cleaner who specializes in mold.

☐ Clean and disinfect basement-floor drains regularly. Before finishing a basement, patch all water leaks and provide outdoor ventilation and adequate heat to minimize condensation. Operate a dehumidifier in the basement if needed to keep humidity levels between 30 and 50 percent.

☐ Moisture control and ventilation are key in preventing mold: Keep air-conditioning and humidifier drip pans clean, and ensure that drain lines are unobstructed. Never put away wet shoes or clothing.

☐ If you are concerned that mold has formed in areas you cannot clean, check with a local building inspector who specializes in mold remediation or visit the EPA website for more information: www.epa.gov/mold/mold _remediation.html.

CHEMICAL POLLUTANTS

VOLATILE ORGANIC COMPOUNDS (VOC)

Many household products release volatile organic compounds after manufacture. VOCs, which are found in concentrations up to ten times higher indoors than outdoors, include a variety of chemicals, some of which may cause short-term health effects, and some of which can cause long-term effects. According to the EPA, VOCs can cause eye, nose, and throat irritations as well as headaches, nausea, and loss of coordination. Eventual side effects can include damage to the liver, the kidneys, and the central nervous system. Some VOCs are known or suspected carcinogens. Offenders include paints and finishes, wood preservatives, pesticides, glues and adhesives, permanent markers, moth repellents, air fresheners, fuels, and dry-cleaning chemicals. The health effects of VOCs vary greatly, due to many factors, such as level of exposure and length of time exposed. To reduce exposure to VOCs, always follow the manufacturer's instructions for storing and using household products, and always ensure there is adequate ventilation by opening windows and running fans when using products that contain solvents, such as paint strippers. Because gases can leak from even sealed containers, do not store unused paints and similar materials inside. Stored fuels and paint supplies can be a source of benzene, which is a known human carcinogen. Dry cleaning that smells strongly of chemicals may still contain perchloroethylene (perc), a solvent known to cause cancer in animals. Ask that perc be removed from clothing; if clothes repeatedly come back with a chemical smell, seek another dry cleaner.

RADON

Radon is an odorless, colorless, radioactive gas produced naturally in soil, water, and rocks by the breakdown of uranium. According to the EPA, radon is the second leading cause of lung cancer deaths in the United States after smoking. It also greatly increases a smoker's risk of lung cancer. Any home, school, or business can have elevated levels of radon; it enters through cracks in the foundation, floor and wall joints, mortar joints, or the water supply. Reliable home tests are available at hardware stores and home centers, or you can hire a qualified tester to evaluate your home (contact your state radon office for a list: www.epa.gov/iaq/whereyoulive.html).

The most common remedy for a house with radon is sealing cracks and installing an exhaust system that will draw radon-contaminated air from beneath the foundation and release it through an exhaust pipe in the roof. You can obtain information on choosing a qualified state-certified radon contractor from your state radon office.

CHEMICAL POLLUTANTS (CONTINUED)

FORMALDEHYDE

According to the EPA, formaldehyde is found in a wide variety of products, from home-building materials to household products, and is a by-product of combustion and other natural processes. Formaldehyde can cause watery eyes, a burning sensation in the eyes and throat, nausea, wheezing and coughing, fatigue, skin rash, and difficulty breathing with high levels of exposure. The most significant sources of formaldehyde are pressed-wood products made using adhesives that contain urea-formaldehyde (UF) resins, including particleboard (used as subflooring and shelving and in cabinetry and furniture); hardwood plywood paneling (used for decorative wall covering and in cabinets and furniture); and medium-density fiberboard (used for drawer fronts, cabinets, and furniture tops).

During the 1970s, many homes were built using urea-formaldehyde foam insulation (UFFI), but this was shown to create high indoor concentrations of formaldehyde and is rarely used today. Formaldehyde is also used in glues and adhesives, as a preservative in some paints and coating products, as well as to add permanent-press qualities to clothing and draperies and home textiles.

The rate at which products such as pressed wood or textiles release formaldehyde can change. When products are new or exposed to humidity or high indoor temperatures, they tend to release more formaldehyde; the levels of emissions decrease as the products age. No one knows for certain how long it takes for formaldehyde fumes to dissipate completely.

Because formaldehyde is classified as a known human carcinogen, it is important to reduce exposure whenever possible. One way is to check with manufacturers before purchasing products to learn if they contain formaldehyde. It is possible that coating wood products containing formaldehyde with polyurethane (one that does not contain formaldehyde) may reduce emissions. Most important, use air conditioners and dehumidifiers to keep temperatures in the home moderate and humidity low. Increase ventilation after bringing home any new furnishings.

COMBUSTION BY-PRODUCTS

Cigarettes, unvented kerosene and gas space heaters, woodstoves, fireplaces, and gas ranges all release toxic gases such as carbon monoxide and nitrogen dioxide. Such gases can also enter the house from chimneys and flues that are improperly installed or maintained, as well as from cracked furnace heat exchangers; combustion gases can reach dangerous levels in weatherized houses that have little or no ventilation. According to the EPA, exposure to combustibles can result in eye, nose, and throat irritations; respiratory infections; headaches; dizziness; sleepiness; and the dangers associated with carbon monoxide poisoning (see Carbon Monoxide, below), and can potentially lead to lung diseases such as emphysema. Tobacco smoke is one of the main indoor sources of benzene, a known human carcinogen.

To reduce exposure, make sure gas appliances are installed and maintained properly and use exhaust fans over gas cooktops. Always read and follow the manufacturer's instructions before using any combustion appliance. Change filters on central heating and cooling systems and portable air purifiers according to the manufacturer's instructions.

CARBON MONOXIDE

Carbon monoxide is a colorless, odorless gas that is lethal in high concentrations. Common sources of carbon monoxide are unvented kerosene and gas heaters, gas ranges, fireplaces, woodstoves, furnaces, gas water heaters, gasoline-powered equipment, automobile exhaust from attached garages, and tobacco smoke.

According to the EPA, exposure can cause fatigue in healthy people and chest pain in those with heart disease. In high concentrations, it can cause impaired vision and coordination, severe headaches, confusion, dizziness, nausea, faintness, reduced brain function, and death. If you experience symptoms you think could be a result of carbon monoxide poisoning, get fresh air immediately and seek medical attention.

Prevent exposure by installing a carbon-monoxide detector (available at hardware stores and home centers) on each floor of your house, with at least one near sleeping areas (this may even be a municipal law where you live). A detector should not be placed within 15 feet of heating or cooking appliances or in or near humid areas such as bathrooms. Replace the batteries twice a year. Any carbon-monoxide detector has a lifespan of only about two years; write the date of purchase on the back so you know when to replace it. Reduce exposure by avoiding products containing methylene chloride (found in products such as paint and varnish removers), which is converted to carbon monoxide in the body. Never leave your car idling inside the garage.

CHEMICAL POLLUTANTS (CONTINUED)

NITROGEN DIOXIDE

Nitrogen dioxide is a highly reactive and corrosive gas. It can be formed when combustion appliances, such as kerosene heaters and gas ranges, are not vented or when vented appliances are installed improperly. Welding and tobacco smoke also release nitrogen dioxide. Exposure can cause eye, nose, and throat irritation; it also has the potential to cause impaired lung function and increased respiratory infections in children, according to the EPA. Low-level exposure can cause problems for asthmatics and decreased lung function in people with chronic pulmonary disease and those with weakened immune systems or increased risk of respiratory infections. Concentrated exposure can lead to pulmonary edema. Proper installation of combustion appliances and ventilation systems are the best way to reduce exposure. Always open flues when fireplaces are in use. Choose woodstoves that are certified to meet Environmental Protection Agency standards. Never leave your car idling inside the garage.

PESTICIDES

Products containing pesticides, which are categorized as semivolatile organic compounds, include insect repellents and cleaning products labeled as disinfectants. The levels of pesticides measured in homes is not due solely to the use of repellents and disinfectants, however. Other sources include contaminated soil or dust that floats in or is tracked in from outside. According to the EPA, exposure can lead to eye, nose, and throat irritation, headache, dizziness, muscular weakness, and nausea as well as damage to the central nervous and endocrine systems, the liver and kidneys, and increased risk of cancer.

Reduce exposure by carefully selecting pest-control methods and using nonchemical methods when possible. If you must use a pesticide or disinfectant, follow manufacturer's instructions and increase ventilation. Always store and dispose of pesticides according to label directions. (You can also contact your local sanitation department for guidelines.)

ASBESTOS

Asbestos is a mineral fiber (similar to fiberglass) that is easily inhaled or swallowed, and was once commonly used in the manufacture of insulation, fireproofing, and acoustical materials, some types of paints, as well as ceiling and floor tiles. Once inhaled, asbestos particles, which are too small to see, accumulate in the lungs and can cause chest and abdominal cancers and other fatal lung diseases. Symptoms do not appear until many years after exposure. As long as asbestos-containing materials are in good condition, with no threat of being disturbed, it is fine to leave them alone. But as soon as any project begins that could disturb it, or if asbestos begins peeling and crumbling from surfaces, it should be removed or sealed by a certified asbestos contractor. Consult your local health or environmental officials for proper handling and disposal procedures.

LEAD

Exposure to lead can occur in a variety of ways, such as through air, drinking water, food, contaminated soil, dust, and, most commonly, deteriorating paint. When it's inhaled or ingested in large concentrations (at or above 80 micrograms per deciliter of blood), lead can cause myriad health problems, including high blood pressure, convulsions, coma, and death. Lower levels can adversely affect the brain, central nervous system, blood cells, and kidneys. According to the EPA, the effect on children and fetuses can be severe, including delays in physical and mental development, lower IQ levels, shortened attention spans, and increased behavioral problems. Children are more likely to be exposed because they are more likely to put lead-dust-covered hands in their mouths.

Housing built before 1978 may contain lead-based paint, which, when it deteriorates and peels, contaminates indoor air. Improper removal of lead-based paint—dry scraping, sanding, or open-flame burning—produces lead dust and therefore creates extremely harmful conditions. If you suspect lead contamination in your home, test children for exposure immediately. Ask your pediatrician, state health department, or the Centers for Disease Control and Prevention (www.cdc.gov) for more information. Keep areas where children play as dust-free as possible. Clean using a solution of warm water and powdered automatic dishwasher detergent, which has a high phosphate content; most all-purpose cleaners will not remove lead in ordinary dust. Launder toys and stuffed animals regularly and make sure children wash their hands before meals, naptime, and bedtime.

Leave lead paint undisturbed if it is in good condition. Never remove lead paint yourself. Do not bring lead dust into your home; if your work or hobby involves lead, change clothes and use doormats before entering your home. Eat a diet rich in calcium and iron to counteract the side effects of lead.

LIGHTING

LIGHTING IS ONE OF the most creative and least expensive ways to make a room look more attractive. A combination of diffuse and direct light sources provides contrast and flexibility. For instance, table lamps with translucent shades cast soft, ambient light, while spotlights in the ceiling can highlight artwork and add focal points to the room's warm glow. Your choices begin with the fixtures themselves: table, floor, and wall lamps, chandeliers, and ceiling-mounted lights. Different types of bulbs, and with varying wattages, produce a palette of hues—from warm pink to pale yellow to brilliant white light. Dimmers are even more effective than low-wattage bulbs in creating warm light, which is well-suited to entertaining or enjoying intimate conversation.

ANATOMY OF AN INCANDESCENT BULB

The incandescent bulb, which is the most common type found in
households, has a simple structure with a classic design (known as an
A shape) that has changed very little since it was first invented.

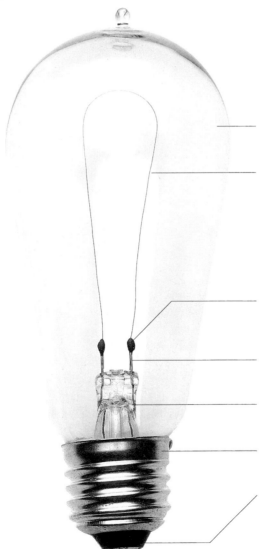

GLASS BULB
This the structural frame that keeps the gas in
and air out.

FILAMENT
Electricity runs through the filament, producing heat,
which forms the light. A filament is typically made
from tungsten because of its high melting point.

GAS
Because filaments must be heated to such a high
degree to produce light, bulbs are usually filled with
an inert gas, such as argon, to slow the degradation
of the glowing metal.

FILAMENT SUPPORTS
Many lightbulbs have these to prevent the filament
from bending due to shock, vibration, or simply its
own weight.

LEAD-IN WIRES
The filament is welded to two electrical leads
embedded in a glass post.

GLASS STEM OR MOUNT
This internal glass post is welded to the bulb and
supports the lead-in wires and filament supports.

SCREW-THREAD CONTACT
One lead-in wire is welded to a side of the interior
of the threaded base.

BASE CONTACT
The second lead-in wire is welded to the bottom of
the base; the bulb and base are soldered together.

HOW TO CHOOSE A LIGHTBULB

Selecting the right bulb is just as important as selecting the right fixture. You'll need to make decisions about wattage, color, and shape.

INCANDESCENT BULBS

These are the most common but least efficient since the majority of the energy they consume is converted into heat, not light. Although inexpensive, they are costly to use and burn for only 750 to 1,000 hours. All incandescent bulbs are full-spectrum (i.e., designed to mimic natural light). They generate light with a greater proportion of energy at the red end of the spectrum and generally cast a warm, yellowish light. Bulbs that are coated in neodymium, a metallic element, produce a whiter light. Clear glass bulbs are most effective in unshaded fixtures, such as carriage lamps; they create defined shadows, and the glitter of the glass is decorative. The standard-shaped bulb is called an A shape and has a medium screw base. Most sockets in the house take bulbs with medium bases. Bulbs for many chandeliers, and some sconces and vanity fixtures, take bulbs with small screw bases, also called a candelabra or chandelier base.

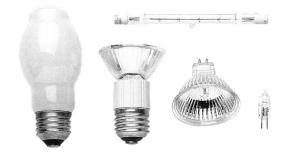

HALOGEN BULBS

These modified incandescent bulbs radiate an intense white light, produced by a chemical process between halogen gases and an electrical filament. They are more energy-efficient than incandescent bulbs, and can last as long as 3,500 hours. They also burn much hotter and must be kept out of children's reach and well away from fabrics. Halogen bulbs are available in the same shape as standard (A) incandescent bulbs with medium screw bases, as well as many other sizes and configurations.

COMPACT FLUORESCENT BULBS

These bulbs are adapted from the fluorescent tubes commonly found in offices. They give off a warm light that is meant to be similar to incandescent, but they are cooler, last up to ten times longer, and use one-third of the electricity to produce the same level of light. Inside the glass, electrodes release free electrons that strike atoms of mercury gas, causing them to give off ultraviolet radiation. This reacts with a phosphorescent coating in the glass, creating light. Bulbs are available in the same shape as standard (A) incandescent bulbs with medium screw bases, as well as many other shapes.

LIGHT-FIXTURE MAINTENANCE

☐ Dust lightbulbs (make sure they're cool first) and light fixtures weekly with a feather duster or a soft cloth as part of your regular cleaning routine.

☐ Routinely check for frayed wires as you dust, and replace them immediately.

☐ Tighten finials so lamp shades are held firmly in place; otherwise, heat from the bulb might cause the shade to burn.

LIGHTING TERMS

WATT
A unit of electrical power that denotes a bulb's rate of energy consumption. The higher the wattage, the whiter the light will be; the lower the wattage, the warmer, or more yellow, it will be.

LUMEN
The amount of light emitted by a bulb; the higher the number, the greater the output. (As a bulb ages or gets dirty, however, it won't output as much light.) A 100-watt incandescent bulb produces about 1,750 lumens.

EFFICACY
The rate at which a lightbulb is able to convert electrical power (watts) into lumens, expressed in terms of lumens per watt (LPW).

AMBIENT LIGHTING
Nonspecific illumination. Overall, general room lighting.

TASK LIGHTING
Augments ambient light for a work area or an activity.

ACCENT LIGHTING
Localized and directional lighting used to highlight an object or an area for decorative effect.

LED
Light-emitting diodes are the tiny lights found on electronic equipment, in traffic signals, and in vehicle indicator lights. They do not have filaments, like incandescent lightbulbs, but are made with semiconductors instead. Lighting manufacturers are experimenting with ways to make LED lighting available for home use (LED Christmas lights are readily available) since it requires a lot less electricity than incandescent lighting and does not emit heat.

DIMMER
A dimmer is an electrical component for varying the amount of electricity sent to a light source, thereby allowing an adjustment of light levels from dim to bright. Dimmers create a warm light, particularly when turned down. A dimmed high-wattage lightbulb radiates warmer light than a low-wattage lightbulb, because the filament doesn't burn but glows instead. Dimming also increases the life of a lightbulb.

TYPES OF LIGHTING

AMBIENT

LIVING ROOM/FAMILY ROOM
A shaded lamp placed beside the television decreases glare and reduces eyestrain.

HALLWAY/STAIRS
For safety in hallways, use several overhead lights to create bright paths. On stairs, lights should be bright enough to clearly define each of the steps.

KITCHEN
Compact fluorescent bulbs in ceiling fixtures will not add appreciably to the heat in a kitchen as other bulbs can.

BEDROOM
To avoid glare when reading in bed, turn off ceiling fixtures and use shaded lamps on nightstands instead.

DINING ROOM
Hang a chandelier 30 to 36 inches above the tabletop and supplement it with wall sconces.

TASK

COUNTERTOP
Hang pendant lights about 2 feet above countertops or mount them under cabinets so they don't shine directly into your eyes.

READING CHAIR
Put a lamp with a translucent shade beside and slightly behind a chair. Too small a shade casts distracting shadows.

MIRROR
Light emanating from above a mirror results in unattractive shadows. Frosted bulbs on both sides give soft, balanced light.

DESK
To spread light over a large area, use a pale-colored lamp shade with a wide bottom. To minimize shadows, consider placing a light on both sides of a desktop.

ACCENT

ARTWORK
Use standard incandescent bulbs that contain neodymium, which cast a bright, white light. Avoid halogen bulbs; the heat they generate can be damaging to artwork.

PLANTS
For decorative illumination of houseplants, use compact fluorescent bulbs, which stay cool.

CHINA CABINET
Miniature incandescent or halogen bulbs used inside a cabinet make glass and china sparkle.

ARCHITECTURE
Position floodlights to wash interior walls with light and to accentuate architectural details.

LIGHT-FIXTURE TERMS

CHANDELIER
A branched, often ornate ceiling fixture. The word "chandelier" derives from the Latin verb meaning "to glisten."

SCONCE
A wall fixture that supplies ambient light. Sconces are the best choice for areas where floor space is limited, such as narrow hallways, bathrooms, or bedrooms with little space for bedside tables.

PENDANT
An overhead hanging fixture, with a shade to prevent glare. Provides task or ambient light for work surfaces such as kitchen counters.

TRACK
A fixed band, generally mounted on the ceiling, that supplies a current to movable light fixtures.

COMMON LAMP SHADE SHAPES

The perfect shade should make a statement, and should be two-thirds the height of the base. Choose a dark shade for accents only. Shades lined in pink create flattering light.

ROUND BELL
Flat, silk-clad ribs emphasize the graceful concave lines of this shade, which is appropriate for formal bases.

COOLIE
This classic shade is triangular in shape, like a coolie hat. Here, the texture of the shade's pleats echoes that of the turnings on its wood base.

DRUM
The pairing of this large silver-trimmed cylinder with a smaller block base demonstrates how unorthodox proportions can work well.

HEXAGONAL EMPIRE
A classic choice where a strong simple profile is called for, the Empire narrows slightly toward the top. Most Empire shades are round.

OVAL BELL
This "fancy" shade has convex panels and is the proper choice for a formal base such as this handsome urn.

SQUARE
Square shapes with cut corners pair well with rounded bases, such as this ginger jar.

HOW TO DUST LAMP SHADES

Lamp shades are notoriously difficult to clean; washing can cause the frame to rust, glue to unstick, fabric to shrink, and colors to bleed or fade. To prolong the life of your lamp shades and keep them from getting dirty and damaged, regular maintenance is key. Here are a few general guidelines:

☐ Dust lamp shades thoroughly—inside and out—about once every two weeks to prevent dirt buildup. Use a soft brush, such as a paintbrush, or an electrostatic duster.

☐ Delicate lamp shades made of paper, silk, or antique fabrics can be dusted with a hair dryer set on a low, cool setting; move it in a downward motion, blowing dust out of crevices. Sweep out any dirt caught in the crevices or pleats with a dry, extrafine paintbrush.

☐ Sturdier shades can be cleaned with a vacuum. Select the smallest brush attachment available, put the vacuum on its lowest setting, and run the brush down the shade. If the vacuum has only one setting, expose the hole on the pipe or hose to lessen the suction.

HOW TO WASH LAMP SHADES

To remove grime from a particularly dirty shade, you can try to use water, but do so cautiously. Test the shade in an inconspicuous spot by dabbing with a damp rag; if the area dries normally, try cleaning the rest of the shade. Keep in mind, though, that some fabrics may discolor, and that too much moisture can cause pleats to lose their shape. To maintain pleated shades, try the gentlest cleaning methods first, and move on to incrementally stronger measures if necessary. If your shade is valuable to you, or if the stains are stubborn, take it to an experienced dry cleaner.

☐ Plastic-coated and laminated shades: Use a barely damp sponge to wipe away dirt. Avoid any trim and other areas with glue. For more stubborn dirt, sponge or brush on the suds of a gentle detergent, such as Woolite or Ivory Snow. Remove suds with a damp sponge, using as little water as possible; dry the shade with a soft cloth. If you try this with a fabric shade, you may cause water spots.

☐ Fabric shades: A well-made, hand-sewn fabric shade can be immersed in water for a thorough cleaning (make sure the shade is completely hand-sewn; if any glue is present, don't use the immersion cleaning method; instead, dust the shade with a duster or paintbrush). Fill a sink or tub with water and a small amount of mild dishwashing liquid. Dip the shade into the water, lift it out, and dip it again. Repeat until the water that runs off the shade is clean; refill the tub if necessary. Then rinse the shade in clean water using the same technique. You can use a blow-dryer for drying the shade; just be sure to aim it toward a white cloth first to make sure it's not blowing out any dust. Keep in mind that if the frame isn't lacquered, rustproof, or wrapped in fabric, it can rust, staining the shade. In that case, leave the cleaning to a dry cleaner experienced with lamp shades.

ENERGY-SAVING TIPS

According to the Department of Energy, lighting accounts for 20 percent of electricity costs in the United States and nearly 15 percent of a household's electricity use, with the average home having thirty light fixtures. To save energy, you can either curtail the amount of electricity consumed by the light source or decrease usage of lights. The following guidelines help also:

☐ Use natural lighting as much as possible. Keep blinds and drapes open to let in the daylight.

☐ Use task lighting instead of lighting an entire room; focus the light where you need it. Optimize it to match the difficulty of the task at hand. For example, sewing requires more light than cooking.

☐ Consider three-way lamps; they make it easier to keep lighting levels low when brighter light is not necessary. Dimmer controls can achieve the same effect for overhead lighting.

☐ Use a single higher-wattage bulb instead of several lower-wattage bulbs in table or floor lamps. Just make sure the higher-wattage bulb doesn't exceed the recommended level for the fixture.

☐ Use a motion or occupancy sensor where you may not notice if a light is left on, such as in a basement, garage, attic, or closet.

☐ Install a photocell (a device that turns a light on or off in response to natural light levels) on a porch light, or switch to low-voltage garden lights.

☐ Dust light fixtures and bulbs often. A heavy coat of dust can block up to 50 percent of the light.

☐ Keep lamps away from thermostats. The heat they produce can cause your furnace to run less than needed or your air conditioner more than needed.

☐ Turn off any lights you're not using. Get into the habit of switching lights off when you leave a room.

LIGHTING SAFETY TIPS

Most lamps do not draw dangerous levels of electrical power; nevertheless, there are a few simple safety rules to keep in mind:

☐ Use lightbulbs that are the proper wattage for your lamp or light fixture. A bulb with a wattage that is too high may overheat.

☐ Always shut off the power at the service panel when working on light fixtures. Test the fixture with a continuity tester (available at hardware stores) to be sure the power is off. Always unplug a lamp before working on it.

☐ Don't change any fixtures yourself if your house has aluminum wiring (bluish silver color), which could be dangerous. Call an electrician to replace the wire ends. Copper or copper-coated wire is safe to work on.

☐ Keep the wires protected from each other. A hot or positive wire (usually black) delivers the current to the lamp or fixture. The neutral wire (usually white) completes the circuit (electrical current must flow through a closed loop). If they touch, a short circuit occurs.

☐ Read the safety section on page 628 in Electricity before taking on any home electrical repairs.

BASIC LIGHTING REPAIRS

Anyone embarking on an electrical repair or improvement project should have a healthy respect for the potential danger, but if you follow certain commonsense rules, you can safely get the job done. The most important rule of electrical repair cannot be overemphasized: Never work on a live wire. Be sure to shut off power at the service panel, and always test for live wires at the light fixture before working on it.

BASIC TOOLS FOR LIGHTING REPAIRS

- [ ] Flashlight
- [ ] Utility knife
- [ ] Combination wire stripper and cutter
- [ ] Phillips and flathead screwdrivers
- [ ] Needle-nose pliers
- [ ] Insulating wire nuts
- [ ] Electrical tape
- [ ] Battery-powered continuity tester
- [ ] Magnetic voltage tester with needle-like probes (which tests for power even with the fixture cover in place)
- [ ] Soldering iron (optional)

A DISASSEMBLED LAMP SOCKET

SHELL   SLEEVE   BODY   TERMINAL SCREW   CAP   SET SCREW   UNDERWRITERS KNOT

A NOTE ABOUT WIRING SAFETY

Working with fixture and lamp wires is easy if you remember a few of the basics. Once the insulating cover has been stripped away, it's best to solder the exposed wires together, but if you don't solder, tightly twist the strands together clockwise. Form the wires into a hook shape before connecting them to a terminal screw. Exposed hot and neutral wires shouldn't touch; this could cause a short circuit, which is a fire hazard. (Hot wires carry the current from the service panel to the fixture; neutral wires carry it back.)

In light fixtures, wire nuts connect and insulate exposed wires. Put the corresponding fixture and circuit wires next to each other, cover the wires with the wire nut, and turn the nut clockwise. If you twist the wires together first, the wire nut may not stay in place, thus leaving the wires exposed.

HOW TO CHANGE A PLUG

Plugs that are cracked, discolored, or warm to the touch when in use should be replaced. Two types of replacement plugs are available: self-clamping plugs and screw-on plugs. Self-clamping plugs are simple to install, but they will not accept cords of every shape and size. To avoid choosing the wrong kind, you may need to ask for help at an electrical-supply store when matching a plug to a cord. Changing plugs for large appliances can be complicated, so amateurs should change only lamp, radio, clock, or other small-appliance plugs. New plugs should only be attached to undamaged or new cords.

SELF-CLAMPING PLUG
To install a self-clamping plug, cut the cord straight across (not at an angle) near the old plug (or further up if there is cord damage). Then open the shell of the new plug. Slip the wire into the shell from behind, and clamp the prongs shut; replace the shell. You don't need to strip the insulation from cords inserted into self-clamping plugs.

SCREW-ON PLUG
To install a screw-on plug, pry the insulating disk from the prongs. Strip the wire back half an inch (after you've cut off the old plug), and twist the strands together tightly. Insert the twisted wire into the plug from behind, and wrap each wire so it goes around a prong for support before it is attached to its terminal screw. Be sure that exposed wires do not touch. If one prong of the plug is larger than the other, the plug is polarized: Connect the positive wire (with a smooth casing) to the terminal screw of the smaller prong (it should be a brass screw); connect the neutral wire (with a ridged casing) to the silver terminal screw of the larger prong. Replace the insulating disk.

REPLACING A SOCKET

The first step of repairing any electrical appliance is to locate the source of the problem. If your lamp doesn't turn on, check that it is plugged into a working outlet and that the bulb is good. Then check the cord and the plug for damage. (If the cord is damaged, follow the steps on the opposite page; for more on changing a plug, turn to page 585.) If the cord and plug look good, it's time to test the socket. The photo on page 584 identifies the parts you will need to locate. The directions below are for a one-way switch only.

1. Unplug the lamp and remove the bulb. Squeeze the socket shell where the word PRESS is imprinted, and lift it off the cap (some lamps will have a small setscrew that needs to be loosened before you can lift off the shell). Lift out the insulating sleeve, loosen the terminal screws, and remove the wires.

2. Now, attach the clip of a continuity tester (available at hardware stores) to the metal part of the socket body, and touch the probe to the silver terminal screw. If the tester lights, the socket is good.

3. The socket switch might be bad, however, so test it next: Attach the clip to the brass terminal screw; with the switch in the "on" position, the tester should light when the probe is touched to the round tab inside the socket. If the socket or switch is bad, buy a new socket just like the old one.

4. To wire a new socket, or to rewire an old working socket to a new cord, first wrap the neutral wire (covered with rigid insulation) clockwise around the silver terminal screw and tighten; wrap the smooth, hot wire clockwise around the brass terminal screw and tighten. Test the connection on the socket with a continuity tester. Snap the socket body into place; replace the insulating cover and the shell.

CHANGING A CORD

If a cord is obviously damaged or worn, it's time to replace it. (You may also need to do this if the tested socket is still functional.) Here's how to change it:

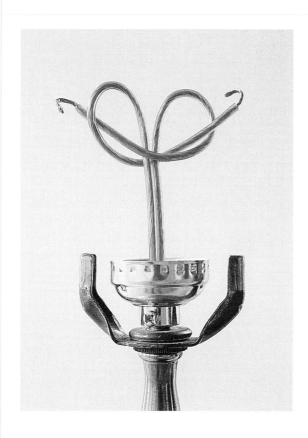

1. Unplug the lamp and remove the bulb. Disconnect the socket, if you haven't done so already, by detaching the wires from the terminal screws. Cut the old cord somewhere between the plug and the base of the lamp. Cords comprise two insulated wires, joined at the middle. Split the top 2 inches of the new cord down the middle, and use a wire stripper to strip ½ inch of insulation from each wire.

2. You may also need to separate and strip the old cord. Twist the old wires and new wires together with a Western Union splice: Make an X shape with the two exposed wires; put your finger at the tip of one of the wires and push it down, wrapping it around the other wire. Repeat with the other wire. Continue until you've made a single row of tight little coils (they should look like the coiled rope on a noose). When covered with electrical tape, a Western Union splice should be able to slip through a lamp or chandelier arm.

3. Lift off the cloth covering on the bottom of the lamp if there is one and pull carefully at the top of the old cord so the new cord will be threaded through the lamp. When the new cord is visible, disconnect the old cord and discard it. If there is enough room in the cap to hold it, tie the ends of the new wire into an underwriters' knot (see photo), which will prevent the cord from being pulled free of the socket by a tug or a jerk at the end of the cord. Proceed with the directions on the opposite page for attaching the new cord to the socket.

HOW TO REPLACE A WALL SWITCH

In some rooms, only one wall switch will control a light fixture; these are called single-pole switches. The following directions describe how to replace this kind of switch. (Switches that control more than one fixture should be left to an electrician.)

1 Shut off power at the service panel. Use a continuity tester to make sure the switch is dead. If it is, unscrew and remove the switch's cover plate.

2 Unscrew the switch's mounting screws and pull the switch out of the electrical box for access.

3 Loosen the terminal screws on the switch, which will free the wires. Remove only the wires attached to the switch's terminal screws. The wires will usually be black. These wires are "hot," meaning they carry the current when power is on at the service panel. Never disconnect the neutral wires in the electrical box; they are usually white.

4 Wrap a black wire clockwise around each terminal screw on the new switch and tighten the screws.

5 Fold the black wires into an S shape and push the switch back into the electrical box, making sure that the Off position on the switch is toward the bottom.

6 Center the switch's mounting flanges on the electrical box's mounting-screw holes; replace and tighten the screws.

7 Install the switch's cover plate. Turn on the power at the service panel, and then try out the switch.

DIMMERS

Most home builders install dimmers only in the dining room, taking a cue from restaurants that lower the lights at dusk and raise them at closing time for cleanup. But other rooms can benefit from dimmers, too. In the kitchen they can soften lights for dining or brighten them for working; in the bathroom, they can be used to create a gentle glow that enhances the luxury of taking a bath.

Retrofitting a switch with a dimmer is easy to do yourself, as long as the light it controls takes a screw-in incandescent bulb. Fluorescent and some halogen fixtures require special apparatus and installation, which is best left to an electrician. Professional expertise is essential if you want a programmable computerized system that governs every light in a room, or throughout a house, from a single panel. Unless specified during house construction or renovation, such systems require major rewiring.

☐ Never use a dimmer to control a bulb that doesn't screw into the socket, such as a fluorescent or halogen bulb with a pin base. If a dimmer is used to control a fixture with more than one bulb, the rating marked on the dimmer must be as high as the bulbs' combined wattage.

☐ Never use a dimmer to control an outlet where you might plug in a motor-driven device, such as a fan or a vacuum cleaner, because the dimmer will burn out the motor.

☐ A dimmer occasionally causes interference in stereos and cordless phones. To avoid this, ask your supplier for a dimmer switch with a good built-in noise filter, and have an electrician check that the circuit is well grounded. If interference occurs nonetheless, the electrician can add a special filter to the wiring.

☐ Another potential annoyance is lamp buzz, which results when the dimmer cycle makes bulb filaments vibrate. Try a lower-wattage bulb or one that's smaller in size.

HOW TO INSTALL A DIMMER

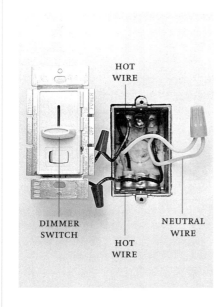

DIMMER SWITCH

HOT WIRE

HOT WIRE

NEUTRAL WIRE

1. Shut off power at the service panel.

2. Take off the wall plate; remove the screws holding the switch in the electrical box, and pull out the switch so it hangs by its wiring.

3. Dimmer switches typically come with wire leads rather than screw terminals. You need to mate these to the wires in the electrical box.

4. There are usually two hot wires (black) connected to brass screws on the switch, and sometimes there's a grounding wire (bare copper) on a green screw. Once you have identified the wires, loosen each terminal screw enough to separate the wires from the old switch. Then join them to the leads on the dimmer with plastic wire nuts (align the ends of each set of wires, cover with the nut, and twist in a clockwise motion). No bare wires should show.

5. Install the dimmer switch's cover plate. Turn on the power at the service panel, and then try out the dimmer.

CHANDELIERS

A chandelier above a dining room table should be low enough to bathe the table in light but not so low as to block anyone's line of vision. For the most pleasing effect, consider the size of the fixture and the proportions of the entire room. A good rule of thumb for a room with 8-foot ceilings is to hang the chandelier with a clearance of approximately 30 inches above the table-top. For higher ceilings, that number would increase—for a 9-foot ceiling, the distance should be about 33 inches, for example. Of course, this will vary according to personal taste; some decorators recommend an allowance of 36 inches or more. It also depends on the style of the fixture: A chandelier that is very delicate can be hung lower than a heavily constructed piece.

Chandeliers should be hung only from ceiling boxes outfitted with a ceiling-box stud, which is a short piece of threaded tubing. Ceiling boxes that will hold very heavy fixtures must also be secured to ceiling joists or a cross brace, the structural support beams inside the ceiling. Have an electrician assess a ceiling box if you're not certain that it can safely hold a fixture. Before removing a chandelier, shut off power at the appropriate breaker or fuse and test the fixture with a continuity tester. To keep the chandelier from dropping, enlist a helper to hold it while you work.

Like chandeliers, most ceiling fixtures and wall sconces that take incandescent bulbs are simple enough for the layperson to replace. Ceiling fixtures can be removed and installed like chandeliers, though they require lighter-weight mounting straps rather than heavy supports like ceiling-box studs. A sconce also requires a metal wall box; if there isn't one, you'll have to have an electrician install one.

HOW TO CLEAN CHANDELIERS

Dust chandeliers weekly with a natural-fiber duster, such as a lamb's-wool or ostrich-feather duster. The oils in these fibers create static electricity that works like a magnet to attract and hold dust. When dusting no longer restores a chandelier to pristine condition, it's time for a thorough cleaning.

☐ Turn the light fixture off; if you are using a liquid cleaner, turn off the power at the service panel.

☐ Cover the table and floor underneath the chandelier with drop cloths.

☐ Remove the bulbs when cool and wipe with a cloth dampened with a solution of 1 part white vinegar and 1 part water, taking care not to wet the metal bases. Dry with a clean soft cloth.

☐ Do not rotate the chandelier while cleaning; instead, move around it.

☐ Spray cleaning products onto a cloth rather than the chandelier.

HOW TO CLEAN A BRASS CHANDELIER

Brass is generally coated with a clear lacquer that maintains its bright finish. Wipe with a cloth dampened in a solution of warm water and mild dishwashing liquid. Follow with a clean, damp cloth to remove any soap film, then dry immediately with a soft clean cloth. Do not use window cleaners containing ammonia; they will damage that protective coating, which will invite tarnish.

HOW TO CLEAN A CRYSTAL OR GLASS CHANDELIER

Wipe the chandelier with a cotton cloth dampened with white vinegar and hot water. Rinse the cloth often and wring it out well. If crystals are removable, take them off the chandelier and hand-wash them. Line the sink with a folded towel to guard against breakage. Wash in a solution of warm water and mild dishwashing liquid and rinse in clean water. Dry the crystals with a soft, clean cloth. Rehang them, wearing cotton gloves to avoid fingerprints.

HOW TO REPAIR OR REPLACE A CHANDELIER

1. Turn off the power at the service panel.

2. Loosen the collar and lower the canopy; test the wiring with a continuity tester for live wires. The main cord (and possibly a ground wire) will run up the center of the chandelier and might be woven through the chain. (Check with an electrician before reweaving the cord; it is against code in some municipalities.) The main cord and ground wire are then fed through a threaded tube (the nipple), which is covered by the canopy; the nipple screws into an adapter called a hickey, which is connected to the ceiling-box stud by a locknut. A second locknut holds the nipple to the hickey.

3. Remove the wire nuts connecting the fixture wires to the circuit wires.

4. Being careful not to snip any wires, cut a link of the chain with chain pliers, and pry it apart. Lift out the link below the opening.

5. Gently lower the chandelier. If some of the sockets on the chandelier don't work, you can replace the nonfunctioning sockets and wiring.

6. Remove the bulb, the sleeve, and the shell; detach the wires from the terminal screws.

7. Unscrew the socket from the chandelier arm.

8. Tape new socket wires (stripped ½ inch at each end) to the old ones. Then remove the cap at the bottom of the chandelier, which gives access to the wire nuts that connect the main cord to the socket wires.

9. Remove the wire nuts, and tug gently on the disconnected socket wires. When you see the taped wires moving at the end of the chandelier arm, pull them through from the bottom, unwrap the tape, and connect the new wires to the main cord with wire nuts.

10. To mount a new chandelier or remount a repaired one, set the chain back in the broken link and twist the broken link back in place.

11. Thread the new fixture wires through the collar, canopy, nipple, and bottom half of the hickey.

12. Reconnect the wires with wire nuts: Attach the neutral cord (which will be ridged) to the white circuit wire, and the hot wire to the black circuit wire.

13. Reset the power and test the polarity of the wires with a continuity tester to be sure the proper circuit wires are connected to the proper fixture wires.

14. Install the fixture canopy, and screw the collar to the nipple.

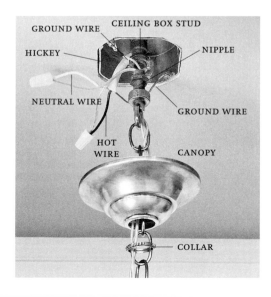

GROUND WIRE   CEILING BOX STUD

HICKEY   NIPPLE

NEUTRAL WIRE

GROUND WIRE

HOT WIRE   CANOPY

COLLAR

WATER SYSTEMS

THE PLUMBING SYSTEM through which water flows into and out of your home is essential to your health and well-being. Caring for and promptly repairing damaged pipes and leaky faucets will make life more comfortable and cut down on costly repairs later. And, perhaps most important, conserving water and monitoring the quality of your drinking water will give you and your family peace of mind.

PLUMBING

Learning the rudiments of your plumbing system and how to make a few simple repairs can save a lot of money in plumbers' bills, and possibly more money by preventing water damage.

HOW PLUMBING WORKS

Fresh water is delivered to the house via a network of pipes; the water is supplied by a city's water supplier or by a private source, such as a well.

Once the water enters the home, it's distributed to different areas and rooms via another network of pipes. Some of it is directed to the water heater, which then sends the water to pipes that run to sinks, showers, dishwashers, and washing machines.

Used water exits the house via a different network of pipes, called the drain-waste-vent (DWV) system. The water flows into the sewer system (or to a home's septic tank), aided only by the force of gravity. Venting pipes are linked to the drain and waste pipes; these pipes release noxious gases through the roof. They also maintain proper drainpipe pressure.

PLUMBING SYSTEM MAINTENANCE

These monthly tasks will keep a plumbing system running smoothly.

☐ Clean drains with a solution of vinegar, boiling water, and baking soda; turn to page 595 for instructions. This will help prevent drains from clogging, and is gentler on pipes than commercial drain cleaner, which should be avoided unless absolutely necessary.

☐ If you have sinks, tubs, showers, or toilets that are rarely used, flush or run the water to keep the pipes in good working order.

☐ Once a month, inspect the network of water pipes in the basement, attic, or crawl space for any signs of leaks.

PLUMBING FIRST-AID KIT

The most common plumbing problems can be fixed with a few simple tools and supplies. Assembling a kit of necessary items will make it easier to do repairs as they arise.

- ☐ Funnel-cup plunger with at least a 6-inch-diameter cup
- ☐ Pipe wrench: an adjustable wrench used to turn pipes and pipe fittings
- ☐ Standard adjustable 10- to 12-inch wrench
- ☐ Basin wrench: a long tool used for setting up faucets and tightening fittings
- ☐ Spud wrench: the tool used for taking out a spud nut, which secures the flush valve on a toilet

- ☐ Phillips and flathead screwdrivers
- ☐ Pair of tongue-and-groove pliers: a tool with angled teeth for gripping round, square, hexagonal, and other shapes of hardware
- ☐ Flexible drain auger
- ☐ Assorted washers and O-rings
- ☐ Thin rubber sheeting
- ☐ Steel hose clamps: tools that attach hoses to fittings
- ☐ Pipe cutter

- ☐ Teflon tape: a nonadhesive tape used to create a water-tight seal when coupling two pipes
- ☐ Masking tape
- ☐ Inspection mirror: a small mirror on a handle, for seeing around corners when working in small spaces
- ☐ Small, powerful flashlight
- ☐ Rubber gloves
- ☐ Utility knife

HOW TO PATCH A LEAKY PIPE

The water in a plumbing system is pressurized; if the pipes are weak, they can develop pinholes. If a leak occurs, it can be patched temporarily until the section of pipe is replaced (contact a plumber to replace it after it's patched).

1. With Teflon tape, wrap the pipe tightly.

2. Cut a piece of rubber sheeting, long enough to wrap around the pipe once.

3. Secure the sheeting around the taped leak with a steel hose clamp: Slip the clamp over the rubber sheeting, then screw the clamp tightly shut.

HOW TO PLUNGE A DRAIN

1. If there is more than an inch of water in a sink, first remove it with a cup and pour it into a bucket. If you have a double-bowl sink, plug one drain with a wet rag or sponge before plunging the other drain—otherwise, water will shoot out of the second drain. Plug the overflow hole if there is one.

2. Fit the funnel cup of the plunger over the drain. Make sure the seal is tight, and then plunge vertically (there's no need to do it rapidly).

3. The plunger will push air and water down into the drain, and then pull water back up with it as you plunge, dislodging the blockage. Don't quit if the results aren't immediate—it may take up to ten minutes to loosen the blockage.

A NOTE ABOUT SHUT-OFF VALVES

From the moment water enters a house, it can be controlled via a series of shut-off valves. Should your pipes burst, for instance, you can stop some of the damage if you turn off the water supply to the house. (All adults living in the house should know how to do this.) A house's main shut-off valve is a wheel-like valve next to the water meter. To stop the flow, turn the valve clockwise; this should be true for every water valve, anywhere in the house. Other useful shut-off valves are adjacent to or under faucets and fixtures. These local shut-off valves allow repair without disrupting the entire household.

HOW TO CLEAN A DRAIN

A stopped or slow drain may not unclog with plunging alone, especially in a tub or shower where the clog may be solid (the culprit may be matted hair that needs to be broken apart). If the drain has a trip plate—a built-in closing mechanism that's usually a circular piece of metal with a lever—unscrew the plate, pull out the stem, and clear the clog that may be hanging from it. If, instead, the drain has a strainer, pull it out, or unscrew it to clean beneath it. Hair is often caught just below, before it disappears into the bend of the pipe.

HOW TO USE AN AUGER

If plunging or cleaning the drain doesn't work, try a drain auger (also called a snake).

1. Feed the auger down into the drain slowly, twisting it as you go to follow the bend of the drainpipe.

2. Once you hit the blockage, push through it steadily and pull the auger back and forth to loosen the block and expand the hole inside.

3. When the blockage is broken, plunging should clear the rest of it.

HOW TO CLEAR A CLOGGED TRAP

The problem with a kitchen or bathroom sink may be a clogged trap, a common site for blockages and where you might find the ring or demitasse spoon you dropped down the drain. The trap is the U-shaped pipe under the sink. Because of its shape, the trap stays filled with water whether the sink is in use or not to prevent sewer gases in the venting pipes from reentering the house. It also traps anything solid that has gone down the drain accidentally. A slip nut at each end of the trap allows easy removal for periodic cleaning. To clear it:

1. Turn off the sink's water supply using the shutoff valve and place a bucket under the trap.

2. Loosen the nuts with a pipe wrench and remove and empty the trap, running a bottlebrush through it to clean the walls.

3. Replace the trap and replace the nuts.

FAUCETS

A compression faucet, the most common type of faucet, develops drips because of problems with its washer. Other, newer types of faucets—disk, ball, and cartridge—have different assemblies that are washerless. Although they develop leaks less often, when they do, the culprit is likely the rubber O-ring or the cartridge, but it can sometimes be another faucet part.

Before repairing a leaky faucet, always line the sink with a towel to protect it, cover the drain so you don't lose any nuts or bolts, and set up a place for laying out disassembled faucet parts. Always lay disassembled parts out carefully in linear sequence, to provide yourself with a diagram for reassembly.

TYPES OF FAUCETS

COMPRESSION

Typically found in older homes, compression faucets are the most affordable but also the most likely to leak and require repairs. The handles for hot and cold are separate, and in order to stop the water flow, you need to screw down, or compress, the handle to close it off. Compression faucets rely on a rubber washer, which opens or closes the valve seat by pressing against it. Over time, as the washer continues to grind against the valve seat, it starts to wear away and will eventually need to be replaced.

BALL

Introduced as the first washerless faucet, a ball faucet is characterized by a ball-shaped cap above the base of the spout, with a single handle on top. Beneath the rounded cap, a slotted plastic or metal ball with slots or chambers controls water flow and temperature. Repairs are more common for this faucet than for other washerless types, most often because of worn inlet seals or O-rings.

CARTRIDGE

These faucets may have one or two handles, and often look like other types. They rely on a hollow plastic or metal stem cartridge in order to function. On a single-handle model, the cartridge moves up and down to control water flow and left or right to monitor temperature. Two-handled cartridge faucets are nearly indistinguishable from compression types, but the difference is that you don't have to tighten the handles to cut off the water flow; instead, a cartridge faucet in the closed position will turn off smoothly, without requiring any additional pressure to the handle.

DISK

These modern faucets are often installed in new and recently remodeled homes, and feature a single handle placed over a wide cylindrical cartridge. Two ceramic disks—one that's fixed in place, and another that moves—permit or block the flow of water. These types of faucets need repairs less often than other types.

HOW TO FIX A COMPRESSION FAUCET

As you twist a faucet handle to turn off water, a stem is lowered in a screwlike motion into what's called a valve seat. A small rubber washer completes the watertight seal. If the washer is old or disintegrating, the faucet will leak when closed, or the washer will wobble loosely when the faucet is on, creating irregular water pressure and banging pipes. To replace the washer:

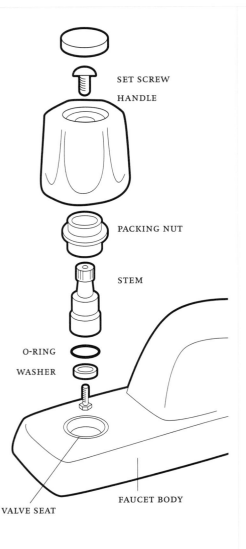

SET SCREW

HANDLE

PACKING NUT

STEM

O-RING

WASHER

VALVE SEAT

FAUCET BODY

1. Turn off the water supply.

2. Remove the handle with a screwdriver or remove the handle set screw and lift off the handle, then use pliers or an adjustable wrench to loosen the faucet's large bonnet or packing nut (which tightens the thread of the faucet stem into the valve seat) in a counterclockwise motion. If the packing nut is chrome or brass-plated, wrap the teeth of the pliers with masking tape to prevent scratches.

3. Hold the faucet body securely to avoid wrenching it loose.

4. With the nut loosened, unscrew the stem from the valve seat. At the end of the stem is the washer, secured by a screw. Remove the screw and the washer, and refit the stem with a new washer from a kit of assorted-size washers, available at hardware stores.

5. Before putting back the stem, you may want to inspect the valve seat for wear. If it's chipped, replace it with a new one. Screw the stem back into the seat, and retighten the packing nut.

HOW TO FIX A BALL FAUCET

A ball faucet leak could be the result of a loose adjusting ring or worn inlet seals, springs, or O-rings, or a worn ball or cam. You can buy a ball-faucet replacement kit at a hardware store and simply replace all of the parts, or inspect the parts after disassembling the faucet and replace only the worn pieces.

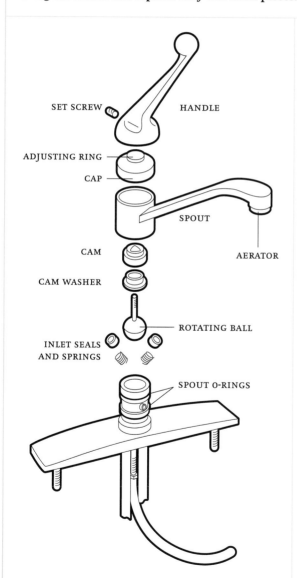

SET SCREW   HANDLE

ADJUSTING RING

CAP

SPOUT

CAM

AERATOR

CAM WASHER

ROTATING BALL

INLET SEALS
AND SPRINGS

SPOUT O-RINGS

1. Turn off the faucet's water supply.

2. With a wrench, unscrew the faucet handle or remove the handle set screw and lift off the handle. If the handle (as opposed to the spout) has been leaking, just tighten the adjusting ring. Otherwise, continue on to the next step.

3. With pliers, take off the adjusting ring and cap.

4. Remove the cam, cam washer, and rotating ball.

5. With needle-nose pliers, remove inlet seals and springs.

6. Cut off the O-rings with a utility knife.

7. Inspect what's worn and replace accordingly, or replace all parts using pieces from a replacement kit.

8. Reassemble the faucet parts.

HOW TO FIX A CARTRIDGE FAUCET

A leaking cartridge faucet is the result of a worn cartridge or O-rings. Buy replacement parts made by the faucet's manufacturer, available at a faucet dealer, when possible.

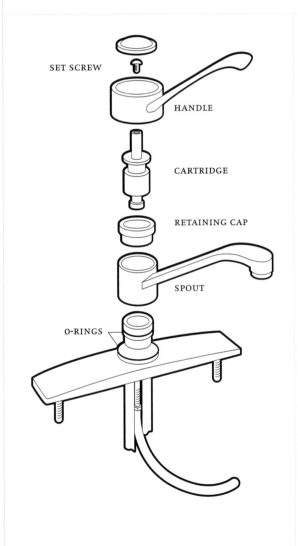

SET SCREW

HANDLE

CARTRIDGE

RETAINING CAP

SPOUT

O-RINGS

1. Turn off the water supply to the faucet.

2. Unscrew the handle, and remove the cartridge.

3. Remove the retaining cap, if it has one, with needle-nose pliers.

4. Remove the spout.

5. With a utility knife, cut off O-rings.

6. Replace the O-rings with new ones; if they're not worn, you may need to replace the cartridge. Certain brands of faucets, such as those made by Moen, require a special tool, called a cartridge remover, to take out the cartridge; the tool is available from a faucet dealer.

7. Reassemble the faucet parts.

HOW TO FIX A DISK FAUCET

This kind of faucet rarely leaks, but if it does, the culprit
is probably a worn cartridge or seals.

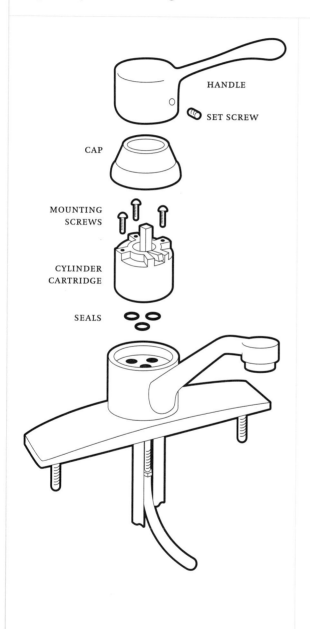

HANDLE

SET SCREW

CAP

MOUNTING
SCREWS

CYLINDER
CARTRIDGE

SEALS

1. Turn off the water supply to the faucet.

2. Remove the set screw from the side of the handle.

3. Unscrew the cylinder.

4. With a screwdriver, lift out the seals from the cylinder. If they are damaged, replace them. If the cylinder is badly worn, replace it; otherwise, clean it with 1 part white vinegar and 1 part water, rinse, and let dry.

5. Reassemble the faucet.

TOILETS

The apparatus inside a toilet tank is simple: The flush handle is connected to a rulerlike trip lever inside the tank, which has a chain on the end of it. The chain descends to either a ball or flapper-style stopper valve, which opens when the handle is pressed, emptying the water in the tank into the bowl and flushing the toilet.

HOW TO FIX COMMON TOILET PROBLEMS

STICKING HANDLE
If the toilet handle sticks or is loose, remove the tank cover and clean the mounting nut, which is located on the inside behind the handle.

FLUSHING PROBLEMS
If the toilet won't flush, and the flush handle doesn't resist slightly when you push on it, the chain between the trip lever and the stopper valve may be disconnected. Rehook it.

OVERFLOW
If the toilet bowl threatens to overflow, remove the tank lid and hold the flapper down on the valve seat to prevent the water in the tank from flowing into the bowl; then turn off the water supply. Most likely, you have a drainage problem, which should be corrected with a plunger or an auger.

HOW TO FIX A CONSTANTLY RUNNING TOILET

If the toilet runs or sweats, the stopper may not be maintaining a tight seal. This can result when the chain gets caught up on the hook or when the seal wears out. Another cause of a constantly running toilet is when the float ball touches the side of the tank. Here's how to fix these problems:

MAINTAINING A TIGHT SEAL
☐ Turn off the toilet's water supply, and then flush the toilet to drain the tank.

☐ Most flapper-style stoppers are attached with hooks to the bottom of the overflow tube, which is a pipe that extends from the bottom to the top of the tank. Detach the flapper and replace it; when you match it at the hardware store, buy two so you'll have a spare.

☐ While the flapper is off, clean the valve's seat with fine steel wool to further secure the seal.

FIXING A FLOAT BALL
☐ Bend the float rod to reposition the float away from the side of the tank.

☐ Lift the float rod above the water level. If the water stops running, gently bend the rod down until the float is at rest (when the water level is about ½ inch below the top of the overflow pipe).

☐ Also check to see if the float ball is leaking. If more than half the float is underwater, it may have a puncture.

☐ If you think the float ball has a leak, turn the water off at the shutoff valve below the tank and flush the toilet to empty the tank.

☐ Unscrew the float and shake it. If you hear water inside, replace it.

WATER HEATERS

Usually located in the basement or garage, water heaters are tanks in which water is heated using either gas or electricity. Both types operate using similar principles, except a gas heater has a burner with a flame and an electric water heater has electric heating elements. In general, set the thermostat between 120°F and 140°F. (Keep it at 120°F if you have small children in your household to prevent accidental scalding.)

Annually, contact a plumber to inspect the water heater. The professional should check the thermostat operation; inspect the flow of combustion and ventilation air; examine the pilot light and clean the burner parts on a gas water heater; drain off water; inspect the anode rod; and check the pressure-relief valve.

WHAT TO DO IF THERE'S NOT ENOUGH HOT WATER

☐ You may not be allowing cold water enough time to reheat. Using hot water in several appliances simultaneously—dishwasher, washing machine, and shower—can use up all of the hot water in the tank before it has time to reheat. Taking extra-long showers may also be the culprit.

☐ Your water heater may be too small for your household. If one long shower or running two appliances at the same time exhausts the supply, it's likely that your tank is too small. Investigate replacing it with a larger one; consult a plumber about sizing and installation.

☐ The water heater's dip tube, a plastic pipe inside the tank that runs vertically and delivers cold water to the bottom of the tank, may be cracked or broken. Cold water may be mixing with heated water in the upper portion of the tank. A plumber can replace it, or the water heater may need to be replaced.

WHAT TO DO IF THERE'S NO HOT WATER

☐ The thermostat may not be set high enough. It should be at least at 120°F. To determine if it's defective, turn it up to the highest setting and then turn on the hot water on a faucet; if the burner doesn't ignite or the electric heating elements don't turn on, contact a plumber.

☐ If you have a gas water heater, the pilot light may have gone out. To check, remove the metal cover at the bottom of the heater. If the pilot light is out, follow the instructions on the side of the tank to relight it. If you have an electric water heater, check the fuse or circuit breaker to make sure the electricity is on. If neither the pilot light nor the electricity is malfunctioning, call a plumber.

☐ If there is a gas smell near the heater, turn the gas valve, which is on the side of the tank, to Off. Ventilate the area. If the smell does not go away, leave the house and call the utility company from a neighbor's house or from your cell phone; it's likely that you have a gas leak.

SEPTIC SYSTEMS

In areas not serviced by municipal sewers—often rural or remote locales—septic tanks are a common means of storing and partially treating household sewage. They are generally buried in your yard. Liquid and solid wastes flow into the tank, where the solids sink to the bottom and eventually decompose with the aid of anaerobic bacteria and enzymes. The result is additional liquid waste and a quantity of nondecomposed solid matter called sludge. The liquid then overflows into a distribution box, from which it flows to rows of perforated pipes in a drainage field of gravel and sand. Some of the liquid evaporates and the rest leaches into the ground. The sludge remains in the tank and must be pumped out periodically.

SEPTIC-SYSTEM MAINTENANCE

Learning how to take care of a septic tank before trouble arises—what to put into it, and what not to, and how often to have it cleaned out—will keep your water flowing smoothly and cut down on repair bills. In addition, maintaining your septic system can prevent damage to the environment. Failed septic systems are a significant source of water pollution and contribute to a process called eutrophication, in which oxygen levels in water go down, causing fish to die.

USE COMMON SENSE

Harsh chemicals, acids, and certain household products will kill the anaerobic bacteria in a septic tank or clog the system. These include strong alkaline drain cleaners, paint thinners and strippers, bug spray, coffee grounds, paper goods other than white toilet tissue, grease, motor oil, gasoline, and paint. Contact your local sanitation or waste-management office for information about how to dispose of these items.

USE LESS WATER

A sudden influx of wastewater may temporarily overwhelm the system, so use water-saving toilets and appliances, spread laundry over a week, minimize the amount of water used for bathing and dishwashing, and fix all faucet and toilet leaks immediately.

CLEAN THE TANK REGULARLY

Have a licensed septic-service professional (look for one in the Yellow Pages under "Septic Tanks") inspect and remove sludge. The tank should be pumped out before it reaches the level of the outflow pipe, or it will cause incoming untreated waste to flow directly into the drainage field, ruining the gravel bed. The frequency depends on the number of people in your household as well as on the capacity of the tank; ask a septic-service professional how often you should clean yours. Keep a record of your septic-system maintenance so you can anticipate your next cleaning.

DON'T ADD MICROBES

Putting extra bacteria, yeast, or enzymes (sold at hardware stores) in septic tanks in an effort to diminish the total volume of solids (and thus reduce the frequency of pumping) is unnecessary and potentially harmful. The microbes already in your tank will degrade the organic matter. Additions will likely clog the drainfield. Pumping is far less costly than rehabilitating a drainfield. And when a septic tank is pumped, the trace of waste residue in the tank is sufficient to seed a new microbe colony.

DON'T ADD PRESSURE

Never allow a car to drive or park over the tank; the weight can cause it to cave in.

SIGNS OF SEPTIC-SYSTEM FAILURE

If you become aware of any of the occurrences noted below, call a septic-tank service company immediately, as all are indications of tank failure.

☐ Odors and surfacing sewage

☐ Wet spots or lush vegetation in the drain-field area

☐ Slow-draining sinks or toilets that aren't otherwise clogged

☐ Plumbing backups

☐ Gurgling sounds in the plumbing system

WATER CONSERVATION

Increasingly, water is in short supply in many areas of the world. In the twentieth century, water consumption grew tenfold, and in many parts of the United States—particularly arid regions such as the Southwest and California—water reserves have become critically low. It's just plain smart to conserve water, and there are easy ways to use less—and cut down on your water bill in the process. Here are a few pointers about how you can conserve water throughout the house—both inside and out.

EASY WAYS TO CONSERVE

☐ Run the dishwasher and clothes washer only with full loads, and use the Economy setting on the dishwasher if it has one.

☐ Don't let the faucet run unnecessarily such as while brushing your teeth or shaving.

☐ Take showers instead of baths, and take shorter showers. A five-minute shower uses about 20 gallons of water whereas a bath uses about 50.

LONG-TERM WAYS TO CONSERVE

☐ Toilets account for 40 percent of residential water use in the United States, so purchase low-flow toilets, which use 1.6 gallons of water per flush. Toilets installed before 1994 consume about 3.5 to 5 gallons of water per flush.

☐ Install low-flow showerheads (showers account for 30 percent of residential water use), which use 2.5 gallons of water per minute. Showerheads installed before 1994 use 4.5 gallons per minute.

☐ Choose water softeners wisely. In particular, reverse-osmosis softeners use extravagant amounts of water: 3 to 9 gallons of water are required to produce 1 gallon of purified water.

☐ Consider Xeriscaping, a landscape method that incorporates drought-tolerant plants and trees, and rocks, rather than grass, which requires frequent watering.

UNDERSTANDING YOUR HOME'S COMPLEXITIES IS ESSENTIAL TO LIVING WELL AND EASILY. BEING ORGANIZED AND KNOWING HOW TO IDENTIFY A TECHNICAL PROBLEM AND WHO TO CALL IN AN EMERGENCY ARE ALL PART OF RUNNING AN EFFICIENT HOME.

IN THE BASEMENT AT BEDFORD

HARD WATER

It's estimated that about 80 percent of U.S. households have hard water. The hardness or softness of your water supply depends on where you live: As water flows underground past rock and materials, it picks up concentrations of minerals along the way. Hard water carries high levels of calcium, magnesium, and iron, while soft water contains low levels of these substances.

HARD WATER VS. SOFT WATER

HARD WATER

Pros In general, hard water tends to taste better than soft (although very hard water can taste metallic), and is also better for you because it contains healthful minerals.

Cons Hard water can create a host of cleaning and appliance problems. Its minerals turn into scale, which is a hardened coating that clogs pipes and can shorten the life of appliances, including washing machines, dishwashers, and water heaters, because scale builds up on heating elements. Scale can also substantially raise repair bills. Hard water can reduce the cleansing power of detergents, dull clothes, and cause them to wear out more quickly. In addition, when minerals mix with soap, they create a scummy residue in bathtubs and showers that can be difficult to remove.

SOFT WATER

Pros Soft water is generally gentler on skin, hair, clothes, and appliances.

Cons It's not as good for you to drink as hard water because of its higher sodium content. Some people think soft water leaves a slimy residue on their skin, although the opposite is true—hard water leaves residue, but most people are so used to the feel of it that the lack of residue when washing with soft water makes skin feel slippery in comparison.

HOW TO TEST WATER HARDNESS

You can obtain a water-quality report from your public water supplier that will indicate how hard your water is, which will help you determine whether or not you should treat it. If your water is supplied privately, you will need to send a sample to a testing laboratory (turn to page 609 for more details).

Water hardness is usually expressed in grains (of mineral) per gallon (GPG); sometimes, it's measured in parts per million (PPM). If the results come back in PPM, you can determine the GPG by dividing the PPM by 17.1.

RATINGS

3 to 3.5 GPG:
Soft to moderately soft

3.6 to 7 GPG:
Moderate

7.1 to 10.4:
Hard

10.5 and above:
Very hard

IF YOU HAVE HARD WATER

If your GPG is below 7, you probably don't need to use water softeners: Most laundry detergents and soaps are now formulated to accommodate moderate to hard water. However, if you've been having problems with dingy-looking clothing, spots on glasses, and dull-looking hair, add a softener, such as borax (available in the laundry aisle at the grocery store) to the washing machine or dishwasher, and a hard-water filter to your showerhead. Some dishwashers are now sold with built-in water softeners.

If your water is above the 10.5 GPG range, consider a whole-house mechanical water softener. Most softeners are ion-exchange units; they are installed as part of your plumbing system and replace the minerals with sodium salts. Ion-exchange units can cost from several hundred dollars to more than a thousand (turn to page 610 for more information). Contact a plumber for prices and installation information. If you do install a mechanical softener, you will also need to install a filter for your drinking water to remove the sodium. You will need to water plants with filtered water, too, as the sodium content in soft water will hamper growth.

WATER QUALITY

Eighty-five percent of Americans draw their tap water from municipal water systems. The 55,000 municipalities that provide this service are overseen by the Environmental Protection Agency (EPA), which determines safe levels of various contaminants and also requires that the water authorities provide detailed annual reports on the quality of their water to consumers. Bottled water must also adhere to these EPA standards. If your water comes from a well, a spring, or a cistern, as it does for the remaining 15 percent of the population, you'll have to gauge the quality of your water yourself on a regular basis.

All tap water contains at least some dissolved contaminants, including materials picked up from the surfaces that it comes in contact with during its long journey to your tap. Contaminants, though, aren't necessarily dangerous. While there are potentially millions of contaminants in water, there are only a few dozen that pose any real risk—and most of these are present in such low levels that they are not dangerous. A few, including lead, pose serious health risks when they are present at high levels.

If you think that your water may be unhealthy, start by asking your public water supplier for a water-quality report. Water departments are required to provide property owners with Consumer Confidence Reports (CCR); the Environmental Protection Agency can help you find yours online (log on to epa.gov/safewater/dwinfo/index.html). Some contaminants,

HOW TO TEST FOR LEAD

Two signs indicate lead pipes: pipes that are a dull gray and scratch easily, and reddish or rust-colored water. Houses built before 1930 are more likely than newer homes to have lead pipes. If you suspect you have lead pipes, send a water sample to a laboratory to have it tested (turn to page 609 for more information). If you do have lead pipes, the best solution is to replace them, although this is very expensive. A plumber can assess the job and offer an estimate. Otherwise, filter drinking water (turn to page 610 for more information).

including many types of pesticides, aren't governed by EPA regulations and therefore won't appear in your CCR, however. Others, like lead, may originate in your home. If you want to know the levels of unregulated contaminants (or if you draw your water from a private source), send a water sample to a lab. (See the opposite page for information.) If you're worried about lead, first examine your pipes (see the previous page for more information) and then consider a laboratory test.

HOW TO READ A CONSUMER CONFIDENCE REPORT

The Consumer Confidence Report supplied by your water provider can be difficult to understand, but for help you can always call your water supplier for clarification or consult the brochure "Making Sense of Drinking Water 'Right to Know' Reports," released by the Campaign for Safe and Affordable Drinking Water (log on to safe-drinking-water.org/rtk.html#make). The information below will help you grasp the basics.

☐ For each contaminant level noted on the CCR, your supplier should provide the EPA's legally binding "maximum contaminant level" (MCL). The CCR should also tell you how much of the contaminant was detected on average, and the range of detected levels. In a few cases, rather than listing levels, the report will note what treatment technique was applied to the problem.

☐ If any contaminant exceeded the MCL, the report should explain the likely source of the contamination, the potential health effects, and the steps the supplier took to fix the problem.

☐ In some cases, you may see that contaminants exceeded EPA standards, but there was no violation. For certain contaminants, such as disinfection by-products, the average of many samples determines whether a violation has occurred. That could mean, for instance, that the contaminant was greater than the standard in some parts of the water system but not others, or that at certain times of year you were exposed to high levels but your average annual exposure was within EPA limits.

TYPES OF COMMON WATER CONTAMINANTS

ARSENIC
Widely recognized as a carcinogen, arsenic occurs naturally in rock and soil. It's expensive to remove from drinking water, whether tap or bottled. The EPA allows 50 parts per billion.

NITRATES
These occur naturally, but are most often the result of fertilizers and sewage migrating into ground water. Nitrates are especially dangerous for children; high levels can reduce oxygen to vital tissues. The EPA regulates the presence of nitrates.

DISINFECTION BY-PRODUCTS (DBP)
Water suppliers often use chlorine to kill disease-causing bugs. Unfortunately, the chlorination process releases by-products that have been linked to cancers in humans. Another common method of disinfection, ozonation, also creates by-products, including formaldehyde and acetaldehyde, that have been linked to cancer. Only some DBPs are regulated by the EPA.

LEAD
Several public-water distribution systems in the United States still have some lead components, and many houses built before 1930 have lead plumbing. Lead can cause anemia, high blood pressure, and kidney problems. It's particularly dangerous for young children because it interferes with brain development. Even though it's EPA regulated, lead can leach into water from lead pipes after it has entered a home; turn to pages 575 and 607 for details.

PATHOGENS
Bacteria, viruses, and other nasty bugs can cause disease and illness. Among the primary culprits in water are microorganisms such as cryptosporidium, giardia, and certain strains of *E. coli*. The EPA regulates the presence of microorganisms.

PESTICIDES AND OTHER HORMONE DISRUPTORS
Various pesticides and chemicals such as polychlorinated biphenyls (PCBs)—mixtures of chlorinated compounds formerly used as coolants and lubricants—can mimic hormones, confusing the body's normal hormone signals. Many pesticides have also been linked to cancer and nervous-system problems. The EPA regulates the presence of these substances.

RADON
A naturally occurring radioactive gas that can leach into drinking water from the surrounding soil and rocks, radon increases the risk of certain cancers. The EPA regulates the presence of radon.

OBTAINING A PRIVATE WATER REPORT

If your water comes from a well or private supplier, or if you're on a public system but want a more comprehensive analysis, you can have your water analyzed. For a list of certified labs nearby, call your town's or state's public health department. The lab will send you a sample bottle and instructions for collecting the water. The cost can be anywhere from $15 to hundreds of dollars, depending on how many contaminants you test for. To determine which tests to pursue, start by asking the lab which contaminants other testers have found in your area. Then contact local environmental advocacy groups to see whether there have been any reported problems with contaminants. If you live in a rural area, nitrates from fertilizers and pesticides may be likely suspects.

TYPES OF WATER TREATMENT

Method	How it works	What it removes	
ACTIVATED CARBON (CHARCOAL) FILTER	The carbon attracts and absorbs and traps impurities. This is an inexpensive, easy-to-maintain option.	Most organic chemicals, including some pesticides and disinfection by-products. It can also absorb lead and the pathogen cryptosporidium.	
BOILING	Contaminants are killed by boiling.	Many pathogens.	
DISTILLATION	Water is boiled and the steam, which becomes liquid, is collected. Heavy inorganic compounds, such as mineral salts, are left behind.	Many pathogens, including arsenic and *E. coli*.	
ION EXCHANGE	Exchanges the ions in the unit with the ions in the water. Often referred to as a water softener.	The minerals that make water hard, such as calcium and magnesium (which are not unhealthy—but they do leave hard-to-clean deposits on appliances, tubs, and sinks). Some ion exchange units will remove radon.	
REVERSE OSMOSIS	This purifying system uses a semipermeable membrane that blocks contaminants but allows water to pass.	The widest swath of contaminants, including organic compounds as well as inorganic chemicals such as nitrates and sodium. Also removes arsenic and pathogens.	

Installation	Special considerations
Three types are available: pour through, faucet mounted, and high volume, which is installed under the sink. For a large family an under-the-sink filter would be most convenient, while a pour-through pitcher would work well for one or two people. All three types can be installed without a plumber; the manufacturer will provide instructions.	Carbon filters must be replaced periodically. If you're treating cryptosporidium, you'll need a carbon filter with an absolute pore size of 1 micron or less (look for the word "absolute" on the label).
N/A	Evaporation can raise the concentration of the contaminants that are left behind—nitrates, lead, and pesticides. If the nitrate levels in your water are high, don't give infants or children boiled water.
Underneath the sink; the manufacturer provides instructions.	Some organic contaminants, such as pesticides, vaporize and recondense into the distilled water. Also, because it removes minerals, distilled water may not be recommended for drinking.
A whole-house system that requires professional installation. Look in the Yellow Pages under "Water Softening Equipment." Typically, a valve connects the unit to the water main.	These units need to be periodically recharged with salt, following the manufacturer's instructions.
The manufacturer will provide instructions for installation, which involves connecting the filter to the sink; if you're not comfortable doing plumbing work, have a plumber install this system. The device usually includes a particle filter, a membrane unit, a water-storage container, and a carbon absorption postfilter.	Although reverse osmosis is often touted as the most effective method for removing pathogens, such systems are expensive and can waste two to four times as much water as they filter, which is a burden on the environment. They also use a lot of electricity.

HOW TO CHOOSE A WATER FILTER

The method of water treatment you choose depends on how you want to change your water—whether you simply want to remove odors and improve the taste, or to eliminate contaminants, or both. Read the fine print on the label before buying a filter. Each treatment removes a different range of contaminants. Not all filters remove lead, for instance. Make sure any filter you choose meets the standards of the American National Standards Institute and National Sanitation Foundation (ANSI/NSF), an independent testing organization.

☐ Jug filters, the pitchers or small tanks that you fill from the tap, cost about $20 and are the most common and affordable option. Make sure that you replace the filter according to the manufacturer's instructions—a filter that's been used too long can release the contaminants it has accumulated back into the water.

☐ Inline filtering systems are more convenient than jug filters and treat larger volumes of water, but they're more expensive. Some connect directly to the faucet; others connect to supply lines under the sink. Refrigerators that dispense water may also have built-in filters. If you plan to buy a filter that connects to supply lines, avoid those with brass components. The Center for Environmental Health discovered that brass alloys in a number of under-the-sink filters sold in California leached lead into the water; though the manufacturers have since agreed to reformulate their filters, it's still advisable to choose filters without brass parts.

☐ New water-filtration technologies are evolving all the time. The following three organizations, which test and certify water filters, along with the information you have from your utility's test results, will guide you to the right filter for your home: NSF International, Underwriters Laboratories (UL), and the Water Quality Association. These organizations all use standards developed by the NSF.

MINIMIZING LEAD IN DRINKING WATER

There are a number of water-filtration methods, but these two strategies can minimize lead coming out of the tap if you have lead pipes.

☐ Run the water for thirty to sixty seconds before drinking or cooking with it, since lead accumulates in water as it stands in your pipes. Run the water a bit longer than that in the morning.

☐ Lead levels are higher in hot water than in cold, so don't drink, cook, or make baby formula with hot tap water.

BOTTLED WATER

Americans spend billions of dollars per year on bottled water, but what they're drinking may not be any safer or better regulated than tap water. Follow these tips to choose a safe bottled water.

☐ Check affiliations. Look for manufacturers that belong to the International Bottled Water Association (IBWA), which requires its members to test water daily and to have bottling plants inspected annually by an independent party. You can find a listing of IBWA member companies on the group's website (www.bottledwater.org).

☐ Scrutinize labels. Labels will reveal the water's source. When a bottled water fails to meet federal regulations, the label must also state that it contains "excessive levels" of the contaminant in question.

☐ Assess packaging. Water in glass bottles or clear plastic bottles made from polyethylene terephthalate (which will be stamped with the numeral 1 on the underside) tastes better than water in milky white jugs made from high-density polyethylene (which will be stamped on the underside with the numeral 2). Avoid polycarbonate, the strong rigid plastic used in five-gallon water bottles. It can leach bisphenol-A, a potential carcinogen and hormone disruptor (polycarbonate bottles will be imprinted with the numeral 7).

BOTTLED-WATER TERMINOLOGY

ARTESIAN WATER
Underground pressure pushes water to the surface once a well is drilled, resulting in water similar to spring water in taste and content. Brands include Avita and Fiji.

MINERAL WATER
Contains at least 250 parts per million of naturally occurring minerals such as calcium, magnesium, sodium, potassium, silica, and bicarbonates. Like spring water, it also comes from an underground source and flows naturally to the earth's surface. Perrier and Vittel are examples.

PURIFIED DRINKING WATER
This term describes bottled water that has been treated by distillation, deionization, or reverse osmosis. The source of the water doesn't need to be named, and it may even be municipal tap water, but the label must say how the water was purified. Common brands include Aquafina and Dasani.

SPRING WATER
Comes from an underground source and flows naturally to the earth's surface. Bottlers can add carbon dioxide to make it bubbly. Brands include Crystal Geyser, Dannon, Evian, Poland Spring, and Trinity.

WELL WATER
Underground water reserves that are pumped to the surface. Typically, bottled well water is sold locally or regionally.

HEATING AND COOLING

THE INVENTION OF CENTRAL HEAT and air conditioning has made our lives much more comfortable. But a constant, even flow of heat or air conditioning isn't something to take for granted. Understanding the rudiments of your system, including familiarizing yourself with a simple regimen of preventive care as well as scheduling professional, routine maintenance will help keep your home pleasant and inviting—and can even cut down on repair bills.

HEATING SYSTEMS

Forced air, steam, and hot water are the three types of heating systems that warm the majority of American homes. All three share the same basic components: a centralized heat source, conduits to move the heat through the house, and appliances that release the heat into rooms. Once your system has delivered heat to these appliances, it is up to you to ensure it is distributed efficiently. Any obstruction—from a sofa to a dust bunny—can impede that flow of air.

Two other systems—radiant-floor and solar heating—are less common. In general, they require less maintenance and are more energy efficient. If you are building a new home, both systems are worth considering. No matter what kind of heating system you have, however, regular upkeep will ensure that your house is comfortable.

TYPES OF HEATING SYSTEMS

FORCED AIR

If your rooms have grates or grilles in floors or walls, your house is probably heated by forced air. Air is heated in a furnace, then blown through ducts into each room, displacing the cold air, which is drawn into return ducts and back to the furnace.

Maintenance

☐ Vacuum the vents—grates and grilles—weekly, using the crevice or dust-brush tool.

☐ Don't block vents with furniture or other objects.

☐ Be careful about shutting doors: In rooms without return vents (more common in older houses), closing the door gives the air no chance to return to the furnace. When that happens, the return-supply cycle is disrupted and the furnace will work overtime, creating hot spots in some areas and drafts in others.

☐ Every two to five years, ask a heating, ventilating, and air-conditioning (HVAC) professional certified by the National Air Duct Cleaners Association to inspect the ductwork in addition to the furnace (for more on furnace inspections, turn to page 618). Smokers and pet owners should have their ducts inspected more often.

Special Considerations

☐ An insufficient number of return vents can cause drafts; a simple upgrade is to trim doors by about an inch so they don't completely seal off a room.

☐ Adding a jumper duct, a device that runs from a room without vents to a return vent, will increase the efficiency of the airflow from the room to the furnace; contact an HVAC professional for information and installation.

☐ Installing additional return vents is another option; an HVAC professional will be able to tell you if this is necessary. It can be an energy-efficient solution; however, new ductwork can be very expensive.

TYPES OF HEATING SYSTEMS (CONTINUED)

HOT WATER

Hot water is pumped through the house from a boiler (a vessel that heats water under pressure). It runs to either baseboard or upright radiators, and then back down to the boiler. These radiators rely on convection—the circulation of air—to heat a room. As cool air comes in contact with either, it is warmed and rises. Older hot-water installations have cast-iron radiators that look like those used with steam heat, except they do not have the steam radiators' whistlelike release vents.

Maintenance

☐ At the start of the cold season, working from the top of the house to the bottom, bleed each heater, one by one, by turning the bleed valve open slightly. Turn off the valve as soon as steam starts to escape.

☐ Vacuum underneath the radiators weekly with the crevice or dust-brush tool.

☐ Vacuum radiators monthly; don't use water or cleaners—the former can cause rust, and the latter can create an unpleasant smell.

☐ Once a year, use a dry bottle brush or radiator brush to clean radiator baffles.

Special considerations

☐ Installing programmable thermostats and automatic valves, which go with them, will increase efficiency if you live in a large house. An HVAC professional can do this for you.

STEAM

A boiler converts water into steam, which then rises through pipes that supply radiators. Once the steam has flowed through the radiator and heated the baffles (the cast-iron sections on the radiator), it condenses into liquid and returns to the boiler. In a one-pipe system, the water returns to the boiler via the same pipe that delivered it, sliding past the rising steam. In a two-pipe system, the water returns via a separate pipe. Steam heat is found in older homes and apartment buildings; it's almost never installed in new homes because it's difficult to control as precisely as other systems.

Maintenance

☐ Vacuum under radiators weekly with the crevice or dust-brush tool.

☐ Vacuum radiators monthly; don't use water or cleaners—the former can cause rust, and the latter can create an unpleasant smell.

☐ Once a year, use a dry bottle brush or radiator brush to clean the baffles.

Special considerations

☐ Clanging pipes is a common complaint. In a one-pipe system, a clogged air vent—which bleeds air as steam enters the radiator—is the likely culprit. To fix it, close the shutoff valve and then unscrew the air vent with a wrench or screwdriver; boil the air vent in 1 part water and 1 part white vinegar for half an hour. If that doesn't work, replace the vent. An HVAC professional can also remedy this problem.

☐ In a two-pipe system, a bad steam trap—the trap is located near the outlet valve and controls steam flow—is the most common cause of a noisy system. Contact an HVAC professional to replace steam traps.

☐ If the radiator emits banging noises when it's warming up, it may be leaning the wrong way (as a result of the house or building shifting over time), causing water to drain in the wrong direction. In a one-pipe system, it should slope toward the pipe; in a two-pipe setup, it should slope toward the steam trap. To correct the problem, insert a shim, a small piece of metal or wood, underneath the radiator so that it is realigned in the correct direction.

RADIANT FLOOR

Radiant-floor heating relies on a system of channels or pipes through which heat is pumped; the pipes are installed under the floor. The heat can come from water, known as hydronic heat, or from electricity. (Most people opt for water because it's more affordable.) Radiant-floor heating has many advantages over forced air: It heats a room evenly, from the bottom up, eliminates any draft and dust problems, and is quiet and invisible.

Maintenance

☐ If you have an electric radiant floor, it doesn't require any maintenance. If the heat goes off, call the manufacturer, who will walk you through a series of tests; the problem may be with the power—in that case, contact an electrician. If there's something wrong with the heating elements underneath the floor, the manufacturer should direct you to an HVAC professional who specializes in radiant-floor systems.

☐ Hydronic radiant floors require no maintenance. However, you will need to maintain the source of the hydronic heat—the boiler (turn to page 618 for information). Don't drill into floors or ceilings, which may puncture a pipe and cause a leak. In the unlikely event that a leak develops, call a plumbing-and-heating professional (a store that sells hydronic heating parts should be able to direct you to a serviceperson).

Special Considerations

☐ Before installing a radiant-floor system, consult an engineer to determine how much weight the floor can bear; you may need to install extra floor support.

☐ A concrete floor with a ceramic-tile top is ideal for conducting heat efficiently via a radiant-heating system. If you'd prefer wood, be sure to choose a laminated type instead of solid wood.

☐ Use carpeting sparingly, since it decreases the heat efficiency.

SOLAR

This system uses the sun's energy to heat water, generate electricity, or heat the house. Some utility companies offer credits to homeowners who install solar heating. There are three basic methods of harnessing the sun's power:

☐ Solar water heaters are usually housed in the basement or garage and hold water that has been pumped through a solar-energy collector mounted on the roof. The heated water may be piped into a standard water heater for household use, or may be stored in another tank (for those not using a standard water heater).

☐ Passive solar heating is a less-costly, non-mechanical system that uses a solar collector—a building material or an architectural feature, such as a masonry floor, that absorbs the sun's energy. For example, a dark stone floor in front of a south-facing window will absorb heat and radiate it back into the room. In the summer, window treatments can be used to block the sun.

☐ Photovoltaic systems consist of large panels that are fastened to the roof, usually in a south-facing direction. These panels are comprised of solar cells that convert sunlight into electricity. The electricity is fed into the house's wiring. If the system produces less power than is needed, power from the utility company makes up the balance. If the system produces too much, the excess flows onto utility wires, your meter turns backward, and the utility company credits your bill. The panels are not especially attractive, but the building industry has begun to incorporate photovoltaic cells into other exterior fixtures, such as skylights and awnings.

Maintenance

☐ If the solar system is connected to a water heater, you'll need to maintain the heater according to the guidelines on page 616. Otherwise, seasonal maintenance consists of checking equipment for wear. Read through the manufacturers' and your installer's recommendations.

Special considerations

☐ Check your local building codes before deciding to install mechanical solar-heating systems, as there may be restrictions.

FURNACES AND BOILERS

The heart of any heating system is the furnace or boiler. Forced-air and some types of radiant-floor systems rely on a furnace; steam and hot-water heat, as well as some types of radiant-floor and solar heating, rely on a boiler. Boilers and furnaces are powered by gas, oil, or electricity. Gas is the most common.

THE FURNACE

Cool air enters a heat exchanger through the return air duct, first passing through a filter. The air is heated by a flame (if the furnace is powered by natural gas) or an electric element. A blower pushes the warm air out of the furnace and into your house via a network of ducts.

Maintenance

☐ During the cold-weather season, clean the furnace filter monthly: First turn it off (the switch should be located next to the thermostat). Most filters are located in a slot between the furnace and the return-air duct; slide it out. To access some filters, you must first open an access panel. If you have a metal or plastic filter, clean it with water from a hose, let it dry, then replace it. If you have a disposable fiberglass filter, replace it with a new one.

☐ Every fall, call an HVAC professional to inspect the furnace. The serviceperson should check the flue (which expells pollutants through a chimney and must not be obstructed); the heat exchanger for possible cracks, which can introduce carbon monoxide into the house; the thermostat for proper operation; the combustion chamber; the fuel output; the airflow; and the belts and motors. He or she should also seal the furnace-duct connections, if necessary, clean off soot, and oil the blower.

THE BOILER

Cold water enters the boiler and flows through a series of coils which are heated by a flame (if the boiler is powered by gas) or an electric element. Steam or hot water then flows through pipes to radiators or under-floor coils to heat the house.

Maintenance

☐ Each fall, the boiler should be drained and refilled with fresh water by an HVAC professional. Once that is complete, the technician will activate the system, then bleed it of air trapped in the lines to allow the hot water or steam to flow properly. For a hot-water heating system, a professional should also inspect the pressure tank and pressure-relief valve, and clean the heat exchanger. For a steam system, the professional should drain the float chamber, check the water, and clean the heat exchanger.

A NOTE ABOUT SPACE HEATERS

Space heaters are generally used when a house's heating system is inadequate and when a particular room needs extra heat. They operate on electricity, propane, or natural gas. A unit that runs on propane or natural gas must be vented outdoors (an unvented heater can release carbon monoxide into the home). Electric heaters do not need to be vented outdoors. If you use an extension cord to plug in an electric space heater, use only a heavy-duty extension cord that's at least 14-gauge, to reduce the risk of fire. (For more information on extension-cord safety, turn to page 630.) No matter what kind of space heater you purchase, be sure to read the chart on the label to ensure you buy the right size for the room.

ENERGY-SAVING STRATEGIES

A thermostat is a temperature-sensitive switch, usually in a box or on a dial mounted to a wall, that controls a heating or cooling system, or both. The thermostat is set to the desired temperature, and sends a signal to your system to warm or cool air. According to the Department of Energy, you can save on fuel costs in the winter if you lower the thermostat when you're asleep or away; 68°F is considered comfortable when you're at home and awake. During the summer, you can follow the same strategy with central air-conditioning by keeping the house warmer than normal when you are away. Programmable thermostats adjust the temperature according to a preset schedule. This is useful if, for example, you tend to forget to turn down the heat before leaving the house for the day. You can also program an automatic thermostat to raise the temperature at specific times of day—say, right before you get home.

COOLING SYSTEMS

Until a century ago, the most anyone could do to keep cool was open a window or use a hand fan. As electric power became common in the 1890s, electric fans offered some relief. Then, in 1902, a young engineer named Willis Carrier invented the modern air conditioner, an expensive and cumbersome system initially used in industrial spaces. Affordable home air conditioners became widespread only after World War II.

There are two main types of air conditioners: room air conditioners, often called window units, and central-air systems, which piggyback on a house's heating system, using parts of the furnace and the ducts for the heating system. There are a few less common types, as well, including freestanding units, which are called spot coolers or portable air conditioners, and ductless mini-split units. All air conditioners operate on the same basic principle: They remove the heat from the air, send the heat outdoors, then recirculate the newly cooled air. The size of your house, climate, and the heating system it relies on dictate which air-conditioning system is best.

The cooling capacity of an air conditioner is generally measured in BTUs, or British thermal units. One BTU is equal to the amount of energy required to raise one pound of water $1°F$. The higher the BTUs, the more powerful the unit. Central systems are also measured in tons—one ton equals 12,000 BTUs per hour. The Association of Home Appliance Manufacturers offers a calculator to help you determine how many BTUs you need in a room air conditioner at www.cooloff.org. When determining the requisite capacity of a central unit, it's best to consult an HVAC professional, who will take your climate, ductwork, and layout into consideration. It's important that any air conditioner you choose is sized appropriately—one that's too small won't remove enough heat and humidity; one that's too large will cycle on and off too frequently, making rooms uncomfortable.

ENERGY EFFICIENCY

Since 1980, all new air conditioners have carried a yellow "Energy Guide" tag that rates the appliance's efficiency compared with other models in its class (as defined by size and features). Room units are assigned an energy-efficiency ratio (EER) that's determined by how much electrical wattage an appliance uses to achieve its cooling output. Central-air conditioners are assigned a seasonal energy efficiency ratio (SEER). The higher the number within the range, the more efficient the unit and the less it will cost to run. Keep in mind that you're not looking for a specific number but for a unit that scores well in its class. Some utility companies offer rebates to consumers who purchase high-efficiency appliances; check with yours to find out.

In addition to the yellow tag, look for an Energy Star label. In order for air conditioners to qualify for an Energy Star label, they must have high-efficiency compressors, fan motors, and heat-transfer surfaces (such as coils). Also, they must exceed minimum federal standards for energy consumption by at least 10 percent. The Energy Star labeling system is the result of a partnership in the mid-1990s between the Environmental Protection Agency and the United States Department of Energy. It was established to identify and promote energy-efficient products, in order to reduce carbon-dioxide emissions.

A NOTE ABOUT AIR-CONDITIONER FILTERS

If you have allergies or are concerned about indoor air pollution, consider replacing the standard fiberglass filter on your central air-conditioning unit with one that removes small particles such as pollen, dust, plant spores, and smoke from the air. Choose from among three types: media filters, electronic filters, and high-efficiency-particulate-air, or HEPA, filters. Dirty coils, caused by low-quality filters, will impede the exchange of heat, resulting in higher energy bills and reduced cooling efficiency, perhaps shortening the life of the air-conditioning system.

TYPES OF AIR-CONDITIONING SYSTEMS

CENTRAL AIR

Central air systems are comprised of an evaporator, or cooling coils, and a condenser unit. The evaporator is often located in the furnace; the condenser unit is located outdoors. Both components can be in a single outdoor unit, as well.

Warm room air is pulled through return air vents; coils in the furnace filled with a refrigerant absorb the heat, which is pumped outdoors, to the condenser unit, where the heat is expelled. The refrigerant then travels back to the furnace, where the cycle starts again. The air, which is now cool, is delivered back into rooms via heat vents in floors and walls.

Usage Tips

☐ Don't repeatedly adjust the temperature. Setting the thermostat lower than the desired temperature when you first arrive home wastes energy and won't cool the house any faster.

☐ Install a programmable thermostat. It will allow you to tailor the system to daily needs, and keep you from adjusting the temperature too often.

☐ Keep heat away from the thermostat. It can sense heat from appliances, floor lamps, or television sets, causing the air conditioner to run longer than necessary.

☐ Don't block vents. Keep furniture, curtains, and plants away from vents so that the air can flow freely.

Maintenance

Weekly

☐ Vacuum vents to remove dust with a crevice or dust-brush tool.

Seasonally

☐ Clear the area around the outside condenser unit of tall grass, weeds, leaves, and other debris, so that air can circulate.

☐ Clean the inside of the condenser unit. First, turn off the power. Next, unscrew or unbolt the protective grille; you will see the metal fins on the condenser coil. (These fins may cover three sides of the unit.) Use a soft brush to clear away dirt and debris, working carefully to avoid bending the fins. If any fins are already bent, straighten them by brushing gently with a fin comb, available from a home center or appliance store. Rinse coils with a hose, spraying in the direction of the airflow (from the inside out) so you don't force the debris deeper into the fins. On most models, this requires removing the top fan grille and spraying through the opening. Finally, clear debris from the base pan on the bottom of the unit so that rainwater will drain.

☐ To clean the cooling coils, generally located in the furnace, first turn off the power. Next, unscrew or unbolt the access panel on the top or front of your furnace. Locate the cold coil—it resembles the letter "A" (which is why it's sometimes called an A coil). Run a cleaning brush across the underside to remove dirt. Clean the condensation tray underneath with a solution of 1 part chlorine bleach to 10 parts water. Let the tray dry before replacing it.

Annually

☐ Before the start of the warm-weather season, have your central-air system checked by an HVAC professional.

Special considerations

☐ Indoor and outdoor components work together. If you're thinking of replacing one or the other, you should replace both—otherwise, your system won't operate at peak efficiency.

ROOM UNITS

Like a central-air system, a room unit—also called a window unit—houses an evaporator or cooling coils and a condenser unit. The evaporator is located near the front of the appliance, and the condenser is in the part that protrudes outdoors. Room units are used in apartments and in houses without ductwork. They can be installed in a window or in a wall.

Usage Tips

☐ Don't repeatedly turn the unit on and off. A room unit shouldn't be switched on for at least five minutes after it has been turned off. Turning it on sooner puts strain on the compressor.

☐ Give it room. Objects blocking a unit, such as plants, may cause it to build up heat, which will cause it to work less efficiently and, over time, shorten its life.

☐ Use fans. If one room air conditioner must cool several rooms, position an electric fan nearby to help direct the air to where it's needed. It's more energy-efficient than turning the unit full blast.

Maintenance

Weekly

☐ Vacuum with a crevice or dust-brush tool to remove dust.

Seasonally

☐ Clean the filter at the beginning of the cooling season and once a month while the unit is operating. This will keep the evaporator coil from getting dirty too quickly, which can decrease the effectiveness of the unit. It's especially important to wash the filter if you have a lot of dust or cats and dogs. First, unplug the unit. Next, pop off or unscrew the front panel for access to the filter and evaporator, which is covered by thin metal fins. Remove the filter. If it's made of metal mesh or foam, wash it in warm water with a mild dishwashing liquid. While it's out, vacuum all accessible surfaces. Let everything dry before re-installing the filter.

☐ If the filter is disposable or extremely dirty, replace it; standard sizes are available at housewares and appliance stores.

Annually

☐ If you see any bent metal fins when you take off the filter, straighten them out by gently running through them with a fin comb, available from a home center or appliance store.

Special considerations

☐ Models with timers, which allow you to program the air conditioner to turn on or shut off at preset times, can cut down on energy use. Programming the unit to turn on consistently at a low temperature an hour before bedtime, for example, is more efficient than running the unit on high to cool the room quickly when you enter it.

TYPES OF AIR-CONDITIONING SYSTEMS (CONTINUED)

PORTABLE AIR CONDITIONERS

Also known as a spot cooler, this machine cools a room the same way as a window unit and central system. Unlike a window system, it's on wheels and can be moved from room to room. Spot coolers are useful in houses and apartments with windows that won't accommodate a room unit. They are also a smart option for the elderly, who might have difficulty removing a window unit at the end of the season. Portable units require little setup, but they do need to be vented to the outside via an exhaust hose that attaches to a coupling in a window or in the wall (you'll need an HVAC professional if you want to vent through the wall).

Usage Tips

☐ Don't repeatedly switch it on and off. For maximum energy efficiency, wait at least three minutes after you've switched off the spot cooler before turning it on again.

☐ Empty the reservoir before moving it. Most units collect condensation in a reservoir, which must be emptied periodically.

Maintenance

Weekly

☐ Unplug the machine and remove the filter according to the manufacturer's instructions; vacuum using a crevice or dust-brush tool, then rinse with water. If the filter is extremely dirty, soak it in lukewarm water and then rinse. Let the filter dry completely before reinserting it.

Seasonally

☐ Wipe the exterior with a damp cloth.

☐ Cover the spot cooler with a dust cover before storing it for the season.

Special considerations

☐ If you're using an extension cord, be sure it is heavy-duty (at least 12 gauge).

DUCTLESS MINI-SPLIT UNITS

Mini-split units have a condenser unit, which is located outdoors, and an air-handling unit, which contains the evaporator, or cooling coil, located indoors. The air-handling unit is installed in a wall or ceiling and looks much like a room air conditioner (except it is only a few inches deep). Several air-handling units can be serviced by one outdoor condenser unit. And instead of having to make a large hole in the wall for installation, as with room air conditioners, only a three-inch opening is required for a power connection, refrigerant tubing, and other lines to link the air-handling unit and condensor (these lines run along the exterior of the house). Some units also provide heat.

Usage Tips

☐ As with all air conditioners, do not obstruct the vents.

Maintenance

Weekly

☐ Vacuum vents to remove dust with a crevice or dust-brush tool.

☐ Wipe the exterior of the air-handling unit with a damp cloth.

Monthly

☐ Remove the filter and wash it in warm, soapy water. Let it dry and replace it.

Seasonally

☐ Check drain pipes for obstructions.

☐ Clean indoor and outdoor coils with a soft brush.

Special considerations:

☐ Because these air conditioners are not as common as other types, it can be difficult to find experienced installers and service people.

ALTERNATIVE COOLING METHODS

Cooling your home mechanically can be expensive and will raise the level of pollutants in the air. Adopting just a few of the strategies below can reduce your dependence on air conditioners—and lead to savings on your energy bill.

WEATHERIZE WINDOWS, DOORS, AND CRACKS

Adding weather stripping, insulation, and caulking will protect your house from summer heat buildup. Start in the attic since it is a major source of heat gain (for more information about insulating your attic, go to page 419).

HANG SHADES AND BLINDS

Shading windows can reduce indoor temperatures by as much as 20 percent. Indoor window coverings and outdoor awnings and shutters both produce effective shading.

VENTILATE

In climates with hot days and cool nights, open windows in the evening. If a house is well insulated, by the time the inside heats up toward evening, the air will be cool again outside. In climates with daytime breezes, create cross-ventilation: Open windows on both sides of rooms, and keep interior doors open.

PLANT TREES

Well-placed plants provide shade. Deciduous trees, which lose their leaves, are best: Selectively situated around a house, they let in light and warmth in the winter and block them in the summer. They also create a microclimate, reducing the temperature of the air around them: During photosynthesis, water vapor escapes through leaves, and the surrounding air is cooled as a result. A lawn is usually cooler than bare ground, but if you live in an arid climate, consider ground covers—small plants and bushes—that require less water than grass.

CUT DOWN ON APPLIANCE USAGE

Ovens, dishwashers, clothes washers and dryers, as well as incandescent lights all contribute to the buildup of heat in your home. They should be used only when necessary, and in the morning or late evening when temperatures are lowest.

PAINT WITH LIGHT COLORS

In hot climates, paint the exterior of your house white or a light color. Light-colored exteriors effectively reflect heat away from your home. Dark-colored exteriors absorb 70 to 90 percent of the radiant energy given off by the sun. That energy is then transferred into your home by conduction. If you live in a predominantly cold climate, a dark exterior may be desirable.

INSTALL CEILING FANS

They don't actually cool air but can make a room feel several degrees cooler. Use one alone, or, if you have central air-conditioning, turn up the thermostat by several degrees when the fan is on. Ceiling fans work best when the blades are 7 to 9 feet above the floor but no more than 8 inches from the ceiling.

ELECTRICITY

MOST OF US GREW UP LEARNING the bare minimum about electrical safety: Unplug appliances before cleaning them, keep appliances and power tools away from water, and steer clear of downed power lines. Many of us, however, have little understanding about just how the electrical systems in houses and apartments work. Along with natural gas and fuel oil, electricity supplies many of the comforts we take for granted. The service panel, wiring, outlets, and switches are your house's circulatory system. When this system is functioning, it's easy to ignore it, but when there's an interruption—and your computer, lights, or air conditioner stop working—a little knowledge can go a long way toward diagnosing the problem and ensuring that it's fixed quickly—and safely.

WIRING

Electricity flows into your house from your utility company's power lines, which are either suspended overhead on poles or buried underground. The electricity in these lines is generated in power plants by a number of fuels, including coal, natural gas, nuclear fusion, oil, and the force of running water (known as hydroelectric power). In rare cases, electricity is generated using wind or solar energy. Electricity, which is generated on demand and can't be stored, travels from power plants to substations, where it's then distributed along smaller lines to your house.

The electricity in these smaller lines passes through your house's meter, which measures your consumption, and then to the service panel, which is the heart of your house's electrical system, usually located in a box on the wall. Here, the electricity is distributed to a number of circuits that provide power to one or to many outlets. Each circuit is designed to handle a specific amount of power. If you overload a circuit by plugging in too many appliances or appliances that draw too much power, the breaker connected to that circuit in the service panel will trip, "breaking" or cutting off the flow of electricity before it damages wiring. Older houses will sometimes have fuses—which "blow" or melt when overloaded.

HOW TO TEST A CIRCUIT

Instead of jogging back and forth between the electrical panel in the basement and the outlet upstairs, enlist your vacuum cleaner as an assistant. Plug the vacuum into the suspect outlet, with its switch turned on. When you have restored power to that circuit, the vacuum will signal with its noise.

COMMON ELECTRICAL TERMS

VOLTAGE

Voltage is equivalent to water pressure—it's the force that pushes electricity through wires. The electricity generated at power plants has to travel long distances, so it's pushed at great pressure along high-voltage lines. This voltage is dramatically decreased at substations along the way. Houses are generally wired with 120- and 240-volt lines. Most lights and appliances use 120 volts; some large appliances, such as water heaters, room air conditioners, ranges, and clothes dryers, require 240 volts.

AMPERAGE

Amperage is equivalent to the size of a water pipe—it's the amount of electricity flowing through wires. Each circuit in your house has an amperage rating, which is determined by the thickness, or gauge, of its wiring. The circuits designed to handle lights and small appliances, such as those feeding outlets in bedrooms, living rooms, and dining rooms, are generally rated for 15 amps. Circuits designed for power-hungry large appliances, such as a range or water heater, are rated for 20 to 50 amps.

WATTAGE

Wattage is equivalent to the number of gallons of water flowing from a water pipe—it's the total amount of power a circuit can handle. To calculate a circuit's wattage capacity, multiply the number of volts times the number of amps. For example, a 15-amp, 120-volt circuit could accommodate 1,800 watts. If that circuit fed four outlets, you could plug one lamp with a 100-watt bulb into each, plus operate a 1,200-watt hairdryer.

ELECTRICAL SAFETY

THROUGHOUT THE HOUSE

☐ Buy electrical appliances and tools that have a safety certification from an independent testing organization such as Underwriters Laboratories (UL), Canadian Standards Association (CSA), or ETL Testing Laboratories.

☐ Keep all electrical equipment away from sinks, bathtubs, and pools, and never touch electrical equipment, outlets, or switches while wet or standing in water. Water and electricity are a dangerous combination.

☐ Never use lightbulbs with a higher wattage rating than is recommended for the fixture.

☐ Don't attempt even simple electrical repairs if your house has aluminum wiring, which is more vulnerable to damage than copper wiring. If you're unsure, consult a qualified electrician.

☐ Do not use small appliances (i.e., hair-dryers, toasters, and radios), computers, or telephones (except in an emergency) during electrical storms. Lightning can cause destructive high-voltage surges in electrical lines.

☐ Use surge protectors on electronic devices, appliances, phones, fax machines, and modems. If the voltage on a circuit surges above 120 volts, the protector diverts the extra power, thereby preventing damage to electronic equipment. (Note: Surge protectors will not prevent damage during an electrical storm.) When buying a surge protector, always choose one with an indicator light, which lets you know that the protection feature is working. One or more surges, which originate with your power company, can destroy the protection capabilities. In that case, the surge protector will need to be replaced.

☐ Keep in mind that surge protectors, power strips, and extension cords do not provide more power, only better access to outlets. Don't overload them with equipment that draws more power than they, or the wall outlet, are designed to handle.

☐ Do not use electric-powered mowers or electric tools in the rain or on wet grass.

☐ Inspect power tools and electric lawn mowers before each use. If power cords, plugs, or the electrical housing is damaged, do not use them.

☐ When working outdoors on a ladder, stay at least 10 feet away from overhead power lines, which carry a deadly amount of voltage.

OUTLETS

- ☐ Ensure outlets and switches are installed flush with walls. Replace any broken cover plates.

- ☐ Use outlet plugs to prevent children from inserting objects into outlets.

- ☐ Plugs should fit securely into outlets; never force a plug into an outlet or modify a plug to fit an outlet. The round hole in a three-prong outlet is for grounding purposes. If the appliance or tool gets a short, the electricity will travel safely down the ground wire rather than through you.

- ☐ Don't overload circuits by plugging too many things into an outlet.

- ☐ Have an electrician install ground fault circuit interrupter (GFCI) outlets in rooms where water is present, including the bathroom, kitchen, laundry room, basement, and workshop. They prevent shocks by shutting down the circuit if they detect an unsafe flow of electricity. Once a month, test GFCI outlets to make sure they are functioning correctly: Push the "reset" button. Plug a hair dryer into the outlet and turn it on. Push the "test" button; the dryer should turn off. Push the reset button; the dryer should go back on. If the dryer does not go on and off as described, call an electrician to check and possibly replace the outlet. It may have been damaged by a power surge or may have been installed incorrectly.

CORDS

- ☐ Periodically check cords to make sure they're in good condition. Replace anything with a cord that's frayed or cracked.

- ☐ Keep cords away from traffic areas.

- ☐ Do not nail or staple cords to walls, baseboards, or other objects.

- ☐ Do not place cords under carpets or rugs or rest furniture on them, all of which are serious fire hazards.

- ☐ Never unplug an appliance by pulling on the cord; always pull on the plug.

- ☐ Keep all portable and countertop appliances unplugged when not in use. This lowers electric bills since plugged-in items consume a small amount of electricity, even when not in use.

THE SERVICE PANEL

- ☐ If you shut off a circuit breaker to do an electrical repair, tape over the breaker and close the panel door. (If you have a fuse box, put the fuse in your pocket so someone doesn't inadvertently replace it while you're working.) Tape a sign to the door reading DO NOT TOUCH! This will reduce the chance that someone will unwittingly turn the power back on.

- ☐ When cutting power to a circuit, always test outlets with a continuity tester, a small tool available at hardware stores that indicates whether the power is indeed off.

EXTENSION-CORD SAFETY

If an appliance draws more electricity than an extension cord can carry, it can overheat and cause a fire. The Consumer Product Safety Commission estimates that about 4,700 residential fires originate in extension cords each year. Use only extension cords that are certified by an independent testing laboratory, such as Underwriters Laboratory. Be sure, too, to heed label information, which will indicate the use, size, and wattage rating. The thicker the cord, the higher the wattage it can accommodate. If you're unsure of the wattage of the appliance or tool you're connecting to an extension cord, consult the user's manual. If the appliance or tool indicates power usage in amps, multiply amps by volts (generally 120) to determine the wattage.

- ☐ Use extension cords only when necessary and only on a temporary basis. Never use them as a permanent substitute for inadequate wiring.

- ☐ Use polarized extension cords with polarized appliances. Polarized plugs have one prong slightly wider than the other and can be inserted only one way into an outlet.

- ☐ Disconnect a cord immediately if any part of it feels warm. Heat indicates the cord is overloaded, which is a fire and shock hazard.

- ☐ Make sure cords do not dangle from counters or tabletops, where they can be pulled down or tripped over.

- ☐ Replace cracked or worn extension cords.

- ☐ Cover unused outlets on extension cords with electrical tape or with outlet covers to prevent a child from inserting a foreign object and making contact with the live circuit.

- ☐ Insert plugs fully so that no part of the prong is exposed when the cord is in use.

- ☐ Plug an appliance or tool into the extension cord, then plug the cord into the wall outlet.

- ☐ Use only three-prong extension cords for appliances with three-prong plugs. Never remove the third (round or U-shaped) prong, which is a safety feature designed to reduce the risk of electrocution.

- ☐ In locations where furniture or beds may be pushed against an extension cord where it joins the plug, use an angle extension cord, which is specifically designed for this.

- ☐ Never use an extension cord while it is coiled or looped.

- ☐ Never cover any part of an extension cord with a rug or anything else.

- ☐ Never place an extension cord where it is likely to be damaged by heavy furniture or foot traffic.

- ☐ Never use an extension cord for a refrigerator.

- ☐ Keep extension cords away from heat sources, such as near a heater or behind a refrigerator.

- ☐ Don't use staples or nails to attach extension cords to a baseboard or to another surface. This could damage the cord, creating a shock or fire hazard.

- ☐ Use special, heavy-duty extension cords for high-wattage appliances such as hair dryers.

- ☐ When using outdoor tools and appliances, use only extension cords labeled for outdoor use.

- ☐ Never keep an extension cord plugged in when not in use; the cord will still conduct electricity.

ELECTRICAL-SYSTEM DANGER SIGNS

If you experience any of the following, you may have dangerous electrical wiring, according to the Electrical Safety Foundation International, and should consult a qualified electrician immediately for an inspection:

☐ Frequent power outages— circuits that trip or fuses that blow repeatedly

☐ Dim or flickering lights

☐ Flashes of light or sparks

☐ Sizzles and buzzes

☐ An odor of burning plastic— which can indicate overheated wires

☐ Hot switch plates or outlet covers

☐ Switch plates or outlet covers discolored from heat buildup

☐ Electrical shocks—even mild ones

☐ Cut, broken, or cracked wire insulation.

HOW TO RESET THE SERVICE PANEL

CIRCUIT BREAKER

☐ Locate the breaker that has its switch leaning toward the off side rather than on. (Some breakers may have a red button, instead of a switch, that pops out if tripped.)

☐ Before resetting the switch or button, check the inside of the panel to determine what circuit the breaker controls and turn off lights or appliances so the circuit isn't overloaded the moment you turn it on; you will want to have at least one item on, however, to see if the circuit is working again. Then reset the breaker switch or button to the on position.

FUSE BOX

☐ Turn off lights or appliances on the circuit before replacing the blown fuse.

☐ Turn off the main power supply, which is done in one of three ways depending on the kind of fuse box. Some boxes have removable fuse blocks containing cartridge fuses. One of these blocks will be marked "main power" and it should be removed before a fuse is replaced. On other fuse boxes, a large lever on the side shuts off power. On the third type, there is no power switch; power should be turned off at the main service panel, located elsewhere in the house or in the apartment building.

☐ Once the power has been shut off, unscrew the fuse, being careful to touch only the insulated rim, and replace it with a new fuse of the same amperage (which will be marked on the fuse). Never substitute an object, such as a coin, for a fuse.

☐ Removable-cartridge fuses power large appliances, such as air conditioners. To change these fuses, shut off the main power supply and remove the fuse block marked "appliance" from the panel. Next, take out the individual cartridge fuses with a tool called a fuse puller, then test each fuse with a continuity tester (both tools are available at hardware stores). If the tester doesn't glow, replace the fuse. If there is a chronic problem with a circuit, call an electrician.

HOME SECURITY

INSTALLING A SECURITY ALARM SYSTEM is a deterrent to intruders (often window decals and lawn signs alone—indicating that your house is protected by an alarm—will be effective). A security system should sound loudly when activated, and should have sensors at exit doors (especially garage and back doors, which provide the most cover) and motion detectors in hallways outside bedrooms and in the main living area. Before installing a system, make sure you research companies carefully and choose one that is well established. Once installed, don't write your pass code on or near the alarm keypad. With or without an alarm, there are several steps you can take to reduce your house's vulnerability to break-ins.

HOW TO SECURE YOUR HOME

☐ Ensure all exterior doors are constructed of solid wood or are metal clad. Hollow-core doors, which can give way with a kick, are suitable only for interiors.

☐ Reinforce key-operated doorknobs with dead bolts. Opt for single-cylinder dead bolts, which operate by key on the outside of the door and a thumb latch on the inside. They are safer in the event of a fire than double-cylinder dead bolts, which are key operated on both sides. A beveled rim prevents the dead bolt from being pulled out with pliers. The bolt (known as the "throw") should extend at least 1 inch when locked to resist heavy blows. Use mounting screws that are at least 3 inches to properly anchor the strike plate (the metal plate installed in the door frame that receives the bolt).

☐ Ensure hinges for outside doors are mounted on the interior of the door frame so intruders cannot pop out the pins to lift the door off the frame.

☐ Choose a peephole with a wide-angle view. For those in wheelchairs or children who can't reach the standard peephole level, install a second peephole at a lower level. A contractor can retrofit peepholes.

☐ In addition to the regular lock, put a dowel in the lower track of a sliding glass door to prevent the door from being forced open. You can also install a metal fold-down device called a charley bar, to prevent sliding doors from being lifted off the track.

☐ Replace glass insets in doors and in windows surrounding a front entry with security glazing. This durable plastic prevents trespassers from breaking the glass and opening the door from inside. Check with a window manufacturer or your local home center about installation.

☐ Create pin locks for double-hung windows by drilling an angled hole through the top and bottom sash and inserting a nail or eyebolt.

☐ Consider safety bars for windows, particularly in urban areas. Look for models with a release mechanism that allows them to be opened in case of fire.

☐ Trim hedges so they are no higher than ground-floor windowsills.

☐ Make sure driveways, pathways, and entry points are well lit to discourage intruders. Illuminating house numbers will help police and emergency vehicles locate your house quickly. Avoid overly bright lighting, however, which will create deep shadows where intruders can hide.

☐ Install motion sensors that will turn on lights automatically to welcome visitors and scare away intruders.

☐ Make an inventory of possessions. Record serial numbers or identifying marks of valuables. Keep the inventory in a safe-deposit box. (Turn to page 634 for more information.)

WHENEVER YOU LEAVE HOME . . .

☐ Lock all doors and windows and activate the alarm if you have one every time you go out, even for a short amount of time.

☐ Don't leave valuables in sight through windows.

☐ Do not leave spare keys in obvious spots, such as in a flowerpot, mailbox, or under a doormat. A better alternative is to leave a set of keys with a trusted neighbor.

☐ Leave your name off your mailbox and front door. This will keep potential thieves from looking you up in the phone book, calling, and discovering that you are not home.

☐ If you have a central station monitoring your alarm, make certain that your response call list is up to date.

☐ When on vacation, set timers for at least two interior lights; stagger when they turn on so the house looks genuinely occupied. Suspend newspaper and mail deliveries (you can do the latter at your post office).

☐ If you will be away for an extended period, in addition to the above, hire someone to maintain the yard (lawn, bushes, and trees) and shovel snow. Inform a trusted neighbor of your trip so they can alert police to suspicious activity and check on your home periodically.

ABOUT NEIGHBORHOOD WATCHES

If you don't already belong to one, join a neighborhood watch. According to the National Crime Prevention Council, such a program—a collaboration between neighbors and local law enforcement that trains citizens how to recognize suspicious activity, how to help one another, and how to work with law enforcement—can significantly reduce crime. If no group exists in your community, contact local law-enforcement agencies about starting one. (For more information about neighborhood watch groups, visit www.usaonwatch.org.)

HOME SAFES

Once you have inventoried your valuables and organized and photocopied your important documents (such as property deeds, car titles, birth certificates, bank information, and insurance policies), the best place to keep the originals is in a safe-deposit box at the bank or in a home safe. Choose one that can be bolted to the floor or built into a wall. For optimum security, purchase a safe that is fireproof as well. Standard UL-listed fireproof home safes are made of concrete sheathed in metal. They come with one-, two-, three-, and four-hour fire ratings, which indicate the amount of time the interior will stay below 350°F. One hour should be sufficient for the average homeowner. Since disks and tapes melt at lower temperatures, "media" safes are available, which maintain a temperature of 125°F.

IDENTITY THEFT AND FRAUD

"Identity theft" and "identity fraud" are terms used to refer to a crime in which someone wrongfully obtains and uses another person's personal data. The Federal Trade Commission and the Department of Justice recommend several precautions you can take to minimize your risk of becoming a victim, including the following:

☐ Order a free copy of your credit report annually from one of the three principal credit reporting companies mentioned in the box below. Ask that only the last four digits of your Social Security number appear on the report. Carefully inspect it to make sure there is no suspicious activity.

☐ Choose different passwords for bank and credit card accounts, and avoid using "easy" passwords, such as consecutive numbers, your birthday, your phone number, your mother's maiden name, or your child's or pet's name.

☐ Shred charge card and ATM receipts, credit card applications, and bank statements before placing them in the trash.

☐ Secure originals of all important documents in a bank safe-deposit box or fireproof safe.

☐ When ordering new checks, pick them up at the bank instead of having them mailed.

☐ Leave your Social Security card in a secure place. Only give out your Social Security number if absolutely necessary; always ask if you can use other types of identifiers.

☐ Ask how personal information is secured in your workplace or other institutions that collect data from you, such as a doctor's office.

☐ Do not give out personal information over the phone, through the mail, or over the Internet unless you are sure you know who you are talking to. If you have been solicited, do not give out any information over the phone; hang up and call the institution through its public line. Do not click URLs or links contained in e-mails asking for information—go directly to the company's website instead.

☐ Carry only the credit or debit cards you need and leave the rest in a secure spot at home.

☐ Update your computer virus software. Viruses have a variety of damaging effects, including introducing program codes that can cause your computer to send out files or other stored information.

☐ Install a firewall program to prevent hackers from accessing your computer.

☐ Use a secure browser that encrypts and obscures personal information to secure your online transactions.

☐ Due to the accessibility of laptops, avoid storing financial information on them. Make your laptop password protected, using a combination of numbers and upper- and lowercase letters.

☐ Before disposing of a computer, overwrite the entire hard drive using a "wipe" utility program. Reformatting your hard drive may not be enough because the files can often be retrieved.

WHAT TO DO IF YOU BECOME A VICTIM OF IDENTITY THEFT

Immediately contact the Federal Trade Commission (FTC) either online (www.consumer.gov/idtheft) or via phone (877-438-4338). You may also need to call the local Postal Inspection Service, the Social Security Administration, and the Internal Revenue Service. Report the fraud to the three principal credit-reporting companies: Equifax (www.equifax.com), Experian (www.experian.com), and Trans Union (www.transunion.com). Contact the security or fraud department of all companies who have had your name used fraudulently. File a report with your local police department or the department in the community where the identity theft occurred. (You may need to submit the police report to creditors as proof of a crime.) Finally, it's important to get a copy of your credit report and monitor your status regularly.

EMERGENCY PREPAREDNESS

FOR SAFETY'S SAKE, every home should have an emergency plan in place. But for any homekeeper, being well-prepared means much more than just having an emergency kit at the ready. It also means taking a few simple steps to ensure a home is safe for children, stocking a first-aid kit (and regularly replenishing it), knowing what to do during a weather advisory (and what to do after a storm)— even keeping plenty of flashlights (and batteries) throughout the house. These measures and others like them go a long way toward making you feel more safe and secure in your own home, which is, after all, another hallmark of good homekeeping.

BASIC EMERGENCY PLANNING

The American Red Cross offers detailed advice on how to be prepared for a disaster,
including the following precautionary steps:

☐ Contact your local Emergency Management Office or American Red Cross chapter to find out which natural disasters could occur in your area and how to prepare for each.

☐ Learn what your community's warning signals sound like and how to react to them.

☐ Familiarize yourself with the disaster plans for your workplace, children's schools or day-care center, and any other place family members spend time.

☐ Post emergency telephone numbers near telephones.

☐ Have an age-appropriate conversation with children to explain the dangers of fire, severe weather, earthquakes, and other emergency situations.

☐ Teach children how and when to call 911.

☐ Explain how everyone should respond to each disaster that could occur.

☐ Draw a floor plan of your house and mark two escape routes from each room.

☐ Pick two meeting places: one spot near your house in case of a fire, and one place outside your neighborhood in case you cannot return home after a disaster.

☐ Pick one out-of-state friend or relative and one local person for family members to call if separated by disaster (it is often easier to call out-of-state than within the affected area).

☐ If you have pets, create a plan for their care—animals may not be allowed in emergency shelters due to health regulations.

☐ Brief everyone on how to evacuate family pets.

☐ If you have elderly or disabled persons in your home, you will need to do additional preparation to ensure their safety. Go to www.redcross.org to download the booklet "Preparing for Disaster for People with Disabilities and Other Special Needs."

☐ Show every family member where the fire extinguishers are kept and how to use them. (Turn to page 657 for more information.)

☐ Learn how to turn off the water and gas mains, and electricity at the circuit breaker or fuse box.

☐ Instruct household members to turn on the radio for emergency information. Keep a transistor radio and batteries on hand.

☐ Take a basic first-aid and CPR class.

☐ Make sure you have adequate insurance to cover the disasters most likely to occur. (For more on insurance, turn to page 234.)

☐ Keep family records in tightly sealed plastic bags in a fireproof safe. (For more on safes, turn to page 634.)

DISASTER-SUPPLIES KIT

If disaster strikes, you may not have time to gather essential belongings. The American Red Cross recommends that you assemble a basic kit—water, food, first-aid supplies, clothing and bedding, tools and medications—and store it in a large duffel bag inside a waterproof container or bin. Include the following items:

WATER

At least a three-day supply (1 gallon per person per day for both drinking and sanitary purposes)

FOOD

A three-day supply (per person) should include only nonperishables that require no cooking and little or no water, such as canned meats, fruits, vegetables, juices, high-energy foods such as energy bars and nuts, baby food or formula for infants, and comfort foods, such as candy bars

FIRST-AID KIT

For instructions on assembling a first-aid kit, turn to page 648.

TOOLS AND SUPPLIES

Disposable plates, cups, and utensils; battery-operated radio and extra batteries; flashlight and extra batteries; cash, traveler's checks, and loose change; nonelectric can opener; small fire extinguisher; tube tent; pliers; duct tape; compass; matches in waterproof container; plastic storage containers; signal flare; paper and pencil; needles and thread; shut-off wrench to turn off household gas and water; whistle; plastic sheeting; map of area; sanitation supplies, such as toilet paper, soap, feminine supplies, plastic bags for waste, bucket with a tight lid, and disinfectant

CLOTHING AND BEDDING

At least one complete change of clothing and footwear per person and sturdy shoes or boots, rain gear, long-sleeve shirts and long pants, hats and gloves, thermal underwear, sunglasses, and blankets or sleeping bags

FAMILY MEDICAL INFORMATION AND SUPPLIES

A list of family physicians and their telephone numbers; special items for specific family members, such as supplies for an infant, prescription medications, or an extra pair of eyeglasses; a list of important family information; the model and serial number of medical devices such as pacemakers

CAR KEYS

Always keep an extra set in your kit so you won't have to hunt for them.

A NOTE ABOUT FLASHLIGHTS

In the event of any power outage, always use a flashlight; never use candles, which can be a fire hazard. It's important to keep flashlights (and a supply of spare batteries) in convenient locations throughout the house. The best solution is to keep at least one flashlight in each room. Consider which drawers or shelves have easiest access in the dark. To ensure that you will be able to see the fuse box when you need to, attach a flashlight to the box itself. You can use magnets for metal flashlights, or strips of Velcro or strong double-sided tape.

PETS AND EMERGENCIES

Be sure you know of a safe place to take your pets should an evacuation ever be necessary, and maintain a list of "pet friendly" hotels and motels, veterinarians, neighbors, and animal shelters. (It will be difficult, if not impossible, to obtain this information in the midst of a disaster.) Animal shelters may be overburdened with animals they already have in their care, so they should be a last resort. And since you may not be home when evacuation orders are issued, find out if a trusted neighbor would be willing to take your pets and meet you at a prearranged location. This person should know where your pet disaster-supplies kit is kept (see below), and have a key to your house. Remember that pets act differently in times of stress; even the most mild-mannered pets may panic, hide, try to escape, or bite and scratch. Keep dogs on leashes and cats in pet carriers until you can get them to safe shelter.

PET DISASTER-SUPPLIES KIT

- [ ] Medications and medical records
- [ ] First-aid kit (see page 664)
- [ ] Leash, harness, and pet carrier
- [ ] Current photos of your pets in case they get lost

- [ ] Food, water, bowls, and cat litter and litter box or pan
- [ ] Information on feeding schedules, medical conditions, and behavioral problems, and your veterinarian's name and number in case you have to board your pets
- [ ] Pet beds and toys, if they are easy to transport

- [ ] Dog and cat collars with securely fastened, up-to-date identification tags. Attach the phone number and address of your temporary shelter, if you know it, or of a friend or relative outside your area.

WHAT TO DO IN CASE OF...

POWER OUTAGE

A power outage of more than two hours can be frustrating, especially when your refrigerator is filled with food. Here is what to do in case of such an event:

☐ Turn off or unplug the appliances or electronics you were using when the power went off. When the power comes back on, it can cause a "surge" or "spike" that can cause damage.

☐ Resist the temptation to open the refrigerator door—an unopened refrigerator will keep foods cold for a couple of hours. A half-full freezer will hold for up to twenty-four hours, and a full freezer will hold for up to forty-eight hours.

☐ If it appears the power will be out for more than two hours, pack milk, dairy products, meats, fish, poultry, eggs, and any other perishable foods into coolers with ice. Either the heavy-duty plastic or disposable Styrofoam types are fine.

☐ Before you go to bed, flip a bedroom light switch on. When the power returns, the light will wake you, reminding you to check on the condition of the foods in your freezer. If freezer foods still display ice crystals, then they can be safely refrozen.

☐ If the power went out while you were away, check the temperature of foods in your refrigerator with an instant-read thermometer. If the internal temperature of any food is above 40°F, throw it out.

FORCED EVACUATION

☐ Listen to NOAA (National Oceanic and Atmospheric Administration) Weather Radio (nws.noaa.gov/nwr/) as well as local radio or television reports to find out if government officials have ordered an evacuation.

☐ Wear long-sleeved shirts, long pants, and sturdy, flat shoes.

☐ Take your disaster-supplies kit and your first-aid kit.

☐ Gather essential documents, such as driver's license, insurance policies, and Social Security card.

☐ Bring pets with you and go to your pre-designated pet-friendly location.

☐ Lock your house.

☐ Use only travel routes specified by local authorities.

☐ Stay alert for downed power lines.

WHAT WATCHES AND WARNINGS MEAN

FLASH FLOOD WATCH AND WARNING
The result of storms dropping large amounts of rain within a brief period. It can occur with little or no warning and can reach peak in a matter of minutes. In the event of a flash flood watch, be ready to evacuate on a moment's notice. When a flash flood warning is issued, evacuate immediately.

FLOOD WATCH
A flood is possible in your area. Move furniture and other valuables to the second story if possible, and fill your car's gas tank in case of an evacuation notice.

FLOOD WARNING
A flood is under way or will soon occur in your area. Stay tuned to radio and TV stations and be prepared to evacuate.

HURRICANE WATCH
Hurricane conditions are possible within thirty-six hours.

HURRICANE WARNING
Hurricane conditions are expected in twenty-four hours or less. Stay tuned to radio or TV for instructions.

TORNADO WATCH
A tornado is possible. Be alert for signs of an approaching storm, often a dark, greenish sky, large hail, a large dark rotating cloud, or a loud roar. Stay tuned to radio and TV for instructions.

TORNADO WARNING
Weather radar has picked up a tornado or one has been sighted. Because tornados strike quickly, take shelter immediately.

WHAT TO DO AFTER A NATURAL DISASTER

☐ Contact your local branch of the American Red Cross. It will provide a voucher to purchase clothing, groceries, medications, bedding, essential furnishings, and other emergency supplies, as well as a cleanup kit (including mop, broom, bucket, and cleaning products).

☐ Call your insurance agent to discuss claims. If the damage is covered, documenting what you own and its condition will be a high priority. Take plenty of pictures. Discuss with your agent whether any of your antique or valuable belongings require professional treatment, and hire a restoration company. Such specialists should be listed in the phone book under "Fire and Water Damage Restoration." They will bring in large fans to dry wet belongings and may save you unnecessary labor. They usually dry upholstered furniture at the same time as the walls and floors, so you can leave the heavy pieces in place.

☐ Listen to the radio for information on assistance that may be available from the state or federal government or other organizations.

EARTHQUAKE PREPAREDNESS

If you live in an earthquake-prone area, here's how to minimize risk
of damage to your house and belongings in the event of a quake.

☐ Have a contractor or structural engineer inspect your house, particularly chimneys, roofs, and wall foundations, for stability and to shore up any weak areas.

☐ Make sure the house is bolted to the foundation.

☐ Bolt bookcases, china cabinets, and other tall furniture to wall studs. Install strong latches on cabinet doors and keep heavy items on lower shelves.

☐ Secure your refrigerator, water heater, and all gas appliances to wall studs. You can buy earthquake-safety straps, fasteners, and adhesives to secure your belongings at hardware stores.

☐ Store flammable liquids outdoors rather than indoors.

☐ Prepare a disaster-supplies kit (page 638) for your home and car.

☐ Ensure you have the appropriate homeowner's insurance. Turn to page 234 for information.

DEALING WITH WATER DAMAGE

The American Institute for Conservation of Historic & Artistic Works and the Heritage
Preservation offer the following general tips for dealing with water-damaged belongings:

☐ If the object is still wet, rinse it with clear, clean water or a fine hose spray. Clean off dry silt and debris with a soft brush or blot it with a damp cloth. Be careful not to grind debris into the object.

☐ Air dry objects indoors if possible. (Sunlight and heat may dry certain materials quickly, causing splits, warpage, and buckling.)

☐ Inhibit the growth of mold and mildew by reducing the level of humidity. Increase airflow with fans, open windows, or air conditioners and dehumidifiers.

☐ Remove heavy deposits of mold from walls, baseboards, floors, and other household surfaces with commercially available disinfectants formulated for mold.

☐ If objects are broken or begin to fall apart, place all broken pieces, bits of veneer, and detached parts in clearly labeled open containers. Do not attempt to repair objects until they are completely dry or, in the case of valuable antiques or objects, until you have consulted with a conservator.

FIRST AID FOR WATER-DAMAGED ITEMS

Item	Preparation	Treatment	Drying
COMPUTER DISKS	Rinse in distilled water.	For professional help, search phone listings for "Document Retrieval."	Dry with lint-free kitchen towel.
ELECTRONICS	Assuming it is safe to proceed, turn off (if necessary) and unplug.	Arrange ultrasonic cleaning. Check Yellow Pages under "Fire and Water Damage Restoration," or ask your insurance agent.	Have the cleaning professional check equipment before switching it back on.
PHOTO ALBUMS	Disassemble album (if it's an heirloom, contact a conservator). If pages are "magnetic," remove plastic covers. Other pages can be dried individually as is.	If ink labels are bleeding onto photographs, remove pictures from pages. Copy information. If you cannot dry within 48 hours, interleave with waxed paper or polyester-web interfacing (Pellon) and freeze.	Dry pages or photos in a single layer on absorbent material, such as paper towels or clean dish towels. Make sure nothing touches the fronts of photographs.
PHOTOGRAPHS	Remove from frames. Rinse with cool, clean water. If stuck together, soak in water until photographs separate.	Do not touch or blot surface. Dry within 48 hours; if you can't, freeze as above.	Lay flat in a single layer as above.
UPHOLSTERED FURNITURE AND BEDDING	Separate colors that may bleed. Decide whether to contract for whole-house drying; if so, the crew will deal with these items.	If drying on your own, rinse off any mud. Remove cushions and other separate pieces. If something must be moved, lift from the bottom of the frame.	Wrap in white cotton towels, and when those become damp, replace them. Use fans to circulate air, but do not aim them directly at furniture or bedding.
WOOD FURNITURE AND OBJECTS	Rinse off mud, and blot dry. Exception: If paint is blistering or flaking, do not rinse or blot; consult a furniture restorer or conservation specialist.	Use weights or clamps to hold veneer in place while drying; use plastic film to protect surface from weights.	Cover loosely with plastic to prevent rapid drying, and lift it periodically to allow air to circulate. If mildew appears, increase circulation with a fan.
BOOKS	To learn how to treat water-damaged books, turn to page 248.		

WINTER ISSUES

A fresh blanket of snow on the ground is beautiful and provides the basis for many fun outdoor activities, but it is also important to keep in mind that there are some safety and maintenance concerns that go along with the snow and freezing temperatures.

WINTER-STORM KIT

If you live in a part of the country prone to severe winter storms, add the following items to the Disaster-Supplies Kit on page 638 to ensure you're ready for a weather emergency.

☐ Extra blankets

☐ Ice scraper and brush

☐ A warm coat, gloves or mittens, hat, and water-resistant boots for every member of the family

WINTER-STORM PREPAREDNESS

Before storm season, have your car winterized by adding snow tires, antifreeze, and good windshield wipers—and stock it with a winter-storm kit such as the one detailed above. During a storm, stay tuned to NOAA (National Oceanic and Atmospheric Administration) Weather Radio (to find your local station listing, visit www.nws.noaa.gov/nwr/) as well as your local television and radio stations for updates.

WHAT WINTER-STORM ADVISORIES MEAN

In the event of a watch or warning, regularly check radio or television news outlets for new information. Stay inside if you can. If you must venture outside, dress in layers, and keep your head and hands covered. Watch out for slippery conditions.

☐ A winter-storm watch means that weather conditions may lead to a winter storm in your area.

☐ A winter-storm warning is issued when weather patterns indicate a winter storm headed your way.

☐ A blizzard warning means that you can expect strong winds, blinding wind-driven snow, and dangerous wind-chill conditions in your area.

SHOVELING SNOW

Shoveling snow is hard work, but don't put it off—it is easiest to shovel freshly fallen snow that is still powdery. When snow buildup on a walkway or driveway becomes compacted, it forms a strong bond with the pavement and will become harder to remove.

☐ Dressing in layers will keep you warmer and make it easy for you to remove clothing as you become warm from exertion.

☐ Use a shovel with a small face, or fill a large shovel less than halfway with snow. Wet or packed snow is heavy; a snow-shovel load can weigh as much as six pounds. Dry, powdery snow weighs about two and a half pounds per shovelful. If you are dealing with a large snowfall, remove the snow in layers from top to bottom.

☐ Scoop up the snow and push it out of the way with your shovel rather than lifting it. This is easier on your back. Newer shovels are designed specifically to push instead of lift snow; they are available at hardware stores. If you do have to lift the snow, stand with your feet hip-distance apart and keep the shovel close to your body. When lifting, always bend from the knees. Your spine should remain straight and relaxed as you work. Practice sitting into the motion as you work. You should feel the exertion in your thighs, the trunk of your body, and your shoulders rather than in your back.

☐ Don't attempt to shovel snow if you have a heart condition or a bad back, as it can put too much strain on both. Hire or enlist the help of someone to shovel the snow for you.

☐ Your home's roof is almost certainly strong enough to carry a snow load typical for your area, but many roofs cannot support the maximum load for an entire season. Heavy loads can cause the wood fibers in rafters to bend at weak points. Remove snow with a snow rake, available at hardware stores, or call a professional.

☐ Gently knock snow off bushes and tree limbs to prevent breakage.

☐ Use a snowblower with caution: Gasoline-powered snowblowers emit toxic exhaust fumes, and electric snowblowers can cause electric shock if the cord gets tangled in the machine.

ABOUT DEICERS

Deicers both prevent ice from forming and soften existing accumulations, so they're easy to remove with a shovel. They can be sprinkled on the pavement before a storm hits to prevent snow and ice from sticking or after precipitation has ended to make cleanup less arduous (they work best on thin layers, however, so you do need to shovel first). They offer peace of mind, making outdoor surfaces less treacherous, but they must be used with care; since they are most commonly made of salts, they can kill shrubs and trees and corrode metals. Be aware that the more you use, the greater the likelihood of damage.

Apply only enough deicer to make ice removal possible, rather than saturating surfaces so ice melts completely. Never pile snow containing deicing salts on top of or near plants or grass. When the ground thaws in spring, water the soil well to flush salts away. Keep deicing salts well away from metal planters or garden furniture and wash your car after every storm.

Gritty materials, such as sand, cat litter, and sawdust, are not considered deicers—they don't melt or prevent ice buildup. They can, however, be added to a deicing salt to improve traction.

TYPES OF DEICERS

CALCIUM CHLORIDE
Calcium chloride works better than other deicing salts, especially at lower temperatures, because it gives off heat as it melts. It is not as toxic to plants as sodium chloride, but it is corrosive. It can cause skin irritation if your hands are moist when using it. It can also burn the pads of pets' feet. Effective in temperatures as low as -25°F.

SODIUM CHLORIDE
Also known as rock salt, sodium chloride is readily available and inexpensive, but toxic to plants and highly corrosive. Most effective in temperatures above 15°F.

UREA
This nitrogen-based fertilizer is available at garden-supply stores and nurseries, and will melt ice just as well as salts do without the adverse effects on plants—as long as it's used sparingly. It's generally safe to use up to 10 pounds of urea per 100 square feet per season. Urea is most effective when the temperatures are only slightly below freezing (25°F to 30°F).

HOW TO THAW A FROZEN LOCK

Heat a key with a lighter and work the warmed key carefully into the lock (never force the key). You may have to reheat the key several times. If that doesn't do the trick, try blowing into a drinking straw aimed at the lock; the warm air will eventually thaw the metal. A mist of WD-40 will also help to loosen the ice.

HOW TO PREVENT FROZEN PIPES

Water expands as it freezes, putting pressure on anything that contains it. When water in pipes freezes, it can cause them to crack. The pipes that are most likely to freeze are those that are exposed to extreme cold, such as outdoor hose bibs, swimming-pool supply lines, sprinkler-system lines, and pipes in unheated areas such as basements, garages, and attics. Pipes that run along exterior walls with no insulation also freeze readily. The Red Cross recommends homeowners do the following to protect pipes:

☐ Close inside valves supplying outdoor hose bibs. Disconnect and drain the hose. Open the outside hose taps to allow water to drain, and keep them open so that any water remaining in the pipe can expand without causing the pipe to break. Drain swimming pool and sprinkler lines.

☐ Insulate hot- and cold-water pipes in the basement, crawl spaces, attic, garage, and under kitchen and bathroom cabinets (a hot-water supply line can freeze if water is not running through the pipe or the water temperature in the pipe is cold). Use a pipe sleeve or UL-listed heat tape or a heat cable. Such products are available at home- and building-supply centers. Secure insulation with heat tape. Follow the manufacturer's instructions for applying and using these products.

☐ Keep garage doors closed if the garage contains water-supply lines.

☐ Open kitchen and bathroom cabinet doors to allow warmer air to circulate around pipes.

☐ In extremely cold weather, let a trickle of water drip from faucets served by exposed pipes (open both hot and cold valves). This will help prevent pipes from freezing.

☐ If you will be going away, leave the household temperature set no lower than 55°F.

☐ If a frozen section of pipe is visible, you can thaw it by applying heat with a hair dryer or by wrapping the pipe in towels soaked in hot water. Keep the faucet open as you work; as the ice begins to melt, water will begin to flow, helping to melt more ice. Never use a blowtorch, a kerosene or propane heater, or any other open flame to thaw a pipe: All are hazardous (they can not only cause the water to boil, bursting the pipe, but also increase the risk of carbon-monoxide poisoning).

HOW TO DEAL WITH ICE DAMS

The frozen ridges that form along the bottom of a pitched roof, called ice dams, are caused by a lack of insulation underneath the roof. Warmth from the house escapes through the roof and melts the thin layer of snow in direct contact with the roof without disturbing the outer layer of snow. Ice then forms in the gutters and along the edges of the roof, causing the dam. Eventually, ice dams obstruct so much melting water that the water seeps through the roof and leaks into the house. This moisture can rot lumber and ruin ceilings, floors, walls, and insulation. If an ice dam forms, take the following steps to prevent damage.

☐ Remove snow from the roof with a roof rake and push broom (or hire a roofing contractor).

☐ Make channels through the ice dam by hosing it with water. The channels will clog within days, however, so they are only a temporary solution.

☐ Have a roofing contractor remove the ice dam. Never do it yourself by using a hammer, axe, or deicers—all of which can damage your roof.

☐ Reduce the likelihood of ice dams by adding insulation. Consult a contractor to evaluate your roof and attic.

FIRST AID

Every home should be equipped with a readily available, fully stocked first-aid kit. Prepackaged kits are widely available, but it's easy to put together your own and tailor it to your needs. (A lightweight tool chest makes a convenient carrying case.) After all, certain activities and hobbies may call for specific additions—a gardener's first-aid kit would include insect repellent, sunscreen, and calamine lotion in case of poison ivy. Be sure, too, to include any essential prescription medications.

In case of emergency, you should always have important phone numbers posted in a prominent place. The list should include doctors, the Poison Control Center, and cell phone and work phone numbers of family members. (It's also a good idea to note severe allergies, especially to medications, foods, and insect bites.)

FIRST-AID KIT

The American Red Cross recommends the following list of items for a basic home first-aid kit. Be sure to check your kit every six months and replace any used, missing, or expired contents.

☐ Activated-charcoal solution to absorb caustic poisons (it should not be used before calling the Poison Control Center or 911)

☐ Adhesive bandages (assorted sizes)

☐ Adhesive tape

☐ Antibiotic cream

☐ Antiseptic cleansing wipes/spray

☐ Blanket

☐ Burn ointment

☐ Chemical cold pack

☐ Cotton balls

☐ Cotton swabs

☐ Disposable gloves

☐ Elastic bandages

☐ Eyewash solution

☐ Fever and pain reducers (over-the-counter), for adults and children

☐ Flashlight and batteries

☐ First-aid pocket guide

☐ Gauze (rolls and pads)

☐ Hand cleaner

☐ Hydrogen peroxide

☐ Plastic bags

☐ Rubbing alcohol

☐ Safety pins

☐ Scissors

☐ Tape

☐ Triangular bandages

☐ Tweezers

BASIC MEDICINE CHECKLIST

Keep the following on hand to deal with common ailments:

☐ Antacids

☐ Antidiarrhea medication

☐ Antihistamines

☐ Anti-itch topical medication, such as hydrocortisone cream or calamine lotion

☐ Aspirin

☐ Cold and/or flu medicines

☐ Cough medicine

☐ Fever and pain reducers

☐ Laxative

☐ Sore-throat spray

☐ Thermometer

A NOTE ABOUT SYRUP OF IPECAC

The American Academy of Pediatrics advises against keeping ipecac in the house. They have concluded that there is no evidence that vomiting helps children who have swallowed poison. Most emergency rooms use activated charcoal instead because it binds to the poison and prevents it from entering the bloodstream. More important, taking ipecac may result in not being able to tolerate the hospital's charcoal or other poison treatments.

STORING MEDICATIONS

Follow these guidelines to ensure medications are stored securely and retain their efficacy. As you would with a first-aid kit, check your medications regularly to make sure you have a ready supply and discard any that have expired.

☐ Most medications are meant to be stored in a cool, dark, dry place because moisture and heat can cause them to lose effectiveness. This is why medications should not be stored in the bathroom.

☐ Do not transfer pills and capsules from their original bottles into other containers. Doing so increases the chance of taking the wrong medicine or taking pills at the wrong time.

☐ Read the label and the printed instructions each time you purchase medication. These instructions provide information about dosage, side effects, and interactions.

☐ Label pill bottles with colored stickers bearing names, so family members can spot their medications instantly.

☐ Dispose of expired medications by taking them to a pharmacy with a take-back program or securing them in a trash bag that is out of reach of children and animals. (Do not flush them down the toilet; doing so is bad for the environment.)

CHILDPROOFING

A child's curiosity is his or her driving force in learning about the world. Caution and restraint develop over time, so it is up to adults to anticipate danger and ensure safety. Whether you have small children at home or others who visit, childproofing is an ongoing endeavor. The requirements will change as a baby grows and learns to crawl, walk, climb, and explore. Reevaluate your childproofing efforts every few months, well in advance of his or her next step, and amend them as necessary.

HOW TO CHILDPROOF YOUR HOME

☐ Use easy-to-install safety latches or locks to secure cabinets and drawers in the kitchen, bathrooms, and other areas of the house where potentially dangerous objects are stored.

☐ Keep all poisons, medicines, knives, and other sharp objects out of the reach of children.

☐ Store all household products in their original containers—never in receptacles that were once used for food, especially empty drink bottles.

☐ Anchor tall furnishings, such as china cabinets and bookcases, to studs in walls to prevent them from toppling.

☐ Use doorknob covers and door locks to keep children away from hazardous areas, such as swimming pools (locks on swimming pool gates and doors should be too high for children to reach).

☐ To prevent burns, set your water-heater temperature to 120°F, and have a plumber outfit faucets and showerheads with antiscald devices.

☐ Install smoke and carbon-monoxide detectors on every level of your house and near bedrooms. For more on detectors, turn to pages 573 and 653.

☐ Cover sharp edges of furniture and other architectural features like stone steps or raised fireplace hearths with soft bumpers.

☐ Install window guards and safety netting to help prevent falls from windows, decks, balconies, and landings. Window screens are not adequate protection, as children can push through them. If you use window guards, make sure that at least one window in each room can be used for escape in case of a fire.

☐ Install safety gates on stairs and at entrances to dangerous areas. For the tops of stairs, use gates that screw into the wall instead of "pressure gates," which can be easily dislodged. New safety gates should display a certification seal from the Juvenile Products Manufacturers Association (JPMA). Gates should attach securely to doorframes without any openings to trap fingers and necks and there should be no more than 1 to 2 inches between the floor and the gate bottom. If you have an older safety gate, be sure it has no gaps or diamond-shape spaces large enough for a child's head to fit through; the vertical slats or rods should be no more than $2\frac{3}{8}$ inches apart. Avoid gates with structures that could give a child a foothold for climbing.

☐ Shield electrical outlets with covers.

☐ Keep hanging wires and appliance cords out of reach.

☐ Cut long window-blind cords and use safety tassels to prevent strangulation. Window-blind cord-safety tassels are available for free from the Consumer Product Safety Commission (log on to www.cpsc.gov for more information).

☐ Use doorstops or door holders (mounted to the door or the wall with a hook latch) to keep doors from slamming shut (and catching fingers and toes).

☐ Avoid toys with buttons or other small embellishments that can pose a choking hazard.

BABYSITTER CHECKLIST

Whenever you leave children in the care of a sitter, make a list of the following telephone numbers and post it in a visible spot, such as on the refrigerator door or by the telephone:

☐ Your location and a cell-phone number

☐ Poison Control Center

☐ Pediatrician

☐ Hospital

☐ Nearby neighbor, friend, or relative

KITCHEN AND BATH SAFETY

IN THE KITCHEN

☐ Never leave a baby or toddler unattended in a high chair. Always fasten the safety belt and straps. Ensure that the straps are independent of the tray and that the tray locks securely.

☐ Use the back burners when cooking, and keep pot handles turned to the back of the cooktop. Install knob protectors to prevent children from turning on the burners and oven.

☐ Never hold a child while handling hot food or water.

☐ Keep household cleaning products, knives, matches, and plastic bags in locked cabinets.

☐ Avoid using tablecloths. With a tug, the cloth—and everything on it—can quickly end up on the floor.

IN THE BATHROOM

☐ Keep toiletries and cleaning products in locked cabinets.

☐ At bathtime, have all bathing supplies, clothes, and towels at hand so you don't need to turn your back while your child is in the water.

☐ Check bath-water temperature with your wrist or elbow before putting your baby in to bathe; this will prevent burns.

☐ Fit the bathtub with spout-bump and drain-bump protectors.

☐ Keep the toilet lid closed.

FIRE SAFETY AND PREVENTION

The most important part of home fire safety is installing and maintaining smoke alarms (most fire casualties are caused by smoke inhalation). The early warning smoke detectors provide is crucial, since most deadly fires occur between midnight and four o'clock in the morning. Eleven out of twelve homes in the United States have at least one smoke detector, although it is estimated that as many as one-third of them don't work. At a minimum, there should be one smoke detector on every level of the house, including the basement, but it's best to have one in every room.

SMOKE DETECTORS

The National Fire Protection Association (NFPA) fire-alarm code now requires that new homes have hardwired smoke detectors that are connected to the house's electrical system (they also have a battery backup) so that homeowners don't need to worry about replacing batteries.

If you don't have hardwired smoke detectors, use battery-operated models. There are two basic types: ionization and photoelectric. Both are easily installed with a screwdriver. According to a study by the National Institute of Standards and Technology (NIST), ionization alarms respond more quickly to flaming fires while photoelectric alarms respond more quickly to smoldering fires. The study concluded that both types, however, provided adequate time for homeowners to escape most residential fires.

Ionization models use a small, safe amount of radioactive material to create an electrical current in the detector. Smoke then ionizes, or changes the electrical charge of air molecules, slowing the current and triggering the alarm.

Photoelectric models use a light sensor. A beam of light is directed across a chamber in front of the sensor. If smoke interrupts the beam, sending it in different directions and toward the cell, the alarm is activated.

Check all battery-operated smoke alarms once a month by pressing the Test button. Twice a year (or if your alarm is making a chirping noise), change the batteries; to make a habit of it, replace them when you reset your clocks for the begining and end of daylight saving time. This is also a good time to clean each unit, since dirt and debris can impede operation: Remove the cover, and wipe it using a soft cloth; carefully dust the inside as well with a can of compressed air.

The U.S. Fire Administration recommends replacing smoke alarms every eight to ten years or as recommended by the manufacturer; write the date of purchase on the inside cover when you install it so you will know when to replace it.

FIRE-PREVENTION TIPS

☐ Ensure all appliances are certified by an independent testing laboratory, such as Underwriters Laboratories (this will be indicated on the packaging).

☐ Keep cooktops and ovens clean to prevent grease fires.

☐ Keep curtains away from cooktops and ovens.

☐ Make sure electric kitchen appliances are clean and that their cords and plugs are in good working order. Replace frayed or worn-out cords and plugs.

☐ Discard frayed or broken extension cords and do not run them under rugs or furniture or nail them into place.

☐ Don't overload circuits by plugging too many appliances into one socket.

☐ Never replace a blown fuse with a fuse of different amperage. Frequently blown fuses or tripped circuit breakers can signal that wiring is inadequate. Consult an electrician.

☐ Clean the lint trap in your clothes dryer after every use—lint is the most common cause of dryer fires. Once a year, remove lint from the hose attached to the back of the dryer. (For instructions, turn to page 371.)

☐ Remove clutter—especially anything flammable—from around the furnace and water heater.

☐ Store gasoline and flammable liquids in air-tight containers—they emit gases that can ignite when they come in contact with a spark or pilot light.

☐ Dispose of oily rags (such as those used to oil furniture or wipe up motor oil) after each use in accordance with your community's sanitation guidelines. They are a fire hazard because as the oil ages, it oxidizes and produces heat, which can lead to spontaneous combustion.

☐ Never store flammable liquids beneath stairways or near exits: If they catch fire, an escape route will be eliminated.

☐ Put a spark screen in front of fireplaces and never lay a rug close to a fireplace. (For more on fireplace safety, turn to pages 198–199.)

☐ Have your chimney cleaned when there is a buildup of ¼ inch of creosote. (For more on fireplace safety, turn to pages 198–199.)

☐ Keep space heaters away from combustible materials, such as curtains, upholstery, bedding, and rugs. Never use one to dry clothing or other combustibles.

☐ If someone smokes cigarettes in your home, dampen the butts before throwing them away.

☐ Never use electrical devices outdoors unless they are designed for that purpose.

☐ Keep matches and lighters out of the reach of children.

☐ Learn to extinguish fires. Place a fire extinguisher in any area of the house where a fire hazard exists: the kitchen, the garage, at the top of the cellar stairs, and even in the bedroom. Teach everyone in your household how to use one.

☐ Never fight electrical or grease fires with water or baking soda. Use an extinguisher.

INSTALLING SMOKE DETECTORS

☐ Equip each floor in your house with at least one detector, including the attic and basement; there should be one near each bedroom.

☐ Place detectors at the highest point and in the center of the room, since smoke rises.

☐ Never place a unit near an air duct, which can dissipate smoke.

☐ Keep the units dust-free, and never paint them.

☐ Don't install detectors near fireplaces, wood-stoves, or ovens, or in bathrooms or garages, all of which can cause false alarms. Although many people install smoke detectors in the kitchen, smoke from burning food can trip them, and even the most patient cook may be tempted to pull out the batteries in a fit of frustration. Install one several feet away from the kitchen door instead.

CREATING A FIRE-ESCAPE PLAN

The best way to ensure your family's safety is to sit down with everyone who lives in the house to map out a plan:

☐ Make sure everyone can hear and recognize the smoke alarm. (There are models equipped with flashing lights for the hearing impaired.)

☐ Draw a plan of every floor of your house noting exits (each room should have two).

☐ Identify and eliminate obstacles: Are windows painted shut? Do screens come out easily? Do antitheft bars on windows have quick-release latches that are easy to operate? Sliding glass doors that have been fortified against intruders must not be designated as fire exits, nor should doors with double-cylinder deadbolts (which require a key for the inside and outside) or windows with key-operated locks.

☐ Teach everyone to recognize the signs that a primary escape route is blocked by fire—smoke seeping under a door or a door that's hot—as well as where the secondary escape route exists. You should also instruct them in how to locate an alternate escape route.

☐ Equip upper-floor rooms with UL-approved escape ladders or ropes.

☐ Hold a fire drill twice a year. Instruct family members to exit quickly, closing doors behind them, without stopping to collect valuables or calling 911 (you should call 911 from a neighbor's phone). Meet at your designated outdoor spot.

FIRE EXTINGUISHERS

Fire extinguishers are readily available at home centers and hardware stores. Before shopping for an extinguisher, familiarize yourself with the four basic fire extinguisher ratings. Some extinguishers are rated for multiple types of fires, such as "AB" or "ABC"; these multipurpose extinguishers are the best ones for home use.

A	B	C	D
For ordinary combustibles such as paper and wood.	For flammable liquids such as grease, paint, and propane.	For electrical fires.	For combustible metals (some metals require specific extinguishers).

Fire extinguishers are generally filled with one of these four extinguishing substances:

DRY CHEMICAL
Usually rated for multiple use.

CARBON DIOXIDE
Carbon dioxide works well for class-B and -C fires. It does not leave residue.

HALON
Halon uses gas to disrupt the chemical reaction of burning fuel. This is commonly used in industries with electrical equipment such as computer installations, as it leaves no residue.

WATER
Water is effective for burning wood and paper and other class-A materials.

After use, the extinguisher may need to be recharged (see below). Keep in mind that you should never try to fight a large blaze. You should leave the house, shutting doors behind you, and call the fire department. Even after extinguishing a small fire, always notify the fire department, as some fires can rekindle.

FIRE-EXTINGUISHER MAINTENANCE

Keep fire extinguishers in accessible areas, but away from heat sources, as the contents may become less effective. Check extinguishers regularly—about once a month—to make sure they are adequately pressurized. When the arrow is in the green area there's enough pressure; if it's in the red, the extinguisher will need to be recharged. Call your local fire department and ask if they will recharge it for you. (Otherwise you'll have to replace it.) Shake the extinguisher once a month to prevent the contents from solidifying.

HOW TO USE A FIRE EXTINGUISHER

To use an extinguisher effectively, aim it at the base of the fire and sweep the area. Once the fire appears to be extinguished, watch carefully, since it may reignite. Just remember the National Fire Protection Association's acronym PASS:

1. <u>P</u>ull the pin.
2. <u>A</u>im the nozzle.
3. <u>S</u>queeze the trigger.
4. <u>S</u>weep the spray back and forth.

HOLIDAY-SAFETY TIPS

Here are tips to make sure the Christmas season remains safe year after year:

☐ Choose a fresh tree with a trunk that is sticky to the touch. If you bounce the trunk on the ground and a lot of needles fall off, it is dry enough to pose a fire hazard.

☐ Leave the tree outside until you are ready to decorate to prevent it from drying out.

☐ Once it's inside, water the tree daily. Trees generally become fairly dry after two weeks.

☐ Keep the tree away from space heaters, fireplaces, or other heat sources.

☐ Use UL-listed lights on your tree and join no more than three strands together.

☐ Inspect your lights every year and discard those with frayed cords, gaps in the insulation, broken or cracked sockets, and excessive kinks or bends.

☐ Avoid overloading wall outlets and extension cords.

☐ Do not leave your lights on unattended.

☐ Never use electric lights on a metallic tree.

☐ Never use candles on a tree, even on an artificial one.

☐ Dispose of your tree according to your community's sanitation guidelines (ask if there is a recycling program that turns trees into mulch). Never burn the tree in your fireplace.

☐ Use only outdoor lights outdoors and indoor lights indoors.

☐ Never use indoor extension cords outside.

LIVING WITH PETS

FOR PET OWNERS, one of the nicest things about coming home is the reception they get from their animals, regardless of whether the absence has been a few days or a few hours. But pets require lots of care—including regular grooming and bathing— as will your home if you share it with animals.

PET-PROOFING

One of the most persistent issues homekeepers who live with pets face is animal hair—on floors, furniture, and clothing. A good way to keep hair off you and your furniture is to provide a designated spot (or perhaps more than one) where your pet is welcome to rest. Dog and cat beds offer comfortable alternatives to furniture.

Still, pets often want to join you on sofas or beds. If this is the case, place an old towel or sheet wherever your pet likes to rest. When tidying up, you can pick up the covering, shake it to remove most of the hair (you should do this outside), and toss it in the washing machine. Keep in mind that regular grooming will help minimize pet-fur accumulations.

There are myriad ways to remove pet hair. You may need to try a few methods to find one that works for you, but regardless of what works, it's important to clean furniture, rugs, and clothing often. As fur builds up, it becomes more and more difficult to remove without blowing it throughout the house.

HOW TO REMOVE PET HAIR

☐ On carpeting, vacuum several times a week using full suction. Use a vacuum with a high-efficiency particulate air (HEPA) filter. (For more on these filters, turn to page 499.)

☐ On wood or other hard floors, use an electrostatic mop. They're more efficient than vacuums since they don't blow the hair around.

☐ On clothing, use a tape roller. Loop a ribbon through the handle and hang one from the doorknob inside closets throughout the house so they're always at the ready.

☐ On upholstery, use the vacuum's upholstery tool or, better still, a hand vacuum with a motorized beater-bar attachment. Lint brushes designed for clothing and dry sponges, sold at pet-supply stores, also work well.

HOW TO REMOVE PET STAINS

Every once in a while, due to illness, stress, old age, or behavioral issues, your pet will have an accident. These stains must be thoroughly removed, or else your pet may continue to return to that spot.

1. First remove any solid residue with a blunt, flat object, such as a dull knife.

2. Blot fresh stains with a clean white cloth. After absorbing as much moisture as possible, apply a solution of ¼ teaspoon clear dishwashing liquid mixed with one cup of tepid water; blot with another clean, dry towel. Rinse by blotting with a towel dampened with tepid water. Continue alternating with a soapy towel and a clean, damp towel until the stain is gone. For stale stains, skip the blotting and move directly to the next step.

3. Apply an enzymatic product designed specifically for pet stains such as Nature's Miracle. The enzymes break down stains effectively and remove odors that might be undetectable to you but can attract your pet to the same area. If odor persists, call a professional carpet cleaner to treat the carpet. (In extreme cases, the carpet and padding underneath—and sometimes even the subfloor—will need to be replaced.)

PROTECTING SURFACES FROM WEAR AND TEAR

Dogs and cats are both likely to gnaw on or claw at household surfaces, expecially furniture. Cats cannot be "trained" out of clawing; this is an instinctual behavior that should not be punished. The key is to give the cat a more attractive target.

- [ ] Since cats' claws are continuously growing, they scratch in order to remove the sheath on the nail. Trimming your cat's nails regularly will help eliminate the need to score your furniture.

- [ ] Purchase a sisal-rope or carpet-covered cat tree or scratching post—some even come baited with catnip. Set them near furniture that you'd like to protect. The posts should be level, stable, and high enough for your cat to stretch her front legs.

- [ ] Place strips of double-stick tape on the corners of sofas and anywhere else the cat likes to scratch. She will be bothered by the stickiness and will eventually move to the scratching post. You can remove the tape once she's made the transition. If she strays, cover the clawed area with tape or cardboard until she is dissuaded again. (Cats like to scratch where they see their own markings.)

- [ ] Trim dogs' nails to help minimize damage to wood flooring. Some breeds need them trimmed as often as once a month. If your pet's nails grow unchecked, they can eventually become ingrown. Dogs have a vein that runs in the nail, so never clip the nails without having your veterinarian or groomer show you how.

- [ ] The best way to prevent puppies from gnawing furniture—as well as electrical wires, shoes, children's toys, and just about everything else—is with constant supervision, and correction when caught in the act. Spray taste deterrents may also work, but mostly as a supplement to your regular routine of supervision and correction.

- [ ] Provide proper chew toys. Never give a puppy an old shoe—it sends the message that any shoe is okay to gnaw on.

GROOMING

Brushing pets regularly minimizes the amount of dirt, hair, and dander (the mixture of saliva and skin cells left on the fur) that they shed throughout the house. If you begin a grooming routine while your pets are young, they will become accustomed to your handling.

Grooming isn't just good homekeeping; this care also benefits your pets' health and well-being. Dogs and cats need brushing so their fur doesn't become matted, so they don't get fur balls that can damage their skin and get stuck in their throats, and so that fleas and skin problems are caught before they become serious. Brushing also brings oil to the coat, improving its appearance. The first few times you are grooming your pet, give her time to sniff the brushes. Groom for only a few minutes, and reward with a treat.

Different types of coats require different care. Long-haired dogs and cats need to be brushed every day to prevent matting; short-haired animals can be brushed about once a week.

TYPES OF PET BRUSHES

When grooming, use a brush made just for pets. If you are unsure which tool is best suited for your pet's coat, ask your veterinarian or follow these general guidelines:

BRISTLE BRUSHES
Bristle brushes are ideal for dogs with short, silky coats, and for short-haired cats.

METAL COMBS
Metal combs are good for gently unsnarling mats or inspecting for fleas. The spacing of the comb's teeth should vary according to the density of the animal's coat: wide tooth for the body and fine tooth for the area around the face. They are good for cats and dogs.

UNDERCOAT RAKES
Undercoat rakes are plastic brushes with thick bristles that are good for troublesome undercoats on cats and dogs. These implements untangle even the deepest layers of fur.

CURRYCOMBS
Currycombs are thick bristled and good for short-haired dogs, such as Dobermans and beagles. Their gentle rubber tips also make them a good choice to use on cats who are skittish about being brushed.

PIN BRUSHES
Pin brushes and shedding blades are ideal for removing clumps of hair, particularly from long-haired cats.

WIRE-BRISTLED SLICKER BRUSHES
To efficiently remove shed fur from all varieties of cats, use one of these brushes.

HOW TO GROOM YOUR PET

1. First, remove your pet's collar, and wipe it down with a damp cloth. Remove identification tags and put them somewhere safe. Place machine-washable collars in small mesh bags—the kind designed to protect lingerie and other fine washables—before laundering. Other collars can be spot-cleaned or washed by hand, depending on the material.

2. On long hair, use a stainless-steel comb, preferably one with varying size teeth to prevent matting; then use a slicker brush to separate each hair. A light mist of water on the fur will allow you to use a brush or comb without breaking the fur. Never yank through matted fur. Not only can you damage the fur, but your pet will also associate grooming with pain. Use a mat splitter instead, working little by little to remove the tangle. If fur is excessively matted, take your pet to a professional groomer or a vet. Never cut matted fur with scissors, as pets' skin is thin and can be cut easily.

3. Brush a short coat in the direction it grows. If steel or metal bristles irritate your pet's skin or make her uncomfortable while brushing, use a rubber-bristle brush instead.

4. Start grooming slowly. If your pet resists your efforts, work in ten-second intervals and brush her gently every day, extending the grooming session each time. Be persistent but never forcibly restrain your pet while grooming.

5. Inspect your pet for the following while grooming: fleas and ticks, lumps under the skin, rashes, bald spots, sores, cuts, punctures, and objects in footpads. If any of these conditions are present, contact your veterinarian.

6. Check the ears for debris or odors. To clean, use a cotton ball dampened in water or a little mineral oil. Never insert anything in your dog's ear canal. Some breeds of dogs need to have hair removed from their ears regularly. This should only be done after a veterinarian or groomer shows you how. Breeds with long or droopy ears tend to have excess wax buildup and should be checked weekly. Dogs who like to swim may also be prone to yeast infections in their ears. Make sure to clean their ears with an ear-cleaning solution that dries the ear canal. Your vet will be able to advise you.

7. Wipe your pet's face with a clean damp cloth. You can do this as often as once a day. Your pets' eyes should be clear and bright with no excessive tearing or mucus discharge. If his eyes are red, this may indicate a possible infection or injury. Consult your veterinarian.

8. Since a dog's food isn't abrasive enough to maintain healthy, infection-free teeth and gums, it is important to brush your pet's teeth at least once a week. Use toothpaste formulated for pets (do not substitute toothpaste designed for people as it's too foamy). Brush using a dog or cat toothbrush, or wrap gauze around your finger and just rub her teeth. Have your vet check for signs of periodontal disease during annual checkups. Your vet can advise you if your dog needs a professional cleaning.

9. Breeds that have skin folds, such as pugs and shar-peis, require special care to prevent fungal infections. Clean the folds weekly and make sure the areas are thoroughly dried.

BATHING

Bathing is required less often than grooming is. The frequency will depend on the type of animal you have and whether she goes outside or stays indoors. Generally, every other month is adequate for most breeds of dogs, often with more baths required during the summertime. Most felines do not need regular baths. But there are some times, such as when a pet is unusually dirty, when a bath may be necessary. All pets should be groomed before being bathed. Water can create tight mats in long hair, and already matted hair will worsen when wet.

HOW TO BATHE CATS AND DOGS

Cats and small dogs may be bathed in the roomy sink of a mudroom or laundry room. It's best to close off the room in which you're bathing your pet, in case she tries to escape. Larger dogs will have to be bathed in the bathtub or outdoors in a large basin. Remove any items from the room that you don't want to get wet, as it is natural for a dog to shake his coat during the bathing process.

Place a towel in the bottom of the sink or tub to give the animal something to grip; cats and dogs become nervous on slippery surfaces and may try to jump if they lose their footing. Help your pet in and out of the tub to avoid catching a leg or hurting a hip joint.

Turn the water on slowly and adjust the temperature and pressure before training the nozzle on your pet; water should be lukewarm. When you're ready to start wetting down your pet, hold the spray nozzle as close as possible to the coat, so the water penetrates. (Most animals find this pressure less frightening than sprinkling from far away.) Completely soak through to the skin. Then start cleaning, working from the head to the legs and tail. Talk to your pet in a soothing voice through the entire process; be gentle but firm.

Keep water out of the ears, eyes, and nose. Use only a damp cloth to wipe the animal's face.

Choose a shampoo made for your breed. (Do not use a shampoo for humans as it will be too drying.) Begin to shampoo at the neck. Make certain you rub it in, through to the skin. Soap up every area, including the backs of legs, underside of the tail, and belly. Don't forget to wash your dog's feet, between toes, in skin folds, and around the rump. Rinse well, again, starting with the head. Make sure to remove all traces of shampoo; leftover suds can cause skin irritation. Squeeze out excess water with your hands. Then blot using a clean towel—or two if your dog has a heavy coat. You may want to do what many professional groomers do—blow-dry the coat, if your pet will stand for it (use a low setting). Be aware that a dog's first instinct is to roll around, even after being toweled off.

FIRST AID

Fleas are not just a minor irritation. They can cause itching and scratching that can result in fur loss and broken skin (which can lead to rashes and infection). A bad infestation will spread from your pet throughout the house and continue to breed and flourish even after your pet's flea baths. Ticks can cause infections such as Lyme disease (dogs are 50 percent more susceptible than humans), Rocky Mountain spotted fever, and ehrlichiosis. Liquid preventive treatments such as Bio Spot, Advantage, and Frontline work well. If your pet has a flea infestation or a tick, consult your veterinarian about the best methods for eradication (particularly if your pet is young or old, pregnant, or debilitated).

Humans aren't the only ones who fall victim to emergencies requiring first aid; our pets sometimes find themselves with scrapes, cuts, bumps, or other mishaps requiring attention. Be sure to keep the telephone numbers of your veterinarian and the closest animal hospital on an emergency list near the telephone. And affix IN CASE OF FIRE stickers to windows and doors to alert firefighters that there are pets living in your home.

FIRST-AID KIT FOR PETS

For minor problems, or to stabilize your pet until she can be brought to a veterinarian, put together a first-aid kit that can address any number of injuries. The kit should include the following items:

- ☐ A booklet on treating pets' injuries, such as the American Red Cross's Pet First Aid
- ☐ Antibiotic cream (those made for people are safe for pets)
- ☐ Blanket
- ☐ Castile soap (which is mild on skin and fur)
- ☐ Chemical cold pack
- ☐ Cotton swabs
- ☐ Disposable gloves
- ☐ Gauze (sterile rolls and pads)
- ☐ Glycerine-based antibacterial cleanser
- ☐ Hydrogen peroxide
- ☐ Penlight
- ☐ Pet thermometer
- ☐ Plunge syringe for administering liquid medication or flushing out eyes or wounds
- ☐ Rags or rubber tubing for a tourniquet
- ☐ Tweezers and scissors

COMMON HOUSEHOLD HAZARDS

Many common household items pose a threat to pets. Although rodenticides and insecticides are the most common sources of poisoning, there are other household hazards that pet owners should be acquainted with and take steps to avoid:

☐ Cleaning products should be tightly sealed when not in use to prevent accidental spills and ingestion.

☐ Certain foods, including onions, grapes, raisins, and macadamia nuts, can present health problems if ingested by pets. Talk to your veterinarian if you have concerns, or visit the ASPCA website (www.aspca.org) for more information.

☐ Stimulants that can raise your dog's heart rate such as chocolate and caffeinated beverages (including coffee, tea, and soft drinks) should be avoided. They not only irritate the gastrointestinal tract but can also cause internal bleeding. Beware of mulches that contain cocoa, because dogs will be attracted to the odor, and ingestion can prove fatal.

☐ Medication, both prescription and over-the-counter, can be fatal. Keep well out of reach.

☐ Fumes from nonstick pots or pans that are heated to the point of smoking as well as self-cleaning ovens can be toxic to birds.

☐ Items containing zinc, such as pennies and even sunblock, are dangerous to both cats and dogs.

☐ Toys with removable parts can pose a choking hazard, while rubber bands, dental floss, and bits of string (including those on the ends of rope toys) and yarn can cause intestinal blockages or strangulation.

☐ Pets should not tread on lawns or gardens treated with fertilizers, pesticides, or herbicides until they are completely dry. Ensure that these items are safely stored out of reach, as well.

☐ Pets should be kept out of garages to prevent them from ingesting toxic chemicals, such as those in motor oil, antifreeze (which has a sweet, attractive odor to pets), and gasoline. Purchase "pet-safe" antifreeze, which contains propylene glycol instead of ethylene glycol.

☐ Close trash cans securely to prevent pets not only from dragging garbage all over the house but also from getting at dangerous bones, metal, or plastic bags.

☐ Keep the dishwasher closed, since pets will be attracted to food residue and may cut themselves on a knife or utensil. Similarly, keep the dryer closed, because pets often like to nap in there when it's warm.

☐ Dangling cords on window shades should be tacked up so as to be unnoticeable.

☐ Several species of plants are also considered toxic to animals. Visit the ASPCA website (www.aspca.org) for a comprehensive list.

PEST CONTROL

PREVENTIVE CARE IS THE most effective strategy against unwanted animals and insects. If you have a problem, start with the gentlest methods, and proceed more aggressively as the need arises. Serious infestations should be dealt with by an exterminator (and health issues, such as stings and bites, should be addressed by a doctor). With a little care and attention to detail, your home can stay pest-free and pleasant.

PREVENTION

Keeping your home clean, inside and out, will go a long way toward keeping pests away. The commonsense approaches listed below and on the following page should be standard practice in every household. They are your first line of defense against a range of common pests.

In order for them to be effective, however, you must insist that everyone in the house does his or her part to follow the instructions consistently.

HOW TO DISCOURAGE PESTS

THE PANTRY

☐ Store food in tightly sealed containers.

☐ Decant dry, often-used items such as flour and sugar into airtight containers, rather than leaving them in their packaging. Cereal, spaghetti, and pet foods are also best stored in resealable containers.

☐ Wipe down oil bottles, honey jars, and syrup bottles after each use.

☐ Dispose immediately of fruits and vegetables that have spoiled.

THE KITCHEN

☐ Wipe up spills immediately, especially if they contain oil or grease.

☐ Wash dishes, glasses, and utensils as soon as possible after preparing and consuming meals.

☐ Keep pet-feeding areas free of excess food and spills.

☐ Sweep the floor daily.

☐ Confine eating to the kitchen or dining room.

BATHROOMS

☐ Clear slow-moving drains as soon as they occur. (For more information about how to clean a drain, turn to page 595.)

CLOSETS

☐ Wash or dry-clean garments thoroughly before storing them for the season in airtight containers. (For more information about storing clothes, turn to page 341.)

HOW TO DISCOURAGE PESTS (CONTINUED)

THE GARBAGE AREA

- ☐ Rinse glass, metal, plastic, and paper food containers and wrappers before recycling them or throwing them away.

- ☐ Clean the inside of garbage and recycling bins monthly. To clean a large garbage can, place it on its side outdoors, and then hose it down. Scrub the inside of the can with an old broom dipped in a disinfecting solution.

- ☐ Store garbage in cans or bins with lids.

THROUGHOUT THE HOUSE

- ☐ Keep corners and crevices clean and dry, paying attention to the attic, basement, and garage.

- ☐ Eliminate clutter, especially when situated alongside an outside wall.

- ☐ Don't stack boxes directly against a wall.

- ☐ Ventilate closed rooms and attics.

- ☐ Manage moisture by sealing all cracks and crevices with silicone caulking.

- ☐ When necessary, use dehumidifiers to control excess moisture.

- ☐ Cover holes in cabinets and under sinks.

- ☐ Add screens to windows and doors, if you don't already have them, and replace screens that are torn or don't fit snugly.

- ☐ Seal any gaps where utility wires or pipes enter your house and around doors and windows.

- ☐ Repair water leaks as soon as you discover them.

- ☐ Always keep new plants separate from others until you are sure they are pest-free. Inspect plants for pests before bringing them inside for the first time.

- ☐ Don't overwater houseplants.

OUTDOOR AREAS

- ☐ Stack firewood away from the house and make sure it is aerated. (For more on how to store firewood, turn to page 472.) Avoid storing large amounts of wood in the garage or anywhere inside.

- ☐ Clear gutters.

- ☐ Direct water from downspouts and drains away from your house. (For more information about exterior drainage, turn to page 421.)

- ☐ Trim trees, shrubs, and flowerbeds when necessary and avoid having them touch the house.

- ☐ Drain and refill birdbaths daily in the summer and weekly in other seasons.

A NOTE ABOUT PANTRY PESTS

An infested package of food isn't always a result of poor housekeeping; often packages are already infested at the grocery store. Flour, cereals, cornmeal, rice, legumes, dried fruits, candies, and boxed cake mixes are all attractive to moths—most often the Indian meal moth—and any number of tiny beetle species, including the common weevil. If you come across an infested package, throw it away; then check all other food packages that were near it. Throw away any more that you find, tie up the garbage bag, and dispose of it outside. Next, remove all items from the shelves where you found the packages, and vacuum corners and crevices. Wipe with mild dishwashing liquid and hot water. Once the shelves have dried, replace cans and packages.

To discourage future infestations, try this trick: drop a dried chili pepper or bay leaf into each jar or package. Both are nontoxic and have insect-repelling properties.

TYPES OF PESTS

ANTS

Many species of ants are beneficial, as they are likely to eat other, more harmful insects such as fleas and bedbugs. The problem with ants is largely aesthetic; they're not likely to cause disease. When ants invade a house, they are generally just looking for food.

TREATMENT

☐ When you spot a line of ants marching toward food, or spilling out of a crevice in the wall, identify what they are after and then mark their point of entry. If they're after food, leave it there—ants are easier to kill if they're in a line. Dip a sponge in soapy water and wipe away the ants. Block the entry point with a smear of petroleum jelly or a square of duct tape, until you can permanently close the hole or crack with silicone caulk.

☐ When ant infestations persist, it may be necessary to attack the ant colony—both the parent and satellite ones. Because ants share food, poisoned baits—usually made of boric acid with a sweet attractant—are effective. Use a commercial boric acid bait, available at hardware stores, in the spring since they become less effective in hot and dry weather. Place bait near the end of the line, not near the nest; follow label directions. Be careful not to disturb trails between any nests and bait stations—otherwise you may prevent ants from carrying the bait back to the colony. Keep bait out of the reach of children.

TYPES OF PESTS (CONTINUED)

BEES
There are about twenty thousand species of bees. The most common ones are:

BUMBLEBEES
These robust bees are densely covered with fuzzy black and yellow hairs. They range in size from about $\frac{1}{2}$ inch to 1 inch long. Bumblebees are social and nest in existing cavities, usually on or in the ground. Abandoned mouse nests and bird nests are attractive to bumblebees.

CARPENTER BEES
These solitary bees are so named because of their habit of boring into wood, in lieu of creating hives, to make homes for their offspring. They measure about $\frac{1}{2}$ to 1 inch, with a blue-black to black body and a green or purplish metallic sheen. Carpenter bees resemble bumblebees because they have yellow or orange hair, but the top surface of their abdomen is bare and shiny. Signs of a carpenter bee infestation include circular holes in wood, with sawdust shavings beneath the holes. Although they prefer softwoods (cedar, redwood, cypress, pine, and fir), these bees will also drill into all species of dry, seasoned wood. Damage is commonly caused to porch and shed ceilings, railings, overhead trim, wooden porch furniture, dead tree limbs, fence posts, wooden shingles, wooden siding, windowsills, and wooden doors. Carpenter bees tend to drill into wood that is at least 2 inches thick.

HONEYBEES
These bees are about $\frac{1}{2}$ inch long and have a fuzzy light brown to black appearance with striped brown and black abdomens. They are considered beneficial as they pollinate plants and produce honey and beeswax.

TREATMENT
☐ Treat infestations with an appropriate insecticide. For bumblebees, spray the nest entrance with a "wasp and hornet" aerosol, and then close the entrance with a handful of moist soil. Treat at dusk, when the bees have retreated to the nest. Always wear protective clothing to safeguard against stings. The best protection against carpenter bee destruction is to paint—not merely stain—all wood surfaces with an oil- or latex-based paint. Pressure-treated wood will also deter nest construction.

☐ Seek immediate medical attention for anyone who is stung and allergic to wasp or bee stings or is not allergic but stung around or within the mouth, nose, or throat, as swelling could close airways. Otherwise, take out the stinger: Dislodge it by scraping across it with a credit or playing card. Do not pull the stinger out by gripping it with tweezers or your fingers, or you could force more venom into the wound. After the stinger is removed, wash the area. A paste of baking soda and water can lessen pain. Ice will reduce swelling.

COCKROACHES

Roaches usually enter homes in paper products such as bags or cardboard boxes, and they prefer to seek refuge in dark, damp places with plenty to eat. Starchy and sugary materials including bookbindings, photographic film, household linens, leather, soap, glue, toothpaste, as well as a variety of foods, all attract cockroaches.

TREATMENT

☐ Water is attractive to roaches, so it's essential to minimize humidity and water leaks, as well as to wipe up spills immediately.

☐ Baits are effective when placed in cracks and crevices near refuge areas. Place baits in the following locations: beneath the sink and drain board, in cracks around the cupboards and cabinets, under toilets, as well as beneath refrigerators, dishwashers, washing machines, and ranges.

☐ Never spray bait stations with other insecticides or cleaning agents, or you may deter roaches from feeding on the bait.

☐ If you want to try a nontoxic alternative to roach baits, the National Wildlife Federation advises making your own by mixing equal parts of sugar and boric acid.

☐ If the baits are ineffective, contact an exterminator.

FRUIT FLIES

Fruit flies can develop anyplace where fermenting organic matter stays moist, such as a slow-moving or seldom-used sink or shower, a floor drain with buildup, or on spoiled produce. Like other flies, fruit flies develop from larvae, and fruit-fly larvae must have moist, fermenting organic matter in order to survive. Therefore, the best protection is to throw away spoiled produce and unclog drains.

TREATMENT

☐ Trap the flies in a jar: First place a small piece of ripe fruit or a few drops liquor or beer in an open jar, and then place a paper funnel (such as a coffee filter with the tip snipped off) in the top. The fruit flies will fly in and become trapped. You can kill them by pouring in boiling water.

☐ Another option is to set out a shallow dish of apple-cider vinegar. Cover the bowl in plastic wrap; using a needle, punch a half dozen holes in the surface at least $1/2$ inch in from the edge of the bowl. As with the paper-funnel method, the fruit flies will fly in and get trapped.

☐ Keep a few sprigs of fresh basil in a bowl or a potted basil plant near fruit and vegetables. Many cooks use this time-honored method with good results; some even find that setting a pot or two of basil outside the kitchen door keeps flies from entering the room.

TYPES OF PESTS (CONTINUED)

MOSQUITOES

Mosquitoes love swampy air and humid weather. They can carry diseases, including West Nile virus, so it's best to take measures to keep them away. Eliminating standing water and cutting tall grass are the most effective preventive measures.

TREATMENT

☐ Eliminate breeding grounds—basically, anywhere stagnant water can accumulate. Don't allow cans, buckets, or wading pools to collect water when it rains. If they have, empty them immediately. Repair leaky air conditioners. Birdbaths, fountains, troughs, and dog dishes should be emptied and refilled daily; saucers beneath potted plants should also be emptied, or filled with sand. If you have a pond, stock it with mosquito fish—a minnow that preys on mosquitoes. (Don't worry about your swimming pool; the chlorine will keep mosquitoes away.)

☐ Citronella, an extract from citronella grass, is often sold as a mosquito repellent, but its effectiveness is debatable. Commonly sold as a component of mosquito-repellent candles, citronella oil is also available and can be burned in tiki torches and other outdoor lanterns.

☐ Wood smoke is another mosquito repellent. Since building a bonfire isn't practical, mimic the effect on a smaller scale by using mosquito coils, also known as smoke coils or cedar coils.

☐ According to *Consumer Reports,* repellents containing DEET (diethyl toluamide) work better than any of the natural products on the market. Many people object to DEET because, in high concentrations, it can cause serious side effects, such as dizziness, blisters, rashes, and confusion. As such, DEET should never be used in concentrations higher than 30 percent (most commercial mixtures are lower). Children should not use repellents with more than 10 percent.

☐ If the infestation is serious, contact your local health department to find a mosquito-control professional in your area.

MICE

October through February is the peak time for mice to enter the home. Mice droppings, nests, evidence of gnawing, stale odors, footprints, and, of course, mouse sightings are evidence of an infestation. If you have a problem, pay special attention to food and garbage cans, and seal off holes and gaps as mentioned in the Prevention section starting on page 667.

TREATMENT

☐ The two most commonly available mechanical mouse traps—the traditional "snapback" trap and the more expensive metal-lever-jaw traps—are both effective if used properly. Wear gloves when handling the traps, since mice can detect human odors.

☐ Use a lot of traps—five to ten per mouse hole—spaced at 2-foot intervals from the hole (mice only forage a short distance from their nests). Set them at right angles to walls, since mice scurry close to baseboards. By placing the traps perpendicular to the wall, the mouse will have open access to the bait area. Keep traps away from children and pets.

☐ Set out the traps unarmed, with bait, for a few days to let the mice get used to eating food from them. For bait, use peanut butter mixed with rolled oats, raisins, or bits of whole-grain bread.

☐ If you decide to use rodenticides and you have pets and/or small children, purchase a tamper-proof bait station.

☐ Wear gloves when disposing of dead rodents.

MOTHS

Moths live in dark, undisturbed areas such as closets, basements, and attics, and tend to congregate in the corners or in folds of fabrics. They produce eggs that hatch into fabric-eating larvae. Clothes-moth larvae feed on animal-based materials, including wool, hair, fur, silk, felt, feathers, and leather. Synthetic fabrics such as polyester and rayon are rarely attacked unless blended with wool, or if they are dirty. Larvae may also infest carpet edges, upholstered furniture, and air ducts where they feed on lint and pet hair. Damage may consist of irregular holes. For more information about preventing and treating moths, turn to page 348.

TREATMENT

☐ If you find holes in clothes, you have a problem. With moth larvae, you may find silky webbing or cigarlike cocoons. Beetle larvae leave dried skins—like tiny rice grains. Remove and treat all infested clothes: Brush them vigorously outdoors with a clothing brush, available at some department stores, paying particular attention to cuffs and collars. Then either wash or dry-clean them. As an alternative to brushing, wrap clothes in plastic bags, squeeze out air, and freeze for a few days. Take the bags out, let them return to room temperature, and then repeat. Dry-clean or launder the clothes, then return to storage, properly wrapped to prevent future infestation.

TYPES OF PESTS (CONTINUED)

SILVERFISH

These tiny silver-gray wingless insects grow to $\frac{1}{2}$ inch long and seek dark, warm, moist environments, such as attics, closets, baseboards, and around bathroom fixtures. Named for their coating of tiny, silvery scales, these bugs like to eat starch from wallpaper, books, and fabric. Signs of silverfish damage include uneven holes in paper as well as small yellow stains on fabric.

TREATMENT

☐ Treat the cracks and crevices wherever the pests seem to be entering. Never apply pesticides or other chemicals directly to paper or textiles, which could be damaged.

☐ Ant and roach sprays are an effective treatment; follow manufacturer's instructions.

☐ Boric acid dust, which is long lasting and low in toxicity, can also be helpful, but is not as easy to apply to crevices as a spray. It is available at hardware stores and home centers.

☐ Isolate valuable objects until you are sure they are completely free of infestation. For example, wrap books or textiles in clear polyethylene sheeting and carefully seal them with tape. If after two or three weeks, no evidence of insect activity is present, the object can be displayed or stored with the rest of your collection.

SPIDERS

Spiders subsist mostly on insects, and generally enter a house for two reasons: to find dark areas for spinning webs and laying eggs, and to prey on household insects. There are a number of folk remedies for getting rid of spiders; in general, there's no need to resort to using insecticides.

TREATMENT

☐ As a deterrent, try leaving scraps of soap, preferably eucalyptus scented, where webs appear.

☐ Spray cotton balls with pennyroyal oil (a variety of mint available at health food stores) or rubbing alcohol, and rub on windowsills, baseboards, and behind appliances.

☐ To make your own bug spray, fill a spray bottle with 8 ounces of water and 3 tablespoons of liquid soap.

SPIDER MITES

These tiny members of the arachnid family thrive in dry, hot weather and are a common problem for both indoor and outdoor plants. When plants are stressed from hot weather and dehydration, they are especially vulnerable to spider mites. They inflict damage to leaves by piercing and eating individual plant cells, leaving behind yellow and white speckles or discolored patches. To check for the presence of spider mites, hold a piece of white paper beneath the leaves of a plant, and gently shake the foliage: If tiny bugs fall onto the paper, there's a problem.

TREATMENT

☐ Start with a natural approach. First, discard infested leaves. Then wipe down both sides of the remaining leaves using a damp cloth; repeat every week or so as long as mites are present. This simple act removes mites, as well as the dust and webbing that act as camouflage for the pests and as a nest for their eggs. As an alternative approach, spray infected plants with a garden hose, which will dislodge mites.

☐ Don't use traditional pesticides; gardeners often attack their plants with bug sprays, only to find their spider mite situation worsen. That's because these insecticides kill the natural predators of spider mites— lady beetles, lacewings, and predatory mites among them. There are specially formulated "miticides" on the market, but because of their toxicity, you should consider these a last resort.

☐ For more severe infestations on outdoor plants, consider biological controls such as introducing predatory insects. Many garden centers sell them.

☐ If these methods aren't sufficient, or if the problem is confined to indoor plants where biological controls are not an option, try "soft pesticides" such as insecticidal soaps. Available at garden centers, these soaps shouldn't have a long-term toxic impact on harmless insects, but they can eliminate spider mites on contact. They are sprayed directly on the mites and work by suffocating them; cover the plant thoroughly for effective treatment.

☐ Heavily infested foliage is often covered with dusty-looking webbing—at this stage, the damage is often irreversible, and the plant should be discarded.

TYPES OF PESTS (CONTINUED)

TERMITES

Termites eat wood and they live in warm, moist soil near food sources such as fallen trees, woodpiles, and houses. They can enter buildings through gaps in masonry as small as $\frac{1}{32}$ of an inch. Termite colonies live in underground nests connected to a network of mud tunnels through which the termites travel to look for food, which they carry back to the nest. Even in homes with little wood in the framing or walls, termites may target wooden doors, window frames, cabinets, or shelves.

Unfortunately, termite damage is usually not obvious until it is significant. To catch it early, examine the masonry foundation inside and outside for mud tunnels (weblike brown streaks). Probe all masonry cracks, holes, and crumbly areas for insects or dirt formations that might be nests. In addition, check all wooden features of the house that are close to the ground, as well as crawl spaces. Use a small knife or pick to poke into any area that appears rotten or decayed. If you can easily penetrate the wood to a depth of $\frac{1}{2}$ inch or more, termites may have damaged the wood. Use the same technique to check all other wooden features of the house and yard, including windowsills, door frames, stairs, fences, trellises, and posts.

TREATMENT

☐ The following three treatments may be used individually or in combination, but the best treatment will depend on the severity of the infestation. Before you try to remedy the situation on your own, consult an exterminator for the most effective solution.

☐ Bait systems perform well but take time to work; they lure termites to the bait, which they then carry back to the colony.

☐ Soil treatments applied around a house's perimeter prevent the termites from getting into the house.

☐ Wood treatments that are applied directly to wood that is infested or is in danger of becoming infested act as a deterrent and kill those that feed on it.

WASPS

Of the three kinds of wasps—Polistes (paper wasps), yellow jackets, and hornets—the latter two are the most dangerous.

POLISTES

Polistes build nests of masticated wood in protected areas such as under eaves. They are not overly aggressive and therefore don't generally disturb people.

YELLOW JACKETS

Yellow jackets are aggressive when provoked and often attack in swarms. (They are easily provoked; just waving them away from food can cause an attack.) They have black and yellow stripes, like bees, but they don't have body hair: bees are fuzzy, wasps are smooth. Their nests are made of masticated wood or leaves and are often found in the crevices of stone walls or in hollow logs.

HORNETS

Hornets are black with white markings. Their nests—constructed in trees or shrubs, or under eaves—are oval-shaped (about the size of a basketball) and covered with whitish papery material.

TREATMENT

☐ Kill wasps in the air by spraying them with wasp spray; hosing them will only make them more aggressive. Since wasps and hornets aggressively defend their nests, the safest method of destroying nests is to call a professional exterminator or wait until October when the queen insect has left and the workers have died. At that time, if nests are aboveground and hang from trees or houses, you can dislodge them with the spray from a hose. If the nests are in the ground or inside a wall, you can dig them up or out.

☐ Seek immediate medical attention for anyone who is stung and allergic to wasp or bee stings or is not allergic but stung around or within the mouth, nose, or throat, as swelling could close airways. Otherwise, take out the stinger: Dislodge it by scraping across it with a credit or playing card. Do not pull the stinger out by gripping it with tweezers or your fingers, or you could force more venom into the wound. After the stinger is removed, wash the area. A paste of baking soda and water can lessen pain. Ice will reduce swelling.

5 MOVING

ALTHOUGH IT CAN BE ONE OF LIFE'S BIGGEST CHALLENGES, moving to a new home also presents the refreshing opportunity to start anew. There's no better time to rid yourself of the clutter that accumulates in even the most well organized household.

On the following pages, you will find a timetable to help prepare for moving day, but you can also begin to plan, pare down, and pack even earlier. For example, if you know in December that you will be moving in June, pack holiday ornaments for moving, not for another year's storage. If you will be moving from a cold climate to a warm one, give away, sell, or donate many of your woolens when spring arrives. If you are moving to a smaller house, you can begin to get rid of furniture long before you move.

If you begin the planning (and packing) process as soon as you know you're moving, you are less likely to make hasty decisions—choosing a moving company without checking references, for example, or packing so haphazardly that things break. Staying focused and organized will keep your move smooth and manageable.

MOVING TIMETABLE

TWO MONTHS BEFORE	☐ Sort through the contents of closets, drawers, and cupboards to weed out what you don't want or need. Hold a yard sale, or donate unwanted items to charity. ☐ Inventory everything of value you plan to move and determine replacement values for insurance purposes. ☐ Obtain estimates from several moving companies and choose one.
SIX WEEKS BEFORE	☐ Finalize real estate or rental needs. ☐ If moving out of town, make travel arrangements. ☐ Notify your children's schools of the move and contact new schools for enrollment information. ☐ Obtain copies of school records, or have them sent to new schools. ☐ Obtain copies of medical records for each family member. ☐ Ask doctors to recommend doctors in your new community. ☐ Consult insurance agents to find out if changes to policies are necessary.
ONE MONTH BEFORE	☐ Alert utility companies to disconnect services the day after you move and to have new services activated several days before you arrive at your new house. Contact the chamber of commerce in your new town for information on utility services. ☐ If necessary, arrange for storage in your new community. ☐ If you're packing your house yourself, order supplies (turn to page 684 for a list) and start packing boxes.

ONE WEEK BEFORE	☐ If you're packing your house yourself, finish packing boxes.
	☐ Confirm travel arrangements, if needed.
	☐ Arrange payment or deposit for movers.
	☐ Get cash to have on hand to tip movers.
	☐ Write directions to your new home for the moving company, confirm delivery date, and give the company your itinerary and cell phone number.
	☐ Complete change-of-address forms at the post office, and send notices to magazine subscriptions, creditors, friends and relatives, alumni organizations, credit cards, banks, and any other necessary companies and organizations.
	☐ Cancel newspaper subscriptions.
	☐ Notify your employers—new and old—of your new contact information.
	☐ Clean rugs and have them packed for moving.
	☐ Obtain health certificates from your vet for pets traveling by air.
	☐ Pack suitcases you plan to move yourself with clothes, toiletries, jewelry, and important financial records and documents.
MOVING DAY	☐ Pack your first-night box (turn to page 685 for a list).
	☐ Accompany the mover as he or she inventories your possessions and makes condition reports.
	☐ Sign the bill of lading (ensure that the address and phone number are correct) and inventory, and keep your copies in a safe place.
	☐ Lock windows, turn off lights, close doors, and take a final tour after the movers have finished to make certain nothing is left behind.

HIRING A MOVER

If you have only a roomful of possessions or are traveling a short distance, moving yourself is probably the easiest and most economical choice. Renting a trailer or truck yourself may save you 30 percent or more over hiring a moving company. Keep in mind, however, that many rental companies charge more in the summer months (peak-season rates), when most moves take place. On the other hand, if you have a large household or will be traveling far, hiring a professional moving company makes sense.

The best way to find a reliable mover is to ask friends, relatives, neighbors, and real estate brokers whom they recommend. Ask whether the movers were reliable, and if the final cost resembled the estimate. If you can't get a referral, look in the Yellow Pages for potential movers. Be sure to ask movers for client references and check them.

QUESTIONS TO ASK A MOVING COMPANY

- ☐ How long has the company been in business?
- ☐ What are the average years of experience of their drivers, movers, and packers?
- ☐ Are they licensed with the state's Department of Transportation?
- ☐ Are they licensed for interstate moves?
- ☐ Do they offer storage?
- ☐ Are their workers bonded?

Visit the Better Business Bureau's website to check whether the companies you're considering have had complaints filed against them, and see if you can determine which companies have the fewest number of complaints. But beware, fewer complaints may not indicate a reliable mover; it may simply mean that a moving company is new.

For interstate moves, get written estimates from at least three national companies. For other moves, get two. To ensure your estimate is as accurate as possible, make an inventory ahead of time of your household goods, and review it at your house with a representative from the moving company, assigning dollar values to each item (this process usually takes a few hours). Don't forget to include everything in the attic, basement, closets, garage, and any off-site storage areas. Antiques should be appraised ahead of time by an accredited appraiser, and photographed. The representative will write an Order of Service—a detailed plan of the move, with a fixed or estimated cost, including insurance.

Moving insurance usually requires that you choose either to be reimbursed for the full replacement value of items broken or by the weight of the items broken. Unless you happen to be moving extremely heavy items, the former method is the best choice.

Movers generally offer two kinds of bids: binding and nonbinding. Both bids are based on the estimated weight of what's to be moved, distance to be traveled, and special services to be rendered, such as packing.

☐ A binding bid means the price agreed to before moving is final, assuming all the agreed-upon conditions remain the same—in other words, last-minute add-ons can inflate the bill. Even if the load weighs more or less than the estimate, you pay the price set forth in the bid.

☐ A nonbinding bid is an approximation of costs based on estimated weight and services requested. The final price will depend on the actual weight of the shipment, but can't exceed the estimate by more than 10 percent. Make sure you read the contract carefully to be sure you understand the terms and conditions before signing it.

BEFORE PACKING

Paring down your belongings before you pack will make that process (as well as unpacking) much easier. Set aside time to sort through possessions, and then hold a tag sale or donate unwanted goods to charity.

The most effective way of getting rid of belongings is to tackle one closet, drawer, or cabinet at a time. Before starting each project, gather several cardboard boxes or large trash bags; you'll need them to transport belongings to the staging area for your sale or to charities, recycling, or the trash. Start by pulling everything out of the closet, drawer, or cabinet, and sort items into three piles: keep, discard, giveaway/sale.

SORTING STRATEGY

KEEP PILE
These are the items you are sure to wear or use and will go with you to your new house.

DISCARD PILE
These are the things that are broken or damaged beyond repair and belong in the trash or recycling bin.

GIVEAWAY/SALE PILE
These are the things to sell or give to either friends or charity. (Many charities are happy to accept bags of clothing and other household items and will often send a truck to pick them up. Registered 501(c)(3) charities will also provide receipts for tax purposes.)

Next assemble basic packing materials to ensure that you have everything at hand so there will be no interruptions to hunt for scissors or extra tape once you start packing. Keep all the materials in one spot, so that everyone in the house knows where to find them.

ESSENTIAL PACKING SUPPLIES

BOXES
They can be purchased from your moving company, a packing-supply store, or you can get them from a grocery, liquor, or office-supply store (make sure boxes have lids and are clean and dry). Wardrobe boxes are the best way to move hanging garments. Measure the number of linear feet of hanging clothing to calculate the quantity you'll need. For the kitchen and dining room, use boxes with preassembled partitions to protect glassware. You can purchase boxes specifically designed to accommodate large items, including glass tabletops, mirrors, artwork, mattresses, and lamps. For books, choose small boxes. Those larger than 12 inches square can be difficult to lift when full.

BOX CUTTERS
To quickly open boxes.

TAPE
Standard packing tape, strapping tape, which is lined with nylon fibers that make it impossible to tear or cut without scissors (for reinforcing the bottoms of heavy boxes), and clear plastic mailing tape (for affixing labels and making them waterproof). Have a tape dispenser for every member of the house.

STRETCH WRAP
For securing doors and drawers on bureaus and cabinets. It sticks to itself, leaving no residue behind.

LABELS
For identifying boxes.

PACKING PAPER
White tissue paper or blank newsprint (avoid newspaper, which can leave ink stains on your valuables). Keep either on hand (both are available from packing-supply companies) to stuff boxes and wrap fragile items before packing them.

BUBBLE WRAP
For padding the bottoms of boxes, and wrapping breakable items. It's most economical to buy it in large rolls, and cut sheets as you need them.

PERMANENT MARKERS
For labeling boxes.

PENS AND A NOTEPAD
For making notes and writing directions.

BASIC TOOL KIT
For furniture disassembly.

SCISSORS
For cutting Bubble Wrap and tape.

SMALL SEALABLE PLASTIC BAGS
For keeping small items together, such as screws and brackets for shelving. (Look for the variety with a white stripe for writing labels.)

LARGE TRASH BAGS

HOW TO PACK A BOX

1. Assemble the box, and secure the bottom seam with tape. For added reinforcement, strap the bottom of the box by applying tape perpendicular to the main seam.

2. Pad the bottom with enough crumpled paper to form a cushion—if you press down on the paper, you should not be able to feel the bottom of the box.

3. Stuff extra paper into corners, since they will take the brunt of the impact if a box is dropped.

4. Wrap each item in paper, then put it in the box, leaving enough room on the sides and top for more paper padding.

5. Don't "underfill" boxes, or they will collapse when stacked. Small gaps can be stuffed with paper, a towel, or clothing.

6. Tape the box shut and label it with your name, the room it belongs in, and general contents. Label the side of each carton rather than the top so that labels are visible when boxes are stacked.

TIPS FOR SUCCESSFUL PACKING

☐ If you are using professional movers, let them pack the fragile items, since companies are usually liable only for things they pack themselves.

☐ Pack one room at a time.

☐ Avoid mixing things from different rooms in the same box; it will make unpacking more time consuming.

☐ Pack clothing and linens in suitcases.

☐ Wrap small items that can be easily lost in brightly colored tissue paper before placing them in boxes.

☐ Clearly label each box with your name, its general contents, an arrow indicating which side is up, "Fragile" if contents are breakable, and which room each box belongs in. Refrain from noting anything valuable, such as silver, on the outside of a box.

☐ Have area rugs professionally cleaned before your move. They will return from the cleaners rolled, wrapped, and ready for shipping.

☐ Assigning color codes to labels and corresponding rooms or family members can make unpacking quicker.

☐ Use small boxes for heavy items, large boxes for light ones, and medium boxes for everything in between. Heavier items should be placed at the bottom, lighter ones on top. A good rule of thumb is that if you can't pick up a box with ease, it's too heavy.

☐ When disassembling furniture, put hardware in a plastic bag and affix it to the corresponding piece (however, do not apply tape or any adhesives directly to polished or painted wood surfaces).

☐ Never pack flammables or combustibles.

PACKING A FIRST-NIGHT BOX

Create a "first-night" box containing essentials. These items, many of which you'll be using on the last morning in your old house and the first night and day in your new one, can be loaded on the truck last; label the boxes appropriately so that they will also be the first boxes off. Keep in mind that you should always carry valuables, jewelry, and important paperwork with you.

☐ Disposable plates, glasses, and cutlery

☐ Napkins and paper towels

☐ Nonperishable snacks

☐ Bed linens for each bed

☐ Towels

☐ Toiletries

☐ Medicine

☐ Change of clothes for every member of the family

☐ Telephone

☐ Lightbulbs

☐ Trash bags

☐ Basic tools

☐ Cleaning supplies

☐ Flashlight

☐ Toys for children and pets

HOW TO PACK HOUSEHOLD GOODS

ELECTRONIC EQUIPMENT

☐ Check owner's manuals for the manufacturer's moving tips—printers, especially, require special packing.

☐ Let equipment cool to room temperature before packing, and once you've unpacked it, let it return to room temperature before plugging it in.

☐ Most electronic equipment, including audio equipment, television sets, DVD players, and computers, are best moved in the manufacturer's original packaging. If you don't have it, double-box them using the method described opposite, under Other Kitchen Items.

☐ When disassembling electronics with numerous cords, place small colored stickers on each cord and the same colored sticker where the cord connects to the device for easy reference.

☐ Make copies of all computer files and store them online or carry them with you in the car (not in the trunk) or in your carry-on luggage (to ensure that they won't get too hot or cold, which can cause damage).

☐ Label boxes containing electronics with only the room they'll end up in or a family member's name to lessen the possibility of theft.

LAMPS

☐ Remove the bulb, harp, and shade.

☐ Pack the base of the lamp in an upright position in a well-padded box.

☐ Wrap the shade in tissue paper (never packing paper) and place it upright in a separate box, lined with crumpled tissue.

☐ Wrap the harp separately and affix it to the inside of the box containing the shade with a piece of tape.

FILES

☐ Transfer the files from your home office into cardboard file boxes. Carry important documents, such as birth certificates and passports, and financial records containing bank account numbers and Social Security numbers with you to guard against identity theft.

FRAMED ITEMS

☐ Wrap in tissue paper and sandwich each item between two layers of $\frac{1}{4}$-inch foam board cut slightly larger than the frame. Secure the corners with foam board and tape. Wrap the bundle in kraft paper.

BOOKS

☐ Pack books flat, alternating bindings, keeping like sizes together. Put a piece of packing paper between valuable books to protect the jackets or covers. Fill empty spaces with paperbacks or crumpled packing paper.

HOW TO PACK KITCHENWARE

SMALL APPLIANCES

☐ Pack each separately in a box close to the appliance's dimensions, rather than bunched together in one box.

☐ Wrap each appliance with packing paper (and Bubble Wrap if it is heavy or fragile), and fit it snugly into its box. Stuff any gaps with crumpled packing paper.

CUPS, GLASSES, AND STEMWARE

☐ Gently stuff cups and glasses with wadded-up packing paper.

☐ Wrap stems and handles with paper, crumpling slightly to create padding, and then wrap each entire piece individually in paper.

☐ Pack cups, glasses, and stemware in an upright position, cushioning them well with crumpled paper, rather than laying them down. Label boxes "Fragile, This Side Up."

OTHER KITCHEN ITEMS

☐ Wrap handles of large objects, such as pitchers, with crumpled packing paper prior to wrapping them individually.

☐ To wrap a teapot, wind rolled-up paper around the handle, then additional paper around the spout. Place the teapot upside down in the bottom corner of a stack of packing paper, and fold a few sheets over it until you have a bundle; secure it with tape. Wrap a teapot lid separately from the pot, but put both together in the same box.

☐ Wrap knives individually in paper, then in Bubble Wrap. (Or wrap them in protective sleeves designed specifically for knives.) Label the bundles so you're mindful of the sharp edges when you unpack it.

DISHES

☐ All china is best packed in cartons made for that purpose.

☐ Place one plate in the center of a stack of packing paper; grasp two or three sheets of the paper at one corner, and fold them over the plate, covering it completely. Place another plate on top of the first, and fold papers over from a second corner. Add a third plate, and fold the two remaining corners over it. Turn the stack upside down on the packing paper, and rewrap the entire bundle, sealing it with tape. (Some office-supply stores carry Bubble Wrap bags designed specifically to fit plates; these bags are more convenient, though they can be expensive.) Place the bundle in a small box, standing dishes on edge on a thick layer of crumpled paper or Bubble Wrap. (Dishes are more likely to break when packed flat.) Add additional bundles until the box is packed snugly. Stuff the top and all four sides with more crumpled paper, and tape shut. Label boxes "Fragile, This Side Up."

☐ Pack pots and pans of graduated sizes in nesting groups; place two or three sheets of packing paper in a large pan, insert a smaller pan, and line that one with more packing paper. Insert an even smaller pan, and so on. Place nested pans upside down on packing paper, and wrap with at least three more sheets of packing paper. Seal the bundle with a piece of tape.

☐ Very fragile items will be safer if you double-box them. Place the paper-wrapped object in a small box, packed well, then pack this box in a larger one, padded with packing paper or Bubble Wrap on all sides. (This is also an excellent method for mailing delicate items.)

☐ Pack only nonperishable food items, and make sure they are kept upright.

TIPS FOR MOVING PETS

☐ Before leaving your old home, securely attach an ID collar on your pet with her name and your new contact information.

☐ If you're moving a short distance, ask a friend or relative to watch your pets for the day. Changing homes can be upsetting, and keeping them away from the action will alleviate some of that stress, as well as prevent them from getting underfoot.

☐ To prepare a pet for air travel, visit a veterinarian for inoculations and any medication your animal may need (and perhaps sedatives, to lessen the stress of travel). Check airline instructions: They may require a health certificate from a licensed vet issued within ten days of travel. If you're moving to another country, contact the appropriate embassy, governmental agency, or consulate at least four weeks in advance for information about potential quarantine requirements. Additional requirements may also exist for international flights.

☐ If flying, choose a nonstop flight, if possible, to avoid excess handling as well as climate and air-pressure changes.

☐ Traveling long distances with animals by car can be difficult; many get carsick, and accommodations must be planned in advance to guarantee that pets will be welcome. Make frequent stops on the way so your pet can drink, eat, and stretch.

☐ Check licensing laws for your destination before departing, and secure copies of medical records and any necessary health certificates from your veterinarian.

☐ Birds and caged pets are susceptible to drafts and changes in temperature, and should therefore travel with a black cloth draped over their cages.

☐ If moving a bird internationally, you must obtain documents from the U.S. Department of Agriculture and the Department of the Interior's Fish and Wildlife Service before leaving the States. Such preparation is critical for birds covered by the Convention on International Trade in Endangered Species.

☐ Once settled, allow your pet to explore your new home; if she seems upset, confine her to one room, and keep food, water, a favorite bed, and a toy (and litter box) there for a day or two.

☐ If you have fish that you would prefer not to part with, ask for advice at your pet store. Some pet shops will store and ship fish, but this is typically an expensive process. Otherwise, it is usually most humane to find a good home for your fish and buy new ones once you've settled.

TIPS FOR MOVING HOUSEPLANTS

Houseplants do not travel well. Temperature and light fluctuations, not to mention the jostling, are intolerable to most houseplants. Many moving companies refuse to transport them, and some states restrict what may be carried across their borders.

☐ If you wish to move a valuable plant to another state, contact its department of agriculture as there may be restrictions. Such regulations guard against introducing insects and pests that may destroy valuable cash crops.

☐ Protect plants from heat, cold, sunlight (which is intensified by car windows), and wind by wrapping them in cones of kraft paper. Stake tall, delicate plants first.

☐ Place wrapped plants in cardboard boxes, leaving the tops open, and stuff crumpled paper around pots so they're snug.

☐ Place plants in the backseat of a car, never the trunk.

☐ When you reach your destination, make tending to plants a priority—unwrap and water them as soon as possible.

AT YOUR NEW DESTINATION

☐ Have a certified check, cashier's check, cash, or a credit card ready for final payment to the moving company.

☐ When the driver arrives, he will list all boxes and loose objects on a new inventory, noting the condition they are in. This inventory will be attached to the bill of lading, or contract; read both carefully, and keep copies.

☐ Designate a couple of helpers. As movers bring boxes inside, one person can check off items against the driver's inventory, and the other can guide the crew to the right rooms. Damage, even on the exteriors of cartons, or missing goods, should be noted on the driver's copy of the inventory.

☐ Before the driver leaves, have him sign the inventory—this will help validate an insurance claim should that be necessary.

☐ If, upon unwrapping and unpacking your things, you discover damage, leave those cartons untouched—do not unpack or unwrap them—until a representative of the moving company can come and inspect them.

☐ Have tools ready for assembling furniture.

MATERIALS GUIDE

IN EVERY HOME THERE ARE MYRIAD BELONGINGS—some purely functional, some designed to provide comfort, and some acquired simply to make the home a more beautiful place. It is these objects that give a home its pleasing complexity and character.

All objects, whether used daily, displayed proudly, or packed away for safekeeping, require specific care. The technique for restoring brightness to a vintage milk glass vase, for example, is different than for the handwoven lace that adorns a set of antique linens. The method for cleaning a lacquered box is different than that for the heirloom strand of pearls it contains.

Understanding the composition of the many objects throughout the house is critical to their care. Some objects are composed of the elements of nature, others are man-made; some are crafted (or painted or woven) by hand, others are assembled in factories. Just as important is the distinction between those objects made from materials that come from plants or animals, defined as organic, and those derived from minerals and metals, which are identified as inorganic (wool, for example, which comes from shorn animal hair, is organic, while glass, made from sand that is heated to a liquid state, is considered inorganic). Objects made from organic materials may at first seem more delicate than things made from inorganic substances, because they are so much more vulnerable to the elements. They may swell and shrink as the humidity climbs and falls, or fade when exposed to direct sunlight. But, in fact, inorganic objects often need gentle care, too. Stone, for example, is porous and subject to staining. Metals can be corroded by moisture.

Fortunately, to learn once about these materials is to understand how to use them, treat them, and care for them over the course of many years. Curators, preservationists, and restorers have discovered much about how time and the elements can destroy valuable or beloved things, from artwork to ceramics to stone. They have learned, too, how to protect and preserve these same things against such damage, with techniques easily adapted for use in the home. The better you care for and store the objects in your home, the better they will serve you (and future generations).

Elsewhere in this book you will find maintenance recommendations for other, more commonplace, household materials, whether you are looking for the best way to treat stains on a marble countertop (page 50), polish a piece of wooden furniture (page 521), or clean a porcelain bathtub (page 316). What follows is a guide to the proper care and preservation of the more unusual materials used to create the treasured objects handed down by parents or grandparents or lovingly collected at tag sales and antique stores. Before delving into the care of each material, it's worth studying the guidelines opposite, which should be applied to every object noted in the pages that follow. These seven tips will help you create a safe environment for all of your treasures, and ensure they withstand the test and conditions of time.

BASIC CARE GUIDELINES

CREATE A STABLE ENVIRONMENT

The best way to protect and preserve your specialty materials is to control the three most damaging elements—light, humidity, and heat.

Light Ultraviolet light is harmful to materials, so keep valuables out of direct sunlight. Use UV-filtering glass on windows and artwork, and regularly rotate anything on display. Choose incandescent lighting over halogen to minimize fading.

Humidity Because it encourages the growth of mold and mildew, moisture should be controlled in any area where organic materials are displayed or stored. Moisture can also corrode metals. In general, a relative humidity of 45 to 55 percent is best for most materials. Use a hygrometer (available at hardware stores) to assess the humidity level, and avoid displaying or storing objects in kitchens, bathrooms, and laundry rooms. Use dehumidifiers and desiccants if necessary. (For more information on air quality, turn to page 560.)

Heat Maintain a temperature of about 72°F; fluctuations will have a bearing on humidity, thus increasing the likelihood of damage. Higher-than-average temperatures can also cause organic materials to deteriorate more rapidly.

HANDLE OBJECTS WITH CARE

Always pick up heavy objects by the base. Don't leave fingerprints on metals and soft stones such as alabaster; the oils and acids from skin can cause corrosion. To be safe, wear clean cotton gloves when handling vulnerable materials.

DISPLAY OBJECTS SENSIBLY

Hanging objects should be secured with sturdy hardware. Items on display should rest firmly on level surfaces (with felt rounds placed beneath them to protect tabletops, mantels, and other surfaces).

KNOW WHEN TO LEAVE SOMETHING ALONE

Sometimes patina is what gives an object its charm—and its value. Antiques dealers and conservators regularly advise owners to forgo rigorous polishing designed to restore a like-new shine. Although there is nothing wrong with making over an everyday flea-market find, you can irreparably damage a fine antique by doing anything more than dusting it and applying a coat of paste wax.

STORE OBJECTS PROPERLY

Wrap large items in clean white cotton sheets. Wrap small items in acid-free tissue paper and use only archival-quality packing materials and boxes (ordinary paper is usually strengthened with lignin, a chemical compound which breaks down over time, releasing acids that can discolor paper and other materials). Similarly, unlined wood shelves, insulation, and carpeting can all release fumes that will cause many materials to deteriorate over time. Line shelves with archival paper, and store objects away from materials that might off-gas. Most important, never store objects in plastic, which can trap moisture, fostering mold growth and corrosion. Finally, label stored belongings for easy identification.

CHECK STORED OBJECTS ANNUALLY

Inspect items in long-term storage for cracks, flakes, or crumbling bits, as well as insect infestation or water damage; remedy the situation immediately if you discover a problem.

KNOW WHEN TO CALL A PROFESSIONAL

Some repairs are do-it-yourself endeavors, while others require a conservator. As a rule, anything you can't replace or can't afford to replace is a candidate for professional care. To find conservators, visit the website of The American Institute for Conservation of Historic and Artistic Works, aic.stanford.edu.

ABALONE A mollusk known for the iridescent lining of its one-piece shell; it is also called mother-of-pearl (which also refers to the linings of mussel, oyster, and snail shells). It is used to adorn furniture, and to make boxes, picture frames, jewelry such as cameos and cuff links, buttons, the keys of some musical instruments, flatware handles, and caviar spoons.

CARE After wearing an abalone item, or as part of regular dusting, wipe it with a soft, dry cloth. For a deep cleaning, use a commercial pearl cleaner that contains no ammonia, dyes, or fragrances (consult a jeweler for sources); apply the product as directed and dry the piece using a soft cloth. Be aware that abalone may be affixed with adhesive potentially weakened by such cleaners; wipe these items with only a soft, dry cloth.

STORAGE Store small items in soft pouches, padded boxes, or on a padded shelf apart from other objects that might scratch them.

AGATE A variety of chalcedony (quartz). Found in rocks or lavas, it is a hard stone that comes in an array of colors, often with striations in the shape of concentric rings. It is found in jewelry and carved into flatware handles, bowls, urns, picture frames, clocks, and boxes.

CARE Use a soft cloth to wipe dust, dirt, and oils from agate. For particularly dirty pieces, use a solution of mild dishwashing liquid and warm water applied with a damp cloth. Agate requires no penetrating sealer or coating; over time, it develops a waxy luster.

STORAGE Agate chips and cracks more easily than many other stones and can break if dropped. Store it in a padded container, or wrapped in a soft, lint-free fabric to guard against scratching. In general, agate items will not be affected by extremes of heat or cold, but colors can fade if pieces are left in direct sunlight. If agate becomes stained, there may be no remedy; consult a jeweler.

ALABASTER A fine-grained variety of gypsum. Because it is soft, it is often carved into ornamental objects, such as sculptures, urns, boxes, compotes, and lamp bases; because of its translucency, it is often used to make chandeliers and sconces. It is usually white, but because it is porous, it can be easily dyed.

CARE Alabaster should be dusted regularly—before a layer of dirt builds up—with a soft-bristled brush or soft untreated cloth. It requires an extremely light touch because it scratches easily and cannot withstand any contact with sharp objects (wrap masking tape around the base of the brush to guard against damage) or abrasives. Never use detergents, alcohols, or corrosives on alabaster. Even plain water can cause iron in the stone to oxidize and form a stain. Never use an alabaster vessel to hold moist or acidic foods, both of which can discolor and etch it. Light, humidity, and normal household temperatures should not affect alabaster, but it is susceptible to water stains and damage from high heat (such as contact from lightbulbs when used in chandeliers and sconces). A restorer can often reverse water stains, but heat can permanently discolor alabaster.

STORAGE Store items in padded containers or wrapped in a soft, lint-free fabric or acid-free tissue paper to prevent scratches.

ALUMINUM A strong, durable lightweight metal with a silvery luster. It is an excellent heat conductor so is often used to make cookware and bakeware. Because aluminum is very malleable and corrosion-resistant, it is fashioned into a host of household products, including utensils, trays, candlesticks, lamp bases, window frames, and outdoor furniture.

CARE In general, aluminum requires little care beyond regular dusting and washing with a solution of water and mild dishwashing liquid. It scratches easily, however, and should not be cleaned with anything abrasive. To avoid discoloration, never use strong detergents, alkalis (including ammonia), or alkaline scouring powders, such as baking soda.

STORAGE Protect pots and pans by placing rounds of felt or paper plates between them when stacking them. Wrap other objects in soft, lint-free fabric or acid-free tissue to prevent scratches.

B

BAKELITE A malleable form of plastic—technically, phenolic resin—used to make colorful buttons, jewelry, billiard balls, clocks, flatware handles, furniture pulls and knobs, napkin rings, and dresser and desk accessories. It was invented accidentally in 1907 by a Belgian-born chemist, Leo Baekeland, who was trying to develop a form of synthetic shellac. Bakelite objects were particularly popular during the 1930s and are highly collectible today. Because it wouldn't melt or catch fire, Bakelite also became a popular insulation for electric wiring and electric plugs.

CARE Bakelite can be brittle, so handle it carefully. Dust regularly and wash pieces as needed using a soft, white cloth and a solution of mild dishwashing liquid and warm water (never use alkaline cleaners such as ammonia or alcohol). Utensils should be hand washed (never put Bakelite in the dishwasher—harsh detergents and high heat can cause drying out to the point of cracking and can dull colors). Bakelite may also benefit from periodic treatment with Novus Plastic Polish, available at hardware stores, a three-step chemical process that deep cleans and polishes plastics. The treatment lasts for one to several years, depending upon how frequently the item is used. Do not let Bakelite jewelry come in contact with hair-care products, deodorant, perfume, moisturizers, or cosmetics, all of which will damage it.

STORAGE Keep Bakelite out of direct sunlight to prevent discoloration, and away from heat sources such as cooktops, which can scorch and dry it. Wrap objects separately in acid-free tissue for long-term storage. Store utensils in divided trays, with metal parts facing in the same direction, to avoid scratching and chipping.

BAMBOO The only woody member of the grass family. Because it grows fast and rejuvenates quickly (it can be harvested every four to five years, as opposed to trees, which can take decades to mature), it is an environmentally friendly alternative to wood. It is, however, often shipped from Asia, which requires a great deal of fossil fuel. Bamboo is widely used for decorative items, including furniture, window blinds, utensils, and serving pieces. Distinguished by its pale color, tight grain, and "knuckles," bamboo is also becoming an increasingly popular floor covering.

CARE Bamboo objects and furniture should be dusted or vacuumed regularly with a dusting-brush attachment. Remove dirt with a sponge dampened with a solution of warm water and a few drops of mild dishwashing liquid; then wipe with a clean cloth dampened with plain water, and dry with a clean cloth. Do not wash bamboo-handled flatware in the dishwasher.

STORAGE Although bamboo is a stable material, it should not be exposed to extremes in temperature or humidity. Extended exposure to direct sunlight will discolor the material and finish (outdoor furniture and objects will weather to a dull gray, like teak). Store bamboo away from sunlight and from heat sources such as radiators and vents. Cover furniture with clean white sheets to keep the dust off.

BONE Animal skeleton used to make objects such as cutlery handles, carvings, buttons, combs, sewing tools, handles and knobs, and game pieces. Although it is sometimes mistaken for ivory, bone is more brittle and decays faster.

CARE Bone must be handled carefully to keep it from warping or absorbing dirt. Do not immerse objects in water; they will swell, crack, and discolor. Dust with a soft-bristled brush or cloth. If dirt remains, wipe with a barely dampened cloth. Always use soft, white cloths, since bone can absorb fabric dyes. For flatware, wipe the metal with a soft cloth dampened in a solution of water and mild dishwashing liquid, but avoid wetting the bone handles and the seam between the blade and the handle, where the adhesives used to bond metal and bone can be weakened. Rinse with a cloth dampened with plain water and dry with a soft, clean cloth. Do not wash bone-handled items in the dishwasher.

STORAGE Store objects in a cool, dry spot and keep them out of direct sunlight. Do not display them in internally lit cases; heat can cause damage. For long-term storage, wrap items in a soft, lint-free white cloth or acid-free tissue paper, or place them in boxes lined with acid-free material.

BRASS An alloy of copper and zinc. Yellowish in color, it is a common material for bed frames, musical instruments, decorative hardware, lighting fixtures, candlesticks, trays, and fireplace andirons.

CARE Because brass tarnishes easily when exposed to air, many brass items are coated with clear lacquer (if you dab a small amount of polish on an inconspicuous spot with a white cloth and the cloth does not turn black, the metal is likely lacquered). As long as the lacquer is in good condition, these pieces will need only dusting or an occasional gentle cleaning with mild dishwashing liquid and tepid water (never use hot water, which can damage lacquer) followed by a thorough drying. Lacquered brass will not tarnish, but the clear coating is fragile, and if it gets nicked or wears away, the metal underneath will tarnish where it has been exposed to air—and you cannot remove the tarnish without removing the lacquer. Consult a conservator about removing lacquer from large or valuable pieces. You can remove lacquer from small pieces yourself, using acetone (available at hardware stores) on a cotton pad, or paint stripper applied with an old paintbrush. After treating, let the piece stand for five minutes, then, wearing protective gloves, remove the stripper with a soft brush. Rinse the item thoroughly, and polish as necessary. You can also apply a new coating of lacquer yourself; use a spray-on gloss lacquer appropriate for metals (also found at hardware stores). It is important to spray in light coats—if it begins to drip, you are using too

much. A layer of paste wax will protect the delicate lacquer, but be sure the object is thoroughly clean before applying it. (For instructions on how to apply wax, turn to page 524.)

Besides dusting, unlacquered brass needs polishing to maintain its shine. Use a commercial polish designed for brass; liquids, polish-soaked cloths, or pastes and creams are all suitable. (For instructions on how to apply polish, turn to page 525.) Heavily corroded brass may require the attention of a conservator. Do not attempt to remove thick corrosion with steel wool, which may scratch the surface.

You may be able to tap out dents in thin-gauge metal with a jeweler's hammer (tap gently from the reverse side), but damage to thicker metals will probably require a conservator's attention.

STORAGE Store brass in a cool, dry environment in acid-free tissue, and if possible, keep objects out of direct contact with unsealed wood (which emits acids that can contribute to corrosion). For long-term storage of large collections, use padded metal shelving. Cotton sheeting draped over large objects helps keep off dust. Tarnish is not harmful to objects being stored, but any pieces displaying corrosion should be stabilized by a conservator.

BRONZE A durable alloy of several metals, including copper and tin, and sometimes other elements, such as zinc. Bronze has been in use for more than six thousand years, and is commonly crafted into decorative objects such as candlesticks, desk accessories, vases, lamp bases, bookends, and indoor and outdoor sculptures. Keepsakes such as baby shoes are often "bronzed," or coated with a metallic surface through electroplating. Bell metal is a type of bronze made from a copper-tin alloy that contains small amounts of silver or other elements to enrich the tone.

CARE Whether indoors or out, bronze usually requires only dusting with a soft-bristled brush (such as an artist's paintbrush) or a light wiping with a soft cloth, as the development of a patina (which ranges from reddish brown to green to black) is desirable.

On smaller, intricately detailed pieces, dust using a can of compressed air (available at office-supply stores). Lacquered bronze (see BRASS for more information on lacquer) needs only an occasional wiping with a cloth dampened with water and mild dishwashing liquid. Dry the object with a soft, clean cloth. Pieces with crevices can be dried with a blowdryer on the lowest setting. Have cracked or peeling lacquer replaced by a professional conservator.

STORAGE See BRASS.

C

CANING The skin of the fast-growing rattan vine, the inner core of which is used to make wicker. Over the centuries, chair seats and backs have been made from woven strips of thin, flat cane because it is light, strong, and durable—even without a protective finish, it can last more than fifty years.

CARE Regularly vacuum cane with the dusting-brush attachment or dust using a paintbrush. To clean or remove stains, wipe with a solution of a few drops of mild dishwashing liquid diluted in warm water (don't use abrasives, or acidic or alkaline cleaners). Dry with a second clean cloth. Stains should lift off newer caning easily. Indelible stains generally occur only on old caning where the protective shellac finish has worn away, allowing stains to penetrate. Reapplying shellac is inadvisable because it is thinned with a drying agent that is damaging to old cane.

Although caning is strong and long lasting, just one broken strand can cause an entire chair seat to unravel. If this occurs, the piece may be restored, by either hand or machine, by a professional caning craftsperson. Excessive dryness can cause caning to break. Regular misting with water—one or two times a month—will remedy this. Apply a fine mist from a distance of 2 feet. (See Caring for Caning and Rush in "Dining Room," on page 153.)

STORAGE Avoid heat sources, which can dry out caning. Use a sheet to keep dust off of furnishings.

CAST IRON Iron that has been cast into a mold. It is inexpensive and easy to produce, making it a popular material for cookware, decorative objects (such as doorstops and garden furniture), lamps, and exterior ornaments. You can identify cast iron by its porous surface and its weight; it is noticeably heavier than other metals. Cast iron has two drawbacks: It is brittle and prone to rust. The best way to protect outdoor cast iron is to apply several coats of high-quality, rust-inhibiting paint. However, coating an antique piece may diminish its value. Cast-iron cookware conducts heat evenly, making it ideal for both long, slow cooking and high-heat searing. Because of its porosity, cast-iron cookware must be seasoned (treated with oil) before using it for the first time and periodically thereafter to prevent food from sticking and to guard against rust. (For instructions on how to season a cast-iron pan, turn to page 68.)

CARE Unpainted, untreated cast iron should be vacuumed using the dust-brush attachment, then wiped with a soft, dry cloth. Do not clean cast iron with water—the metal absorbs moisture and will rust rapidly. If grease or grime are resistant to a dry cloth, wearing rubber gloves, dampen the cloth in mineral spirits (paint thinner available at hardware stores). Use this technique only on untreated pieces that will not have contact with food and first test for discoloration on an inconspicuous spot. Rust can be removed by lightly rubbing the affected area with a fine (0000) steel wool. Flaking rust can be removed with an X-Acto knife, putty knife, or wire brush. If rust removal leaves pitting, consider having the item attended to by a conservator. Use caution when cleaning painted pieces—even mild cleaning solutions can remove paint. Consult a conservator about especially grimy pieces.

Pieces that have begun to corrode must be stripped of both paint and rust, neutralized, and then repainted. Although these procedures can be done at home, keep in mind that vintage pieces may be coated with lead paint, which is best stripped by a professional.

STORAGE If storing a cast-iron pan for an extended period, apply a thin layer of edible-grade mineral oil instead of vegetable oil, which can turn rancid. Ensure there is sufficient padding between cast iron and other objects to prevent chips and cracks. Handle pieces as little as possible, as salt and oils from your skin can damage cast iron.

CELLULOID A plastic commonly known as French ivory, composed of wood or cotton fibers and various acids. It was developed in the mid-nineteenth century for use as imitation ivory, but since it takes pigment well, colors vary beyond the traditional creamy white. It was also used to imitate other exotic materials, including marble, amber, tortoise, and horn. It is fashioned into small household items such as handles for utensils, trays, boxes, grooming tools, mirrors, picture frames, game pieces, buttons, jewelry, toys, and clocks. Unlike modern plastics, celluloid has a warm smoothness that's pleasant to the touch and polishes to a high sheen. To determine whether a piece is celluloid, warm the piece by rubbing it with your hand and then sniff. If you detect the chemical smell of camphor (a major component), it is celluloid. The material develops a satiny, light ocher patina over time from exposure to light and air. Such exposure actually darkens, rather than fades, celluloid. Before you buy a piece at a flea market or antiques store, peel back price tags or labels to make sure there is not a lighter spot underneath, since this discoloration is permanent.

CARE Dust celluloid regularly. Wipe with a cloth dampened with mild dishwashing liquid and water to remove surface dirt. A plastic polish, such as Novus Plastic Polish, may be effective on seriously soiled pieces. For detailed pieces, dust using a can of compressed air (available at office-supply stores). While it is chip resistant, celluloid is highly flammable and vulnerable to ammonia, alcohol, and perfume—one drop will permanently mar the surface.

STORAGE Display celluloid in a cool environment, as it has a tendency to warp when left in direct sun-

light. A few weeks near a radiator can cause permanent deformation. Wrap pieces in acid-free tissue for long-term storage—other packing materials may cause celluloid to disintegrate.

CERAMICS The word "ceramic" comes from the Greek word *keramos,* meaning "potter" or "pottery." It is used to describe any object shaped from clay that has been fired to render it hard. There are three main categories of ceramics: earthenware, stoneware, and porcelain.

EARTHENWARE

Earthenware is a kind of clay fired at low heat, such as terra cotta. It does not vitrify, or become glassy. It is thick, porous, and opaque. Earthenware dishes are generally coated with a nonporous glaze. Chips in the glaze reveal the clay body underneath. Earthenware has been produced since ancient times.

STONEWARE

Stoneware clay is fired at high heat. It is vitrified, heavy, opaque, and nonporous. Like earthenware, stoneware has been produced since ancient times. It came into widespread use in Europe in the fourteenth century.

PORCELAIN

Porcelain is a clay to which kaolin, a fine white or gray mineral, and feldspar, a crystalline mineral, have been added for strength and translucency. It is fired at high heat, which vitrifies it and makes it nonporous. It is thinner, lighter, and more durable than earthenware or stoneware. Porcelain was first produced in China in the seventh century. Its popularity as an import ware in Europe (which led to the words "china" and "porcelain" becoming synonymous) prompted the creation of imitation porcelain (known as soft-paste) in the seventeenth and eighteenth centuries. Potters added ground glass to the clay to render it thin and hard instead of kaolin, which they had not yet discovered. The first true European porcelain (known as hard paste) was produced in Meissen in the early eighteenth century. Bone china is a porcelain to which bone ash has been added for translucency and whiteness. It was developed in the eighteenth century in Britain.

There are many styles of antique ceramics. Among the most collectible are ironstone, lusterware, majolica, transfer ware, and yellow ware.

IRONSTONE

Ironstone is a variety of stoneware developed in Staffordshire, England, in the early 1800s. English potters produced most of the vast quantities of ironstone sold in the United States until the 1870s. After the Civil War, technical innovation and expanding railways enabled American entrepreneurs to outsell foreign rivals. Ironstone may be patterned (as with transfer ware), but in the United States it has been most popular in its white-glazed form. This solid, sturdy, mass-produced pottery, also referred to as white granite, was designed to withstand the rigors of daily use. By the 1890s, however, in middle-class households where it had once radiated respectability, white ironstone acquired the stigma of "farmer's ware" and was replaced at table by dainty porcelain and bone china.

LUSTERWARE

Developed at the start of the nineteenth century in England, lusterware uses a glazing formula that lends earthenware, stoneware, or porcelain a metallic, mother-of-pearl luminescence. (Other glazing techniques that lend an iridescent sheen stretch back to the ninth century.) The three basic colors of English luster pottery are silver (derived from platinum in the glaze) and copper and pink (derived from gold in the glaze). Around the turn of the twentieth century, thanks to its broad popularity, lusterware was widely manufactured. Wares from Japan, Germany, and Czechoslovakia took on a new look, with orange, purple, green, and blue glazes and more fanciful forms.

MAJOLICA

This tin-glazed, hand-painted earthenware originated in fifteenth-century Spain. The name is likely derived from the island of Majorca, where the first of these pieces was made. Later they were also crafted in Italy and France (where they were called faenza and faience, respectively, after the Italian city of Faenza, famous for its pottery). Majolica, in forms ranging from elegant to outlandish, was popular throughout Europe for centuries. Collectors particularly covet quirky Victorian English wares covered in lush flora and fauna.

TRANSFER WARE

Developed in England in the eighteenth century, transfer ware features detailed storytelling images, often of the Far East. The images were printed rather than hand-painted, first on soft-paste porcelain and later, around 1840, on more durable ironware pottery. Cobalt blue ink was used initially because it was inexpensive and could survive the firing process; by 1820, transfer ware could be made with red, green, black, brown, purple, and yellow inks.

YELLOW WARE

A staple of American households for more than a century, yellow ware derived its color from the plentiful clay that lines riverbanks from New Jersey to Ohio. This stalwart ceramic runs the gamut from light corn yellow to deep mustard and is often peppered with flecks and slight imperfections. The ceramic made its debut in England in the late eighteenth century, and by the 1830s it was being manufactured in the United States for the mass market. Because it was mass produced, only some 5 to 10 percent of wares ever carry a potter's mark.

CARE Dust display pieces regularly with a soft cloth or feather duster. Always check ceramics carefully before immersing them in water. If a piece shows evidence of a repair, wipe it gently with a cloth dampened with water and mild dishwashing liquid rather than soaking it or running it under the tap (many old repairs were done with water-soluble glue). Treat earthenware pieces with cracked or chipped glaze in the same way to prevent moisture from penetrating the exposed clay body. Antique and vintage ceramics in good condition can be hand washed in warm water and a few drops of mild dishwashing liquid. To guard against chips, wash items in a plastic washtub or line the bottom of the sink with a thick towel. Never treat stains on ceramics with chlorine bleach, which can cause irreparable damage (consider stains part of a piece's patina and learn to live with them instead). Modern ceramics, whether earthenware, stoneware, or porcelain, can generally go in the dishwasher. The exceptions include unglazed earthenware or ceramics with metallic or hand-painted decorations; these are best washed by hand.

STORAGE To guard against chipping, wrap objects in acid-free tissue and space them out on shelves so there's no danger of them knocking against other objects. You can protect dinnerware by placing it in zippered, padded storage containers (available at home-supply stores). Do not nest cups, which can cause handles to break. Instead, store them on their bases (rather than their rims) in a single layer or stack them with saucers in between each cup. Sturdy cups without repairs can also be hung from cuphooks. Put paper plates, coffee filters, paper towels, or felt rounds between stacked bowls and plates to prevent scratching. Always put pieces with repairs on top, and only stack plates of the same size together, no more than four to six to a group. To secure lidded pieces, wrap twine in a figure eight around both vessel handles and over the lid, then tie gently. Although most ceramics are not susceptible to damage from direct sunlight, painted pieces may fade.

CLOISONNÉ An ancient decorative technique in which layers of colored enamel are separated by thin strips of metal soldered onto a base metal, often in intricate patterns. It is used to adorn jewelry, vases, lamps, and small boxes. It is thought to have originated in the Near East. It is also found on objects made in the Middle Ages, and later in China, where it is still made today.

CARE Regularly dust pieces with a soft, dry, lint-free cloth to remove dirt and oils. If pieces are particularly dirty, use a cloth dipped in a solution of mild dishwashing liquid and warm water (never soak cloisonné). Dry thoroughly to prevent corrosion. Do not put cloisonné jewelry in an ultrasonic cleaner.

STORAGE Cloisonné is prone to chipping. If a section of enamel becomes chipped, have the piece repaired by a jeweler or antiques dealer specializing in cloisonné rather than trying to glue it yourself.

Store cloisonné objects in acid-free tissue paper and padded boxes to guard against chipping.

COPPER A soft metal with a distinctive pink color, copper was one of the first metals used by humans, and remains a common household material. It conducts heat and electricity well and so is often used to make cookware and electrical wiring. Copper acquires black or brown tarnish over time, which eventually turns green. Moisture in the air accelerates this process. Decorative pieces (which are not designed for food) are often coated with clear lacquer, which retards tarnishing. For more on lacquer finishes, see BRASS, page 696.

CARE Outside of the kitchen, copper is frequently left to develop its familiar brown-green patina. This coating, which won't harm the metal, is desirable on many decorative objects, and in some cases, removing it will diminish the value of the piece. Dusting with a soft-bristled brush or a can of compressed air (available at office-supply stores) will remove dirt without affecting the patina. Wipe copper objects using a damp cloth and a solution of water and mild dishwashing liquid. Most pieces shouldn't be submerged in water. Dry the piece inside out, minding all the nooks and crannies. A blow-dryer on the lowest setting can be used to accelerate the drying process. Do not, however, place copper on top of a radiator or in direct sunlight; both may cause staining.

If you opt to remove the tarnish, select a commercial polish that's specially formulated for copper and follow the manufacturer's directions, making sure to test in an inconspicuous spot before proceeding. For more on polishing metal, turn to page 525. Especially heavy accumulations of tarnish should be removed by a conservator.

STORAGE See BRASS.

CORAL The skeletal remains of a branchlike marine creature, the coral polyp (when millions live together in colonies, they create coral reefs) is made up of calcium carbonate (just like eggshells and seashells). Coral is used in jewelry and as decorative *objets*. The species of coral chosen for jewelry are smoother, more compact relatives of common reef coral. Colors range from pale pink (known as angel skin) to salmon to deep red (or oxblood) to black. Soft and malleable compared with gemstones, this type of coral lends itself well to intricate carving. Coral jewelry was the finery of choice for dressy daywear in the Victorian era. During its heyday, legions of craftsmen (usually Italian, as coral was once abundant in the Mediterranean Sea) cut it into beads, cameos, and flowers. By the turn of the nineteenth century, supplies in the Mediterranean were dwindling due to overfishing and coral was harvested in the waters surrounding Japan, Hawaii, and Australia. Although experts differ on which color and type is most precious, most agree that the more consistent the color, the greater the worth. Because many coral reefs around the world are in jeopardy due to pollution and climate change, a number of countries now limit the collection and sale of coral.

CARE The soft and porous coral used in jewelry must be treated gently. Put coral on only after you have applied cosmetics, perfume, or hairspray. Never wear it in the pool, when cleaning, or when cooking with vinegar, all of which are damaging. Clean it by wiping with a soft clean cloth or quickly rinsing it in warm, soapy water. Do not soak it, immerse it in jewelry dips, or use an ultrasonic cleaner. Blow the dust off pieces of decorative coral using a can of compressed air (available at office-supply stores); such pieces can also be rinsed under the faucet and dried with a soft cloth.

STORAGE Store coral jewelry individually in pouches or in the compartment of a jewelry box to keep the surfaces from becoming scratched by other pieces. Wrap larger pieces of coral in tissue to keep them from knocking or scratching objects around them.

CORK The dead outer bark of cork oak trees grown primarily in Portugal and Spain. Harvested when the bark naturally loosens every decade or so, much of it is used for wine-bottle stoppers. It is also ground up for use as soundproofing, and made into bulletin boards, shoe soles, and flooring (for sheet, tiles, and tongue-and-groove planks).

CARE Cleaning methods vary depending on how (or whether) cork is sealed. Because cork is soft and absorbent, cork objects are sometimes sealed with polyurethane, acrylic, or wax during the manufacturing process. Dust sealed cork regularly with a soft cloth and wipe with a cloth dampened with water and a pH-neutral all-purpose cleaner or mild dishwashing liquid.

The cork used for wall and ceiling tiles, bulletin boards, coasters, and trivets is often unsealed, and therefore vulnerable to stains, so be sure to wipe spills immediately. A set stain cannot be removed. Dust weekly using the dust-brush attachment or a barely damp cloth.

STORAGE Cork objects are subject to shrinkage and swelling due to moisture, so keep them in a dry environment.

DIAMONDS The only gem mineral composed of a single element—carbon. They are the hardest known natural material and can only be scratched by other diamonds. Colored blue-white to sooty black, most are slightly yellowish; the rarest, known as "fancies," are red, green, pink, purple, and blue. Jewelers grade diamonds according to the four C's—cut, which refers to the shape; clarity, the number of microscopic flaws; carat, which is the weight; and color, the scale of which ranges from D (virtually colorless) to Z (traces of yellow or brown). Fancies are not rated on the D-to-Z scale. Diamonds temporarily lose their distinctive sparkle when dirty; hand lotions, cosmetics, oils from your skin, and soaps can all cloud their surface. They are, however, easy to clean.

CARE Place paper towels over the drain to prevent jewelry from falling into it. Mix mild dishwashing liquid with warm water, and scrub with a soft toothbrush. Rinse under warm running water, and dry with a soft, lint-free cloth. If you have a diamond that has not been fracture-filled and contains no other gemstones in the setting, you can also soak it in equal parts household ammonia and cold water for five minutes. Remove, rinse, and dry as directed above. Diamond jewelry can also be safely cleaned in an ultrasonic cleaner.

STORAGE Store diamonds separately from other jewelry, to prevent scratching, in fabric-lined drawers or boxes. Remove diamond rings while doing heavy work. Have settings and prongs checked once a year by a professional jeweler to ensure the diamonds are secure.

E

EMERALDS The green variety of the mineral beryl and the world's most valuable gemstone by weight. Emeralds contain many internal fissures and fractures. Even though these flaws are routinely filled with colorless oils and resins to improve clarity, emeralds are brittle and fragile, and must be treated with the utmost care. They can develop internal cracks if banged hard or exposed to extreme temperature changes. Remove an emerald ring before doing any chores or even washing your hands, and do not wear emerald jewelry while applying lotion, makeup, or hairspray.

CARE Wipe emeralds clean with a damp cloth. If a stone is particularly dirty, rinse it quickly with lukewarm, soapy water. Never use ammonia, chemical or ultrasonic cleaners, or hot water, which can damage the stone. Resetting and conditioning should be undertaken only by experienced jewelers.

STORAGE Store emeralds in velvet-lined boxes or drawers, separate from other jewelry, to prevent scratching.

ENAMELWARE Metal kitchenware made of thin sheets of iron, steel, or aluminum and coated with enamel, which has been baked on in a hot oven. Popular from the 1870s until the 1930s, enamel-

ware was commonly used to make pots and pans, bowls, canisters, biscuit cutters, ladles, pitchers, trays, picnic sets, bread boxes, and muffin pans. Sometimes called graniteware or agate ware, many pieces feature a splatter pattern or a swirl pattern in vibrant colors mixed with white.

CARE Enamelware chips easily, and rust may develop on these spots (and seams). If you plan to eat or cook with enamelware, make sure that the enamel coating is intact on any surfaces coming in contact with food. It's best to wash enamelware by hand using mild dishwashing liquid and a soft cloth. If necessary, use a plastic scouring pad or wooden spoon to remove burnt-on food, or soak the piece in a solution of 2 teaspoons baking soda and 1 quart water. Avoid using abrasive cleansers or steel wool. After washing, always dry enamelware thoroughly, inside and out; water can seep into chips and cracks and rust the metal underneath.

STORAGE Store enamelware in a dry place. Put paper towels between pans when stacking them to prevent scratches.

F

FEATHERS Bird feathers, which are made of a protein called keratin, are used decoratively in the manufacture of quill pens, holiday ornaments and trees, and mask and hat trimmings. The type of feather most commonly used in decorative applications is the contour feather, which comes from the tail and wings. These strong, stiff feathers cover the down feathers, which are the soft, fluffy feathers that keep birds warm. The greatest enemy of feathers is dust, which attracts moisture from the atmosphere and, if not removed, can hasten deterioration. Prevent dirt buildup by displaying feather items under glass or in shadow boxes. In general, they should be handled as little as possible, both to keep their structure intact and maintain their natural coating of oil.

CARE When on display, feathered items should be dusted weekly with a soft-bristled brush. Follow the direction of the vane, the flat surface on either side of the quill, when dusting. Don't wash or dry-clean feathers. To treat fresh spills, dab the area—do not rub—with an absorbent, white cloth (such as a terry towel) to pick up excess liquids and solids. Allow the feather to air dry. Set stains should be cleaned by a professional conservator.

STORAGE Keep feathers out of direct sunlight, which will cause them to fade and dry out, accelerating decay. When storing feathers, use acid-free tissue paper and roomy acid-free boxes.

FELT A dense, extremely warm, water-resistant fabric made from wool, which is often mixed with other fibers, including rayon and polyester. During the manufacturing process, heat, water, and a lubricant such as soap are used to relax and stretch combed wool, coaxing the shinglelike scales on the surface of each fiber to open. Pounding, rolling, and drying cause the wool to shrink and coil, making the scales catch on one another and close tight. Wool's felting power is so strong that even when blended with 90 percent other materials, it still felts. It is used to make blankets, pool table covers, slippers, hats, dolls and doll accessories, and Christmas stockings and tree skirts.

CARE Regular dusting with a dry sponge, available at home-supply stores, will help prevent stains from setting. Blot spills immediately with an absorbent white cloth (such as a terry towel). Some felt items can be hand washed in cold water, but if there is no care label it's best not to risk damage (felt can shrink and dyes can run). Felt can be freshened with a handheld steamer, followed by gentle brushing with a clothes brush. Cleaners designed for felt hats (such as cowboy hats) can be useful when tackling greasy stains, such as fingerprints.

STORAGE Felt does not unravel, so it rarely requires mending; however, pure wool felt is susceptible to moth damage. Store such objects as you would a wool sweater; ensure items are clean and dry. For short-term, seasonal storage, reclosable plastic bags or bins are best for keeping out pests. For long-term storage—years rather than months—it's best to use canvas or another material that allows ventilation, since some plastics can degrade fabrics over time. For more on mothproofing, turn to page 348.

FUR Fur rugs, blankets, and garments are extremely warm and durable. A pelt usually includes short, dense fur, known as underfur, and longer, straighter outer fur, called guard hair, which is the fur you see on the surface of the pelt. The term "fur" includes sheep and lamb skins that have intact hair.

CARE Fur should be shaken regularly to dislodge dust. It should not be vacuumed, as the force of the suction can break the individual strands. In the event of a spill, coat the liquid immediately with baking soda and remove it using a clean cloth once it is dry or brush it out using a soft-bristled brush. Once a year, furs should be cleaned by a professional furrier. They will be tumbled in a drum with a material that absorbs dirt and oils. They may also be treated with a glaze to enhance their luster. Although plain water will not harm it, fur should never be laundered or dry-cleaned.

STORAGE Store fur rugs in a cool, dry environment. Furriers keep storage vaults at between 40° and 50°F, with humidity at 45 to 55 percent. Keep the dust off garments by draping them with a cotton sheet or placing them in a canvas bag; never use plastic. Roll fur rugs in a clean sheet.

GALVANIZED METAL Most commonly steel or iron that has been coated with a thin layer of zinc, which protects the underlying metal from corrosion. The zinc outer layer oxidizes over many years, developing the characteristic dull, silvery patina. Although the galvanizing process was developed during the mid-eighteenth century, it didn't come into widespread use until a hundred years later when large-scale manufacturing and population growth made demand skyrocket. It was used to make common building materials such as corrugated roofing as well as farm implements. Tabletops, garden pots, watering cans, buckets, wash tubs, and garbage bins are often also made from galvanized metal.

CARE Wash with mild dishwashing liquid and water. To keep the zinc coating intact—which will keep rust at bay—avoid abrasives. For indoor surfaces, a coat of paste wax can give some protection and shine to the surface and help prevent staining. (For instructions on how to wax, turn to page 524.) If a galvanized metal item has rusted, remove the rust with a stiff brush. Then paint or coat with a clear finish, such as polyurethane, to prevent the rust from returning.

STORAGE Avoid storing galvanized metal in damp or poorly ventilated areas. Moisture can lead to white, gray, or black spots. Sea air can accelerate spotting.

GLASS Most is made from three primary ingredients: silica, soda, and lime. These components (and occasionally some additives) are heated at high temperatures until they melt and are then formed into objects of all sorts, either by machine-pressing or blowing the molten glass into molds or by drawing it (the process used to create sheet glass). Sometimes, lead is added to glass to make it more brilliant and easier to cut. Leaded glass, also known as crystal, is readily distinguished from regular soda-lime glass by its unmistakable tone—if you tap the edge of a crystal glass, it will ring like a bell. Full leaded crystal must contain 24 percent lead (for more on crystal stemware, turn to page 172). Another common additive is boric oxide, which makes glass able to tolerate high heat without breaking. This glass often used for bakeware, such as Pyrex, is called borosilicate glass.

Glass has been produced for thousands of years (the ingredients and techniques have, in fact, changed little over time), but it was the Romans who perfected the art of glassblowing in the first century. During the Renaissance, Venice was the center of glass production and innovation and the techniques developed there eventually spread to the rest of Europe. Manufacturing continued as a craft until the Industrial Revolution. It was not until the first quarter of the twentieth century that glass production was truly mechanized; prior to that, glass was generally mouth-blown into molds or otherwise shaped by hand.

There are many styles of vintage and antique glass. Among the most popular types of collectible glass are jadeite, mercury, milk, and Venetian.

JADEITE

First made in the 1930s, jadeite takes its name from its beautiful color, which ranges from milky green to deep emerald. Jadeite dinnerware, serving and mixing bowls, citrus reamers, and vases became household staples in the U.S. in the 1940s and 1950s. Many earlier jadeite pieces are not heatproof and can't be placed in the oven (they should be used only for display or to serve foods that have been cooled), but Anchor Hocking's Fire-King line of jadeite, which it marketed as Jade-ite, is dishwasher and oven safe (but can't be used in the microwave).

MERCURY GLASS

Despite the name, there is no mercury in mercury glass. It is, in fact, a clear glass mold-blown into double-walled shapes, then coated on the inside, through a hole in the bottom, with a silvering formula made of silver nitrate, alcohol or ammonia, and oil of cassia or tartaric acid (depending on which recipe you read) it is also called silvered glass. First discovered in early-nineteenth-century Germany and used as an inexpensive, tarnish-free substitute for silver objects, mercury glass quickly gained favor in France, England, and the United States. Much vintage glass found today is damaged. Air enters through the hole in the bottom (the original methods for plugging the holes proved less than permanent), causing the silver coating to flake off or oxidize. You can slow the damage by shaving a cork to fit the hole and plugging it, or by covering the hole with a plug of malleable wax.

MILK GLASS

Milk glass almost always refers to the opaque white glass that was popular from 1835 through the 1980s in America and England. It originally addressed the desire of an expanding middle class for the finer things in life. It was porcelain for the masses, an inexpensive substitute for the luxurious tableware made by such companies as Wedgwood and Spode, whose designs it sometimes shamelessly imitated. Early manufacturers added arsenic to the standard glass recipes, which yielded a faintly grayish color but a nicely opalescent effect. Some older glass also contains quantities of lead, which gives it a bell tone when tapped. Later glassmakers used tin oxide, feldspar, and other additives to achieve the denser whiteness they desired. Milk glass should be used only for display or for foods that have cooled.

VENETIAN GLASS

After a long period of dominance during the Renaissance, the Venetian glass industry eventually fell into decline. It was revived in the 1860s when Venice officially became part of Italy and every region was called on to manufacture products for the collective good. Ancient formulas and techniques, which had never totally died out, were revived. Venetian glassblowers, unlike their colleagues in northern Europe, used a sodium-based formula—not the lead-based formula used in making crystal. Because soda glass takes longer to harden than lead glass, they were able to fashion much more complex designs. After World War II, Venetian glassblowers began to take inspiration from the modern art movements of the day, producing objects in strong, contemporary shapes and bright colors along with the more familiar forms modeled after pieces from antiquity and the Renaissance.

CARE Dust display pieces regularly with a soft cloth or feather duster. Always check glass objects carefully before immersing them in water. If a piece shows evidence of a repair, wipe it gently with a cloth dampened with water and mild dishwashing liquid rather than soaking it or running it under the tap (many old repairs were done with water-soluble glue). Treat glass pieces with surface decoration—such as hand painting or opalescent coatings—in the same way and do not use anything abrasive on them. Antique and vintage glass in good condition can be hand-washed in warm water and a few drops of mild dishwashing liquid. To guard against chips, wash items in a plastic washtub or line the bottom of the sink with a thick towel. Wash especially delicate pieces one at a time. Dry glassware with a soft, lint-free cloth. Modern glass can generally go in the dishwasher. The exceptions are fine stemware or glass with metallic or hand-painted decorations; these are best washed by hand.

STORAGE To guard against chipping, wrap objects in acid-free tissue and carefully twist tissue around handles, stems, and necks to provide additional protection. Space them out on shelves so there's no danger of them knocking against other objects. Store drinking glasses on their bases rather than their rims to protect against chipping. Although most glass is not susceptible to damage from direct sunlight, painted pieces may fade.

GOLD One of three precious metals (the others are silver and platinum). Pure gold is soft enough to mold like stiff clay, which is why it is mixed with another metal. The alloying metal also lends color. Although gold's true color is warm yellow, the addition of nickel, silver, or zinc can result in white gold; adding copper creates a pinkish gold known as rose gold. By law, gold jewelry has to exhibit a hallmark indicating the percentage of gold: 24 carat gold is 99.99 percent pure. The lowest permitted percentage in the United States is 10 carat (10 parts pure to 14 parts alloy). Gold does not corrode like other metals, but it can become brittle. It must be handled carefully to prevent scratching.

CARE Wash in warm water mixed with a few drops of mild dishwashing liquid. For intricate pieces, scrub gently with a soft toothbrush. Rinse, and shine with a soft cloth or chamois.

Remove jewelry when doing heavy work to minimize scratching, and when swimming in a chlorinated pool or cleaning with chlorine bleach. Chlorine can pit and discolor gold. If gold is scratched or bent, it can usually be polished and reshaped by a jeweler. Prongs should be checked for wear by a jeweler once a year.

STORAGE To prevent scratching, store items individually in compartmentalized boxes or velvet bags.

GOLD LEAF Gold that has been beaten into very thin sheets (a stack of 250,000 is only an inch high). It is applied to many different objects and surfaces, including ceilings, walls, picture frames, trays, and lamps. Glassware, fabrics, and leather may also be embellished with gold leaf. There are two methods of application: water gilding and oil gilding. If a piece has been water gilded, the application of any water will disolve the binding, and the gold will come off. If a piece was oil gilded, you'll have the same problem if you use a solvent-based cleaner. Any cleaning liquids or chemicals might well destroy the beautiful patina gold leaf develops over time. Only a professional has the expertise to discern the original method of gilding.

CARE The only cleaning advisable is regular dusting with a sable brush (available at art supply stores) or a feather duster.

STORAGE Do not keep gold-leafed items in direct sunlight or in areas with extreme temperature or humidity fluctuations. If wood under gilding swells or shrinks, the bond between the gilding and surface can be weakened, causing flaking and cracking.

H

HORN Typically from a buffalo, sheep, or cow and used to make decorative items—cutlery handles, tumblers, bowls, and decorative inlays. Horn consists mainly of keratin, which is a protein. It has a plasticlike texture but it can display shallow holes from insect attacks, which helps to distinguish it from plastic.

CARE Dust regularly with a soft, clean cloth. Dampen the cloth with lukewarm water, if necessary, to remove grime. Flatware and other tableware should be handwashed with mild dishwashing liquid (do not put horn in the dishwasher). Do not soak horn or expose it to excessive dampness, both of which will cause it to swell and crack. Do not wax or oil horn; these treatments will eventually yellow, discolor, and cause the material to become brittle.

STORAGE Horn fares best in a stable, cool, low-light environment. Displaying horn objects in direct sunlight and extremes in temperature or humidity can cause warping and discoloration.

I

IVORY From the tusks and teeth of a variety of creatures, including elephants, mammoths, narwhal (an Arctic whale), hippopotamuses, and walrus. Generally, only an expert can distinguish among them. Historically, ivory has been crafted into many objects, including picture frames, buttons, combs, cutlery handles, game pieces, billiard balls, inlays for furniture, and piano keys. Many types of ivory are now subject to international bans. It has been illegal to trade in sperm whale and killer whale teeth since the early 1970s and in African elephant tusks since 1989. All animal-derived ivory has a multilayered structure, and is therefore especially vulnerable to cracking and splitting. Vegetable ivory, derived from the seeds of the South American ivory palm, is very smooth, as is French ivory, which is made of celluloid (for more, see CELLULOID on page 698).

CARE Dust regularly with a soft cloth or a feather duster. Wipe ivory clean with a damp cloth—always use a white cloth, since ivory can pick up dyes from fabrics. Dry with another cloth. Never immerse ivory in water, not even ivory-handled flatware. The absorption and release of moisture causes ivory to shrink and expand, which can lead to irreparable cracks. To clean flatware, wipe the metal with a soft cloth with water and mild dishwashing liquid. Avoid wetting the handles and the seam between the blade and the handle; on antique pieces, animal glue was often used to join the two parts, and it can weaken in water. (For information on cleaning piano keys, turn to page 215.) Ivory is very sensitive to light: bright daylight will bleach it, and darkness will cause it to darken. Rotate pieces frequently to maintain an even coloration. Ivory will also darken if it is frequently handled because of the oils in skin.

STORAGE Ivory is easily affected by its environment. Dryness will cause it to shrink and split; humidity will cause it to swell. Wrap items individually in acid-free tissue and store them where conditions are stable. Never store ivory on colored fabric or in proximity to wood. Both can cause staining and damage.

JADE There are two stones called jade: nephrite and jadeite. Nephrite is the more common; it's found in shades of green and milky white. Jadeite displays a wide range of color variation, the most familiar of which is bright emerald green. It may also be gray, yellow, pink, or lavender. Both nephrite and jadeite are extremely fine-grained and hard. Jade is used in jewelry-making and is often carved into intricate *objets d'art*. It is not particularly porous, nor is it affected by changes in temperature and humidity. It is brittle, however, and must be handled with care.

CARE Dust regularly with a soft brush or cloth. Use a can of compressed air (available at office-supply stores) to blow dust out of the crevices of carved pieces. Clean a dirty piece with a soft cloth, dampened with water. Do not clean jade with solvents or other cleaners, including ultrasonic cleaners.

STORAGE Jade jewelry should be stored separately from other pieces in velvet-lined boxes or bags.

Wrap objects in acid-free tissue and store on a padded shelf or surface.

JET Also known as lignite, jet is a fossilized wood that takes a high polish. "Hard" jet refers to fossils formed under saltwater conditions; "soft" jet refers to fossils formed in fresh water. Its inky color inspired the phrase "jet black." Although it's been used in jewelry for thousands of years, it became popular in the nineteenth century when Queen Victoria wore it with her mourning clothes after the death of her husband, Albert. There are many jet imitations, including epoxy resin and black glass. Jet will leave a brown streak if rubbed against an unglazed porcelain surface. And unlike glass, it is warm to the touch. Some of the best-quality jet comes from mines near Whitby, a town in the northeast of England.

CARE Dust jet objects regularly, and wash as needed in a solution of warm water and mild dishwashing liquid. Dry thoroughly with a soft cloth. Shine can be restored with a few drops of mineral oil.

STORAGE Store jet jewelry in individual pouches or bags to prevent it from being scratched by harder stones and metals. Jet is flammable and should be kept away from heat sources.

LACE Fine cotton, silk, or linen thread that has been formed into a decorative openwork design by twisting and sometimes knotting. It is used to trim fine linens and clothing, and to make curtains, tablecloths, bedding, wedding veils, and coasters and doilies. It was first developed in sixteenth-century Europe and was often named for its place of origin, such as Alençon and Chantilly, towns in France. Lace was originally made by hand using bobbins or needles, but today is made by machine.

CARE Clean vintage cotton or linen lace by soaking it overnight in plain, tepid water. This will rehydrate it and rinse away old detergent and dust. Line a tub or large sink with a white towel and fill it with a few inches of water. (Keep in mind that you should not attempt to clean lace that's made of silk, multicolored, or more than one hundred years old yourself; contact a conservator.) To wash lace (which must be done after soaking), swish it gently in tepid, soapy water (use a mild detergent such as Ivory Snow or Orvus Paste). Do not wring or rub the lace as you wash it. Drain and rinse it well in fresh water, without running the water directly on it. Repeat until the rinse water runs clear. Roll the lace in a white towel—again, without wringing—to absorb excess moisture, then dry flat on towels indoors.

Yellowed lace may be soaked in a solution of 2 to 3 gallons of hot water to ½ cup oxygen bleach until the fabric looks brighter. Make certain the bleach is completely dissolved before placing the lace in the water.

A baking-soda-and-water paste may be an effective spot treatment for food stains; a mix of baking soda, mild detergent, and dry oxygen bleach may lighten grease stains. For rust stains, apply salt and lemon juice and set the piece out in the sun to dry. Blot stains with a clean sponge; do not rub. Follow all stain treatments with the washing method above. When ironing lace, place a thick white towel beneath and on top of the lace, and use a dry iron. If you iron lace-trimmed linens, press the linens when they are still slightly damp.

STORAGE Drape items made entirely of lace, such as tablecloths, on hangers and cover with acid-free tissue; or roll onto acid-free tubes to store horizontally; or fold with as few creases as possible (place acid-free tissue between folds to minimize creasing). Whether hung, rolled, or folded, lace should be protected from dust, which can soil and permanently damage the material. (Dust is especially harmful to fine linens; it is abrasive and will cut the delicate fibers.) Cover with a clean sheet or canvas bag; do not use plastic.

LACQUER A water- or solvent-based finish, either clear or colored, that can be polished to a high sheen. It is applied in layers and provides a durable, protective surface. The Chinese and Japanese first perfected the art of lacquering centuries ago, using varnish made from the sap of the tree *Rhus vernicifera*. This type of lacquer is very hard and resistant to water, heat, and acids. When the technique was adopted in the West in the seventeenth and eighteenth centuries, it became known as japanning. Artisans used varnish rather than Asian lacquers to achieve the high-gloss decorative effect. The term "lacquer" is also used for a modern spray-on clear finish widely used in the furniture industry. For more on this finish, turn to page 526.

CARE Dust regularly using a barely damp soft cloth, being careful not to snag it on any chips. A particularly dirty piece can be wiped with a solution of water and a few drops of mild dishwashing liquid. Be sure to test first on an inconspicuous spot. Do not attempt to wipe down an antique piece that shows cracks or damage, however. If moisture reaches the wood or substructure under the lacquer, the damage can be exacerbated. Furnishings and objects in good condition can benefit from a coat of protective paste wax. For instructions on how to wax, turn to page 524. Talk to a conservator about stabilizing valuable pieces that are cracked. Wash lacquer tableware by hand in tepid water and mild dishwashing liquid. Do not soak objects or put them in the dishwasher. Keep all lacquerware out of direct sunlight, which can cause it to fade.

STORAGE Do not store lacquered items in areas with extreme temperature or humidity fluctuations. If the wood under lacquer swells or shrinks, the bond between the lacquer and surface can be weakened, causing cracking. Wrap small pieces in acid-free tissue to guard against chipping.

LEAD A dull gray and dense metal, with a wide variety of industrial uses. Lead is also used to make sculpture and garden ornaments. It is soft and malleable; pieces are easily scratched, bent, and dented. Lead is a toxin—ingestion of lead dust can cause serious health problems, particularly in children. (For more on lead safety, turn to page 575.)

CARE Objects coated with lead paint, such as small decorative antiques, should not be washed, as they can easily peel. Dust other lead objects as necessary with a slightly dampened paper towel (discard it when you're finished). Do not use detergent on lead. Wash your hands thoroughly with soap and water immediately after handling it. If a piece shows signs of corrosion—white powder and pitting—keep it out of reach of children as it is extremely poisonous, and contact a conservator who specializes in restoring metals.

Lead is also added to glass to lend it brilliance—crystal is glass containing 8 to 24 percent lead—and to ceramic glazes, particularly on handcrafted pieces made abroad.

Drinking out of lead crystal does not pose any risk for healthy adults, but children, pregnant women, and those in poor health should avoid it. (For more information, turn to page 174.) Because more significant amounts of lead can leach into liquids stored in lead crystal for extended periods, do not decant liquid into crystal unless it is lined with a protective coating.

Since 1980, the Food and Drug Administration has required that new ceramic products made with unsafe glazes sold in the United States be labeled: "Not for Food Use—May Poison Food." Ceramics from other countries and antiques do not have such warnings and should not be used for food storage or service.

STORAGE Keep lead objects away from heat, as lead melts easily. Painted objects, wood, and wood products such as cardboard encourage corrosion. Do not wrap lead objects in plastic, which can trap moisture and lead to corrosion. Instead, store lead on metal shelves lined with acid-free tissue or foam padding.

LLOYD LOOM A wicker woven using lengths of twisted kraft paper. The wicker fabric is woven on a machine and then attached to a wooden frame. The American inventor Lloyd Marshall Burns patented the process in 1917 and his company,

Lloyd Manufacturing Co., which merged with the Heywood-Wakefield Co. in 1921, produced furniture and baby carriages. The same materials and technique are still used today by a number of companies to produce furniture for both indoor and outdoor use.

CARE Vacuum Lloyd Loom weekly with the dust-brush attachment to remove dust, or brush with a counter broom. If soil builds up, wipe with a solution of mild dishwashing liquid and warm water. Do not use copious amounts of water on the wicker. Rinse with a clean, damp cloth and allow to dry out of direct sunlight; fast drying can cause the wicker to become misshapen.

STORAGE Outdoor Lloyd Loom pieces should be used only on covered porches or other protected areas, and stored indoors when not in use.

LUCITE A trade name for methyl methacrylate, a clear plastic also known by the trade name Plexiglas. The common name is acrylic. Lucite was introduced by DuPont in 1931 (the Rohm and Haas company developed Plexiglas at about the same time), and put into large-scale production during World War II for use on fighter planes. After the war, Lucite and other acrylic products were fashioned into a host of household objects, from chandeliers to coffee tables. The glossy surface is hard and stain-resistant but scratches easily.

CARE Dust weekly, or as necessary, with a soft, clean, damp cotton or microfiber cloth. Use only the lightest pressure to avoid scratching. If soil has built up, wash the item with mild dishwashing liquid and water. Never use a dry cloth, which can grind the dirt into the surface, causing a fine mesh of scratches, which will give the acrylic a dull appearance, and avoid cleaners containing ammonia, which will dull the surface. Fine scratches can be buffed out with a product designed for plastic such as Novus Plastic Polish.

STORAGE Wrap acrylic items individually in acid-free tissue to keep dust off and prevent scratches.

MIRROR Sheets of glass coated on one side with metal, usually either silver or aluminum. The metal surface, which is what makes the mirror reflective, is covered by a layer of paint to guard against oxidation. Some of the earliest mirrors, which date back to 6200 B.C.E., were simply highly polished pieces of stone or metal. The practice of covering glass with metal was first widely practiced in sixteenth-century Venice. The majority of mirror glass used throughout the house is flat, but mirrors can also have a concave or convex surface. Concave mirrors enlarge the reflection and are useful for applying makeup and shaving. Convex mirrors are generally used only for decorative effect, but can be useful outdoors at driveways to see around corners and curves. Antique and vintage mirrors sometimes display a rippling or waviness, which is a result of the way glass was manufactured prior to the 1950s, when it was of a less uniform thickness than it is today. As time goes by, the reflective backing of a mirror will wear away, causing subtle streaks and uneven dark spots known as foxing. This appearance is treasured by some collectors (you can speed up the process by spraying ammonia on the reflective materials on the back); if you want to repair it, you will need the services of a professional re-silverer. (Look in the Yellow Pages under "Mirrors.") The result will probably not make the mirror look like new, but it will eliminate dark patches.

CARE Clean mirrors weekly with a microfiber cloth dampened with water or a soft cotton cloth (an old T-shirt is ideal) dampened with glass cleaner. Spray cleaner on the cloth rather than on the mirror to prevent moisture from seeping into the joints where it can damage the backing. Be sure to wipe away all of the cleaning product to prevent streaks.

STORAGE High humidity can damage a mirror's reflective coating, so it's important to store mirrors in locations with stable humidity and temper-ature levels. Store them upright, but do not lean them against uninsulated walls (such as in the attic or basement), which can harbor dampness. Wrap a mirror in acid-free tissue to protect the glass from scratches, then sandwich it between two layers of $\frac{1}{4}$-inch foam board cut slightly larger than the frame. Secure the corners with small strips of foam board and tape.

O

OILCLOTH Originally a fabric treated with linseed oil and paint to render it waterproof. It was once a staple in middle-class kitchens, where it was used as a table covering. Although original oilcloth is hard to find—it fell out of style, and what remained either disintegrated or was discarded—modern versions have a loyal following. Today's oilcloth is made of plastic or vinyl woven with cotton. It is used to make tablecloths and place mats, aprons, bibs, upholstery, shower curtains, and outdoor apparel. It is useful wherever a washable cloth surface is needed.

CARE Wipe oilcloth with a damp sponge or cloth. To remove stains, use a cloth dampened with a solution of warm water and mild dishwashing liquid. Avoid solvents, which will damage the protective surface. Do not dry-clean oilcloth. The material becomes stiffer and less flexible with age and may even permanently crack along creases. Unfortunately, tears are irreparable, but you may be able to salvage a damaged piece of oilcloth by sewing on patches.

STORAGE Roll oilcloth (the fabric can crack along creases) and store in a cool, dry location.

ONYX A variety of chalcedony (quartz) related to agate. It is a hard stone primarily used for jewelry and cameos. Although it is generally thought of as black, it is found in white, brown, and reddish brown varieties, which are sometimes referred to as chalcedony.

CARE Wipe gently with a soft, dry cloth to remove dust, dirt, and oils. Do not expose onyx to harsh chemicals or detergents. Avoid letting it come into contact with hair spray or perfume. Take off onyx jewelry before swimming or bathing. For particularly grimy pieces, use a solution of mild dishwashing liquid and warm water applied with a damp cloth. Do not use chemical jewelry dips or an ultrasonic cleaner. Onyx requires no penetrating sealer or coating; over time it develops a waxy luster.

STORAGE Onyx chips and cracks more easily than many other stones and can break if dropped. Store it in a padded container, or wrapped in acid-free tissue to guard against scratching. In general, onyx items will not be affected by extremes of heat or cold, but colors can fade if onyx is left in direct sunlight. If onyx becomes stained, there may be no remedy; consult a jeweler.

OPAL Stones composed of water and silicon dioxide—the substance that makes up quartz and sand—known for their fiery iridescence. Most of the world's iridescent opals are mined in Australia, and their color ranges from milky white to "black," which is actually a very rare (and very expensive) dark blue. Colored but translucent "jelly" opals are a variety usually found in the United States and Mexico. The high water content in both kinds of opals makes them very delicate and vulnerable to cracking.

CARE Wipe opals clean with a damp cloth. Especially dirty pieces may be rinsed with lukewarm soapy water (do not soak them). Never use chemicals such as ammonia or ultrasonic cleaners, which will dim some of their iridescence.

Remove opal jewelry before applying makeup or perfume, washing your hands, doing dishes, or cooking; exposure to oils and alcohol can damage opals, and steam can crack them. Avoid exposing opals to any extremes in heat or humidity. Wear gloves over opal rings in cold weather.

STORAGE Store opal pieces individually in cloth bags or padded boxes. Never store opals in a plastic bag, or they will dry out, become dull, and possibly crack.

PAPIER-MÂCHÉ A mixture of paper and a binder, such as starch or flour, that becomes malleable when moistened, and dries strong and hard. It originated in China during the Han Dynasty (202 B.C.E.–220 A.D.). By the mid-eighteenth century, it was being used in Europe to make architectural embellishments. In the early nineteenth century, the process was mechanized and papier-mâché was fashioned into a large number of household products, including trays, snuffboxes, clock cases, and even furniture. These pieces were generally japanned, a lacquering process involving numerous coats of varnish that resulted in a smooth, glossy surface. (For more, see LACQUER on page 708.)

CARE Dust papier-mâché objects with a clean cotton cloth or feather duster, taking care not to abrade lacquer finishes. Do not use water, detergents, or polishes.

STORAGE Store papier-mâché in a cool, dry location away from direct sunlight; prolonged exposure to light can darken and discolor finishes. Dramatic changes in humidity and temperature can cause papier-mâché to swell and shrink, which can lead to cracking.

PEARL Pearls grow inside certain types of mollusks, such as oysters and mussels. They develop when a wayward particle, such as a parasite or grain of sand, gets stuck in the soft tissue, and the mollusk responds by coating it with calcium carbonate, the same substance that forms the interior of its shell (known as mother-of-pearl). The vast majority of pearls are cultivated—or cultured—rather than natural. The technique of culturing pearls was developed by Kokichi Mikimoto in Japan in the late nineteenth century. Prior to that, pearls were so rare that they were available only to the very wealthy. Cultured pearls are made by placing a mother-of-pearl bead in the tissue of a mollusk, which is then placed in a cage; about two to three years later the cultured pearl is harvested. Pearls cultivated in saltwater are generally rounder and more expensive than pearls cultivated in freshwater. Pearls come in a wide range of colors, including cream, pink, gray, blue, and green.

CARE Pearls are relatively soft and susceptible to damage from the environment and cosmetics. Once pearls have lost their luster, the glow cannot be recaptured. Put pearl jewelry on only after you've applied perfume, cosmetics, and hair spray. Never wear pearls in the pool, when cleaning, or when cooking with vinegar; chlorine, ammonia, and vinegar can all damage pearls. Body oils and perspiration are also harmful, so wipe pearls with a soft, damp cloth every time you take them off. Do not use jewelry dips or ultrasonic cleaners.

If pearls are particularly dirty, you can rinse them in a solution of water and mild dishwashing liquid (do not soak them). Lay necklaces on a clean towel to allow the string to dry thoroughly.

The silk or nylon thread used to string pearls can weaken and stretch, so jewelers recommend having pearls restrung as often as once a year, depending on how often you wear them.

STORAGE Store pearls in a soft pouch separate from other jewelry to prevent scratches. Never store pearls in plastic bags, which can cause them to dry out, resulting in yellowing.

PEWTER Made primarily of tin, which is alloyed, or mixed, with a number of other metals, including copper, antimony, bismuth, and sometimes lead. Pewter was to the eighteenth century what plastic is to ours—it was used to make plates, platters, mugs, even baby bottles and nipples. It was the main material for tableware before china imports became popularized. Whether antique or modern, pewter has a lovely, muted luster that is easy to maintain—unlike silver, it does not tarnish. Prolonged exposure to moisture, however, can cause it to develop scale—oxidation similar to rust, that cannot be repaired.

CARE Wash pewter pieces by hand with mild dishwashing liquid and water, then dry them thoroughly. Pewter should never be put in the dishwasher or the oven (it melts at 450° F). Pewter will naturally develop a dark, spotty patina over time, which is considered desirable by collectors. It isn't meant to take a bright shine. If you do polish your pewter, choose a polish designed specifically for it. All-purpose metal polishes and those designed for silver can contain abrasives that can scratch pewter.

STORAGE Store objects in acid-free tissue, and, if possible, keep them out of direct contact with wood (which emits acids and gases that can contribute to corrosion).

PLASTIC A polymer, which is a material formed by large molecules made up of many small molecules. Natural polymers include rubber and cellulose. The first synthetic polymer was Bakelite, which was invented in 1907 (see page 695). During the first half of the twentieth century, the plastics that make up many of the household items we count on daily—from polyethelene milk jugs to polyvinyl chloride pipe fittings—were developed and put into widespread production. Plastics share a number of characteristics: They are chemically resistant, impact resistant, and lightweight. There are two general categories: thermoset, which can't be softened by heat (a polyurethane cushion, for example) and thermoplastic, which softens when heated (such as a water bottle).

CARE All plastics benefit from gentle care; they scratch easily and should never be cleaned with abrasive tools or cleansers. Solvents will dull the finish of many plastics. Day to day, dust plastics with a soft, clean cloth. Dampen the cloth with a solution of water and mild dishwashing liquid for dirtier pieces. Outdoor items can be scrubbed with a soft-bristled brush instead of a cloth. Most decorative and vintage plastics (including Bakelite, and acrylics such as Lucite and Plexiglas) can be polished with Novus Plastic Polish (available at hardware stores). Follow the manufacturer's instructions. Do not use strong alkalis, such as ammonia, or products containing ammonia, such as window cleaner, on acrylics.

Avoid placing plastic storage containers and lids in the bottom rack of the dishwasher. They may crack and melt in the intense heat. Remove odors and greasy film from food storage containers with a thick paste of baking soda and water.

STORAGE Store plastic objects away from heat sources.

PLATINUM One of the three precious metals (along with gold and silver). It gets its name from the Spanish word *platina,* which means "little silver," because it was thought that it was nothing more than a difficult-to-work version of that precious metal. However, once properly refined, platinum is a shiny silver-white metal that is malleable, making it ideal for jewelry. It is generally 95 percent pure; it is hypoallergenic and won't cause skin reactions. Because it is inert, it won't tarnish or corrode, which is why it is also used to make surgical and lab equipment as well as electrical wires. It is the rarest and most expensive of the precious metals. Platinum jewelry reached the peak of its popularity during the 1920s with the emergence of the Art Deco style and increased wealth throughout the United States. Platinum was banned for civilian use during World War II and it was not until the late 1990s that it again became a metal of choice for engagement and wedding rings.

CARE Polish platinum with a soft cloth and wash it in warm water mixed with a few drops of mild dishwashing liquid. It can be cleaned using a commercial jewelry dip or ultrasonic cleaner (though you should not use either if the stones in a platinum setting are too delicate to tolerate these cleaning methods).

STORAGE Store jewelry in individual fabric bags or a compartmentalized jewelry box to guard against scratches.

R

RUBBER Natural rubber comes from the sap of the rubber tree (*Hovea brasilienesis*), which is native to the Amazon. It was first used by pre-Columbian civilizations. Rubber was exported to North America and Europe in the nineteenth century. One of its early uses was as a coating on textiles; Charles Macintosh created the first rubberized raincoat in Scotland in the 1820s. In the 1830s, Charles Goodyear, an American, invented the technique of vulcanization, in which sulfur was combined with rubber to make it more elastic and durable. It was after this advance that rubber became widely used in products for the household and industry. There are two main kinds of rubber: dry and dipped. The former is used for items such as erasers, balls, hoses, and gaskets. Dipped rubber starts out as a liquid and is turned into stretchy products such as balloons and latex gloves. The first synthetic rubber, called neoprene, was developed by DuPont in 1930. Synthetic rubbers are more resistant to heat, solvents, and oil than natural rubber.

CARE Petroleum or oil should never be used on rubber, as they will degrade it. Oiling the rubber belt on a sewing machine, for instance, will ruin it. Clean rubber with mild dishwashing liquid and water.

STORAGE Avoid prolonged exposure to sunlight, which will cause rubber to break down.

RUBY A variety of the mineral corundum, rubies are second only to diamonds in hardness. Most are from Southeast Asia; the finest are from Myanmar (formerly Burma). Rubies are commonly treated with heat, which improves their color and clarity, and cavities and fractures are filled with resin or oil. Large, high-quality rubies are extremely rare, and can command higher prices than diamonds. Much lore surrounds this gem, which is thought to be a symbol of health, wealth, wisdom, passion, and triumph in love.

CARE Clean with a soft, old toothbrush that has been dipped in soapy water. Avoid chemical dips and ultrasonic cleaning, which can damage stones with oil or resin fillings.

STORAGE Store jewelry individually in pouches or in the compartments of a jewelry box to prevent scratches.

S

SHAGREEN A pale gray-green, pebbly-surfaced leather made from the skin of sharks or rays (it is also known as sharkskin and galuchat). It was first used in Europe by the French cabinetmaker Jean-Claude Galuchat in the eighteenth century. In the 1920s, shagreen was a signature detail in the Art Deco furniture of Emile-Jacques Ruhlmann. It's used as a fancy decorative flourish on such items as boxes, books, notebooks, and humidors; because of its rough texture, it was also used for the grips of swords.

CARE Shagreen is durable and should not be treated with dressings or preservatives. Dust as necessary; do not use moisture or cleaners.

STORAGE Store objects in cool, dry, moderately lit spaces. Prolonged exposure to direct sunlight and heat may fade or otherwise degrade skins.

SILVER One of the three precious metals (gold and platinum are the others). Like gold, pure silver is very malleable and is generally alloyed with other metals (usually copper) to lend durability. It is used to make jewelry, flatware, tableware, and mirrors, and in a variety of industrial applications, including photography. Although it is prized for its bright luster and reflectivity, it tarnishes easily. There are a number of different kinds of silver, such as sterling, silver plate, Venetian and Nevada, coin, and hotel.

STERLING

To qualify as sterling, silver has to be at least 92.5 percent pure. This standard—92.5 parts silver to 7.5 parts copper alloy, which strengthens softer silver—was established by the English in the twelfth century and later adopted by most of the world, including the U.S. in 1868.

SILVER PLATE

Silver plate is a coating of pure silver set on top of a base metal such as copper or nickel silver, which is actually an alloy of nickel, copper, and zinc. Various forms date to the eighteenth century. Electroplating processes were invented in England in the 1830s and 1840s; this method is still used today.

VENETIAN AND NEVADA SILVER

Venetian and Nevada silver are alloys consisting of nickel and silver. Although both are solid metal rather than plated, they contain less silver than sterling does. These lower-grade compounds are often less costly than silver plate, but don't polish up as brightly.

COIN SILVER

Some of the oldest American silver is coin silver, which contains an amount of the precious metal that was set by the U.S. Mint for coinage after the American Revolution. Coin made from 1792 to 1837 is composed of at least 89.2 percent silver, and thereafter, 90 percent. Many people think of coin as much less valuable than sterling, but it has only about 2 percent less silver and, in some cases, may even contain more.

HOTEL SILVER

Hotel silver is electroplated silver that was manufactured for use on trains and steamships and in restaurants and hotels. You can dent a sterling silver bowl very easily, but a similar piece of hotel silver can be dropped without much harm because the underlying base metal—often nickel—is stronger than silver. The majority of hotel silver is rather plainly shaped, partly because the base metal is so stiff, partly for economic reasons: the more exotic and decorated the form, the more difficult the silver is to clean, which would have slowed down service.

To distinguish among the different types, you must rely on hallmarks, a variety of emblems stamped on silver to attest to its purity. England's system of hallmarks is one of the oldest and most detailed (the laws governing them date to the fourteenth century). A lion symbolized British sterling; a symbol for the city of origin might include an anchor for Birmingham or a crown for Sheffield (since 1975, a rose). Another mark is the head of the reigning monarch. A letter provides the date of manufacture, and initials indicate the name of the silversmith. American marks aren't as systematic or elaborate. Early pieces may bear the maker's name and nothing else. Eventually, manufacturers also started using the word "coin." With the adoption of sterling standards after the Civil War, silversmiths continued to stamp their own names as well as the word "sterling" or the numbers 92.5 or 925, all of which indicate sterling quality. Some companies used symbols as a commercial logo.

Silver plate has its own codes. The maker or company name is usually stamped on the back, along with acronyms or phrases—A1, AA, EP, EPNS, "sterling inlaid," or "silver soldered"—indicating that the piece is plated.

CARE Although tarnish is inevitable, it is merely unsightly and not harmful to silver; it does not penetrate beyond the very surface of the metal. In some cases, as with an intricately engraved piece, tarnish actually contributes to the beauty (and sometimes the value), by providing shading to the design, lending it a sense of venerability. For this reason—and more important, because a little bit of metal is worn away with each polishing—silver should be cared for with a light touch. Clean silver jewelry with a polish designed specifically for that purpose (they are available from jewelers). Apply just a small dab with a soft cotton cloth and rub gently. Rinse in hot water to prevent spotting and dry with another soft cloth. Silver flatware and objects should be polished with a liquid or cream made for silver. Avoid commercially available acid baths, called silver dips, for heavily tarnished pieces. They remove a layer of metal and are much too harsh. For instructions on how to polish silver, turn to page 170. With many years of use, silver will develop a foggy sheen that many collectors find desirable. Often called a "butler finish," it is a mesh of thousands of microscopic scratches dulling the original mirror brightness, suggesting that a piece has been well used by previous generations.

STORAGE Store jewelry, flatware, and other objects in tarnish-inhibiting flannel bags, available from jewelers or at home-supply stores (you can also buy treated flannel by the yard at fabric stores). Never store silver in plastic bags, which trap moisture, or in rubber bands, which contain sulfur, which encourages tarnish. Rotate place settings in and out of use to ensure a consistent appearance over time.

T

TAXIDERMY The craft of preserving mammals, birds, insects, and fish in a lifelike manner so they can be mounted for display. Collecting taxidermy was especially popular in the nineteenth century, when creatures were amassed for educational purposes by hobbyists. It was also prized for its ornamental value and as an indicator of wealth and status—country houses were often decorated with mounts shot on their grounds or during expeditions to exotic locales. The methods used to preserve animals vary greatly. Generally, the skins of mammals and birds are tanned and then fitted over a padded form. With older mounts, the form may be made of sawdust or wood shavings reinforced with a wire armature called a manikin. For newer pieces, the form may be constructed out of synthetic materials such as polyurethane or fiberglass. Insects are often simply dried. Fish, because of their delicate skins, are the most difficult creatures to preserve; the skins are sometimes used, but in modern taxidermy, more often a mold is taken and the fish is re-created using a synthetic material.

CARE To keep the dust off of small specimens, put them under glass—either in a cabinet or under a cloche—and dust them annually using a soft paintbrush, following the growth pattern of the feathers or fur. Exposed mounts should be dusted monthly. You can also blow dust off sturdy specimens with a hair dryer set on low. Never use a vacuum; the strong suction can damage feathers and fur. Fur in good condition can also be gently wiped with a barely damp cloth (if the specimen has loose, torn, or ripped fur, do nothing more than dust it). Clean the "eyes" (real eyes are replaced by the taxidermist with glass or plastic replicas) with a damp cotton swab; do not use glass cleaner, which can dull eyes made of plastic. Fish mounts, which are generally protected with a clear coating such as varnish, can be dusted with a feather duster and gently wiped with a soft cloth. Horns should not be oiled or otherwise dressed; antlers can be wiped with a small amount of linseed oil once a year to restore their luster. Mammals, birds, and fish (with skin intact) are extremely vulnerable to insect damage. Evidence of an infestation includes bald patches, bore marks, and small piles of fur or debris under or around the animal. If you suspect a specimen is contaminated, consult a taxidermist about a course of treatment immediately.

STORAGE Taxidermy must be stored in an environment with stable humidity. Moisture can lead quickly to mold and insect infestation. Dry air can cause hides to shrink and split. When not on display, keep dust off by draping mounts with clean white sheets or wrapping them loosely in acid-free tissue. Never wrap taxidermy in plastic, which can trap moisture and lead to rapid decay.

TERRA COTTA "Baked earth" in Italian, terra cotta is made from clay and fired at low temperatures. It is found both glazed and unglazed, and is made into a range of products, from floor tile to flower pots to serving pieces. Unglazed terra cotta is very porous and stains easily—so unglazed floor tiles require the application of sealers or coatings to ensure a durable surface (for more on sealing terra-cotta tile, turn to page 531).

CARE Wash terra-cotta pots every time they are emptied, before anything else is replanted, and before they are put up for storage at the end of the season. Washing removes fungal diseases and any insect larvae that might be harmful to new plantings. Washing also loosens any buildup of crusty minerals that may have leached into the porous surface. Fill a large bucket or tub with a solution of 1 part bleach to 10 parts water and set it aside. Prepare your terra-cotta pots by brushing off and rinsing away any loose soil still clinging to them. Add the pots to the bleach solution and leave them to soak overnight. (You should always wear old clothing, gloves, and eye protection when working with bleach.) The next morning, scrub the pots with a scouring pad or a stiff-bristled brush (a bottle brush is ideal). Using soap is unnecessary—the absorbent nature of terra cotta makes its residue difficult to rinse out. Allow pots to thoroughly air dry before storing them. Glazed terra-cotta cookware and serving ware can be washed in the dishwasher. However, since these pieces are very soft and subject to chipping, washing by hand is recommended. Unglazed pieces should not be put in the dishwasher. Hand-wash them in warm water with a scant amount of mild dishwashing liquid.

STORAGE Never stack terra-cotta pots—changes in temperature and humidity will make them swell, causing them to stick together and guaranteeing breakage when you try to pull them apart. Similarly, avoid nesting terra-cotta cookware to minimize the chance of chipping. Lay small pots on their sides, one tucked loosely inside another in a shallow crate. Store large pots upright; conserve space by storing pots on top of one another rim to rim or base to base. Protect them from freezing temperatures, which can cause pots to crack.

TIN A soft, silver-white metal that is frequently alloyed with other metals (tin has been alloyed with copper since ancient times to create bronze). In its pure state, tin can take a high polish and resists tarnish and rust. It was frequently used as a plating material to protect other metals. Beginning in the early nineteenth century, everything from tea and tobacco to crackers and candies came packaged in boxes made from tin-plated iron or steel. These containers' exteriors were decorated with company logos and designs that make them especially appealing to collectors today. Colorful tin toys were also widely produced during the nineteenth and first half of the twentieth centuries. So-called tin ceilings had their heyday in the late nineteenth century (they were generally made of steel). Taking their cue from the embellished ceilings of Europe, craftsmen used presses to imprint thin sheets of metal with designs. These panels were installed in buildings of all kinds, including homes, theaters, schools, and churches. The panels were attractive as well as practical—because metal is a noncombustible material, buildings with these ceilings cost less to insure. Production of metal ceilings declined during World War I, when metal was diverted to military use.

CARE Rust is the scourge of tin-plated objects. Moisture trapped in nooks can rust the iron or steel under the tin plating. One way to stave it off is to apply a coat of clear lacquer (spray and brush-on lacquer are available at hardware and paint stores) to inside and outside surfaces. It's important to do a test first, as lacquer can dissolve certain inks in surface decoration. Alternatively, you can apply a thin coat of paste wax (for instructions on waxing, turn to page 524). Both surface coatings will block moisture and inhibit rust, but may require periodic reapplications. Keep in mind, however, that tin toys can be extremely valuable; applying any coating can diminish their worth significantly. If you plan to use tin containers to hold food, line them with parchment paper or aluminum foil beforehand. Wipe tin surfaces with a clean, dry cloth and protect them from moisture. Vintage tin ceilings should be dusted with a dry cloth or dust mop; steel rusts easily and moisture will hasten the process (even if they are painted, moisture can seep into fissures and seams). Modern tin ceilings are often made from aluminum, which does not rust, and can be wiped with a damp cloth or mop.

STORAGE Store tin objects in a dry location out of direct sunlight, which can fade painted surfaces.

TOLE Painted tin-plated iron, commonly found in the form of trays, lamps, and baskets. It typically features a black background, although red, yellow, green, white, and imitation wood and tortoiseshell designs were also fashionable. It often included colorful floral or fruit patterns, flowers and birds, urns, swags, or pastoral scenes. The earliest tole dates back to the mid-eighteenth century, when the technique was invented in Wales. It was meant to serve as an inexpensive substitute for the lustrous lacquered wooden pieces, typically red and black, being imported from Asia. The tin surface was brushed with a rust-inhibiting varnish made from coal tar. The finish, called japan, was baked on and cooled, then decorated, polished, and sealed with clear varnish. Its lacquered finish and the tin plating beneath it are resistant to rust, but if they have worn away, the exposed iron is vulnerable to rust.

CARE Dust with a soft brush, and, if necessary, wipe tole by hand with a damp cloth. Do this carefully, without wetting the piece, then dry it thoroughly to prevent rust; use a blow-dryer on a low setting to dry corners and crevices. Applying a thin coating of paste wax (for instructions on how to wax, turn to page 524) provides a barrier against moisture and rust, as well as a little protection against dirt.

STORAGE A damp environment encourages rust, so tole is best kept in a dry area, out of direct sunlight and away from other objects, which can scratch the paint.

TORTOISESHELL Derived from the hawksbill sea turtle, which is found in tropical and subtropical regions of the Atlantic, Pacific, and Indian Oceans and the Caribbean Sea. The trade in hawksbill is now banned internationally. Throughout the nineteenth and most of the twentieth centuries, tortoiseshell was crafted into a number of household objects and ornaments, including combs, brushes, boxes, and furniture inlays. The Japanese have a long tradition of crafting objects out of tortoiseshell, which they call *bekko*. Often, a piece called tortoiseshell is made from plastic, which is generally more fragile than the natural material.

CARE The same cleaning recommendations apply to both natural and faux tortoiseshell: regular dusting with a soft cloth, or wiping with a damp cloth. Plastic will suffer more readily from exposure to heat and sunlight.

STORAGE Keep tortoiseshell away from direct sunlight and do not expose it to extremes in temperature or humidity to guard against cracking.

V

VINYL RECORDS The first vinyl records (made of polyvinyl chloride, or PVC) were introduced in 1948. Although recording technology has been changing ever since, many collectors and music aficionados value vinyl's unique sound quality. The best way to preserve sound quality is to keep records dust-free. If dust settles into the grooves it can permanently mar the surface of the record, resulting in a crackling sound when played.

CARE Handle records by the outside edges only, to prevent fingerprints and scratches. Dust records in concentric circles with a record brush, which has angled bristles, before playing them. Should you discover a mildewed or musty record, wipe it with a soft, clean cloth dampened with distilled water or record cleaner (available online; search for "vinyl record cleaner"), being careful not to wet the label. Dry with another clean cloth, wiping in concentric circles. Use only lint-free cloth (old T-shirts work well).

STORAGE Store records vertically, never flat, and never leaning to one side; don't store them too tightly together. They should be stored in a cool, dry place, away from direct sunlight, to prevent them from warping. Remove shrinkwrap, which could also cause warping. Always keep them in their dust jackets to prevent scratches and keep them clean. Many record collectors place the jackets (with vinyl records inside) in specially made plastic sleeves, for added protection from dust and abrasion.

Z

ZINC A metal often used to coat rust-prone metals such as steel and tin, which are then used to cover countertops and work surfaces, and to make garbage cans, downspouts, and gutters. This process is called galvanizing. Zinc is durable, will not corrode, and does not react to most chemicals. There are two methods for coating metal with zinc: electroplating and dipping the base metal in molten zinc. Electroplating produces the smoother, more durable finish and is the technique used for countertops and work surfaces (for more on zinc countertops, turn to page 53).

CARE Clean zinc surfaces with mild dishwashing liquid and water. To keep zinc shiny, avoid abrasives. Buff after wiping using a soft, white nylon pad. Apply a thin coat of wax (for instructions on how to wax, turn to page 524). If rust is present, remove it with a stiff brush.

STORAGE Avoid storing zinc in damp or poorly ventilated areas. Moisture can lead to white, gray, or black spots. Sea air can accelerate spotting.

REFERENCE

SOURCES

Listed below are products and companies mentioned throughout this book. Some of the websites offer online shopping; others will list retailers where products can be purchased.

ALL-IN-ONE MOP
LEIFHEIT MR. MISTER SPRAY MOP, 866-695-3434 or www.leifheitusa.com

ARCHIVAL STORAGE SUPPLIES
CONSERVATION RESOURCES INTERNATIONAL, 800-634-6932 or www.conservationresources.com

GAYLORD BROTHERS, 800-448-6160 or www.gaylord.com

LIGHT IMPRESSIONS, 800-828-6216 or www.lightimpressionsdirect.com

ELECTRONIC LABEL MAKER
P-TOUCH, 877-478-6824 or www.brother-usa.com/ptouch/

ENZYME LAUNDRY PRE-SOAK
BIZ, 866-447-3369 or www.bizisbetter.com

ENZYME PET-STAIN REMOVER
NATURE'S MIRACLE, 800-645-5154 or www.eightinonepet.com

KNIFE SHARPENER
CARBORUNDUM SHARPENING STONE, www.carborundumabrasives.com

LEATHER CLEANER
LEATHER MASTER, 540-772-3878 or www.leatherworldtech.com

METAL POLISH
CAMEO COPPER, BRASS & PORCELAIN CLEANER, 800-524-1328 or www.churchdwight.com

GODDARD'S SILVER FOAM, www.goddards.com

RED BEAR POLISH, 800-966-5489 or www.scandicrafts.com

MILD LAUNDRY DETERGENT
DREFT, www.dreftbaby.com

IVORY SNOW, www.ivory.com

ORVUS QUILT SOAP, available on www.amazon.com

MILD LIQUID SOAP
DR. BRONNER'S, 877-786-3649, www.drbronner.com

MILDLY ABRASIVE CLEANSER
BON AMI, 816-842-1230 or www.bonami.com

NONAMMONIATED GLASS CLEANER
ECOVER, 800-449-4925 or www.ecover.com

MRS. MEYER'S, 877-865-1508 or www.mrsmeyers.com

SEVENTH GENERATION, 800-456-1191 or www.seventhgeneration.com

OXYGEN BLEACH
CLOROX OXI MAGIC, www.oxygenaction.com

ECOVER, 800-449-4925 or www.ecover.com

PIANO POLISH
CORY CARE PRODUCTS, 800-552-2679 or www.corycare.com

PLASTIC CLEANER AND POLISH
NOVUS PLASTIC POLISH, 800-668-8760 or www.noscratch.com/novus

PUTTY FOR ANCHORING FRAGILE ITEMS
MUSEUM PUTTY, www.containerstore.com

RUST REMOVER
NAVAL JELLY, 800-321-0253 or www.loctiteproducts.com

ROVER RUST REMOVER, 800-227-4224 or www.hach.com

SHOE CLEANER
LINCOLN E-Z CLEANER, 408-732-5120 or www.lincolnshoepolish.com

SPECIALTY BRUSHES
FULLER BRUSHES, 620-792-1711 or www.fuller.com

STAINLESS-STEEL COOKWARE CLEANER
BAR KEEPERS FRIEND POWDERED CLEANSER, 800-433-5818 or www.barkeepersfriend.com

SURFACE PROTECTORS
EZ GLIDE, 800-654-5744 or www.ezglide.com

WAX
BUTCHER'S WHITE DIAMOND BOWLING ALLEY PASTE WAX, available at 800-569-0394 or www.bwccompany.com

RENAISSANCE WAX, 800-229-5530 or www.restorationproduct.com

ACKNOWLEDGMENTS

A book of this length and scope does not come together overnight. The *Homekeeping Handbook,* which represents the focus of my career as an author, editor, and teacher in the subject of the domestic arts, has been in development for many years. And it has involved the hard work, cooperation, and dedication of dozens of staff members who very ambitiously and carefully researched, collected, edited, wrote, and fact-checked so much of the information within on everything having to do with homekeeping. I am grateful to them and to all of the industry professionals and experts who provided us with suggestions, advice, and guidance for the very best ways to care for any home and its contents.

Ellen Morrissey, my executive book editor, worked tirelessly assembling everything into a coherent whole, at the same time giving birth to two beautiful children, and overseeing and editing several other books, including *The Martha Stewart Baking Handbook.* We are so fortunate that William van Roden lent his considerable talent and impeccable design sense to the creation of this book; Will's design is flawless, making even the most "homey" advice and material flow in a way that is at once dynamic, easy to follow, and beautiful to behold. We were equally lucky that Kelly Tagore came on board to edit the project; with her extensive knowledge of all things home-related, Kelly helped shape an enormous amount of information into a concise and ultimately very useful resource. Amy Conway kindly took time from her editing duties at *Martha Stewart Living* to help with the project, and her careful eye lends accuracy and style to every page. Designer Matt Papa ably assisted with the overall look of the book.

This project introduced us to the fine work of photographer Ellen McDermott, who shot the majority of the photographs in the book over the course of a few years. We were delighted by her talent, hard work, and good cheer at every photo shoot. The work of dozens of other favorite photographers (the list appears on page 724) makes up the rest of the photos. We are very grateful to each of them. Special thanks must go to Victoria Pearson, who photographed my portrait for the cover.

I would also like to offer my sincerest thanks to the wonderful group of housekeepers, all women, who have worked with me over the years as I developed my own personal style of homekeeping: Necy Guimares, my first housekeeper, who taught me so much about cleaning techniques; Laura Acuna, who still works long hours brightening my homes and my life; Luisa Santos, who cared not only for my home, but also so lovingly for my pets; Lily Pei Mei, who organizes and directs better than anyone; Esperanza Franco, who cares for Lily Pond; Torie Hallock, who cared for Skylands and taught me the secrets of cleaning an enormous and beautiful home; Peggy Knox and Gretchen Sweet, who are presently keeping Skylands shining and bright; and Odette Schooley, Li Peng, and Edna Coelho, and the wonderful cadre of helpful housekeepers at *Martha Stewart Living*'s three offices in New York City.

Many other members of our editorial and art departments lent time and energy in myriad ways; they include Jennifer Aaronson, Elizabeth Alsop, Matthew Axe, Rachel Boyle, Sarah Carey, Denise Clappi, Christine Cyr, Paul Dobrowolski, James Dunlinson, Thomas Eberharter, Sandra Rose Gluck, Melañio Gomez, Heloise Goodman, Meesha Diaz Haddad, Jennifer Jarett, Fritz Karch, Melissa Morgan, Debra Puchalla, Madhu Puri, Anthony Santelli, Lucinda Scala Quinn, Kevin Sharkey, Alison Vanek, Laura Wallis, and Bunny Wong.

Many thanks to Eric A. Pike for his careful guidance over the book's design, and to Margaret Roach for her editorial direction. And special thanks as well to my longtime colleagues Gael Towey and Lauren Podlach Stanich.

As much as we relied on our own homekeeping experts and editors, there were many instances throughout the research for this book when we had to rely on the expertise of others. We are indebted to the following helpful institutions and individuals:

Abstract Masonry Restoration, Air Temp Heating & Air Conditioning, the American Academy of Pediatrics, the American Gas Association, the American Institute for Conservation of Historic & Artistic Works, the American Red Cross, the American Society for the Prevention of Cruelty to Animals, American Standard, Baxter & Liebchen, Best Buy, the Better Sleep Council, Brother P-Touch Labels, the Carpet and Rug Institute, the Centers for Disease Control and Prevention, Conserval Engineering, the Consumer Product Safety Commission, the Consumers Union, the Cornell Human Factors and Ergonomics Research Group, Electrical Safety Foundation International, the Environmental Protection Agency, the Environmental Working Group, EZ Glides, the Federal Emergency Management Association, the Federal Trade Commission, the Food Marketing Institute, the Hearth, Patio, and Barbecue Association, Hi Valley Supply, the Home Ventilating Institute, the Juvenile Products Manufacturers Association, Kohler, Madame Paulette, the Marble Institute of America, James C. McGoldrick and Mark McGoldrick of McGoldrick Plumbing, Meurice Garment Care, the National Air Duct Cleaners Association, the National Closet Group, the National Fire Protection Association, the National Kitchen & Bath Association, the Piano Technicians Guild, the Propane Education and Research Council, Rethinkit, the Rubber Manufacturers' Association, Roland Schmidt, Seventh Generation, the Soap and Detergent Association, the Stone Partnership, TileDealer, the Smithsonian Center for Materials Research and Education, the U.S. Department of Agriculture, the U.S. Fire Administration, and Wilsonart.

As always, we are grateful to our friends at Crown and Clarkson Potter for their dedication and enthusiasm for this project, including Jenny Frost, Lauren Shakely, Doris Cooper, Jane Treuhaft, Marysarah Quinn, Mark McCauslin, Amy Boorstein, Linnea Knollmueller, Andrea Peabbles, Tina Constable, Amy Corley, Sydney Webber, Maria Gagliano, and Adrienne Jozwick.

And finally, an especially heartfelt thanks to the readers of our magazines, viewers of our television shows, and consumers of our home products, who continue to inspire us and to remind us that caring for our homes is what brings us the greatest pleasure and comfort every single day.

CREDITS

WILLIAM ABRANOWICZ vi, 35, 144, 152, 182, 197, 216, 224, 237, 244, 245 (left and center), 258, 266, 291, 323, 460, 467

ANTONIS ACHILLEOS 81, 118 (bench scraper), 120 (mandoline), 151

ANTHONY AMOS 259–261, 416, 424, 472, 473

SANG AN 112 top, 123 (timer), 254, 277, 278, 281, 298, 299, 302, 340

JAMES BAIGRIE 294

CHUCK BAKER 146 left

FERNANDO BENGOECHEA 584–587, 591

ANDREW BORDWIN 305, 426

MONICA BUCK 40

ANITA CALERO 113

JACK COBLE 462

JONN COOLIDGE 270 top

REED DAVIS 100 left, 282, 589

MATT DUCKLO 458

TODD EBERLE 55, 171, 308 right

CARLOS EMILIO 255 left

SCOTT FRANCES 554

JÜRGEN FRANK 365 bottom

FORMULA Z/S 418, 577, 578

DANA GALLAGHER 447 left, 469

GENTL & HYERS 6–7, 30, 56, 100 right, 167–169, 270 bottom, 334 left

JOHN GRUEN 356

MATTHEW HRANEK 1, 363 bottom

LISA HUBBARD 95, 142

THIBAULT JEANSON 231, 451, 454

DAVID JOSEPH 186

KARL JUENGEL 178, 189 bottom left, 192 bottom left

JOHN LAWTON 428, 429, 549

STEPHEN LEWIS 161, 172, 249, 311, 457

CHARLES MARAIA 76, 579

ELLEN McDERMOTT Back cover, frontispiece, 11, 32, 33, 36, 44, 47, 66, 69, 70, 98, 99, 102, 103, 105–109, 114, 116, 118 (all but bench scraper), 119, 120 (all but mandoline), 121, 122, 123 (all but timer), 124–128, 139, 140 top, 141, 143, 146 right, 150 top, 153, 157, 159, 162, 164, 165, 170, 177, 179, 181 bottom, 184, 192 (all but bottom left), 198, 206, 212, 214, 215, 218, 219, 221, 226–228, 248, 250, 252, 264, 269, 271, 293, 306, 308 left, 338, 357, 360, 362, 363 top, 365 top, 375, 379, 390 top right and bottom left, 391, 401–405, 407, 409–412, 445, 447 right, 450, 483–485, 487, 489–491, 493, 494, 497, 498, 500, 507–509, 515–518, 541, 619, 719

STEVEN McDONALD 364, 381, 382

DAVID MEREDITH 336, 342, 343, 346, 535

JAMES MERRELL 452

MINH+WASS 189 (all but bottom left), 196, 297, 387, 396

JENS MORTENSEN 232

VICTORIA PEARSON Front cover, 385, 390 top left and bottom right

ERIC PIASECKI 225, 241, 257, 394–395, 437, 448, 605

CON POULOS 474, 475

DAVID PRINCE 154, 255 right, 273, 312, 374, 439, 441, 442, 444, 495, 581

MARIA ROBLEDO 334 right, 351–353

DAVID SAWYER 149, 150 bottom, 180, 181 top

CHARLES SCHILLER 319

ANNIE SCHLECHTER 318

JASON SCHMIDT 245 right, 256 top, 358, 471

VICTOR SCHRAGER 112 bottom, 140 bottom, 173, 175, 425

MATTHEW SEPTIMUS 553

LUCA TROVATO 256 bottom, 344, 355, 413, 414

PIA TRYDE 268

WILLIAM WALDRON 200

SIMON WATSON 236, 242

WENDELL T. WEBBER 163, 432–435

MARK WEISS 45

ANNA WILLIAMS 400

BRUCE WOLF 88, 527

WILLIAM VAN RODEN 210, illustrations 597–600

JAY ZUKERKORN 220

INDEX